2824B: Implementing Microsoft® Internet Security and Acceleration Server 2004

First Printing

Course Number: 2824B
Part Number: X11-00106
Released: 04/2005

END-USER LICENSE AGREEMENT FOR OFFICIAL MICROSOFT LEARNING PRODUCTS – STUDENT EDITION

PLEASE READ THIS END-USER LICENSE AGREEMENT ("EULA") CAREFULLY. BY USING THE MATERIALS AND/OR USING OR INSTALLING THE SOFTWARE THAT ACCOMPANIES THIS EULA (COLLECTIVELY, THE "LICENSED CONTENT"), YOU AGREE TO THE TERMS OF THIS EULA. IF YOU DO NOT AGREE, DO NOT USE THE LICENSED CONTENT.

1.   **GENERAL.** This EULA is a legal agreement between you (either an individual or a single entity) and Microsoft Corporation ("Microsoft"). This EULA governs the Licensed Content, which includes computer software (including online and electronic documentation), training materials, and any other associated media and printed materials. This EULA applies to updates, supplements, add-on components, and Internet-based services components of the Licensed Content that Microsoft may provide or make available to you unless Microsoft provides other terms with the update, supplement, add-on component, or Internet-based services component. Microsoft reserves the right to discontinue any Internet-based services provided to you or made available to you through the use of the Licensed Content. This EULA also governs any product support services relating to the Licensed Content except as may be included in another agreement between you and Microsoft. An amendment or addendum to this EULA may accompany the Licensed Content.

2.   **GENERAL GRANT OF LICENSE.** Microsoft grants you the following rights, conditioned on your compliance with all the terms and conditions of this EULA. Microsoft grants you a limited, non-exclusive, royalty-free license to install and use the Licensed Content solely in conjunction with your participation as a student in an Authorized Training Session (as defined below). You may install and use one copy of the software on a single computer, device, workstation, terminal, or other digital electronic or analog device ("Device"). You may make a second copy of the software and install it on a portable Device for the exclusive use of the person who is the primary user of the first copy of the software. A license for the software may not be shared for use by multiple end users. An "Authorized Training Session" means a training session conducted at a Microsoft Certified Technical Education Center, an IT Academy, via a Microsoft Certified Partner, or such other entity as Microsoft may designate from time to time in writing, by a Microsoft Certified Trainer (for more information on these entities, please visit www.microsoft.com). WITHOUT LIMITING THE FOREGOING, COPYING OR REPRODUCTION OF THE LICENSED CONTENT TO ANY SERVER OR LOCATION FOR FURTHER REPRODUCTION OR REDISTRIBUTION IS EXPRESSLY PROHIBITED.

3.   **DESCRIPTION OF OTHER RIGHTS AND LICENSE LIMITATIONS**

   3.1   *Use of Documentation and Printed Training Materials.*

            3.1.1   The documents and related graphics included in the Licensed Content may include technical inaccuracies or typographical errors. Changes are periodically made to the content. Microsoft may make improvements and/or changes in any of the components of the Licensed Content at any time without notice. The names of companies, products, people, characters and/or data mentioned in the Licensed Content may be fictitious and are in no way intended to represent any real individual, company, product or event, unless otherwise noted.

            3.1.2   Microsoft grants you the right to reproduce portions of documents (such as student workbooks, white papers, press releases, datasheets and FAQs) (the "Documents") provided with the Licensed Content. You may not print any book (either electronic or print version) in its entirety. If you choose to reproduce Documents, you agree that: (a) use of such printed Documents will be solely in conjunction with your personal training use; (b) the Documents will not republished or posted on any network computer or broadcast in any media; (c) any reproduction will include either the Document's original copyright notice or a copyright notice to Microsoft's benefit substantially in the format provided below; and (d) to comply with all terms and conditions of this EULA. In addition, no modifications may made to any Document.

            Form of Notice:

            Copyright undefined.

            © 2005. Reprinted with permission by Microsoft Corporation. All rights reserved.

            Microsoft and Windows are either registered trademarks or trademarks of Microsoft Corporation in the US and/or other countries. Other product and company names mentioned herein may be the trademarks of their respective owners.

   3.2   *Use of Media Elements.* The Licensed Content may include certain photographs, clip art, animations, sounds, music, and video clips (together "Media Elements"). You may not modify these Media Elements.

   3.3   *Use of Sample Code.* In the event that the Licensed Content include sample source code ("Sample Code"), Microsoft grants you a limited, non-exclusive, royalty-free license to use, copy and modify the Sample Code; if you elect to exercise the foregoing rights, you agree to comply with all other terms and conditions of this EULA, including without limitation Sections 3.4, 3.5, and 6.

   3.4   *Permitted Modifications.* In the event that you exercise any rights provided under this EULA to create modifications of the Licensed Content, you agree that any such modifications: (a) will not be used for providing training where a fee is charged in public or private classes; (b) indemnify, hold harmless, and defend Microsoft from and against any claims or lawsuits, including attorneys' fees, which arise from or result from your use of any modified version of the Licensed Content; and (c) not to transfer or assign any rights to any modified version of the Licensed Content to any third party without the express written permission of Microsoft.

3.5   *Reproduction/Redistribution Licensed Content.* Except as expressly provided in this EULA, you may not reproduce or distribute the Licensed Content or any portion thereof (including any permitted modifications) to any third parties without the express written permission of Microsoft.

4.   **RESERVATION OF RIGHTS AND OWNERSHIP.** Microsoft reserves all rights not expressly granted to you in this EULA. The Licensed Content is protected by copyright and other intellectual property laws and treaties. Microsoft or its suppliers own the title, copyright, and other intellectual property rights in the Licensed Content. You may not remove or obscure any copyright, trademark or patent notices that appear on the Licensed Content, or any components thereof, as delivered to you. **The Licensed Content is licensed, not sold.**

5.   **LIMITATIONS ON REVERSE ENGINEERING, DECOMPILATION, AND DISASSEMBLY.** You may not reverse engineer, decompile, or disassemble the Software or Media Elements, except and only to the extent that such activity is expressly permitted by applicable law notwithstanding this limitation.

6.   **LIMITATIONS ON SALE, RENTAL, ETC. AND CERTAIN ASSIGNMENTS.** You may not provide commercial hosting services with, sell, rent, lease, lend, sublicense, or assign copies of the Licensed Content, or any portion thereof (including any permitted modifications thereof) on a stand-alone basis or as part of any collection, product or service.

7.   **CONSENT TO USE OF DATA.** You agree that Microsoft and its affiliates may collect and use technical information gathered as part of the product support services provided to you, if any, related to the Licensed Content. Microsoft may use this information solely to improve our products or to provide customized services or technologies to you and will not disclose this information in a form that personally identifies you.

8.   **LINKS TO THIRD PARTY SITES.** You may link to third party sites through the use of the Licensed Content. The third party sites are not under the control of Microsoft, and Microsoft is not responsible for the contents of any third party sites, any links contained in third party sites, or any changes or updates to third party sites. Microsoft is not responsible for webcasting or any other form of transmission received from any third party sites. Microsoft is providing these links to third party sites to you only as a convenience, and the inclusion of any link does not imply an endorsement by Microsoft of the third party site.

9.   **ADDITIONAL LICENSED CONTENT/SERVICES.** This EULA applies to updates, supplements, add-on components, or Internet-based services components, of the Licensed Content that Microsoft may provide to you or make available to you after the date you obtain your initial copy of the Licensed Content, unless we provide other terms along with the update, supplement, add-on component, or Internet-based services component. Microsoft reserves the right to discontinue any Internet-based services provided to you or made available to you through the use of the Licensed Content.

10.   **U.S. GOVERNMENT LICENSE RIGHTS**. All software provided to the U.S. Government pursuant to solicitations issued on or after December 1, 1995 is provided with the commercial license rights and restrictions described elsewhere herein. All software provided to the U.S. Government pursuant to solicitations issued prior to December 1, 1995 is provided with "Restricted Rights" as provided for in FAR, 48 CFR 52.227-14 (JUNE 1987) or DFAR, 48 CFR 252.227-7013 (OCT 1988), as applicable.

11.   **EXPORT RESTRICTIONS.** You acknowledge that the Licensed Content is subject to U.S. export jurisdiction. You agree to comply with all applicable international and national laws that apply to the Licensed Content, including the U.S. Export Administration Regulations, as well as end-user, end-use, and destination restrictions issued by U.S. and other governments. For additional information see <http://www.microsoft.com/exporting/>.

12.   **TRANSFER.** The initial user of the Licensed Content may make a one-time permanent transfer of this EULA and Licensed Content to another end user, provided the initial user retains no copies of the Licensed Content. The transfer may not be an indirect transfer, such as a consignment. Prior to the transfer, the end user receiving the Licensed Content must agree to all the EULA terms.

13.   **"NOT FOR RESALE" LICENSED CONTENT.** Licensed Content identified as "Not For Resale" or "NFR," may not be sold or otherwise transferred for value, or used for any purpose other than demonstration, test or evaluation.

14.   **TERMINATION.** Without prejudice to any other rights, Microsoft may terminate this EULA if you fail to comply with the terms and conditions of this EULA. In such event, you must destroy all copies of the Licensed Content and all of its component parts.

15.   **DISCLAIMER OF WARRANTIES.** TO THE MAXIMUM EXTENT PERMITTED BY APPLICABLE LAW, MICROSOFT AND ITS SUPPLIERS PROVIDE THE LICENSED CONTENT AND SUPPORT SERVICES (IF ANY) *AS IS AND WITH ALL FAULTS,* AND MICROSOFT AND ITS SUPPLIERS HEREBY DISCLAIM ALL OTHER WARRANTIES AND CONDITIONS, WHETHER EXPRESS, IMPLIED OR STATUTORY, INCLUDING, BUT NOT LIMITED TO, ANY (IF ANY) IMPLIED WARRANTIES, DUTIES OR CONDITIONS OF MERCHANTABILITY, OF FITNESS FOR A PARTICULAR PURPOSE, OF RELIABILITY OR AVAILABILITY, OF ACCURACY OR COMPLETENESS OF RESPONSES, OF RESULTS, OF WORKMANLIKE EFFORT, OF LACK OF VIRUSES, AND OF LACK OF NEGLIGENCE, ALL WITH REGARD TO THE LICENSED CONTENT, AND THE PROVISION OF OR FAILURE TO PROVIDE SUPPORT OR OTHER SERVICES, INFORMATION, SOFTWARE, AND RELATED CONTENT THROUGH THE LICENSED CONTENT, OR OTHERWISE ARISING OUT OF THE USE OF THE LICENSED CONTENT. ALSO, THERE IS NO WARRANTY OR CONDITION OF TITLE, QUIET ENJOYMENT, QUIET POSSESSION, CORRESPONDENCE TO DESCRIPTION OR NON-INFRINGEMENT WITH REGARD TO THE LICENSED CONTENT. THE ENTIRE RISK AS TO THE QUALITY, OR ARISING OUT OF THE USE OR PERFORMANCE OF THE LICENSED CONTENT, AND ANY SUPPORT SERVICES, REMAINS WITH YOU.

16.   **EXCLUSION OF INCIDENTAL, CONSEQUENTIAL AND CERTAIN OTHER DAMAGES.** TO THE MAXIMUM EXTENT PERMITTED BY APPLICABLE LAW, IN NO EVENT SHALL MICROSOFT OR ITS SUPPLIERS BE LIABLE FOR ANY SPECIAL, INCIDENTAL, PUNITIVE, INDIRECT, OR CONSEQUENTIAL DAMAGES WHATSOEVER (INCLUDING, BUT NOT

LIMITED TO, DAMAGES FOR LOSS OF PROFITS OR CONFIDENTIAL OR OTHER INFORMATION, FOR BUSINESS INTERRUPTION, FOR PERSONAL INJURY, FOR LOSS OF PRIVACY, FOR FAILURE TO MEET ANY DUTY INCLUDING OF GOOD FAITH OR OF REASONABLE CARE, FOR NEGLIGENCE, AND FOR ANY OTHER PECUNIARY OR OTHER LOSS WHATSOEVER) ARISING OUT OF OR IN ANY WAY RELATED TO THE USE OF OR INABILITY TO USE THE LICENSED CONTENT, THE PROVISION OF OR FAILURE TO PROVIDE SUPPORT OR OTHER SERVICES, INFORMATION, SOFTWARE, AND RELATED CONTENT THROUGH THE LICENSED CONTENT, OR OTHERWISE ARISING OUT OF THE USE OF THE LICENSED CONTENT, OR OTHERWISE UNDER OR IN CONNECTION WITH ANY PROVISION OF THIS EULA, EVEN IN THE EVENT OF THE FAULT, TORT (INCLUDING NEGLIGENCE), MISREPRESENTATION, STRICT LIABILITY, BREACH OF CONTRACT OR BREACH OF WARRANTY OF MICROSOFT OR ANY SUPPLIER, AND EVEN IF MICROSOFT OR ANY SUPPLIER HAS BEEN ADVISED OF THE POSSIBILITY OF SUCH DAMAGES. BECAUSE SOME STATES/JURISDICTIONS DO NOT ALLOW THE EXCLUSION OR LIMITATION OF LIABILITY FOR CONSEQUENTIAL OR INCIDENTAL DAMAGES, THE ABOVE LIMITATION MAY NOT APPLY TO YOU.

17. **LIMITATION OF LIABILITY AND REMEDIES.** NOTWITHSTANDING ANY DAMAGES THAT YOU MIGHT INCUR FOR ANY REASON WHATSOEVER (INCLUDING, WITHOUT LIMITATION, ALL DAMAGES REFERENCED HEREIN AND ALL DIRECT OR GENERAL DAMAGES IN CONTRACT OR ANYTHING ELSE), THE ENTIRE LIABILITY OF MICROSOFT AND ANY OF ITS SUPPLIERS UNDER ANY PROVISION OF THIS EULA AND YOUR EXCLUSIVE REMEDY HEREUNDER SHALL BE LIMITED TO THE GREATER OF THE ACTUAL DAMAGES YOU INCUR IN REASONABLE RELIANCE ON THE LICENSED CONTENT UP TO THE AMOUNT ACTUALLY PAID BY YOU FOR THE LICENSED CONTENT OR US$5.00. THE FOREGOING LIMITATIONS, EXCLUSIONS AND DISCLAIMERS SHALL APPLY TO THE MAXIMUM EXTENT PERMITTED BY APPLICABLE LAW, EVEN IF ANY REMEDY FAILS ITS ESSENTIAL PURPOSE.

18. **APPLICABLE LAW.** If you acquired this Licensed Content in the United States, this EULA is governed by the laws of the State of Washington. If you acquired this Licensed Content in Canada, unless expressly prohibited by local law, this EULA is governed by the laws in force in the Province of Ontario, Canada; and, in respect of any dispute which may arise hereunder, you consent to the jurisdiction of the federal and provincial courts sitting in Toronto, Ontario. If you acquired this Licensed Content in the European Union, Iceland, Norway, or Switzerland, then local law applies. If you acquired this Licensed Content in any other country, then local law may apply.

19. **ENTIRE AGREEMENT; SEVERABILITY.** This EULA (including any addendum or amendment to this EULA which is included with the Licensed Content) are the entire agreement between you and Microsoft relating to the Licensed Content and the support services (if any) and they supersede all prior or contemporaneous oral or written communications, proposals and representations with respect to the Licensed Content or any other subject matter covered by this EULA. To the extent the terms of any Microsoft policies or programs for support services conflict with the terms of this EULA, the terms of this EULA shall control. If any provision of this EULA is held to be void, invalid, unenforceable or illegal, the other provisions shall continue in full force and effect.

Should you have any questions concerning this EULA, or if you desire to contact Microsoft for any reason, please use the address information enclosed in this Licensed Content to contact the Microsoft subsidiary serving your country or visit Microsoft on the World Wide Web at http://www.microsoft.com.

Si vous avez acquis votre Contenu Sous Licence Microsoft au CANADA :

DÉNI DE GARANTIES. Dans la mesure maximale permise par les lois applicables, le Contenu Sous Licence et les services de soutien technique (le cas échéant) sont fournis *TELS QUELS ET AVEC TOUS LES DÉFAUTS* par Microsoft et ses fournisseurs, lesquels par les présentes dénient toutes autres garanties et conditions expresses, implicites ou en vertu de la loi, notamment, mais sans limitation, (le cas échéant) les garanties, devoirs ou conditions implicites de qualité marchande, d'adaptation à une fin usage particulière, de fiabilité ou de disponibilité, d'exactitude ou d'exhaustivité des réponses, des résultats, des efforts déployés selon les règles de l'art, d'absence de virus et d'absence de négligence, le tout à l'égard du Contenu Sous Licence et de la prestation des services de soutien technique ou de l'omission de la 'une telle prestation des services de soutien technique ou à l'égard de la fourniture ou de l'omission de la fourniture de tous autres services, renseignements, Contenus Sous Licence, et contenu qui s'y rapporte grâce au Contenu Sous Licence ou provenant autrement de l'utilisation du Contenu Sous Licence. PAR AILLEURS, IL N'Y A AUCUNE GARANTIE OU CONDITION QUANT AU TITRE DE PROPRIÉTÉ, À LA JOUISSANCE OU LA POSSESSION PAISIBLE, À LA CONCORDANCE À UNE DESCRIPTION NI QUANT À UNE ABSENCE DE CONTREFAÇON CONCERNANT LE CONTENU SOUS LICENCE.

EXCLUSION DES DOMMAGES ACCESSOIRES, INDIRECTS ET DE CERTAINS AUTRES DOMMAGES. DANS LA MESURE MAXIMALE PERMISE PAR LES LOIS APPLICABLES, EN AUCUN CAS MICROSOFT OU SES FOURNISSEURS NE SERONT RESPONSABLES DES DOMMAGES SPÉCIAUX, CONSÉCUTIFS, ACCESSOIRES OU INDIRECTS DE QUELQUE NATURE QUE CE SOIT (NOTAMMENT, LES DOMMAGES À L'ÉGARD DU MANQUE À GAGNER OU DE LA DIVULGATION DE RENSEIGNEMENTS CONFIDENTIELS OU AUTRES, DE LA PERTE D'EXPLOITATION, DE BLESSURES CORPORELLES, DE LA VIOLATION DE LA VIE PRIVÉE, DE L'OMISSION DE REMPLIR TOUT DEVOIR, Y COMPRIS D'AGIR DE BONNE FOI OU D'EXERCER UN SOIN RAISONNABLE, DE LA NÉGLIGENCE ET DE TOUTE AUTRE PERTE PÉCUNIAIRE OU AUTRE PERTE

DE QUELQUE NATURE QUE CE SOIT) SE RAPPORTANT DE QUELQUE MANIÈRE QUE CE SOIT À L'UTILISATION DU CONTENU SOUS LICENCE OU À L'INCAPACITÉ DE S'EN SERVIR, À LA PRESTATION OU À L'OMISSION DE LA 'UNE TELLE PRESTATION DE SERVICES DE SOUTIEN TECHNIQUE OU À LA FOURNITURE OU À L'OMISSION DE LA FOURNITURE DE TOUS AUTRES SERVICES, RENSEIGNEMENTS, CONTENUS SOUS LICENCE, ET CONTENU QUI S'Y RAPPORTE GRÂCE AU CONTENU SOUS LICENCE OU PROVENANT AUTREMENT DE L'UTILISATION DU CONTENU SOUS LICENCE OU AUTREMENT AUX TERMES DE TOUTE DISPOSITION DE LA U PRÉSENTE CONVENTION EULA OU RELATIVEMENT À UNE TELLE DISPOSITION, MÊME EN CAS DE FAUTE, DE DÉLIT CIVIL (Y COMPRIS LA NÉGLIGENCE), DE RESPONSABILITÉ STRICTE, DE VIOLATION DE CONTRAT OU DE VIOLATION DE GARANTIE DE MICROSOFT OU DE TOUT FOURNISSEUR ET MÊME SI MICROSOFT OU TOUT FOURNISSEUR A ÉTÉ AVISÉ DE LA POSSIBILITÉ DE TELS DOMMAGES.

LIMITATION DE RESPONSABILITÉ ET RECOURS. MALGRÉ LES DOMMAGES QUE VOUS PUISSIEZ SUBIR POUR QUELQUE MOTIF QUE CE SOIT (NOTAMMENT, MAIS SANS LIMITATION, TOUS LES DOMMAGES SUSMENTIONNÉS ET TOUS LES DOMMAGES DIRECTS OU GÉNÉRAUX OU AUTRES), LA SEULE RESPONSABILITÉ 'OBLIGATION INTÉGRALE DE MICROSOFT ET DE L'UN OU L'AUTRE DE SES FOURNISSEURS AUX TERMES DE TOUTE DISPOSITION DEU LA PRÉSENTE CONVENTION EULA ET VOTRE RECOURS EXCLUSIF À L'ÉGARD DE TOUT CE QUI PRÉCÈDE SE LIMITE AU PLUS ÉLEVÉ ENTRE LES MONTANTS SUIVANTS : LE MONTANT QUE VOUS AVEZ RÉELLEMENT PAYÉ POUR LE CONTENU SOUS LICENCE OU 5,00 $US. LES LIMITES, EXCLUSIONS ET DÉNIS QUI PRÉCÈDENT (Y COMPRIS LES CLAUSES CI-DESSUS), S'APPLIQUENT DANS LA MESURE MAXIMALE PERMISE PAR LES LOIS APPLICABLES, MÊME SI TOUT RECOURS N'ATTEINT PAS SON BUT ESSENTIEL.

À moins que cela ne soit prohibé par le droit local applicable, la présente Convention est régie par les lois de la province d'Ontario, Canada. Vous consentez Chacune des parties à la présente reconnaît irrévocablement à la compétence des tribunaux fédéraux et provinciaux siégeant à Toronto, dans de la province d'Ontario et consent à instituer tout litige qui pourrait découler de la présente auprès des tribunaux situés dans le district judiciaire de York, province d'Ontario.

Au cas où vous auriez des questions concernant cette licence ou que vous désiriez vous mettre en rapport avec Microsoft pour quelque raison que ce soit, veuillez utiliser l'information contenue dans le Contenu Sous Licence pour contacter la filiale de succursale Microsoft desservant votre pays, dont l'adresse est fournie dans ce produit, ou visitez écrivez à : Microsoft sur le World Wide Web à http://www.microsoft.com

Contents

About This Course

This section provides you with a brief description of the course, audience, suggested prerequisites, and course objectives.

Description

This five-day, instructor-led course directly addresses the Microsoft Certified Systems Administrator (MCSA) and Microsoft Certified Systems Engineer (MCSE) skills paths for information technology (IT) professional security practitioners. This course provides students with the current standard best practices and a clear understanding of how Microsoft® Internet Security and Acceleration (ISA) Server 2004 fits into the larger security infrastructure. Additionally, students will be able to identify security threats and vulnerabilities and respond to and recover from security incidents.

The course will cover security concepts that are unique to ISA Server and will teach implementation of security concepts that are specific to Microsoft products and technologies. After completing this course, students will be prepared to successfully implement and manage ISA Server 2004.

This course also maps directly to Exam 70-350: *Implementing Microsoft Internet Security and Acceleration Server 2004.*

Exam 70-350 is an elective exam for the MCSA and the MCSE certifications and a core exam for the MSCE: Security and MCSA: Security certifications.

Audience

This course is intended for IT professionals who are responsible for Internet edge firewalls, departmental or back end firewalls, branch office firewalls, back-to-back perimeter networks, integrated firewall and caching servers, or application layer firewalls.

This course is also intended for IT managers and technology implementers. Key needs include simplifying ongoing management and reducing support costs by eliminating hacks, outages, viruses, and security breaches due to misconfiguration.

This course is also intended for anyone who wants to pursue a security specialist role and associated credential.

Job role:	Systems administrator or systems engineer
Skill level:	200-300
Product and technology experience:	Experience implementing a Microsoft Windows® 2000/2003 Active Directory® environment. Experience with security concepts such as firewalls, caching/proxy, and administrative scripting. Experience with organizational resources such as Web, FTP, and Microsoft Exchange servers (students not expected to have detailed knowledge) and with shared resources and network services such as DHCP, DNS, and WINS.
Preferred learning style:	Instructor presentation with facilitated guided discovery labs.

Student prerequisites   This course requires that students meet the following prerequisites:

- Successful completion of Course 2810: *Fundamentals of Network Security* or equivalent knowledge of networking security.

- Successful completion of Course 2273: *Managing and Maintaining a Microsoft Windows Server™ 2003 Environment* or equivalent knowledge of the Windows Server 2003 operating system and network concepts, or equivalent knowledge of the Windows 2000 Server operating system and network concepts.

- Experience implementing network resources such as Web, FTP, and Exchange servers. Detailed knowledge about deploying these resources is not required.

Course objectives   After completing this course, the student will be able to:

- Describe the functionality provided by ISA Server 2004, and explain valid deployment scenarios for ISA Server 2004.

- Install and maintain ISA Server 2004, and install and configure ISA Server clients.

- Configure secure access to Internet resources for internal network clients using ISA Server 2004.

- Configure ISA Server 2004 as a firewall between the Internet and the internal network.

- Configure secure access to internal network resources for Internet clients who are using Web and server publishing rules.

- Configure ISA Server to provide secure access to Exchange Server for servers and clients located on the Internet.

- Implement application and Web filters on ISA Server 2004.

- Implement a virtual private network (VPN) for remote clients and remote networks using ISA Server 2004.

- Implement Web proxy caching on ISA Server 2004.

- Monitor server performance, security, and usage on ISA Server 2004.

- Implement ISA Server 2004 Enterprise Edition.

Student Materials Compact Disc Contents

The Student Materials compact disc (CD) contains the following files and folders:

- *Autorun.inf*. When the CD is inserted into the CD drive, this file opens StartCD.exe.

- *Default.htm*. This file opens the Student Materials Web page. It provides you with resources pertaining to this course, including additional reading, review and lab answers, lab files, multimedia presentations, and course-related Web sites.

- *Readme.txt*. This file explains how to install the software for viewing the Student Materials CD and its contents, and how to open the Student Materials Web page.

- *StartCD.exe*. When the CD is inserted into the CD drive, or when you double-click the **StartCD.exe** file, this file opens the CD and allows you to browse the Student Materials CD.

- *StartCD.ini*. This file contains instructions to launch StartCD.exe.

- *Addread*. This folder contains additional reading pertaining to this course.

- *Appendix*. This folder contains appendix files for this course.

- *Flash*. This folder contains the installer for the Macromedia Flash browser plug-in.

- *Fonts*. This folder contains fonts that may be required to view the Microsoft Word documents that are included with this course.

- *Media*. This folder contains files that are used in multimedia presentations for this course.

- *Mplayer*. This folder contains the file to update the codecs for Microsoft Windows Media Player.

- *Webfiles*. This folder contains the files that are required to view the course Web page. To open the Web page, open Windows Explorer, and in the root directory of the CD, double-click **StartCD.exe**.

- *Wordview*. This folder contains the Word Viewer that is used to view any Word document (.doc) files that are included on the CD.

Document Conventions

The following conventions are used in course materials to distinguish elements of the text.

Convention	Use
Bold	Represents commands, command options, and syntax that must be typed exactly as shown. It also indicates commands on menus and buttons, dialog box titles and options, and icon and menu names.
Italic	In syntax statements or descriptive text, indicates argument names or placeholders for variable information. Italic is also used for introducing new terms, for book titles, and for emphasis in the text.
Title Capitals	Indicate domain names, user names, computer names, directory names, and folder and file names, except when specifically referring to case-sensitive names. Unless otherwise indicated, you can use lowercase letters when you type a directory name or file name in a dialog box or at a command prompt.
ALL CAPITALS	Indicate the names of keys, key sequences, and key combinations—for example, ALT+SPACEBAR.
`monospace`	Represents code samples or examples of screen text.
[ ]	In syntax statements, enclose optional items. For example, [*filename*] in command syntax indicates that you can choose to type a file name with the command. Type only the information within the brackets, not the brackets themselves.
{ }	In syntax statements, enclose required items. Type only the information within the braces, not the braces themselves.
|	In syntax statements, separates an either/or choice.
▶	Indicates a procedure with sequential steps.
...	In syntax statements, specifies that the preceding item may be repeated.
. . .	Represents an omitted portion of a code sample.

Introduction

Contents

Introduction

- Name
- Company affiliation
- Title/function
- Job responsibility
- Network security experience
- Microsoft® Internet Security and Acceleration Server 2000 experience
- Expectations for the course

Course Materials

> - Name card
> - Student workbook
> - Student Materials compact disc
> - Course evaluation

The following materials are included with your kit:

- *Name card*. Write your name on both sides of the name card.

- *Student workbook*. The student workbook contains the material covered in class, in addition to the hands-on lab exercises.

- *Student Materials compact disc (CD)*. The Student Materials CD contains the Web page that provides you with links to resources pertaining to this course, including additional readings, review and lab answers, lab files, multimedia presentations, and course-related Web sites.

> **Note** To open the Web page, insert the Student Materials CD into the CD-ROM drive, and then in the root directory of the CD, double-click **StartCD.exe**.

- *Assessments*. There are assessments for each lesson, located on the Student Materials CD. You can use them as pre-assessments to identify areas of difficulty, or you can use them as post-assessments to validate learning.

- *Course evaluation*. You will have the opportunity to provide feedback on the course, training facility, and instructor by completing an online evaluation near the end of the course.

To provide additional comments or feedback on the course, send e-mail to support@mscourseware.com. To inquire about the Microsoft Certified Professional (MCP) program, send e-mail to mcphelp@microsoft.com.

Prerequisites

* Completion of Course 2810: *Fundamentals of Network Security*, or equivalent knowledge and skills

* Completion of Course 2273: *Managing and Maintaining a Microsoft® Windows Server™ 2003 Environment*, or equivalent knowledge and skills

* Experience implementing network resources such as Web, FTP, and Microsoft Exchange servers

This course requires that you meet the following prerequisites:

■ Successful completion of Course 2810: *Fundamentals of Network Security*, or equivalent knowledge of networking security.

■ Successful completion of Course 2273: *Managing and Maintaining a Microsoft® Windows Server™ 2003 Environment*, or equivalent knowledge of the Windows Server 2003 operating system and network concepts, or equivalent knowledge of Microsoft Windows® 2000 Server operating system and network concepts.

■ Experience implementing network resources such as Web, FTP, and Microsoft Exchange servers. Detailed knowledge about deploying these resources is not required.

Course Outline

- **Module 1: Overview of Microsoft ISA Server 2004**
- **Module 2: Installing and Maintaining ISA Server**
- **Module 3: Enabling Access to Internet Resources**
- **Module 4: Configuring ISA Server as a Firewall**
- **Module 5: Configuring Access to Internal Resources**

Module 1, "Overview of Microsoft ISA Server 2004," provides an introduction to the core functionality provided by Microsoft Internet Security and Acceleration (ISA) Server 2004: proxy and caching, firewall service, and VPN server. This module also presents an overview of how ISA Server integrates with other security practices in providing a defense-in-depth approach to network security. This module also describes the most common deployment scenarios for ISA Server 2004.

Module 2, "Installing and Maintaining ISA Server," explains how to install and perform the initial configuration and maintenance of ISA Server 2004. The module explains how to install and configure the ISA clients, as well.

Module 3, "Enabling Access to Internet Resources," describes how to use ISA Server 2004 to provide secure access to Internet resources for internal network clients. ISA Server 2004 provides several configuration options for providing this secure access.

Module 4, "Configuring ISA Server as a Firewall," provides information on how to configure ISA Server 2004 to act as a firewall between the Internet and the internal network. ISA Server can use multiple layers of inspection to filter the network traffic.

Module 5, "Configuring Access to Internal Resources," describes how to use Web and server publishing rules to publish internal network resources to the Internet without compromising internal network security. Web publishing rules determine how ISA Server deals with HTTP requests from the Internet that are intended for internal Web servers. Server publishing rules define how ISA Server responds to requests from the Internet for other network resources on the internal network.

Course Outline *(continued)*

> - **Module 6: Integrating ISA Server 2004 and Microsoft Exchange Server**
> - **Module 7: Advanced Application and Web Filtering**
> - **Module 8: Configuring Virtual Private Network Access for Remote Clients and Networks**
> - **Module 9: Implementing Caching**
> - **Module 10: Monitoring ISA Server 2004**

Module 6, "Integrating ISA Server 2004 and Microsoft Exchange Server," explains how to use ISA Server 2004 to provide, from the Internet, secure access to Microsoft Exchange Server. ISA Server 2004 provides several options for securing Exchange Server and for securing client connections to Exchange.

Module 7, "Advanced Application and Web Filtering," describes how application and Web filtering work in ISA Server 2004. By implementing these filters, ISA Server administrators can configure very specific filtering of traffic that flows through the ISA server. For example, HTTP filtering can be enabled to block traffic based on file extensions or on specific virus signatures.

Module 8, "Configuring Virtual Private Network Access for Remote Clients and Networks," describes how to use ISA Server 2004 to implement a virtual private network (VPN) solution to provide secure access to internal network resources for remote users or for users in other company locations. ISA Server 2004 provides an integrated VPN solution that includes a network quarantine solution.

Module 9, "Implementing Caching," explains how ISA Server 2004 can be configured to cache much of the content that clients request from the Internet. This content is stored on the ISA server, so that the next time a user requests the same information, it is provided to the client from the ISA server cache. This provides a quicker response to the client.

Module 10, "Monitoring ISA Server 2004," describes how to monitor ISA Server 2004. This monitoring might include real-time monitoring and configuring alerts that provide detailed information about the current activity on the ISA server. This monitoring also includes configuring logging and reports that provide documentation of server utilization.

Course Outline *(continued)*

- **Module 11: Implementing ISA Server 2004 Enterprise Edition**
- **Module 12: Implementing ISA Server 2004 Enterprise Edition: Back-to-Back Firewall Scenario**
- **Module 13: Implementing ISA Server 2004 Enterprise Edition: Site-to-Site VPN Scenario**

Module 11, "Implementing ISA Server 2004 Enterprise Edition," describes the differences between ISA Server 2004 Standard Edition and ISA Server 2004 Enterprise Edition and then provides details about the Enterprise Edition features that enhance scalability. This module also includes details about how to install and manage ISA Server 2004 Enterprise Edition.

Module 12, "Implementing ISA Server 2004 Enterprise Edition: Back-to-Back Firewall Scenario," describes one of the deployment scenarios for ISA Server 2004 Enterprise Edition. This module introduces the complexities of implementing a back-to-back firewall configuration and then provides guidelines for deploying this configuration. In the lab, the students will implement and test a back-to-back firewall scenario.

Module 13, "Implementing ISA Server 2004 Enterprise Edition: Site-to-Site VPN Scenario" describes a second deployment scenario for ISA Server 2004 Enterprise Edition. This module describes how to implement network load balancing for a site-to-site VPN and how to implement a Configuration Storage server and configure firewall policies in a branch office scenario. In the lab, the students will implement and test a site-to-site deployment.

Demonstration: Using Virtual PC

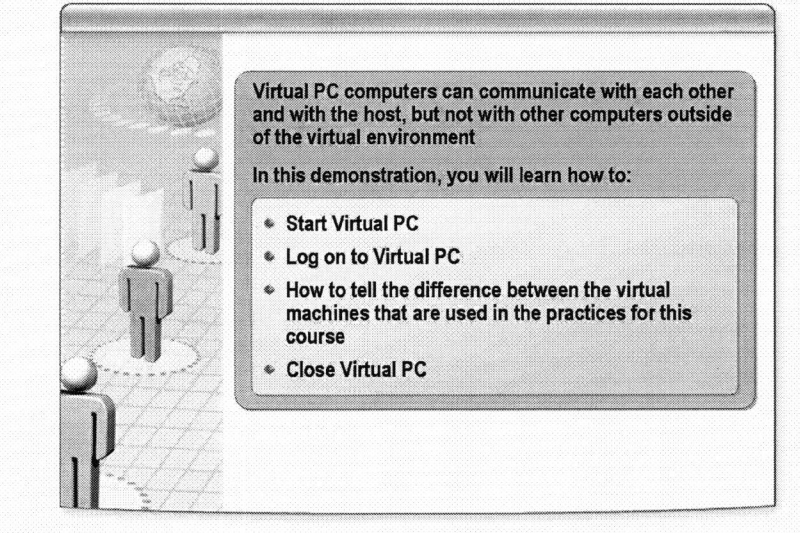

In this demonstration, your instructor will help familiarize you with the Microsoft Virtual PC environment in which you will work to complete the practices and labs in this course. You will learn:

- How to start Virtual PC.

- How to log on to Virtual PC.

- How to tell the difference between the virtual machines used in the practices and those used in the labs for this course.

- That the virtual machines can communicate with each other and with the host computer, but not with computers outside of the virtual environment. (For example, no Internet access is available from the virtual environment.)

- How to close Virtual PC.

Microsoft Learning

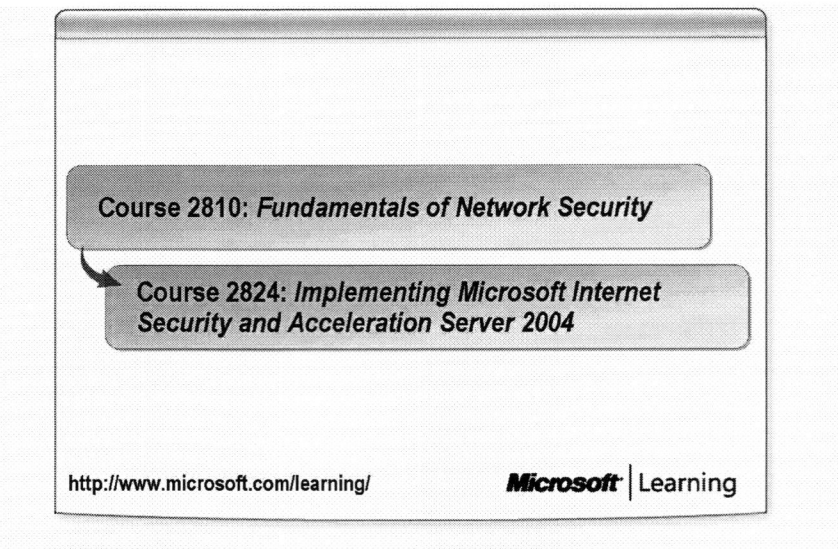

Introduction

Microsoft Learning develops Official Microsoft Learning Products for computer professionals who design, develop, support, implement, or manage solutions with Microsoft products and technologies. These learning products provide comprehensive, skills-based training in instructor-led and online formats.

Additional recommended courses

Each course relates in some way to another course. A related course might be a prerequisite, a follow-up course in a recommended series, or a course that offers additional training.

It is recommended that you take the following course:

- 2810: Fundamentals of Network Security

Other related courses might become available in the future, so for up-to-date information about recommended courses, visit the Microsoft Learning Web site.

Microsoft Learning information

For more information, visit the Microsoft Learning Web site at http://www.microsoft.com/learning/.

Microsoft Learning Product Types

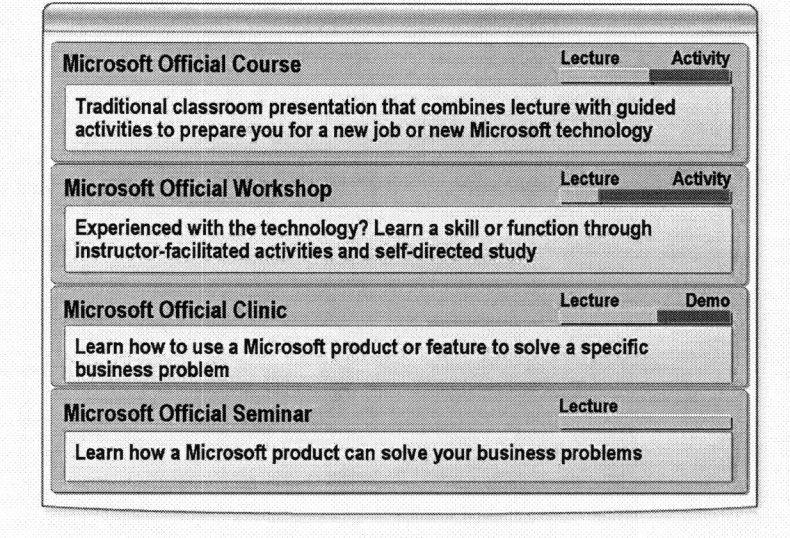

Microsoft Learning offers four instructor-led product types. Each type is specific to a particular audience type and level of experience. The different product types also tend to suit different learning styles. These types are as follows:

- Microsoft Official Courses are for information technology (IT) professionals and developers who are new to a particular product or technology, and for experienced individuals who prefer to learn in a traditional classroom format. Courses provide a relevant and guided learning experience that combines lecture and practice to deliver thorough coverage of a Microsoft product or technology. Courses are designed to address the needs of learners engaged in planning, design, implementation, management, and support phases of the technology adoption lifecycle. They provide detailed information by focusing on concepts and principles, reference content, and in-depth, hands-on lab activities to ensure knowledge transfer. Typically, the content of a course is broad, addressing a wide range of tasks necessary for a job role.

- Microsoft Official Workshops are for knowledgeable IT professionals and developers who learn best by doing and exploring. Workshops provide a hands-on learning experience in which participants use Microsoft products in a safe and collaborative environment based on real-world scenarios. Workshops are the learning products where students learn by doing, through scenario, troubleshooting hands-on labs, targeted reviews, information resources, and best practices, with instructor facilitation.

- Microsoft Official Clinics are for IT professionals, developers, and technical decision makers. Each clinic offers a detailed "how to" presentation that describes the features and functionality of an existing or new Microsoft product or technology and showcases product demonstrations and solutions. Clinics focus on how specific features will solve business problems.

- Microsoft Official Seminars are for business decision makers. Through featured business scenarios, case studies, and success stories, seminars provide a dynamic presentation of early and relevant information on Microsoft products and technology solutions that enable decision makers to make critical business decisions. Microsoft Official Seminars are concise, engaging, direct-from-the-source learning products that show how emerging Microsoft products and technologies help our customers serve their customers.

Microsoft Certified Professional Program

Exam number and title	Core exam for the following track	Elective exam for the following track
70-350: *Implementing Microsoft Internet Security and Acceleration Server (ISA) 2004*	MCSA: Security MCSE: Security	MCSA MCSE

http://www.microsoft.com/learning/

Microsoft
C E R T I F I E D
Professional

Introduction

Microsoft Learning offers a variety of certification credentials for developers and IT professionals. The Microsoft Certified Professional (MCP) program is the leading certification program for validating your experience and skills, keeping you competitive in today's changing business environment.

Related certification exams

This course helps students prepare for Exam 70-350: *Implementing Microsoft Internet Security and Acceleration Server (ISA) 2004.*

Exam 70-350 is an elective exam for the MCSA and the MCSE certifications and a core exam for the MSCE: Security and MCSA: Security certifications.

MCP certifications

The MCP program includes the following certifications.

- MCSA on Microsoft Windows Server 2003

  The Microsoft Certified Systems Administrator (MCSA) certification is designed for professionals who implement, manage, and troubleshoot existing network and system environments based on the Windows Server 2003 platform. Implementation responsibilities include installing and configuring parts of systems. Management responsibilities include administering and supporting systems.

- MCSE on Microsoft Windows Server 2003

  The Microsoft Certified Systems Engineer (MCSE) credential is the premier certification for professionals who analyze business requirements and design and implement the infrastructure for business solutions based on the Windows Server 2003 platform. Implementation responsibilities include installing, configuring, and troubleshooting network systems.

- MCAD

  The Microsoft Certified Application Developer (MCAD) for Microsoft .NET credential is appropriate for professionals who use Microsoft technologies to develop and maintain department-level applications, components, Web or desktop clients, or back-end data services, or work in teams developing enterprise applications. The credential covers job tasks ranging from developing to deploying and maintaining these solutions.

- MCSD

  The Microsoft Certified Solution Developer (MCSD) credential is the premier certification for professionals who design and develop leading-edge business solutions with Microsoft development tools, technologies, platforms, and the Windows DNA architecture. The types of applications MCSDs can develop include desktop applications and multi-user, Web-based, N-tier, and transaction-based applications. The credential covers job tasks ranging from analyzing business requirements to maintaining solutions.

- MCDBA on Microsoft SQL Server™ 2000

  The Microsoft Certified Database Administrator (MCDBA) credential is the premier certification for professionals who implement and administer SQL Server databases. This certification is appropriate for individuals who derive physical database designs, develop logical data models, create physical databases, create data services by using Transact-SQL, manage and maintain databases, configure and manage security, monitor and optimize databases, and install and configure SQL Server.

- MCP

  The Microsoft Certified Professional (MCP) credential is for individuals who have the skills to successfully implement a Microsoft product or technology as part of a business solution in an organization. Hands-on experience with the product is necessary to successfully achieve certification.

- MCT

  Microsoft Certified Trainers (MCTs) demonstrate the instructional and technical skills that qualify them to deliver Official Microsoft Learning Products through Microsoft Certified Technical Education Centers (Microsoft CTECs).

Certification requirements

The certification requirements differ for each certification category and are specific to the products and job functions addressed by the certification. To become a Microsoft Certified Professional, you must pass rigorous certification exams that provide a valid and reliable measure of technical proficiency and expertise.

For More Information   See the Microsoft Learning Web site at http://www.microsoft.com/learning/.

You can also send e-mail to mcphelp@microsoft.com if you have specific certification questions.

Acquiring the skills tested by an MCP exam

Official Microsoft Learning Products can help you develop the skills that you need to do your job. They also complement the experience that you gain while working with Microsoft products and technologies. However, no one-to-one correlation exists between Official Microsoft Learning Products and MCP exams. Microsoft does not expect or intend for the courses to be the sole preparation method for passing MCP exams. Practical product knowledge and experience is also necessary to pass MCP exams.

To prepare for MCP exams, use the preparation guides available for each exam. Each Exam Preparation Guide contains exam-specific information such as a list of the topics on which you will be tested. These guides are available on the Microsoft Learning Web site at http://www.microsoft.com/learning/.

Facilities

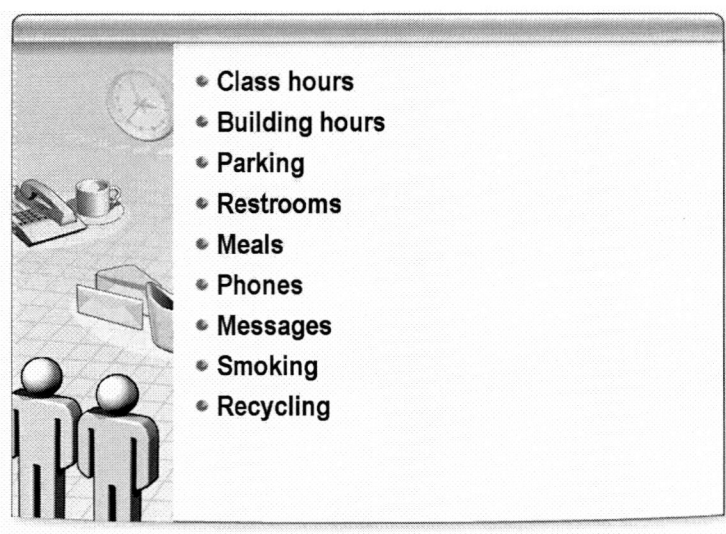

- Class hours
- Building hours
- Parking
- Restrooms
- Meals
- Phones
- Messages
- Smoking
- Recycling

Microsoft®

Module 1:
Overview of Microsoft
ISA Server 2004

Contents

Overview

- Introducing Microsoft ISA Server 2004
- Deployment Scenarios for ISA Server 2004

Introduction

Creating a secure networking environment is one of the most important tasks that network administrators must perform. Microsoft® ISA Server 2004 is a critical component in creating this secure network. To deploy ISA Server 2004, you must first understand the functionality provided by ISA Server 2004. The first part of this module introduces the core functionality provided by ISA Server 2004. ISA Server 2004 can be configured as a proxy and caching server, firewall, and virtual private network (VPN) remote access and gateway server. As well, this module describes the most common deployment scenarios for ISA Server 2004.

Objectives

After completing this module, you will be able to:

- Discuss the features and functionality available in ISA Server 2004 Standard Edition.

- List common deployment scenarios for ISA Server 2004.

Lesson: Introducing ISA Server 2004

* What Are the Benefits of ISA Server 2004?
* Multimedia: Overview of ISA Server 2004 Functionality
* ISA Server 2004 Management Interface
* ISA Server 2004 Enterprise Edition Features
* Differences Between ISA Server 2000 and ISA Server 2004

Introduction

ISA Server 2004 offers a complete solution for providing an access point between the Internet and the corporate internal network. ISA Server 2004 can operate as a firewall, limiting access to and from the internal organization network. ISA Server 2004 also provides a proxy and caching server enabling access to resources on the Internet to internal network clients. In addition, it provides a virtual private network (VPN) server and gateway providing access to internal network resources. This lesson provides an overview of this core functionality provided by ISA Server, the management interface that is used to administer it, and the differences between ISA Server 2004 and ISA Server 2000.

Lesson objectives

After completing this lesson, you will be able to:

- List the benefits of deploying ISA Server 2004.
- Describe the firewall, VPN server, and caching features of ISA Server 2004.
- Identify the management tools available to manage ISA Server 2004.
- Describe the ISA Server Enterprise Edition features.
- Describe the differences between ISA Server 2004 and ISA Server 2000.

What Are the Benefits of ISA Server 2004?

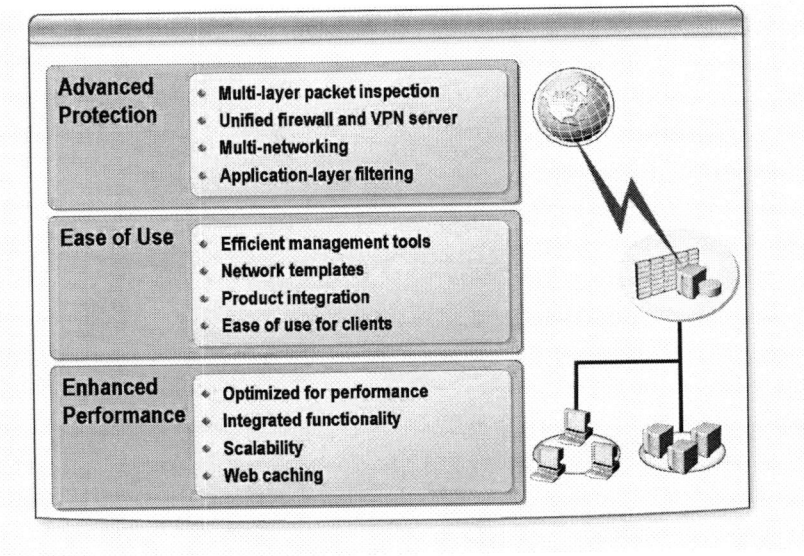

Introduction

ISA Server 2004 provides an advanced, multilayer firewall, virtual private network (VPN), and Web proxy and cache solution that can be used to create a secure connection between the Internet and the company's internal network.

Advanced protection

One of the benefits of deploying ISA Server 2004 is that it provides advanced protection for your network. Features include:

- *Multilayer packet inspection.* ISA Server 2004 operates as a firewall that examines every packet flowing through the ISA Server. The inspection includes packet filtering, stateful filtering, and application filtering. This multilayer inspection helps protect Internet Information Server (IIS), Exchange Server, Microsoft SharePoint®, and other internal network resources from hackers, viruses, and unauthorized use.

- *Application-layer filtering.* Most new security threats happen at the application layer. ISA Server 2004 provides advanced application-layer filtering that enables complex application traffic to the Internet while ensuring high levels of security, performance, and protection against these types of attacks.

- *Unified firewall and VPN server.* ISA Server 2004 provides a single management point for configuring VPN access to the internal network and integrates the firewall and VPN server functionality and management. As a VPN server, ISA Server 2004 is the VPN endpoint which means that it can inspect network packets and enable VPN quarantine.

- *Multi-networking.* ISA Server 2004 supports multiple networks and enables the configuration of network and firewall rules that filter the flow of traffic between all networks.

Ease of use

ISA Server 2004 also includes features that make it easy to use:

- *Efficient management tools.* The ISA Server management console is easy to learn and provides a single interface for its configuring and monitoring. ISA Server also provides a single rule base, so that all firewall rules can be viewed and modified in a single location. This makes it easier for new security administrators to deploy ISA Server 2004 while making it easier to avoid security breaches due to firewall misconfiguration.

- *Network templates.* ISA Server provides network templates that make its deployment easy into existing IT environments as an edge, departmental, or branch office firewall. Multiple firewall rules can be configured by applying the network template.

- *Product integration.* ISA Server's integration with Microsoft Windows® Active Directory® directory service, third-party VPN solutions, and other existing security products simplifies the task of securing corporate applications, users, and data.

- *Ease of use for clients.* By integrating ISA Server 2004 with your Active Directory infrastructure or by using a Remote Authentication Dial-In User Service (RADIUS) server to provide authentication, you can make the use of ISA Server 2004 transparent to internal clients. For external clients, ISA Server provides single sign-on capability through multiple Internet-standard authentication mechanisms.

Enhanced performance

ISA Server 2004 provides fast and secure access to corporate applications and data, such as Microsoft Exchange Server and internal Web servers.

- *Optimized for performance.* ISA Server is designed to provide high-performance infrastructure for enabling both inbound and outbound Internet access. The firewall architecture is designed to optimize packet inspection at multiple layers.

- *Integrated functionality.* ISA Server provides an integrated single-server solution that puts only the necessary services at the edge of the network, including firewall security, VPN, and Web cache.

- *Scalability.* As your network grows, ISA Server supports scalability with a flexible multi-network architecture and options for deploying multiple ISA Servers, either in the same company location, or across multiple locations.

- *Web caching.* ISA Server 2004 enhances network performance and reduces bandwidth usage for Internet access with Web caching so that frequently accessed information from the Internet is stored on the ISA Server.

Multimedia: Overview of ISA Server 2004 Functionality

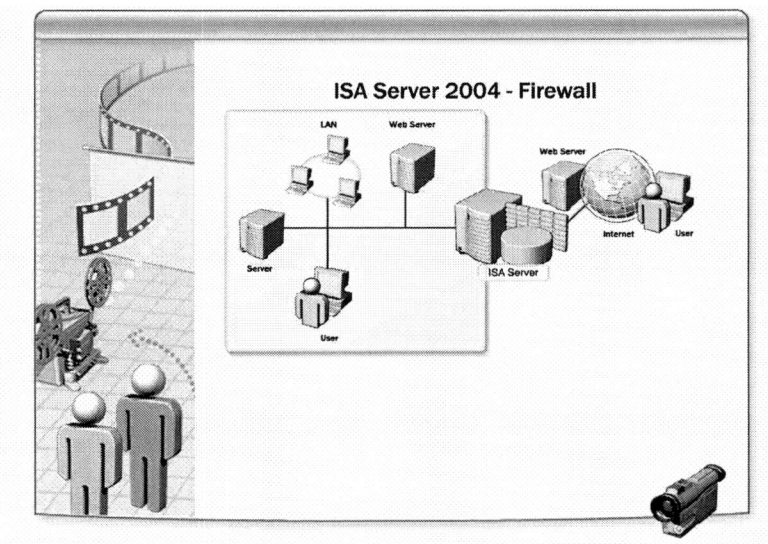

This animation presents a high-level overview of the core functionality provided by ISA Server 2004.

Tip To view the Overview of ISA Server 2004 presentation later on your own, open the Web page on the Student Materials compact disc, click **Multimedia**, and then click the title of the presentation.

ISA Server 2004 Management Interface

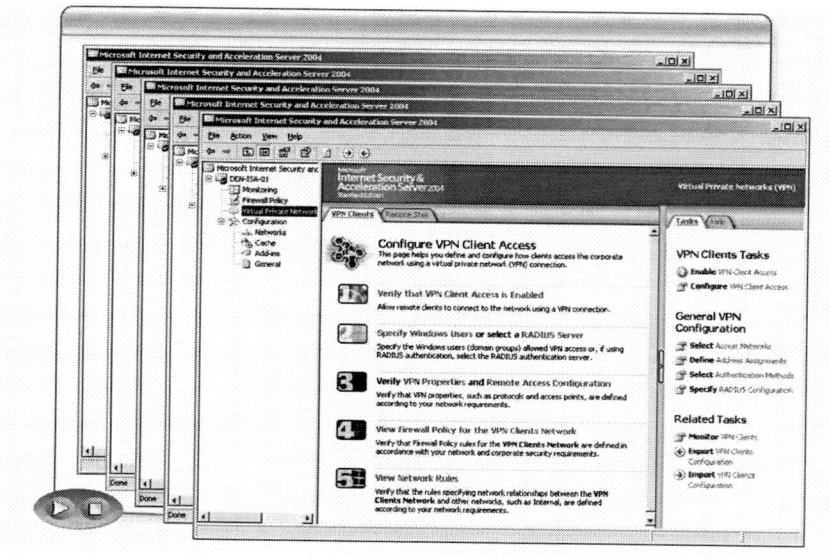

Introduction

One of the features of ISA Server 2004 is the new management interface. The ISA Server management interface provides a single interface for monitoring and managing ISA Server 2004.

Management console features

The new management interface has a number of features:

- *Uses the Microsoft Management Console (MMC).* Many of the components that are common to all MMCs include the tree view for navigation with the details pane for detailed information, configuration wizards, context-sensitive help, and typical dialog boxes. Because the MMC is already a familiar interface for most administrators, the ISA Server management interface does not require any additional learning time.

- *Getting Started page.* The ISA Server management console opens to a Getting Started page when it is first opened. This page provides an overview of the steps required to configure ISA Server with links to the specific locations within the interface where the configuration actions will be performed. By following the steps outlined on the Getting Started page, you can implement a secure deployment of ISA Server 2004.

- *Monitoring Dashboard.* The management console provides a single interface for monitoring the ISA Server performance and security-related information. The dashboard provides additional tabs that can be accessed to provide detailed monitoring information.

- *Single firewall rule base and policy editor.* All system policy and firewall rules are displayed in a single interface. From this interface, you can also create or modify all firewall or system policy rules as well as manage server publishing rules.

- *Context-sensitive task lists*. Most console pages provide a context-sensitive task list that provides a list of all relevant tasks that you can perform within the specific context. The task list includes links to wizards or dialog boxes where you can complete the task.

- *Context-sensitive toolbox*. Many console pages also include a context-sensitive toolbox. The toolbox presents a list of relevant objects that you can modify based on the context.

- *Network templates*. Much of the management of ISA Server 2004 can be done through scenario-based wizards. One example of these types of wizards is the network template wizard, which enables you to pick a network scenario that matches your deployment scenario, and then you can use the wizard to configure many of the firewall rules that are appropriate for that network template.

- *Consolidated VPN management*. ISA Server 2004 uses and extends the Routing and Remote Access Service (RRAS) on Windows 2000 Server or Microsoft Windows Server™ 2003 to enable VPN access. However, all VPN configuration is performed in the ISA Server management interface.

ISA Server 2004 Enterprise Edition Features

* ISA Server 2004 Enterprise Edition provides enhanced scalability by:
  * Providing centralized storage and configuration of the ISA Server configuration data
  * Supporting CARP for distributed caching
  * Providing NLB integration

Introduction

ISA Server 2004 is available in two versions, Standard Edition and Enterprise Edition. The two editions provide similar functionality. The most significant difference between the two versions is that Enterprise Edition provides enhanced scalability. Specifically, ISA Server 2004 Enterprise Edition enhances scalability by:

- Providing centralized storage and configuration of the ISA Server configuration data.
- Supporting Cache Array Routing Protocol (CARP) for distributed caching.
- Providing Network Load Balancing (NLB) integration.

Centralized storage of configuration data

One of the primary differences between Standard Edition and Enterprise Edition is the manner in which the two versions store their configuration information. Standard Edition stores its configuration information in the local computer registry. This means that if you want to deploy two computers running Standard Edition with the same ISA Server configuration, you must install and configure one server, export the configuration, and then import it into the second server. If you need to change the configuration, you must make the changes on both servers.

ISA Server Enterprise Edition stores its configuration information in a separate directory. When you install Enterprise Edition, you must configure one or more Configuration Storage servers. The Configuration Storage server uses Active Directory Application Mode (ADAM) to store the configuration information for all ISA Server computers in the organization. Because ADAM can be installed on multiple servers and the data can be replicated between the servers, you can have multiple Configuration Storage servers.

You can configure enterprise policies on the Configuration Storage server. Enterprise policies define firewall policies and policy elements that can be applied to one or more arrays in the organization. You can also configure arrays and array policies. Arrays are groups of ISA Server computers that share the same array policy. After installing the Configuration Storage server and creating the enterprise and array policies, you can install the ISA Server services on a computer and assign the computer to a specific array. The enterprise and array policies will be assigned automatically to each ISA Server computer in the array.

To change the ISA Server Enterprise Edition configuration, you simply change the information in the Configuration Storage server. The Enterprise Edition computers periodically access the Configuration Storage server to check whether there are any configuration changes. If there are changes, the servers will update their local (registry-based) storage to reflect the recent changes.

Support for the Cache Array Routing Protocol

ISA Server 2004 Enterprise Edition provides enhanced scalability by enabling shared Web caching across all the ISA Server computers in an array. With Enterprise Edition, multiple ISA Server computers can be configured as a single logical cache so that the caching capacity for all of the ISA Server computers is combined.

To enable this feature, ISA Server uses the Cache Array Routing Protocol (CARP). When a user requests a page from the Internet, CARP determines which ISA Server in the array will retrieve and cache the requested item. When another user requests the same page, CARP again determines which ISA Server computer in the array has cached the page, and the client request is sent to that ISA Server. ISA Server uses CARP to optimize Web caching, which means that the ISA Server caching can be scaled to almost any size.

Integration of Network Load Balancing

The third additional feature available with Enterprise Edition is the integration of network load balancing (NLB) with ISA Server. NLB is a Windows network component available with Windows 2000 Server and Windows Server 2003 that enables load balancing of IP traffic across a number of hosts, helping to enhance the scalability and availability of IP-based services. NLB also provides high availability by detecting host failures and automatically redistributing traffic to surviving hosts. With NLB, several computers can be clustered so that the entire group of servers shares a single IP address. When client computers connect to the NLB cluster, the client connections are automatically distributed across all of the servers in the cluster. If one of the servers is not available, the client connections are redirected to the available servers.

With ISA Server 2004 Standard Edition, you can configure NLB manually. With Enterprise Edition, NLB is integrated so that NLB can be managed by means of ISA Server management. ISA Server also provides NLB health monitoring and manages the failover from one ISA Server computer in the cluster to another. During NLB failover, all of the functionality provided by one of the computers in the cluster is transferred to another computer or computers in the cluster.

Note   Module 11, "Implementing ISA Server 2004 Enterprise Edition," in Course 2824, *Implementing Microsoft Internet Security and Acceleration Server 2004*, provides detailed information about these ISA Server Enterprise Edition features. In Module 12, "Implementing ISA Server 2004 Enterprise Edition: Back-to-Back Firewall Scenario," and Module 13, "Implementing ISA Server 2004 Enterprise Edition: Site-to-Site VPN Scenario," you will use Enterprise Edition to implement two ISA Server deployment scenarios.

Differences Between ISA Server 2000 and ISA Server 2004

* Multiple network support
* Policies assigned per network
* Routed and NAT network relationships
* Extended protocol support
* Advanced application filtering
* Enhanced authentication options
* VPN and quarantine integration
* Stateful inspection for VPN
* Export and import
* Delegated permissions wizard for firewall administrator roles

Introduction

ISA Server 2004 provides numerous enhancements over the functionality provided by ISA Server 2000.

New features in ISA Server 2004

The following table provides an overview of the new features available in Server 2004.

Feature	Description
Multiple network support	ISA Server 2004 supports multiple networks, each with distinct relationships to other networks. ISA Server 2000 supported only three networks, the internal network defined by the local address table (LAT), the external network, and the perimeter network (also known as demilitarized zone and DMZ). ISA Server 2004 includes a VPN and VPN quarantine network. You can configure an unlimited number of networks on ISA Server 2004.
Policies assigned per network	In ISA Server 2004, all access policies are defined relative to the networks, and not just relative to the internal network. Because of limited network support in ISA Server 2000, all access policies defined access to or from the internal network or use static packet filters to configure access between the perimeter network and the external network. In ISA Server 2004, you can define distinct access rules for each network on the server. For example, you can create a perimeter network that is separate from the internal network and configure different access rules for this network.

(continued)

Feature	Description
Routed and NAT network relationships	ISA Server 2004 supports both routed and network address translation (NAT) relationships between networks. In some cases, you may want more secure, less transparent communication between the networks; for these scenarios you can define a NAT relationship. In other scenarios, you may want to route traffic through ISA Server 2004; in this case, you can define a routed relationship.
Extended protocol support	ISA Server 2004 extends ISA Server 2000 functionality by letting you control access and usage of any protocol, including Internet Protocol (IP)-level protocols. This enhancement enables features such as publishing Point-to-Point Tunneling Protocol (PPTP) servers. In addition, Internet Protocol security (IPSec) tunnel-mode traffic can be used to create site-to-site VPN connections.
Advanced application filtering	ISA Server 2004 provides enhanced application filtering by controlling application-specific traffic with application command and data-aware filters. Traffic can be accepted, rejected, redirected, and modified based on its contents through intelligent filtering of VPN, Hypertext Transfer Protocol (HTTP), File Transfer Protocol (FTP), Simple Mail Transfer Protocol (SMTP), Post Office Protocol 3 (POP3), Domain Name System (DNS), H.323 conferencing, streaming media, and remote procedure call (RPC) traffic.
Enhanced authentication options	ISA Server 2004 supports authentication using built-in Windows, Remote Authentication Dial-In User Service (RADIUS), and RSA SecurID authentication. You can define different authentication rules to users or user groups in any namespace.
VPN and quarantine integration	ISA Server 2004 extends Routing and Remote Access Service to provide VPN access. ISA Server 2004 also enables VPN quarantine, which can be used to provide limited network access to VPN clients until they pass a security check. ISA Server uses the Windows Server 2003 Resource Kit tools to manage VPN quarantine client connections.

(continued)

Feature	Description
Stateful inspection for VPN	VPN clients are configured as a separate network in ISA Server 2004. Therefore, you can create distinct policies for VPN clients. The rules engine checks requests from VPN clients, statefully inspects these requests, and dynamically opens connections based on the access policy.
Export and import	ISA Server 2004 enables the option to export and import configuration information. You can use this feature to save configuration parameters to an Extensible Markup Language (XML) file and then import the information from the file to another server or use this file for disaster recovery.
Delegated permissions wizard for firewall administrator roles	ISA Server 2004 includes the Administration Delegation Wizard, which helps you assign administrative roles to user and groups. These predefined roles delegate the level of administrative control users are allowed over specified ISA Server 2004 services.

Lesson: Deployment Scenarios for ISA Server 2004

* How ISA Server Works as an Internet Edge Firewall
* How ISA Server Works as a Back-End Firewall
* How ISA Server Works as a Branch Office Firewall
* How ISA Server Works as an Integrated Firewall, Proxy, and Caching Server
* How ISA Server Works as a Proxy- and Caching-Only Server

Introduction

ISA Server 2004 is used to meet an organization's requirements for providing secure and scalable access to the Internet and for providing access to internal network resources for Internet users. The organizational requirements are going to be different depending on what ISA Server will be used for and where it will be deployed. This lesson describes the most common deployment scenarios for ISA Server.

Lesson objectives

After completing this lesson, you will be able to:

- Describe how ISA Server functions as an Internet edge firewall.
- Describe how ISA Server functions as a back-end firewall.
- Describe how ISA Server functions as a branch office firewall.
- Describe how ISA Server functions as an integrated firewall, proxy, and caching server.
- Describe how ISA Server functions as a proxy- and caching-only server.

How ISA Server Works as an Internet Edge Firewall

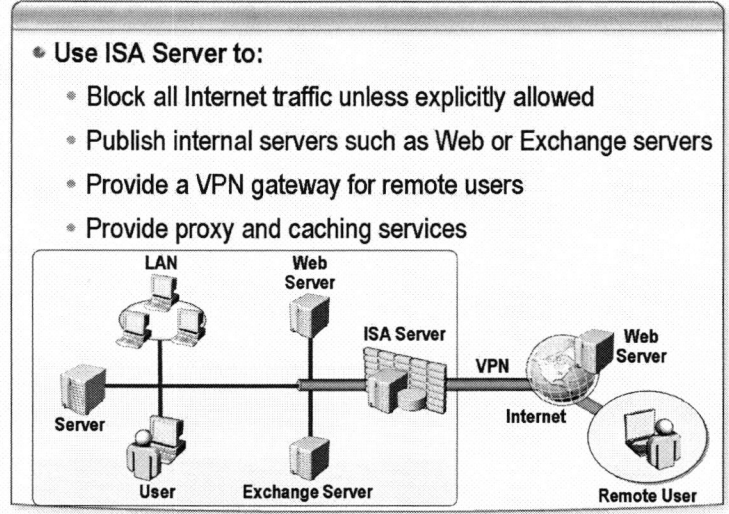

Use ISA Server to:

- Block all Internet traffic unless explicitly allowed
- Publish internal servers such as Web or Exchange servers
- Provide a VPN gateway for remote users
- Provide proxy and caching services

Introduction

One of the primary deployment scenarios for ISA Server 2004 is as an Internet edge firewall. In this scenario, ISA Server provides both a secure gateway for users to access resources on the Internet and a firewall that prevents unauthorized access and malicious content from entering the network.

Deploying ISA Server as an Internet edge firewall

As an Internet edge firewall, ISA Server is the one entry point as well as the primary security boundary between the internal network and the Internet. ISA Server is deployed with one network interface card connected to the Internet and a second network interface card connected to the internal network. In some cases, ISA Server may have a third network interface card that is connected to a perimeter network.

In this scenario:

- ISA Server blocks all Internet traffic from entering the organization's network unless the traffic is explicitly allowed. Because ISA Server is the primary security boundary, all components of ISA Server firewall functionality are implemented including multi-layered traffic filtering, application filtering, and intrusion detection. In addition, the operating system on the ISA Server must be hardened to prevent operating system–level attacks.

- ISA Server is used to make specified servers or services on the internal network accessible to Internet clients. This access is configured by publishing the server or by configuring firewall access rules. ISA Server filters all inbound requests and allows only the traffic specified by the access rules.

- ISA Server may also be the VPN access point to the internal network. In this case, all VPN connections from the Internet are routed through ISA Server. All access rules and quarantine requirements for VPN clients are enforced by ISA Server.

- All client requests for resources on the Internet pass through ISA Server. ISA Server enforces the organization's policies defining which users are allowed to access the Internet, which applications and protocols can be used to access the Internet, and which Web sites can be accessed on the Internet.

How ISA Server Works as a Back-End Firewall

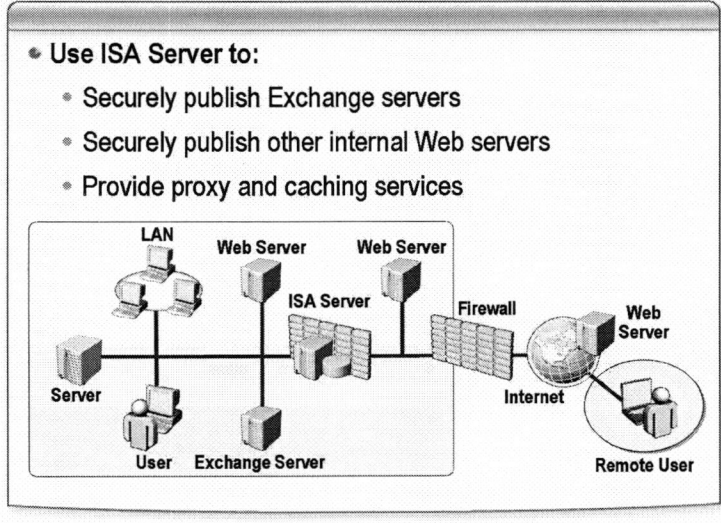

Introduction

In some cases, an organization may choose to deploy ISA Server as a second firewall in a multiple firewall configuration. This scenario enables organizations to use their existing firewall infrastructure but also enables the use of ISA Server as an advanced application-filtering firewall.

Deploying ISA Server as a back-end firewall

Many organizations implement a back-to-back firewall configuration. In this configuration, one firewall is directly connected to the Internet while the second network adapter on the firewall is connected to the perimeter network. The second firewall is connected to the perimeter network and the internal network. All network traffic must flow through both firewalls and through the perimeter network to pass between the Internet and the internal network.

For organizations that already have a hardware-based firewall deployed as the Internet edge firewall, ISA Server can provide valuable additional functionality as the back-end firewall. In particular, the advanced application-filtering functionality of ISA Server can ensure that specific applications are published securely.

In this scenario:

- ISA Server can be used to provide secure access to the organization's Exchange servers. Because computers running Exchange Server must be members of an Active Directory domain, some organizations prefer not to locate the Exchange servers in a perimeter network. ISA Server enables access to the Exchange servers on the internal network through secure Microsoft Outlook® Web Access publishing; secure SMTP server publishing, including spam filtering and secure Exchange RPC publishing for Outlook clients; and through remote procedure call (RPC) over HTTP connections.

- ISA Server may also be used to publish other secure Web sites or Web applications. If the Web servers are located on the internal network, ISA Server can be configured to publish the Web servers to the Internet. In this case, the advanced application filters on ISA Server can be used to inspect all network traffic being forwarded to the Web server.

- ISA Server may also be used as a Web proxy and caching server in this scenario. In this case, all client requests for resources on the Internet or within the perimeter network pass through ISA Server. ISA Server enforces the organization's policies for secure Internet access.

How ISA Server Works as a Branch Office Firewall

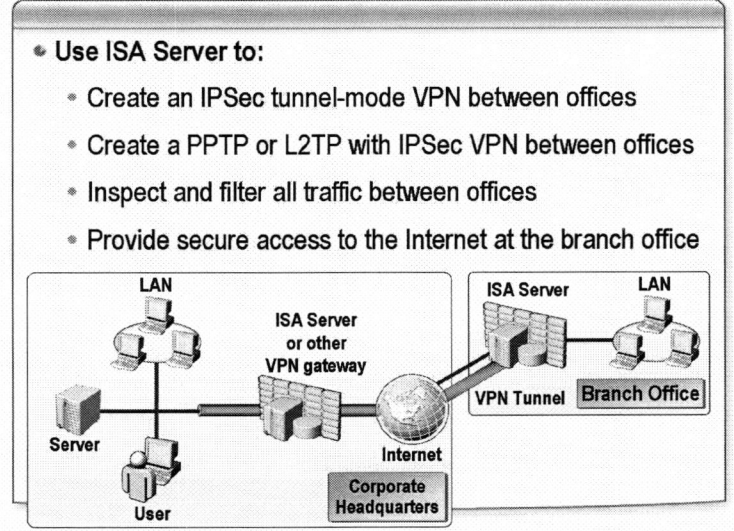

* Use ISA Server to:

  * Create an IPSec tunnel-mode VPN between offices

  * Create a PPTP or L2TP with IPSec VPN between offices

  * Inspect and filter all traffic between offices

  * Provide secure access to the Internet at the branch office

Introduction

A third deployment scenario for ISA Server is as branch office firewall. In this scenario, the ISA Server can be used to secure the branch office network from external threats as well as connect the branch office networks to the main office using site-to-site VPN connections.

Deploying ISA Server as a branch office firewall

For organizations with multiple locations, ISA Server can function as a branch office firewall, possibly in conjunction with additional ISA Servers at other locations. If the branch office has a direct connection to the Internet, ISA Server may operate as an Internet edge firewall for the branch, securing the branch office network and also publishing server resources to the Internet. If the branch office only has a dedicated WAN connection to the other offices, the ISA Server can also be used to publish servers such as SharePoint Portal Server or a local Exchange Server.

One of the benefits of using ISA Server as a branch office firewall is that ISA Server can operate as a VPN gateway that connects the branch office network to the main office network using a site-to-site VPN connection. The site-to-site VPN provides a cost-effective and secure method to connect the branch office to other locations in the organization.

In this scenario:

- ISA Server can be used to create a VPN from the branch office to other office locations using IPSec tunnel mode. The VPN gateway at the other sites can be either additional ISA servers or third-party VPN gateways. Alternatively, ISA Server can be configured to create a VPN from the branch office to other office locations using Point-to-Point Tunneling Protocol (PPTP) and Layer Two Tunneling Protocol (L2TP) over IPSec. In this case, the destination location must also deploy a Microsoft VPN gateway.

- ISA Server can perform stateful inspection and application-layer filtering of the VPN traffic between the organization's locations. This can be used to limit which remote networks can access the local network and to ensure that only approved network traffic can access the local network.

How ISA Server Works as an Integrated Firewall, Proxy, and Caching Server

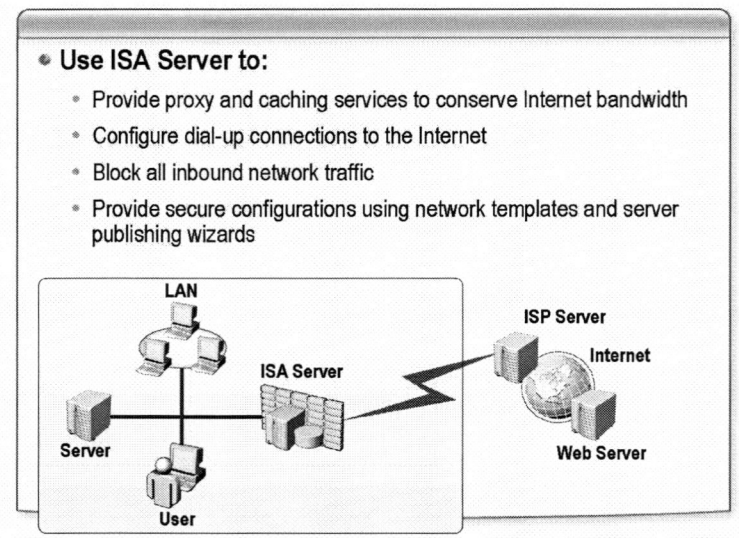

Use ISA Server to:

- Provide proxy and caching services to conserve Internet bandwidth
- Configure dial-up connections to the Internet
- Block all inbound network traffic
- Provide secure configurations using network templates and server publishing wizards

Introduction

In a small or medium organization, a single ISA Server may provide all Internet access functionality. The ISA Server is used to create a secure boundary around the internal network, and to provide Web proxy and caching services for internal users.

Deploying ISA Server as an integrated firewall, proxy and caching server

Small or medium organizations often have significantly different Internet access requirements than larger organizations. Small organizations may have dial-up or other slow connections to the Internet. Almost all organizations provide at least some level of access to the Internet for employees, but these offices may need to limit access because of the slow network connections. Some organizations do not require any services published on the Internet because their ISP may be hosting both their organization's Web site and the e-mail servers. Other organizations may have much more complex requirements, including requirements for SMTP, FTP, and HTTP server publishing as well as VPN access. Another unique situation faced by most small or medium organizations is that a single network administrator must perform all network administration tasks. This means that the administrator is usually not a firewall or Internet security expert.

ISA Server is flexible enough to meet almost any small or medium-organization requirements:

- Configuring caching on ISA Server means that Web pages are cached on the ISA Server hard disk. This can reduce the use of the slow Internet connection or reduce the cost of a connection where cost is based on bandwidth usage.

- ISA Server supports the option of using dial-up connections to access the Internet or other networks. You can configure ISA Server to automatically dial the connection when a request is made for access to Internet resources.

- The default installation of ISA Server is secure out of the box. By default, ISA Server 2004 will not accept any connections from the Internet after installation. This means that if the organization does not require any resources to be accessible from the Internet, the administrator does not need to configure ISA Server to block all incoming traffic. All the administrator has to do in this scenario is configure the server to enable access for internal users to access Internet resources and the configuration is complete.

- ISA Server provides network templates and server publishing wizards that can be used to configure most required settings. Configuring ISA Server to provide access to Internet resources can be as simple as applying a network template and using the wizard to configure the security settings. ISA Server provides several server publishing wizards that make it easy to securely publish internal servers to the Internet.

How ISA Server Works as a Proxy- and Caching-Only Server

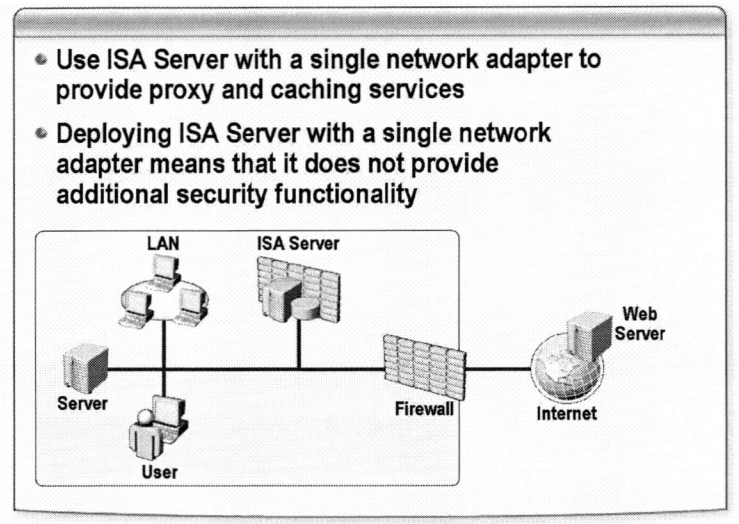

Introduction

A final deployment scenario for ISA Server 2004 is as a proxy- and Web-caching server only. In this scenario, ISA Server is not used to provide a secure boundary between the Internet and the internal network, but only used to provide Web proxy and caching services.

Deploying ISA Server as a proxy and web caching only server

In most cases, computers running ISA Server are deployed with multiple network adapters to take advantage of the ability of ISA Server to connect multiple networks and to filter network traffic between multiple networks. However, if ISA Server is deployed as a Web proxy- and caching-only server, you can deploy the server with a single network adapter. When ISA Server is installed on a computer with a single adapter, it recognizes only one network—the internal network.

If an organization already has a firewall solution in place, it can still take advantage of the proxy and caching functionality of ISA Server. To deploy ISA Server as a proxy and caching server, you only need to configure it to allow users to access resources on the Internet. You would then configure the Web browsers on all client computers to use the computer running ISA Server as a Web proxy server.

When you install ISA Server on a computer with a single adapter, the following ISA Server features cannot be used:

- Firewall and SecureNAT clients
- Virtual private networking
- IP packet filtering
- Multi-network firewall policy
- Server publishing
- Application-level filtering

All of these restrictions mean that ISA Server provides very few security benefits for the network.

Lab: Designing an ISA Server 2004 Implementation

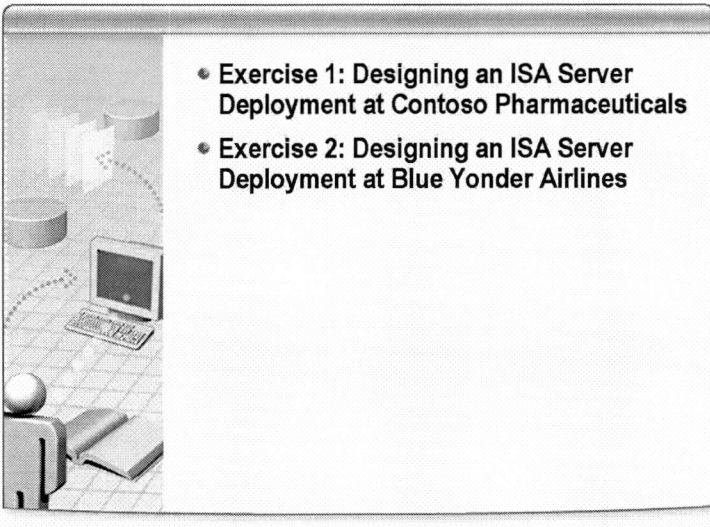

- Exercise 1: Designing an ISA Server Deployment at Contoso Pharmaceuticals
- Exercise 2: Designing an ISA Server Deployment at Blue Yonder Airlines

Objectives

After completing this lab, you will be able to:

- Describe where an ISA Server should be deployed within an organization's network.

- Describe which features should be configured on an ISA server.

Note This lab focuses on the concepts in this module and as a result may not comply with Microsoft security recommendations.

Lab Instructions

This lab presents two scenarios describing the current networking environment and future requirements for two organizations. Review both of the corporate scenarios, including the network diagrams. Then, using the network diagrams, identify where to install one or more computers running ISA Server. For each computer running ISA Server that you deploy, describe the functionality that you would enable. You can work on this lab individually or with a partner. When you complete the exercise, the instructor will lead a class discussion. Be prepared to explain your choices.

Estimated time to complete this lab: 45 minutes

Exercise 1
Designing an ISA Deployment for Contoso Pharmaceuticals

In this exercise, you will create a design for an ISA Server 2004 deployment for Contoso Pharmaceuticals, an international corporation involved in drug manufacturing and sales.

Scenario

Contoso Pharmaceuticals has two main offices: the European headquarters located in Berlin and the North American headquarters located in Toronto. Contoso Pharmaceuticals also has offices in Johannesburg, Atlanta, and São Paolo.

Contoso Pharmaceuticals is planning to deploy ISA Server 2004 and has the following deployment requirements:

- All current firewalls will be replaced by computers running ISA Server. Additional computers running ISA Server will be deployed if required.

- There should be no restrictions on the flow of network traffic between any of the office locations. The existing WANs between offices will not be replaced.

- All Internet traffic flows through either Berlin or Toronto. Because the WAN links between the offices are 70–80 percent utilized during business hours, this configuration needs to be changed. New Internet connections will be installed in Johannesburg, Atlanta, and São Paolo. These Internet connections must be as secure as possible.

- All company Exchange servers are located at Berlin and Toronto. All inbound and outbound e-mail must flow through these locations.

- Each office hosts a public Web site as well as a secure Web site that is used by customers. These Web sites must be available through the local Internet connection.

- Contoso Pharmaceuticals is deploying a new sales application at the Toronto office. This application must be accessible to sales personnel whether they in or out of the office. When outside the office, the sales personnel must connect to the Toronto office using a VPN before getting access to the application. You must be able to filter all traffic that flows between this application server and other servers on the internal network. Sales personnel should not be able to access any resources on the company network except for the sales application using the VPN unless the computer they are using passes all security requirements.

- All users need to be able to access their e-mail on the Exchange servers from the Internet using a Web browser.

Contoso Pharmaceuticals Network Diagram

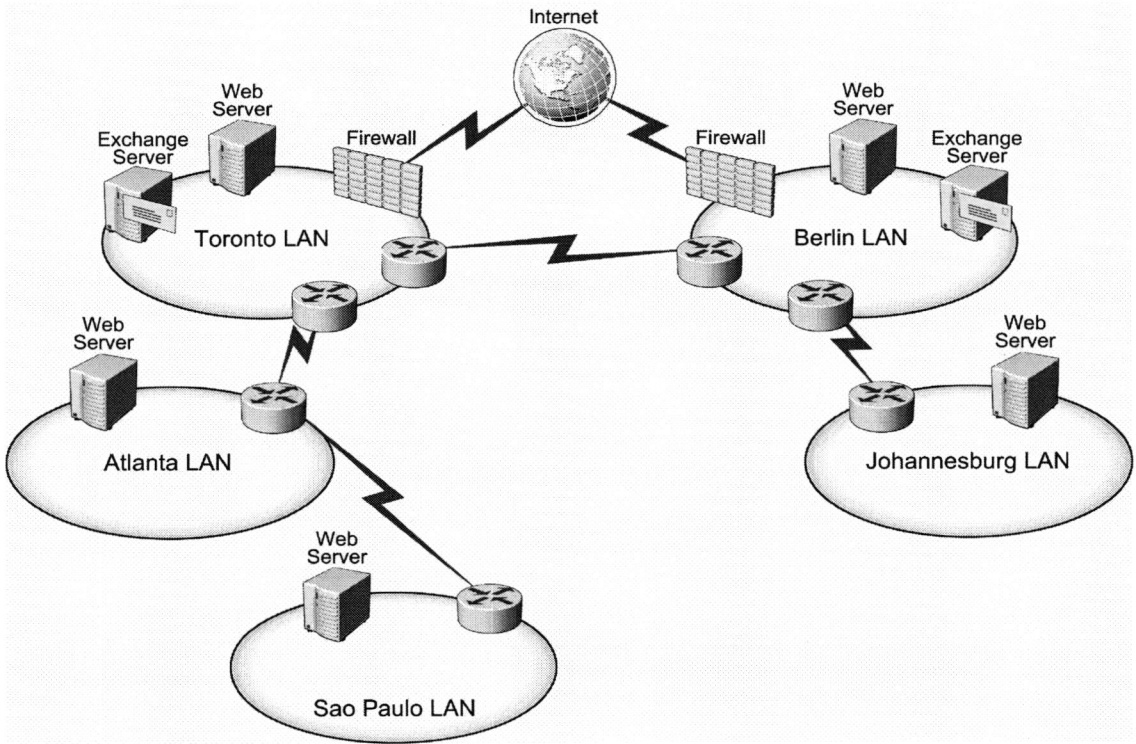

Exercise 2
Designing an ISA Server Deployment for Blue Yonder Airlines

In this exercise, you will create a design for an ISA Server deployment at Blue Yonder Airlines.

Scenario

Blue Yonder Airlines is an airfreight company with locations in Asia and Australia. The company headquarters are located in Tokyo. The company has branch offices in Beijing, Hong Kong, Melbourne, and Singapore.

Blue Yonder Airlines is planning to deploy ISA Server 2004 and has the following deployment requirements:

- The current firewall will not be replaced. This firewall performs packet filtering and stateful filtering of all packets that arrive from the Internet.

- All users in all company locations use the Internet extensively as part of their work. All Internet traffic from the branch offices flows through the head office. Although the Internet connection at Tokyo is over 60 percent utilized during business hours, this configuration should not be modified for any branch office except Melbourne.

- The WAN connections between the branch offices and the head office are over 90 percent utilized at times during business hours. This bandwidth usage should be minimized as much as possible.

- The cost of the WAN connection between Tokyo and Melbourne is scheduled to double within six months. If possible, this WAN connection should be replaced with a secure connection through the Internet.

- The company Web server is located in the Tokyo head office and connected to the internal network. New security specifications for this Web server state that it must not be connected to the internal network. It must, however, be protected from the Internet by a firewall.

- All company Exchange servers are located in Tokyo. All inbound and outbound e-mail must flow through Tokyo. All users with laptop computers should be able to access their e-mail on the Exchange server using Microsoft Outlook®.

Blue Yonder Airlines Network Diagram

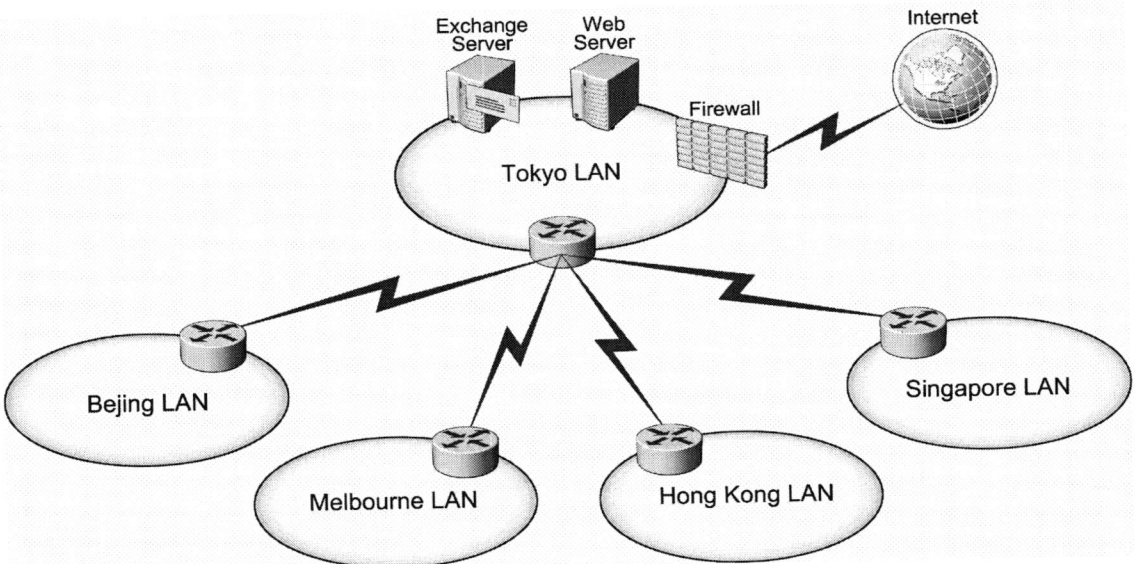

Module 2: Installing and Maintaining ISA Server

Contents

Overview

- Installing ISA Server 2004
- Choosing ISA Server Clients
- Installing and Configuring Firewall Clients
- Advanced Firewall Client Configuration
- Securing ISA Server 2004
- Maintaining ISA Server 2004

Introduction

Part of an ISA Server administrator's job is to install Internet Security and Acceleration (ISA) Server 2004. In most cases, companies also deploy ISA Firewall Clients on client computers or configure Web Proxy clients on the network, so the administrator also needs to know how to install and configure these ISA Server clients. As well, the ISA Server administrator needs to know how to secure and maintain ISA Server after it is deployed. This module provides information on how to perform all of these tasks.

Objectives

After completing this module, you will be able to:

- Install ISA Server 2004.
- Choose the appropriate ISA Server clients and configure Web Proxy and SecureNAT clients.
- Install and configure the ISA Server Firewall client.
- Configure advanced settings for Firewall clients.
- Secure ISA Server 2004.
- Maintain ISA Server 2004.

Lesson: Installing ISA Server 2004

* System and Hardware Requirements for ISA Server 2004
* Installation Types and Components
* Configuration Choices During Installation
* How to Perform an Unattended Installation of ISA Server 2004
* How to Verify an Installation of ISA Server 2004
* Default Configuration for ISA Server 2004
* How to Modify the ISA Server Installation
* Upgrade Options from ISA Server 2000 to ISA Server 2004

Introduction

This lesson describes the hardware and environment requirements for the successful installation of ISA Server 2004 and explains how to install ISA Server 2004. This lesson also describes how to verify and troubleshoot an ISA Server installation. Finally, this module provides an overview of how to migrate from ISA Server 2000 to ISA Server 2004.

Lesson objectives

After completing this lesson, you will be able to:

- List the system and hardware requirements for ISA Server 2004.
- Identify installation types and components.
- Identify installation choices to be made during setup.
- Perform an unattended installation of ISA Server 2004.
- Verify a successful installation of ISA Server 2004.
- Verify the default configuration of ISA Server 2004.
- Modify the ISA Server installation options after installation.
- Describe how to migrate from ISA Server 2000 to ISA Server 2004.

System and Hardware Requirements for ISA Server 2004

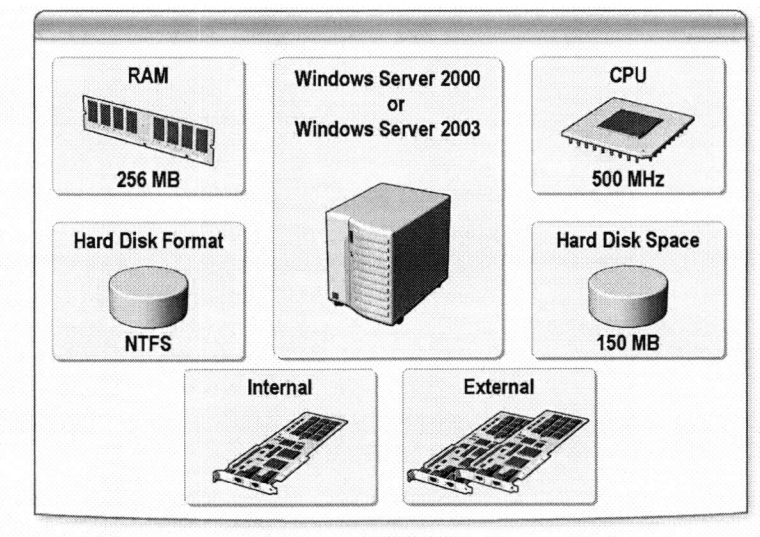

Introduction

In order to install ISA Server 2004, you need to ensure that you have the correct operating system and hardware configurations.

Operating system requirements

ISA Server 2004 can be installed only on computers running a Microsoft® Windows® 2000 Server or Microsoft Windows Server™ 2003 operating system. When installing ISA Server 2004 on a Windows 2000 Server operating system, note the following additional requirements.

- You must install Microsoft Windows 2000 Service Pack 4.

- You must install Microsoft Internet Explorer 6.

- If you installed Windows 2000 from media that included the Service Pack (SP4) files, install the hotfix specified in article KB821887, "Events for Authorization Roles Are Not Logged in the Security Log When You Configure Auditing for Windows 2000 Authorization Manager Runtime," in the Microsoft Knowledge Base at http://support.microsoft.com/default.aspx?scid=kb;en-us;821887.

Note If you are installing ISA Server on a server running Windows 2000, the following options are not supported:

- Configuring the Layer 2 Tunneling Protocol (L2TP) IPSec pre-shared key is not supported.

- Quarantine mode for virtual private network (VPN) clients is not supported when using Remote Authentication Dial-In User Service (RADIUS) policy.

Hardware Requirements

The minimum hardware requirements for installing ISA Server 2004 are:

- A personal computer with a 500 megahertz (MHz) or higher Pentium III–compatible CPU.

- 256 megabytes (MB) of memory.

- One network adapter for communication with the internal network.

- An additional network adapter for each network directly connected to the ISA Server 2004 computer.

- One local hard disk partition that is formatted with the NTFS file system and that has at least 150 megabytes (MB) of available hard disk space. If you enable caching and logging, you will need additional hard disk space.

Scaling ISA Server

ISA Server can be scaled to support almost any size organization, either by increasing the hardware level on individual ISA Servers or by deploying multiple ISA Servers. The following factors should influence your choice in hardware configuration:

- *Bandwidth of the Internet connection.* ISA Server is designed to provide very fast data throughput, even if each packet is inspected at multiple layers. In most cases, ISA Server's throughput will exceed the Internet connection throughput.

- *Firewall policy configuration.* The number of firewall rules and the complexity of the rules will affect server performance. For example, advanced application filtering requires more server resources than packet filtering.

- *Logging requirements.* The level of logging that you require will affect the server resources, particularly hard disk space. If you have thousands of clients connecting through the server, and have configured a high level of logging, you will require up to 10 gigabytes (GB) of disk space to maintain the logs. During a widespread virus or worm attack, the disk space required for the logs will increase significantly.

- *Number and type of published servers.* The more servers you publish on the ISA Server, the more server resources are needed. This is especially true if you publish secure Web sites because of the extra resources required to decrypt and encrypt Secure Sockets Layer (SSL) traffic.

The following table provides general guidelines, depending on the Internet link bandwidth available.

Internet Bandwidth	Recommended Server Configuration
Up to 1.5 megabytes per second (Mbps)	Minimum hardware requirements with additional disk space for logging and caching
Up to 25 Mbps	Single Pentium 4 2.0–3.0 GHz processor 512 MB RAM 2–3 GB of disk space for logging with additional space for caching
Up to 45 Mbps	Dual Xeon 2.0–3.0 GHz processors 1 GB RAM 8–10 GB of disk space for logging with additional space for caching

Note For more information on scaling ISA Server, see ISA Server 2004 Performance Best Practices at http://www.microsoft.com/technet/prodtechnol/isa/2004/plan/bestpractices.mspx.

Installation Types and Components

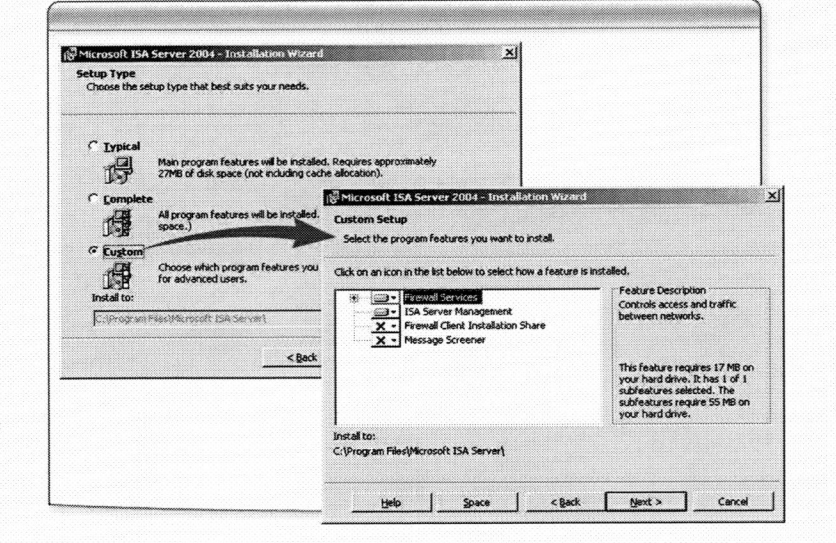

Introduction

When you install ISA Server 2004, you need to choose the type of installation to perform and determine the components to install.

Important   Before installing ISA Server 2004, review the Release Notes file that is located on the ISA Server 2004 installation CD-ROM. This file contains important information on installation issues that you may encounter.

Installation types

When you start the ISA Server installation, you are given a choice of three installation types:

- *Typical Installation*. This type installs ISA Server Services and ISA Server Management.

- *Full Installation*. This type installs all four ISA Server components.

- *Custom Installation*. This type enables you to select which components will be installed.

Installation components

If you choose to perform a custom installation, you can select the following components:

- *Firewall Services*. The services that control access and traffic between networks.

- *ISA Server Management*. The ISA Server Management user interface enables you to use the management console to centrally manage ISA Server.

- *Firewall Client Installation Share.* This option installs a shared folder named *ServerName**mspclnt*, from which client computers can install the Firewall Client software. The client installation files are typically installed on a computer other than the ISA Server computer, so it is not part of the Typical Installation option. You can install the Firewall Client share on computers running Windows Server 2003, Windows 2000 Server, or Windows XP.

- *Message Screener.* This feature performs content filtering on Simple Mail Transfer Protocol (SMTP) traffic arriving on an ISA Server. Configure this component to screen e-mail messages for keywords and attachments. You can install this feature on the computer running ISA Server only if the IIS SMTP service is installed on the computer.

Configuration Choices During Installation

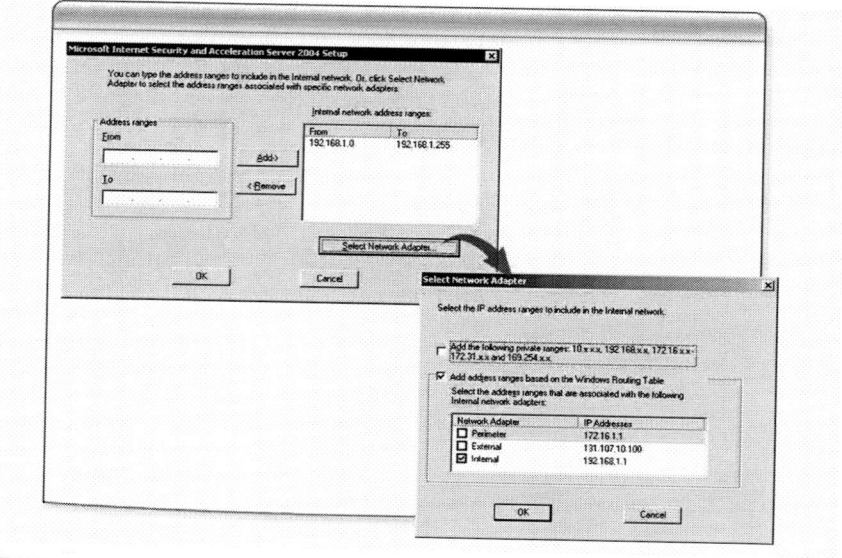

Introduction

When you install ISA Server 2004, you need to configure the IP addresses associated with the internal network as well as be aware of other installation choices.

Configuring the Internal network

One of the options that you need to configure during the installation is the Internet Protocol (IP) addresses in the internal network. The internal network can contain the IP addresses associated with all the network adapters on the ISA Server computer except the network adapter connected to the Internet. You can also configure the internal network to contain a set of IP addresses associated with only one network adapter, while the IP addresses assigned to other network adapters are used to create additional networks. By default, ISA Server setup also assigns the private IP address ranges defined by Internet Assigned Numbers Authority (IANA) as part of the internal network.

During ISA Setup, you can configure the internal network to use the IP addresses assigned to a specific network adapter. When ISA Server setup constructs the internal network based on the network adapter, it uses the Windows routing table to determine which address ranges are internal. If the routing table is not set correctly, the ISA Server internal network may not be built correctly. This can result in a client request for an internal IP address being routed to the Internet or being redirected through the Microsoft Firewall service. Before starting the installation of ISA Server, ensure that the routing table on the server is correct.

Allowing earlier versions of Firewall Client software

One of the choices that you need to make during the ISA Server installation is whether to allow earlier versions of the Firewall Client. ISA Server supports earlier versions of the Firewall Client software, including Firewall Client for ISA Server 2000 and the Winsock Proxy client (from Microsoft Proxy Server 2.0). However, these clients cannot use encryption when connecting to the ISA Server, so you may want to prevent these versions of the Firewall Client software installed on earlier versions of Windows operating systems from connecting to your ISA Server computer. By default, the ISA Server 2004 installation does not allow non-encrypted Firewall Client connections. To enable older clients, select the option **Allow non-encrypted Firewall client connections** and **Allow Firewall clients running earlier versions of the Firewall client software to connect to the ISA Server** during the installation.

Note   When you enable encryption, only the network traffic sent using the control channel is encrypted. When a Firewall client connects to the firewall service on ISA Server, information such as authentication credentials, name resolution queries and port negotiations are sent along the control channel. Firewall clients use TCP and UDP Port 1745 to connect to the control channel.

Stopping and disabling services

As part of the ISA Server 2004 installation process, the following services are disabled:

- Internet Connection Firewall or Internet Connection Sharing
- IP Network Address Translation

In addition, the following services are stopped during installation:

- Simple Network Management Protocol (SNMP) service
- File Transfer Protocol (FTP) Publishing service
- Network News Transfer Protocol (NNTP)
- Internet Information Server (IIS) Admin service
- World Wide Web Publishing service

Important   In most cases, it is recommended that you do not run Internet Information Services or any of the Internet Protocol services on the ISA Server. This is particularly important if you are deploying ISA Server as an Internet edge firewall.

Installing ISA Server using Remote Desktop

You can install ISA Server 2004 on a server running Windows 2000 using Terminal Services, or on a server running Windows Server 2003 using Remote Desktop. The installation process is the same as if you perform the installation from the server console, except that the System Policy on the ISA Server will be configured to allow remote administration only from the computer that you used to install the ISA Server.

The Microsoft SQL Server™ Desktop Engine (MSDE) component is not properly installed when you use Terminal Services in application server mode to remotely install ISA Server on a server running Windows 2000. Use Terminal Services in administration mode to properly install MSDE. The MSDE component is properly installed if you install ISA Server 2004 using Remote Desktop on a server running Windows Server 2003.

Practice: Installing ISA Server 2004

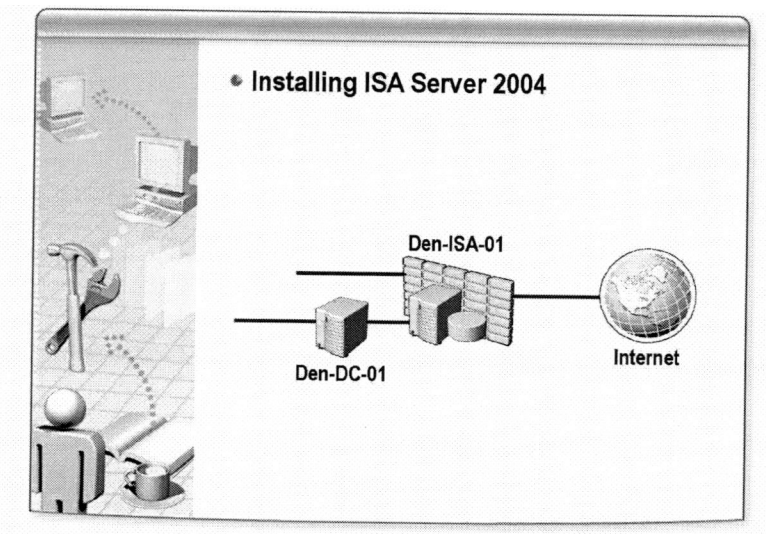

Introduction

In this practice, you will install ISA Server 2004 on the Den-ISA-01 virtual machines.

Important You must complete this practice to complete other practices in this course.

Practice

▶ **To prepare for this practice**

1. You will need the Den-DC-01 virtual machine and the Den-ISA-01 virtual machine for this practice.

2. If necessary, start or resume the required virtual machines and then, on Den-ISA-01, log on to the cohovineyard domain with a user name of **Administrator** and a password of **P@ssw0rd**.

Note When you start the Den-DC-01 virtual machine, a Service Control Manager warning dialog box may appear stating that at least one service or driver failed during system startup. Click **OK** to close the dialog box.

▶ **Installing ISA Server 2004**

1. Open **Windows Explorer** and browse to C:\Program Files\ Microsoft Learning\2824\Setup.

2. Double-click **isaautorun.exe**.

3. On the **Microsoft ISA Server 2004 Setup** page, click **Install ISA Server 2004**.

4. On the **Welcome to the Installation Wizard for Microsoft ISA Server 2004 Setup** page, click **Next**.

5. On the **License Agreement** page, review the terms and conditions stated in the end-user license agreement. Then click **I accept the terms in the license agreement**, and then click **Next**.

6. On the **Customer Information** page, accept the defaults, and then click **Next**.

7. On the **Setup Type** page, click **Custom**. Click **Next**.

8. On the **Custom Setup** page, click **Firewall Client Installation Share**, click the menu for **Firewall Client Installation Share**, and then click **This feature will be installed on local hard drive**. Click **Next**.

9. On the **Internal Network** page, click **Add**.

10. Click **Select Network Adapter**.

11. Click **Internal** and clear the check box for **Add the following private ranges:** and then click **OK** twice.

12. Review the **Internal network address ranges**, and then click **OK**.

13. On the **Internal Network** page, click **Next**.

14. On the **Firewall Client Connections Settings** page, click **Next**.

15. On the **Services** page, click **Next**.

16. On the **Ready to Install the Program** page, click **Install**.

17. On the **Installation Wizard Completed** page, click **Finish**.

18. Click **Yes** to restart the computer.

Important   To install ISA Server 2004, you must be a member of the local Administrators group.

How to Perform an Unattended Installation of ISA Server 2004

* Why Use an Unattended Installation of ISA Server?
* Modifying the Msisaund.ini File

```
[Setup Property Assignment]
PIDKEY=xxxxxxxxxxxxxxxxxxxxxxxxx
INTERNALNETRANGES=1 192.168.1.0-192.168.1.255
INSTALLDIR=C:\Program Files\Microsoft ISA
Server
COMPANYNAME=Coho Vineyards
DONOTDELLOGS=1
DONOTDELCACHE=1
ADDLOCAL=MSFirewall_Management,MSFirewall_
Services,Message_Screener,MSDE
```

* Running an Unattended Setup

```
D:\Setup.exe /V" /qn FULLPATHANSWERFILE=
\"c:\MSISAUND.INI\""
```

Why use an unattended setup?

There are several scenarios in which you may want to use an unattended rather than a manual installation of ISA Server 2004:

- To ensure an identical and error-free installation. If you are deploying multiple ISA Servers that all require the same configuration, you can configure the installation information file once, and then you can use that file repeatedly to ensure all servers are installed the same way.

- To rapidly rebuild a failed server. If a server fails, you can use the installation information file that you used to build the server to rapidly install ISA Server on another server. You can configure the installation file to use an exported XML file to configure the ISA Server settings.

In order to perform the unattended installation, you need to create or modify the Msisaund.ini file and then configure the ISA Server installation process to use this file when completing the setup.

Modifying the Msisaund.ini file

The Msisaund.ini file contains the configuration information that is used by ISA Server setup in unattended mode. The following table describes the entries and values in the Msisaund.ini file of the server. If a value is not specified in this file, a default value is used.

File Entry	Description
PIDKEY	Specifies the product key. This is the 25-digit number located on the back of the ISA Server CD-ROM case.
INTERNALNETRANGES	Specifies the range of addresses in the internal network. Msisaund.ini must specify at least one Internet Protocol (IP) address. Otherwise, setup fails. The syntax specifies the number of internal networks and the network numbers. For example, if you have two internal network ranges, you would use a line like: INTERNALNETRANGES=2 192.168.1.0 – 192.168.1.255, 192.168.2.0 – 192.168.2.255.

(*continued*)

File Entry	Description
InstallDir = {install_directory}	Specifies the installation directory for ISA Server. If not specified, it defaults to the first disk drive with enough space. The syntax is Drive:\Folder. The default folder is: %Program Files%\Microsoft ISA Server.
COMPANYNAME = Company_Name	Specifies the name of the company installing the product.
DONOTDELLOGS = {0|1}	If set to 1, log files on the computer are not deleted. The default is 0.
DONOTDELCACHE = {0|1}	If set to 1, cache files on the computer are not deleted. The default is 0.
ADDLOCAL = {MSFirewall_Management}, {MSFirewall_Services}, {Message_Screener}, {Publish_Share_Directory}, {MSDE}	Specifies a list of components (delimited by commas) that should be installed on the computer. To install all the components, set ADDLOCAL = ALL.
REMOVE = {MSFirewall_Management}, {MSFirewall_Services}, {Message_Screener}, {Publish_Share_Directory}, {MSDE}	Specifies a list of components (delimited by commas) that should be removed from the computer. To remove all the components, set REMOVE = ALL.
IMPORT_CONFIG_FILE = Importfile.xml	Specifies a configuration file to import. This can be used to apply an ISA Server Configuration to the server after installation.

Running an unattended setup

After modifying the Msisaund.ini file, open command prompt, and type:

```
PathToISASetup\Setup.exe [/[X|R]] /V" /Q[b|n]
FULLPATHANSWERFILE=\"PathToINIFile\MSISAUND.INI\""
```

Parameters for unattended setup are described in the following table:

Parameter	Description
PathToISASetup	The path to the ISA Server 2004 installation files. The path may be the root folder of the ISA Server CD-ROM or a shared folder on the network that contains the ISA Server files.
/Q [b|n]	Performs a quiet, unattended setup. If b is specified, the exit dialog box displays when setup completes. If n is specified, no dialog boxes are displayed.
/R	Performs an unattended reinstallation.
/X	Performs an unattended uninstallation.
/V	Provide verbose logging during the installation.
PathToINIFile	The path to the folder containing the unattended installation information.

Tip   A sample answer file (Msisaund.ini) is provided on the ISA Server Installation CD, in the FPC folder.

How to Verify an Installation of ISA Server 2004

* Verify that the ISA Server services are installed and started
* Verify that the MSDE services are installed and started
* Review the setup log files
* Check the Application Log in the Event Viewer
* Check for ISA Server Alerts

Introduction

After completing the ISA Server installation, the next step is to verify that the installation was successful and that all components were installed.

Verifying the installation

There are several steps that you can perform to verify that the ISA installation completed successfully. These steps include:

- Verify that the ISA Server services are installed and started. Performing a default installation of ISA Server creates and starts the following services:
  - Microsoft Firewall
  - Microsoft ISA Server Control
  - Microsoft ISA Server Job Scheduler
  - Microsoft ISA Server Storage
- Verify that the MSDE services are installed and started. The ISA Server installs the MSDE and adds the following services:
  - MSSQL$MSFW – This service is started and set for automatic start.
  - MSSQLServerADHelper – This service is not started and is set for manual start.

  Installing the MSDE service also creates the initial log files for ISA Server. By default, these log files are located in C:\Program Files\ Microsoft ISA Server\ISALogs.
- The ISA Server installation creates three setup log files. These files are located in the %windir%/temp directory and are named ISAWRAP_###, ISAMSDE_###, and ISAFWSV_### where ### is a three-character number. The ISAWRAP file contains a summary of the installation, including a statement on whether the installation was successful or not. The other two files provide detailed information about the installation of MSDE and ISA Server.

- Check the Application Log in the Event Viewer. If the installation fails, error messages may be written to the Application Log that provides useful information for troubleshooting the error. If the installation was a success, the Event Log will include events indicating that the ISA Services started successfully.

- Using the ISA Server Management console, check for ISA Server Alerts. If the installation completed successfully, an ISA Server alert is created showing that the Firewall Service started.

Important By default, the ISA Server computer will deny all access to Internet resources after the installation. This means that you cannot use a client to test access through the ISA Server computer until you have configured a firewall rule enabling access.

Default Configuration for ISA Server 2004

* Only Administrators can modify firewall policies
* Traffic is routed between the ISA Server and all other networks
* Traffic between the Internal network, the VPN network, the VPN Quarantine network, and the Internet will use network address translation
* Traffic is routed between the VPN network and the Internal network
* System policy permits access to the ISA Server but access rules deny all network traffic through the ISA Server
* No servers are published
* Web Proxy requests will be retrieved directly from the Internet
* Caching is disabled
* A rule enabling access to the Firewall Client installation share is configured if you install the Firewall Client installation files

Introduction

After a standard installation, ISA Server starts with a default installation that is secure and does not allow access to any Internet or internal resources.

ISA Server Default Configuration

The ISA Server default configuration is listed in the following table:

ISA Server Feature	Default Configuration
User permissions	Members of the Administrators group on the local computer can configure all ISA Server settings. If the ISA Server is a member of a domain, the Domain Admins group is a member of the local Administrators group so the Domain Admins also has full ISA Server management rights.
Network settings	The following network relations are created: • *Local Host Access.* Defines a network rule that states that all traffic between the Local Host and all networks will be routed. This does not enable the routing of traffic, but it states that traffic between the ISA Server and any other network will be routed rather than using Network Address Translation (NAT). • *Internet Access.* Defines a NAT network relationship from the internal network, the Quarantined VPN Clients network, and the VPN Clients network, to the External network. Again, this does not grant any access; it only states that NAT will be used for traffic flowing between these networks. • *VPN Clients to Internal Network.* Defines a routed network relationship between the VPN Clients and the Internal network.

(continued)

ISA Server Feature	Default Configuration
Access rules	The following default rules are created: • *System policy rules*. A series of rules that enable interaction between the ISA Server and other network resources. • *Default rule*. This rule denies all traffic between all networks. Because this is the only firewall access rule that is created by default, all traffic between different networks on the ISA Server is blocked.
Publishing	No internal servers are accessible to external clients.
Web routing	The default rule specifying that all Web Proxy client requests are retrieved directly from the Internet.
Caching	The cache size is set to 0. All caching is therefore disabled.
Firewall Client Install Share	When you install the Firewall Client Share, a system policy rule named **Allow access to firewall client share to trusted computers**, which allows clients on the Internal network to access the share, is enabled. This rule must be enabled to allow the clients to install the software from the share.

The default configuration of a newly installed ISA Server means that traffic can flow between the ISA Server and other networks. For example, Lightweight Directory Access Protocol (LDAP) traffic is permitted from the ISA Server to the internal network. This enables the ISA Server to operate as a member of a Microsoft Active Directory® directory service domain. However, by default, no traffic is permitted to flow through the ISA Server from one network to another. Some ISA Server settings, such as the network settings and Web-routing settings, define how traffic will flow, but until an access rule is created that enables the traffic flow, all traffic is blocked.

Note The system policy rules define the network traffic that is allowed to flow from the computer running ISA Server to other networks. For more information on how system policy rules work and how to modify the default settings, see Module 4, "Configuring ISA Server as a Firewall," in Course 2824, *Implementing Microsoft® Internet Security and Acceleration Server 2004.*

Practice: Verifying the Installation and Default Configuration of ISA Server 2004

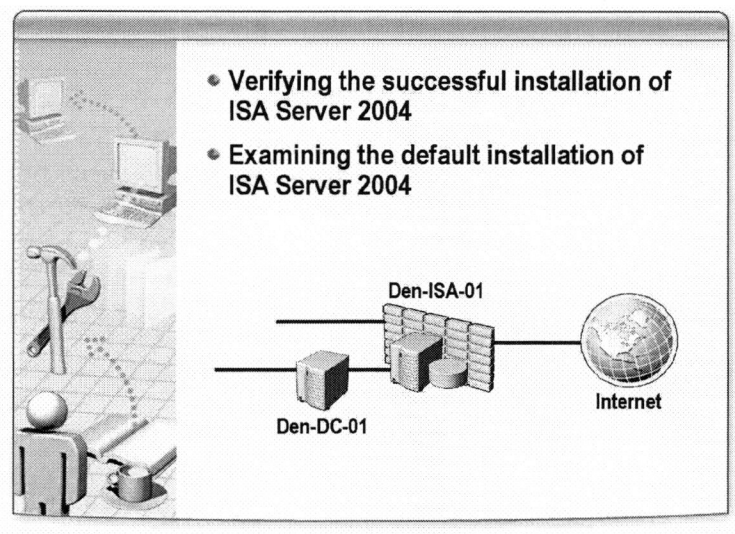

Introduction

In this practice, you will verify the installation of ISA Server on the Den-ISA-01 virtual machine and examine the default configuration.

▶ **To prepare for this practice**

1. You will need the Den-DC-01 virtual machine and the Den-ISA-01 virtual machine for this practice.

2. If necessary, start or resume the required virtual machines and then, on Den-ISA-01, log on to the cohovineyard domain with a user name of **Administrator** and a password of **P@ssw0rd**.

Practice

▶ **Verifying the successful installation of ISA Server 2004**

1. In the **Internet Explorer** dialog box, click **In the future, do not show this message** and click **OK**.

2. Close **Internet Explorer**.

3. Open the **Services** management console from the **Administrative Tools** folder. Ensure that the following services are installed and running:

   a. Microsoft Firewall

   b. Microsoft ISA Server Control

   c. Microsoft ISA Server Job Scheduler

   d. Microsoft ISA Server Storage

   e. MSSQL$MSFW

4. Ensure that the MSSQLServerADHelper is installed but not running. Close the **Services** management console.

5. On the desktop, ensure that the MSDE icon is displayed in the System Tray. To remove the MSDE icon from the System Tray, right-click the icon and click **Exit**.

6. Open Windows Explorer and browse to the C:\Program Files\Microsoft ISA Server\ISALogs folder. Ensure that several .mdf and .ldf files are located in this folder.

7. Browse to the C:\Windows\Temp folder. Open the ISAWRAP_###.log file (where ### is a three-character number). Review the log file, ensuring that the log indicates that the firewall installation ended successfully. Close all open windows.

8. Open the **Event Viewer** from the **Administrative Tools** folder. Open the **Application** log and review the events listed. You may see two error messages from the Microsoft Firewall service indicating network routing errors. These error messages can be safely ignored. Close the **Event Viewer**.

9. Open **ISA Server Management** from the **All Programs\Microsoft ISA Server** folder. Expand **DEN-ISA-01**. Click **Monitoring** and then click **Alerts**. Review the alerts that were created during the installation. If a configuration error alert is listed that indicates the same network routing error as was displayed in the **Application** log, it can be safely ignored.

▶ **Examining the default installation of ISA Server 2004**

1. Right-click DEN-ISA-01 and click Administration Delegation.

2. On the **Welcome to the ISA Server Administration Delegation Wizard** page, click **Next**.

   What roles have been assigned to the following groups?

   a. Cohovineyard\Administrator ____ISA Server full Administrator____

   b. Builtin\Administrators _____

   Click **Cancel**.

3. Expand **Configuration** and click **Networks**. In the details pane, click **Network Rules**.

4. Review the **Network Rules**. List the network relationships between the networks listed below:

   a. Local Host and All Networks _____Route_____

   b. Quarantined VPN Clients, VPN Clients, and Internal _____

   c. Quarantined VPN Clients, VPN Clients, Internal and External _____

5. Click **Web Chaining**. Double-click **Last Default** rule. Click the **Action** tab. What default behavior will ISA Server apply to all requests? Click **OK**.

   _____

6. In the console tree, click **Firewall Policy**. What rule or rules are listed? Describe the rule configuration.

   _____

7. On the **Tasks** tab, click **Show System Policy Rules**. Locate the rule named **Allow access from trusted computers to the Firewall Client installation share on ISA Server**. Double-click the rule. What does this rule enable? What network is included in this rule? Click **OK**.

   _____

8. In the console tree, expand **Configuration** and click **Cache**. Under **Tasks**, click **Define Cache Drives**. What is the default size of the **Maximum cache size**? What does this indicate about the default cache configuration? Click **OK**.

   _____

9. Close all open windows. If you receive a message about **Unsaved Changes**, click **Discard Changes**.

▶ **To prepare for the next practice**

- Start the Den-Clt-01 virtual machine by selecting **Den-Clt-01** in the Virtual PC Console and clicking **Start**.

How to Modify the ISA Server Installation Options

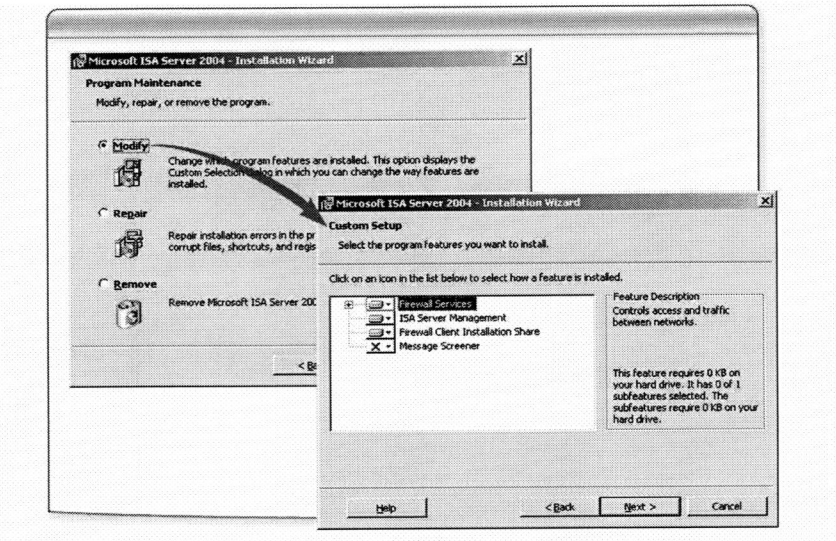

Introduction

You can change the ISA installation options after you complete the ISA Server installation by running ISA Server setup from Add/Remove Programs in the Control Panel.

Modifying the ISA Server installation options

To change ISA Server installation options:

1. On computers running Windows Server 2003, click **Start**, click **Control Panel**, and then double-click **Add/Remove Programs**.

2. Click **Microsoft ISA Server 2004**, and then click **Add/Remove**.

3. On the **Welcome** page, click **Next**.

4. On the **Program Maintenance** page, select **Modify**.

5. On the **Custom Setup** page, in **Click on an icon in the list below to select how a feature is installed** box, choose one or more of the following:

   - **Firewall Services**. If you select this option, all the ISA Server services will be installed.

   - **ISA Server Management**. If you select this option, the management console used to centrally manage ISA Server will be installed.

   - **Firewall Client Installation Share**. If you select this option, a folder with all the files necessary to install the Firewall Client software will be created on the ISA Server computer. The folder will be shared to the Everyone group, thereby allowing anyone access to install the software.

   - **Message Screener**. If you select this option, the Message Screener will be installed. This component must be installed on an SMTP server, which is typically not your ISA Server computer.

6. Click **Next**, and then click **Install** to begin the installation.

Upgrade Options from ISA Server 2000 to ISA Server 2004

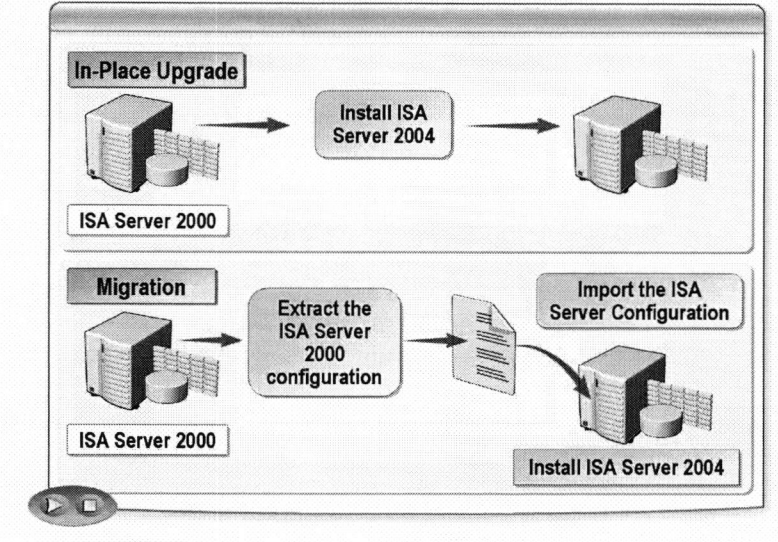

Introduction

ISA Server 2004 supports a full upgrade path for ISA Server 2000. Most ISA Server 2000 rules, network settings, monitoring configuration, and cache configuration will be upgraded to ISA Server 2004.

Options for Upgrading

There are three options for upgrading from ISA Server 2000 to ISA Server 2004:

- *In-place upgrade.* In this scenario, you install ISA Server 2004 on the same computer running ISA Server 2000. Most of the configuration settings are migrated to ISA Server 2004. You do not have to run any migration tools.

- *Migrate ISA Server 2000 configuration to a new ISA Server 2004.* In this scenario, you either install ISA Server 2004 on a different computer, or completely remove ISA Server 2000 before installing ISA Server 2004. In either case, you must use the Migration Tool to export the ISA Server 2000 configuration, and then transfer the configuration information to ISA Server 2004.

- *Migrate Routing and Remote Access configuration.* In this scenario, you may have previously configured virtual private networking using Routing and Remote Access (RRAS). You can use the Migration Tool to copy most of the RRAS VPN information to ISA Server 2004.

In-place upgrade

To perform an in-place upgrade, you install ISA Server 2004 on the server currently running ISA Server 2000. The server may be running Windows 2000 or Windows Server 2003. If the server is running Windows 2000, ensure that all prerequisites for installing ISA Server 2004 are met on the server. You must also ensure that ISA Server Service Pack 1 (SP1) or later is installed on the computer.

When you perform an in-place upgrade, ISA Server 2000 is removed from the computer and ISA Server 2004 is installed with the migrated configuration. Almost all configuration options from ISA Server 2000 are upgraded to ISA Server 2004 with the exception of the following ISA Server 2000 objects and configuration settings:

- Bandwidth rules are no longer supported in ISA Server 2004.

- Permission settings, such as system access control lists (SACLs), are not upgraded.

- Logging and reporting configuration and information are not migrated.

ISA Server 2000 Feature Pack 1 introduced several new features, which are included in ISA Server 2004. Most ISA Server 2000 Feature Pack 1 configuration information is migrated directly to ISA Server 2004.

Note   For detailed information on how to upgrade or migrate from ISA Server 2000 to ISA Server 2004, see Upgrading from Microsoft Internet Security and Acceleration (ISA) Server 2000 Standard Edition. This document is included on the ISA Server 2004 CD-ROM and can be accessed by selecting **Read Migration Guide** from the Autorun startup screen. The document includes detailed information on how configuration options and settings are migrated from ISA Server 2000 to ISA Server 2004.

Migrating an ISA Server 2000 configuration

To migrate the ISA Server 2000 configuration to ISA Server 2004, complete the following high-level steps:

1. Run the ISA Server Migration Wizard on the ISA Server 2000 computer. The wizard creates an .xml file with the configuration information.

2. If you are moving the ISA Server to another server, install Microsoft ISA Server 2004 on the new server. If you are installing ISA Server 2004 on the same server, completely uninstall ISA Server 2000 and then install ISA Server 2004.

3. Import the .xml file to the ISA Server 2004 computer. Before you import the .xml file, you should perform a full backup of the current settings on the ISA Server 2004 computer.

Migrating Routing and Remote Access configuration

If you have a Windows Server providing VPN access through Routing and Remote Access (RRAS), you can upgrade some of the VPN settings to ISA Server 2004. If you install ISA Server 2004 on a server running RRAS, the VPN configuration is automatically migrated into ISA Server. The server does not need to be running ISA Server 2000.

You can also use the ISA Server Migration Wizard to migrate the RRAS settings to a new installation of ISA Server 2004. Use the same steps as previously outlined to complete this migration.

For details on which RRAS VPN configuration is upgraded to ISA Server 2004, see the **Migration Guide** on the ISA Server 2004 CD-ROM.

Lesson: Choosing ISA Server Clients

* Types of ISA Server Clients
* How to Configure a SecureNAT Client
* How to Configure Web Proxy Clients
* Guidelines for Choosing an ISA Server Client

Introduction

The second part of deploying an ISA Server infrastructure is choosing which ISA Server clients to use within your network. ISA Server supports three different clients, including SecureNAT, Firewall client, and Web Proxy clients. This lesson describes these clients and provides guidance to choose the client that best meets your organization's requirements.

Lesson objectives

After completing this lesson, you will be able to:

- Describe the three types of clients supported by ISA Server 2004.
- Configure SecureNAT clients.
- Configure Web Proxy clients.
- Choose the best client for your organization.

Types of ISA Server Clients

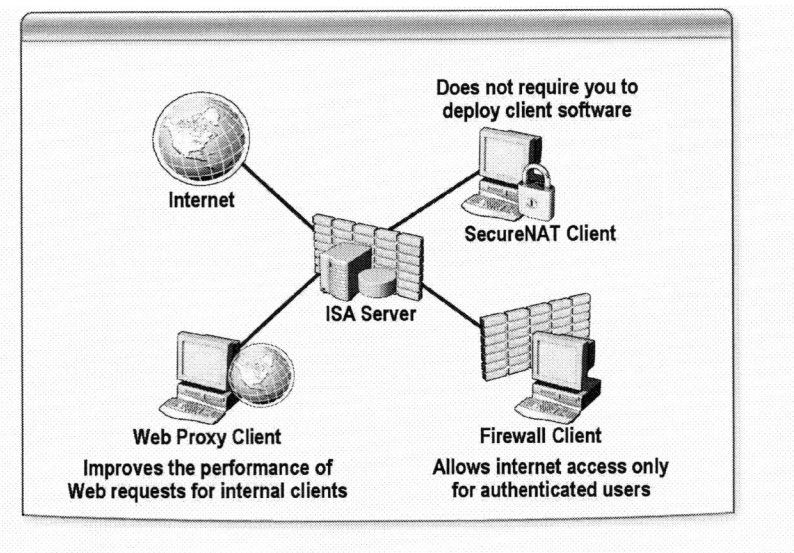

Introduction

An ISA Server client is a client computer that connects to resources on another network by going through ISA Server. ISA Server 2004 supports three different types of clients. The type of client you use on your network depends on your security requirements and whether you want to deploy Firewall Client software to each client computer on your network.

Types of clients

ISA Server provides secure access to the Internet for all of its clients. ISA Server supports three types of clients: Firewall clients, SecureNAT clients, and Web Proxy clients.

- *Firewall clients.* Firewall clients are computers that have Firewall Client software installed and enabled. When a computer with the Firewall Client software installed makes a request for resources on the Internet, the request is directed to the Firewall service on the ISA Server computer. The Firewall service will authenticate and authorize the user and filter the request based on Firewall rules and application filters or other add-ins. The Firewall service may also cache the requested object or serve the object from the ISA Server cache by using the Web Proxy filter. Firewall clients provide the highest level of functionality and security.

- *SecureNAT clients*. SecureNAT clients are computers that do not have Firewall Client software installed. Instead, SecureNAT clients are configured to route all requests for resources on other networks to an internal IP address on the computer running ISA Server. If the network includes only a single segment, the SecureNAT client is configured to use the internal IP address on the computer running ISA Server as the default gateway. Requests from SecureNAT clients are directed first to the network address translation (NAT) driver, which substitutes the ISA Server's external IP address for the internal IP address of the SecureNAT client. The client request is then directed to the Firewall service to determine if access is allowed. Finally, the request may be filtered by application filters and other extensions. The Firewall service may also cache the requested object or deliver the object from the ISA Server cache. The SecureNAT clients are easiest to configure because you need to configure only the default gateway on the client computers.

- *Web Proxy clients*. Web Proxy clients are any computers that run CERN-compatible Web applications such as Web browsers. Requests from Web Proxy clients are directed to the Firewall service on the ISA Server computer to determine if access is allowed. The Firewall service may also cache the requested object or serve the object from the ISA Server Web cache. Because most client computers already run Web Proxy–compatible applications, Web Proxy clients do not require any special software to be installed. However, the Web application must be configured to use the ISA Server.

Regardless of client type, when ISA Server receives a Hypertext Transfer Protocol (HTTP) request, the client is treated as if it is a Web Proxy client. Even when a Firewall client or a SecureNAT client makes an HTTP request, the client is considered a Web Proxy client.

Both Firewall client computers and SecureNAT client computers may also be Web Proxy clients. If the Web application on the computer is configured explicitly to use ISA Server for proxy services, all HTTP, FTP, and Secure HTTP (HTTPS) are sent to the Web Proxy listener on ISA Server.

Client characteristics   The following table compares the ISA Server clients.

Feature	SecureNAT Client	Firewall Client	Web Proxy Client
Client installation	No client installation but some client configuration	Client installation required	No client installation but application configuration
Operating system support	All operating systems that support TCP/IP	Only Windows clients	All operating systems that support compatible Web applications
Protocol support	Application filters required for multi-connection protocols	All Winsock applications	HTTP, HTTPS, and FTP over HTTP
User level authentication	Yes for VPN clients only	Yes	Yes

How to Configure a SecureNAT Client

* SecureNAT clients do not require client installation or client configuration

* On a single subnet network, configure the IP address of the internal network interface as the SecureNAT client default gateway

* On a multiple subnet network, configure the IP address of the router as the SecureNAT client default gateway

Introduction

Client computers that do not have Firewall Client software are SecureNAT clients if they are configured to use the internal address of the ISA Server as their default gateway. You do not need to deploy or configure a client application on a SecureNAT client which makes the SecureNAT client the easiest client to implement.

Because requests from SecureNAT clients are handled by the Microsoft Firewall service, SecureNAT clients benefit from the Firewall service security features. All ISA Server access rules can be applied to SecureNAT clients, with the exception of user-level authentication. Policies regarding protocol usage, destination, and content type are also applied to SecureNAT clients.

Configuring default gateways for SecureNAT clients

Although SecureNAT clients do not require special software, you must configure the default gateway so that all traffic destined for the Internet is sent through the ISA Server. You can configure clients manually or by using the Dynamic Host Configuration Protocol (DHCP) service.

To configure SecureNAT clients on a network without routers, set the SecureNAT client's IP default gateway settings to the IP address of the ISA Server computer's internal network interface.

To configure SecureNAT clients on a network with routers, set the default gateway settings to the router closest to the SecureNAT client. Ensure that the router is configured to forward IP packets to the Internet so that all packets are routed through the ISA Server computer. Optimally, routers should use a default gateway that routes along the shortest path to the ISA Server computer.

How to Configure Web Proxy Clients

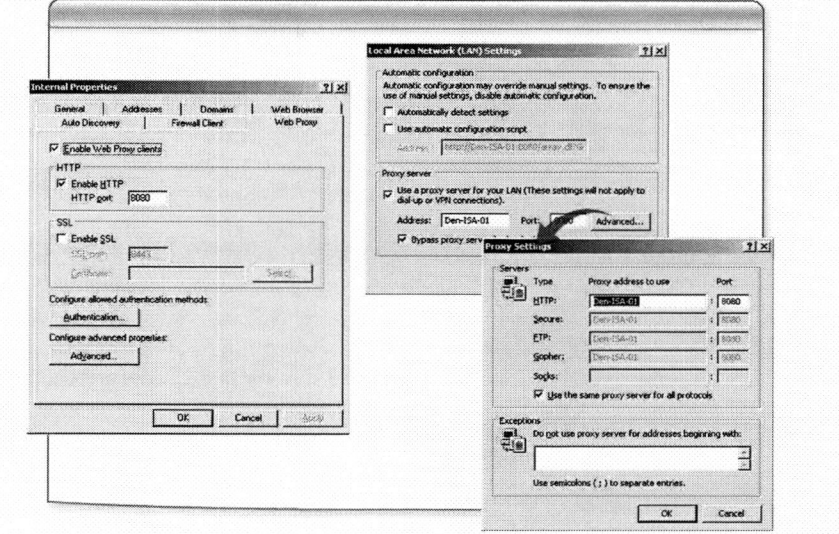

Introduction

A Web Proxy client is a client computer that has a Web Proxy application installed and configured to use the ISA Server as a proxy server. The most common type of Web Proxy application is a Web browser.

Configuring the ISA Server for Web Proxy clients

The first step in enabling Web Proxy clients is to configure the ISA Server to allow connections from these clients. To do this, use the following procedure:

1. In the console tree of **ISA Server Management**, expand **Configuration**, and click **Networks**.

2. In the details pane, click the **Networks** tab and select the applicable network.

3. On the **Tasks** tab, click **Edit Selected Network**.

4. On the **Web Proxy** tab, click **Enable Web Proxy clients**.

5. Configure the HTTP and SSL ports and the authentication options for Web Proxy clients.

6. Click **OK**.

Web Proxy client configuration

You do not have to install any software to configure Web Proxy clients. However, you must configure the Web applications on the client computers to use the ISA Server computer as the proxy server. To configure the Web Proxy settings on Internet Explorer 6, use the following procedure:

1. Open Internet Explorer, click the **Tools** menu, and then click **Internet Options**.

2. On the **Connections** tab, click **LAN Settings**.

3. On the **LAN Settings** page, click **Use a proxy server for your LAN**. In the **Address** box, type the name or IP address of the proxy server. In the **Port** box, type the port number that the client will use to connect to the proxy server.

4. Select **Bypass proxy server for local addresses** to configure the Web Proxy to bypass the proxy server when accessing resources on the local network. When this option is selected, Internet Explorer sends requests directly to Web servers located on the same network segment as the client rather than forwarding the request to the proxy server.

5. To configure additional settings, click **Advanced**. On the **Proxy Settings** page, you can configure different proxy servers for various types of servers, and specify addresses that the Web Proxy client should connect to directly rather than through the proxy server.

Automatic configuration of the Web Proxy client

You can set an option on the Web Proxy client so that the client automatically downloads a configuration script, located on the ISA Server computer, every time a Web browser is opened. By enabling the automatic configuration on the Web Proxy client, you can modify the Web Proxy configuration on the ISA Server without having to reconfigure each individual Web browser.

To configure the client to be configured automatically, use the following procedure:

1. Open Internet Explorer, click the **Tools** menu, and then click **Internet Options**.

2. On the **Connections** tab, click **LAN Settings**.

3. On the **LAN Settings** page, click **Automatically detect settings** and **Use automatic configuration script**. In the **Address** box, type in the URL for the configuration script. The default configuration URL is http://*ISA_Server*/array.dll?Get.Routing.Script, where *ISA_Server* is the fully qualified domain name or IP address of the ISA Server computer.

Using the Firewall Client to configure Web Proxy settings

If you have the Firewall Client installed on a client computer, you can also use the Firewall Client to configure the Web browser settings. These settings can be configured automatically or disabled altogether. To enable this, you use ISA Server Management to configure the following Firewall Client settings and Web browser settings:

■ ISA Server computer and port to which the client will connect

■ Automatic discovery settings

■ Computers that the Firewall client's Web browser will access directly

■ Backup route, if the ISA Server computer is unavailable

When the Firewall Client software is installed—and with every user connection to the ISA Server—the Web browser on the client computer is configured with those settings.

Guidelines for Choosing an ISA Server Client

If you need to...	Then use...
Avoid deploying client software	SecureNAT clients
Use ISA Server only for forward caching	SecureNAT or Web Proxy clients
Allow access only for authenticated clients	Firewall clients or Web Proxy clients
Publish servers on your internal network	SecureNAT clients
Improve Web performance for non-Windows operating systems	SecureNAT or Web Proxy clients

Introduction

One of the choices that you need to make as you deploy ISA Server 2004 is which ISA Server client you will deploy. Each client has advantages and disadvantages.

Choosing an ISA client

Use the following guidelines to determine which clients to deploy for ISA Server.

If you need to	Then use
Avoid deploying client software or configuring client computers	SecureNAT clients. SecureNAT clients do not require any software or specific configuration. Firewall clients require that you deploy Firewall Client software and Web Proxy clients require that you configure Web applications on client computers.
Use ISA Server only for forward caching of Web objects	SecureNAT or Web Proxy clients. If you use SecureNAT clients in this scenario, you will not have to deploy any special software or configure the client computers. Instead, client requests are transparently passed to ISA Server for caching.
Allow access only for authenticated clients	Firewall clients or Web Proxy clients. For Firewall clients, you can configure user-based firewall policy rules. You can also configure user-based rules for Web Proxy clients, but the rule will be effective only if the Web application can pass the authentication information.

(*continued*)

If you need to	Then use
Publish servers that are located on your Internal network	SecureNAT clients. Internal servers can be published as SecureNAT clients. This eliminates the need for creating special configuration files on the publishing server.
Improve Web performance in an environment with non-Windows operating systems	SecureNAT clients or Web Proxy clients. Any client computer that supports TCP/IP can be a SecureNAT client. SecureNAT client requests are transparently passed to the Firewall service and can also be cached. Most operating systems also support Web Proxy–compatible applications.

Important Some protocols and applications require secondary connections. For example, when you use FTP, by default, the client initiates a primary connection to the server and the server then initiates a secondary connection to the client. ISA Server must use an application filter that edits the data stream to allow SecureNAT clients to use such protocols and applications. ISA Server includes several application filters, such as an FTP filter and an H.323 filter. If ISA Server does not include the appropriate application filter for a protocol or application, SecureNAT clients cannot use this protocol or application.

Practice: Configuring SecureNAT and Web Proxy Clients

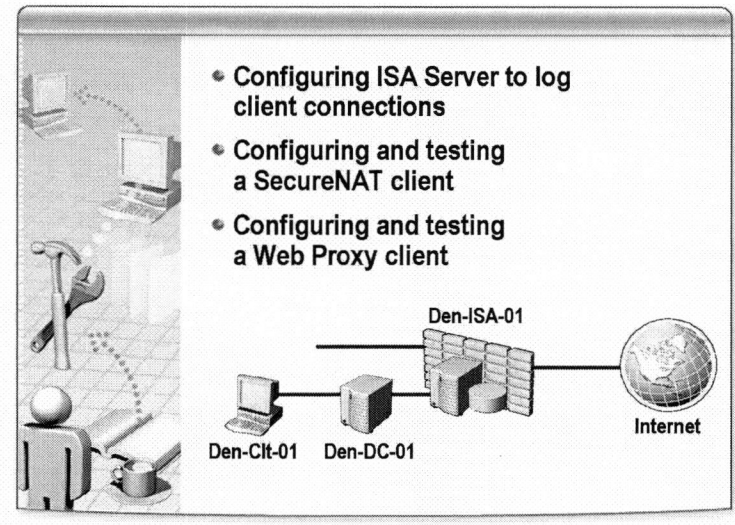

- Configuring ISA Server to log client connections
- Configuring and testing a SecureNAT client
- Configuring and testing a Web Proxy client

Den-ISA-01

Internet

Den-Clt-01   Den-DC-01

Introduction

In this practice, you will configure logging on the ISA Server to monitor client connections to the server. You will then configure a SecureNAT client and a Web Proxy client and test the client connections.

▶ **To prepare for this practice**

1. You will need the Den-DC-01 virtual machine, the Den-Clt-01 virtual machine and the Den-ISA-01 virtual machine for this practice.

2. If necessary, start or resume the required virtual machines and then, on Den-ISA-01, log on to the cohovineyard domain with a user name of **Administrator** and a password of **P@ssw0rd**.

Practice

▶ **Configuring ISA Server 2004 to log client connections**

1. Open **ISA Server Management**, expand Den-ISA-01, and then click **Monitoring**.

2. On the **Logging** tab, in the **Details** pane click **Start Query**.

▶ **Configuring and testing a SecureNAT client**

1. Switch to the Den-DC-01 virtual machine, and log on to the cohovineyard domain with a user name of **Administrator** and a password of **P@ssw0rd**.

2. Open a **Command Prompt** and type **IPConfig /all**. Notice that the server does not have a default gateway configured.

3. Click **Start**, point to **Control Panel**, point to **Network Connections**, and then click **Local Area Connection**. Click **Properties**.

4. Click **Internet Protocol (TCP/IP)**, and then click **Properties**.

5. In the **Default gateway** box, type **192.168.1.1**. Click **OK**, and then click **Close** twice.

6. Open **Internet Explorer**. If you receive an Internet Explorer error message select **In the future, do not show this message** and then click **OK**. Try connecting to http://131.107.1.200. The connection will fail.

7. Close the open windows.

8. Switch to the Den-ISA-01 virtual machine and locate the events logged that used the **HTTP** protocol. Confirm that the HTTP request was denied by the **Default rule**.

▶ **Configuring and testing a Web Proxy client**

1. Switch to the Den-Clt-01 virtual machine, and log on to the cohovineyard domain with a user name of **Administrator** and a password of **P@ssw0rd**.

2. Open **Internet Explorer**. Click **Tools**, and then click **Internet Options**.

3. In the **Internet Options** dialog box, click **Connections** tab.

4. Click **LAN Settings**. On the **LAN Settings** page, click **Use a proxy server for your LAN**. In the **Address** box, type **Den-ISA-01**. In the **Port** box, type **8080**.

5. Select **Bypass proxy server for local addresses**. Click **OK** twice.

6. In the **Address** box, type **web.cohovineyard.com**. If you receive an Internet Explorer error message, click **OK**. The connection will fail.

7. Review the Proxy Message.

8. Switch to the Den-ISA-01 virtual machine and locate the events logged that used the **HTTP** protocol and the **Destination Port** of 8080. Confirm that the request was denied by the **Default rule**.

9. On the **Tasks** tab, click **Stop Query**. Close all open windows.

Lesson: Installing and Configuring Firewall Clients

* How to Configure Firewall Client Settings
* The Firewall Client Installation and Configuration Process
* Options for Automating the Firewall Client Installation

Introduction

In addition to the SecureNAT and Web Proxy clients, ISA Server also supports Firewall clients. Firewall clients provide the highest level of functionality and security, but also require a client installation on each computer. This lesson describes how to install and configure the Firewall Client software.

Lesson objectives

After completing this lesson, you will be able to:

- Configure the Firewall Client settings on the ISA Server
- Install and configure the Firewall Client
- Identify options for automating the installation of the Firewall Client

How to Configure Firewall Client Settings

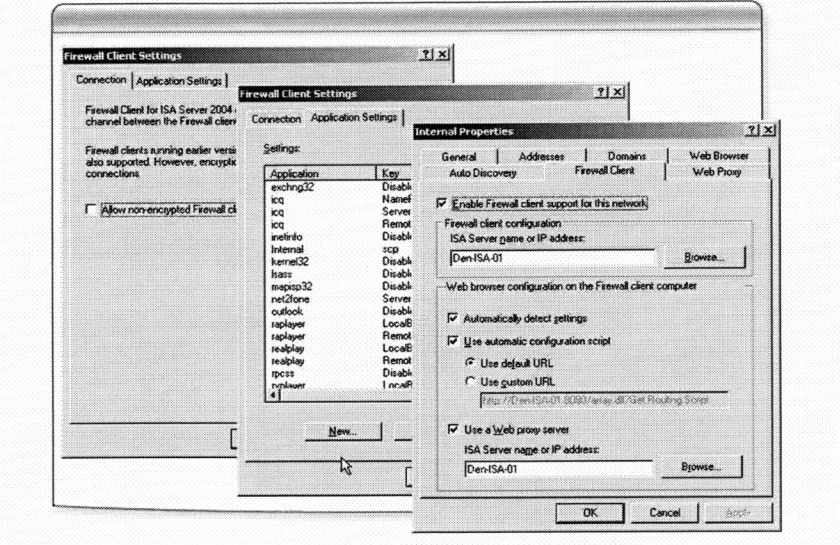

Introduction

When a computer running the Firewall Client connects to the ISA Server, the Firewall Client checks for any new client configuration settings on the server. This means that you can modify the Firewall Client by configuring the settings using ISA Server Management. The settings are then applied to the client when the client connects, or updated every six hours on the client computer if the client computer stays connected.

Firewall Client settings

You can configure the following Firewall Client settings:

- *Application settings*. These settings define how the Firewall Client connects to ISA Server for specific applications.

- *Internal network and local domains*. These settings define the set of IP addresses and domains that the Firewall Client recognizes as local. The Firewall Client will connect to resources in these locations directly, without going through the ISA Server.

- *Automatic discovery*. By enabling automatic discovery, Firewall clients will automatically discover the appropriate ISA Server computer.

- *Web browser settings for the Firewall client*. The Firewall Client application can automatically update the Web Proxy settings on the Firewall Client computer. These settings are obtained from ISA Server when the Firewall Client settings are updated. You can configure how the Web browser will be set on the Firewall Client computer.

ISA Server supports earlier versions of the Firewall Client software, including Firewall Client for ISA Server 2000 and the Winsock Proxy client (from Microsoft Proxy Server 2.0). You can enable support for these clients on the ISA Server.

How to configure Firewall Client versions and application settings

The Firewall Client settings are configured in two different locations within the ISA Server Management Firewall.

To configure the versions of Firewall Client supported and the application settings, use the following procedure:

1. Open **ISA Server Management**, expand the **Configuration** folder, and click **General**.

2. Click **Define Firewall Client Settings**.

3. On the **Connection** tab, configure whether earlier versions of the Firewall Client software are supported.

4. On the **Application Settings** tab, configure the application settings for applications. To configure a specific application, click the application name and click **Edit**.

How to configure the Firewall client settings for a network

To configure the other Firewall Client settings, use the following procedure:

1. Open **ISA Server Management**, expand the **Configuration** folder and click **Networks**.

2. In the details pane, click the **Networks** tab.

3. To edit the internal network settings, click **Internal**.

4. On the **Tasks** tab, click **Edit Selected Network**.

5. To configure the internal addresses, click the **Addresses** tab and do one of the following:

    a. To add a specific range of IP addresses, click **Add**. Then, type the first address of the network address range in **Starting address** and the last address of the network address range in **Ending address**.

    b. To add IP addresses associated with a specific adapter, click **Add Adapter** and then, in **Network Interfaces**, select one or more adapters.

    c. To add private address ranges, click **Add Private** and then select a range from the list.

6. To configure the internal domains, click the **Domains** tab and click **Add** to add the domain names for the internal network.

7. To configure the Web browser settings, click the **Firewall Client** tab and verify that the **Enable Firewall Client support for this network** check box is selected.

    a. Select **Automatically detect settings** if the client computer should automatically attempt to find the ISA Server computer.

    b. Select **Use automatic configuration script** if the Web browser on the Firewall Client computer should use configuration information that is contained in the specified automatic configuration script. If you select this option, specify **Use default URL** or **Use custom URL**.

    c. Select **Use a Web proxy server** to specify the ISA Server name.

The Firewall Client Installation and Configuration Process

The Firewall Client:

- Uses a common Winsock service provider that other Winsock applications use to connect to application servers
- Intercepts Winsock client application calls for remote application servers and redirects the request to ISA Server

Install the Firewall Client:

- From the Firewall Client share on computer running ISA Server or another network share

Introduction

A Firewall Client is a computer with Firewall Client software installed and enabled.

How the Firewall client works

The Firewall Client computer runs Winsock applications that use the Microsoft Firewall service of ISA Server 2004. Setting up a Firewall Client does not configure individual Winsock applications. Instead, it uses a common Winsock service provider that the other applications use. When the client computer initiates a Winsock application, the Firewall Client intercepts the application calls. The Firewall Client checks the destination computer name or IP address and determines whether to route the request to the ISA Server computer or to server on the local network. If the address is in the range of addresses included in the specific network, then the application request is sent directly to the application server.

If the destination computer is not considered local, the request is sent to the Firewall service on the ISA server. The Firewall service handles the request, forwarding it to the appropriate destination as permitted.

You can specify whether Firewall Client support is enabled for a specific network. If Firewall Client support is enabled, ISA Server will accept incoming requests on TCP or UDP port 1745.

Installing Firewall Client

One of the options available when installing ISA Server is to install the Firewall Client Share on the ISA Server. You can also copy the Firewall Client installation files to a shared folder on another server on the network. To install the Firewall Client, users connect to the share and run the setup program.

After installing the client software, users can modify the server name to which the client connects by specifying a different name either on the ISA Server computer to which the client currently connects or by changing the name in the Firewall Client software. The configuration changes take effect after the firewall configuration is refreshed.

You must be a member of the Administrators group on the client computer to install the Firewall Client. To install the Firewall Client software from a shared folder, use the following procedure:

1. Connect to the shared folder that contains the Firewall Client installation files. If you are using the shared folder on the ISA Server, the default share name is *ISA_Server_name*/MSPClnt.

2. Right-click **MS_FPC.msi** and click **Install**. Alternatively, you can double-click **Setup.exe**.

3. On the **Welcome to the Install Wizard for the Microsoft Firewall Client** page, click **Next**.

4. On the **Destination Folder** page, review the default installation folder location. Click **Change** if you want to change the installation folder. Click **Next** to continue.

5. On the **ISA Server Computer Select** screen, you can select how the Firewall Client will locate the ISA Server. To manually configure the server name or IP Address, select **Connect to this ISA Server** and type the ISA Server name or IP address. To enable automatic discovery of the ISA Server, select **Automatically detect the appropriate ISA Server computer**. Click **Next**.

6. On the **Ready to Install the Program** page, click **Install**.

7. When the installation wizard finishes, click **Finish**.

After the installation is complete, the Firewall Client application is enabled. The Microsoft Firewall Client Management icon is added to the system tray. To configure the Firewall Client configuration on the client, right-click the icon and click **Configure**. On the **General** tab, you can enable or disable the Firewall Client and configure the Client to automatically detect the ISA Server or manually configure the ISA Server. On the **Web Browser** tab, you can enable or disable automatic configuration of the Web browser.

Note   You can install Firewall Client software on client computers that run Microsoft Windows Server 2003, Windows 2000 Server, Windows XP, Windows 98 Second Edition, Windows Millennium Edition, or Microsoft Windows NT® 4.0. You cannot install Firewall Client software on the ISA Server computer.

Practice: Installing the Firewall Client

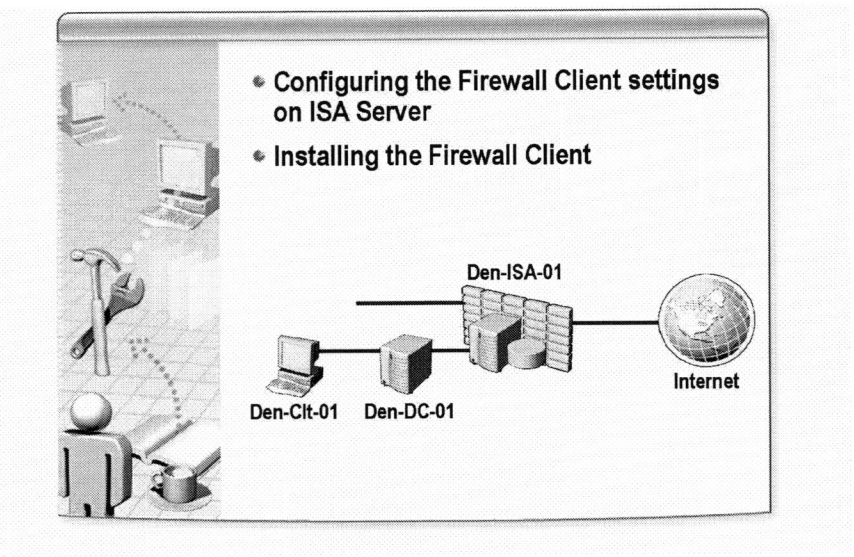

Introduction

In this practice, you will configure the Firewall Client settings on the ISA Server and then install the Firewall Client software from a shared folder on the ISA Server.

▶ **To prepare for this practice**

1. You will need the Den-DC-01 virtual machine, the Den-Clt-01 virtual machine and the Den-ISA-01 virtual machine for this practice.

2. If necessary, start or resume the required virtual machines and then, on Den-ISA-01, log on to the cohovineyard domain with a user name of **Administrator** and a password of **P@ssw0rd**.

Practice

▶ **Configuring the Firewall Client settings on the ISA Server**

1. Open **ISA Server Management**, expand **Configuration** if it is not expanded, and click **General**.

2. Click **Define Firewall Client Settings**.

3. On the **Connection** tab, click **Allow Non-Encrypted Firewall Client Connections**. Click **OK**.

4. Click **Apply** to apply the changes and click **OK** when the changes have been applied.

5. In **ISA Server Management**, under **Configuration**, click **Networks**.

6. In the details pane, click the **Networks** tab and then click **Internal**.

7. On the **Tasks** tab, click **Edit Selected Network**.

8. Click the **Domains** tab, and click **Add** to add the domain names for the internal network. Type ***.cohovineyard.com**, and click **OK**.

9. Click the **Firewall Client** tab and verify that the **Enable Firewall Client support for this network** check box is selected.

   a. Clear the **Automatically detect settings** option.

   b. Clear the **Use automatic configuration script** option.

   c. Ensure that **Use a Web proxy server** is selected and **Den-ISA-01** is listed in the **ISA server name or IP address** box.

10. Click **OK**.

11. Click **Apply** to apply the changes and click **OK** when the changes have been applied.

▶ **Installing the Firewall Client**

1. Switch to the Den-Clt-01 virtual machine.

2. On the **Start** menu, click **Run**. Type **\\Den-ISA-01\MSPClnt** and click **OK**.

3. Right-click **MS_FWC** and click **Install**.

4. On the **Welcome to the Install Wizard for the Microsoft Firewall Client** page, click **Next**.

5. On the **Destination Folder** page, review the default installation folder location. Click **Next** to continue.

6. On the **ISA Server Computer Select** screen, select **Connect to this ISA Server** and type **Den-ISA-01**. Click **Next**.

7. On the **Ready to Install the Program** page, click **Install**.

8. On the **Install Wizard Completed** page, click **Finish**. Close all open windows.

Options for Automating the Firewall Client Installation

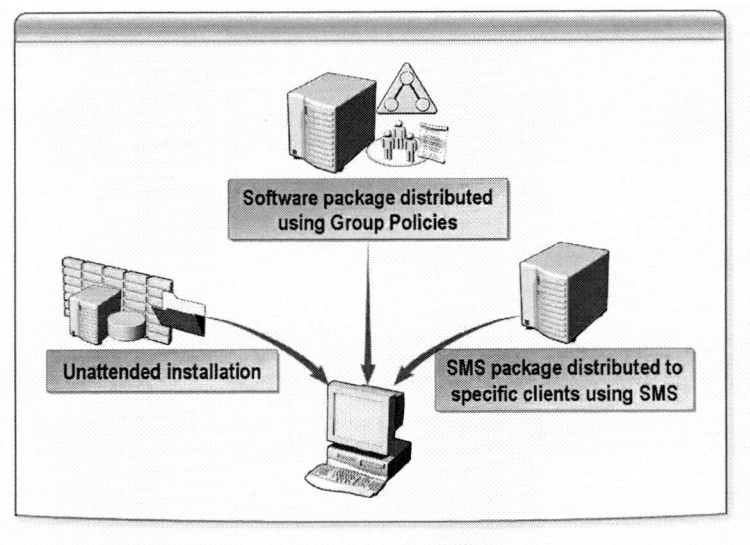

Introduction

If you are deploying the Firewall Client to a large number of clients, you may choose to automate the Firewall Client installation. You can perform an unattended installation; use Group Policy, or Systems Management Server (SMS) to automate the installation.

Before deploying Firewall Client, configure the Firewall Client settings using ISA Server Management. By configuring these settings first, all the clients will get the desired Firewall Client configuration.

Creating an unattended install of the Firewall Client

To complete an unattended installation of Firewall Client, at the command prompt, use the following syntax:

```
Path\Setup.exe /v " [SERVER_NAME_OR_IP=ISA_Server_Name]
[ENABLE_AUTO_DETECT={1|0}] [REFRESH_WEB_PROXY={1|0}]/qn "
```

where:

- Path is the path to the shared ISA Server 2004 client installation files.

- ISA_Server_Name is the name of the ISA Server computer to which the Firewall Client should connect.

- ENABLE_AUTO_DETECT=1 specifies that the Firewall Client should automatically detect which ISA Server computer to connect to.

- REFRESH_WEB_PROXY=1 indicates that the Firewall Client configuration should be updated with the Web Proxy configuration specified on the ISA Server computer.

To automate the unattended installation of the Firewall Client, you can provide users with a link that will run the unattended installation from a network location. Users must be logged on as local Administrators in order to install the Firewall Client.

Using Active Directory Group Policy

You can also use the Software Installation option in Active Directory Group Policy to automate the installation of the Firewall Client. To distribute the Firewall Client using this option:

1. Copy the Firewall Client installation files to a network share.

2. Determine whether you wish to distribute the client software to users or computers. If you distribute the software to users, the software will be installed the next time the user logs on or the user can initiate the installation from **Add/Remove Programs**. If you distribute the software to computers, the software will be installed the next time the computer restarts.

3. Create a new software distribution package. Configure the software distribution package to use the installation files on the shared folder. You can also configure the distribution options for the software package.

4. When users log on or the client computers reboot, the Firewall Client is installed. The Firewall Client will then automatically discover the ISA Server and download the configuration information.

Using Systems Management Server 2003

Organizations that have deployed Microsoft Systems Management Server (SMS) 2003 can use the software distribution feature of SMS to distribute the ISA Firewall Client. Software distribution in SMS 2003 provides the ability to deploy Windows Installer (.msi) or Package Definition Format (.pdf, .sms) files to any computer that is assigned to the SMS environment. To deploy the ISA Firewall Client using SMS:

1. Create a collection that includes any computer that is to receive the ISA Firewall Client software. A collection is a logical group of resources such as computers or users that are gathered together to be managed within SMS. You can set specific requirements such as IP address, hardware configuration, or add clients directly by name to group all resources that are to have the ISA Firewall Client installed.

2. Create an SMS package by importing the ISA Firewall Client Windows Installer file (MS_FWC.msi). The Windows Installer file automatically creates a number of attended and unattended installation program options that can be deployed on a per-system or per-user basis. Programs are also created to uninstall the client if the need arises. The per-system programs are configured to install the client with administrative rights whether or not the user is logged on. The per-user programs install the client using the credentials of the logged-on user.

3. Create an SMS advertisement, which specifies the target collection and program to install. In order to control deployment, you can schedule a time for the program to be advertised to collection members.

Lesson: Advanced Firewall Client Configuration

- Advanced Firewall Client Configuration Options
- Firewall Client Configuration Files
- What is the Automatic Discovery Feature?

Introduction

In most organizations, you can deploy the Firewall Client and then use the configuration options on the ISA Server to manage any client configurations. In some cases, however, you may need to configure specific settings on a Firewall Client, or you may want to automate the process by which Firewall Client acquire a configuration from the ISA Server. This lesson explains how to perform these advanced configuration options.

Lesson objectives

After completing this lesson, you will be able to:

- Describe the advanced Firewall Client configuration options.
- Modify the Firewall Client configuration files.
- Configure automatic discovery.

Advanced Firewall Client Configuration Options

Locallat.txt:

- A client computer-specific file that defines local addresses for that client
- The client uses its own routing table, the server-specific settings, and the Locallat.txt file to determine the local IP addresses

Advanced Firewall Client settings:

- Can configure locally for each user and for each computer
- Configure changes to Firewall Client .ini files

Introduction

In addition to the Firewall Client settings that you can configure on the ISA Server for distribution to all clients, there are also advanced settings that you configure on the client computer running the Firewall Client. In most cases, these settings will be specific to a particular client.

Configuring local addresses

One of the advanced options that you can configure is the local address table. By default, Firewall Client considers all addresses on the network for which it is configured, as well as the addresses specified in the local routing table on the Firewall client computer, as local. Each time a Winsock application on that client attempts to establish a connection to an IP address, the Firewall Client uses this information plus the internal network information on the ISA Server to determine whether the IP address is on the local network.

You can modify this client behavior by creating a client computer–specific file that defines local addresses for that client. Using a text editor, you can create a custom client local address table (LAT) file named Locallat.txt and place it in the \Documents and Settings\All Users\Application Data\Microsoft\Firewall Client 2004 folder on the Firewall Client computer. You can add additional IP address ranges that the client recognizes as part of the local network. If this file exists, the client uses its own routing table, the server-specific settings, and the Locallat.txt file to determine the IP addresses that are part of the local network.

Example

When you create the Locallat.txt file, enter IP address pairs in the file. Each address pair defines either a range of IP addresses or a single IP address. The following example shows a Locallat.txt file that has two entries. The first entry is an IP address range and the second entry is a single IP address. Note that the second entry is an IP address and not a subnet mask.

10.51.0.0   10.51.255.255

10.52.144.103   10.52.144.103

Advanced Firewall Client settings

When you install the Firewall Client software, it uses the settings configured on the ISA Server 2004 computer that the client connects to. These server settings determine settings such as automatic Web Proxy configuration, ISA Server name, ISA Server automatic detection, and others. The Firewall Client settings are updated from the ISA Server updates each time a client computer is restarted, and every six hours after an initial refresh is made.

For most Winsock applications, the default Firewall Client configuration works with no need for further modification. However, in some cases, you will need to add client configuration information. Firewall Client can be configured locally for each user, and for each computer, on the Firewall Client computer. The configuration is done by making changes to Firewall Client .ini files, which are installed on the Firewall Client computer.

Firewall Client Configuration Files

```
Application.ini
    [FW_Client_App]
    Disable=0
    NameResolution=R
    LocalBindTcpPorts=7777
    LocalBindUdpPorts=7000-7022, 7100-7170
    RemoteBindTcpPorts=30
    RemoteBindUdpPorts=3000-3050
    ServerBindTcpPorts=100-300
    ProxyBindIp=80:192.168.10.20, 82:192.168.10.30
    KillOldSession=1
    Persistent=1
    ForceCredentials=1
    NameResolutionForLocalHost=L
```

Introduction

The Firewall Client configuration information is stored in a set of files, which are installed on the Firewall Client computer. Specifically, when Firewall Client is installed on the computer, the files listed in the following table are created on the Firewall client computer:

File name	Configuration settings
Common.ini	Specifies the common configuration for all applications
Management.ini	Specifies Firewall Client Management configuration settings
Application.ini	Specifies application-specific configurations settings

These files are created for all users logged on to the computer and can also be manually created for each specific user on the computer. The per-user settings override the general configuration settings. These files are created in different locations, depending on the operating system. For example, on Windows XP computers, the files may be located in one of two locations:

- \Documents and Settings\All Users\Application Data\Microsoft\ Firewall Client 2004 folder

- \Documents and Settings*user_name*\Local Settings\Application Data\ Microsoft\Firewall Client 2004 folder

The settings in these files are applied as follows:

1. The .ini files in the user's folder take precedence. Any configuration settings here are used by Firewall Client to determine how the application will function.

2. The .ini files in the All Users folder are applied next. If a specified configuration setting contradicts the user-specific settings, it is ignored.

3. Finally, Firewall Client examines the server-level settings. Any configuration settings specified on ISA Server are applied. If a specified configuration setting contradicts the user-specific or computer-specific settings, it is ignored.

Firewall Client configuration sample files

If a specific client computer requires unique Firewall Client settings, you can modify these .ini files to meet the client requirements.

The Common.ini file specifies common configuration for all applications. In most cases, the common.ini file very simply consists of lines like the following:

```
[Common]
ServerName=Den-ISA-01
Disable=0
Autodetection=0
```

By default, the management.ini file contains only a setting that specifies whether the Firewall Client is enabled to modify the Web Proxy settings on the client.

The Application.ini file is a more complicated file and also the file that is most often modified. This file specifies configuration settings for specific applications and, in most cases, it is these specific applications that require a unique setting that must be configured on the Firewall Client. For example, you may have several users on your network running a Winsock application, but only a subset of those users should be able to use that application to access Internet resources. One way to enable this is to configure the application.ini files on the client computers used by the users that should use the application to gain access to Internet resources.

The following is an example of part of an Application.ini file showing possible configuration settings for an application:

```
[FW_Client_App]
Disable=0
NameResolution=R
LocalBindTcpPorts=7777
LocalBindUdpPorts=7000-7022, 7100-7170
RemoteBindTcpPorts=30
RemoteBindUdpPorts=3000-3050
ServerBindTcpPorts=100-300
ProxyBindIp=80:192.168.10.20, 82:192.168.10.30
KillOldSession=1
Persistent=1
ForceCredentials=1
NameResolutionForLocalHost=L
```

Note For detailed information on all the settings that you can configure in the .ini files, see the Advanced Firewall Client Configuration Settings topic in ISA Server Online Help.

What Is the Automatic Discovery Feature?

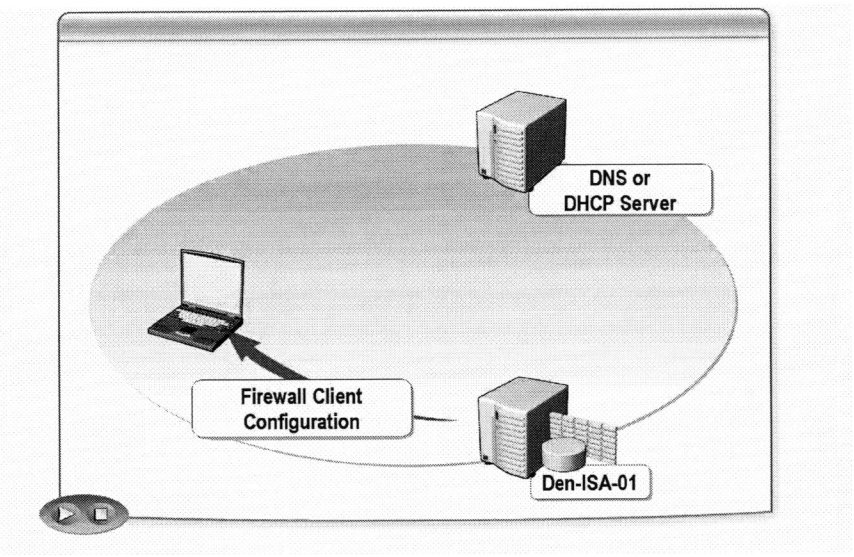

Introduction

For a Web Proxy client or a Firewall Client to connect to an ISA Server computer, you must configure the browser or Firewall Client to forward Internet requests to a specific ISA Server computer. If the ISA Server computer becomes unavailable or you want to use a different ISA Server computer, you must change this configuration before the client will connect to an ISA Server.

Why use automatic discovery?

When you enable automatic discovery, Firewall clients and Web Proxy clients can automatically find an ISA Server computer on the network. Using automatic discovery can help you minimize the time spent troubleshooting connection problems on client computers. Web Proxy clients enable automatic discovery by using Web Proxy AutoDiscovery Protocol (WPAD) information. Firewall clients use the Winsock Proxy AutoDetect Protocol (WSPAD). Both clients connect to an ISA Server computer and request configuration information after locating the ISA Server computer by using a WPAD entry on the Dynamic Host Configuration Protocol (DHCP) server or the Domain Name System (DNS) server.

Automatic discovery is especially useful when you move your computer from one network to another. For example, if you use a laptop computer at home and at work, both the Firewall Client and Microsoft Internet Explorer use ISA Server when you are connected to the corporate network, but you can gain access to the Internet directly when you are working at home.

How automatic discovery works

The automatic discovery process works as follows:

1. When automatic discovery is enabled, the Firewall Client or the Web Proxy client requests an object from the ISA Server computer that is configured to fulfill requests. If the ISA Server computer does not respond and if automatic discovery is enabled for the client, it starts the automatic discovery process.

2. A client connects to a DNS or DHCP server for the ISA Server location information.

3. The client uses a WPAD entry to locate an ISA Server computer.

4. The client connects to the ISA Server computer specified in the WPAD entry to retrieve configuration information by using the WPAD protocol or the WSPAD protocol. The connection uses TCP port 80.

5. The client configures itself by using the configuration information that it retrieved.

How to enable automatic discovery

To enable automatic discovery, complete these steps:

1. Enable the ISA Server to publish automatic configuration information.

2. Configure the DHCP server or DNS server to provide automatic discovery server names for ISA Server clients.

Note The automatic discovery values need to be assigned on each DHCP server or scope that will be used by ISA Server clients. With a DNS server, the DNS values are assigned to DNS zones. This means you must configure each DNS zone, including delegated zones, that the ISA Server clients use.

Practice: Configuring Automatic Discovery

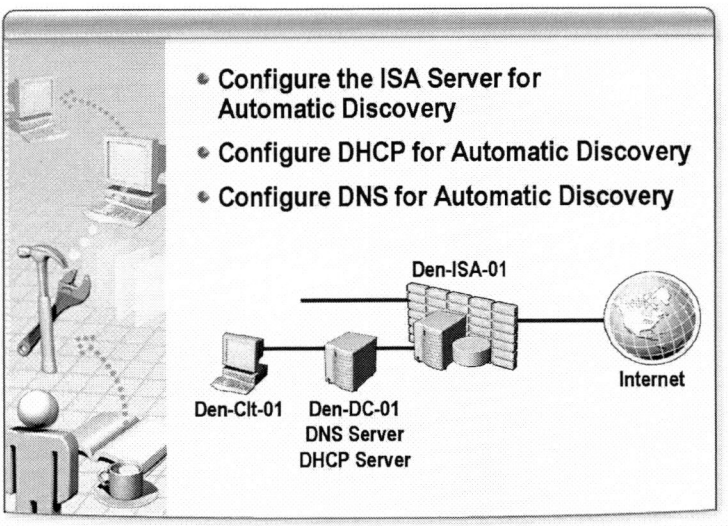

Introduction

In this practice, you will configure the ISA Server to publish automatic discovery information, and then configure both DNS and DHCP to enable automatic discovery.

Practice

▶ **To prepare for this practice**

1. You will need the Den-DC-01 virtual machine, the Den-Clt-01 virtual machine and the Den-ISA-01 virtual machine for this practice.

2. If necessary, start or resume the required virtual machines and then, on Den-ISA-01, log on to the cohovineyard domain with a user name of **Administrator** and a password of **P@ssw0rd**.

▶ **To prepare the ISA Server for automatic discovery**

1. Open **ISA Server Management** (if it is not already open), expand **Configuration**, and click the **Networks** tab.

2. Click **Internal** and, on the **Tasks** tab, click **Edit Selected Network**.

3. On the **Auto Discovery** tab, click the **Publish automatic discovery information** check box and then click **OK**.

4. Click **Apply** to apply the changes and click **OK** when the changes have been applied.

▶ **To prepare the DHCP Server for automatic discovery**

1. Switch to the Den-DC-01 virtual machine. Log on to Den-DC-01 using **CohoVineyard\Administrator** with a password of **P@ssw0rd**.

2. Open **DHCP** from the **Administrative Tools** folder.

3. Expand **Den-DC-01** and then right-click the server name. Click **Set Predefined Options**.

4. In the **Predefined Options and Values** dialog box, click **Add**.

5. In the **Option Type** dialog box, specify the following information:

   a. In the **Name** box, type **WPAD**.

   b. In the **Data** type box, click **String**.

   c. In the **Code** box, type **252**. Click **OK**.

6. In the **Value** area, in the String box, type **http://den-isa-01.cohovineyard.com:80/wpad.dat**. Click **OK**.

7. Expand the **Head Office** scope. Right-click **Scope Options**, and then click **Configure Options**. Select the check box for **252 WPAD**, and then click **OK**.

8. Close the DHCP console.

▶ **To prepare the DNS server for automatic discovery**

1. Open **DNS** from the **Administrative Tools** folder.

2. Expand **Den-DC-01**, expand **Forward Lookup Zones**, expand **cohovineyard.com**, right-click the domain name, and then click **New Alias**.

3. In the **New Resource Record** dialog box, in **Alias** name, type **WPAD**.

4. In **fully qualified domain name (FQDN) for target host**, type **den-isa-01.cohovineyard.com**. Click **OK**.

5. Close the DNS console.

Lesson: Securing ISA Server 2004

- ISA Server and Defense in Depth
- About Using Security Templates to Secure the Server
- Methods for Implementing Security Updates
- Guidelines for Enabling Only Required Services
- How to Secure the Network Interfaces
- Configuring Administrative Roles
- Best Practices for Securing the Server

Introduction

ISA Server is a core component in your organization's overall security strategy. If you deploy ISA Server as an Internet edge firewall, your ISA Server is accessible to everyone on the Internet. In this scenario, a security compromise on the ISA Server can have very significant repercussions for your entire network.

This lesson introduces you to the tasks that an administrator would perform to secure ISA Server 2004 and explains how to perform these tasks.

Lesson objectives

After completing this lesson, you will be able to:

- Describe the relationship between ISA Server and a defense in depth approach to security.
- Implement security templates on ISA Server 2004.
- Implement security updates.
- Describe which services to enable on ISA Server.
- Configure the network interfaces on ISA Server.
- Configure administrative roles.
- Apply best practices for securing ISA Server 2004.

ISA Server and Defense in Depth

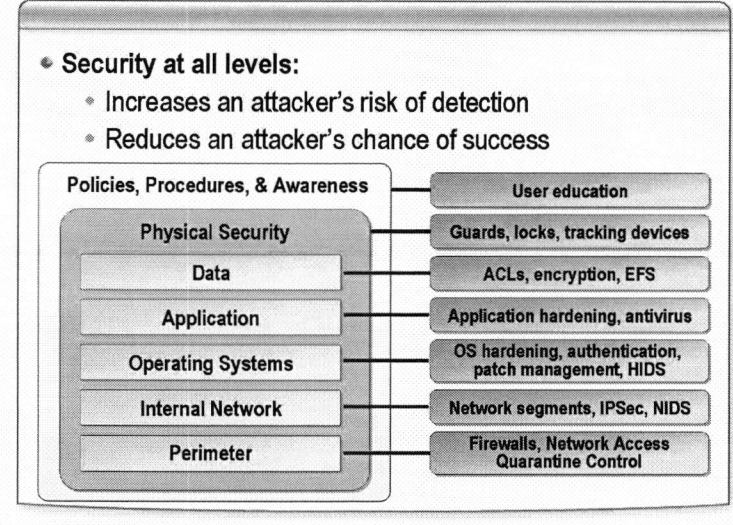

* **Security at all levels:**
  * Increases an attacker's risk of detection
  * Reduces an attacker's chance of success

Policies, Procedures, & Awareness	User education
Physical Security	Guards, locks, tracking devices
Data	ACLs, encryption, EFS
Application	Application hardening, antivirus
Operating Systems	OS hardening, authentication, patch management, HIDS
Internal Network	Network segments, IPSec, NIDS
Perimeter	Firewalls, Network Access Quarantine Control

Introduction

Deploying ISA Server 2004 is a critical component in an organization's overall security design. However, just deploying ISA Server 2004 at the perimeter of the network does not guarantee security throughout the network. To provide security throughout the network, you need to implement a defense-in-depth security strategy.

What is defense in depth?

A defense-in-depth security strategy means that you use multiple levels of defense to secure your network. If one level is compromised, it does not necessarily mean that your entire organization is compromised. As a general guideline, design and build each level of your security using the assumption that that level is the final level preventing an attacker from gaining access to resources on your network. If you assume that every other layer has been breached, you will ensure that each layer is as secure as possible.

Benefits of a defense-in-depth strategy

Using a defense-in-depth strategy increases an attacker's risk of detection and reduces an attacker's chance of success. Because you are monitoring for illegitimate activity at many levels, you are more likely to detect the attacker's actions. In addition, because you are monitoring at many levels, you can correlate related events from various monitoring sources to identify the attack and determine which levels have been compromised.

The defense-in-depth strategy also reduces the attacker's chance of success. The attacker may use a particular strategy to defeat one level of defense but then need to use a completely different strategy to compromise the next level.

Levels in the defense-in-depth strategy

Each level in the defense-in-depth strategy forms part of the overall strategy:

- *Policies, procedures, and awareness.* Many network attacks are successful because an organization's employees deliberately or inadvertently create a breach. This means that one of the first components in creating the security strategy is to develop organization policies dealing with security and then to train users.

- *Physical security.* Another component in a defense-in-depth strategy is securing critical network resources so that only authorized personnel can gain physical access to the resources. Options for providing this security include security guards, locked server rooms, and requiring multiple forms of authentication to gain access to the resources.

- *Perimeter.* Almost all companies provide some form of access to the Internet. This makes it critical that the connecting point between the Internet and the internal network is as secure as possible. Options for providing this security include firewalls or multiple firewalls, secure virtual private network access that uses quarantine procedures, and secure server publishing to provide required access to internal resources.

- *Internal networks.* Even if the perimeter is secure, you still need to ensure that the internal networks are secure for those cases in which the perimeter is compromised or when the attacker is internal to the organization. Options include network segmentation to isolate networks that carry highly confidential network traffic, using Internet Protocol security (IPSec) to encrypt network traffic, and network intrusion-detection systems (NIDS) at each network entrance.

- *Operating systems.* Many of the security attacks take advantage of security breaches that are available within the operating system. These attacks can be prevented by hardening server and client operating systems, ensuring that all security updates are efficiently deployed, requiring strong authentication methods, and using host-based intrusion-detection systems (HIDS).

- *Applications.* Security attacks also take advantage of breaches in application security. These attacks can be mitigated by ensuring that applications are designed with security in mind, hardening the applications so that the applications are secure and run with the least possible permissions, and ensuring that appropriate antivirus software is deployed on each application server. As well, using a firewall like ISA Server 2004 with application filtering functionality can help secure applications.

- *Data.* The final level in the defense-in-depth strategy is protecting the data that is located on network resources. This data can be protected by using access control lists (ACLs), and using a data encryption mechanism such as Encrypting File System (EFS) to ensure that only authorized users can gain access to the data.

ISA Server and defense in depth

ISA Server 2004 is a critical component in the overall defense-in-depth security strategy. When designing your ISA Server implementation, you need to consider how ISA Server will fit into your defense-in-depth strategy. In some cases, ISA Server 2004 is the tool that you use to implement the security requirements at a specific defense-in-depth level. In other cases, ISA Server may complement the defense-in-depth strategy for another layer.

About Using Security Templates to Secure the Server

- Configure one security template and then apply it to multiple computers, or reapply the template occasionally to the same computers to ensure that the security settings are not changed

- Apply the security template through Group Policies at a domain or organizational unit level

- Use the Security Templates MMC snap-in to apply the security templates to ISA Servers

Introduction

All Windows Servers have a security policy applied to them. The policy may not set any security restrictions or it may set very strict security restrictions. For computers that are part of a domain, the server security settings may be configured by domain security policies. On computers that are not part of a domain, the policy is stored in the local security policy.

What are security templates?

Security templates are pre-configured sets of security settings that can be applied to users and computers. Security templates are useful in that you can configure one security template and then apply that template to multiple computers, or reapply the template occasionally to the same computers to ensure that the security settings are not changed.

Security templates can be used to configure the following:

- Audit Policy settings specify the security events that are recorded in the Event Log. You can monitor security-related activity such as who accesses, or attempts to access an object, when a user logs on to or off a computer, or when changes are made to an Audit Policy setting.

- User Rights Assignment settings specify which users or groups have logon rights or privileges on the member servers in the domain.

- Security Options settings are used to enable or disable security settings for servers, such as digital signing of data, administrator and guest account names, driver installation behavior, and logon prompts.

- Event Log settings specify the size of each event log and actions to take when each event log becomes full.

- System Services settings specify the startup behavior and permissions for each service on the server.

Implementing security templates

If your computer is a member of an Active Directory domain, you can apply the security template through Group Policies at a domain or organizational-unit level. If your computer is not a member of a domain, you can use the Security Configuration and Analysis or the Secedit command line tool. These tools can be used to compare the local policy on a server with a specified security template. You can also use these tools to apply the settings in a specific security template to a server. Secedit combines the functionality of the Security Configuration and Analysis tool with the ability to use scripting to apply security template settings to servers.

Microsoft has released the Windows Server 2003 Security Guide, which includes several templates that you can use to secure servers on your network. The templates are grouped into three categories:

- Enterprise Client templates designed for most networking environments that contain only Windows 2000 or later computers

- Legacy Client templates designed for networking environments that contain older computers

- High Security templates designed to be deployed only in networks that require very high security

___

Caution The High Security templates set very restrictive security policies that may interfere with network functionality. These policies should be deployed only in environments that require this level of security, and only after thorough testing.

___

The Security Guide also provides multiple templates based on server roles.

- For member servers in a domain, the Security Guide recommends that you first apply the Member Server Baseline template. This template provides a set of baseline security settings that can be applied to all member servers in the domain.

- After you have applied baseline security settings, you can use additional security templates provided in the Security Guide to apply additional, incremental, security settings to member servers that perform specific roles, such as infrastructure servers, file servers, print servers, and Internet Information Services (IIS) servers.

___

Note The Windows Server 2003 Security Guide can be found at http://www.microsoft.com/technet/Security/prodtech/win2003/w2003hg/sgch00.mspx.

___

ISA Server and security templates

Security templates are the ideal means to configure the security settings on an ISA Server. By applying these templates, you can ensure a high and consistent level of security on the ISA Server. To apply the security templates to the ISA Server:

1. Using the Security Templates Microsoft Management Console (MMC) snap-in, analyze the security templates included with the Windows Server 2003 Security Guide and determine which template most closely meets your organization's requirements. Modify those parts of the template that do not match your requirements.

2. Apply the security templates to your ISA Server(s). If your ISA Servers are members of an Active Directory domain, create an organizational unit (OU) that contains just the ISA Servers and then create a Group Policy Object to apply the security template to the servers. If your ISA Server is not a member of the domain, use the Security Analysis and Configuration tool to apply the security policy to the ISA Server.

Methods for Implementing Security Updates

- Monitor security updates is to know what security updates are available and the security issues each update is designed to fix

- Use tools like Microsoft Baseline Security Analyzer, Windows Update Service, Microsoft Windows Update Services, and Systems Management Server to implement security updates

- Implement security updates on ISA Server only after thorough evaluation and testing

Introduction

Another critical component in keeping your ISA Server secure is to ensure that all security updates are applied to the server. Security updates are product updates that eliminate known security issues such as those caused by or exploited by viruses. When a security update becomes available, you should quickly evaluate your system to determine if the update is relevant to your current situation.

Most security updates are released for client software such as Web browsers; however, updates are also occasionally released to protect server software. To keep ISA Server secure, you must ensure that the security updates for both ISA Server and the operating system are current by installing the latest security fixes. If the operating system is vulnerable, ISA Server is also vulnerable.

Monitoring security updates

The first step in applying security updates is to be aware of which security updates are available and the security issues that each update is designed to fix. Resources that help you stay aware include:

- Microsoft and many third-party antivirus vendors include services that periodically release security bulletins that enable you to stay current on security issues and fixes. To receive the Microsoft notifications, register at Microsoft Security Notification Service, which is located at http://www.microsoft.com/technet/security/bulletin/notify.mspx.

- Monitor the Microsoft Security Web site, which is located at http://www.microsoft.com/security.

- For ISA Server–specific information, monitor the Microsoft Internet Security and Acceleration Security Center located at http://www.microsoft.com/technet/security/prodtech/isa/default.mspx.

Implementing security updates

Microsoft provides several tools that can be used to implement security updates:

- *Microsoft Baseline Security Analyzer (MBSA).* This utility checks for missing updates, blank or weak passwords, and security issues on each server that is running Windows 2000 or later. MBSA uses the Microsoft Network Security Hotfix Checker (Hfnetchk.exe) tool to scan for missing security updates and SPs for Windows, Internet Explorer, IIS, SQL Server, Exchange, and Microsoft Windows Media® Player. You can download the latest MBSA from http://www.microsoft.com/technet/security/tools/mbsahome.mspx. Although MBSA does not scan for ISA Server–specific security issues, it does scan the host operating system and other applications that may be running on the server.

- *Windows Update Service.* Windows Update Service is a Web site maintained by Microsoft that contains all the latest updates for all Microsoft operating systems. Use the Web site if you need to update individual computers. You can configure Windows to automatically download and install updates from the Windows Update site. In most cases, you should disable this on the ISA Servers to ensure that you can test each update before deployment.

- *Microsoft Windows Update Services (formerly known as Software Update Services, or SUS).* This utility simplifies the process of keeping Windows-based computers and servers up to date with the latest critical updates by automating update deployment. Windows Update Service is recommended for medium enterprises with one or more locations. Windows Update Service is a free download from the Microsoft Web site.

- *Microsoft Systems Management Server.* This utility automates the distribution and installation of the recommended security fixes for large companies with multiple locations and a large number of Windows-based client and server computers. Systems Management Server enables you to determine which computers need security fixes, and then enables you to deploy the fixes to the appropriate resources.

ISA Server and security updates

Because ISA Server security is critical, you need to ensure that the most recent security updates for the operating system, ISA Server, and other components such as MSDE are installed on the ISA Server. At the same time, you need to ensure that you do not install a security update that breaks something else on the ISA Server or prevents users from using the ISA Server. Follow these guidelines when deploying security updates on your ISA Server:

- *Evaluate the security update severity and risk.* When a new security update is released, evaluate the severity of the security issue that it is fixing and evaluate the risk to your organization. If the security update is fixing a security issue that is extremely difficult to exploit, or if the fix is for a feature that you have not implemented, you may choose to wait till the next service pack to apply the update. However, if the update fixes a critical security issue that directly affects your organization, you should immediately begin implementing the update.

- *Apply the security update in a test environment.* You should maintain a test environment that closely mirrors your production environment. Install the update in this environment first to see if it will disrupt any ISA Server functionality.

- *Monitor others' experiences with the security update.* Monitor the Internet newsgroups and forums to see if other people are having problems with the update. This will not only reveal problems with the update itself but also reveal problems with the update installation.

- *Deploy the security update in the production environment.* Once you are confident that the update will not interfere with the functionality in the production environment, deploy the updates to the production ISA Servers.

Guidelines for Enabling Only Required Services

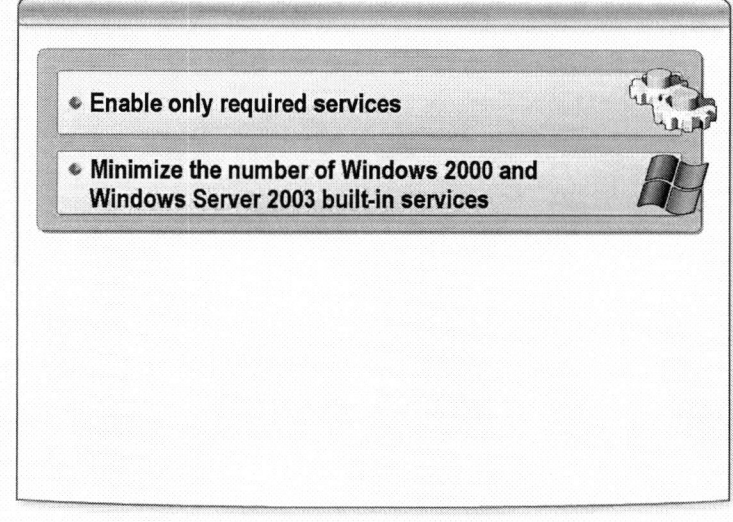

* Enable only required services

* Minimize the number of Windows 2000 and Windows Server 2003 built-in services

Introduction

One of the most important steps in securing the computer running ISA Server is to ensure that only the required applications or services are running on the server. The server should, ideally, only run the ISA Server itself. The more services or applications running on the ISA Server, the more options there are for hackers to attack the computer.

Services and applications that should not be installed on ISA Server

Every service and application potentially has a weakness. The more services and applications you run to the ISA Server computer, the more potential weaknesses you introduce. Examples of services and applications that you should avoid putting on the ISA Server, particularly if the ISA Server is an Internet edge server, are:

- DHCP
- DNS
- Windows Internet Naming Service (WINS)
- Certificate Services
- IIS Services: WWW, SMTP, NNTP, FTP
- Mail servers such as Exchange
- Third-party FTP servers
- Mail clients such as Microsoft Outlook® and Outlook Express
- Active Directory domain controllers

Services that should be disabled on ISA Server

You should also minimize the number of Windows 2000 and Windows Server 2003 built-in services that run after installing ISA Server. Some of those services that ISA Server does not require include:

- Alerter
- Clipbook
- Computer Browser
- Distributed File System
- File Replication
- Indexing Service
- Internet Connection Sharing
- Intersite Messaging
- Kerberos Key Distribution Center
- License Logging Service
- Messenger
- Microsoft NetMeeting® Remote Desktop Sharing
- Network DDE
- Print Spooler
- Removable Storage
- RunAs
- Telnet

One of the features of Windows Server 2003 is that only services that are required on the server are enabled by default. If you are running Windows Server 2003, you should not enable any services that are currently disabled. Windows 2000 enables most of these services by default so disable all services that are not required.

How to Secure the Network Interfaces

* **Secure the External Network Interface**
  * Disable File and Printer Sharing for Microsoft Networks and Client for Microsoft Networks
  * Disable NetBIOS over TCP/IP
  * Disable LMHOSTS lookup
  * Disable automatic DNS name registration
* **Configure the Internal Network Interface**
  * Disable components if not required

Introduction

Another component in securing the ISA Server is to secure the network interfaces. This is particularly important for the interface that is connected to the Internet, but can also be applied to the internal network interface.

Securing the external interface

The external interface of your ISA Server is likely to be directly attached to the Internet. This means that this interface may be exposed to any attack from anywhere on the Internet.

By default, network interfaces in both Windows 2000 and Windows Server 2003 are configured to make it easy for other computers on the network to connect. This means that you need to change the interface configuration considerably if you want to secure the network interface connected to the Internet.

To secure the external interface on the ISA Server, complete the following actions:

- *Disable File and Printer Sharing for Microsoft Networks and Client for Microsoft Networks*. File and Printer Sharing for Microsoft Networks allows the machine to share Server Message Block/Common Internet File System (SMB/CIFS) resources. The Client for Microsoft Networks allows the machine to access SMB/CIFS resources. These options enable NetBIOS and/or Direct Hosting ports, both of which are used for conventional file sharing and access on Microsoft networks. Both of these options must be disabled on the external interface.

- *Disable NetBIOS over TCP/IP*. NetBIOS over TCP/IP is needed if the computer needs to be configured as a WINS client, needs to send out NetBIOS broadcasts, needs to send out browser service announcements, or needs to access NetBIOS resources on the Internet. The ISA Server should not be sending or receiving any NetBIOS packets to the Internet, so this can be disabled.

- *Disable the LMHOSTS lookup option.* The LMHOSTS file is used to enable NetBIOS name lookups and the ISA Server should not be connecting to any computers on the Internet using NetBIOS. Computers running Windows 2000 and later operating systems use DNS for computer name resolution.

- *Disable automatic DNS name registration.* By default, Windows 2000 and Windows Server 2003 computers attempt to register their IP addresses with a DNS Server. The ISA Server should not register the IP address for its external interface with DNS servers on the Internet or with DNS servers inside the network.

Configuring the internal interface

In addition to securing the external interface, you should also secure the internal interface on the computer running ISA Server.

- You will need to leave File and Printer Sharing for Microsoft Networks enabled on the internal interface if you want internal network clients to access the Firewall Client software. If the client installation files are stored on another computer, you can disable File and Printer Sharing.

- The Client for Microsoft Networks also needs to be enabled if you wish to access resources on the internal network or authenticate to internal resources.

- You can disable NetBIOS over TCP/IP if you do not have any legacy client computers or NetBIOS-based applications on the network that need access to the ISA Server. Test the effect of disabling this option before you implement the change.

- You should leave automatic DNS name resolution enabled on the internal network interface so that the ISA Server's IP address is registered in DNS. If you do not have automatic updates enabled on the DNS zone, then you can disable this option and manually configure the host record in DNS.

Note   The practice at the end of this lesson will describe how to configure each of these options.

Configuring Administrative Roles

ISA Server Administrative Roles

Role	Description
ISA Server Basic Monitoring	• Monitor ISA Server and network activity • Cannot configure monitoring functionality
ISA Server Extended Monitoring	• Can perform all monitoring tasks • Can modify monitoring configuration
ISA Server Full Administrator	• Can perform all administrative tasks

Introduction

Another component to securing the ISA Server is to ensure that users do not have more administrative permissions on the ISA Server than they require. As a general rule, user accounts should always be configured with the minimum privileges necessary to perform a specific task. Administrators should use an account with restrictive permissions to perform routine, non-administrative tasks, and use an account with higher levels of permissions only when performing specific administrative tasks.

ISA Server provides an Administration Delegation Wizard that can be used to assign appropriate roles on the ISA Server.

Administrative roles on the ISA Server

You can use role-based administration to organize your ISA Server administrators into separate, predefined roles, each with its own set of privileges and corresponding tasks. The roles assigned in ISA Server are based on Windows users and groups. If the ISA Server is a member of a domain, these users and groups can be either local accounts or domain accounts. If the ISA Server is not a member of a domain, you must assign local users and groups to the roles.

The following table describes the ISA Server roles.

Role	Description
ISA Server Basic Monitoring	Users and groups assigned this role can monitor the ISA Server computer and network activity, but cannot configure specific monitoring functionality.
ISA Server Extended Monitoring	Users and groups assigned this role can perform all monitoring tasks, including log configuration, alert-definition configuration, and all monitoring functions available to the ISA Server Basic Monitoring role.
ISA Server Full Administrator	Users and groups assigned this role can perform any ISA Server task, including rule configuration, application of network templates, and monitoring.

Roles and activities

Each ISA Server role has a specific list of ISA Server tasks associated with it. The following table lists some ISA Server administration tasks along with the roles in which they are performed.

Activity	ISA Server Basic Monitoring	ISA Server Extended Monitoring	ISA Server Full Administrator
View Dashboard, alerts, connectivity, sessions, services	X	X	X
Acknowledge alerts	X	X	X
View log information		X	X
Create alert definitions		X	X
Create reports		X	X
Stop and start sessions and services		X	X
View firewall policy		X	X
Configure firewall policy			X
Configure cache			X
Configure VPN			X

Configuring administrative roles

To assign administrative roles, use the following procedure:

1. In the console tree of **ISA Server Management**, click the ISA Server computer name.

2. On the **Tasks** tab, click **Define Administrative Roles**.

3. On the **Welcome to the ISA Server Administration Delegation Wizard** page, click **Next**.

4. On the **Delegate Control** page, to add groups, click **Add**.

5. On the **Administration Delegation** page, click **Browse** to locate the group or user account.

6. On the **Select User or Group** page, click **Locations** and select the appropriate directory location. Click **OK**.

7. Type the name of the user or group that you want to add, and click **OK**.

8. In the **Role** box, select the ISA Server role that you want to assign to this user or group. Click **OK**.

9. Click **Next**, review the changed roles, and then click **Finish**.

Best Practices for Securing the Server

```
Securing ISA Server

  ⬥ Do Not Install ISA Server on a Domain Controller
  ⬥ Avoid Installing an Internet Edge Server on a
    Domain Member
  ⬥ Rename the Administrator Account
  ⬥ Disable Unused Functionality
  ⬥ Apply Window Server Security Best Practices
```

Introduction

In addition to the security practices included in this lesson, there are several other best practices that you should implement when securing your ISA Server.

Best practices for securing the ISA Server

The best practices include:

- Do not install ISA Server on a domain controller. There are several reasons for this. First, Windows domain controllers require many different ports to be accessible to client computers, resulting in a very complicated configuration. Second, the domain information for your organization is critical information. If an attacker can gain access to the domain database, he or she may be able to compromise all users' accounts, or he or she may be able to damage the database so that no one can log on.

- If possible, avoid installing ISA Server deployed as Internet edge firewalls on domain member servers. The potential for damage to your network is significantly higher if a member server is compromised than if a stand-alone server is compromised. Installing ISA Server as a stand-alone server can make it more challenging to configure authentication, but ISA Server can be configured to use RADIUS authentication rather than domain authentication.

- Rename the built-in Administrator account name and change its descriptions and passwords to prevent malicious use. Ensure that the Guest account is disabled.

- Ensure that the ISA Server computer is stored in a physically secure location. Physical access to a server is a high security risk. Physical access to a server by an intruder could result in unauthorized access or modification, as well as installation of hardware or software designed to circumvent security. To maintain a secure environment, you must restrict physical access to the ISA Server computer.

- Apply the principle of reduced attack surface, disabling functions not critical to the current task. Disable ISA Server features that you do not use. Configure a system policy suited specifically to your network needs.

- In addition, follow the security recommendations for the operating system running on the ISA Server computer. For detailed information and prescriptive guidance on securing the operating system, review the following documentation:

  - For Windows Server 2003, see the Windows Server 2003 Security Guide at http://www.microsoft.com/technet/Security/prodtech/win2003/w2003hg/sgch00.mspx.

  - For Windows 2000 Server, see the Security Operations Guide for Windows 2000 at http://www.microsoft.com/downloads/details.aspx?FamilyID=f0b7b4ee-201a-4b40-a0d2-cdd9775aeff8&DisplayLang=en.

Practice: Securing the ISA Server

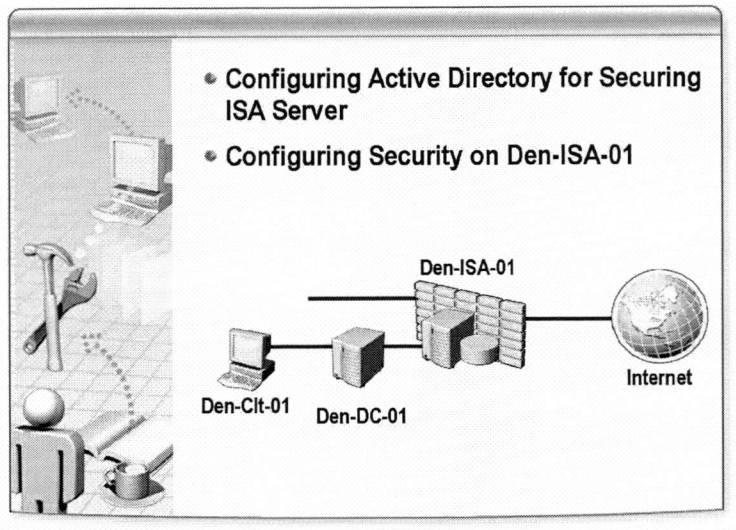

Introduction

In this practice, you will configure Active Directory to support the use of security templates to secure the ISA Server and to enable ISA Management on a non-administrator account. You will then apply a security template to the ISA Server, secure the ISA Server's external network interface, and assign the non-administrator account as an ISA Server Full Administrator.

Practice

▶ **To prepare for this practice**

1. You will need the Den-DC-01 virtual machine, the Den-Clt-01 virtual machine and the Den-ISA-01 virtual machine for this practice.

2. If necessary, start or resume the required virtual machines and then, on Den-ISA-01, log on to the cohovineyard domain with a user name of **Administrator** and a password of **P@ssw0rd**.

▶ **Configuring Active Directory for securing ISA Server**

1. On Den-DC-01, if necessary, log on to the cohovineyard domain with a user name of **Administrator** and a password of **P@ssw0rd**.

2. Open **Active Directory Users and Computers** from the **Administrative Tools**.

3. Right-click the **Users** container. Point to **New**, and then click **User**.

4. In the **New Object – User** dialog box, type your first name and last name in the appropriate boxes. Type your first name and first initial of your last name in the **User Logon Name** box. Click **Next**.

5. Type a password in the **Password** and **Confirm Password** boxes. Clear the check box for **User must change password at next logon**. Click **Next**.

6. Clear the check box for **Create an Exchange mailbox**, click **Next** and then click **Finish**.

7. Right-click the **Users** container. Point to **New**, and then click **Group**.

8. In the **Group Name** box, type **ISA Admins**. Click **Next** twice and then click **Finish**.

9. Select *yourusername*, then right-click *yourusername* and click **Add to a group**. In the **Enter the object name to select** box, type **ISA Admins** and click **OK** twice.

10. Right-click **cohovineyard.com** and point to **New**, and then click **Organizational Unit**.

11. In the **New Object – Organizational Unit** dialog box, in **Name**, type **ISA Servers**. Click **OK**.

12. Right-click **ISA Servers** and click **Properties**.

13. On the **Group Policy** tab, click **New**.

14. Type **ISA Server Security Settings** and then click **Edit**.

15. Expand **Computer Configuration** and then click **Windows Settings**.

16. Right-click **Security Settings** and select **Import policy**.

17. In the **Import Policy From** dialog box, browse to the **C:\Program Files\ Microsoft Learning\2824\Security Templates** folder. Click **High Security-Member Server Baseline** and click **Open**.

Note The High Security-Member Server Baseline security template is designed for servers that require a high level of security. However, you need to modify a few settings to enable the ISA Services to run.

---

18. Expand **Security Settings** then click **System Services**. Double-click **Remote Access Connection Manager**.

19. Click **Automatic** and click **OK**.

20. Double-click **Routing and Remote Access**.

21. Click **Automatic** and click **OK**.

22. Double-click **Telephony**.

23. Click **Automatic** and click **OK**.

24. Close the **Group Policy Object Editor** and close the **ISA Servers Properties** page.

25. Select the **Computers** container, and right-click **DEN-ISA-01**.

26. Click **Move**, click **ISA Servers**, and then click **OK**.

27. Close all open windows.

▶ **Configuring security on Den-ISA-01**

1. Switch to Den-ISA-01 and, if necessary, log on to the cohovineyard domain with a user name of **Administrator** and a password of **P@ssw0rd**.

2. Open **Computer Management** from the **Administrative Tools** folder.

3. Expand **Local Users and Groups** and then click **Groups**.

4. Right-click **Administrators** and then click **Add to Group**.

5. In the **Administrators Properties** dialog box, click **Add**. In the **Select Users, Computers and Groups** dialog box, in the **Enter the object names to select** box, type **ISA Admins**. Click **OK** twice.

6. Close **Computer Management**.

7. Open a command prompt and type **gpupdate**. This command forces a refresh of the Group Policies.

8. After you receive the message that the group policies have been refreshed, type **gpresult**.

9. Under **Computer Settings**, check the **Applied Group Policy Objects**. Confirm that the **ISA Server Security Settings** policy is listed. Close the command prompt.

Note It can take several minutes for the Group Policy to refresh. If the ISA Server Security Settings policy is not listed, wait a few minutes and run the gpresult command again.

---

10. Open **ISA Server Management**. Right-click **Den-ISA-01** and click **Administration Delegation**.

11. On the **Welcome to the ISA Server Administration Delegation Wizard** page, click **Next**.

12. On the **Delegate Control** page, click **Add**.

13. In the **Administration Delegation** dialog box, click **Browse**. Click **Locations**, expand **Entire Directory** and then click **cohovineyard.com**. Click **OK**.

14. In the **Enter the object name to select** box, type **ISA Admins** and then click **OK**. Select **ISA Server Full Administrator** from the **Role** drop-down box. Click **OK**.

15. On the **Delegate Control** page, click **Next**.

16. On the **Completing the Administration Delegation Wizard**, click **Finish**.

17. Click **Apply** to apply the changes and click **OK** when the changes have been applied. Close all open windows.

18. Log off **Den-ISA-01** and log back on using your user name. In the login dialog box, click **OK**.

19. On the **Manage Your Server** page, select **Don't display this page at logon** and close the window.

20. Point to **Start**, then point to **Control Panel**, then point to **Network Connections**, then click **External**. Click **Properties**.

21. On the **External Properties** page, clear the check box for **Client for Microsoft Networks** and **File and Printer Sharing for Microsoft Networks**.

22. Click **Internet Protocol (TCP/IP)** and click **Properties**.

23. Click **Advanced**. On the **DNS** tab, clear the check box for **Register this connection's address in DNS**.

24. On the **WINS** tab, clear the check box for **Enable LMHOSTS lookup** and select **Disable NetBIOS over TCP/IP**. Click **OK** twice and close all open windows.

Lesson: Maintaining ISA Server 2004

* About Monitoring the Server Running ISA Server
* About Exporting and Importing the ISA Server Configuration
* About Backing Up and Restoring the ISA Server Configuration
* Remote Administration Options for ISA Server

Introduction

After the ISA Server has been deployed and secured, the ISA Server administrator needs to maintain it. This lesson introduces the tasks that an administrator would perform to maintain ISA Server 2004 and explains how to perform these tasks.

Lesson objectives

After completing this lesson, you will be able to:

■ Describe the activities included in monitoring the server running ISA Server 2004.

■ Import and export the ISA Server configuration.

■ Back up and restore the ISA Server configuration.

■ Describe the options for performing remote administration of ISA Server 2004.

About Monitoring the Server Running ISA Server

ISA Server monitoring tasks include

Task	Description
Monitor Event Viewer	• Includes information about service failures, application errors, and warnings
Use the ISA Server Dashboard	• Single interface for ISA alerts and performance
Review the ISA Server Alerts	• Includes information about service conditions and error conditions
Monitor Connectivity to Network Services	• Monitor connectivity to Active Directory, DNS servers, internal Web servers, and selected Internet Web servers
Monitor Server Performance	• Use the pre-configured ISA Server Performance Monitor console

Introduction

Monitoring is the daily task of ensuring that critical ISA Server services are running properly and ensuring that the ISA Server is providing the required security and functionality. The goal of daily monitoring is to identify problems before they impact your users. In addition, monitoring will also allow you to identify trends that can indicate future problems or allow you to plan for future growth.

Daily monitoring tasks

Monitoring tasks that you must perform on a daily basis allow you to determine what is normal for your ISA Server and when abnormal events occur. These tasks include:

- *Monitor Event Viewer*. Use Event Viewer to obtain information about service failures, application errors, and warnings when system resources such as virtual memory or available disk space are running low. Using Event Viewer enables you to identify problems that must be resolved and trends that will require future action.

- *Use the ISA Server Dashboard*. The ISA Server Dashboard provides a single interface that provides a high-level view of the ISA Server performance and alerts. Use the dashboard to monitor the ISA Server frequently throughout the day.

- *Review the ISA Server Alerts*. These alerts provide you with information about service conditions and error conditions on the ISA Server. If you have intrusion detection configured, the alerts also provide information about attacks on the ISA server.

■ *Monitor connectivity to network services.* ISA Server provides the option to configure connectivity monitoring between the ISA Server and other servers. Configure the ISA Server to monitor connectivity to Active Directory, DNS servers, internal Web servers published by the ISA Server, and selected servers on the Internet.

■ *Monitor server performance.* When you install ISA Server, a pre-configured ISA Server Performance Monitor console is created. This console includes the critical ISA Server counters. Use this console to monitor server performance. Performance data can be viewed in a report or in various graph and log formats. A performance log can be useful in monitoring counters over an extended period of time. Performance alerts can be configured to create an event as a result of counters reaching certain values. These events could include a log entry, sending a network message, or running a program.

Note For more details on monitoring ISA Server, see Module 10, "Monitoring ISA Server 2004," in Course 2824, *Implementing Microsoft® Internet Security and Acceleration Server 2004.*

About Exporting and Importing the ISA Server Configuration

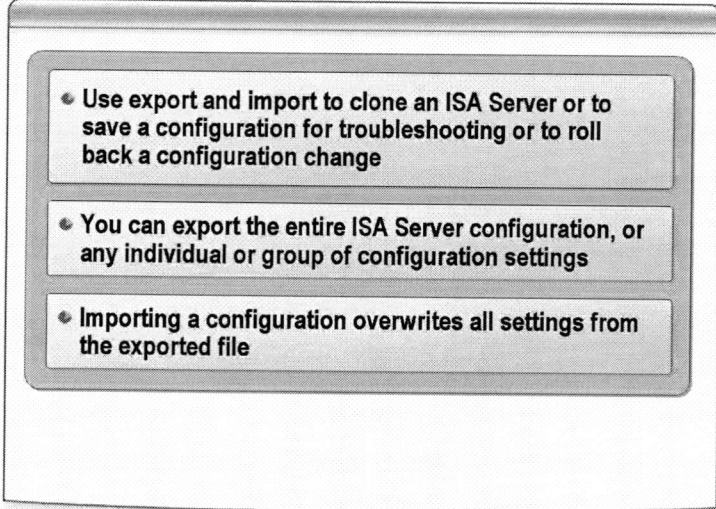

* Use export and import to clone an ISA Server or to save a configuration for troubleshooting or to roll back a configuration change

* You can export the entire ISA Server configuration, or any individual or group of configuration settings

* Importing a configuration overwrites all settings from the exported file

Introduction

ISA Server 2004 includes export and import features that enable you to save and restore most ISA Server configuration information. The configuration parameters can be exported and stored in an .xml file.

Why use import and export?

The import and export features can be useful in several scenarios:

- Cloning a server. You can export a configuration from one ISA Server computer to another computer, thereby easily duplicating a server setup. For example, after configuring an ISA Server computer at one branch, you can export the configuration to an .xml file. Then you can import it to another computer at another branch.

- Saving a partial configuration. You can export a single rule, an entire policy, or an entire configuration. This is helpful, for example, when you want to copy all the firewall policy rules, but not the monitoring configuration, to another ISA Server computer.

- Sending a configuration for troubleshooting. You can export your configuration information to a file and send it to support professionals for analysis and troubleshooting.

- Rolling back a configuration change. As a best practice, before modifying any ISA Server settings, you should export the specific component that you are modifying. If your modification is not successful, you can easily restore the previous configuration by importing the policy file.

Export the ISA Server configuration

You can export the entire ISA Server configuration, or just parts of it, depending on your specific needs. You can export the following objects:

- Entire ISA Server configuration

- All the connectivity verifiers or one selected connectivity verifier

- All the networks or one selected network

- All the network sets or one selected network set

- All the network rules or one selected network rule
- All the Web chaining rules or one selected Web chaining rule
- Cache configuration
- All the content-download jobs or one or more selected content-download jobs
- Entire firewall policy or one selected rule

The system policy rules are not exported when you export the firewall policy. (To export the system policy, select the Export System Policy task.)

When you export an entire configuration, all general configuration information is exported. This includes access rules, publishing rules, rule elements, alert configuration, cache configuration, and ISA Server properties. In addition, you can select to export user permission settings and confidential information such as user passwords. Confidential information included in the exported file is encrypted.

When you export an entire configuration, certificate settings are also exported. However, if you import the configuration to an ISA Server computer with different certificates, the Microsoft Firewall service will fail to start and an event message will be logged.

Caution Ensure that you save the exported files to a secure location on the local server or on a network share. Only administrators of the ISA Server computer should have read permissions to the location.

Importing the ISA Server configuration

When you import a previously exported file, all properties and settings defined in the file are imported, overwriting the current configuration on the ISA Server. However, if you export only a specific component, such as a specific firewall rule, the file import will overwrite only that particular rule.

When you import the configuration, the configuration file must be imported at the appropriate node. For example, after you export a rule, you must import the configuration file at the Firewall Policy node level or by selecting another rule.

Note The practice at the end of this lesson will provide detailed steps for exporting and importing an ISA Server configuration.

About Backing Up and Restoring the ISA Server Configuration

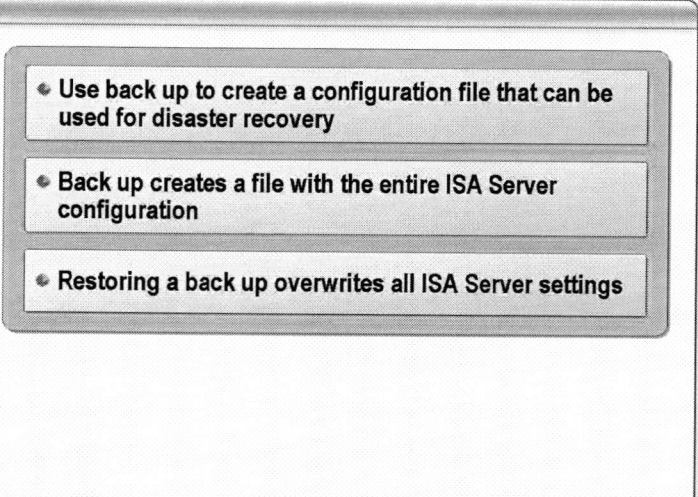

- Use back up to create a configuration file that can be used for disaster recovery
- Back up creates a file with the entire ISA Server configuration
- Restoring a back up overwrites all ISA Server settings

Introduction

ISA Server 2004 also includes backup and restore features that enable you to save and restore the ISA Server configuration information. The backup functionality also stores the configuration information in an .xml file.

Why use backup and restore?

The primary use of backup and restore functionalities in ISA Server is for disaster recovery. You should regularly back up the configuration on the ISA Server computer so that you can restore the computer with the same settings in case of a computer failure. The backup functionality saves the appropriate information to ensure that an identical configuration can be restored.

Backing up the ISA Server configuration

Backing up an ISA Server configuration backs up the server's general configuration information. This includes firewall policy rules, rule elements, alert configuration, cache configuration, and VPN configuration. One of the differences between backing up the server configuration and exporting the configuration is that you can only backup the entire ISA Server configuration, not individual components or groups of components.

Restoring the ISA Server configuration

The restore process reconstructs the configuration information that was backed up. By restoring a backup, you can rebuild the ISA Server configuration or restore it after a configuration error.

Note   The practice at the end of this lesson will provide detailed steps for backing up an ISA Server configuration.

Remote Administration Options for ISA Server

- Use remote administration to manage physically secured servers or servers in other offices

- Use Remote Desktop or Terminal Services to manage all settings on the server running ISA Server

- Use the ISA Server Management MMC to manage ISA Server settings remotely

- Configure the server running ISA Server to enable Remote Desktop and configure System Policy to enable remote MMC management

Introduction

ISA Server 2004 enables you to administer ISA Server computers from other computers. You can perform all ISA Server administrative tasks remotely, either from a computer running Remote Desktop Connection or from a Microsoft Management Console (MMC) installed on the remote computer.

Why use remote administration?

In most organizations, you will not be performing ISA Server administration directly from the ISA Server console. The ISA Server computer in most cases is located in a physically secure server room and you may be performing the administration from your client computer. If your organization has multiple locations with ISA Servers installed in each location, you may need to manage all of the servers from your desktop. Remote administration enables you to administer ISA Server in all of these cases.

Remote administration options

You have two options for remotely administrating ISA Servers. You can use a Terminal Services or Remote Desktop connection to administer the server, or you can install the ISA Server Management MMC console on another computer and use it to manage an ISA Server. If you have more than one ISA Server installed, you can manage an ISA Server from another server using the MMC console.

If you have installed ISA Server on a server running Windows 2000, you can use Terminal Services to manage the ISA Server. If the ISA Server is installed on a computer running Windows Server 2003, you can use Remote Desktop in the same way. When you use Terminal Services or Remote Desktop to administer the ISA Server computer, you can view the desktop of the ISA Server computer as if you were in front of the monitor attached to the ISA Server computer. This results in faster refresh rates than using the MMC because the work of refreshing the view is done by the ISA Server computer, and only the information that composes the picture on the monitor has to be transmitted to the remote computer.

To enable remote administration of ISA Server on computers running Windows Server 2003, you must be a member of the Administrators group or Remote Desktop Users group on the ISA Server computer, or be granted permission to use Remote Desktop to connect to the server. To enable remote administration of an ISA Server running on a Windows 2000 computer, you must install Terminal Services on the server, in either Application or Remote Administration mode. Then the user properties must be configured to allow remote connections.

You can also perform remote administration of ISA Servers using the ISA Server Management MMC snap-in. To install the MMC snap-in on a computer not running ISA Server, you perform a custom installation, installing only ISA Server Management. After installation, you can connect to any computer with ISA Server installed.

There are advantages to remote administration with ISA Server Management. Using ISA Server Management, you can connect to and display information from many ISA Server computers at once. This is useful for central administration of geographically dispersed ISA Server computers.

To run ISA Server Management, you need:

- A personal computer with a 300 megahertz (MHz) or higher Pentium II–compatible CPU

- Windows Server 2003, Windows 2000 Server or Workstation, or Windows XP

- 256 megabytes (MB) of memory

- 19 MB of available hard disk space

Configuring remote administration on the ISA Server

When you install ISA Server, the default system policy allows remote administration from all members of a computer group named Remote Management Computers. By default, no computers are in this group, so no computers can connect to the ISA Server for remote management. To enable remote management on the ISA Server, you need to configure remote administration by editing the appropriate MMC or Terminal Server configuration group in the System Policy editor. You can configure the system policy configuration groups to apply to specific network objects. For example, you may want to limit the system policy rule to apply only to the IP address of the specific remote management computer rather than to all the computers in the internal network.

Practice: Maintaining ISA Server 2004

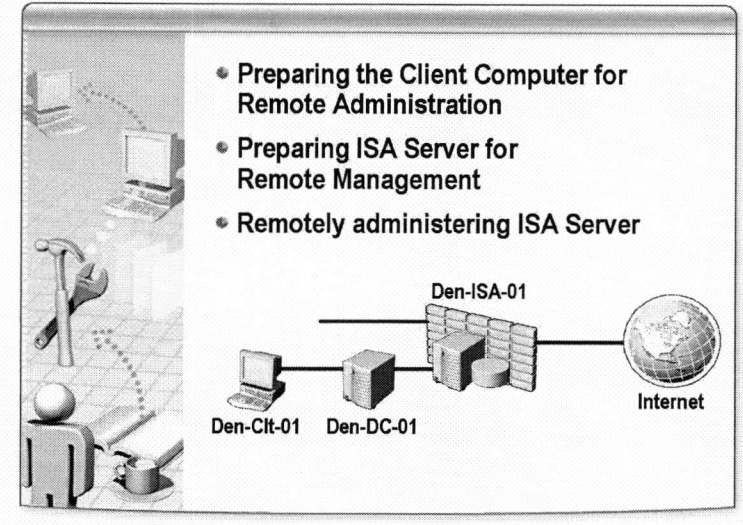

* Preparing the Client Computer for Remote Administration
* Preparing ISA Server for Remote Management
* Remotely administering ISA Server

Introduction

In this practice, you will enable remote administration of the ISA Server and install the ISA Server Management Console on a client computer. You will then use remote administration to perform other maintenance tasks on the ISA Server.

Practice

▶ **To prepare for this practice**

1. You will need the Den-DC-01 virtual machine, the Den-Clt-01 virtual machine and the Den-ISA-01 virtual machine for this practice.

2. If necessary, start or resume the required virtual machines.

▶ **Preparing the client computer for remote administration**

1. On Den-Clt-01, log on to the cohovineyard domain with a user name of **Administrator** and a password of **P@ssw0rd**.

2. Click **Start**, right-click **My Computer**, and click **Manage**.

3. Expand **Local Users and Groups** and then click **Groups**.

4. Right-click **Administrators** and click **Add to Group**.

5. In the **Administrators Properties** dialog box, click **Add**. In the **Select Users or Groups** dialog box, in the **Enter the object names to select** box, type **ISA Admins**. Click **OK** twice.

6. Close **Computer Management**.

7. Log off **Den-Clt-01** and log back on using your user name.

8. Open **Windows Explorer** and browse to C:\Program Files\Microsoft Learning\2824\Setup.

9. Double-click **isaautorun.exe**.

10. On the **Microsoft ISA Server 2004 Setup** page, click **Install ISA Server 2004**.

11. On the **Welcome to the Installation Wizard for Microsoft ISA Server 2004 Setup** page, click **Next**.

12. On the **License Agreement** page, review the terms and conditions stated in the end-user license agreement. Then click **I accept the terms in the license agreement** and click **Next**.

13. On the **Customer Information** page, click **Next**.

14. On the **Installation requirements summary** page, review the features that will not be available and click **Next**.

15. On the **Custom Setup** page, ensure that **ISA Server Management** is configured to be installed on the local hard drive and click **Next**.

16. On the **Ready to Install the Program** page, click **Install**.

17. When the program is installed, click **Finish**. Close all open windows.

18. Point to **Start**, then point to **All Programs**, then point to **Accessories**, then point to **Communications**, then point to **Remote Desktop Connection**.

19. In the **Remote Desktop Connection** screen, in the **Computer** box, type **Den-ISA-01** and click **Connect**. The connection will fail.

20. When the **Remote Desktop Disconnected** message appears, review the contents of the message and click **OK**.

▶ **Preparing ISA Server for remote administration**

1. Switch to the Den-ISA-01 virtual machine and log on to the cohovineyard domain using your user name and password.

2. Click **Start**, right-click **My Computer**, and click **Properties**.

3. On the **Remote** tab, select the check box for **Allow users to connect remotely to this computer**. Click **OK** to clear the **Remote Sessions** warning.

4. Click **Select Remote Users**. Notice that your user account already has access.

5. Click **OK** twice.

6. Switch back to the **Den-Clt-01** virtual machine. In the **Remote Desktop Connection** box, click **Connect**. The connection will fail again.

7. When the **Remote Desktop Disconnected** message appears, review the contents of the message and click **OK**.

8. Switch back to the **Den-ISA-01** virtual machine. Open ISA Server Management.

9. If necessary, expand **Den-ISA-01**. Click **Firewall Policy**. On the **Tasks** tab, click **Show System Policy Rules**.

10. Double-click the rule named **Allow remote management from selected computers using Terminal Server**.

11. On the **From** tab, click **Remote Management Computers** and then click **Edit**.

12. Click **Add** and then click **Subnet**. In the **New Subnet Rule Element** dialog box, in the **Name** box, type **Internal Computers**.

13. In the **Network address** box, type **192.168.1.0**. In the **Network mask** box, type **255.255.255.0**. Click **OK** twice.

14. Click **OK** to close the **System Policy Editor** dialog box.

15. Click **Apply** to apply the changes and click **OK** when the changes have been applied. Close all open windows.

16. Switch back to the **Den-Clt-01** virtual machine. In the **Remote Desktop Connection** box, click **Connect**. The connection should succeed. In the login warning dialog box, click **OK**.

17. Log in using your user name and password.

▶ **Remotely administering ISA Server**

1. Within the Remote Desktop, open **ISA Server Management**.

2. Expand **Configuration**, click **Networks**, select the **Tasks** tab, and then click **Export Existing Networks**.

3. In the **Export Configuration** dialog box, in the **File** name box, type **Networks Export**. Click **Export**.

4. After the export completes, click **OK**.

5. Click **Internal** and then click **Edit Selected Network**. On the **Addresses** tab, remove all **Address ranges**. Click **OK**.

6. Click **Apply** to apply the new configuration and then click **OK** in the **Apply New Configuration** screen.

7. Click **Networks** and on the **Tasks** tab, click **Import Networks**.

8. Select **Networks Export.xml** and click **Import**. Click **OK** to acknowledge the successful import.

9. Click **Apply** to apply the new configuration and then click **OK** in the **Apply New Configuration** screen.

10. Notice that all of the Address ranges have been restored to the internal network. Close all open windows and log off the Remote Desktop connection.

11. Open **ISA Server Management**.

12. On the **Tasks** tab, click **Connect to a Local or Remote ISA Server**.

13. In the **Connect To** dialog box, in the **Another computer (remote management)** box, type **Den-ISA-01** and click **OK**.

14. Click **DEN-ISA-01**. On the **Tasks** tab, click **Backup this ISA Server Configuration**.

15. In the **Backup Configuration** dialog box, in the **File name** box, type **Den-ISA-01 Backup** and click **Backup**.

16. In the **Set Password** dialog box, type **P@ssw0rd** in the **Password** and **Confirm password** boxes. Click **OK**.

17. When the backup is complete, click **OK**. Close all open windows.

▶ **To prepare for the lab**

1. You will need the Den-DC-01 virtual machine, the Den-ISA-01 virtual machine and the Den-ISA-02 virtual machine for the following lab.

2. Shut down Den-Clt-01. As the virtual machine shuts down, select the option to **Commit changes to the virtual hard disk**.

3. Start the Den-ISA-02 virtual machines.

Lab: Installing and Configuring ISA Server 2004

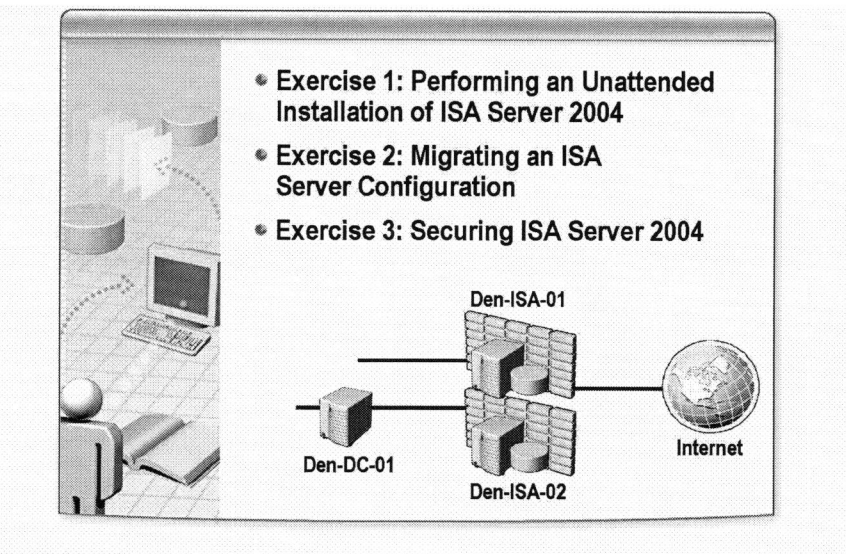

Objectives

After completing this lab, you will be able to:

- Perform an unattended installation of Internet Security and Acceleration (ISA) Server 2004.

- Export and import an ISA Server configuration.

- Configure security templates on a stand alone server.

- Configure an ISA Server for remote administration using Remote Desktop.

Note This lab focuses on the concepts in this module and, as a result, may not comply with Microsoft security recommendations. For instance, this lab does not comply with the recommendation that the Administrator accounts have highly complex passwords.

Scenario

You are deploying an additional ISA Server at Coho Vineyards. At this point, you are going to be using the server primarily for testing but you anticipate that the server will be deployed in another office location to provide site-to-site virtual private network (VPN) access. Because you will need to install multiple servers with almost the same configuration, you would like to use an unattended installation that you can reuse when you install more servers. You would also like to configure the new ISA Server with the same configuration as the current ISA Server. Because you are not sure whether all ISA Servers in the remote offices will be members of the Active Directory directory service domain, you need to install this server as a stand-alone server.

Estimated time to complete this lab: 30 minutes

Exercise 1
Performing an Unattended Installation of ISA Server 2004

In this exercise, you will perform an unattended installation of ISA Server 2004.

Tasks	Detailed steps
1. Start the Den-DC-01 virtual machine, the Den-ISA-01 virtual machine, and the Den-ISA-02 virtual machine if they are not already started. 2. Log on to Den-ISA-02 as local Administrator with a password of **P@ssw0rd**.	

3. Modify the default Msisaund.ini file to meet your installation requirements.
 	
• Install only the Firewall Services, the ISA Server Management, and the MSDE.
 	
• Configure one internal network range. The range is 192.168.1.0 to 192.168.1.255.
 	
• Company name is Coho Vineyards.
 	
• Accept other defaults.
	a. The Msisaund.ini file is located in the C:\Program Files\ Microsoft Learning\2824\Setup\FPC folder.
	
	b. Remove the semicolon from the following lines and modify the lines as listed below:
	
	  • ADDLOCAL=MSFirewall_Management,MSFirewall_ Services,MSDE
	
	  • INTERNALNETRANGES =1 192.168.1.0-192.168.1.255
	
	  • COMPANYNAME=Coho Vineyards
	
	c. Save the file as C:\Msisaund.ini.

4. Perform an unattended installation of the ISA Server. • The ISA Server installation files are located at C:\Microsoft Learning\ 2824\setup.	a. Use the following command to perform the install: • "C:\Program Files\Microsoft Learning\2824\Setup\FPC\ Setup.exe" /V /Qb FULLPATHANSWERFILE= "\C:\MSISAUND.INI" b. Wait for Den-ISA-02 to reboot. It can take several minutes to finish the installation and reboot.

(continued)

Tasks	Detailed Steps
5. After the server reboots, verify that the ISA Server is installed.	**a.** Check the Application Log for events indicating that the ISA Services have started. **b.** Use the Services management console to ensure that the following services are installed and running. • Microsoft Firewall • Microsoft ISA Server Control • Microsoft ISA Server Job Scheduler • Microsoft ISA Server Storage • MSSQL$MSFW **c.** Browse to the C:\Windows\Temp folder. Open the ISAWRAP_###.log file (where ### is a three-character number}. Review the log file, ensuring that the log indicates that the setup was successful.

Exercise 2
Migrating an ISA Server Configuration

In this exercise, you will export the ISA Server Configuration on an ISA Server and then import that configuration on another ISA Server.

Tasks	Detailed steps
1. Export the ISA Server configuration on Den-ISA-01. 2. Import the ISA Server configuration to Den-ISA-02.	a. Switch to the Den-ISA-01 virtual machine. Log in using your user name. b. Use ISA Server Management to export the ISA Server configuration. Do not export user permissions or confidential information. c. Save the configuration file in the My Documents folder on Den-ISA-01. d. Copy the configuration file from the My Documents folder to the desktop of your host computer. e. Switch to the Den-ISA-02 virtual machine. f. Copy the configuration file from the desktop of your host computer to the My Documents folder. g. Use ISA Server Management to import the ISA Server configuration. h. Confirm that the new configuration settings from Den-ISA-01 are imported correctly. For example, confirm that the System Policy is configured to enable remote desktop connections. i. Apply the changes to the ISA Server and restart the services.

Exercise 3
Securing ISA Server 2004

In this exercise, you will apply a security template to an ISA Server 2004, configure the external network interface on the ISA Server, and configure the ISA Server for Remote Management.

Tasks	Detailed steps
1. Apply the High Security – Member Baseline Template to Den-ISA-02. • Because this server is not a member of the domain, you will need to use the Security Configuration and Analysis tool to apply the template. • Before importing the template, modify the template to allow the Firewall Services to run. • The Windows Server 2003 Security Templates are located at C:\Security Templates.	a. Open a new Microsoft Management Console (MMC) and add the **Security Configuration and Analysis** snap-in. b. Right-click **Security Configuration and Analysis** and click **Open Database**. c. Type **ISA Server Configuration** and click **Open**. d. In the **Import Template** dialog box, browse to C:\Program Files\ Microsoft Learning\2824\Security Templates. Select **High Security – Member Server Baseline** and click **Open**. e. Right-click **Security Configuration and Analysis** and click **Analyze Computer Now**. In the **Perform Analysis** dialog box, click **OK**. f. Expand **Security Configuration**, then click **System Services** and double-click **Remote Access Connection Manager**. Under **Select service startup mode**, select **Automatic** and click **OK**. g. Double-click **Routing and Remote Access**. Under **Select service startup mode**, select **Automatic** and click **OK**. h. Double-click **Telephony**. Under **Select service startup mode**, select **Automatic** and click **OK**. i. Right-click **Security Configuration and Analysis** and click **Configure Computer Now**. In the **Configure System** dialog box, click **OK**.
2. Configure the External Interface card on the ISA server to make it more secure.	▪ Configure the external network interface on the server to disable **Client for Microsoft Networks** and **File and Printer Sharing for Microsoft Networks**, to disable automatic registration with DNS server, and to disable NetBIOS over TCP/IP and LMHOSTS lookup.

To Prepare for the Next Lab

As you finish this lab, shut down all of the virtual machines that you used in the lab. As the virtual machines shut down, select the option to Commit changes to the virtual hard disk.

After shutting down the virtual machines, start Den-ISA-01, Den-DC-01, Den-Clt-01, and Gen-Web-01 in preparation for the next module.

Module 3: Enabling Access to Internet Resources

Contents

Overview

- ISA Server 2004 as a Proxy Server
- Configuring Multi-Networking on ISA Server
- Configuring Access Rule Elements
- Configuring Access Rules for Internet Access

Introduction

One of the primary deployment scenarios for Microsoft® Internet Security and Acceleration (ISA) Server 2004 is to provide secure access to Internet resources for internal users. ISA Server 2004 provides a complete solution for providing this secure access. The ISA Server administrator needs to understand the functionality provided by ISA Server and how to configure secure access to Internet resources.

Objectives

After completing this module, you will be able to:

- Describe how ISA Server 2004 works as a proxy server.
- Configure multiple networks on ISA Server.
- Configure access rule elements.
- Configure ISA Server to provide secure access to Internet resources.

Lesson: ISA Server 2004 as a Proxy Server

- How ISA Server Enables Secure Access to Internet Resources
- Why Use a Proxy Server?
- How Does a Forward Web Proxy Server Work?
- What Is a Reverse Web Proxy Server?
- How to Configure ISA Server as a Proxy Server
- DNS Configuration for Internet Access
- How to Configure Web Chaining
- How to Configure Dial-Up Connections

Introduction

One of the primary deployment scenarios for ISA Server 2004 is as a proxy server that enables secure access to Internet resources. This lesson provides an overview of what a proxy server is and how ISA Server 2004 operates as a proxy server.

Lesson objectives

After completing this lesson, you will be able to:

- Describe how ISA Server enables secure access to Internet resources.
- Describe why use a proxy server.
- Describe how a forward Web proxy server works.
- Describe how a reverse Web proxy works.
- Configure ISA Server 2004 as a proxy server.
- Configure DNS for Internet access.
- Configure Web chaining.

How ISA Server Enables Secure Access to Internet Resources

Introduction

In many organizations, ISA Server is deployed to provide secure Internet access for internal clients. ISA Server provides several different options for enabling this secure access.

Secure access components

ISA Server provides the following functionality to enable secure access:

- *Using ISA Server as a firewall.* ISA Server provides a complete firewall solution that enables multi-layer filtering. As a firewall, ISA Server secures access to the Internet by ensuring that no unauthorized traffic can enter the internal network.

- *Using ISA Server as a proxy server.* When Firewall clients and Web proxy clients connect to the ISA Server computer to gain access to Internet resources, ISA Server acts as a proxy server. ISA Server accepts the client request for Internet content, and then creates a new request that it sends to the Internet server. ISA Server hides the details of the internal network from the Internet. Only the ISA Server's external Internet Protocol (IP) address is transmitted on the Internet. ISA Server also hides the network details for SecureNAT clients by using NAT to translate the internal IP addresses to the external IP address for the ISA Server computer.

- *Using ISA Server to implement the organization's Internet Usage Policy.* ISA Server can be used to implement almost any Internet-use restrictions including:

  - *Restrictions based on users and groups.* ISA Server can limit access to the Internet based on users and groups. These user or group accounts can be defined in Active Directory, on a RADIUS server, or on RSA SecurID servers.

  - *Restrictions based on computers.* ISA Server can limit access to specific computers, a group of computers, or all computers on a particular network. For example, you can set restrictions for Internet access from servers on the network, or for computers located in a public location.

- *Restrictions based on protocols*. ISA Server can enable or disable access to the Internet based on the protocols used to access the Internet. For example, you can enable access only for HTTP or HTTPS and disable all other protocols. Or you can enable all protocols, and define the exceptional protocols which will not be allowed.

- *Restrictions based on Internet destinations*. ISA Server can limit access based on Internet destinations. You can block or enable destinations based on domain names or URLs.

- *Restrictions based on content being downloaded from the Internet.* ISA Server can also scan all network packets coming in from the Internet to ensure that users are not downloading inappropriate or dangerous content.

Why Use a Proxy Server?

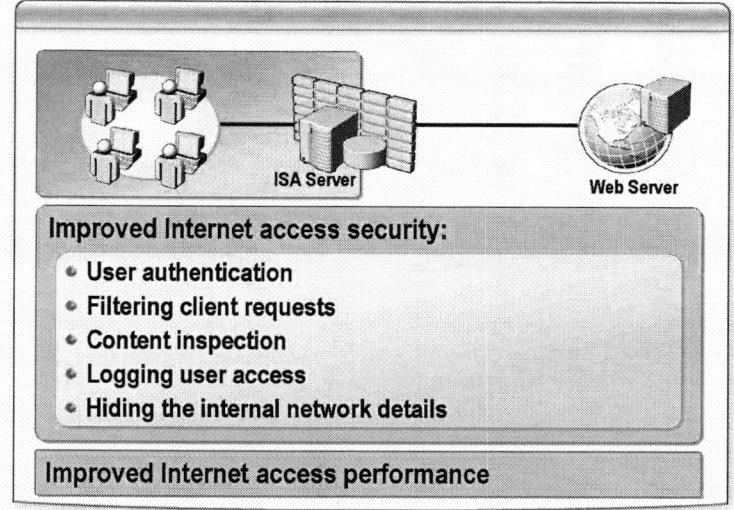

Introduction

A *proxy server* is a server that is situated between a client application, such as a Web browser, and a server that the client is connecting to. All client requests and all server responses pass through the proxy server. A proxy server can provide enhanced security and performance for Internet connections.

Improving Internet access security

The most important reason for using a proxy server is to make the user's connection to the Internet more secure. Proxy servers make the Internet connection more secure in the following ways:

- *User authentication.* When a user requests a connection to an Internet resource, the proxy server can require that the user authenticate, either by forcing the user to enter a user name and password or by using the cached credentials stored on the client computer. The proxy server can then grant or deny access to the Internet resource based on the authenticated user.

- *Filtering client requests.* The proxy server can use multiple criteria to filter client requests. In addition to filtering the request based on the user who is making the request, the proxy server can filter requests based on the IP address, the protocol or application that is being used to access the Internet, the time of day, and the Web site or Uniform Resource Locator (URL) the user is requesting.

- *Content inspection.* Proxy servers can inspect all traffic flowing in and out of the Internet connection and determine if there is any traffic that should be denied. This may include examining the traffic content for inappropriate words, scanning for viruses, or scanning for file extensions. Based on the criteria configured on the proxy server, all content can be inspected and filtered.

■ *Logging user access.* Because all traffic is flowing through the proxy server, the server can log everything the user does. For HTTP requests, this can include logging every URL visited by each user. The proxy server can be configured to provide detailed reports of user activity that can be used to ensure compliance with the organization's Internet usage policies.

■ *Hiding the internal network details.* Because all requests for Internet resources are coming from the proxy server rather than from the internal client computer, the details of the internal network are hidden from the Internet. In almost all cases, no client computer information such as computer name or IP address is sent to the Internet resource. In some cases, such as when creating a Remote Desktop Protocol connection to a server on the Internet, the client computer name is transmitted on the Internet.

Improving Internet access performance

Another benefit of using a proxy server is to improve Internet access performance. The Web proxy server improves performance by caching requested Internet pages on the Web proxy server hard disk. When another user requests the same information, the proxy server provides the page from the cache rather than retrieving it from the Internet.

Note For more information about configuring proxy server caching on ISA Server, see Module 9, "Implementing Caching," in Course 2824, *Implementing Microsoft Internet Security and Acceleration Server 2004.*

How Does a Forward Web Proxy Server Work?

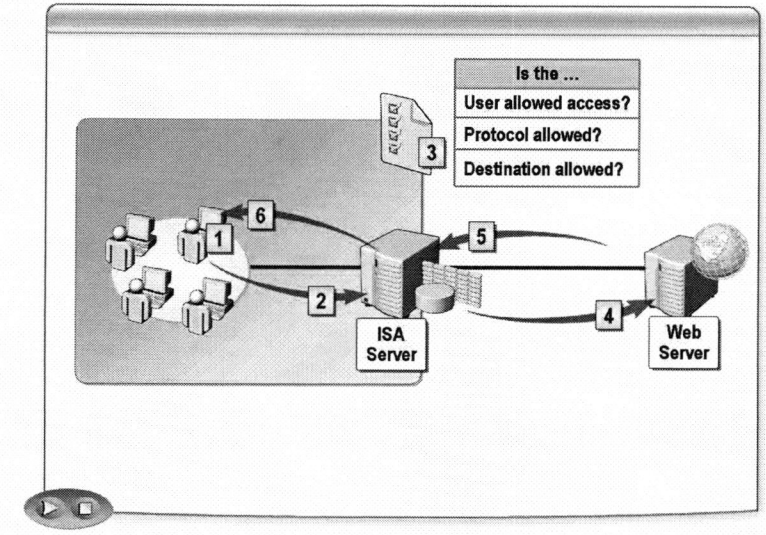

Introduction

Forward Web proxy servers are usually located between a Web application running on a client computer on the internal network and a Web server located on the Internet.

You must configure the Web application on the client computer to use the Web proxy server to gain access to the Internet. The Web proxy service may be running at the connection point between the Internet and the internal network; the client computers may have no physical connection to the Internet other than through the proxy server. In other cases, a firewall may be deployed between the Internet and the proxy server, but all client computers will still use the proxy server because of the Web application configuration.

How does a forward proxy server work?

The following steps outline how a forward Web proxy server works.

1. A client application such as a Web browser makes a request for an object located on a Web server. The client application checks its Web proxy configuration to determine whether the request destination is on the local network or on an external network.

2. If the requested Web server is not on the local network, then the request is sent to the proxy server.

3. The proxy server checks the request to confirm that there is no policy in place that blocks access to the requested content.

4. The proxy server also checks if the requested object already exists in its local cache. If the object is stored in the local cache and it is current, the proxy server sends the object to the client from the cache. If the page is not in the cache, the proxy server sends the request to the appropriate server on the Internet.

5. The Web server response is sent back to the proxy server. The proxy server filters the response based on the filtering rules configured on the server.

6. If the content is not blocked, ISA Server saves a copy of the content in its cache and then the object is returned to the client application that made the original request.

What Is a Reverse Web Proxy Server?

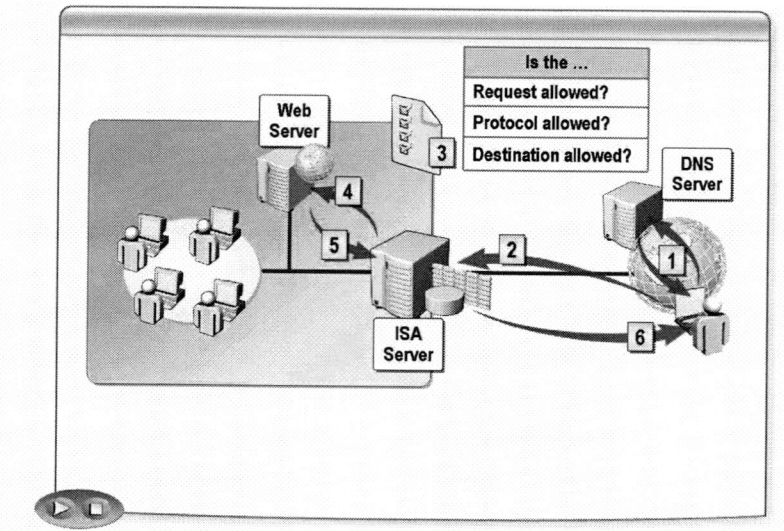

Introduction

A *reverse Web proxy server* operates in much the same way as a forward Web proxy server. However, instead of making Internet resources accessible to internal clients, reverse proxy makes internal resources accessible to external clients.

How a reverse proxy works

The following steps outline how a reverse Web proxy server works.

1. A user on the Internet makes a request for an object located on a Web server that is on an internal network protected by a reverse proxy server. The client computer performs a Domain Name System (DNS) lookup using the fully qualified domain name (FQDN) of the hosting server. The DNS name will resolve to the IP address of the external network interface on the proxy server.

2. The client application sends the request for the object to the external address of the proxy server.

3. The proxy server checks the request to confirm that the URL is valid and to ensure that there is no policy in place that blocks access to the requested content.

4. The proxy server also checks if the requested object already exists in its local cache. If the object is stored in the local cache and it is current, the proxy server sends the object to the client from the cache. If the page is not in the cache, the proxy server sends the request to the appropriate server on the internal network.

5. The Web server response is sent back to the proxy server.

6. The object is returned to the client application that made the original request.

Note Before ISA Server 2004 will operate as a reverse proxy server you need to configure Web publishing rules. Web publishing is covered in detail in Module 5, "Configuring Access to Internal Resources," in Course 2824, *Implementing Microsoft Internet Security and Acceleration Server 2004*.

How to Configure ISA Server as a Proxy Server

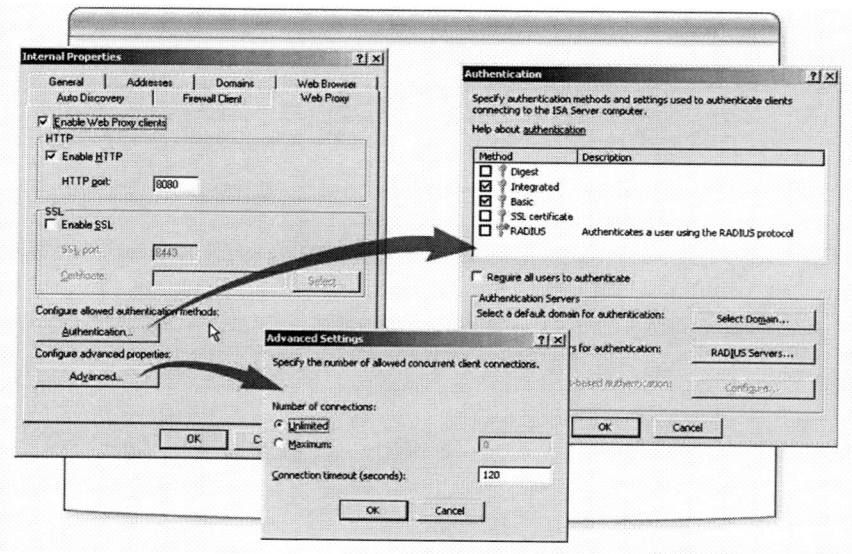

Introduction

You can deploy ISA Server 2004 as a Web proxy and a Winsock proxy server. In fact, as soon as you enable access to Internet resources for internal clients, ISA Server begins to operate as a Web proxy server. However, there are also several Web proxy server settings that you can modify on ISA Server.

All HTTP requests pass through the Web proxy component on ISA Server. This is because regardless of client type, when ISA Server receives a request from a client using one of these protocols, the client connection is treated as if it were coming from a Web proxy client.

Configuring ISA Server as a proxy server

You can configure several Web proxy settings on ISA Server.

1. In the Microsoft **ISA Server Management** console tree, expand the **Configuration** node and select **Networks**.

2. Click the network whose Web access properties you want to configure. This would usually be the internal network. Click **Edit Selected Network**.

3. On the **Web Proxy** tab, ensure that **Enable Web Proxy Clients** is selected.

The following table describes Web proxy configuration settings:

Dialog box	Choose this setting	To:
Web Proxy tab	Enable HTTP	Configure ISA Server to listen on for HTTP connections on the specified port number.
Web Proxy tab	Enable SSL	Configure ISA Server to listen on for HTTPS connections on the specified port number. If you enable SSL, you must also configure a **Certificate** that will be used for SSL authentication and encryption. Web browsers cannot use this setting but it can be used for Web chaining scenarios.
Authentication	Authentication method	Configure the method or methods of authentication supported on ISA Server .
Authentication	Require all users to authenticate	Configure ISA Server to allow only authenticated users to access other networks. If you choose this option, SecureNAT clients will not be able to access the Internet using this ISA Server.
Select Domain	Authentication domain	Configure the default domain that will be used for authentication when using Basic, Digest, or Remote Authentication Dial-In User Service (RADIUS) authentication.
RADIUS Servers	Server name and port	Configure the RADIUS server that will be used for authentication.
Advanced Settings	Number of connections	Configure the number of users that can connect to the ISA Server at one time.
Advanced Settings	Connection timeout (seconds)	Configure a connection timeout for idle connections.

DNS Configuration for Internet Access

- If no internal DNS server is available to resolve Internet addresses, configure the ISA Server clients to use an Internet DNS server

- Configure ISA Server clients to use an internal DNS server if the DNS server can resolve Internet addresses

- ISA Server can proxy DNS requests for Web proxy and Firewall clients but not for SecureNAT clients

- ISA Server includes a DNS cache that caches the results of all DNS lookups performed through ISA Server

Introduction

In order to connect to resources on the Internet, client computers must be able to resolve the Domain Name Service (DNS) names for servers on the Internet to IP addresses. To enable this, a DNS infrastructure must be in place to provide name resolution services.

Configuring DNS resolution

Many companies deploy DNS servers on the internal network that can resolve both internal and Internet names. In an Active Directory® environment, all client computers running Microsoft Windows® 2000 or later must be able to resolve the DNS names for the domain controllers. Often these DNS servers are also configured to resolve Internet DNS names, either by forwarding the requests to DNS servers on the Internet or by configuring the DNS servers to use the Internet root hints. In this type of scenario, you can just configure the ISA Server client computers to use the DNS server on the internal network.

Some organizations have not deployed internal DNS servers. In these organizations, the clients must be configured to use the DNS servers on the Internet for name resolution. In this scenario, you also need to create an access rule that allows the client computers to access the Internet using the DNS protocol. As well, with this configuration, you cannot use DNS to resolve the IP addresses for internal network resources.

DNS resolution and ISA Server clients

If you are using Web Proxy and Firewall clients, the ISA Server computer can function as a DNS proxy server to resolve Internet DNS requests on the client's behalf. When Web Proxy and Firewall clients connect to the ISA Server computer, ISA Server informs the clients which domain names are considered local. When a client requests the IP address for any server that is not local, the ISA Server computer attempts to resolve the IP address by using DNS servers on the Internet. To enable this, you must configure the ISA Server computer with the IP addresses for DNS servers that can resolve Internet hosts.

SecureNAT clients cannot use ISA Server for DNS name resolution. The SecureNAT client must be configured with the IP address of a DNS server that can resolve both internal and external host names. If you do not need to resolve internal host names (for example, if you use WINS to resolve internal names), you can configure the SecureNAT clients with the IP address of a DNS server on the Internet. In this scenario, you also need to create an access rule that allows the client computers to access the Internet by using the DNS protocol. In addition, with this configuration, you cannot use DNS to resolve the IP addresses for internal network resources.

DNS cache

If you are using ISA Server to resolve DNS names for Web Proxy and Firewall client computers, ISA Server uses its own DNS cache component that is built on top of the Windows DNS resolver. Whenever a DNS name is resolved by a DNS client on the internal network, ISA Server caches the lookup result. The purpose of the cache is to reduce the number of DNS queries that exit the firewall boundaries.

The DNS cache consists of three separate caches:

- A cache of DNS name-to-address resolutions.

- A cache of DNS address-to-name resolutions (also called a reverse cache).

- A cache of failures to perform DNS address-to-name resolutions. This cache is also called "negative cache." Its purpose is to mitigate possible DOS attacks on the reverse cache. After a failure to locate an entry in the reverse cache, the negative cache is consulted; if the entry is found there, the firewall will not attempt to do a reverse DNS query against the Windows DNS resolver.

Entries are removed from the three caches in one of the following events:

- When ISA Server retrieves an entry from the DNS cache it checks the time-to-live (TTL) on the entry. If the TTL has expired, ISA Server removes the entry from the cache. ISA 2004 uses the TTL given by the DNS server, though if it is lower than six minutes it is changed to six minutes, or if it is higher than six hours it is changed to six hours.

- When the cache size reaches the maximum threshold defined by the **DnsCacheSize** registry setting, 25 percent of the entries will be removed from the cache, according to the ones whose TTL is earlier. By default, the DNSCacheSize is set to 3000.

- The firewall service also traverses the three caches once every 30 minutes, and removes cache entries whose TTL has been reached.

How to Configure Web Chaining

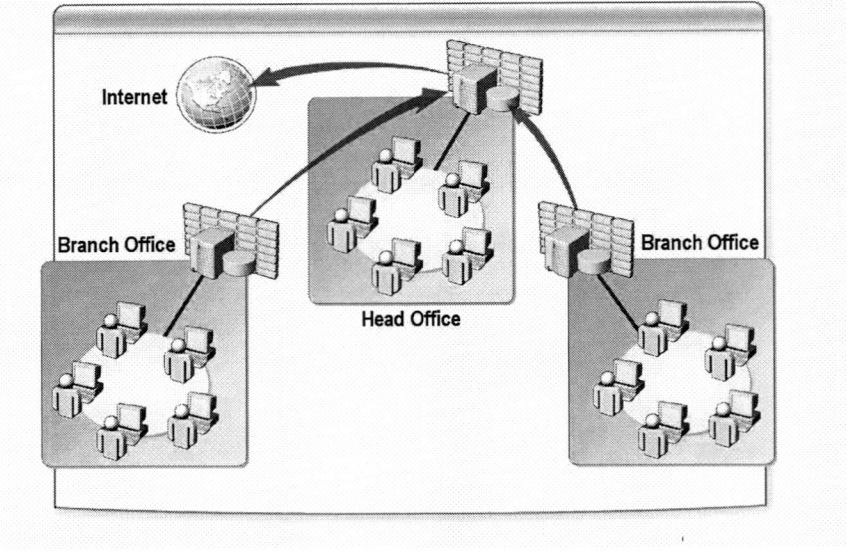

Introduction

ISA Server 2004 supports chaining multiple servers running ISA Server together to provide flexible Web proxy services. These servers can be chained in a hierarchical manner so that one ISA Server routes Internet requests to another ISA Server rather than routing the request directly to the Internet.

Why use Web chaining?

You might use Web chaining when your organization has multiple branch office locations, but all Internet requests are routed through one Internet connection at the head office. In this scenario, you can install ISA Server in each office and then configure ISA Server at the branch offices to route all Internet requests to the server running ISA Server at the head office.

You can configure flexible rules for conditionally routing Internet requests, depending on the destination server. For example, if one of the branch offices has a direct Internet connection and many of the sites used by users in that branch office are in the same country as the branch office, you may choose to have ISA Server route all requests for specific domain names directly to the Internet. You can still have the branch office server route all other requests to the head-office ISA Server.

One of the benefits of using Web chaining is the accumulated caching on ISA Server. If all the servers running ISA Server in the branch offices are configured to forward their requests to the head-office ISA Server, the head-office ISA Server will develop a large cache that contains many requested items. The combination of caching at the local branch office and at head office increases the chances that the Internet content can be delivered to the client with the least use of network bandwidth.

Another benefit of Web chaining is for configuring a test lab. Many organizations run a test lab that needs to be isolated from the production environment but may also need access to the Internet. By configuring ISA Server at the edge of the test lab network, and configuring it to forward all Internet requests to the production ISA Server, you can accomplish both goals.

Configuring Web chaining rules

To configure Web chaining rules, use the following procedure.

1. In the Microsoft **ISA Server Management** console tree, expand the **Configuration** node and select **Web Chaining**.

2. To create a new Web chaining rule, click **Create New Web Chaining Rule**.

3. On the **Welcome to the New Web Chaining Rule Wizard** page, in the **Web chaining rule name** box, type a name for the Web chaining rule. Click **Next**.

4. On the **Web Chaining Rule Destination** page, click **Add** to specify the destinations that will be affected by this rule.

5. In the **Add Network Entities** dialog box, select the destinations that this rule will apply to. For example, if the rule should apply to all Internet requests, expand **Networks**, then click **External**. Click **Close**.

6. On the **Web Chaining Rule Destination** page, click **Next**.

7. On the **Request Action** page, select how the request should be processed. You have three options:

   a. **Retrieve requests directly from the specified destination**. In this case, the Web request is routed directly to the Internet.

   b. **Redirect requests to a specified upstream server**. In this case, the Web request is routed to the server that you specify.

   c. **Redirect requests to**. In this case, the request is routed to the specified Web site.

8. You may also select **Allow delegation of basic authentication credentials**. In this case, ISA Server will forward the basic credentials provided by the client to the upstream server. If the client is required to authenticate, upstream server must be able to authenticate the client using the supplied credentials or the connection will be rejected.

9. To configure Web chaining, select **Redirect requests to a specified upstream server** and click **Next**.

10. On the **Primary Routing** page, in the **Server** box, type the name of the server to which this server will send the requests. You can also specify the port numbers for HTTP and SSL and configure an account that will be used to authenticate at the upstream ISA Server. Click **Next**.

11. On the **Backup Action** page, configure what ISA Server should do if the upstream ISA Server is unavailable. You have three choices:

    a. **Ignore requests**. In this case, ISA Server will not respond to client requests.

    b. **Retrieve requests directly from the specified destination**. In this case, ISA Server will route the request to the Internet.

    c. **Route requests to an upstream server**. In this case, you can specify an alternative upstream server.

    d. Select the option you require and click **Next**.

12. On the **Completing the New Web Chaining Rule Wizard** page, review the configuration and click **Finish**.

How to Configure Dial-Up Connections

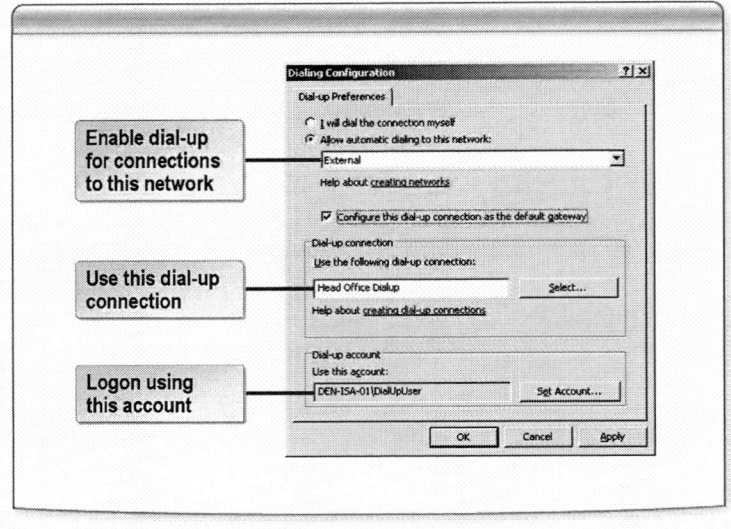

Introduction

ISA Server 2004 also supports the use of a dial-up connection to another network. For example, if you do not have a dedicated Internet connection that is always available, you can configure a dial-up connection so that when a user makes a request for a resource on the Internet, ISA Server can automatically dial an Internet connection. You can also configure the dial-up connection as a backup route, so that the dial-up connection is only used if the primary Internet connection is not accessible. In a Web chaining scenario, either the primary or backup route can also be a dial-up connection.

How to configure dial-up connections

To configure an automatic dial-up connection, use the following procedure:

1. In the Microsoft **ISA Server Management** console tree, expand the **Configuration** node and select **General**.

2. In the details pane, select **Specify Dial-Up Preferences**.

The following table describes dial-up configuration settings:

Choose this setting	To:
Allow automatic dialing to this network	Configure ISA Server to automatically use the dial-up connection to connect to the specified network.
Configure this dial-up connection to be the default gateway	Configure this connection as the primary way connection to the Internet, If you choose this option, all ISA Server traffic intended for the external network is sent on the connection.
Use the following dial-up connection	Specify the name of the dial-up connection.
Use this account	Specify the name and password used to authenticate the dial-up connection. Normally, this is a dial-up account assigned by an ISP.

After you configure the dial-up connection, you can specify this connection when configuring Web chaining rules.

Practice: Configuring ISA Server as a Web Proxy Server

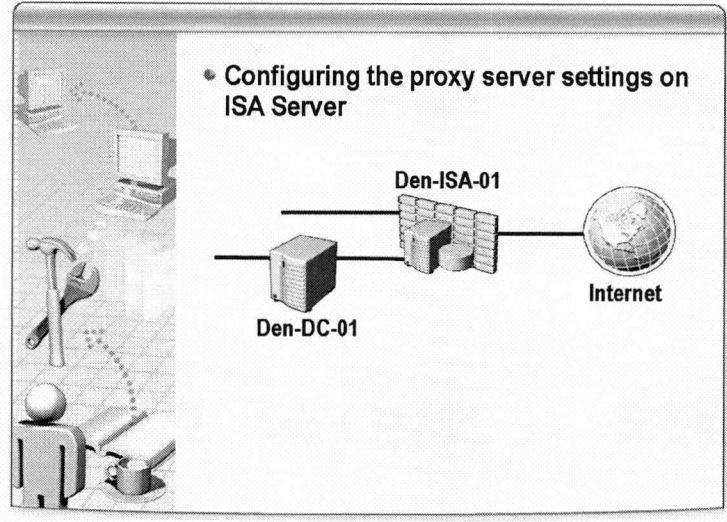

Introduction

In this practice, you will configure ISA Server 2004 to operate as a Web proxy server.

▶ **To prepare for this practice**

1. You will need the Den-DC-01 virtual machine, and the Den-ISA-01 virtual machine for this practice.

2. If necessary, start or resume the required virtual machines and then, on Den-ISA-01, log on to the cohovineyard domain with your user name and password.

Practice

▶ **Configuring the Proxy Server settings on ISA Server**

1. In the Microsoft **ISA Server Management** console tree, expand **Den-ISA-01**, then expand the **Configuration** node and select **Networks**.

2. On the **Networks** tab, click the **Internal** network. On the Tasks pane, click **Edit Selected Network**.

3. On the **Web Proxy** tab, ensure that **Enable Web Proxy Clients** and **Enable HTTP** are selected. Ensure the **HTTP port** is 8080.

4. To configure the authentication options, click **Authentication**.

5. In the **Authentication** dialog box, ensure that **Integrated** is selected and then select **Digest**. Read the warning message and then click **Yes**.

6. Click **Select Domain**. In the **Select Domain** dialog box, in the **Domain Name:** box, type **cohovineyard.com** and click **OK**.

7. Click **OK** to close the **Authentication** dialog box. Click **OK** to close the **Internal Properties** dialog box.

8. Click **Apply** to apply the changes and then click **OK** when the changes have been applied.

Lesson: Configuring Multi-Networking on ISA Server

* How Does ISA Server 2004 Support Multiple Networks?
* Default Networks Enabled in ISA Server
* About Network Objects
* How to Create and Modify Network Objects
* What Are Network Rules?

Introduction

One of the most significant enhancements to ISA Server 2004 is the support for multiple networks. These networks can be used when configuring many of the ISA Server settings, including when configuring access to Internet resources. This lesson provides an overview of how multi-networking is implemented in ISA Server 2004 and how to manage network objects.

Lesson objectives

After completing this lesson, you will be able to:

- Describe how ISA Server 2004 supports multiple networks.
- List the networks enabled by default in ISA Server 2004.
- Configure a dial-up connection.
- List the default network objects.
- Create and modify network objects.
- Describe network rules.

How Does ISA Server 2004 Support Multiple Networks?

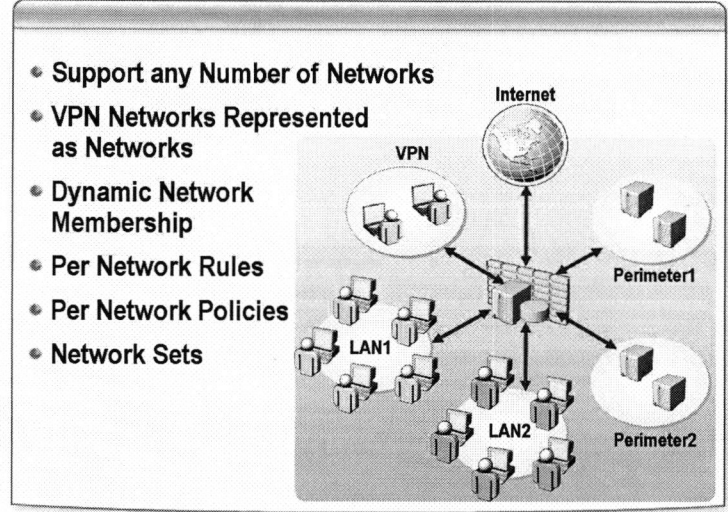

* Support any Number of Networks
* VPN Networks Represented as Networks
* Dynamic Network Membership
* Per Network Rules
* Per Network Policies
* Network Sets

Introduction

ISA Server 2004 supports multi-networking. This means that you can configure an unlimited number of networks on ISA Server. You can then configure access rules to manage the flow of network traffic between all of the networks.

What is multi-networking?

Multi-networking means that you can configure multiple networks on ISA Server, and then configure network and access rules that inspect and filter all network traffic between all networks.

Multi-networking examples

Multi-networking enables flexible options for network configuration. One of the most common network configurations is a three-legged firewall where you create three networks:

- The servers that are accessible from the Internet are usually isolated on their own network, such as a perimeter network.

- The internal client computers and servers that are not accessible from the Internet are located on an internal network.

- The third network is the Internet.

ISA Server multi-networking functionality supports this configuration. You can configure how clients on the corporate network access the perimeter network, and how external clients access the network. You can also configure the relationships between the various networks, defining different access policies between each network.

You might also want to configure a more complicated network environment. For example, you might have two different categories of servers that need to be accessible from the Internet. Perhaps you are deploying some servers that are domain members and other servers that are stand-alone servers. The domain members need to be able to communicate with domain controllers that are located on your internal network. In this scenario, you could configure a second perimeter network for the servers that need to be members of the domain. Because ISA Server supports per-network policies, you can configure two different policies for access from the perimeter networks to the internal networks.

You might also need a second internal network. You might have a group of client computers that needs to access the Internet using a different application or with different security rules than the other client computers. You can create an additional internal network and configure specific Internet access rules for each network.

Multi-networking features

ISA Server 2004 supports several multi-networking features:

- You can create an unlimited number of networks on ISA Server.

- The VPN Clients and Quarantined VPN Clients' networks are represented as networks, which means you can configure network access policies for the traffic flowing from these networks to the other networks.

- The client's membership in a network is automatically assigned. A computer becomes a member of a network based on its IP address (in the case of local area network [LAN]–connected clients) or based on its connection method (in the case of VPN clients).

- You can configure network rules by specifying a route or Network Address Translation (NAT) relationship between networks.

- You can configure per-network access policies so that each network's interaction with other networks can be unique.

- You can group several networks together into network sets, which means that you can define an access policy that applies to an entire network set.

Default Networks Enabled in ISA Server

Default Network	Includes
Local Host	• The ISA Server
Default External	• All IP addresses not associated with another network
Internal	• All IP addresses specified as internal during installation
VPN Clients	• All IP addresses for currently connected VPN clients
Quarantined VPN Clients	• All IP addresses of connected VPN clients that have not cleared quarantine

Introduction

When you install ISA Server 2004 on a server with at least two network cards, it is preconfigured with a default set of networks.

Default networks

ISA Server comes preconfigured with the following networks that cannot be deleted:

- *Local Host*. This network represents the ISA Server computer. Use this network to control all traffic that comes from or goes to ISA Server rather than traffic that flows through ISA Server. As with any network, you can define access rules that define what network traffic can flow to and from the Local Host network. Typically, ISA Server needs to be able to access services on other networks. For example, ISA Server may need to be able to access a domain controller, RADIUS server, or DNS server on the internal network. ISA Server is preconfigured with a set of system policies that enable this type of access. The Local Host network cannot be modified.

- *Default External*. This network includes all computers (IP addresses) that are not explicitly associated with any other network. The external network is generally considered an untrusted network and represents all hosts on the Internet. The Default External network cannot be modified.

- *Internal*. This network includes all computers (IP addresses) that were specified as internal during the installation process.

- *VPN Clients*. This network contains addresses of currently connected VPN Clients. The range of possible addresses is configured when you configure the virtual private network (VPN) properties.

- *Quarantined VPN Clients*. This network contains addresses of VPN Clients that have not yet cleared quarantine.

About Network Objects

Network Object	Includes
Network	• All computers connected to a single network interface
Network Set	• One or more networks
Computer	• A single computer identified by an IP address
Computer Set	• All computers included in specified computer, subnet or address range objects
Address Range	• All computers identified by continuous IP addresses
Subnet	• All computers on a specified subnet
URL Set	• All specified URLs
Domain Name Set	• All specified domain names
Web Listener	• The IP address on which the ISA Server listens for connections

Introduction

In addition to networks, ISA Server enables several other options for configuring groups of computers. You do this by configuring different network objects. For example, you can create a network set that includes multiple networks, and then use the network set when creating a network rule or access rule, or you can create a computer object, or computer set object, to configure a network or access rule based on a specific computer or group of computers.

Default network objects

ISA Server provides the following network objects. These network objects can be used as rule elements when creating network rules or access rules.

- *Network.* A network rule element represents a network, which is all of the computers connected (directly or through one or more routers) to a single ISA Server computer network adapter. When configuring a network rule, you can use any of the default networks, or any networks that you have configured on ISA Server.

- *Network set.* A network-set rule element represents a grouping of one or more networks. You can use this rule element to apply rules to more than one network. By default, ISA Server includes two network sets: All Networks, which includes all of the networks attached to ISA Server, and All Protected Networks, which includes all networks except the external network. You can also create network sets that include any combination of networks on the server.

- *Computer.* A computer rule element represents a single computer, identified by its IP address.

- *Computer set.* A computer set includes a collection of computers identified by their IP addresses, a subnet object, or an address-range object.

- *Address range.* An address range is a set of computers represented by a continuous range of IP addresses.

- *Subnet.* A subnet represents a network subnet, specified by a network address and a mask.

- *URL set*. A URL set rule element is a set of URLs such as http://www.adatum.com or http://www.fabrikam.com/tools/*.

- *Domain name set*. A domain name set rule element is a set of one or more domain names, in the format *.fabrikam.com.

- *Web listener*. A Web listener rule element is an IP address on which the ISA Server computer will listen for Web requests.

Note URL sets, domain name sets, and Web listener rule elements are used only when creating firewall access rules, not for creating network rules. Web listeners are used only for creating server publishing rules.

How to Create and Modify Network Objects

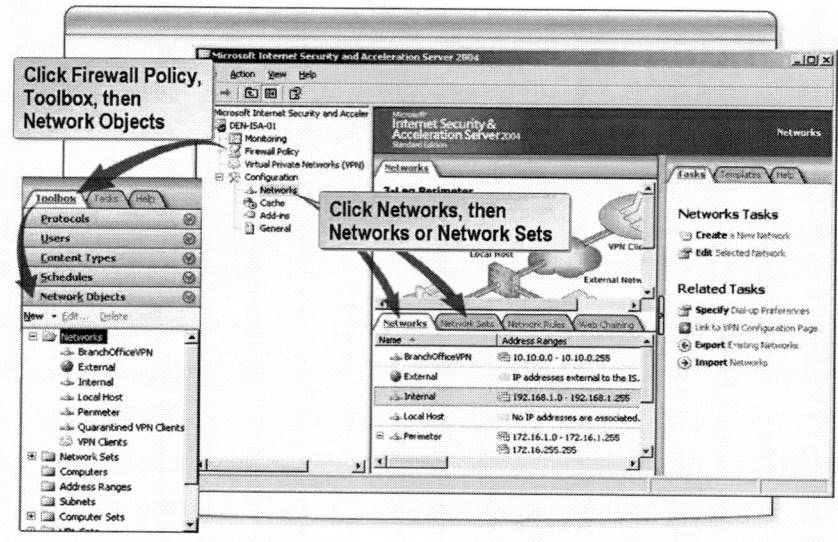

Introduction

For a small organization with a fairly simple network, the default network objects may provide all the configuration options required. However, in a larger organization with a more complex network environment and more complicated requirement, you may need to create and modify the network objects.

Creating and modifying network objects

To create network objects, use the following procedures.

▶ **To create a new network**

1. In the Microsoft **ISA Server Management** console tree, expand the **Configuration** node and click **Networks**.

2. In the details pane, click the **Network** tab.

3. On the **Tasks** tab, click **Create a New Network**.

4. On the **Welcome to the New Network Wizard** page, in the **Network name:** box, type the name for the network. Click **Next**.

5. On the **Network Type** page, select the type of network you are creating. Select one of the following options:

   a. **External Network**

   b. **Internal Network**

   c. **Perimeter Network**

   d. **VPN Site-To-Site Network**

6. After selecting the network type, click **Next**.

7. If you selected an internal, perimeter, or external network type, on the **Network Addresses** page, click **Add**.

8. In the **IP Address Range Properties** page, type the starting and ending addresses. Click **OK**.

9. On the **Completing to the New Network Wizard** page, review the settings and click **Finish**.

To modify a network, click the network in **ISA Server Management** and click **Edit Selected Network**.

▶ **To create a new network set**

1. In the Microsoft **ISA Server Management** console tree, expand the **Configuration** node and click **Networks**.

2. In the details pane, click the **Network Sets** tab.

3. On the **Tasks** tab, click **Create a New Network Set**.

4. On the **Welcome to the New Network Set Wizard** page, in the **Network set name:** box, type the name for the network set. Click **Next**.

5. On the **Network Selection** page, select whether this network set:

   a. Includes all selected networks,

      - or -

   b. Includes all networks except the selected networks.

6. Click the appropriate networks and click **Next**.

7. On the **Completing to the New Network Set Wizard** page, review the settings and click **Finish**.

To modify a network set, click the network in **ISA Server Management** and click **Edit Selected Network Set**.

▶ **To create or modify other network objects**

1. In the Microsoft **ISA Server Management** console tree, click **Firewall Policy** and, in the task pane, select the **Toolbox** tab.

2. Click **Network Objects**.

3. To create a new network object, click **New** and then click the type of network object you are creating. Configure the network object properties and then click **OK**.

4. To modify a network object, expand the network object type that you want to modify. Click the network object you are modifying and click **Edit**. Configure the network object properties and then click **OK**.

Important   After modifying any ISA Server setting, you need to apply the setting before it will take effect. To apply the setting, click **Apply** at the top of the details pane.

What Are Network Rules?

Route connection:

- A route relationship is bidirectional
- If a routed relationship is defined from network A to network B, a routed relationship also exists from network B to network A

NAT connection:

- A NAT relationship is directional
- Addresses from the source network are always translated when passing through ISA Server

Introduction

When you enable multiple networks or network objects on ISA Server, you can configure network rules that define how network packets will be passed between networks or between computers.

Network rule relationships

Network rules determine whether there is a relationship between two network entities and what type of relationship is defined. Network relationships can be configured as follows:

- *Route*. When you specify this type of connection, client requests from the source network are directly routed to the destination network. The source client address is included in the request. A route relationship is bidirectional. That is, if a routed relationship is defined from network A to network B, a routed relationship also exists from network B to network A.

- *Network AddressTtranslation (NAT)*. When you specify this type of connection, ISA Server replaces the IP address of the client on the source network with its own IP address. A NAT relationship is directional. It indicates that the addresses from the source network are always translated when passing through ISA Server. For example, by default a NAT network relationship is defined between the Internet and the internal network. When a client makes a request on the Internet, the IP addresses of the internal client computer are replaced by the address on the ISA Server computer before the request is passed to the server on the Internet. On the other hand, when a packet from the Internet is returned to the client computer, the address of the server is not translated. Client computers on the internal network can access the actual addresses of computers on the Internet, but computers on the Internet cannot access the internal IP addresses.

When no relationship is configured between networks, ISA Server drops all traffic between the two networks.

Default network rules

Upon installation, the following default network rules are created:

- *Local Host Access*. This rule defines a route relationship between the Local Host network and all other networks.

- *VPN Clients to Internal Network*. This rule defines a route relationship among the internal network and the Quarantined VPN Clients and the VPN Clients networks.

- *Internet Access*. This rule defines a NAT relationship among the internal network, the Quarantined VPN Clients, and the VPN Clients networks and the external network.

Creating network rules

To create a new network rule, use the following procedure:

1. In the Microsoft **ISA Server Management** console tree, expand the **Configuration** node and click **Networks**.

2. In the details pane, click the **Network Rules** tab.

3. On the **Tasks** tab, click **Create a New Network Rule**.

4. On the **Welcome to the New Network Rule Wizard** page, in the **Network rule name:** box, type the name for the network rule. Click **Next**.

5. On the **Network Traffic Sources** page, click **Add**.

6. On the **Add Network Entities** page, select the network entity that this rule will apply to. Click **Add**, and then click **Close**.

7. On the **Network Traffic Sources** page, click **Next**.

8. On the **Network Traffic Destinations** page, click **Add**.

9. On the **Add Network Entities** page, select the **Network Entity** that this rule will apply to. Click **Add**, and then click **Close**.

10. On the **Network Traffic Destinations** page, click **Next**.

11. On the **Network Relationship** page, click **Network Address Translation** or **Route**. Click **Next**.

12. On the **Completing to the New Network Rule Wizard** page, review the settings and click **Finish**.

Note Network rules are applied in a specific order. To determine the address relationship between two computers on different networks, ISA Server processes network rules according to priority order, looking for a rule that matches the computer addresses. The first rule that matches the computer addresses defines the network relationship. This means that you may have a routing relationship configured between two networks, but a NAT relationship configured between a specific computer on the network and the other network. In this case, the network rule defining the NAT relationship should be listed first to ensure that this specific rule is applied.

Practice: Managing Network Objects

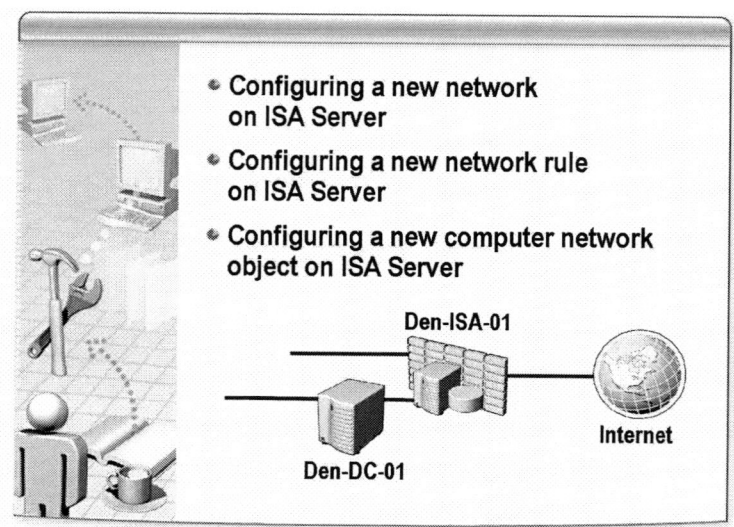

* Configuring a new network on ISA Server

* Configuring a new network rule on ISA Server

* Configuring a new computer network object on ISA Server

Den-ISA-01

Den-DC-01

Internet

Introduction

In this practice, you will configure an additional network on the server running ISA Server, configure network rules for the new network, and configure network objects.

Practice

▶ **To prepare for this practice**

1. You will need the Den-DC-01 virtual machine, and the Den-ISA-01 virtual machine for this practice.

2. If necessary, start or resume the required virtual machines and then, on Den-ISA-01, log on to the cohovineyard domain with your user name and password.

▶ **Configuring a new network on ISA Server**

1. Open **ISA Server Management** if necessary.

2. In the Microsoft **ISA Server Management** console tree, expand the **Configuration** node and click **Networks**.

3. In the details pane, click the **Networks** tab.

4. On the **Tasks** tab, click **Create a New Network**.

5. On the **Welcome to the New Network Wizard** page, in the **Network name:** box, type **Perimeter Network**. Click **Next**.

6. On the **Network Type** page, click **Perimeter Network**, and then click **Next**.

7. On the **Network Addresses** page, click **Add**.

8. In the **IP Address Range Properties** page, type **172.16.1.0** as the starting address and **172.16.1.255** as the ending address. Click **OK**.

9. On the **Network Addresses** page, click **Next**.

10. On the **Completing to the New Network Wizard** page, review the settings and click **Finish**.

11. Click **Apply** to apply the changes and then click **OK** when the changes have been applied.

▶ **Configuring a new network rule on ISA Server**

1. In the details pane, click the **Network Rules** tab.

2. On the **Tasks** tab, click **Create a New Network Rule**.

3. On the **Welcome to the New Network Rule Wizard** page, in the **Network Rule Name:** box, type **Perimeter to External Network Rule**. Click **Next**.

4. On the **Network Traffic Sources** page, click **Add**.

5. On the **Add Network Entities** page, expand **Networks**, click **Perimeter Network**, and click **Add**; then click **Close**.

6. On the **Network Traffic Sources** page, click **Next**.

7. On the **Network Traffic Destinations** page, click **Add**.

8. On the **Add Network Entities** page, expand **Networks**, click **External** and click **Add**; then click **Close**.

9. On the **Network Traffic Destinations** page, click **Next**.

10. On the **Network Relationship** page, click **Network Address Translation**. Click **Next**.

11. On the **Completing to the New Network Rule Wizard** page, review the settings and click **Finish**.

12. Click **Apply** to apply the changes and then click **OK** when the changes have been applied.

▶ **Configuring a new computer network object on ISA Server**

1. In the Microsoft **ISA Server Management** console tree, click **Firewall Policy** and, in the task pane, select the **Toolbox** tab.

2. Click **Network Objects**.

3. Click **New** and then click **Computer**.

4. In the **New Computer Rule Element** dialog box, in the **Name** box, type **Den-DC-01**. In the **Computer IP Address** box, type **192.168.1.10**. Click **OK**.

5. Click **Apply** to apply the changes and then click **OK** when the changes have been applied.

Lesson: Configuring Access Rule Elements

- What Are Access Rule Elements?
- How to Configure Protocol Elements
- How to Configure User Elements
- How to Configure Content Type Elements
- How to Configure Schedule Elements
- How to Configure Domain Name Sets and URL Sets

Introduction

Configuring access to Internet resources involves the configuration of several components within ISA Server 2004. One set of components is the access rule elements. Access rule elements enable the administrator to create objects such as user objects, schedule objects, or protocol objects. These objects can then be used when creating the access policy rules to apply a rule controlling Internet access.

Lesson objectives

After completing this lesson, you will be able to:

- Describe what firewall rule elements are.
- Configure protocol elements.
- Configure user elements.
- Configure content type elements.
- Configure schedule elements.
- Configure network objects.
- Configure domain name sets and URL sets.

What Are Access Rule Elements?

Access Rule Element	Used to Configure
Protocols	• The protocols that will be allowed or denied by an access rule
Users	• The users that will be allowed or denied by an access rule
Content Types	• The content type that will be allowed or denied by an access rule
Schedules	• The time of day when Internet access will be allowed or denied by an access rule
Network Objects	• The computers or destinations that will be allowed or denied by an access rule

Introduction

By default, ISA Server denies all network traffic between networks other than limited traffic between the Local Host Network (the server running ISA Server) and other networks. Configuring an *access rule* is the only way to configure ISA Server so that it will allow traffic to flow between networks. An access rule defines the conditions for when traffic will be allowed or denied between networks. An access rule element is one of the configuration options in an access rule.

Why use access rule elements?

Access rule elements are configuration objects in ISA Server that you can use to create specific access rules. For example, you may want to create an access rule that allows only HTTP traffic. To do this, ISA Server provides a Protocols access rule element that defines HTTP traffic. You can configure an access rule that uses this Protocols element.

Some organizations want to limit access to the Internet to certain users or computers. To enable this, you can create a subnet or users rule element, and then use this element in an access rule to limit access to the Internet to only computers on the specified subnet, or to only the specified users.

Access rule element types

There are five types of rule elements:

- *Protocols*. This rule element contains protocols that you can use to define the protocols that will be used in an access rule. For example, you can allow or deny access on one or more protocols. You may want to allow all protocols with the exception of streaming media protocols.

- *Users*. In this rule element, you can create a user set to which a rule will be explicitly applied, or which can be excluded from a rule. For example, you may want to create a rule that enables Internet access to all users within an organization with the exception of all temporary staff. By using an Active Directory® directory service domain or RADIUS server for authentication, you can configure an access rule that grants the Domain Users group access to the Internet, but denies the TempEmployees group access.

- *Content types*. This rule element provides common content types to which you may want to apply a rule. For example, you can use a content type rule element to block all content downloads that include .exe or .vbs extensions.

- *Schedules*. This rule element allows you to designate hours of the week during which the rule applies. If you need to define an access rule that allows access to the Internet only during specified hours, you can create a schedule rule element that defines those hours, and then use this schedule rule element when creating the access rule.

- *Network objects*. This rule element allows you to create sets of computers to which a rule will apply, or which will be excluded from a rule. You can also configure URL sets and domain name sets that you can use to allow or deny access to specific URLs or domains.

How to Configure Protocol Elements

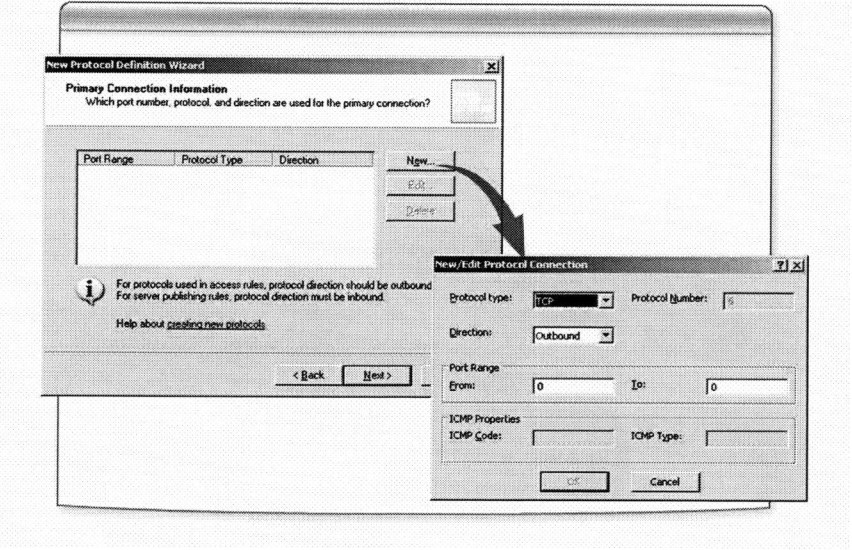

Introduction

In most cases, you may want to create an access rule that allows or denies access to the Internet depending on which protocol the client is using. To do this, you can use one of the protocol elements provided with ISA Server or create your own protocol definition.

Creating new protocols

ISA Server includes a wide variety of preconfigured protocols that you can use when you create access rules. In almost all cases, the preconfigured protocols provide all the flexibility you need when configuring access rules. The protocols included with ISA Server cannot be deleted. You can modify which application filters are applied to the preconfigured protocols, but you cannot modify any other settings.

You can also create new protocols by using ISA Server Management. For example, you may be using a custom application that requires a specific port number. You can create a protocol element that uses this port number and then use the protocol in an access rule. User-defined protocols can be edited or deleted.

When you create a protocol, you specify settings listed in the following table:

Settings	Explanation
Protocol type	This includes TCP-, UDP-, Internet Control Message Protocol (ICMP)–, or IP-level protocol types.
Direction	For UDP, this includes Send, Receive, Send Receive, or Receive Send. For TCP, this includes Inbound and Outbound. For ICMP and IP, this includes Send and Receive.
Port range	For TCP and UDP protocols, this is a range of ports between 1 and 65535 that is used for the initial connection.
Protocol number	For IP-level protocols, this is the protocol number.

(continued)

Settings	Explanation
ICMP properties	For ICMP protocol, this is the ICMP code and type.
Secondary connections	This setting is optional; it is the range of ports, protocol types, and direction used for additional connections or packets that follow the initial connection. You can configure one or more secondary connections.

To create a new protocol object, use the following procedure.

1. In the Microsoft **ISA Server Management** console tree, click **Firewall Policy**.

2. On the **Toolbox** tab, click **Protocols**.

3. Click **New**, and then click **Protocol** or **RPC Protocol**. For this example, choose **Protocol**.

4. On the **Welcome to the New Protocol Definition Wizard**, in the **Protocol definition name:** box, type the protocol name. Click **Next**.

5. On the **Primary Connection Information** page, click **New** to configure the protocol type, direction, and port numbers for the protocol. Click **OK**, and then click **Next**.

6. On the **Secondary Connections** page, select whether you want to use secondary connections. If the protocol requires secondary connections, click **Yes**, and then click **New** to configure the protocol type, direction, and port numbers for the secondary connection. Click **OK**, and then click **Next**.

7. On the **Completing to the New Protocol Definition Wizard**, review the configuration and click **Finish**.

To modify an existing protocol definition, click the protocol in the **Protocols** box, and click **Edit**.

How to Configure User Elements

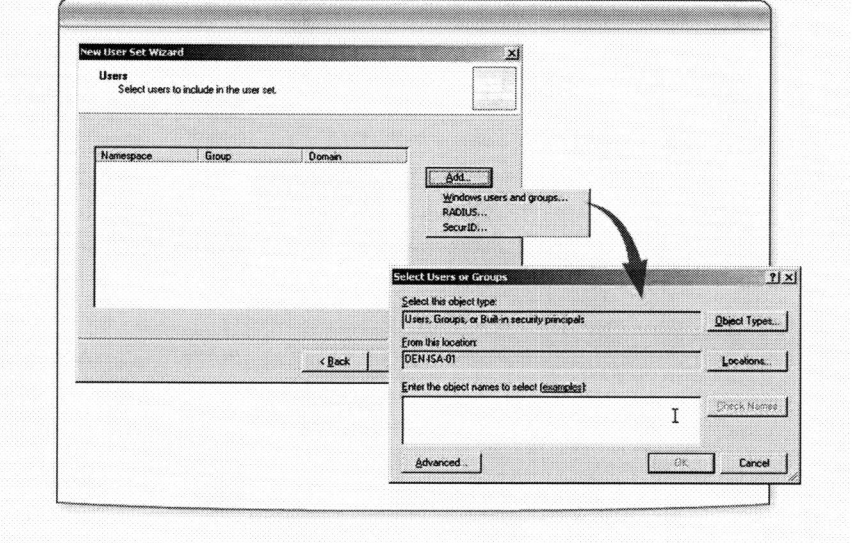

Introduction

The second criterion that you may want to apply to an access rule is which users will be allowed or denied access by the access rule. You can configure this by creating user elements and then applying the user element to an access rule.

Configuring user sets

To limit access to Internet resources based on users or groups, you need to create a user element. When you limit an access rule to specific users, the user must authenticate before they will be granted access. For each group of users, you can define what type of authentication is required. You can mix different types of authentication within a user's set. For example, a user set might include a Windows user based on domain membership, a user from a RADIUS namespace, and another user from the SecurID namespace.

ISA Server comes preconfigured with the following user sets:

- *All Authenticated Users*. This set includes all users who have authenticated using any type of authentication. SecureNAT clients are not authenticated unless they are connecting through a VPN. This means that this group does not include non-VPN SecureNAT clients.

- *All Users*. This set includes all users, both authenticated and unauthenticated.

- *System and Network Service*. This user set includes the Local System service and the Network service on the server running ISA Server. This user set is used in some system policy rules.

To create a new user set, use the following procedure.

1. In the Microsoft **ISA Server Management** console tree, click **Firewall Policy**.

2. On the **Toolbox** tab, click **Users**.

3. Click **New**. On the **Welcome to the New User Sets Wizard**, in the **User set name:** box, type the protocol name. Click **Next**.

4. On the **User** page, click **Add** and then click the type of user that you are adding to the set. There are three options:

   a. **Windows Users and Groups**. Use this option to add users and groups from a Windows domain or from the local accounts on the server running ISA Server.

   b. **RADIUS**. Use this option to add specific users or all users from a specific RADIUS name space.

   c. **SecurID**. Use this option to add specific users or all users from a specific SecureID name space.

5. Click **OK** and then click **Next**.

6. On the **Completing to the New User Sets Wizard**, review the configuration and click **Finish**.

To modify an existing user set, click the user set in the **Users** box, and click **Edit**.

How to Configure Content Type Elements

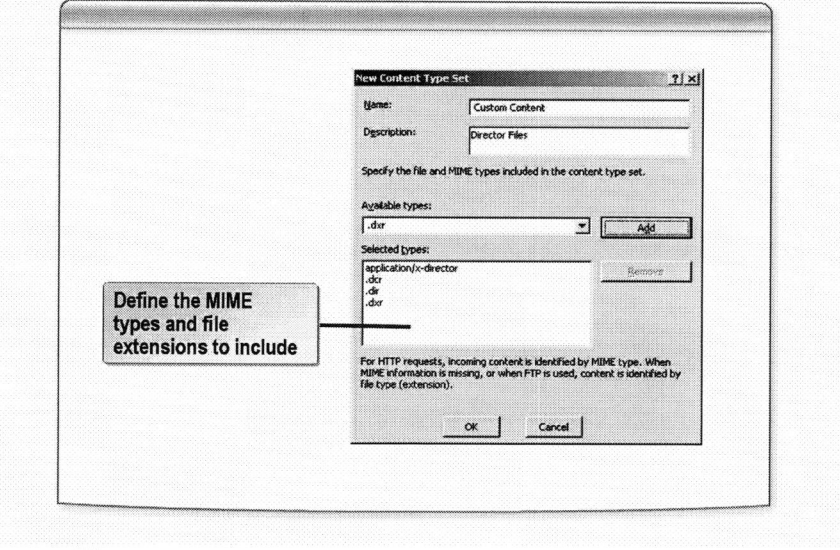

Define the MIME types and file extensions to include

Introduction

You may also want to limit the types of content that users can access on the Internet. To do this, create a new content type element, or use one of the existing content type elements when you create an access rule.

Configuring content type elements

Content type elements define Multipurpose Internet Mail Extensions (MIME) types and file name extensions. When a client like Microsoft Internet Explorer downloads information from the Internet using HTTP or File Transfer Protocol (FTP), the content is downloaded in either MIME format or as a file with a specified file name extension.

Content type elements apply only to HTTP and FTP traffic that is tunneled in an HTTP header. FTP traffic is tunneled in an HTTP header when a client is configured as a Web Proxy client.

- When a client requests FTP content, ISA Server checks the file name extension of the requested object. ISA Server determines if a content type that includes the file extension is linked to the access rule. If a content type applies, ISA Server applies the rule.

- When a client requests HTTP content, ISA Server sends the request to the Web server. When the Web server returns the object, ISA Server checks the object's MIME type or its file name extension, depending on the header information returned by the Web server. ISA Server determines if a rule applies to a content type that includes the requested file name extension, and processes the rule accordingly.

ISA Server is preconfigured with the following content types: Application, Application data files, Audio, Compressed files, Documents, Hypertext Markup Language (HTML) documents, Images, Macro documents, Text, Video, and Virtual Reality Modeling Language (VRML). In most cases, you will not need to configure additional content types but can just apply the existing types.

When you configure a content type and specify the MIME type, you can use an asterisk (*) as a wildcard character. For example, to include all application types, enter application/*. The asterisk wildcard character can be used only with MIME types and not with file extensions. The asterisk can be specified only once, at the end of the MIME type after the slash mark (/).

To create a new content type object, use the following procedure.

1. In the Microsoft **ISA Server Management** console tree, click **Firewall Policy**.

2. On the **Toolbox** tab, click **Content Types**.

3. Click **New**.

4. In the **New Content Type Set** dialog box, fill in the following information:

   a. **Name**. Type the content type set name.

   b. **Available types**. Select the appropriate content types from the drop-down list. You can choose either MIME types or application extensions. Click **Add**.

5. Click **OK**.

To modify an existing content type set, click the content type set in the **Content Types** box, and click **Edit**.

How to Configure Schedule Elements

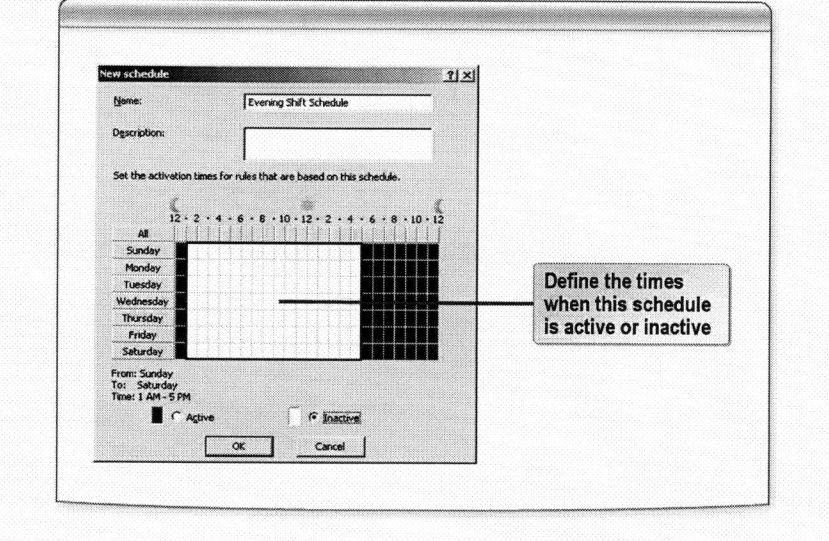

Define the times when this schedule is active or inactive

Introduction

In some cases, you may also want to configure access to the Internet based on time of day. To do this, configure a schedule element and apply it or one of the existing schedules to an access rule.

Configuring schedule elements

Schedule elements define a schedule that you can use to grant or deny Internet access as part of an access rule.

ISA Server 2004 is preconfigured with the following two schedules:

- *Weekends*. Defines a schedule that configures all times on Saturday and Sunday as active

- *Work Hours*. Defines a schedule that configures the hours between 09:00 (9:00 A.M.) and 17:00 (5:00 P.M.) on Monday through Friday as active

To create a new schedule element, use the following procedure.

1. In the Microsoft **ISA Server Management** console tree, click **Firewall Policy**.

2. On the **Toolbox** tab, click **Schedules**.

3. Click **New**.

4. In the **New schedule** dialog box, fill in the following information:

    a. **Name**. Type the content type set name.

    b. Configure the schedule by selecting the times when the rule will be active or inactive and then clicking **Active** or **Inactive**.

5. Click **OK**.

To modify an existing schedule element, click the schedule element in the **Content Types** box, and click **Edit**.

How to Configure Domain Name Sets and URL Sets

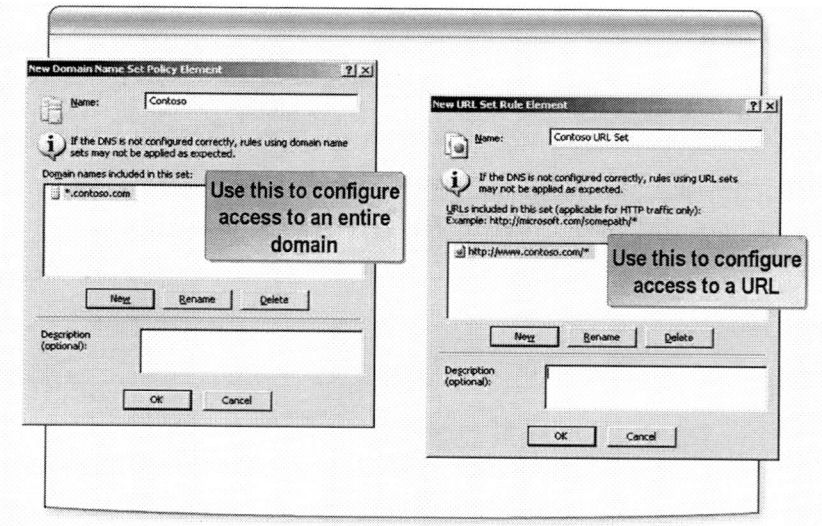

Introduction

You may also want to define which Web sites users can or cannot access. You can configure this by creating either a domain name set or a Uniform Resource Locator (URL) set and then applying these sets to an access rule.

Configuring domain name and URL sets

Domain name and URL sets are both network objects that can be used when defining access rules, but not for defining network rules. Domain name sets define one or more domain names as a single set, so that you can apply access rules to the specified domains. URL sets specify one or more URLs grouped together to form a set. URL sets can be used in access rules to allow or deny access to specified Web sites.

- *Specifying domain names.* When specifying the domain name, you can use an asterisk (*) to specify a set of host names. For example, to specify all hosts in the contoso.com domain, type the domain name as *.contoso.com. The asterisk can appear only at the start of the domain name, and can be specified only once in the name. You must use the fully qualified domain name (FQDN) when specifying a domain name.

- *Specifying URLs.* When you create a URL set, you can specify one or more URLs in URL format. For example, you specify a URL such as http://www.contoso.com. You can also specify a path and use wildcard characters in the path, but only at the end. For example, www.contoso.com/* is acceptable. However, www.contoso.com/*/sales is not.

ISA Server processes rules that apply to URL sets only for client requests for HTTP or FTP over HTTP. When a client uses any other protocol, ISA Server does not process rules that apply only to a URL set.

ISA Server includes the following predefined domain name sets:

- *Microsoft Error Reporting Sites*. A predefined domain name set used to allow error reporting.

- *System Policy Allowed Sites*. A predefined domain name set used to allow access to trusted sites for maintenance and management.

To create a new domain element or URL element, use the following procedure.

1. In the Microsoft **ISA Server Management** console tree, click **Firewall Policy**.

2. On the **Toolbox** tab, click **Network Objects**.

3. To create a new domain name set, click **New**, and then click **Domain Name Set**.

4. In the **New Domain Name Set Policy Element** dialog box, fill in the following information:

   a. **Name**. Type the domain name set name.

   b. **Domain names included in this set**. Click **New** and then type the domain name.

5. Click **OK**.

6. To create a new URL set, click **New** and then click **URL Set**.

7. In the **New URL Set Rule Element** dialog box, fill in the following information:

   a. **Name**. Type the URL set name.

   b. Specify the URLs included in this URL set. Click **New** and then type the domain name.

8. Click **OK**.

To modify an existing domain name or URL set, click the domain name or URL set in the **Network Objects** box, and click **Edit**.

Practice: Configuring Firewall Rule Elements

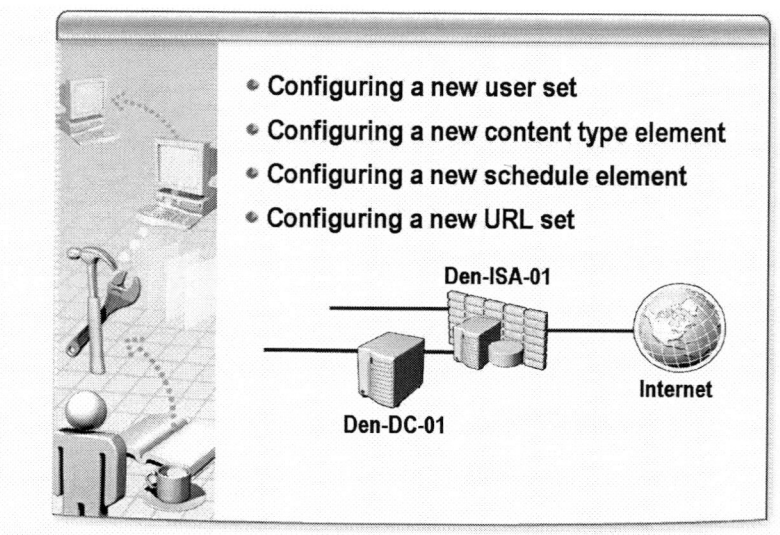

Introduction

In this practice, you will configure several new user elements that can be used to configure access rules for Internet access.

Practice

▶ **To prepare for this practice**

1. You will need the Den-DC-01 virtual machine, and the Den-ISA-01 virtual machine for this practice.

2. If necessary, start or resume the required virtual machines and then, on Den-ISA-01, log on to the cohovineyard domain with your user name and password.

▶ **Configuring a new user set**

1. In the Microsoft **ISA Server Management** console tree, click **Firewall Policy**.

2. On the **Toolbox** tab, click **Users**.

3. Click **New**. On the **Welcome to the New User Sets Wizard**, in the **User set name:** box, type **Managers**. Click **Next**.

4. On the **Users** page, click **Add** and then click **Windows Users and Groups**.

5. In the **Select Users and Groups** dialog box, click **Locations**. In the **Locations** dialog box, expand **Entire Directory**, then click **cohovineyard.com** and click **OK**.

6. In the **Select Users and Groups** dialog box, in the **Enter the object names to select:** box, type **Managers**.

7. Click **OK**, and then click **Next**.

8. On the **Completing to the New User Set Wizard**, review the configuration and click **Finish**.

▶ **Configuring a new content type element**

1. On the **Toolbox** tab, click **Content Types**.

2. Click **New**.

3. In the **New Content Type Set** dialog box, in the **Name:** box, type **Powerpoint Content**. In the **Available types** drop-down list, click **.ppt**. Click **Add**. Repeat for the following available types: **application/vnd.ms-powerpoint, application/x-mspowerpoint, .pot, .pps.**

4. Click **OK**.

▶ **Configuring a new schedule element**

1. On the **Toolbox** tab, click **Schedules**.

2. Click **New**.

3. In the **New schedule** dialog box, in the **Name:** box, type **Night Shift Schedule**. Configure the **Active** time on the schedule to be from midnight to 8 A.M. every weekday.

4. Click **OK**.

▶ **Configuring a new URL set**

1. On the **Toolbox** tab, click **Network Objects**.

2. To create a new URL set, click **New**, and then click **URL Set**.

3. In the **New URL Set Rule Element** dialog box, in the **Name:** box, type **Contoso URL**. Click **New** and then, in the **URLs included in this URL set** box, type **http://www.contoso.com/***.

4. Click **OK**.

5. Click **Apply** to apply the changes and then click **OK** when the changes have been applied.

▶ **To prepare for the next practice**

1. You will need the Den-DC-01 virtual machine, the Den-Clt-01 virtual machine, the Gen-Web-01 virtual machine and the Den-ISA-01 virtual machine for the next practice.

2. If necessary, start or resume the required virtual machines.

Lesson: Configuring Access Rules for Internet Access

* What Are Access Rules?
* How Network Rules and Access Rules Are Applied
* About Authentication and Internet Access
* How to Configure Access Rules
* How to Configure HTTP Policy
* How to Troubleshoot Access to Internet Resources

Introduction

Access rules define how ISA Server 2004 will deal with traffic moving from one network to another. To enable access to the Internet, you must configure one or more access rules that allow this type of access. The access rules make use of network objects and access rule elements to create the rules. This means that you can create rules that define which users or computers can access the Internet and when they can connect to the Internet as well as what information can be accessed on the Internet.

Lesson objectives

After completing this lesson, you will be able to:

- Describe access rules.
- Explain how access rules work.
- Describe how authentication works for Internet access.
- Create and modify access rules.
- Configure HTTP Filtering.

What Are Access Rules?

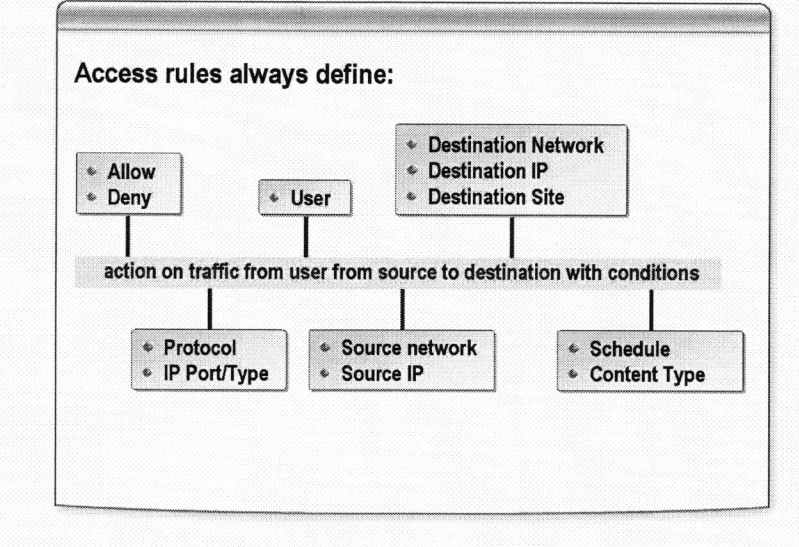

Introduction	Access rules determine how clients on a source network can access resources on a destination network. To enable access to Internet resources for users on your internal network, you need to configure an access rule that enables this access.
Access rule format	Access rules are used to configure all traffic flowing through ISA Server, including all traffic from the internal network to the Internet, and from the Internet to the internal network.

All access rules have the same overall structure as shown in the following table.

Access rules define	Explanation
An action	Access rules are always configured to either allow or deny access.
To be performed on specified traffic	Access rules can be applied to specific protocols or port numbers.
From a particular user	Access rules can be applied to specific users or all users, whether they have authenticated or not.
Coming from a particular computer	Access rules can be applied to specific computers based on their network locations or IP addresses.
Going to a particular destination	Access rules can be applied to specific destinations, including networks, destination IP addresses, and destination sites.
Based on particular conditions	Access rules can set additional conditions, including schedules and content-type filtering.

How Network Rules and Access Rules Are Applied

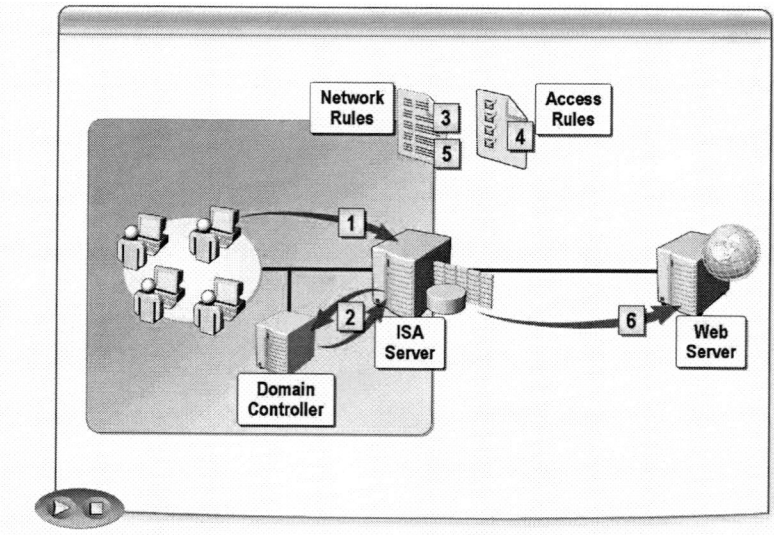

Introduction

When a client computer on the internal network requests a resource located on the Internet, the request is passed through ISA Server. When the request arrives at the server running ISA Server, it evaluates the request based on the configured network rules and access rules. If the network rules and access rules specify that access should be granted, the user request is forwarded. In all other cases, the client request is refused.

How access rules are applied

All of the network rules and access rules make up the firewall policy. The firewall policy is applied in the following way:

1. A user using a client computer sends a request for a resource located on the Internet.

2. If the request comes from a Firewall Client computer, the user is transparently authenticated using Kerberos or NTLM if domain authentication is configured. If the user cannot be transparently authenticated, ISA Server requests the user credentials. If the user request comes from a Web proxy client, and the access rule requires authentication, ISA Server requests the user credentials. If the user request comes from a SecureNAT client, the user is not authenticated, but all other network and access rules are still applied.

3. ISA Server checks the network rules to verify that the two networks are connected. If no network relationship is defined between the two networks, the request is refused.

4. If the network rules define a connection between the source and destination networks, ISA Server processes the access rules. The rules are applied in order of priority as listed in the ISA Server Management interface. If an allow rule allows the request, then the request is forwarded without checking any additional access rules. If no access rule allows the request, the final default access rule is applied, which denies all access.

5. If the request is allowed by an access rule, ISA Server checks the network rules again to determine how the networks are connected. ISA Server checks the Web chaining rules (if a Web proxy client requested the object) or the firewall chaining configuration (if a SecureNAT or Firewall Client requested the object) to determine how the request will be serviced.

6. The request is forwarded to the Internet Web server.

How to assign access rule priorities

Because access rules are evaluated in order based on the priority assigned in the ISA Server Management interface, it is important that you assign these priorities correctly. In general, you should apply all the deny rules first, followed by the more specific rules, followed by general rules. For example, you may have the following requirements when configuring Internet access:

■ All computers should be able to access the Internet except for selected file servers.

■ All users should be able to access the Internet except temporary employees.

■ Users who access the Internet from a public kiosk computer located in the organization's reception area should be able to use only HTTP and HTTPS to access the Internet.

■ Users should be able to access the Internet using all protocols.

To configure the access rules in this scenario, you could configure the rules with the following priorities.

1. Create an access rule that blocks Internet access to a computer set that includes all the file servers.

2. Create an access rule that blocks Internet access to the domain group that contains all temporary employees.

3. Create an access rule that allows only HTTP or HTTPS traffic from the public kiosk computer to access the Internet.

4. Create an access rule that allows all users to access the Internet using any protocol.

Note ISA Server includes one default access rule. This rule denies access to all traffic. This rule cannot be modified, and it is always the last rule to be applied.

About Authentication and Internet Access

* **Authentication and ISA Server Clients**
* **Authentication Methods**
  * Basic authentication
  * Digest authentication
  * Integrated Windows authentication
  * Digital certificates authentication
  * RADIUS authentication
  * RSA SecureID authentication

Introduction

In order to configure access rules based on users, you must configure ISA Server to require authentication. You have several options when configuring authentication on ISA Server 2004.

Authentication and ISA Server clients

The ISA Server authentication that you use depends on the type of client you use:

- *SecureNAT clients*. For SecureNAT clients, there is no user-based authentication. You can restrict access to the Internet based only on network rules and other access rules.

- *Firewall clients*. When ISA Server authenticates a Firewall client, it uses the credentials of the user making the request on the computer running the Firewall client. Because Firewall client authentication is automatic, no client configuration is required to enable authentication of users who gain access to ISA Server by using a Firewall client.

- *Web proxy clients*. Web proxy clients do not automatically send authentication information to ISA Server. By default, ISA Server requests credentials from a Web proxy client to identify a user only when processing a rule that restricts access based on a user element. You can configure which method the client and ISA Server use for authentication. You can also configure ISA Server to require authentication for all Web requests.

Authentication methods

You can configure which authentication method ISA Server will use to authenticate users. ISA Server supports the following authentication methods:

- *Basic authentication*. Prompts users for a user name and password before allowing Web access. Basic authentication sends and receives user information as plaintext and does not use encryption. Basic authentication is not a secure authentication method unless the network traffic is encrypted by using SSL. Because basic authentication is part of the HTTP specification, most browsers support it.

- *Digest authentication.* Passes authentication credentials through a process called hashing. Hashing creates a string of characters based on the password but does not send the actual password across the network, ensuring that no one can capture a network packet containing the password and impersonate the user. Digest authentication currently works only in a domain in which all of the domain controllers are running Windows 2000 or Windows Server 2003 and users are using Internet Explorer 5 or later. Digest authentication works only if the domain controller has a reversibly encrypted copy of the requesting user's password stored in Active Directory. This is not the default configuration and you must enable this. ISA Server 2004 also supports a new version of Digest authentication named WDigest authentication. WDigest does not require that passwords be stored in reversible encryption. WDigest is supported only for ISA Server computers running on Windows Server 2003. When both ISA Server and the domain are based on Windows Server 2003, the default authentication is WDigest. This means that when you select Digest authentication in a Windows Server 2003 environment, you are actually selecting WDigest.

- *Integrated Windows authentication.* Uses either the Kerberos V5 authentication or NTLM protocols, which do not send the user name and password across the network. Integrated Windows authentication works with Internet Explorer 2.0 or later. Use Integrated Windows authentication when all of the client computers use Internet Explorer. Integrated Windows authentication is the default authentication method used by members of the Windows 2000 and Windows Server 2003 family.

- *Digital certificates authentication.* Requests a client certificate from the client before allowing the request to be processed. Users obtain client certificates from a certification authority that can be internal to your organization or a trusted external organization. Client certificates usually contain identifying information about the user and the organization that issued the client certificate. Use client certificate authentication when your organization requires certificates for user authentication. Web proxy clients do not support client certificate authentication, but this option can be used in a Web chaining configuration.

- *Remote Authentication Dial-In User Service.* RADIUS is an industry-standard authentication protocol. A RADIUS client (typically a dial-up server, virtual private network [VPN] server, or wireless access point) sends user credentials and connection parameter information in the form of a RADIUS message to a RADIUS server. The RADIUS server authenticates the RADIUS client request, and sends back a RADIUS message response. RADIUS authentication is more frequently used to provide authentication for accessing resources on the internal network from the Internet.

- *RSA SecureID authentication.* ISA Server 2004 enables the option to authenticate users based on authentication credentials from the RSA SecurID product from RSA Security, Inc. The SecurID product enforces a requirement that a remote user must have two factors of authentication to gain access to protected resources. These two factors are something that the user knows, (a personal identification number, or PIN), and something that a user has (a physical token). Neither the PIN nor the token will grant access in isolation from each other. Both are required. RSA SecureID authentication is more frequently used to provide authentication for accessing resources on the internal network from the Internet.

How to Configure Access Rules

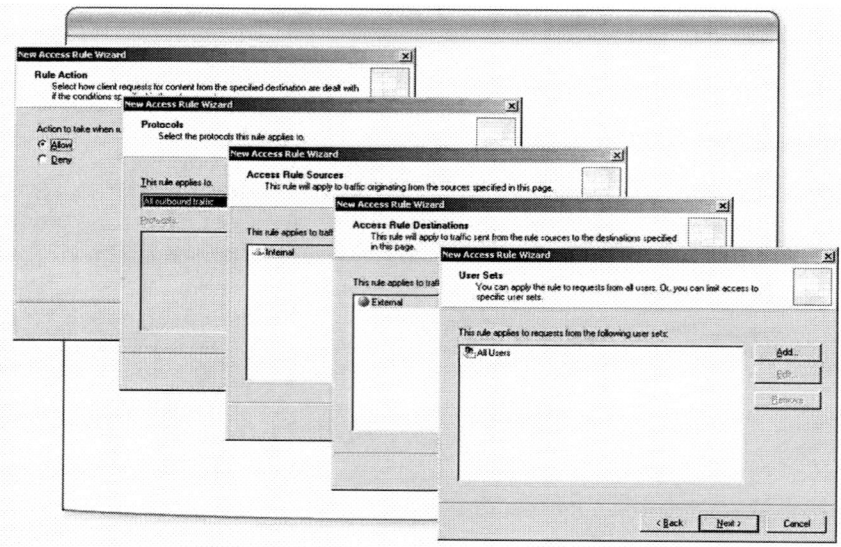

Introduction

To enable access for internal clients to access the Internet, you must configure an access rule that grants this type of access. You can configure the access rule using the access rule elements.

Configuring a new access rule

To configure a new access rule that grants users access to the Internet, use the following procedure:

1. In the **ISA Server Management** console tree, select **Firewall Policy**.

2. In the task pane, on the **Tasks** tab, select **Create New Access Rule**.

3. On the **Welcome to the New Access Rule** page, in **Access rule name**, enter the name for the access rule; then click **Next**.

4. On the **Rule Action** page, click **Allow** if you are allowing access, or **Deny** if you are denying access, and then click **Next**.

5. On the **Protocols** page, configure the protocols that this access rule applies to. You have three options in the **This rule applies to**: drop-down list:

   a. **All outbound protocols**. If you choose this option, the access rule applies to all protocols.

   b. **Selected protocols**. Click the **Add** button to add the specific protocols elements from the **Add Protocols** dialog box.

   c. **All outbound protocols except selected**. Click the **Add** button to add the specific protocols elements from the **Add Protocols** dialog box.

6. When you have made these selections, click **Next**.

7. On the **Access Rule Sources** page, click **Add** to open the **Add Network Entities** dialog box. Select the network object or objects that you want, click **Add**, and then click **Close**. On the **Access Rule Sources** page, click **Next**.

8. On the **Access Rule Destinations** page, click **Add** to open the **Add Network Entities** dialog box, click **Networks**, select the **External** network (representing the Internet), click **Add**, and then click **Close**. On the **Access Rule Destinations** page, click **Next**.

9. On the **User Sets** page, if you want to grant access to the Internet for all users, you can leave the user set **All users** in place and proceed to the next page of the wizard. If the rule applies to specific users, select **All users** and click **Remove**. Then, use the **Add** button to open the **Add Users** dialog box, from which you can add the user set to which the rule applies. The **Add Users** dialog box also provides access to the **New User Sets Wizard** through the **New** menu item. When you have completed the user set selection, click **Next**.

10. On the **Completing the New Access Rule Wizard** page, review the information on the wizard summary page, and then click **Finish**.

11. To configure the content types for the access rule, double-click the access rule. On the **Content Types** tab, either accept the default setting that applies the rule to all content types or select the content types that the rule applies to.

12. To configure the schedule, on the **Schedule** tab, select the appropriate schedule from the **Schedule** list or click **New** to configure a new schedule element. Click **OK**.

13. To change the order of your access rules, select the access rule on the **Firewall Policy** tab and click **Move Selected Rules Up** or **Move Selected Rules Down**.

14. In the **Firewall Policy** details pane, click **Apply** to apply the new access rule.

How to Configure HTTP Policy

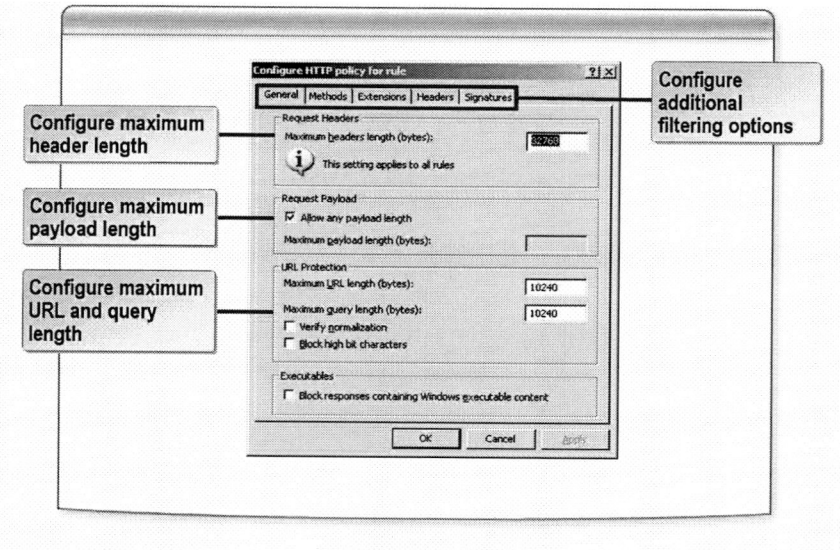

Introduction

You can configure an additional level of security for outbound HTTP requests by configuring an HTTP policy as part of the access rule.

Configuring HTTP policy

ISA Server is an application layer firewall, and applies an application filter to HTTP traffic. Because ISA Server can examine HTTP requests, you can block specific applications from being tunneled through HTTP. The HTTP application filter provides granular control over the HTTP requests allowed by your firewall policy.

HTTP policy includes the following configuration options:

Option	Use this setting to:
Request header maximum length	Limit the maximum HTTP header size for a client request.
Request payload length	Limit the maximum HTTP request body size for a client request.
URL protection	Limit the maximum URL size for client requests.
Executable blocking	Prevent the downloading of any executable content using HTTP.
Denied methods	Specify which HTTP methods will be blocked.
Specified actions for specific file extensions	Prevent the downloading of information based on file extension.
Deny specific headers	Filter client requests and server responses based on information included in the HTTP header.
Modify server and via headers	Specify how server headers will be returned or forwarded when the server responds to the client.
Deny specific signatures	Block server responses based on specific strings in the response header or body.

To configure HTTP policy, follow this procedure.

1. In **ISA Server Management**, click **Firewall Policy**. Double-click the access rule and select the **Protocols** tab.

2. Click **Filtering** and select **Configure HTTP** to open the **Configure HTTP policy for the rule** dialog box.

3. Select the appropriate tab and configure the policy settings.

Note For more details on configuring HTTP filtering, see Module 7, "Advanced Application and Web Filtering," in Course 2824, *Implementing Microsoft Internet Security and Acceleration Server 2004.*

Practice: Managing Access Rules

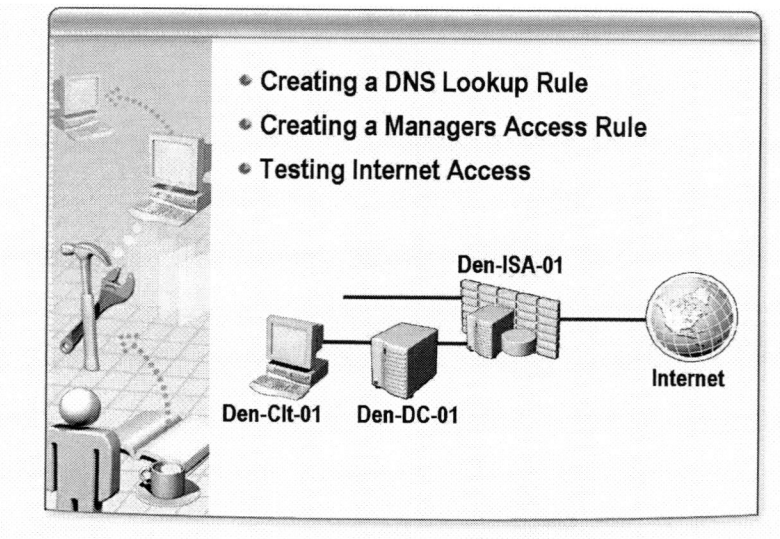

Introduction

In this practice, you will configure a firewall rule that grants the Managers group unlimited access to the Internet using any protocol. You will test the Internet access.

Practice

▶ **To prepare for this practice**

1. You will need the Den-DC-01 virtual machine, the Den-Clt-01 virtual machine, the Den-ISA-01 virtual machine, and the Gen-Web-01 virtual machine for this practice.

2. If necessary, start or resume the required virtual machines and then, on Den-ISA-01, log on to the cohovineyard domain with your user name and password.

▶ **Creating a DNS lookup rule**

All clients on the Coho Vineyard network are configured to use Den-DC-01 as a DNS server. In order for these clients to be able to access resources on the Internet, Den-DC-01 must be able to resolve DNS requests for Internet resources. To enable this, you need to enable an access rule that enables DNS lookups on the Internet from Den-DC-01.

1. In the Microsoft **ISA Server Management** console tree, click **Firewall Policy**.

2. In the task pane, on the **Tasks** tab, click **Create New Access Rule**.

3. On the **Welcome to the New Access Rule Wizard**, type **Domain Controller Policy** as the **Access rule name**, and then click **Next**.

4. On the **Rule Action** page, click **Allow**, and then click **Next**.

5. On the **Protocols** page, in the **This rule applies to:** drop down box, click **Selected Protocols**, and then click **Add**.

6. In the **Add Protocols** dialog box, expand **Common Protocols**, click **DNS**, and click **Add**. Click **Close**.

7. On the **Protocols** page, click **Next**.

8. On the **Access Rule Sources** page, click **Add**.

9. In the **Add Network Entities** dialog box, expand **Computers**, click **Den-DC-01, and** then click **Add**. Click **Close**. Click **Next**.

10. On the **Access Rule Destinations** page, click **Add**.

11. In the **Add Network Entities** dialog box, expand **Networks**, click **External, and** then click **Add**. Click **Close**. Click **Next** twice.

12. On the **Completing the New User Sets Wizard** page, review the settings and click **Finish**.

▶ **Creating a Managers access rule**

1. In the task pane, on the **Tasks** tab, click **Create New Access Rule**.

2. On the **Welcome to the New Access Rule Wizard**, type **Managers Access Policy** as the **Access rule name**, and then click **Next**.

3. On the **Rule Action** page, click **Allow**, and then click **Next**.

4. On the **Protocols** page, ensure that the rule applies to **All outbound traffic**. Click **Next**.

5. On the **Access Rule Sources** page, click **Add**.

6. In the **Add Network Entities** dialog box, expand **Networks**, click **Internal**, and then click **Add**. Click **Close**. Click **Next**.

7. On the **Access Rule Destinations** page, click **Add**.

8. In the **Add Network Entities** dialog box, expand **Networks**, click **External**, and then click **Add**. Click **Close**. Click **Next**.

9. On the **User Sets** page, click **All Users**, and then click **Remove**.

10. Click **Add** and click **Managers**, and then click **Add**. Click **Close**. Click **Next**.

11. On the **Completing the New Access Rule Wizard** page, review the settings and click **Finish**.

12. Ensure that the **Managers Access Policy** is listed after than the **Domain Controller Policy**. If it is not, right click the **Managers Access Policy** and click **Move Down**.

13. In the details pane, click **Apply**. After the new configuration has been applied, click **OK**.

► **Testing Internet access**

Jay Adams is a member of the Managers group. Use his account to test Internet access.

1. Switch to the Den-Clt-01 virtual machine and log on to the cohovineyard domain with a user name of **Jay** and password of **P@ssw0rd**.

2. Open Internet Explorer and attempt to connect to www.contoso.com.

3. Attempt to connect to www.tailspintoys.com.

4. To view the directory listing of an FTP site when connecting to the FTP site through ISA Server, you need to disable the folder view for FTP sites in Internet Explorer. To do this, click **Tools**, and click **Internet Options**. In the **Internet Options** dialog box, on the **Advanced** tab, clear the check box for **Enable folder view for FTP sites**. Click **OK**.

5. Attempt to connect to ftp://ftp.contoso.com. All connections should be successful.

6. Log off the Den-CLT-01 virtual machine and on log on to the cohovineyard domain with your user name and password.

7. Open Internet Explorer and attempt to connect to www.contoso.com.

8. Attempt to connect to www.tailspintoys.com.

9. Attempt to connect to ftp://ftp.contoso.com. All connections should be unsuccessful because only the Managers group has been enabled for Internet access.

How to Troubleshoot Access to Internet Resources

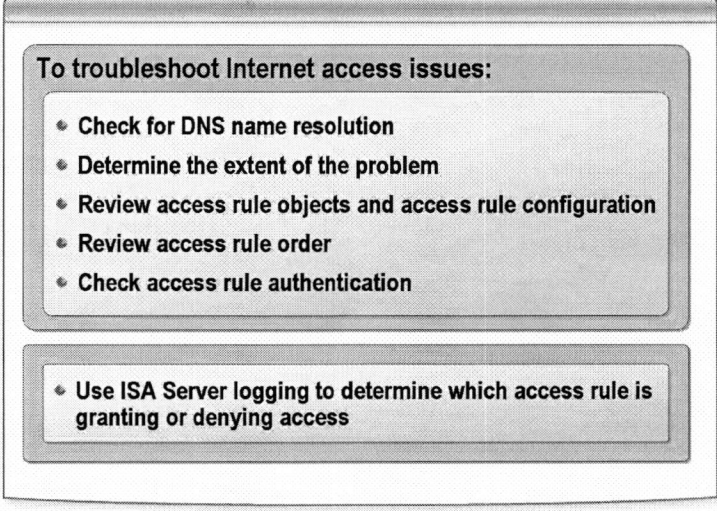

To troubleshoot Internet access issues:

- Check for DNS name resolution
- Determine the extent of the problem
- Review access rule objects and access rule configuration
- Review access rule order
- Check access rule authentication

- Use ISA Server logging to determine which access rule is granting or denying access

Introduction

ISA Server uses access rules to grant internal users access to Internet resources. In some cases, you may need to troubleshoot these access rules to ensure that user can access the required resources.

Troubleshooting Internet access

Use the following guidelines to troubleshoot Internet access issues:

- *Check DNS name resolution.* If the client cannot resolve the DNS name of the Internet resource, the client will not be able to connect to the resource. To check if the client can resolve the DNS name, ping the fully qualified domain name (FQDN) of the Internet resource. Even if you can not ping the server, you can use the ping to determine if the client resolved the FQDN to the correct IP address. If the client did not resolve the DNS name correctly, then check the client DNS configuration and the DNS server used by the client. Also check the access rules on ISA Server to ensure that DNS queries from the internal network can be forwarded to the Internet DNS servers. If the client is a Web proxy client, then ensure that the ISA Server computer can resolve the Internet DNS names.

- *Determine the extent of the problem.* An important troubleshooting step is to attempt to identify the cause of the problem by isolating who is affected by the problem. For example, if only one user or group of users is affected then the issue is likely a configuration error on an ISA Server access rule. If only one Web site is inaccessible, then the problem may be with an access rule configuration, or the Web site may be down. If all computers are affected, rather than just one computer, then you need to check the ISA Server configuration and network connectivity. If only one computer is affected, then check the network connectivity and client configuration on that one computer.

- *Review access rule objects and access rule configuration.* After determining the extent of the problem, review the access rule configurations that specifically relate to the affected users. For example, if a group of users is affected, then look for access rules or access rule elements that apply specifically to that group.

- *Review access rule order*. ISA Server evaluates access rules in the order listed in ISA Server Management. The first rule that matches the client request is applied to the request. For example, if an access rule that allows access to all Web sites using HTTP is listed first, other access rules that set restrictions on which Web sites can be accessed will not be evaluated.

- *Check access rule authentication*. If an access rule requires authentication, then ensure that the ISA Server clients support the authentication protocol configured for the access rule. As well, ensure that all users are using Web proxy or Firewall clients because secureNAT clients do not support authentication. The access rule order is also important when using access rules that require authentication. For example, if an access rule that allows Internet access using all protocols but only for members of a particular group is evaluated first, all users that are not members of that group will not be able to access the Internet.

Using ISA Server logging to troubleshoot Internet access

One of the useful tools provided with ISA Server for troubleshooting access to resources on other networks is the logging feature. By default, ISA Server logs all Web proxy and Firewall Client connections to the Internet. You can use these logs to determine which access rules are allowing or blocking access.

To view the information logged by ISA Server, complete the following steps:

1. In **ISA Server Management**, click **Monitoring**.

2. Click the **Logging** tab.

3. To view the information being logged at the current time, click **Start Query**. To use this option, start the query and then attempt to access the Internet resource from the client computer. You can view the client connection attempts in the log viewer.

4. To view archived information or to limit the number of entries in the log viewer, configure a filter to view specific information contained within the log files. For example, you could configure a filter that allowed you to view all of the client connection attempts from a specific client computer over a specified period of time.

Note For more details on configuring and using ISA Server monitoring tools including logging, see Module 10, "Monitoring ISA Server 2004," in Course 2824, *Implementing Microsoft Internet Security and Acceleration Server 2004*.

Lab: Enabling Access to Internet Resources

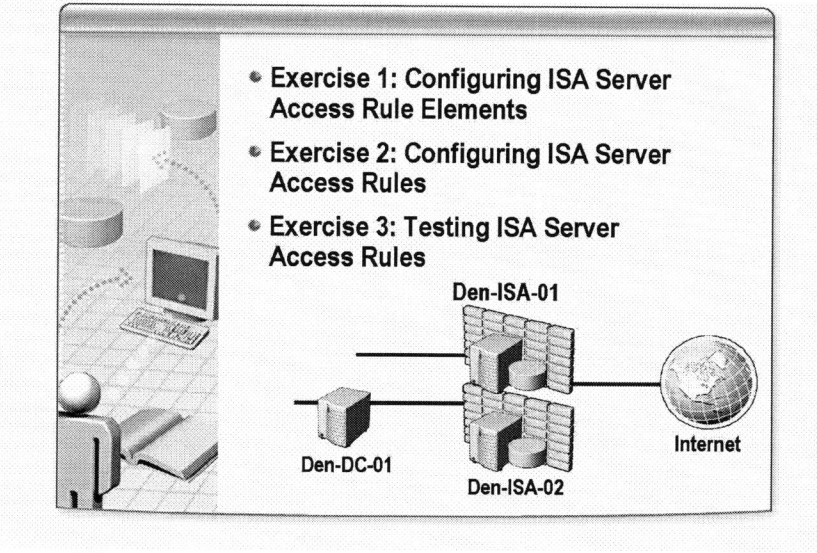

Objectives

After completing this lab, you will be able to:

- Configure Microsoft Internet Security and Acceleration (ISA) Server rule elements that can be used to configure access rules.

- Configure ISA Server access rules that limit access to the Internet based on access rule elements.

- Test an ISA Server access rule configuration to ensure that all organizational requirements are met.

Note This lab focuses on the concepts in this module and, as a result, may not comply with Microsoft security recommendations. For instance, this lab does not comply with the recommendation that the Administrator account be renamed and the user account passwords are not as complex as recommended. Additionally, most of the actions performed in this lab are performed while logged in as an Administrator. The recommended security practice is to log in as a normal user and use the Runas option to start administrative applications.

Scenario

You have deployed ISA Server at cohovineyard.com and configured it to enable access to Internet resources for just the Managers group. You now need to apply additional restrictions to the use of the Internet at cohovineyard.com. The organization's Internet usage policy specifies the following restrictions on Internet usage:

- Users logged on to the domain controllers should be able to use only Hypertext Transfer Protocol (HTTP) and Hypertext Transfer Protocol Secure (HTTPS) to access the Internet.

- Users who work the night shift should only be able to access the Internet between the hours of midnight and 8 A.M.

- Managers should be able to access all sites on the Internet, at any time of day, using any application or protocol.

- Members of the ISA Admins group and the Domain Admins group should have the same access to the Internet as the Managers group.

- Sales personnel should be able to access the Internet only between 9 A.M. and 5 P.M. every day.

- No users, including managers, should be able to download .exe files from any location using HTTP.

- No users except managers and ISA administrators should be able to download Microsoft PowerPoint® files from any location using HTTP.

- Sales users should not be able to access any HTTP or File Transfer Protocol (FTP) sites at Contoso.com.

To prepare for this lab:

1. You will need the Den-DC-01 virtual machine, the Den-ISA-01 virtual machine, the Den-Clt-01 virtual machine, and the Gen-Web-01 virtual machine for this lab.

2. If necessary, start or resume the required virtual machines and then, on Den-ISA-01, log on to the cohovineyard domain with your user name and password.

Estimated time to complete this lab: 60 minutes

Exercise 1
Configuring ISA Server Access Rule Elements

In this exercise, you will configure the access rule elements needed to configure the required access rules. You should use the rule elements and access rules created in the practices in this module whenever possible. The rule elements and access rules that you created in this module are:

- Managers user set
- Powerpoint Content content type
- Night Shift Schedule
- Den-DC-01 computers object
- Contoso, Ltd., URL set
- Domain Controller Policy access rule
- Managers access rule

Tasks	Detailed steps
1. Configure the required user sets.	**a.** Configure a Sales user set. Use the Sales group from the cohovineyard.com domain. **b.** Configure a Night Shift Workers user set. Use the Night Staff group from the cohovineyard.com domain. **c.** Create an ISA Admins user set. Use the ISA Admins group from the cohovineyard.com domain. **d.** Create an Administrators user set. Use the Domain Admins group from the cohovineyard.com domain.
2. Configure the required content types.	■ Configure a Block Executables content type. To block the download of executables by HTTP, configure the content type to block the application/octet-stream MIME type and the .exe file extension.
3. Configure the required domain name sets.	■ Configure a Block contoso.com domain name set. Configure the domain name set to include *.contoso.com.

Exercise 2
Configuring ISA Server Access Rules

In this exercise, you will configure the ISA Server access rules to ensure that all security requirements in the Internet usage policy are met.

Tasks	Detailed steps
1. Configure an access rule that ensures users logged on to the domain controllers can use only HTTP and HTTPS to access the Internet.	a. Modify the Domain Controller Policy access rule to include the HTTP and HTTPS protocols for connections coming from the domain controller. b. Configure Den-DC-01 as a Web Proxy client using Den-ISA-01 as the proxy server and port 8080.
2. Configure an access rule that ensures that users who work the night shift can only access the Internet between the hours of midnight and 8 A.M.	▪ Configure a Night Shift access rule that enables access only during the required times. Use the Night Shift Schedule object to configure the access rule.
3. Configure an access rule that ensures that Sales personnel can access the Internet only between 9 A.M. and 5 P.M. every day and that Sales users cannot access any HTTP or FTP sites at Contoso.com.	▪ Configure a Sales staff access rule that enables access only during the required times and that blocks the contoso.com Web sites. Use the preconfigured Work hours schedule and the Block contoso.com domain name set to configure the access rule.
4. Configure an access rule that ensures no users, including managers, can download .exe files from any location using HTTP.	▪ Configure a Block Executables access rule that blocks the download of all executables using HTTP. Use the Block Executables content type to configure the access rule.
5. Configure an access rule that ensures no users, except managers, can download PowerPoint files from any location using HTTP.	▪ Configure a Block PowerPoint access rule that blocks the download of all PowerPoint files using HTTP. Use the Powerpoint Content content type to configure the access rule.
6. Configure an access rule that ensures ISA Admins and the Domain Admins groups have the same access to the Internet as the Managers group.	▪ Implement the most efficient way to ensure that this requirement is met.

Exercise 3
Testing ISA Server Access Rules

In this exercise, you will test your ISA Server configuration to ensure that all the requirements specified in the Coho Vineyard Internet usage policy are met. Use the following information to test the configuration:

- Doris Hartwig (login name: Doris, password: P@ssw0rd) is a member of the Night Staff group.

- Martin Weber (login name: Martin, password: P@ssw0rd) is a member of the Sales group.

- Jay Adams (login name: Jay, password: P@ssw0rd) is a member of the Managers group.

- Use your user account to test access for the ISA Admins group.

- You can access HTTP sites at www.contoso.com and www.tailspintoys.com.

- Use the FTP site at ftp.contoso.com to test ftp access.

- To test downloading an executable, you can download an executable by clicking **Click here** to download a sample game on the first page of the Tailspin Toys Web site.

- To test downloading a PowerPoint file, you can download a PowerPoint slide by clicking **Click here** to download the Organizational Chart on the Executive Organizational Chart page of the Tailspin Toys Web site.

- Test the domain controller access rule by logging on to Den-DC-01 using Cohovineyard\Administrator.

- Perform all other testing from the Den-Clt-01 client computer. You will need to log in as various users to perform the tests.

Tasks	Detailed steps
1. Configure logging on the ISA Server to monitor all client connections. Use this logging information to troubleshoot client connections.	a. On Den-ISA-01, open **ISA Server Management**. b. Click **Monitoring**. c. On the **Logging** tab, click **Start Query**. All client connections to the ISA Server will now be shown in the details pane.
2. Test whether users logged on to the domain controllers can use only HTTP and HTTPS to access the Internet.	a. Can Cohovineyard\Administrator access www.contoso.com? b. Can Cohovineyard\Administrator access ftp.contoso.com?
3. Test whether users who work the night shift can access the Internet only between the hours of midnight and 8 A.M.	▪ Can Doris Hartwig access www.contoso.com?
4. Test whether Sales personnel can access the Internet only between 9 A.M. and 5 P.M. every day and that Sales users cannot access any HTTP or FTP sites at Contoso.com.	a. Can Martin Weber access www.tailspintoys.com? b. Can Martin Weber access www.contoso.com? c. Can Martin Weber access ftp.contoso.com?

(continued)

Tasks	Detailed steps
5. Test whether no users, including managers, can download .exe files from any location using HTTP.	**a.** Can Martin Weber download the executable from the first page of the Tailspin Toys Web site? **b.** Can Jay Adams download the executable from the first page of the Tailspin Toys Web site? **c.** Can you download the executable from the first page of the Tailspin Toys Web site, using your account?
6. Test whether no users, except managers, ISA Admins and Administrators, can download PowerPoint files from any location using HTTP.	**a.** Can Martin Weber download the PowerPoint file from the Executive Organizational Chart page of the Tailspin Toys Web site? **b.** Can Jay Adams download the PowerPoint file from the Executive Organizational Chart page of the Tailspin Toys Web site? **c.** Can you download the PowerPoint file from the Executive Organizational Chart page of the Tailspin Toys Web site, using your account?
7. Test whether Managers and ISA Admins can access all sites on the Internet, at any time of day, using any application or protocol.	**a.** Can Jay Adams access www.contoso.com? **b.** Can Jay Adams access ftp.contoso.com? **c.** Can you access these sites using your user account?
8. When you finish testing stop ISA Server logging.	**a.** On Den-ISA-01, open **ISA Server Management**. **b.** Click **Monitoring**. **c.** On the **Logging** tab, click **Stop Query**. All client connections to the ISA Server will now be shown in the details pane.

Note The 2824_Lab3_Export.xml file located in the C:\Program Files\Microsoft Learning\2824\ LabFiles\Answers folder on Den-ISA-01 contains an ISA Server export of one set of rules that meets the company requirements. If you are not able to complete the lab, you can import this file to review the access rule configuration.

To Prepare for the Next Lab

As you finish this lab, shut down all of the virtual machines that you used in the lab. To shut down the virtual machines, click **Close** from the **Action** menu. Select **Turn off and delete changes** and click **OK**.

After shutting down the virtual machines, restart the Den-ISA-01 virtual machine, the Den-DC-01 virtual machine, the Den-Clt-01 virtual machine, and the Gen-Web-01 virtual machine in preparation for the next module.

Module 4: Configuring ISA Server as a Firewall

Contents

Overview

- Using ISA Server as a Firewall
- Examining Perimeter Networks and Templates
- Configuring System Policies
- Configuring Intrusion Detection and IP Preferences

Introduction

One of the primary roles for Microsoft® Internet Security and Acceleration (ISA) Server 2004 is to act as a firewall between the Internet and the internal network. Firewalls limit the flow of network traffic from one network to another. Ideally, a firewall should block all traffic except the traffic that is explicitly allowed. Because many organizations will deploy it as a firewall, the ISA Server administrator needs to know how to configure ISA Server 2004 as a firewall.

Objectives

After completing this module, you will be able to:

- Describe the core functionality provided by firewalls and how this functionality is implemented in ISA Server 2004.

- Describe the different types of perimeter network types and use ISA Server network templates to deploy perimeter networks.

- Configure system policies.

- Configure intrusion detection and IP preferences on ISA Server 2004.

Lesson: Using ISA Server as a Firewall

- What Is a TCP/IP Packet?
- What Is Packet Filtering?
- What Is Stateful Filtering?
- What Is Application Filtering?
- What Is Intrusion Detection?
- How ISA Server 2004 Filters Network Traffic
- Implementing ISA Server 2004 as a Firewall

Introduction

Firewalls are used to limit network traffic from one network to another. To distinguish between network traffic that should be allowed and network traffic that should be blocked, firewalls use packet filters, stateful filters, application filters, and intrusion detection. This lesson describes this core functionality provided by firewalls and how this functionality is implemented in ISA Server 2004.

Lesson objectives

After completing this lesson, you will be able to:

- Describe Transmission Control Protocol/Internet Protocol (TCP\IP) packets.
- Describe packet filtering and the benefits of using packet filtering.
- Describe stateful filtering and the benefits of using stateful inspection.
- Describe application filtering and the benefits of using application filtering.
- Describe intrusion detection and the benefits of using intrusion detection.
- Describe how ISA Server 2004 filters network traffic.
- List the steps involved in implementing ISA Server as a firewall.

What Is a TCP/IP Packet?

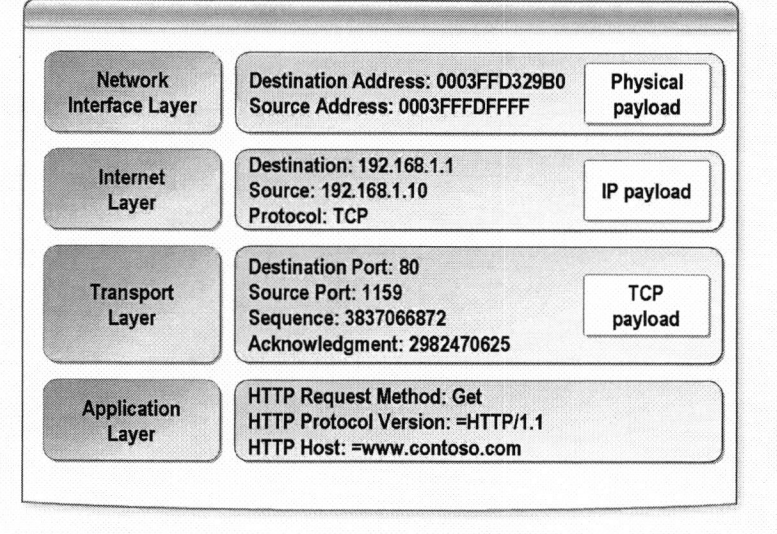

Introduction

All network communication on the Internet uses TCP/IP as its communication protocol. To configure ISA Server as a firewall, you must understand the characteristics of TCP/IP communication.

TCP/IP layers

Each TCP/IP packet is made up of multiple components. The components correspond to the following four protocol layers:

- *Network Interface Layer*. This layer handles placing TCP/IP packets on the network medium and receiving TCP/IP packets off the network medium. TCP/IP was designed to be independent of the network interface layer. The network interface layer header includes addressing information required for the physical devices connected to the network to communicate with each other.

- *Internet Layer*. This layer handles addressing packets, fragmentation and reassembly of packets, and routing packets between networks. The most important protocol at this layer is the Internet Protocol (IP).

- *Transport Layer*. This layer provides session and datagram communication services. The core protocols of the transport layer are the Transmission Control Protocol (TCP) and the User Datagram Protocol (UDP).

- *Application Layer*. This layer lets applications access the services of the other layers and defines the protocols that applications use to exchange data. Hypertext Transfer Protocol (HTTP), File Transfer Protocol (FTP), Simple Mail Transfer Protocol (SMTP), Telnet, and Domain Name System (DNS) are all examples of application layer protocols.

Internet Protocol   IP is a network layer protocol primarily responsible for addressing and routing packets between hosts. An IP packet consists of an IP header and an IP payload. The following table describes the key fields in the IP header.

IP Header Field	Function
Source address	The IP address of the original source of the IP datagram
Destination address	The IP address of the final destination of the IP datagram
Protocol	Informs IP at the destination host whether to pass the packet up to TCP, UDP, Internet Control Message Protocol (ICMP), or other protocols

TCP   TCP is a reliable, session-oriented delivery service. Session-oriented means that a session must be established before hosts can exchange data. Reliability is achieved by assigning a sequence number to each segment transmitted. An acknowledgment is used to verify that the data is received. TCP provides a one-to-one, session-oriented, reliable communications service.

The following table describes the key fields in the TCP header.

TCP Header Field	Function
Source port	TCP port of sending host
Destination port	TCP port of destination host
Sequence number	Sequence number of the first byte of data in the TCP segment
Acknowledgment Number	Sequence number of the byte the sender expects to receive next from the other side of the connection

UDP   UDP provides a sessionless datagram service that offers unreliable, best-effort delivery of data transmitted in messages. This means that neither the arrival of datagrams nor the correct sequencing of delivered packets is guaranteed. UDP does not recover from lost data through retransmission. The UDP header contains a source port and destination port, but does not include sequence information or acknowledgment. Ensuring that UDP packets are delivered is the responsibility of the application layer protocols that use UDP as a transport.

Windows Sockets

Most Internet applications running on Microsoft Windows® use Windows Sockets to communicate with the lower protocol layers. Windows Sockets provides services that allow applications to bind to a particular port and IP address on a host, initiate and accept a connection, send and receive data, and close a connection.

A socket is defined by a protocol and an address on the host. In TCP/IP, the address is the combination of the IP address and port. Two sockets, one for each end of the connection, form a bidirectional communications path.

To communicate, an application specifies the protocol, the IP address of the destination host, and the port of the destination application. After the application is connected, information can be sent and received.

Note For detailed information on TCP/IP, see TCP/IP Technical Reference, one of the technical references located at http://www.microsoft.com/resources/documentation/WindowsServ/2003/all/techref/en-us/Default.asp.

What Is Packet Filtering?

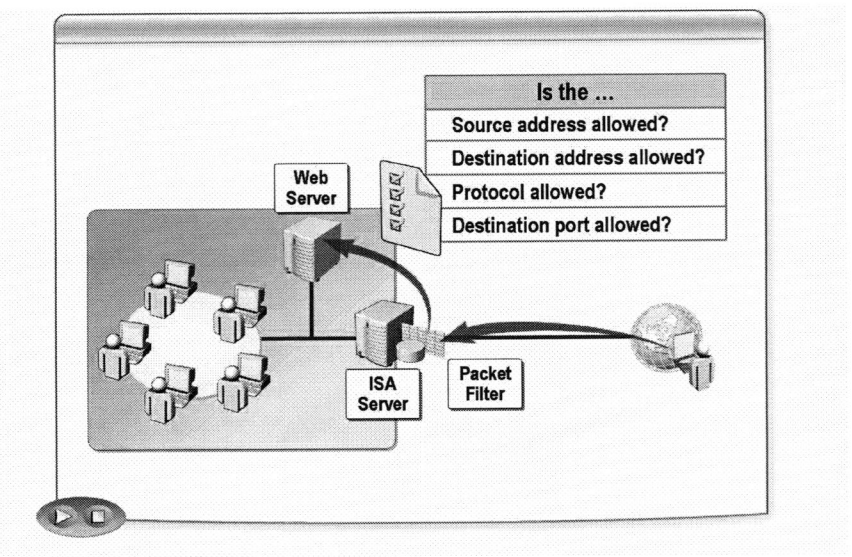

Introduction

The primary role of a firewall is to prevent network traffic from entering an internal network unless the traffic is explicitly permitted. One of the ways in which a firewall ensures this is through packet filtering.

What is packet filtering?

Packet filters control access to the network at the network layer by inspecting and allowing or denying the IP packets to transfer through the firewall. When the firewall inspects an IP packet, it examines only information in the network and transport layer headers, including the packet's source and destination information, and its protocol and port numbers.

The firewall can evaluate IP packets using the following criteria:

- *Destination address*. The destination address may be the actual IP address of the destination computer in the case of a routed relationship between the two networks being connected by ISA Server. The destination may also be the external interface of ISA Server in the case of a Network Address Translation (NAT) network relationship.

- *Source address*. This is the IP address of the computer that originally transmitted the packet.

- *IP Protocol and protocol number*. You can configure packet filters for TCP, UDP, ICMP, and any other protocol. Each protocol is assigned a number. For example, TCP is protocol 6, and the Generic Route Encapsulation (GRE) protocol for Point-to-Point Tunneling Protocol (PPTP) connections is protocol 47.

- *Direction*. This is the direction of the packet through the firewall. In most cases, the direction can be defined by inbound, outbound, or both. For some protocols, such as FTP or UDP, the directional choices may be Receive only, Send only, or Both.

- *Port numbers*. A TCP or UDP packet filter defines a local and remote port. The local and remote ports can be defined by a fixed port number, or as a dynamic port number.

Advantages and disadvantages of packet filtering

Packet filtering has a number of advantages and disadvantages. Some of the advantages include:

■ Packet filtering has to inspect only the network and transport layer headers, so packet filtering is very fast.

■ Packet filtering can be used to block a particular IP address or to allow a particular IP address. If you detect an application-level attack from an IP address, you can block that IP address at the packet-filter level. Or, if you need to enable access to your network and you know that all access attempts will be coming from a particular address, you can enable access only for that source address.

■ Packet filtering can be used for ingress and egress filtering. Ingress filtering blocks all access on the external interface of the firewall to packets that have a source IP address that is logically on the internal network. For example, if your internal network includes the 192.168.20.0 network, an ingress filter will block a packet arriving at the external interface that claims to be coming from 192.168.20.1. An egress filter prevents packets from leaving your network that have a source IP address that is not on the internal network.

Packet filtering also has some disadvantages:

■ Packet filters cannot prevent IP address spoofing or source-routing attacks. An attacker can substitute the IP address of a trusted host as the source IP address and the packet filter will not block the packet. Or the attacker can include routing information in the packet that includes incorrect routing information for return packets so that the packets are not returned to the actual host, but to the attacker's computer.

■ Packet filters cannot prevent IP-fragment attacks. An IP-fragment attack splits a single IP packet into multiple fragments. Most packet-filtering firewalls check only the first fragment and assume that the other fragments of the same packet are acceptable. The additional fragments may contain malicious content.

■ Packet filters are not application aware. You may be blocking the default Telnet port (port 23) on your firewall, but allowing access to the HTTP port (port 80). If an attacker can configure a Telnet server to run on port 80 on your network, the packets would be passed to the server.

ISA Server 2004 and packet filtering

ISA Server 2004 does not have an option to directly configure packet filtering. However, ISA Server does operate as a packet filter firewall inspecting traffic at the network and transport layers. For example, if you define a firewall access rule that enables all protocol traffic from a computer on one network to a computer on another network, ISA Server uses a packet filter to allow that traffic. Or, if you configure a firewall access rule that denies the use of the default Telnet port (TCP port 23), ISA Server will use a packet filter to block that port. ISA Server 2000 supported direct configuration of packet filters. If you upgrade to ISA Server 2004 from ISA Server 2000, packet filters are replaced by access rules.

What Is Stateful Filtering?

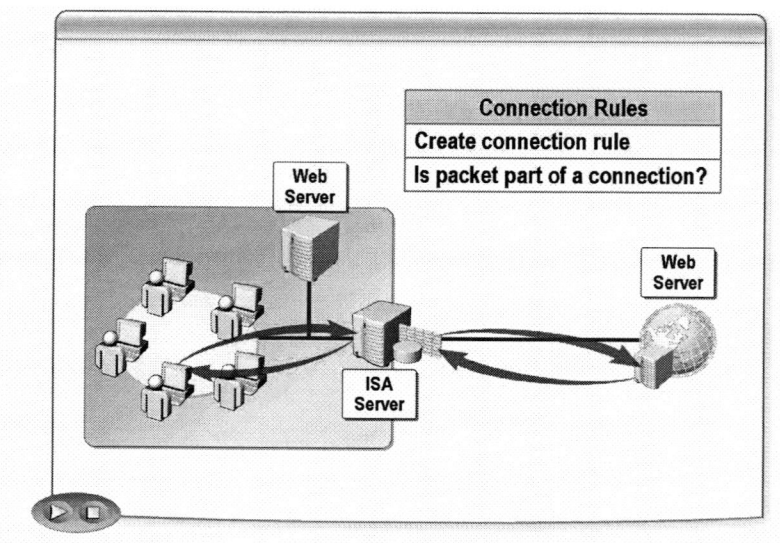

What is stateful filtering?

When a firewall uses stateful filtering, it not only examines the packet header information, but also examines the status of the packet. For example, the firewall can inspect a packet at its external interface and determine whether the packet is a response to a request from the internal network. This check can be performed at both the transport and application layers.

Stateful filtering uses information about the TCP session to determine if a packet should be blocked or allowed through the firewall. TCP sessions are established using the TCP three-way handshake. The purpose of the three-way handshake is to synchronize the sequence number and acknowledgment numbers of both sides of the connection and exchange other information defining how the two hosts will exchange packets. The following steps outline the process:

1. The initiator of the TCP session, typically a client, sends a TCP segment to the server with an initial sequence number for the connection. For example, the client may send a packet that includes the following information:

```
TCP: Control Bits: ....S., len:    0, seq:3837066871-
3837066872, ack:        0, win:16384, src: 1159  dst:    80
TCP: Sequence Number = 3837066871 (0xE4B4FE77)
TCP: Acknowledgement Number = 0 (0x0)
   TCP: ......1. = Synchronize sequence numbers
```

In this example, the client is sending its sequence number and has requested that the server provide its sequence numbers (by setting the SYN bit to 1).

2. The responder of the TCP session, typically a server, sends back a TCP segment containing its chosen initial sequence number and an acknowledgment (ACK) of the client's sequence number. For example, the server may send a packet that includes the following information:

```
TCP: Control Bits: .A..S., len:    0, seq:2982470624-
2982470625, ack:3837066872, win:17520, src:   80 dst: 1159
TCP: Sequence Number = 2982470624 (0xB1C4E3E0)
TCP: Acknowledgement Number = 3837066872 (0xE4B4FE78)
   TCP: ...1.... = Acknowledgement field significant
   TCP: ......1. = Synchronize sequence numbers
```

The server is providing its sequence number and acknowledging that it has received the client's sequence number. Both the SYN and ACK bits are set.

3. The initiator sends the server a TCP segment containing an acknowledgment of the server's sequence number. The client responds with a packet that includes the following information:

```
TCP: Control Bits: .A...., len:    0, seq:3837066872-
3837066872, ack:2982470625, win:17520, src: 1159  dst:   80
TCP: Sequence Number = 3837066872 (0xE4B4FE78)
TCP: Acknowledgement Number = 2982470625 (0xB1C4E3E1)
   TCP: ...1.... = Acknowledgement field significant
```

Now that the client and server have agreed on the sequence numbers, they will use the sequence numbers to track all packets. TCP uses the information to recover from errors such as packets arriving out of order, or packets not arriving at all.

TCP uses a similar handshake process to end a connection. This guarantees that both hosts have finished transmitting and that all data was received.

A firewall uses this TCP information to perform stateful filtering. When a client on the internal network sends out the first packet in the three-way handshake, the server forwards the packet and records the fact that the packet has been sent. When the response comes back from the server, the firewall accepts the packet because it is in response to an internal request. If a packet arrives with just the SYN bit set, or with the SYN and ACK bits set, but the firewall does not have a record of a client request, the firewall blocks the packet.

The firewall can also use other characteristics of TCP session to control traffic. For example, when the client initiates the session, the firewall can set a timer and keep the session open only as long as specified by the timer.

The firewall can also analyze application-level data to perform stateful filtering. For example, when a client sends a GET command for a specific Uniform Resource Locator (URL) on a Web server, the firewall can track the request and allow a response. An HTTP packet that arrives without a corresponding client request is dropped.

Advantages and disadvantages of stateful filtering

One of the advantages of stateful filtering is that it ensures that all network traffic forwarded by the firewall is part of an existing session, or matches the rules for creating a new session.

Another advantage is that stateful filtering implements dynamic packet filtering, which ensures that specific ports are available only when a valid session exists. For example, if a client requests that the server respond on port 1159 (as shown in the previous example), ISA Server will listen on port 1159 only as long as the connection exists.

However, stateful filtering still does not provide enough protection against the threats to network security. Many of the newest attacks happen at the application level. For example, a client computer may download malicious code in an HTTP packet that is part of a legitimate session. Only application layer stateful inspection can block these types of attacks.

ISA Server connection rules

ISA Server uses connection rules to keep track of sessions. Whenever a packet arrives at the server, ISA Server attempts to associate the packet with a connection rule, based on the protocol, source, and destination. A connection rule has the following attributes:

- Protocol number
- Source (IP address and port/endpoint)
- Destination (IP address and port/endpoint)
- Source address translation (used for NAT connections)
- Destination address translation (used for NAT connections)
- Statistics (number of bytes transferred, last access time)
- Misc. (checksum delta, used when doing address translation)

If the packet matches a connection rule, the packet is forwarded. If the packet does not match a connection rule, ISA Server checks the firewall access rules to determine if a new connection rule can be created. If no firewall access rule blocks the creation of the connection rule, then ISA Server creates the connection and forwards the packet. If a firewall rule blocks the creation of the connection rule, then the packet is dropped.

What Is Application Filtering?

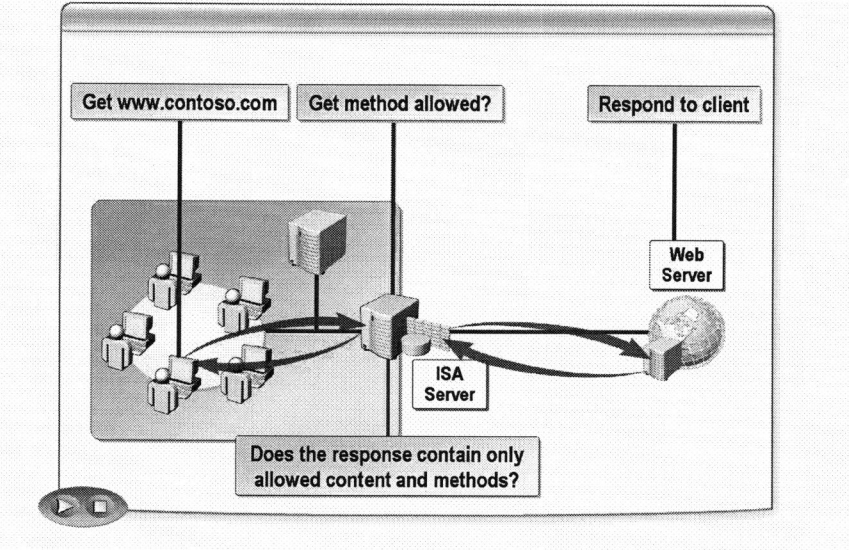

What is application filtering?

Application filtering enables the firewall to open up the entire TCP/IP packet and inspect the application data for unacceptable commands and data. For example, an SMTP filter intercepts communication on port 25 and inspects it to make sure the SMTP commands are authorized before passing the communication to the destination server. An HTTP filter performs the same function on all HTTP packets. Firewalls that are capable of application-layer filtering can stop dangerous code at the edge of the network before it can do any damage.

Application-layer filtering can also be used to stop attacks from sources such as viruses and worms. Most worms look like legitimate software code to the packet-filtering firewall. The headers of the packets are identical in format to those of legitimate traffic. It is the payload that is malicious; only when all the packets are put together can the worm be identified as malicious code, so these exploits often travel straight through to the private network because the firewall allowed what looked like normal code.

Advantages and disadvantages of application filtering

The advantages of application-layer filtering go beyond the prevention of attacks. It can also be used to protect your network and systems from the harmful actions that unaware employees often take. For example, you can configure filters that prevent potentially harmful programs from being downloaded via the Internet, or ensure that critical customer data does not leave the network in an e-mail.

Application-layer filtering can also be used to more broadly limit employee actions on the network. You can use an application filter to restrict common types of inappropriate communication on your network. For example, you can block peer-to-peer file-exchange services. These types of services can consume substantial network resources and raise legal liability concerns for your organization.

The most significant disadvantage of application-filtering firewalls is performance. Because an application-filtering firewall examines the actual payload of each packet, it is usually slower than packet or stateful filtering.

ISA Server and application filtering

The most important benefit of implementing ISA Server 2004 is that it is a powerful and complete application-layer firewall. ISA Server includes many built-in application filters. In addition, ISA Server 2004 includes powerful and flexible interfaces with which administrators can create custom filters to detect virtually any attack. ISA Server is also highly extensible. This means your in-house programmers or third-party vendors can extend much of its functionality, including its filtering capabilities.

What Is Intrusion Detection?

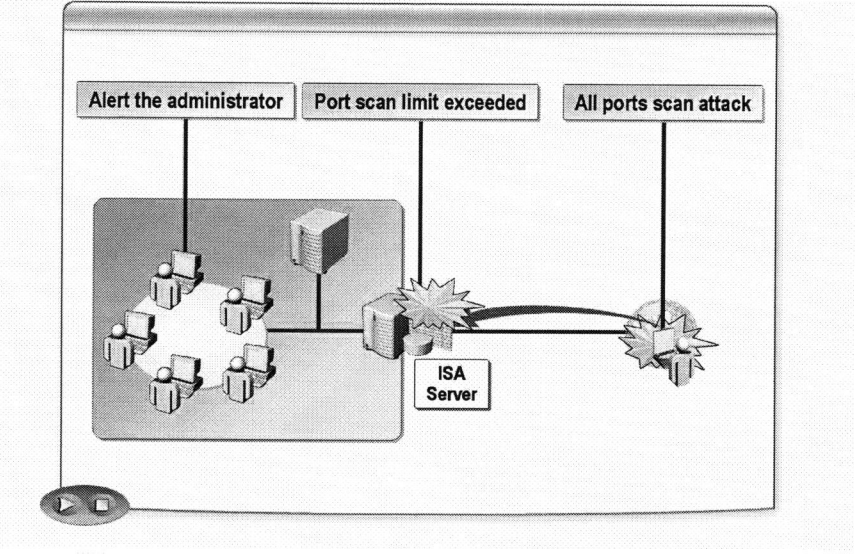

Introduction

If you detect an intrusion attempt early enough, you may be able to prevent a successful intrusion. If an intrusion does occur, you need to be alerted as soon as possible to reduce the potential impact of the intrusion and to eliminate the vulnerability in your network security.

What is an intrusion detection system?

An intrusion detection system (IDS) that is located at the edge of a network inspects all traffic in and out of the network and identifies patterns that may indicate a network or system attack. An IDS is usually configured with information about a wide variety of known attacks. It then monitors the network traffic for signatures that indicate that a known attack is occurring. An IDS can also be configured with information about normal network traffic and then be configured to detect variations from the normal traffic.

A complete IDS also includes several layers. One device may be located at the network perimeter and monitor all traffic entering and leaving the network. Additional devices may be deployed on the internal networks, or on routers connecting networks. A final layer of protection is provided by host-based systems in which an IDS is configured on individual computers. The most sophisticated IDS can collect information from all the layers and correlate data to make the most accurate intrusion detection decisions.

Intrusion detection systems also provide options for configuring alerts or responses to intrusion attempts. At the very least, an IDS should alert an administrator when an attack is detected. More sophisticated IDSs provide additional responses to attacks, including shutting down or limiting the functionality of the systems under attack.

Although they both relate to network security, an IDS differs from a firewall in that a firewall looks out for intrusions to stop them from happening. The firewall limits the access between networks to prevent intrusion and does not signal an attack from inside the network. An IDS evaluates a suspected intrusion once it has taken place and signals an alarm. An IDS also watches for attacks that originate from within a system.

ISA Server and intrusion detection

ISA Server includes intrusion detection that monitors for several well-known vulnerabilities. ISA Server detects intrusions at two different network layers. First, ISA Server detects intrusions at the network layer. This enables ISA Server to detect vulnerabilities that are inherent to the IP protocol. Second, ISA Server uses application filters to detect intrusions at the application layer. You can use third-party application filters to add more intrusion detection or create your own application filters using the filter application programming interfaces (APIs) defined in the ISA Server software development kit (SDK).

How ISA Server 2004 Filters Network Traffic

Introduction

ISA Server 2004 is designed to provide all of the firewall filtering functionality using a layered architecture.

ISA Server filtering architecture

When a network packet arrives at the firewall, it goes through one or more components in the ISA Server architecture. The network packets may be inspected and allowed or denied by each of the following components:

1. *Packet filtering.* The firewall engine, which runs in kernel mode, receives the packets as they pass through the network layer. The packets are associated with a connection rule, and then the packets are filtered. The firewall engine applies the packet filters. If no packet filters apply, the packet is passed to the firewall service.

2. *Stateful and protocol filtering.* The firewall service, which runs in user mode, performs protocol and stateful filtering. The firewall service creates and manages firewall connections. The firewall service also handles communication with and connections via Firewall Client. If an application filter or Web filter is associated with the connection protocol, the packet is passed to the appropriate application filter or Web filter.

3. *Application filtering.* The application filters expand the network packet and inspects the application data. If the packet uses the HTTP or Hypertext Transfer Protocol Secure (HTTPS) protocols, the message is passed through the Web proxy filter to a HTTP Web filter, which inspects the application data. The Web proxy filter also manages and accesses the Web cache.

4. *Kernel mode data pump.* If the data entering the firewall engine can be associated with an existing connection rule, the data is forwarded through ISA Server using the kernel mode data pump. This means that data that will be accepted by the higher layers in the architecture can be passed through ISA Server without ever leaving the kernel mode driver.

The rules engine communicates with all of the other major components, including with both the firewall engine and the firewall service, as well as with application and Web filters.

Implementing ISA Server 2004 as a Firewall

> **To configure ISA Server as a firewall:**
>
> * Determine perimeter network configuration
> * Configure networks and network rules
> * Configure system policy
> * Configure intrusion detection
> * Configure access rule elements and access rules
> * Configure server and Web publishing

Introduction

In many organizations, ISA Server is deployed as a firewall. ISA Server provides a secure firewall solution that can be deployed in many different firewall configurations.

Configuration components

Configuring ISA Server as a firewall includes the following steps.

- *Determine perimeter network configuration*. The primary role for a firewall is to protect the network perimeter. The first step in deploying ISA Server as a firewall is to design the perimeter network configuration and determine the role of ISA Server in that configuration.

- *Configure networks and network rules*. The second step in deploying ISA Server as a firewall is to configure networks and network rules based on your perimeter network design. You can use network templates in ISA Server to simplify this process.

- *Configure system policy*. System policy is used in ISA Server to define how the ISA Server will be managed. One step in your deployment should be to ensure that the system policy enables only required functionality.

- *Configure intrusion detection*. ISA Server provides built-in intrusion detection. Configure intrusion detection so that you can be alerted when an attack occurs on your ISA Server.

- *Configure access rule elements and access rules*. To grant users access to the Internet, you need to configure access rule elements and access rules.

- *Configure server and Web publishing*. The final step in configuring ISA Server as a firewall is to enable server and Web publishing. This step makes internal resources accessible from the Internet.

Practice: Applying Firewall Concepts

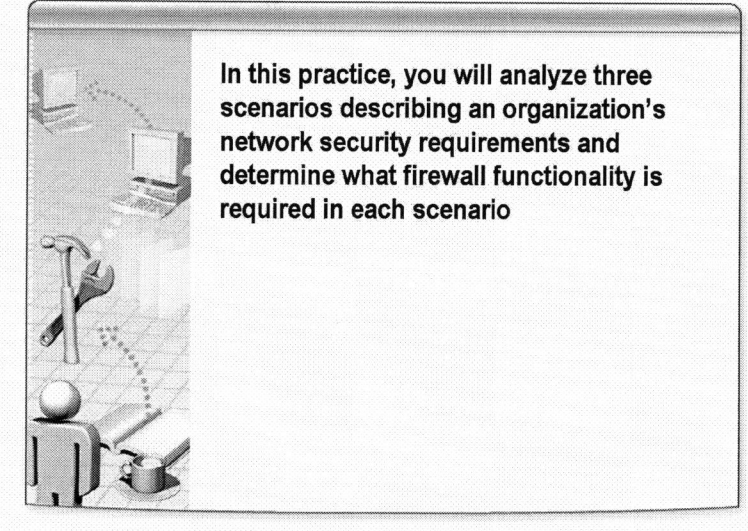

In this practice, you will analyze three scenarios describing an organization's network security requirements and determine what firewall functionality is required in each scenario

Introduction

The following three scenarios all describe an organization's security requirements. Determine what type of firewall functionality is required to address each security concern in the scenario. Discuss your answers with a partner. When you and your partner have agreed on solutions to the scenarios, discuss your solutions with the rest of the class.

Scenario 1

Contoso, Ltd is implementing a new firewall solution. The organization needs to provide access to the Internet for all internal employees using any protocol. However, the organization must be able limit what types of content and files users can download from the Internet. Contoso, Ltd has a Web site that is located on a perimeter network behind the firewall. The security logs indicate that 80 percent of attack attempts on the Web site come from five IP addresses on the Internet. The organization wants to prevent any network connections from those IP addresses, but also needs to be alerted when any other attack attempts occur.

_____

_____

_____

_____

Scenario 2

Tailspin Toys is implementing a new firewall solution. The organization needs to provide access to the Internet for all internal employees using any protocol. Tailspin Toys has an internal Web site that is located on a perimeter network behind the firewall. This internal Web site should be accessible only to employees of a partner organization, and only when the users are in the partner organization's office. The security logs indicate that the previous firewall frequently received packets that were not part of a current connection with a client inside the network. The organization needs to ensure that this type of attack will not succeed in the future.

_____

_____

_____

Scenario 3

Fabrikam, Inc. is implementing a new firewall solution. The organization needs to provide access to the Internet for all internal employees using any protocol. In the past, several employees have been reprimanded for accessing inappropriate Web content. The organization must be able to limit which Web sites employees can connect to and must be able to log all user access to Web sites. Fabrikam, Inc has a Web site that is hosted by an ISP, so there is no need for any HTTP or HTTPS traffic originating from the Internet to enter the company network. The organization does have an internal SMTP server. In the past, several security breaches have occurred when users received viruses by e-mail, so the organization needs to be able to prevent this from happening again.

_____

_____

_____

_____

Lesson: Examining Perimeter Networks and Templates

- ● What Is a Perimeter Network?
- ● Why Use a Perimeter Network?
- ● Network Perimeter Configurations
- ● About Network Templates
- ● How to Use the Network Template Wizard
- ● Modifying Rules Applied by Network Templates

Introduction

Perimeter networks are used to isolate servers and resources from both the Internet and the internal network. In most cases, servers that need to be accessible from the Internet are placed in the perimeter network behind a firewall. However, these servers might also be separated from the internal network by a firewall. ISA Server 2004 is designed to be a full-featured firewall that provides advanced perimeter security. ISA Server enables the configuration of almost any firewall rule and perimeter network configuration. To simplify the task of implementing ISA Server as a firewall, ISA Server 2004 provides several network templates. This lesson describes how to implement a perimeter network with ISA Server 2004.

Lesson objectives

After completing this lesson, you will be able to:

- ■ Describe what a perimeter network is.
- ■ Determine when to use a perimeter network.
- ■ Describe the perimeter network types.
- ■ Describe the ISA Server network template options.
- ■ Implement network templates.
- ■ Modify the rules applied by network templates.

What Is a Perimeter Network?

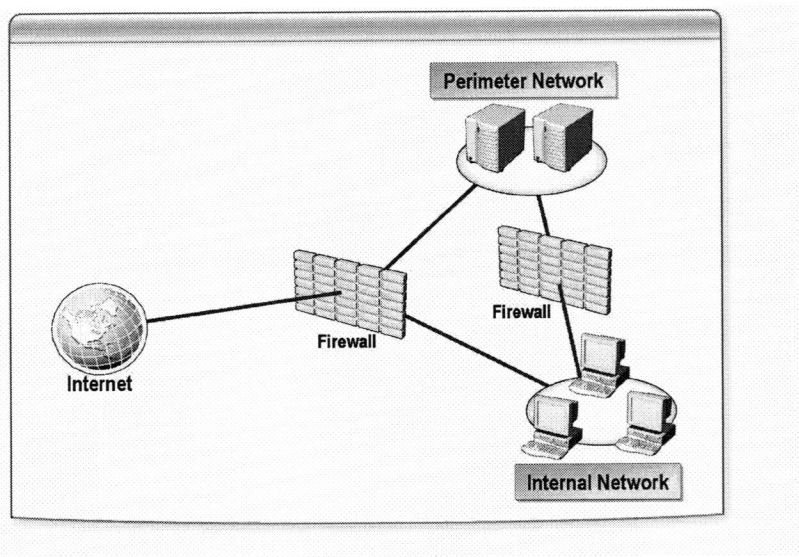

Introduction

A perimeter network, also known as a demilitarized zone (DMZ), or screened subnet, is a network that you set up separately from an internal network and the Internet. Perimeter networks allow external users to gain access to specific servers that are located on the perimeter network while preventing direct access to the internal network.

Perimeter network characteristics

Perimeter networks have the following characteristics:

- *Protected by one or more firewalls.* Perimeter networks are separated from the Internet by one or more firewalls or routers. The perimeter network is usually also separated from the internal network by a firewall. The firewall protects the servers in the perimeter network from the Internet and filters traffic between the perimeter network and the internal network.

- *Contain publicly accessible servers and services.* The servers in the perimeter network are usually accessible to users from the Internet. The types of servers or services that are often located in the perimeter network include virtual private network (VPN) servers and clients, remote access servers (RAS) and clients, Web servers, application front-end servers, SMTP gateway servers, and proxy servers. These servers should be secured and configured to support only their specific applications, and all other services and applications should be disabled.

- *Must be accessible from the Internet.* Because the servers on the perimeter network must be accessible from the Internet, the firewall protecting the perimeter network must allow network traffic from the Internet. This traffic needs to be filtered to ensure that only legitimate traffic enters the perimeter network. Because almost all network traffic will flow from the Internet to the perimeter network, most firewall rules can be configured to allow only inbound traffic.

■ *Require network connectivity to the internal network.* Frequently, the computers on the perimeter network must be able to connect to resources on the internal network. For example, VPN or RAS clients connect to the VPN or RAS server, but then must gain access from that server to the internal network. An SMTP gateway server will need to be able to forward messages to internal e-mail servers. An application front-end server may need to connect to a database server on the internal network. Often, users on the internal network must also be able to connect to servers in the perimeter network. This means that you must configure firewall access rules on the firewall between the perimeter network and the internal network to enable the required network traffic.

■ *Require some level of network protection.* The servers on the perimeter network must be partially isolated both from the Internet and the internal network. The firewalls on both sides of a perimeter network should not forward all traffic, but should filter traffic flowing in both directions. Only required network traffic should be allowed to pass between networks.

Why Use a Perimeter Network?

A perimeter network provides an additional layer of security:

* Between the publicly accessible servers and the internal network

* Between the Internet and confidential data or critical applications stored on servers on the internal network

* Between potentially nonsecure networks such as wireless networks and the internal network

Use defense in depth in addition to perimeter network security

Introduction

Perimeter networks provide an additional layer of network security by protecting publicly accessible servers from unauthorized access while also partially isolating these servers from the internal network.

Benefits of using a perimeter network

The main reason for using a perimeter network is to provide an additional layer of security. A perimeter network is commonly used for deploying publicly accessible servers, such as e-mail servers and Web servers, while servers that should never be accessed from the Internet are located on the internal network. In this way, even if an attacker penetrates the perimeter network security, only the perimeter network servers are compromised.

The servers in the perimeter network usually do not contain confidential or private organization data. This data and critical applications are located on the internal network. By implementing a perimeter network, you ensure that there is an additional layer of security between the Internet and the internal servers.

The perimeter network can also be used to secure other connections to the internal network. For example, many organizations are using mobile clients such as wireless devices or cell phones to access information such as e-mail on the internal network. These devices greatly increase the security risks; one way to reduce that risk is to install the wireless access servers for these devices in the perimeter network and then use the internal firewall to filter traffic from these servers to the internal network. VPN servers and clients can be secured using the same method.

Important   Although a well-designed perimeter network can greatly enhance your network's security, you need to ensure that it is not your only level of defense. Because of the importance of the Internet both for providing services to customers and for providing access to business partners, many organizations are deploying multiple servers in the perimeter network. Often the configuration of the access rules on both the external and internal networks can be quite complicated. This can lead to configuration errors or reduced security because of the number of ports that must be open. To reduce the risk, you need to implement all other defense-in-depth components.

Network Perimeter Configurations

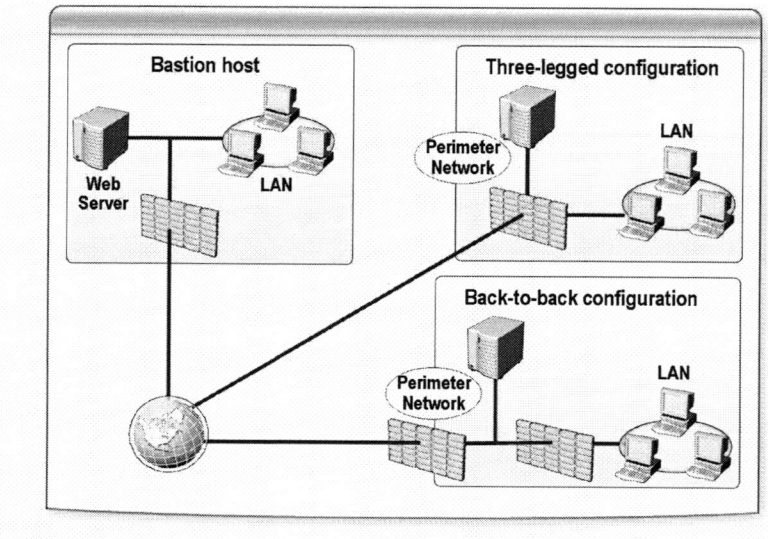

Introduction

The design of a secure network perimeter includes protection for the internal network as well as for servers that need to be accessible from the Internet.

Network perimeter configurations

There are three broad types of network perimeter configurations:

■ *Bastion host.* In this configuration, there is only a single firewall between the Internet and the internal network. The bastion host acts as the main connection for computers on the internal network that are accessing the Internet. As a firewall, the bastion host is designed to defend against attacks that are aimed at the internal network. A bastion host uses two network adapters, one connected to the internal network and one connected to the Internet. This configuration physically isolates the internal network from potential intruders on the Internet. However, the bastion host is only a single line of defense between an internal network and the Internet.

■ *Three-legged configuration.* A three-legged configuration creates a perimeter network that gives users on the Internet limited access to network resources on the perimeter network while preventing unwanted traffic to computers that are located on the internal network. A three-legged configuration uses a firewall with three network adapters—one connected to the internal network, one connected to a perimeter network, and one connected to the Internet. Frequently, the servers in the perimeter network each have IP addresses that are routable on the Internet, so the firewall routes traffic to the perimeter network. The firewall will screen and route packets to the perimeter as defined by the firewall configuration. However, the firewall computer does not allow direct access to resources that are located on the internal network. One advantage of a three-legged firewall is that it gives you a single point of administration to configure access to both your perimeter network and your internal network. A disadvantage of a three-legged firewall is that it presents a single point of access to all parts of your network. If the firewall is compromised, both the perimeter network and the internal network might be compromised.

■ *Back-to-back configuration*. This perimeter network configuration places the perimeter network between two firewalls. The two firewalls are connected to the perimeter network with one firewall connected to the Internet and the other firewall connected to the internal network. In this configuration, there is no single point of access from the Internet to the internal network. To reach the internal network, an attacker would need to get past both firewalls. It is common to use two different firewall vendors in this configuration for maximum security. This dual-vendor configuration prevents an exploit on one firewall from being easily exploited on both firewalls. A back-to-back configuration allows the creation of very granular rules for internal and external access to the network. For example, you can create rules that allow only HTTP and SMTP traffic access to the screened subnet from the Internet and rules that allow only Internet Protocol Security (IPSec)–encrypted traffic access to the back-end servers on the internal network from the screened subnet.

About Network Templates

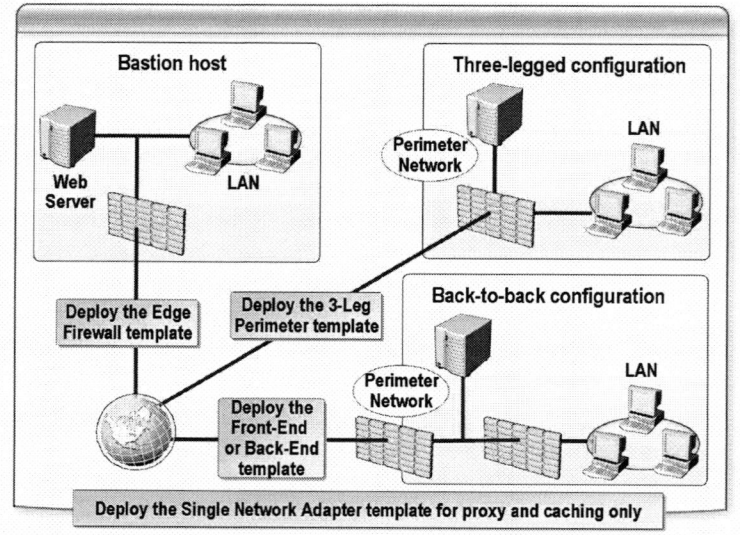

Introduction

ISA Server 2004 can be deployed in any of the perimeter network configurations. To simplify the deployment, ISA Server includes network templates that you can use to configure the firewall policy for traffic between networks.

ISA Server templates

ISA Server 2004 includes several network templates that you can use to configure ISA Server based on one of the perimeter network scenarios. A network template is stored in an XML file that includes:

- Networks and network sets

- Network rules that describe the relationships between networks and network sets

- Access rule elements

- Access rules

To apply a network template, you run the appropriate Network Template Wizard. When you run the Wizard, you can choose the level of access that will be enabled between networks. For example, you may want internal users to be able to access resources on the Internet using all protocols, but only use HTTP or HTTPS to access the perimeter network. The access rules created by the wizard are based on the level of access you grant. When you apply a network template, the Network Template wizard overwrites your current ISA Server configuration with the settings provided in the template.

ISA Server template types

ISA Server 2004 provides the following templates:

- *Edge Firewall.* This template assumes a network topology with ISA Server configured as a bastion host. One network interface is connected to the internal network, the other is connected to an external network (Internet). When you select this template, you can allow all outgoing traffic, or limit outgoing traffic to allow only Web access.

- *3-Leg Perimeter.* This template assumes a network topology with ISA Server configured as the firewall for a 3-leg perimeter configuration. In this configuration, ISA Server has three network interfaces, one connected to the internal network, one connected to the external network, and one connected to a perimeter network.

- *Front End.* This template assumes a network topology with ISA Server at the edge of a network, with another firewall configured at the back end, protecting the internal network.

- *Back End.* This template assumes a network topology with ISA Server deployed between a perimeter network and the internal network, with another firewall located between the perimeter network and the Internet.

- *Single Network Adapter.* This template assumes a single network adapter configuration within a perimeter or corporate network. In this configuration, ISA Server is used as a Web proxy and caching server.

How to Use the Network Template Wizard

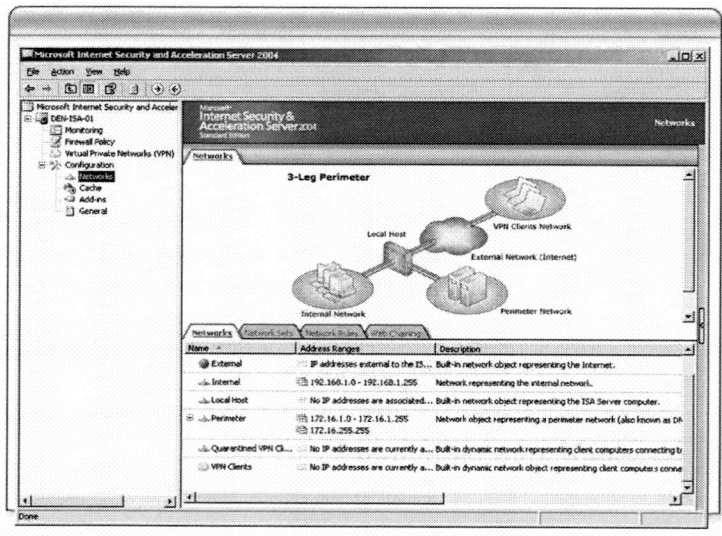

Applying the edge firewall template

One of the templates provided with ISA Server is the edge firewall template. This template assumes that ISA Server is the firewall at the edge of your network, protecting the network from being accessed by others, while at the same time allowing specific access by users on the corporate network.

When you apply the edge firewall template, you can select a firewall access policy that best matches your corporate security guidelines. The following table lists the firewall policies available when you select the edge firewall network template and also details the rules that are created when you select the policy.

Policy Name	Description	Rules Created
Block all	This policy blocks all network access through ISA Server. This option does not create any access rules other than the default rule that blocks all access. Use this option when you want to define firewall policy on your own.	None
Block Internet access, allow access to Internet service provider (ISP) network services	This policy blocks all network access through ISA Server except for access to external network services such as DNS. This option is useful when services are provided by your ISP. Use this option when you want to define firewall policy on your own.	Allow DNS from internal network and VPN Clients network to external network (Internet).
Allow limited Web access	This policy allows limited Web access using HTTP, HTTPS, and FTP only. All other network access is blocked.	Allow HTTP, HTTPS, and FTP from internal network to external network.

(*continued*)

Policy Name	Description	Rules Created
Allow limited Web access and access to ISP network services	This policy allows limited Web access using HTTP, HTTPS, and FTP, and allows access to ISP network services. All other network access is blocked.	Allow HTTP, HTTPS, and FTP from internal network and VPN clients network to external network. Allow DNS from internal network and VPN Clients network to external network (Internet). Allow all protocols from VPN Clients network to Internal network.
Allow unrestricted access	This policy allows unrestricted access to the Internet through ISA Server. ISA Server will prevent access from the Internet to protected networks.	Allow all protocols from Internal network and VPN clients network to external network (Internet). Allow VPN clients network to internal network.

To apply the Internet edge template, use the following procedure.

1. In the **ISA Server Management** console tree, select **Networks**.

2. In the task pane, on the **Templates** tab, click **Edge Firewall**.

3. In the Welcome to the Network Template Wizard, click **Next**.

4. On the **Export the ISA Server Configuration** page, click **Export** to export the network configuration before modifying it.

5. In the **Export Configuration** dialog box, choose a location and name for the .xml file and click **Export**. When the export finishes, click **OK**.

6. On the **Export the ISA Server Configuration** page, click **Next**.

7. On the **Internal Network IP Address** page, confirm that all internal network addresses are listed. Modify the address ranges if required. Click **Next**.

8. On the **Select a Firewall Policy** page, select the appropriate firewall policy. Click **Next**.

9. On the **Completing the Network Template Wizard** page, review the configuration and click **Finish**.

10. In the details pane, click **Apply** to apply the new access rule.

Modifying Rules Applied by Network Templates

You may need to modify the rules applied by a network template to:

* Modify Internet access based on user or computer sets
* Modify Internet access based on protocols
* Modify network rules to change network relationships

You can either change the properties of one of the rules configured by the network template, or you can create a new access rule to apply a specific setting

Introduction

Network templates simplify the configuration of ISA Server 2004. However, in most cases, the access rules applied by the template may not exactly meet your requirements. In these cases, you need to modify the access rules implemented by the template.

Modifying network template rules

There are many scenarios in which you may need to define Internet access more precisely by modifying the access rules. Following are some examples:

■ *Modifying Internet access based on user or computer sets.* The default network template defines the same access rules for all users and all computers on the internal network. If all client computers are Firewall clients or Web proxy clients and you want to ensure that all users authenticate before gaining access to the Internet, you may want to change the rule created by the wizard to apply to All Authenticated Users. If you want to apply more or less restrictive policies based on user or computer groups, you can create a user set or computer set, and then create a new access rule that applies the settings you need.

■ *Modifying Internet access for different protocols.* The network template either allows all protocols, or a selected group of the most common Internet protocols. If you want to allow all users to use a different set of protocols, you can modify the default rule created by the network template. If you want a selected user group to be able to use other protocols, create the user set, then create a new access rule granting the required access.

■ *Modifying network rules to change network relationships.* In some cases, you may also need to change the default network rules that are created by the network templates. For example, the 3-leg perimeter template creates a route relationship between the perimeter network and the external network and a NAT relationship between the perimeter network and the internal network. If you use private IP addresses in the perimeter network, you must change the perimeter network to external network rule to a NAT relationship.

To simplify the configuration of the additional access rules, choose the network template that most closely meets your requirements when you run the wizard. For example, if you are implementing a three-legged perimeter network configuration where almost all users need to be able to access the Internet using all protocols, then choose the 3-leg perimeter network template and enable unrestricted access when you run the wizard. Then create additional access rules that apply the exceptions. For example, you may need to create a more restrictive policy for some users.

Practice: Implementing Network Templates

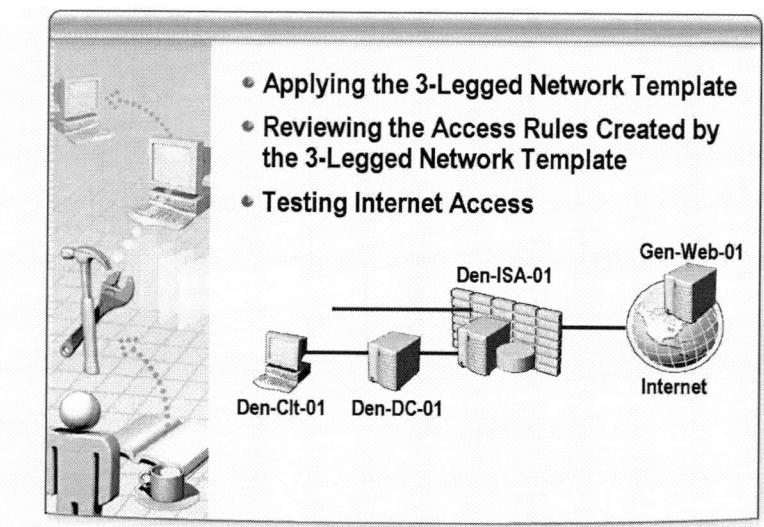

* Applying the 3-Legged Network Template
* Reviewing the Access Rules Created by the 3-Legged Network Template
* Testing Internet Access

Introduction

In this practice, you will use the 3-leg perimeter template to configure restricted Internet access for all users at Coho Vineyard. You will also review the firewall rules created by the wizard and then test the Internet access.

Practice

▶ **To prepare for this practice**

1. You will need the Den-DC-01 virtual machine, the Den-Clt-01 virtual machine, the Den-ISA-01 virtual machine, and the Gen-Web-01 virtual machine for this practice.

2. If necessary, start or resume the required virtual machines and then, on Den-ISA-01, log on to the cohovineyard domain with your user name and password.

▶ **Applying the 3-Leg Perimeter Template**

1. In the **ISA Server Management** console tree, expand **Den-ISA-01**, then expand **Configuration**, and then click **Networks**.

2. In the task pane, on the **Templates** tab, click **3-Leg Perimeter**.

3. In the **Welcome to the Network Template Wizard**, click **Next**.

Note Before implementing a significant change to the ISA Server configuration, you should export the firewall settings. The export performed during the network template wizard exports the entire ISA Server configuration, including networks and network rules.

---

4. On the **Export the ISA Server Configuration** page, click **Export** to export the network configuration before modifying it.

5. In the **Export Configuration** dialog box, type **Network Configuration Pre-Template** in the **File name** box. Click the check boxes for **Export user permission settings** and **Export confidential information (encryption will be used)** and then click **Export**.

6. Type **P@ssw0rd** in the **Password** and **Confirm password** boxes. Click **OK**. When the export finishes, click **OK**.

7. On the **Export the ISA Server Configuration** page, click **Next**.

8. On the **Internal Network IP Address** page, confirm that the **Start Address** is 192.168.1.0 and the **End Address** is 192.168.1.255. Click **Next**.

9. On the **Perimeter Network IP Addresses** range page, click **Add Adapter**.

10. In the **Select Network Adapters** dialog box, click **Perimeter** and click **OK** and then click **Next**.

11. On the **Select a Firewall Policy** page, click **Allow limited Web access and access to ISP network services**. Click **Next**.

12. On the **Completing the Network Template Wizard** page, review the configuration and click **Finish**.

13. Click **Apply** to apply the changes and then click **OK** when the changes have been applied.

▶ **Reviewing the firewall rules created by the 3-Leg Perimeter Template**

1. In the **ISA Server Management** console tree, click **Firewall Policy**.

2. In the task pane, double-click **Web Access Only**. Examine the properties of the access rule. What protocols are allowed by the access rule? What networks are configured as source networks? What networks are configured as destination networks? Click **OK**.

3. In the task pane, double-click **Allow DNS to the Internet**. Examine the properties of the access rule. What protocols are allowed by the access rule? What networks are configured as source networks? What networks are configured as destination networks? Click **OK**.

4. In the task pane, double-click **VPN Clients to Internal Network**. Examine the properties of the access rule. What protocols are allowed by the access rule? What networks are configured as source networks? What networks are configured as destination networks? Click **OK**.

5. Click **Networks**. In the details pane, click **Networks Rules**.

6. Double-click the **Perimeter Configuration** network rule. What networks are configured as source networks? What networks are configured as destination networks? What is the network relationship defined by this rule? Click **OK**.

7. Double-click the **Perimeter Access** network rule. What networks are configured as source networks? What networks are configured as destination networks? What is the network relationship defined by this rule?

8. Because we are using a private IP address range in the Perimeter network we will change the network rule for traffic flowing between the External network and the Perimeter network to a NAT relationship. To do this, on the **Network Relationship** tab, select **Network Address Translation (NAT)**. Click **OK**.

9. Click **Apply** to apply the changes and then click **OK** when the changes have been applied.

▶ **Testing Internet access**

1. Switch to the Den-Clt-01 virtual machine and log on to the cohovineyard domain as *yourusername*.

2. Open Internet Explorer and attempt to connect to www.contoso.com.

3. Attempt to connect to www.tailspintoys.com.

4. Attempt to connect to ftp://ftp.contoso.com. You may need to clear the **Enable folder view for FTP sites** on the **Advanced** tab in **Internet Options** to view the FTP directory listing. All connections should be successful.

Lesson: Configuring System Policies

* What Is System Policy?
* System Policy Settings
* How to Modify System Policy Settings

Introduction

When ISA Server 2004 is installed, a default system policy is configured on the server. This system policy includes a wide variety of access rules that provide an initial configuration for ISA Server 2004. This lesson explains what the default system policies are and when and how to modify the policies.

Lesson objectives

After completing this lesson, you will be able to:

- Describe system policies.
- Examine system policy settings.
- Modify system policy settings.

What Is System Policy?

System policy is:

- A default set of access rules applied to the ISA Server to enable management of the server
- A set of predefined rules that you can enable or disable as required

Modify the default set of rules provided by the system policy to meet your organization's requirements. Disable all functionality that is not required

---

Introduction

When you install ISA Server 2004, it is configured with a default system policy. The system policy is a set of firewall policy rules that control how the ISA Server computer interacts with the connected networks.

What is the system policy?

The system policy is used primarily to enable sufficient access between the ISA Server computer and the connected networks so that you can manage ISA Server. All of the system policies define access between the Local Network, which is the ISA Server computer itself, and the connected networks rather than defining access between networks.

The system policy defines many firewall access rules that function the same way as other access rules. However, the implementation of the system policy rules is different. When you create a new access rule, you need to define all components for that rule. The system policy rules are predefined; all you need to do is decide whether or not to enable the rule and then choose which networks are affected by the rule.

Some system policy rules are enabled by default. These rules enable the management of the ISA Server environment and provide the most common network functionality.

Modifying system policy

After installing ISA Server, you should analyze the default system policy configuration and modify the policy to meet your organization's requirements. If your organization does not require a specific type of functionality enabled by the system policy, then disable the rule that enables the functionality. For example, the default system policy enables remote access to all computers in the Remote Management Computers group. If no one is going to be accessing ISA Server remotely, then disable this rule. In general, it is recommended that all system policy rules that are not required to manage the infrastructure be disabled.

System Policy Settings

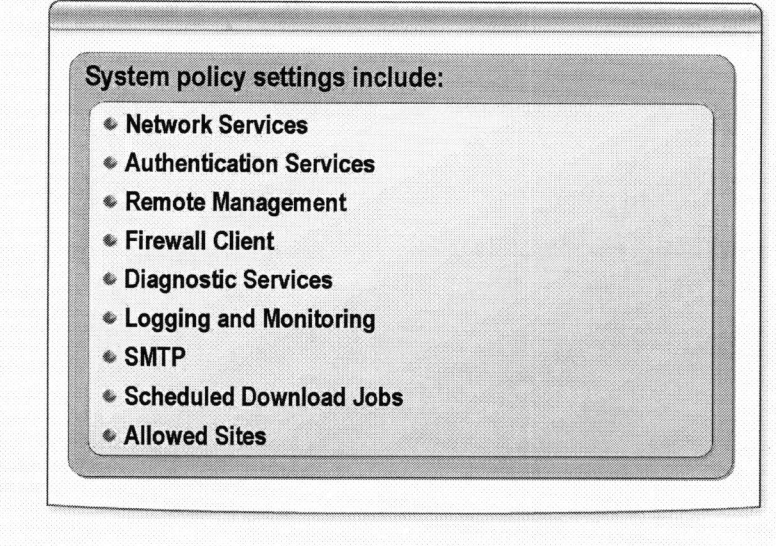

System policy settings include:

- Network Services
- Authentication Services
- Remote Management
- Firewall Client
- Diagnostic Services
- Logging and Monitoring
- SMTP
- Scheduled Download Jobs
- Allowed Sites

Introduction

The default system policy that is applied when you install ISA Server 2004 enables the functionality needed to manage the ISA Server and provide network functionality.

Default system policy settings

The following table summarizes the default system policy configuration:

Configuration Group	Configuration Options
Network services	Defines which networks are accessible from the ISA Server for DNS, Dynamic Host Configuration Protocol (DHCP), and Network Time Protocol (NTP). You can modify the system policy so that only particular computers on the internal network can be accessed, or add networks if the services are found on a different network.
Authentication services	To authenticate users, ISA Server must be able to communicate with the authentication servers. By default, ISA Server can communicate with Active Directory® directory service servers (for Windows authentication) and with Remote Authentication Dial-In User Service (RADIUS) servers located on the internal network. You can modify which networks are accessible for authentication as well as limit which authentication options can be used.
Remote management	By default, ISA Server can be managed by running a remote Microsoft Management Console (MMC) snap-in or by using Terminal Services on any computer in the built-in Remote Management Computers computer set. When ISA Server is installed, this empty computer set is created. Add all computers that will remotely manage ISA Server to this set. Until this is done, remote management is not available from any computer.

(continued)

Configuration Group	Configuration Options
Firewall Client	If the Firewall Client Share component was installed when you installed ISA Server, the Firewall Client Installation Share configuration group is enabled by default. All computers on the Internal network can access the shared folder.
Diagnostic services	The system policy rules that allow access to diagnostic services are enabled, with the following permissions: • *ICMP is allowed to all networks*. This service is important for determining connectivity to other computers. • *Windows networking*. This allows NetBIOS communication to computers on the Internal network. • *Microsoft error reporting*. This allows HTTP access to the Microsoft Error Reporting sites URL set to allow reporting of error information. By default, this URL set includes specific Microsoft sites.
Logging and monitoring	These system policy rules allow remote logging and monitoring. The following configuration groups are disabled by default: • *Remote Logging (NetBIOS)* • *Remote Logging (SQL)* • *Remote Performance Monitoring* • *Microsoft Operations Manager*
SMTP	The SMTP configuration group is enabled, allowing SMTP communication from ISA Server to computers on the Internal network. This is required, for example, to send alert information in an e-mail message.
Scheduled download jobs	The scheduled download jobs feature is disabled. When a content download job is created, the administrator will be prompted to enable this system policy rule. ISA Server will be able to access the sites specified in the content download job.
Allowed sites	By default, the allowed-sites configuration group is enabled, allowing ISA Server to access content on specific sites that belong to the System Policy Allowed Sites URL set. This URL set includes various Microsoft Web sites by default. The URL set can be modified to include additional Web sites, which ISA Server will be allowed to access.

How to Modify System Policy Settings

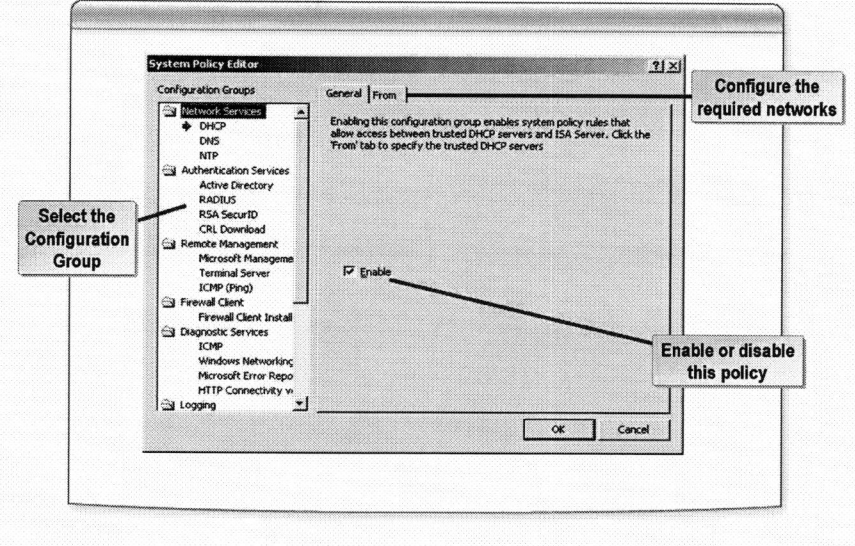

Introduction

The default system policy enables more options than are required for most organizations. For example, the default system policy enables both RADIUS and Active Directory authentication, and most organizations will use one or the other. You can modify the default settings to match your organization's requirements.

Modifying system policy settings

To modify the default system policy, use the following procedure:

1. In the console tree of **ISA Server Management**, click **Firewall Policy**.

2. On the **Tasks** tab, click **Edit System Policy**.

3. Click the configuration group that you want configure. For example, to configure the DHCP settings, click **DHCP** in the **Configuration Groups** box.

4. On the **General** tab, click **Enable** to enable the configuration group.

5. On the **From** tab, configure the source of network traffic. You can use any network entity to configure the source network. You can also define exceptions to the rule.

> **Note**   The system policy settings all configure traffic to or from the Local Host network. For some configuration groups, such as **DHCP**, you define the source network for the traffic on the **From** tab. For other configuration groups, such as **Active Directory** authentication, you configure the destination network on the **To** tab.

6. When you finish configuring the system policy, click **OK**.

7. When you enable a system policy setting, ISA Server configures one or more system policy rules. To display the system policy rules, click **Firewall Policy** in **ISA Server Management** and then, on the **Tasks** tab, click **Show System Policy Rules**.

Practice: Modifying System Policy

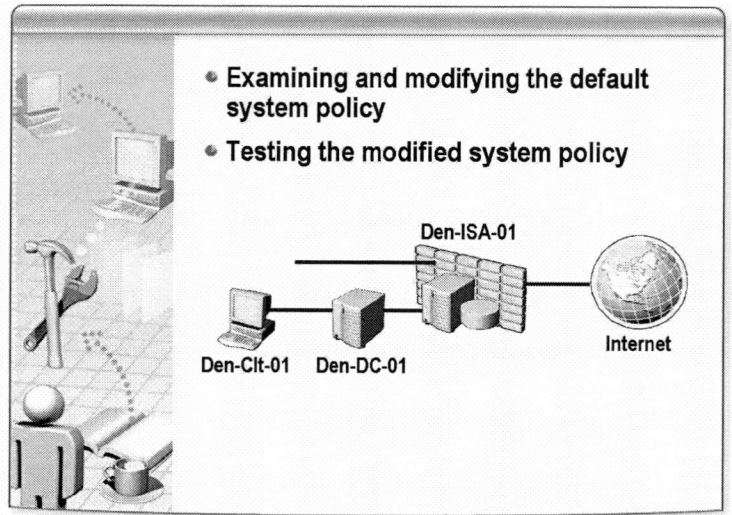

Introduction

In this practice, you will review the default system policy configuration on ISA Server 2004. You will then modify the default system policy and test the results.

Practice

▶ **To prepare for this practice**

1. You will need the Den-DC-01 virtual machine, the Den-Clt-01 virtual machine, and the Den-ISA-01 virtual machine for this practice.

2. If necessary, start or resume the required virtual machines and then, on Den-ISA-01, log on to the cohovineyard domain with your user name and password.

▶ **Examining and modifying the default system policy**

1. In the **ISA Server Management** console tree, click **Firewall Policy**.

2. On the **Tasks** tab, click **Edit System Policy**.

3. In the **Configuration Groups** box, ensure that **DHCP** is selected. On the **From** tab, ensure that **Internal** is listed in the **This rule applies to traffic from these sources** box.

4. On the **General** tab, clear the check box for **Enable**.

5. In the **Configuration Groups** box, click **Microsoft Management Console**. On the **From** tab, ensure that **Remote Management Computers** is listed in the **This rule applies to traffic from these sources** box.

6. Click **Remote Management Computers**, and then click **Edit**. Ensure that the **Internal Computers** computer set is listed in the **Computers, address ranges and subnets included in this computer set** box. Click **OK**.

7. On the **General** tab, clear the check box for **Enable**.

8. In the **System Policy Editor** dialog box, click **OK**.

9. Click **Apply** to apply the changes and then click **OK** when the changes have been applied.

▶ **Testing the modified system policy**

1. In the Microsoft **ISA Server Management** console tree, click **Firewall Policy**.

2. On the **Tasks** tab, click **Show System Policy Rules**.

3. Locate the rule named **Allow DHCP requests from ISA Server to all networks**. Right click the rule and click **Properties**. Confirm that you cannot modify the rule. Click **OK**.

4. Switch to Den-Clt-01.

5. If necessary, open **Internet Explorer** and then attempt to access www.tailspintoys.com. Have the system policy changes affected your ability to access the site? Why or why not? Close **Internet Explorer**.

6. Open **ISA Server Management**. Can you connect to Den-ISA-01? Have the system policy changes affected your ability to access the server using the MMC? Why or why not?

7. Click **Yes**. Close **ISA Server Management**.

8. Switch to Den-ISA-01.

9. In the **ISA Server Management** console tree, click **Firewall Policy**.

10. On the **Tasks** tab, click **Edit System Policy**.

11. In the **Configuration Groups** box, click **Microsoft Management Console**. Select **Enable**.

12. In the **System Policy Editor** dialog box, click **OK**.

13. Click **Apply** to apply the changes and then click **OK** when the changes have been applied.

14. Switch to Den-Clt-01.

15. Open **ISA Server Management**. Can you connect to Den-ISA-01? Have the system policy changes affected your ability to access the server using the MMC? Why or why not?

16. Close all open windows and log off Den-Clt-01.

Lesson: Configuring Intrusion Detection and IP Preferences

* About Intrusion Detection Configuration Options
* How to Configure Intrusion Detection
* About IP Preferences Configuration Options
* How to Configure IP Preferences

Introduction

Two additional options available on ISA Server 2004 to provide security are intrusion detection and IP preferences. These options are used to configure how ISA Server will respond to various attacks or malformed IP packets. This lesson describes how to configure these options.

Lesson objectives

After completing this lesson, you will be able to:

- Describe the intrusion detection configuration options.
- Configure intrusion detection.
- Describe the IP preferences configuration options.
- Configure IP preferences.

About Intrusion Detection Configuration Options

> **Intrusion detection on ISA Server 2004:**
>
> * Compares network traffic and log entries to well-known attack methods and raises an alert when an attack is detected
> * Detects well-known IP attacks
> * Includes application filters for DNS and POP that detect intrusion attempts at the application level

Introduction

To fully protect your network, you will also need to know how to configure your ISA Server for intrusion detection. The purpose of intrusion detection is to detect network attacks as early as possible to ensure that appropriate corrective actions can be taken.

How does ISA Server perform intrusion detection?

Intrusion detection identifies when an attack is attempted against your network and performs a set of configured actions, or alerts, in case of an attack. To detect unwanted intruders, ISA Server compares network traffic and log entries to well-known attack methods. When ISA Server detects suspicious activities, it triggers an alert. You can configure the actions that ISA Server will perform in the event of an alert. These actions include connection termination, service termination, e-mail alerts, logging, and others.

Intrusion detection at the IP level

ISA Server provides intrusion detection for well-known IP attacks listed in the following table:

IP Attack	Description
Windows out-of-band attack	This alert notifies you that there was an out-of-band denial-of-service attack attempted against a computer protected by ISA Server. An out-of-band attack occurs when a Windows system receives a packet with the "URGENT" flag set. The system expects data will follow that flag. The exploit consists of setting the URGENT flag, but not following it with data. The port most susceptible is TCP Port 139, the Netbios Session Service port. If mounted successfully, this attack causes the computer to fail or causes a loss of network connectivity on vulnerable computers.
Land attack	This alert notifies you that a TCP SYN packet was sent with a spoofed source IP address and port number that match those of the destination IP address and port. If the attack is successfully mounted, it can cause some TCP implementations to go into a loop that causes the computer to fail.

(continued)

IP Attack	Description
Ping-of-death attack	This alert notifies you that an IP fragment was received with more data than the maximum IP packet size. If the attack is successfully mounted, a kernel buffer overflows, which causes the computer to fail.
Port scan	This alert notifies you that an attempt was made to access more than the preconfigured number of ports. You can specify a threshold, indicating the number of ports that can be accessed.
IP half scan	This alert notifies you that repeated attempts to send TCP packets with invalid flags were made. During an IP half scan attack, the attacking computer does not send the final ACK packet during the TCP three-way handshake. Instead, it sends other types of packets that can elicit useful responses from the target host without causing a connection to be logged. This is also known as a stealth scan, because it does not generate a log entry on the scanned host. If this alert occurs, log the address from which the scan occurs. If appropriate, configure the ISA Server rules to block traffic from the source of the scans.
UDP bomb	This alert notifies you that there is an attempt to send an illegal User Datagram Protocol (UDP) packet. These UDP packets will cause some older operating systems to fail when the packet is received. If the target machine does fail, it is often difficult to determine the cause.

Intrusion detection at the application layer

ISA Server also provides built-in application filters that detect DNS and Post Office Protocol (POP) protocol intrusions. The DNS intrusion detection filter detects the following known DNS exploits:

- *DNS host name overflow*. A DNS host name overflow occurs when a DNS response for a host name exceeds a certain fixed length (255 bytes). Applications that do not check the length of the host names may overflow internal buffers on the server when copying this host name, allowing a remote attacker to execute arbitrary commands on a targeted computer. This filter inspects the response that an internal client receives from an external DNS server.

- *DNS length overflow*. DNS responses for Internet Protocol (IP) addresses contain a length field, which should be 4 bytes. By formatting a DNS response with a larger value, some applications executing DNS lookups will overflow internal buffers, potentially allowing a remote attacker to execute arbitrary commands on a targeted computer. This filter inspects the response that an internal client receives from an external DNS server.

- *DNS zone transfer*. A malicious user executes a zone transfer to gather a list of all the host names in a domain. This filter detects when an Internet user attempts to execute a zone transfer from an internal DNS server through ISA Server. If you are using a secondary DNS server on another network, you may need to allow DNS zone transfers to the secondary DNS server.

The Post Office Protocol (POP) filter intercepts and analyzes POP traffic destined for the published servers. The application filter checks for POP buffer overflow attacks. A POP buffer overflow attack occurs when a remote attacker attempts to gain root access to a POP server by overflowing an internal buffer on the server.

How to Configure Intrusion Detection

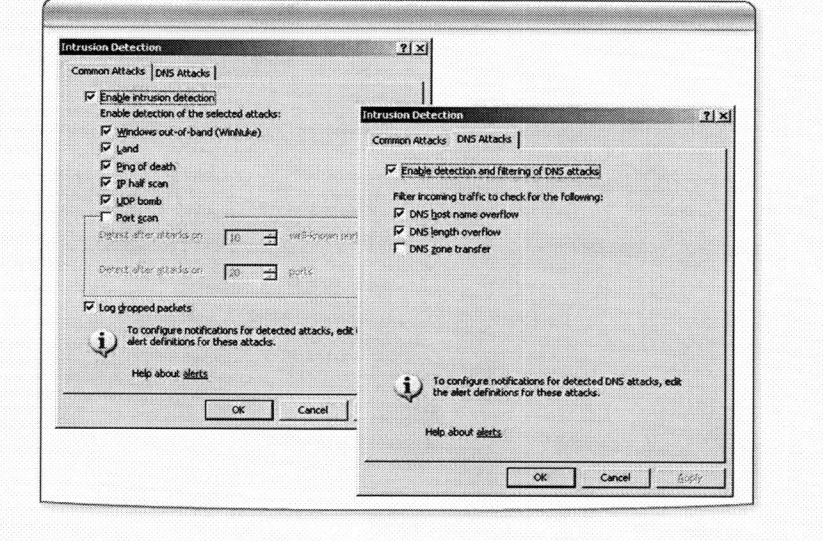

Introduction

By default, ISA Server is configured with most of the intrusion detection options already enabled.

How to Configure Intrusion Detection

To configure intrusion detection of common attacks, use the following procedure:

1. In the console tree of **ISA Server Management**, click **General**.

2. In the details pane, click **Enable Intrusion Detection and DNS Attack Detection**.

3. On the **Common Attacks** tab, ensure that **Enable intrusion detection** is selected.

4. Select one or more of the attack options. The only option that is not configured by default is the **Port Scan**. If you select this option, you can also specify when the alert will be raised. You can choose to raise the alert after a specified number of attacks on well-known ports or after a specified number of attacks on all ports.

5. To enable intrusion detection of DNS attacks, click the **DNS Attacks** tab, and then click **Enable detection and filtering of DNS attacks**.

6. Select one or more of the attack options. The only option that is not enabled by default is **DNS zone transfer**.

7. When you finish configuring intrusion detection, click **OK**.

Note After configuring intrusion detection, you can also configure the alert settings. For more information on configuring alerts and responses to alerts, see Module 10, "Monitoring ISA Server 2004," in Course 2824, *Implementing Microsoft Internet Security and Acceleration Server 2004*.

About IP Preferences Configuration Options

IP preferences are used to:

* **Block or enable network traffic that has an IP option flag set**
  * You can block all packets with IP options, or selected packets
* **Block or enable network traffic where the IP packet has been split into multiple IP fragments**
  * Blocking IP fragments may affect streaming audio and video, and L2TP over IPSec traffic
* **Enable or disable IP routing**
  * With IP routing enabled, ISA Server forwards IP packets between networks without recreating the packet

---

Introduction

Another option on ISA Server 2004 that you can use to improve security is to configure the IP preferences.

Definition

IP preferences are used to configure how ISA Server will handle IP packets. Configuring IP preferences is more complicated than configuring intrusion detection because, in most cases, IP preferences can be used to block normal packets that may or may not be used by attackers. You can configure the following IP preferences on ISA Server:

- *IP options.* You can configure ISA Server to refuse all packets that have the IP options flag set in the header, or you can configure ISA Server to drop packets with only specific IP options enabled. The IP options flags that are most commonly used by attackers are the source routing options. The source route option in the IP header allows the sender to override routing decisions that are normally made by the routers between the source and destination machines. An attacker can use source routing to reach addresses on the internal network that normally are not reachable from other networks, by routing the traffic through another computer that is reachable from both the other network and the internal network. Because source routing can be used in this way, you should disable source routing on your ISA Server.

- *IP fragments.* You can also configure ISA Server to drop all IP fragments. A single IP datagram can be divided into multiple datagrams of smaller sizes known as IP fragments. If you enable this option, then all fragmented packets are dropped when ISA Server filters packet fragments. A common attack that uses IP fragments is the teardrop. In this attack, multiple IP fragments are sent to a server. However, the IP fragments are modified so that the offset fields within the packet overlap. When the destination computer tries to reassemble these packets, it is unable to do so. It may fail, stop responding, or restart. Enabling IP fragment filtering can interfere with streaming audio and video. In addition, Layer Two Tunneling Protocol (L2TP) over IPSec connections may not be successfully established because packet fragmentation may take place during certificate exchange.

- *IP routing*. When IP routing is enabled, ISA Server sends the original network packet from one network to another. ISA Server can filter the network packet. When IP routing is disabled, ISA Server sends only the data (and not the original network packet) to the destination. Also, when IP routing is disabled, ISA Server sends each packet through the firewall in user mode. Disabling IP routing is more secure, but can also decrease router performance.

How to Configure IP Preferences

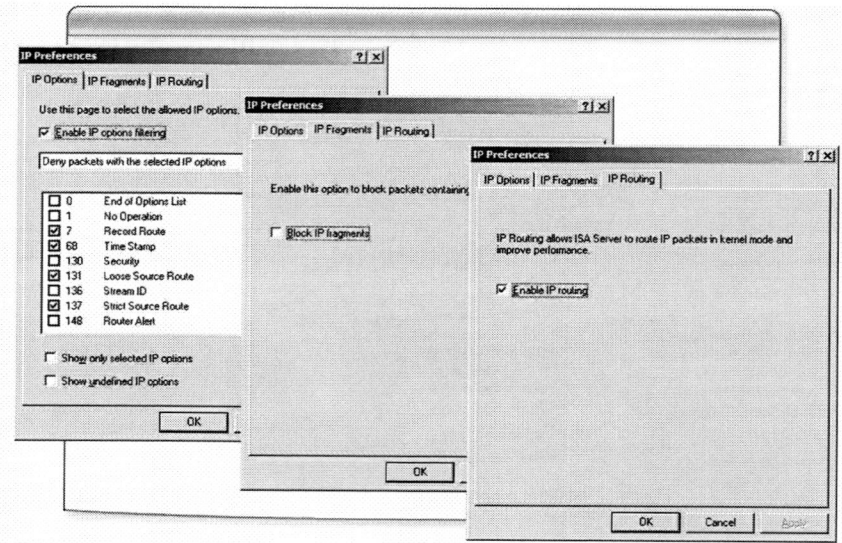

Introduction

By default, ISA Server is configured with the most important IP preferences set. You can modify the default settings.

How to Configure IP Preferences

To configure IP preferences, use the following procedure:

1. In the console tree of **ISA Server Management**, click **General**.

2. In the details pane, click **Define IP Preferences**.

3. On the **IP options** tab, ensure that **Enable IP options filtering** is selected. You can then configure the level of IP options filtering by denying all packets with the IP option flag configured or by denying packets with specific IP options set. By default, packets with IP options **Record Route**, **Time Stamp**, **Loose Source Route**, and **Strict Source Route** are denied.

4. On the **IP Fragments** tab, click **Block IP fragments** to block all IP fragments. By default, this option is not enabled.

5. On the **IP Routing** tab, clear the check box for **Enable IP Routing** to disable IP routing. By default, IP routing is enabled.

Practice: Configuring Intrusion Detection

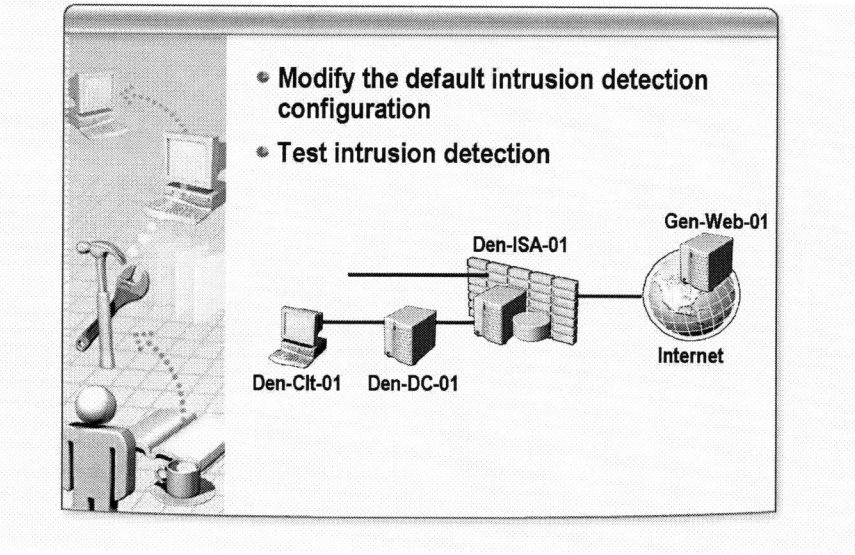

In this practice, you will modify the intrusion detection configuration on ISA Server 2004. You will then test the intrusion detection configuration.

Practice

▶ **To prepare for this practice**

1. You will need the Den-DC-01 virtual machine, the Den-ISA-01 virtual machine, and the Gen-Web-01 virtual machine for this practice.

2. If necessary, start or resume the required virtual machines and then, on Den-ISA-01, log on to the cohovineyard domain with your user name and password.

▶ **Modifying the default intrusion detection**

1. In the **ISA Server Management** console tree, expand **Den-ISA-01**, then expand **Configuration**, and then click **General**.

2. In the details pane, click **Enable Intrusion Detection and DNS Attack Detection**.

3. On the **Common Attacks** tab, ensure that **Enable intrusion detection** is selected.

4. Select **Port Scan** and configure ISA Server to detect after five attacks on well known ports.

5. On the **DNS Attacks** tab, select **DNS zone transfer**. Click **OK**.

6. Click **Apply** to apply the changes and then click **OK** when the changes have been applied.

▶ **Testing intrusion detection**

1. Switch to the Gen-Web-01 virtual machine and log in as **Administrator** with a password of **P@ssw0rd**.

2. Open a command prompt and ensure that the user context is in the C:\Program Files\Windows Resource Kits\Tools folder.

3. Type **portqry.exe –n 131.107.1.100 –r 1:20**.

4. Switch to the Den-ISA-01 virtual machine.

5. In the Microsoft **ISA Server Management** console tree, click **Monitoring**.

6. On the **Alerts** tab, locate the **Intrusion Detected** alert. You may need to wait a few minutes for the alert to appear. Expand the alert and read the **Alert information** at the bottom of the details pane.

7. Close all open windows.

8. Switch to Gen-Web-01 and close the command prompt window.

Lab: Configuring ISA Server as a Firewall

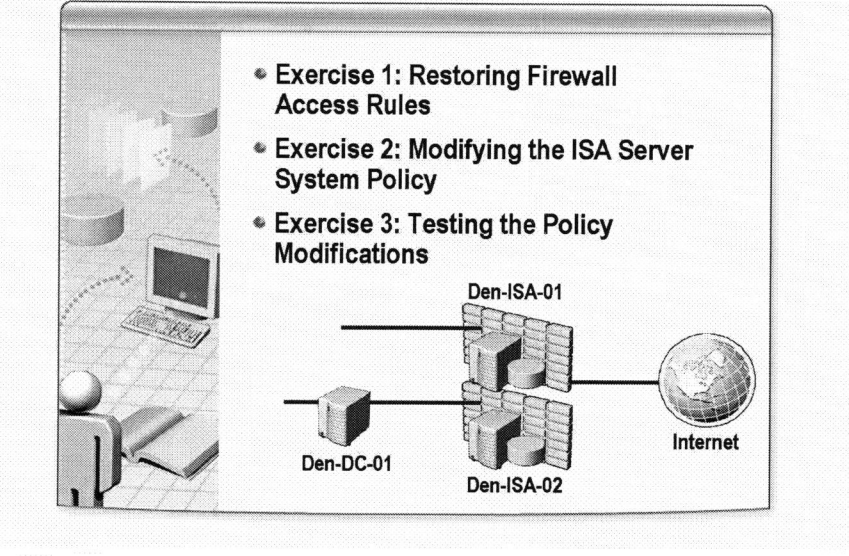

Objectives

After completing this lab, you will be able to:

- Restore and test firewall rule configuration.
- Modify the default system policy.

Note This lab focuses on the concepts in this module and as a result might not comply with Microsoft security recommendations. For example, the Administrator passwords are not as complex as recommended. Additionally, most of the actions performed in this lab are performed while logged in as an Administrator. A better security practice would be to log in as a normal user and use the Runas option to start administrative applications.

Scenario

You have deployed ISA Server at Coho Vineyards. You have applied the 3-leg perimeter network template to enable limited access to Internet resources for all users. You notice that the 3-leg perimeter template overwrote all of the access rules that you had previously applied to the ISA Server. You need to restore those access rules to ensure that the ISA Server configuration meets your company requirements. The default access rules applied by the network template should apply to all Internet access that is not specifically configured by another firewall rule.

You also need to modify the default system policy settings. You need to disable or modify the functionality enabled by the system policy that is not required in your organization. The corporate security policy specifies the following settings that need to be implemented using the system policy:

- The company has not deployed any RADIUS servers so the RADIUS functionality on the ISA Server should be disabled.

- All remote management of the ISA Server should be done through Remote Desktop. The system policy must be modified to ensure that only Remote Desktop can be used to remotely manage the ISA Server.

- Administrators need the ability to remotely monitor the ISA Server performance from the internal network only.

To prepare for this lab:

1. You will need the Den-DC-01 virtual machine, the Den-Clt-01 virtual machine, the Den-ISA-01 virtual machine, and the Gen-Web-01 virtual machine for this practice.

2. If necessary, start or resume the required virtual machines and then, on Den-ISA-01, log on to the cohovineyard domain with your user name and password.

Estimated time to complete this lab: 45 minutes

Exercise 1
Restoring Firewall Access Rules

In this exercise, you will restore the firewall access rules that were overwritten by the application of the 3-leg perimeter template. You will then modify the access rule order to ensure that the default access rule created by the network template is applied only to those users who are not included in other, more specific, access rules.

Tasks	Detailed steps
1. Restore the firewall access rules.	a. Open **ISA Server Management**, and click **Firewall Policy**. b. On the **Task** tab, click **Import Firewall Policy**. c. Import the **2824_Lab3_Export.xml** file located in the **C:\Program Files\Microsoft Learning\2824\LabFiles\Answers** folder.
2. Modify the access rule order so that the default policies created by the network template are applied only to the appropriate users.	a. Select the **Allow DNS to the Internet** rule and move it so that it is the second last rule in the **Firewall Policy**. b. Select the **Web Access Only** rule and move it so that it just above the **Allow DNS to the Internet** rule. c. Modify the **Web Access Only** rule by adding the **Night Shift Workers** and **Sales** user sets to the **Exceptions** list on the **Users** tab. d. Click **Apply** to apply the changes and then click **OK** when the changes have been applied.

Exercise 2
Modifying the ISA Server System Policy

In this exercise, you will configure the ISA Server system policy to ensure that all security requirements are met.

Tasks	Detailed steps
1. Modify the system policy so that the ISA Server cannot connect to any RADIUS servers.	▪ Modify the **RADIUS** configuration group to remove this functionality.
2. Modify the system policy so that all remote management of the ISA Server can only be done using Remote Desktop.	▪ Modify the **Microsoft Management Console (MMC)** configuration group to ensure that the ISA Server will not accept remote connections using the ISA Server Management MMC.
3. Modify the system policy so that Administrators can remotely monitor the ISA Server performance but only from the internal network.	a. Modify the **Remote Performance Monitoring** configuration group to enable this functionality. b. Click **Apply** to apply the changes and then click **OK** when the changes have been applied.

Exercise 3
Testing the Policy Modifications

In this exercise, you will test your ISA Server configuration to ensure that the modifications you implemented meet the company requirements. The company requirements specify that:

- Users who work the night shift should only be able to access the Internet between the hours of midnight and 8 A.M.

- Managers should be able to access all sites on the Internet, at any time of day, using any application or protocol.

- Sales personnel should be able to access the Internet only between 9 A.M. and 5 P.M. every day.

- Sales users should not be able to access any HTTP or FTP sites at contoso.com.

Use the following information to test the configuration:

- Shu Ito (login name: Shu, password: P@ssword) is a member of the Domain Users group.

- Jay Adams (login name: Jay, password: P@ssword) is a member of the Managers group.

- Doris Hartwig (login name: Doris, password: P@ssword) is a member of the Night Staff group.

- Martin Weber (login name: Martin, password: P@ssword) is a member of the Sales group.

Tasks	Detailed steps
1. Test Internet access. Ensure that the specific group based rules are applied before the default policies created by the network template. Log on to Den-Clt-01 to test each user's access.	**a.** Can Doris Hartwig access www.contoso.com? **b.** Can Martin Weber access www.contoso.com? **c.** Can Martin Weber access www.tailspintoys.com? **d.** Can Jay Adams access www.contoso.com? **e.** Can Jay Adams access ftp.contoso.com? **f.** Can Shu Ito access www.contoso.com? **g.** Can Shu Ito access ftp.contoso.com?
2. Test the system policy configuration. Log on to Den-Clt-01 with your user name to test the functionality.	**a.** Can you connect to Den-ISA-01 using the ISA Server Management MMC? **b.** Can you connect to Den-ISA-01 using the Remote Desktop? **c.** Can you connect to the Firewall Client Installation share on Den-ISA-01? **d.** Can you use the Performance MMC to monitor counters on Den-ISA-01? To test this, open **Performance** from the **Administrative Tools** folder located in the **Control Panel**. Add a counter and type Den-ISA-01 in the **Select counters from computer:** box.

Note The 2824_Lab4_Export.xml file located in the C:\Program Files\Microsoft Learning\2824\ LabFiles\Answers folder on Den-ISA-01 contains an ISA Server export of one set of rules that meets the company requirements and includes the network template. If you are not able to complete the lab, you can import this file to review and test the access rule configuration. To import the file, click **Den-ISA-01** and click **Import from an Exported ISA Server Configuration File**.

To Prepare for the Next Lab

As you finish this lab, shut down all of the virtual machines that you used in the lab. To shut down the virtual machines, click **Close** from the **Action** menu. **Select Turn off and delete changes** and click **OK**.

After shutting down the virtual machines, restart the Den-DC-01 virtual machine, the Den-ISA-01 virtual machine, the Den-Clt-01 virtual machine and the Gen-Web-01 virtual machine in preparation for the next module.

Microsoft®

Module 5: Configuring Access to Internal Resources

Contents

Overview

- Introduction to Publishing
- Configuring Web Publishing
- Configuring Secure Web Publishing
- Configuring Server Publishing
- Configuring ISA Server Authentication

Introduction

Microsoft® Internet Security and Acceleration (ISA) Server 2004 uses Web and server publishing rules to publish internal network resources to the Internet without compromising internal network security. Web publishing rules determine how ISA Server deals with Hypertext Transfer Protocol (HTTP) and Hypertext Transfer Protocol Secure (HTTPS) requests from the Internet intended for internal Web servers. Server publishing rules define how ISA Server responds to requests from the Internet for other network resources on the internal network. The ISA Server administrator needs to know how to use these rules to securely publish internal network resources to the Internet.

Objectives

After completing this module, you will be able to:

- Describe how ISA Server 2004 can be used to configure access to internal resources.

- Configure Web publishing.

- Configure secure Web publishing.

- Configure server publishing.

- Configure ISA Server authentication.

Lesson: Introduction to Publishing

- Multimedia: Using ISA Server 2004 to Enable Access to Internal Network Resources
- What Are Web Publishing Rules?
- What Are Server Publishing Rules?
- DNS Configuration for Web and Server Publishing

Introduction

This lesson introduces the concept of publishing internal network resources to the Internet by using ISA Server 2004. It introduces the concepts of Web publishing and server publishing. It also provides an overview of how to configure Domain Name System (DNS) to enable Web and server publishing.

Lesson objectives

After completing this lesson, you will be able to:

- Describe how ISA Server 2004 enables access to internal network resources.
- Describe what a Web publishing rule is.
- Describe what a server publishing is.
- Describe how to integrate DNS with the Web publishing scenarios.

Multimedia: Using ISA Server 2004 to Enable Access to Internal Network Resources

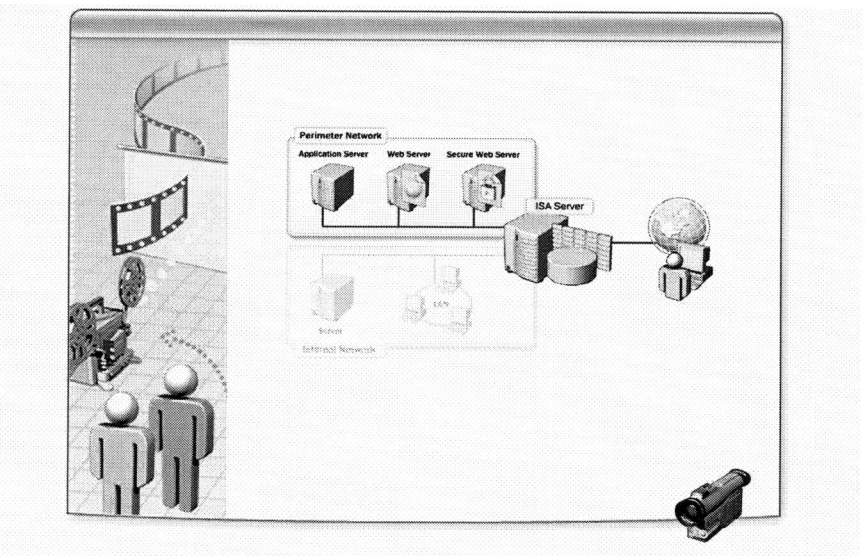

This animation presents an overview of how ISA Server 2004 can be used to provide secure access to internal network resources from the Internet.

Tip To view the Using ISA Server 2004 to Enable Access to Internal Network Resources presentation later on your own, open the Web page on the Student Materials compact disc, click **Multimedia**, and then click the title of the presentation.

What Are Web Publishing Rules?

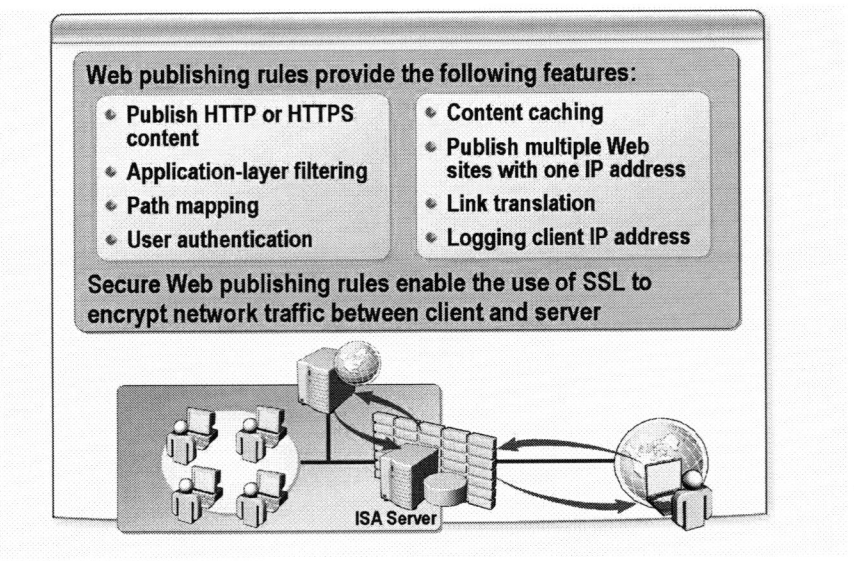

Web publishing rules

ISA Server uses Web publishing rules to make Web sites available to users on the Internet. A Web publishing rule is a firewall rule that specifies how ISA Server will route incoming requests to internal Web servers.

Functions of Web publishing rules

Use Web publishing rules to provide:

- *Access to Web servers running HTTP protocol.* When you configure a Web publishing rule, you configure ISA Server to listen for HTTP requests from the Internet and to forward that request to a Web server on a protected network. To publish servers using any other protocols, you need to use a server publishing rule.

- *Application-layer filtering.* Application-layer filtering enables ISA Server to inspect the application data in each packet passing through ISA Server. This includes filtering of Secure Sockets Layer (SSL) packets if you enable SSL bridging. This provides an additional layer of security not provided by server publishing rules.

- *Path mapping.* Path mapping enables you to hide the details of your internal Web site configuration by redirecting external requests for parts of the Web site to alternate locations within the internal Web site. This means that you can limit access to only specific areas within a Web site.

- *User authentication.* You can configure ISA Server to require that all external users authenticate before their requests are forwarded to the Web server hosting the published content. This protects the internal Web server from authentication attacks. Web publishing rules support several methods of authentication including Remote Authentication Dial-In User Service (RADIUS), integrated, basic, digest, digital certificates, and RSA SecurID.

- *Content caching.* The content from the internal Web server can be cached on ISA Server, which improves the response time to the Internet client while decreasing the load on the internal Web server.

- *Support for publishing multiple Web sites using a single Internet Protocol (IP) address.* You can configure multiple Web publishing rules that can make multiple internal Web sites available to Internet clients.

- *Link translation.* With link translation, you can provide access to complex Web pages that include references to other internal Web servers that are not directly accessible from the Internet. Without link translation, any link to a server that is not accessible from the Internet would appear as a broken link. Link translation can be used to publish complex Web sites providing content from many servers while hiding the complexity from the Internet users.

- *Support for logging of the Internet client's IP address.* By default, when you publish a server using Web publishing, the source IP address that is received by the internal Web server is the IP address of the ISA Server internal interface. If you need to be able to log access to the Web server based on the IP address of the client computer on the Internet, you can modify the default setting.

Functions of secure Web publishing rules

Secure Web publishing rules are a special type of Web publishing rule that increases the security of the Web site by encrypting network traffic using SSL. ISA Server supports both SSL tunneling and SSL bridging.

- *SSL tunneling.* With SSL tunneling, ISA Server forwards encrypted packets between the client and the Web server. In this scenario, ISA Server cannot inspect the content of the packets.

- *SSL bridging.* With SSL bridging, ISA Server can encrypt and decrypt all network traffic between the server and client. In this scenario, ISA Server can accept SSL requests from clients, and can then convert them to HTTP and forward them to the published Web server. ISA Server can also be configured to re-encrypt the traffic sent to the publishing Web server to provide additional security. In a SSL bridging scenario, ISA Server can inspect the HTTP packets while they are not encrypted.

What Are Server Publishing Rules?

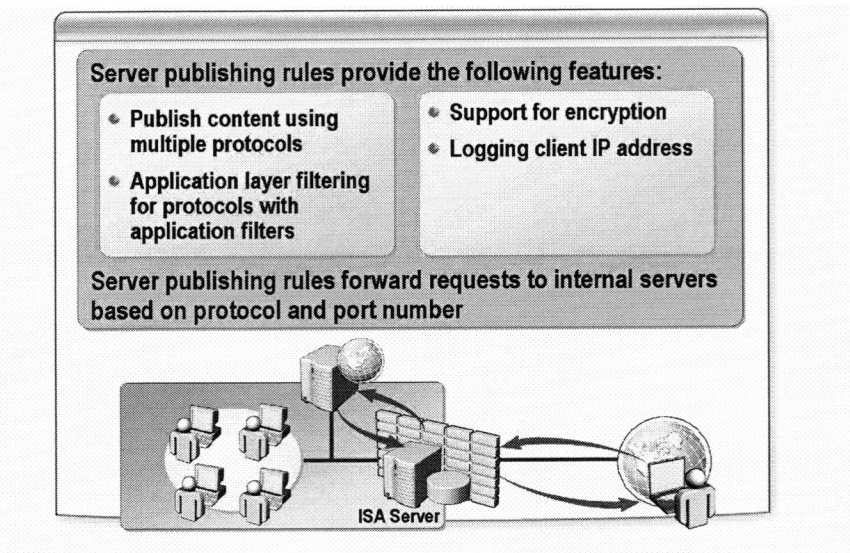

Server publishing rules

ISA Server uses server publishing rules to make servers on protected networks available to users on the Internet. Server publishing rules are firewall rules that specify how ISA Server will route incoming requests to internal servers.

Functions of server publishing rules

Use server publishing rules to provide:

- *Access to multiple protocols*. Server publishing rules provide access to protocols that Web publishing rules cannot. Web publishing rules can only publish servers using HTTP or HTTPS, for all other protocols you must use a server publishing rule. ISA Server comes pre-configured with a number of protocol definitions for commonly used protocols that can be used for server publishing rules. You can also create custom protocol definitions. Any protocol definition in which the primary connection is defined as inbound can be used for a server publishing rule.

- *Application-layer filtering for specified protocols* Application-layer filtering enables ISA Server to inspect the application data in each packet passing through ISA Server. ISA Server can apply application-layer inspection for server publishing when an application filter is registered for a specific protocol. For all other network traffic, ISA Server can apply packet and stateful filtering. ISA Server cannot inspect incoming SSL packets for servers published by server publishing rules.

- *Support for encryption*. Some of the protocol definitions provided with ISA Server are secure protocols. For example, ISA Server includes definitions for secure Internet Message Access Protocol (IMAPS) and secure Post Office Protocol (POPS). When a server publishing rule is configured to use these protocols, ISA Server can forward encrypted data between the client computer and the internal published server.

- *IP address logging for the client computer*. By default, when you publish a server using server publishing rule, the source IP address that is received by the internal Web server is the IP address of the client computer on the Internet.

What are server publishing rules?

Server publishing rules differ from Web publishing rules in that they do not use the Web Proxy filter. A server publishing rule for a particular protocol just forwards the client request to the published server. With a server publishing rule, ISA Server maps a socket on an external interface to an internal server socket. When ISA Server receives a request on the external IP address for a specific port, it passes the request to the internal server based on the port number. So, if you have an internal File Transfer Protocol (FTP) server that you want to make accessible from the Internet, you create a server publishing rule that maps requests for Transmission Control Protocol (TCP) port 21 on an external interface of ISA Server to the internal IP address of the FTP server.

Server publishing rules also differ from Web publishing rules in that server publishing rules forward all requests using the appropriate port number to published server. With a Web publishing rule, you can publish just one virtual directory on a Web server. When you configure a server publishing rule to forward a specific protocol, all requests using that protocol will be forwarded to the published server.

When you use a server publishing rule to publish a server, the client request is always NAT'd by the computer running ISA Server, even if a route relationship is defined between the source and destination network.

DNS Configuration for Web and Server Publishing

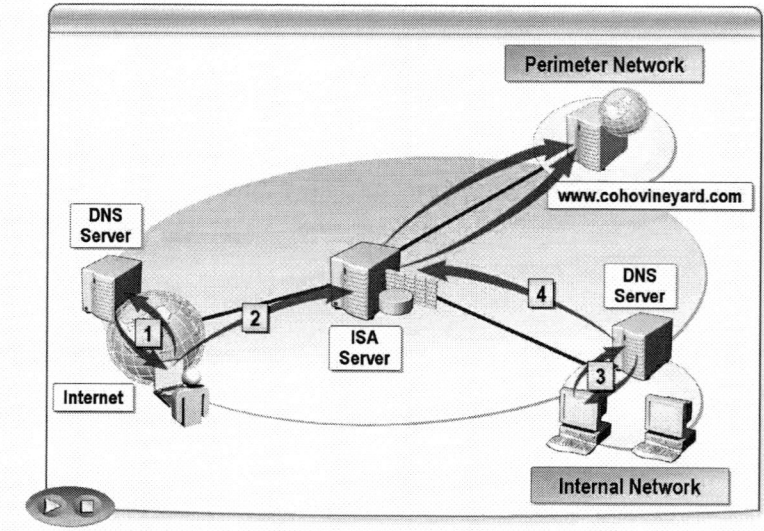

Introduction

One of the complicating issues when publishing internal Web servers as well as other servers to the Internet is DNS name resolution. Often, clients from the internal network, as well as clients from the Internet, need to connect to the same internal server using the same DNS name. However, the internal clients usually need to connect to a different IP address than the external clients. The solution is to deploy a split DNS.

What is a split DNS?

A *split DNS* uses two different DNS servers with the same DNS domain name to provide name resolution for internally and externally accessible resources. Both DNS servers are authoritative for the same domain name. For example, Coho Vineyard may deploy a Web server in its perimeter network named www.cohovineyard.com that needs to be accessible to users on the internal network and on the Internet. However, when users on the Internet access this site, they should be directed to the IP address of the external interface of server running ISA Server. Internal users should be directed to the actual IP address or addresses of the Web server. Split DNS is also used in a server publishing scenario. Users from the Internet will connect to a server like ftp.cohovineyard.com using a different IP address than internal users.

Note   Firewall clients and Web proxy clients do not require a split DNS configuration to access the internal Web sites as they can use the external Internet IP address to access the internal server. In this configuration, the Web requests are passed through ISA Server. However, SecureNAT clients cannot connect to the internal Web servers using an Internet IP address. If you do implement a split DNS, you should configure the Web Proxy clients to access the internal Web servers directly rather than through ISA Server.

Implementing a split DNS

Implementing a split DNS requires two DNS servers that both host the same DNS domain name. For example, in a Web publishing scenario, one DNS server, used by all the internal clients, has a host record for the Web server that points to the actual IP address of the Web server. The second DNS server, accessible to Internet clients, has a host record for the Web server that points to the IP address of the external interface of the server running ISA Server.

With a split DNS, users from both the Internet and the internal network can access the Web site in the following way:

1. When the Internet client wants to access the Web server, it needs to resolve the name www.cohovineyard.com. The client sends a query to the DNS server on the Internet. The server will respond with the IP address of the external interface of the server running ISA Server.

2. The client will then send the Web request to the IP address provided by the DNS server, and ISA Server will forward the request to the Web server.

3. When the internal client wants to access the Web server, it will query the internal DNS server for the IP address of www.cohovineyard.com. The internal DNS server will provide the client with the actual IP address of the Web server.

4. The internal client will then directly connect to the internal Web server. If the Web server is located on a perimeter network, the request will be passed through ISA Server.

Note The scenario described here assumes a Network Address Translation (NAT) relationship between the external network and the perimeter network and a route relationship between the internal network and the perimeter network. If the network relationships were reversed, then the host record on the external DNS would point to the actual IP address for the Web server, while the host record on the internal DNS would point to the IP address of the internal network interface on ISA Server.

Practice: Configuring DNS

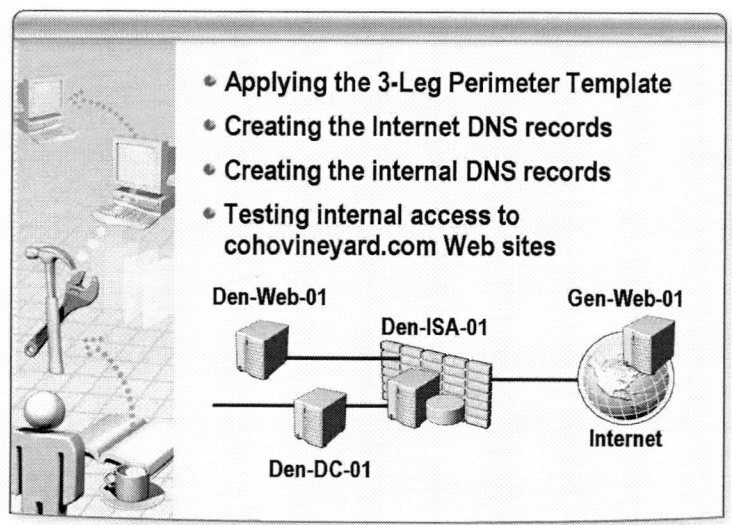

* Applying the 3-Leg Perimeter Template
* Creating the Internet DNS records
* Creating the internal DNS records
* Testing internal access to cohovineyard.com Web sites

Den-Web-01   Den-ISA-01   Gen-Web-01

Den-DC-01   Internet

Introduction

In this practice, you will configure both internal and external DNS records for the Web servers and other servers that will be accessible at Coho Vineyard.

> **Note** For the practices and lab in this module and the following modules, you will be using Gen-Web-01 as an Internet client. This server is also the Internet-accessible DNS server.

▶ **To prepare for this practice**

1. You will need the Den-DC-01 virtual machine, the Den-Web-01 virtual machine, the Den-ISA-01 virtual machine, and the Gen-Web-01 virtual machine for this practice.

2. If necessary, start or resume the required virtual machines and then, on Den-ISA-01, log on to the cohovineyard domain with a user name of **Administrator** and a password of **P@ssw0rd**.

Practice

▶ **Applying the 3-Leg Perimeter Template**

1. In the **ISA Server Management** console tree, expand **Den-ISA-01**, then expand **Configuration**, and then click **Networks**.

2. In the task pane, on the **Templates** tab, click **3-Leg Perimeter**.

3. On the **Welcome to the Network Template Wizard** page, click **Next**.

4. On the **Export the ISA Server Configuration** page, click **Next**.

5. On the **Internal Network IP Address** page, confirm that the **Start Address** is 192.168.1.0 and the **End Address** is 192.168.1.255. Click **Next**.

6. On the **Perimeter Network IP Addresses** range page, click **Add Adapter**.

7. In the **Select Network Adapters** dialog box, click **Perimeter**, click **OK**, and then click **Next**.

8. On the **Select a Firewall Policy** page, click **Allow limited Web access and access to ISP network services.** Click **Next**.

9. On the **Completing the Network Template Wizard** page, review the configuration and click **Finish**.

10. On the **Networks Rules** tab, double-click the **Perimeter Access** network rule. On the **Network Relationship** tab, select **Network Address Translation (NAT)**. Click **OK**.

11. Click **Apply** to apply the changes and then click **OK** when the changes have been applied.

► **Creating the Internet DNS records for cohovineyard.com**

1. Switch to the Gen-Web-01 virtual machine.

2. Log on to Gen-Web-01 with a user name of **Administrator** and a password of **P@ssw0rd**.

3. Open the **DNS** management console from the **Administrative Tools** folder.

4. Expand **Forward Lookup Zones** and then expand **cohovineyard.com**.

5. Right-click **cohovineyard.com** and click **New Host (A)**.

6. In the **New Host** dialog box, type **www** in the **Name** box. Type **131.107.1.100** in the **IP address** box. Click **Add Host**.

7. In the **DNS** dialog box, click **OK**.

8. Click **Done**. Close the **DNS** management console.

► **Creating the internal DNS records for cohovineyard.com**

1. Switch to the Den-DC-01 virtual machine.

2. Log on to the cohovineyard domain with a user name of **Administrator** and a password of **P@ssw0rd**.

3. Open the **DNS** management console from the **Administrative Tools** folder.

4. Expand **Forward Lookup Zones** and then expand **cohovineyard.com**.

5. Right-click **cohovineyard.com** and click **New Host (A)**.

6. In the **New Host** dialog box, type **www** in the **Name** box. Type **172.16.1.11** in the **IP address** box. Click **Add Host**.

7. In the **DNS** dialog box, click **OK**.

8. Click **Done**, then close the **DNS** management console.

▶ **Testing internal access to cohovineyard.com Web sites**

1. Open Internet Explorer and type **www.cohovineyard.com** into the **Address** box.

2. Connect to Den-Web-01.cohovineyard.com and ftp.cohovineyard.com. All connections should be successful. To view the directory listing of an FTP site when connecting to the FTP site through ISA Server, you need to disable the folder view for FTP sites in Internet Explorer. To do this, click **Tools**, click **Internet Options**. In the **Internet Options** dialog box, on the **Advanced** tab, clear the check box for **Enable folder view for FTP sites**.

Lesson: Configuring Web Publishing

- Web Publishing Rules Configuration Components
- How to Configure Path Mapping
- How to Configure Web Listeners
- How to Configure Link Translation
- How to Configure a New Web Publishing Rule

Introduction

Web publishing is a secure and flexible way to publish the content on internal Web servers to the Internet. This lesson describes how to configure Web publishing.

Lesson objectives

After completing this lesson, you will be able to:

- Identify Web publishing rules configuration components.
- Configure path mapping.
- Configure Web listeners.
- Configure link translation.
- Configure Web publishing.

Web Publishing Rules Configuration Components

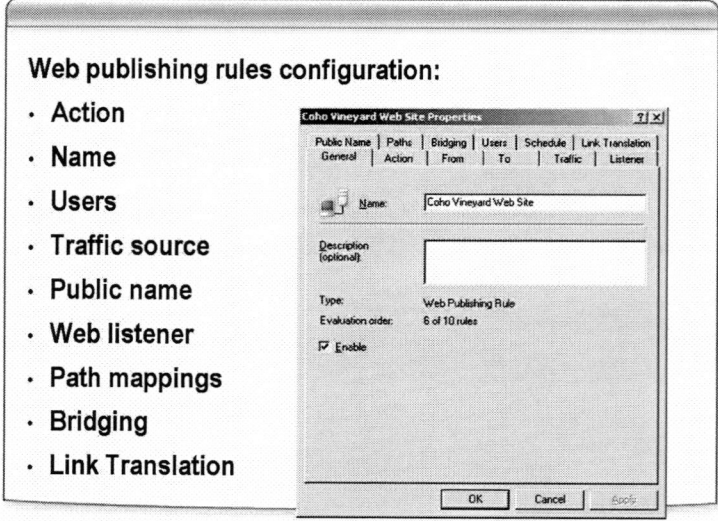

Web publishing rules configuration:
- Action
- Name
- Users
- Traffic source
- Public name
- Web listener
- Path mappings
- Bridging
- Link Translation

Introduction

Web publishing rules map incoming requests to the appropriate Web servers located on the internal or perimeter network. Web publishing rules determine how ISA Server will intercept incoming requests for HTTP objects on a Web server, and how ISA Server will respond on behalf of the Web server. Requests are forwarded to the Web server located on the internal or perimeter network. If caching is enabled on ISA Server, the request may be serviced from the ISA Server cache.

Web publishing configuration options

When you configure Web publishing rules, you need to configure the components listed in the following table:

Configuration option	Explanation
Action	Defines whether the Web publishing rule will allow or deny access.
Name (or IP address)	Defines the name or IP address of the Web server that is published by this rule.
Users	Defines which users can access the Web site.
Traffic source	Defines the network objects that can access the published Web server. The network objects that you specify must also be included in the Web listener specified for this Web publishing rule.
Public name	Defines the Uniform Resource Locator (URL) or IP address that is made accessible by this rule. You can configure ISA Server to allow access based on a specific URL or allow access to all URLs. If you specify a URL, ISA Server will respond only to requests using that URL. If you allow access to all URLs, ISA Server will respond to all requests using the appropriate protocol.

(*continued*)

Configuration option	Explanation
Web listener	Defines the network interface and IP address on the computer running ISA Server that listens for requests from clients.
Path mappings	Defines how ISA Server will modify the external path specified in the request and map it to a corresponding internal path.
Bridging	Defines how HTTP requests are forwarded to the published server. You can configure the requests so that they are redirected using HTTP, SSL, or FTP.
Link translation	Defines how ISA Server updates Web pages that include references to internal server names.

How to Configure Path Mapping

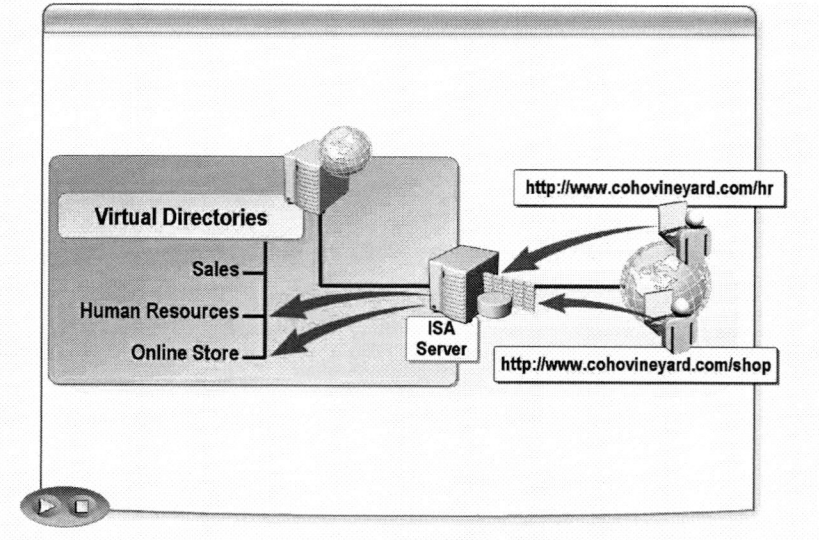

Introduction

Path mapping is an ISA Server feature that enables ISA Server to redirect user requests to multiple internal Web servers or to multiple locations on the same Web server. Path mapping is used for Web and secure Web publishing rules. Path mapping is used on ISA Server to hide the complexity of the internal Web server configuration from the Internet.

How path mapping works

In an organization with multiple Web servers or complex Web sites, the actual data that is being requested by the client may be located in several different locations. As the user browses the Web site, the data may need to come from several different locations on the internal servers. However, this complexity needs to be hidden from the user, for both security and usability reasons. To provide the level of accessibility required for Internet users to access multiple Web sites on the corporate network, ISA Server needs to be able to forward requests based on the names and paths included in the user requests. This feature is often required when Web sites contain links that use the same domain name, but a different path than that used by the remote user.

When a user connects to a Web site protected by ISA Server, the user types a specific URL. Before forwarding a request to the published Web server, ISA Server checks the URL specified in the request. If path mapping is configured, ISA Server will replace the path specified in the request with the corresponding path name.

For example, an organization may have multiple Web servers on the corporate network but a single domain name that it uses to provide Internet access. To allow Internet users access to these servers, the corporate Web site operators want to use different paths and the same fully qualified domain name (FQDN). You can do this with ISA Server 2004 firewalls by redirecting incoming requests to different servers on the corporate network based on path statements. When users request the URL http://www.cohovineyard.com/sales, they can be directed to the Sales virtual directory on one Web server. When users request the URL http://www.cohovineyard.com/catalog, they are redirected to another server. You can configure ISA Server to redirect requests with different folder names. The URL http://www.cohovineyard.com/catalog may be redirected to a virtual folder named CurrentCatalog on the Web server.

ISA Server 2004 performs this redirection transparently. Internet users see only that they are connecting to the Web sites and paths they entered into the browsers or accessed by clicking links to those URLs. ISA Server tracks these requests and forwards them to the appropriate Web server.

Configuring path mapping

To configure path mapping, use the following procedure:

1. In the **ISA Server Management** console tree, click **Firewall Policy**.

2. In the details pane, click the applicable Web publishing rule.

3. On the **Tasks** tab, click **Edit Selected Rule**.

4. On the **Paths** tab, click **Add**.

5. In the **Path Mapping** dialog box, type the path on the Web server. This path is the actual internal path to which the ISA Server will send the request.

6. Under **External Path**, select one of the following:

   - **Same as published folder**. If the path specified in the user request is identical to the path on the published Web server.

   - **The following folder**. If the path specified in the user request needs to be mapped to a virtual directory with a different name on a Web server. Type the path to which requests on the published Web server will be mapped. When specifying the internal path to which the request will be mapped, use this format: /path/*.

7. Click **OK** to close the Web publishing rule properties dialog box.

How to Configure Web Listeners

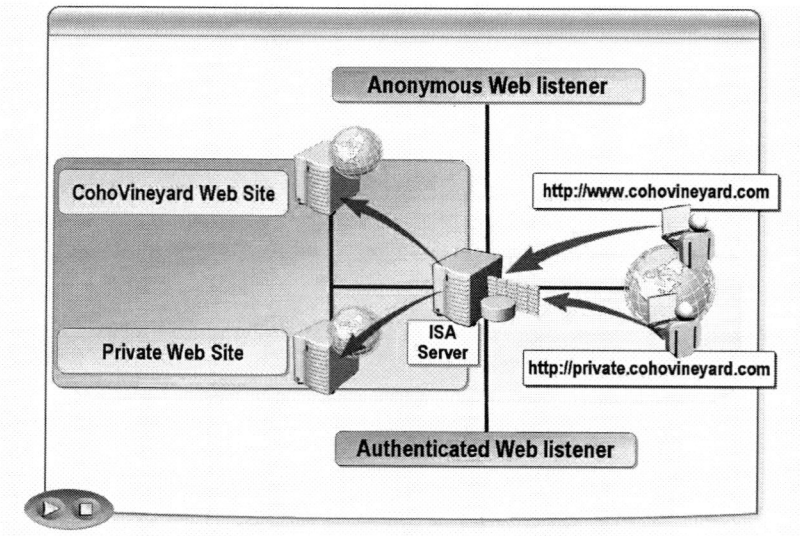

Introduction

Web listeners are used by Web and secure Web publishing rules. A *Web listener* is an ISA Server configuration object that defines how the ISA Server computer listens for HTTP requests and SSL requests. The Web listener defines the IP address and the port number on which ISA Server listens for client connections.

Web listener configuration options

Unless you configure a Web listener for incoming requests, ISA Server discards all of the incoming Web requests before applying Web server publishing rules. If the computer running ISA Server has multiple network adapters or IP addresses, you can configure the same listener configuration for all IP addresses, or you can configure separate listener configurations for different IP addresses. A Web listener can be used in multiple Web publishing rules.

To configure a Web listener, you must configure the following options:

- *Network.* This option specifies the network on which ISA Server will listen for incoming Web requests. The network that you select depends on where the Web requests will be coming from. For example, if the published Web site allows client requests from the external network (Internet), then the external network should be selected for the Web listener. After selecting a network, you can also specify whether the Web listener will listen for requests on all IP addresses on ISA Server that are part of that network, or on specified IP addresses.

- *Port numbers.* This option specifies the port number on which the Web listener will listen for incoming Web requests. By default, ISA Server listens on port 80 for HTTP requests, but this setting can be modified. You can also enable the Web listener to listen for SSL requests (the default is port 443). If you choose SSL, an appropriate certificate must be installed on the computer running ISA Server so that the computer running ISA Server can authenticate itself to the client.

■ *Client authentication methods*. This option specifies the supported authentication methods if you are going to require authentication on the Web listener. If you select the option to require authentication, all users must authenticate using one of the authentication methods specified for the incoming Web requests. The authentication that you configure for the computer running ISA Server is in addition to any authentication that the published Web server requires. ISA Server authentication determines whether a request is passed on to the Web server. The authentication method that you configure for the Web server determines whether a user is allowed to gain access to content on the Web server.

■ *Client Connection Settings*. This option specifies the number of concurrent client connections and connection timeout values for the Web listener.

Configuring a Web listener

To configure Web listener settings, use the following procedure:

1. In the **ISA Server Management** console tree, click **Firewall Policy**.

2. On the **Toolbox** tab, expand **Network Objects** and then expand **Web Listeners**.

3. Double-click the **Web Listener** object. The following table summarizes the configuration options:

Choose this configuration option	To produce this action
Networks tab	Configure the networks on which the Web listener will listen for connections.
Listener IP selection (click Address on the Networks tab)	Configure the IP address or addresses from the selected network on which the Web listener will listen.
Preferences tab	Configure the HTTP and SSL port numbers.
Authentication	Configure the authentication options.
Advanced settings	Configure concurrent client connections and timeout values.
RSA SecurID tab	Configure the RSA SecurID authentication options.

How to Configure Link Translation

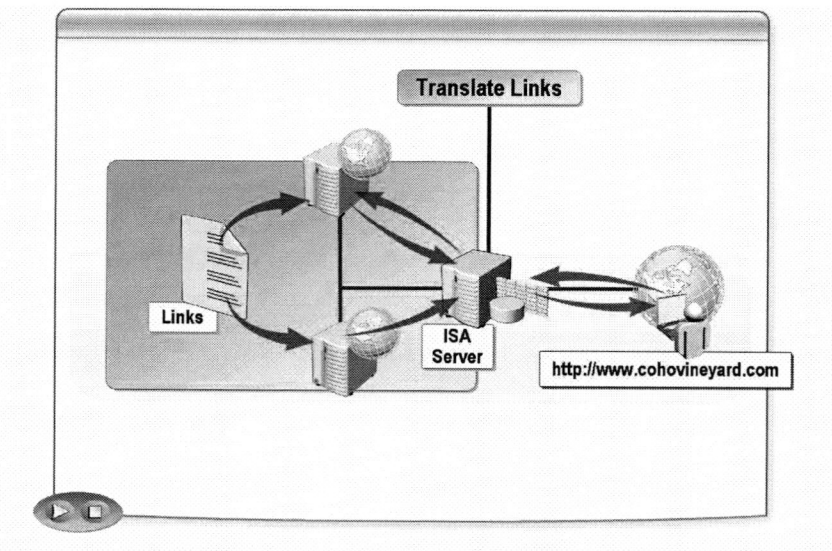

Introduction

Link translation is used by Web and secure Web publishing rules. *Link Translation* is an ISA Server configuration object that enables ISA Server to replace internal server names on Web pages with server names that are accessible from this Internet.

Some published Web sites may include references to internal names of computers. These internal computer names are not accessible to clients outside the network, so these references could appear as broken links. ISA Server includes a link translation feature to ensure that the information on these servers is accessible to Internet clients without requiring that the internal server names be revealed or accessible.

Link translation levels

ISA Server provides several levels of link translation functionality so that you can provide the appropriate level of link connectivity:

- *Header link translation.* Header link translation ensures that any URL returned in a header to the client is translated to an externally recognizable URL. When the user accesses the link, it is recognized by the Web publishing rule and forwarded to the correct internal server. This link translation is always enabled by default in any Web publishing rule.

- *Translation of links in the body of a returned Web page.* This functions in the same manner as the header link translation, but includes links returned in the body of Web pages, not just in the header. To enable this link translation, you need to enable the replacement of absolute links in Web pages on a Web publishing rule.

■ *Translation of links to other internal Web pages.* Link translation works only for links to the Web server specified in the Web publishing rule. If you want links to other internal Web servers to also be translated, you have to provide information about how to translate each link. This information is stored by ISA Server in a link dictionary.

For example, Coho Vineyard may have two internal Web servers named Web-01, hosting www.cohovineyard.com, and Web-02. The www.cohovineyard.com Web site may include cross-references to content on Web-02. For example, a Web page may have a reference to http://Web-02/images/image.gif. This link will not work on the Internet. You can create a link translation dictionary entry for the www.cohovineyard.com Web publishing rule substituting any reference to Web-02 with www.cohovineyard.com.

Configuring link translation

To configure link translation, use the following procedure:

1. In the **ISA Server Management** console tree, click **Firewall Policy**.

2. In the details pane, click the applicable Web publishing rule.

3. On the **Link Translation** tab, click **Replace links in Web pages** to enable link translation. Clicking this option enables link translation for Web page bodies.

4. To enable link translation to other internal Web pages, click **Add** to open the **Add/Edit Dictionary Item** dialog box.

5. In **Replace this text**, provide the internal name of the server to be translated, such as Web-02. In **With this text**, provide the replacement value, such as www.cohovineyard.com. Click **OK**.

6. Click **OK** to close the Web publishing rule properties dialog box.

How to Configure a New Web Publishing Rule

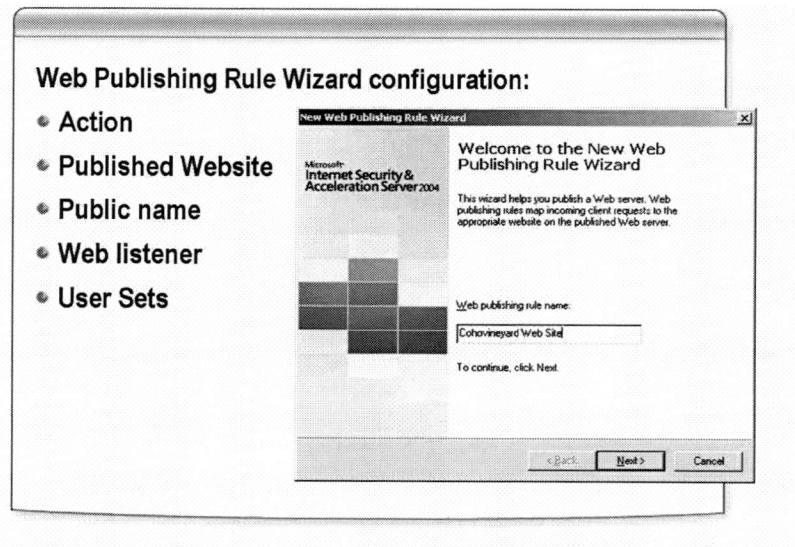

Web Publishing Rule Wizard configuration:

* Action
* Published Website
* Public name
* Web listener
* User Sets

Configuring a new Web publishing rule

The following steps provide a high-level overview of the process of creating a Web publishing rule; the detailed steps are included in the subsequent practice.

1. In **ISA Server Management**, click **Firewall Policy**, and then click **Publish a Web Server** to start the **New Web Publishing Rule Wizard**.

2. Configure a rule action.

3. Configure the options listed in the following table to define which Web site to publish.

Configuration option	Explanation
Computer name or IP Address	Specifies the Web server computer name or IP address for the server that hosts the Web site that you want to publish.
Forward the original host header instead of the actual one	Specifies that ISA Server forward the host header that it received from the client. By default, ISA Server substitutes a host header that it uses to refer to the internal Web server, rather than sending the original host header that ISA Server received. This means that a client request that includes the host header of Host: www.cohovineyard.com is replaced with Host: Den-Web-01.cohovineyard.com as specified in the Web publishing rule. All requests are then routed to the same Web site on the published server.
	To publish more than one Web site on a Web server, configure the Web publishing rule to forward the original host header to the published server. For example, if client requests for www.cohovineyard.com and www.cohowineries.com need to be forwarded to two different Web sites on the same internal server, configure the Web publishing rule to forward the original host header.

(continued)

Configuration option	Explanation
Folder	Specifies the Web site folder that you want to publish, such as Sales. If you leave this field blank, you will be publishing the entire site.

4. Configure a public name, which defines what requests will be received by the ISA Server computer and forwarded to the Web server. You have two options:

   - **Any domain name.** This option means that any request that is resolved to the IP address of the external Web listener of the ISA Server computer will be forwarded to your Web site.

   - **This domain name (type below).** This option means that the ISA Server will forward only requests for a specific URL. To configure this, type the specific domain name in **Public Name**. You can also specify a specific folder in **Folder** that would also be required in the request. For example, if you configure the www.cohovineyard.com as the public name and Sales as the folder, then only requests for www.cohovineyard.com/sales will be forwarded by this rule.

5. Select an existing Web listener or create a new Web listener.

6. Configure the user sets that will have access to the server.

7. Complete the **New Web Publishing Rule Wizard** and apply the changes you have made.

Practice: Configuring Web Publishing

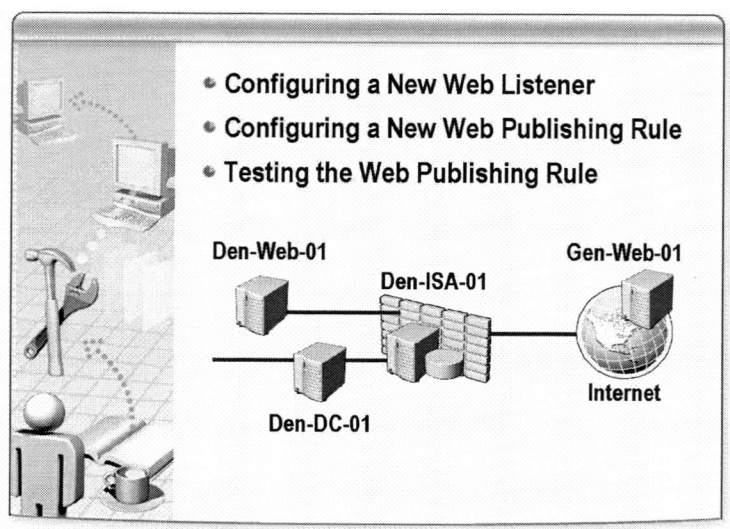

Introduction

In this practice, you will configure a new Web listener to accept HTTP requests on the external interface for the Web server. You will then use this Web listener to configure a Web publishing rule to publish the www.cohovineyard.com site to the Internet. Finally, you will test the Web publishing rule.

▶ **To prepare for this practice**

1. You will need the Den-DC-01 virtual machine, the Den-Web-01 virtual machine, the Den-ISA-01 virtual machine, and the Gen-Web-01 virtual machine for this practice.

2. If necessary, start or resume the required virtual machines and then, on Den-ISA-01, log on to the cohovineyard domain with your user name and password.

Practice

▶ **Configuring a new Web listener**

1. Open **ISA Server Management**, if necessary expand **Den-ISA-01**, and then click **Firewall Policy**.

2. On the **Toolbox** tab, expand **Network Objects**, click **New**, and then click **Web Listener**.

3. On the **Welcome to the New Web Listener Wizard** page, in the Web listener name field, type **HTTP Listener** and then click **Next**.

4. On the **IP Addresses** page, select **External** and then click **Next**.

5. On the **Port Specification** page, ensure that **Enable HTTP** is selected and that **HTTP port** is 80. Click **Next**.

6. On the **Completing to the New Web Listener Wizard** page, review the configuration and click **Finish**.

7. Click **Apply** to apply the changes and then click **OK** when the changes have been applied.

▶ **Configuring a new Web publishing rule**

1. On the **Tasks** tab, click **Publish a Web Server**.

2. On the **Welcome to the New Web Publishing Rule Wizard** page, in the **Web publishing rule name** field, type **Coho Vineyard Web Site** and click **Next**.

3. On the **Select Rule Action** page, ensure that the default **Allow** is selected. Click **Next**.

4. On the **Select Web Site to Publish** page, in the **Computer name or IP Address** box, type **www.cohovineyard.com**. Accept the default settings for the other options and click **Next**.

5. On the **Public Name Details** page, in the **Accept requests for** list, click **This domain name (type below)**. In the **Public Name** box, type **www.cohovineyard.com** and then click **Next**.

6. On the **Select Web Listener** page, click **HTTP Listener** in the **Web listener** list. Click **Next**.

7. On the **User Sets** page, accept the default. Click **Next**.

8. On the **Completing the New Web Publishing Rule Wizard** page, review the configuration settings and click **Finish**.

9. If you receive an **ISA Server Error** message, click **Continue**.

10. Click **Apply** to apply the changes and then click **OK** when the changes have been applied.

▶ **Testing Internet access to the www.cohovineyard.com Web site**

1. Switch to the Gen-Web-01 virtual machine.

2. If necessary, log on to Gen-Web-01 with a user name of **Administrator** and a password of **P@ssw0rd**.

3. Open **Internet Explorer** and type **www.cohovineyard.com** into the **Address** box. The connection should be successful. Close **Internet Explorer**.

Lesson: Configuring Secure Web Publishing

- What Is Secure Sockets Layer?
- How to Prepare ISA Server for SSL
- How SSL Bridging Works
- How SSL Tunneling Works
- How to Configure a New Secure Web Publishing Rule

Introduction

Secure Web publishing provides an additional layer of security when publishing an internal Web site by enabling the option to use Secure Sockets Layer (SSL) to encrypt all network traffic to and from the Web site. This lesson describes how to configure secure Web publishing.

Lesson objectives

After completing this lesson, you will be able to:

- Describe SSL.
- Prepare ISA Server 2004 for SSL.
- Describe SSL bridging.
- Describe SSL tunneling.
- Configure secure Web publishing.

What Is Secure Sockets Layer?

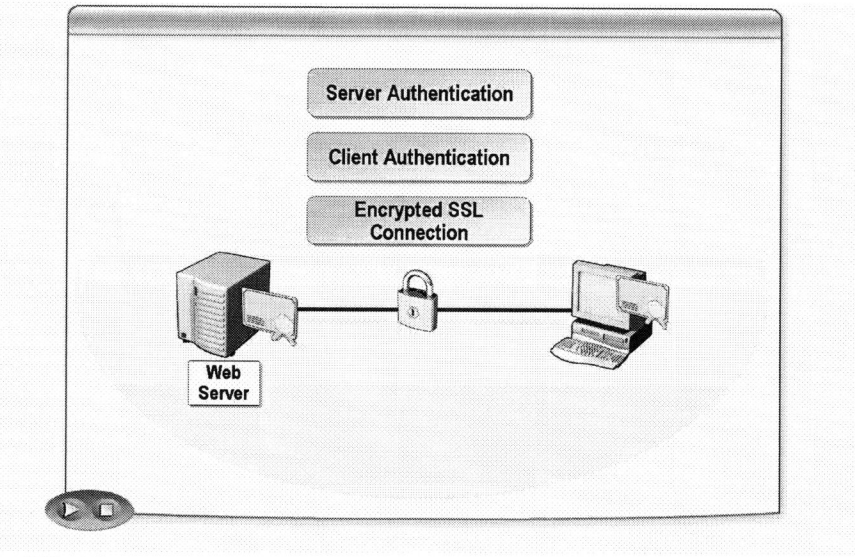

Introduction

Secure Sockets Layer (SSL) is used to validate the identities of two computers involved in a connection across a public network, and to ensure that the data sent between the two parties cannot be read by anyone else on the network.

SSL features

SSL includes the following features:

- *Server authentication.* Server authentication allows a user to confirm a server's identity. SSL-enabled client software can use standard techniques of public-key cryptography to check that a server's certificate and public ID are valid and have been issued by a certificate authority (CA) that the client is configured to trust.

- *Client authentication.* Client authentication allows a server to confirm a user's identity. Using the same techniques as those used for server authentication, SSL-enabled server software can check that a client's certificate and public ID are valid and have been issued by a certificate authority (CA) listed in the server's list of trusted CAs. Client authentication is optional for most secure Web sites.

- *Encrypted SSL connection.* All network traffic, including the confidential parts of the authentication process, is sent using an encrypted SSL connection that is created between the client and server. In addition, the client and server will automatically detect if the data sent over an encrypted SSL connection has been altered in transit.

Enabling SSL

To enable SSL on ISA Server, you must obtain a digital server certificate issued by a certificate authority. You can obtain a certificate from a public CA, or deploy a CA inside your organization by using Microsoft Windows® 2000 Server or Microsoft Windows Server™ 2003. If users from outside your organization will be accessing the Web site, you should obtain the certificate from a commercial CA because their client software will not be configured to trust your internal CA.

If you want to require client authentication, you must also distribute certificates to all clients that will be connecting to the Web site.

How to Prepare ISA Server for SSL

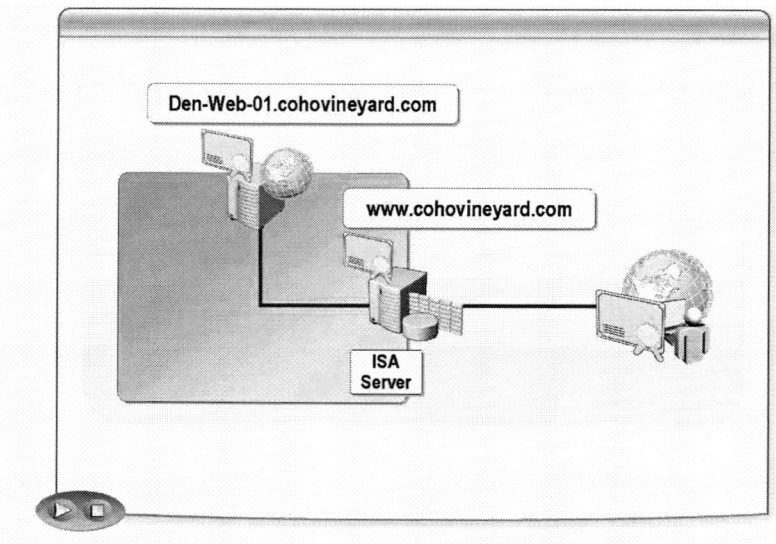

Introduction

SSL can be used in several different ways when publishing Web sites on ISA Server. First, SSL can be used to secure the connection from the Internet to the server running ISA Server. SSL can also be used to secure the connection from ISA Server to the internal Web server. One or both of these options can be used in a Web publishing scenario.

Preparing ISA Server for SSL

Before you can use SSL, you must install a server certificate on ISA Server. Depending on the required configuration, you may also need to install a certificate on the internal Web server.

To install SSL certificates in a Web publishing scenario, follow these high-level steps:

1. Request and install a server certificate on the server running ISA Server. The common name on the certificate must be the fully qualified domain name (FQDN), such as www.cohovineyard.com, that users use to access the Web site. If the common name on the certificate does not match the FQDN used by client computers to access the Web site, clients will receive an error message when they send HTTPS requests. You must install this certificate before ISA Server can accept secure client connections.

   The procedure for installing a server certificate on the computer running ISA Server varies depending on the CA you are using and on the ISA Server configuration.

   a. If you are using an internal CA that provides a Web site for clients to obtain certificates, you can connect to the Web site from the ISA Server and apply for and install the certificate.

b. If you are using an external CA, you need to create a certificate request and forward it to the external CA. You can create the certificate request on the server running ISA Server. However, this requires that IIS be installed on the computer running ISA Server. This is not recommended, so you should prepare the request and install the certificate on the Web server computer, then export it and import it to the ISA Server computer. Remember that this certificate must bear the fully qualified domain name that client computers will use to access the Web site.

2. Request and install a server certificate on the Web servers. The name on the certificate must be the FQDN that ISA Server uses to access the Web site. For example, if the Web publishing rule specifies Web-01.cohovineyard.com as the internal server name, then this must be the FQDN on the certificate. You must install this certificate before the Web servers can accept SSL tunneling connections and before the Web servers can accept secure connections from ISA Server.

3. If you are going to configure ISA Server or the internal Web server to require client certificate authentication, then you need to deploy client certificates to all computers that will be SSL clients. If you are using an internal CA, you may also want to take this step to ensure that the client computers are configured to trust your internal CA.

How SSL Bridging Works

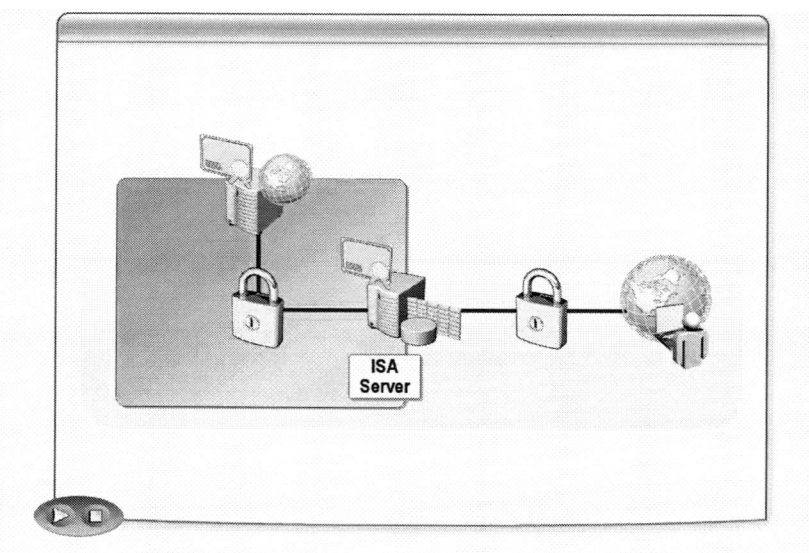

Introduction

One of the options that ISA Server provides for securing network traffic is SSL bridging. SSL bridging means that the ISA Server operates as the end point for an SSL connection. The SSL connection could be between ISA Server and the client or between ISA Server and the internal Web server. The primary benefit of using SSL bridging is that it enables application filtering of SSL traffic.

How SSL bridging works

SSL bridging is used when ISA Server ends or initiates an SSL connection. This connection can be with the client computer, with the internal Web server, or both.

A common scenario in which SSL bridging is used is in a Web publishing scenario.

1. An external client uses HTTPS to request an object from a Web server located on the internal network. By default, the client connects to ISA Server on the standard SSL port (port 443). ISA Server responds with a server-side SSL certificate to the client and the client authenticates the server. After authentication, the client and server create a secure encryption channel.

2. ISA Server accepts the client's request and decrypts it, terminating the SSL connection. If the object is in the cache, ISA Server returns the object to the client.

3. If the object is not in the cache, ISA Server forwards the request to the internal Web server specified in the Web publishing rule. The Web publishing rule also defines how ISA Server communicates the request to the published Web server (FTP, HTTP, or SSL). If the secure Web publishing rule is configured to forward the request using HTTPS, ISA Server initiates a new SSL connection with the Web server, sending a request to port 443. Because the ISA Server computer is now an SSL client, the Web server responds with a server-side certificate. If the Web server requires a client certificate, ISA Server must respond with the appropriate certificate.

4. After the SSL connection has been created, the Web Server responds by sending the requested object back to ISA Server.

5. ISA Server receives the object and decrypts it. ISA Server then re-encrypts the object and passes it to the requesting client.

One of the most important benefits of using SSL bridging is that it allows stateful inspection of SSL connections and application-layer filtering of the contents of HTTPS packets. Because ISA Server decrypts each packet, it can inspect the application-layer data before re-encrypting the packet. This prevents attackers from hiding malicious code inside SSL packets.

SSL bridging options

ISA Server supports three SSL bridging options:

- *SSL bridging from ISA Server to the client.* A client requests an SSL object. ISA Server decrypts the request and forwards it to the Web server. The Web server returns the HTTP object to ISA Server. ISA Server encrypts the object and sends it to the client. In this scenario, SSL is used to secure only the connection between ISA Server and the client.

- *SSL bridging from ISA Server to the Web server.* A client requests an HTTP object from an internal Web server. ISA Server accepts the request, encrypts it, and forwards it to the Web server. The Web server returns an encrypted object to ISA Server. Then, ISA Server decrypts the object and sends it to the client. In this scenario, SSL is used to secure only the connection between ISA Server and the Web server.

- *SSL bridging from client to Web Server.* The client requests an SSL object. ISA Server decrypts the request, and then encrypts it again and forwards it to the Web server. The Web server returns the encrypted object to ISA Server. ISA Server decrypts the object and then encrypts it again and sends it to the client. In this scenario, SSL is used to encrypt all connections.

How SSL Tunneling Works

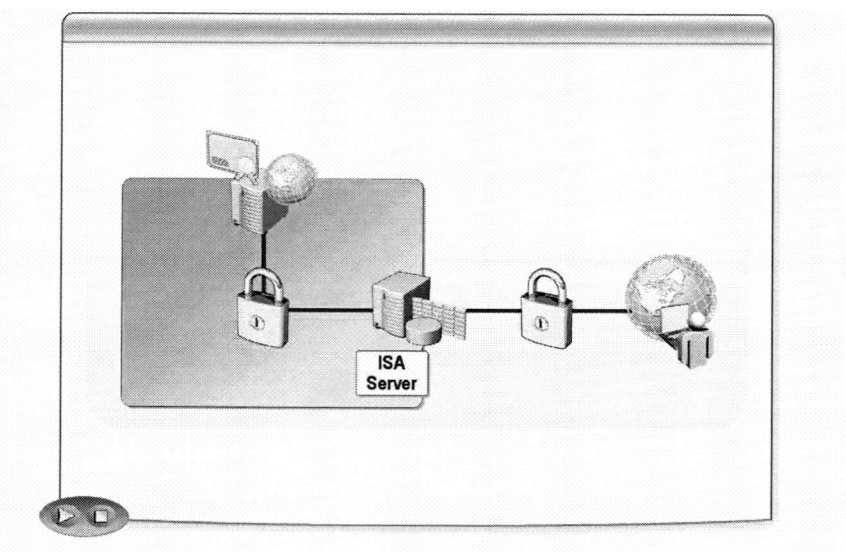

Introduction

In an SSL tunneling scenario, ISA Server does not encrypt or decrypt packets, but simply forwards SSL packets from the client to the Web server. SSL tunneling means that ISA Server does not need to decrypt SSL packets, but it also means that the encrypted packets cannot be inspected by ISA Server.

How SSL tunneling works

In SSL tunneling mode, a client can establish a tunnel through the computer running ISA Server directly to the internal Web server. In tunneling mode, the connection between the client and the Web server is encrypted, but ISA Server does not inspect the contents of the connection. Because ISA Server does not decrypt the packet, it cannot inspect the application-layer contents of the packet. Therefore, no policy or filtering is applied.

SSL tunneling can also be used in a Web publishing scenario:

1. An external client uses HTTPS to request an object from a Web server located on the internal network. The request is sent to an external IP address on ISA Server.

2. ISA Server checks the Web publishing rule for the request. If the rule specifies SSL tunneling mode, ISA Server forwards the request to the internal Web server without decrypting the packet.

3. The Web server responds with a server-side SSL certificate to the client and the client authenticates the server. After authentication, the client and server create a secure encryption channel.

4. The Web server then encrypts the requested object and sends it to ISA Server, which forwards it to the client.

How to Configure a New Secure Web Publishing Rule

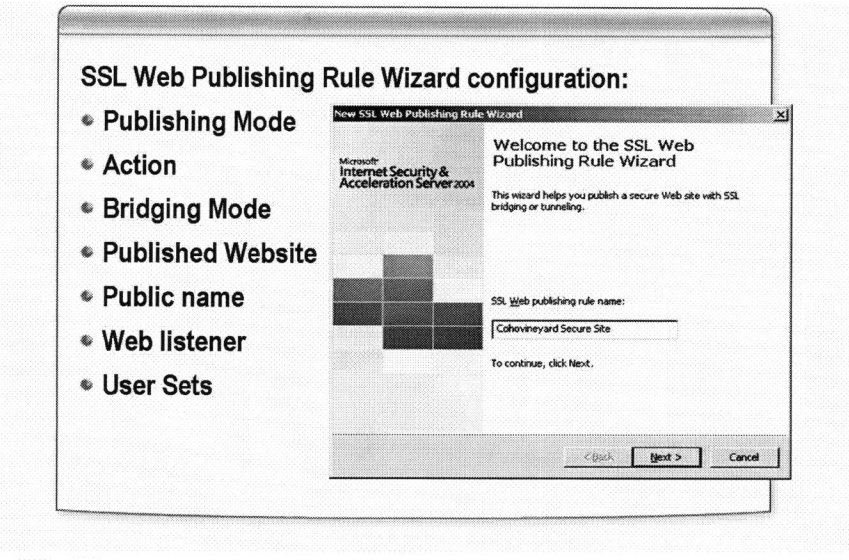

SSL Web Publishing Rule Wizard configuration:

- Publishing Mode
- Action
- Bridging Mode
- Published Website
- Public name
- Web listener
- User Sets

Configuring a new secure Web publishing rule

The following steps provide a high-level overview of the process of creating a new secure Web publishing rule; the detailed steps are included in the subsequent practice.

1. From **ISA Server Management**, run the **New Web Publishing Rule Wizard**.

2. Configure the publishing mode to use either SSL bridging or SSL tunneling.

3. If you selected SSL bridging, then configure a bridging mode. Choose one of the options listed in the following table.

Configuration option	Explanation
Secure connection to clients	When you select this mode, ISA Server establishes a secure HTTPS connection with the client, but forwards the request as standard HTTP to the published Web server.
Secure connection to Web server	When you select this mode, ISA Server establishes a standard HTTP connection with the client, but forwards the request as secure HTTPS to the published Web server.
Secure connection to client and Web server	When you select this mode, ISA Server establishes a secure HTTPS connection with the client, and also forwards the request as secure HTTPS to the published Web server.

4. Configure the Web site that you are publishing using the options listed in the following table.

Configuration option	Explanation
Computer name or IP address	Specifies the Web server computer name or IP address for the server that hosts the Web site that you want to publish.
Forward the original host header instead of the actual one	Specifies that ISA Server forward the host header that it received from the client. By default, ISA Server substitutes a host header that it uses to refer to the internal Web server, rather than sending the original host header that ISA Server received. When you are publishing a secure Web site, the host header passed to the Web Server must match the common name assigned to the digital certificate on the published Web server.
Folder	Specifies the Web site folder that you want to publish, such as Sales. If you leave this field blank, you will be publishing the entire site.

5. Configure a public name, which defines what requests will be received by the computer running ISA Server and forwarded to the Web server. You have two options:

   - **Any domain name.** This option means that any request that is resolved to the IP address of the external Web listener of the computer running ISA Server will be forwarded to your Web site. This option is less secure than using is specific domain name.

   - **This domain name (type below).** This option means that ISA Server will forward only requests for a specific URL. To configure this, type the specific domain name in **Public Name**. You can also specify a specific folder in **Folder** that would also be required in the request. For example, if you configure the www.cohovineyard.com as the public name and Sales as the folder, then only requests for www.cohovineyard.com/sales will be forwarded by this rule.

6. Select an existing Web listener or create a new Web listener.

7. Configure the user sets that will have access to the server.

8. Complete the **New SSL Web Publishing Rule Wizard** and apply the changes.

Practice: Configuring Secure Web Publishing

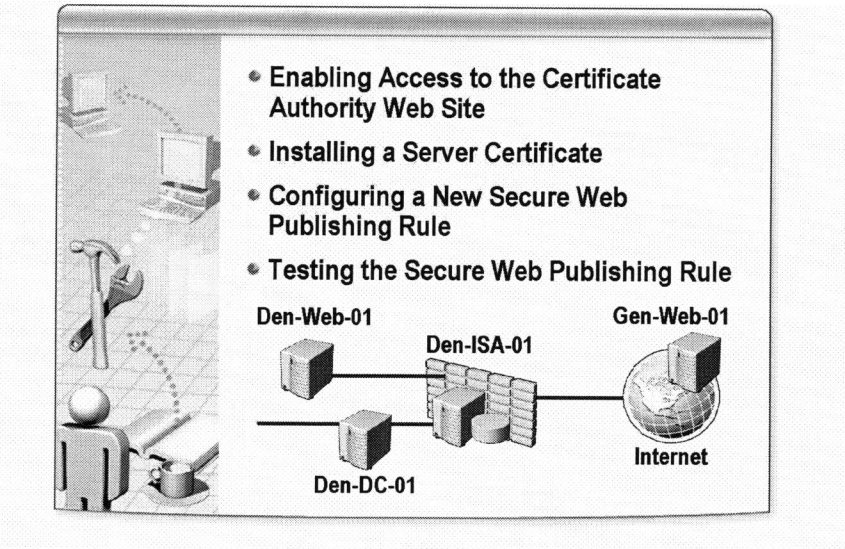

Introduction

In this practice, you will install a server certificate required for SSL on ISA Server. You will also configure a new secure Web publishing rule to publish the store.cohovineyard.com site to the Internet. Then you will test the Web publishing rule.

Note The Den-DC-01 virtual machine is configured as an Enterprise Root CA.

The server certificates must be installed on all servers that will accept SSL connections. In the case of secure Web publishing, this will be the computer running ISA Server, and may also include the Web server computer. In the case of server publishing, this will only be the server computer that you are publishing. If you installed a stand-alone root CA rather than an enterprise root CA, there are also actions that take place on the certification authority.

▶ **To prepare for this practice**

1. You will need the Den-DC-01 virtual machine, the Den-Web-01 virtual machine, the Den-ISA-01 virtual machine, and the Gen-Web-01 virtual machine for this practice.

2. If necessary, start or resume the required virtual machines and then, on Den-ISA-01, log on to the cohovineyard domain with your user name and password.

Practice

▶ **Enabling access to the certificate authority Web site**

1. Open **ISA Server Management**.

2. Ensure **Firewall Policy** is selected under the **DEN-ISA-01** computer node.

3. On the **Tasks** tab, click **Edit System Policy**.

4. In the **System Policy Editor** dialog box, in **Configuration Groups**, under **Various**, click **Allowed Sites**.

5. On the **To** tab, click **System Policy Allowed Sites** and then click **Edit**.

6. Click **New**, and type ***.cohovineyard.com**.

7. Click **OK** and then click **OK** again to close the **System Policy Editor**.

8. Click **Apply** to apply the changes and then click **OK** when the changes have been applied.

▶ **Installing a certificate on ISA Server**

1. Open Internet Explorer.

2. If you receive an Internet Explorer message, click **In the future do not show this message** and click **OK**.

3. In the **Address** bar, type **http://Den-DC-01.cohovineyard.com/certsrv**.

4. Log in as **cohovineyard\administrator** with a password of **P@ssw0rd**.

5. On the **Welcome** page, under **Select a task**, click **Request a certificate**.

6. On the **Request a Certificate** page, click **advanced certificate request**.

7. On the **Advanced Certificate Request** page, click **Create and submit a request to this CA**.

8. On the **Advanced Certificate Request** page, in the **Certificate Template** drop-down list, click **Web Server**. Complete the form using the following information:

   • Name: **Secure.cohovineyard.com**

   • E-Mail: **Administrator@cohovineyard.com**

   • Company: **Coho Vineyard**

   • Department: **IT**

   • City: **Denver**

   • State: **Colorado**

   • Country/Region: **US**

9. Under **Key Options**, select **Store Certificate in the local computer certificate store**.

10. Submit the request by clicking **Submit**. Review the two warning dialog boxes that appear, and click **Yes** for both.

11. Click **Install this certificate**. Review the warning dialog box that appears, and then click **Yes**. When you receive the message that the certificate is successfully installed, close **Internet Explorer**.

▶ **Configuring a new secure Web publishing rule**

1. In **ISA Server Management**, ensure that **Firewall Policy** is selected under the **DEN-ISA-01** node.

2. On the **Tasks** tab, click **Publish a Secure Web Server**.

3. On the **Welcome to the SSL Web Publishing Rule Wizard** page, in the **SSL Web publishing rule name** field, type **Coho Vineyard Store Site** and click **Next**.

4. On the **Publishing Mode** page, accept the default configuration of **SSL Bridging** and click **Next**.

5. On the **Select Rule Action** page, ensure that the default **Allow** is selected. Click **Next**.

6. On the **Bridging Mode** page, click **Secure connection to clients**. Click **Next**.

7. On the **Select Web Site to Publish** page, in the **Computer name or IP Address** box, type **Den-Web-01.cohovineyard.com**. Accept the default settings for the other options and click **Next**.

8. On the **Public Name Details** page, ensure **This domain name (type below)** is selected in the **Accept requests from** box. Then type **Secure.cohovineyard.com** in the **Public Name** box. Click **Next**.

9. On the **Select Web Listener** page, click **New** to create a new Web listener.

10. On the **Welcome to the New Web Listener Wizard** page, in the **Web listener name** field, type **HTTPS Listener** and click **Next**.

11. On the **IP Addresses** page, click **External** and then click **Next**.

12. On the **Port Specification** page, clear the check box for **Enable HTTP** and select the check box for **Enable SSL**. Ensure that the **SSL port** is **443**. Click **Select**.

13. In the **Select Certificate** dialog box, select the certificate from the CohovineyardCA and then click **OK**.

14. Click **Next**.

15. On the **Completing to the New Web Listener Wizard** page, review the configuration and click **Finish**.

16. On the **Select Web Listener** page, click **Next**.

17. On the **User Sets** page, accept the default, **All Users**. Click **Next**.

18. On the **Completing the New SSL Web Publishing Rule Wizard** page, review the configuration settings, and click **Finish**.

19. Click **Apply** to apply the changes and then click **OK** when the changes have been applied.

▶ **Testing the secure Web publishing rule**

1. Switch to the Gen-Web-01 virtual machine.

2. Open **Internet Explorer** and type **https://secure.cohovineyard.com** into the **Address** box.

3. If you receive an **Internet Explorer Security Alert**, click **OK**. The connection should be successful.

Lesson: Configuring Server Publishing

* Server Publishing Configuration Options
* How Server Publishing Works
* How to Configure a Server Publishing Rule
* How to Publish Media Services
* How to Publish Microsoft SharePoint Portal Server
* How to Troubleshoot Web and Server Publishing

Introduction

Server publishing is a secure and flexible way to publish the content or services provided by internal servers to the Internet. This lesson describes how to configure server publishing.

Lesson objectives

After completing this lesson, you will be able to:

- List server publishing configuration options.
- Describe how server publishing works.
- Configure a new server publishing rule.
- Describe how media services can be published by using ISA Server.
- Describe how Microsoft SharePoint® Portal Server can be published by using ISA Server.
- Troubleshoot Web and server publishing.

Server Publishing Configuration Options

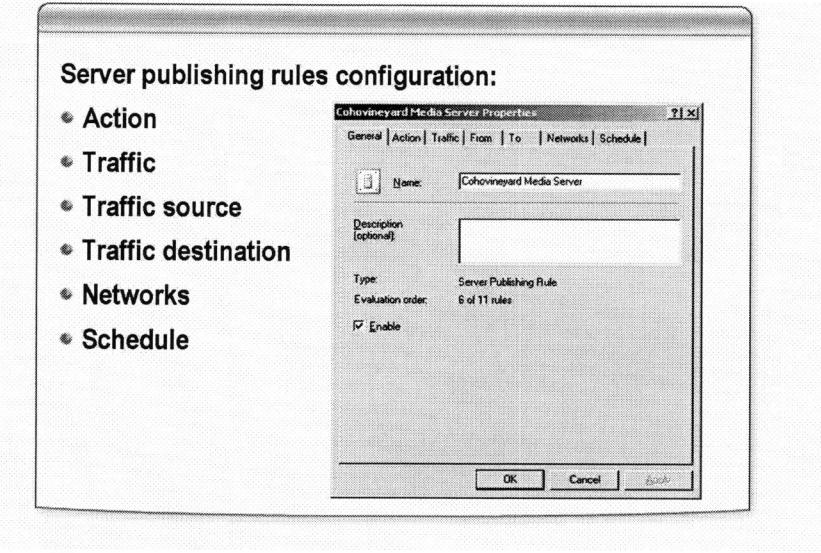

Server publishing rules configuration:

* Action
* Traffic
* Traffic source
* Traffic destination
* Networks
* Schedule

Introduction

Web publishing rules are used on ISA Server to enable access to HTTP and HTTPS content on internal Web servers. Server publishing rules are used to enable access to internal content using other protocols. Before you can create a server publishing rule for a particular protocol, however, a protocol definition for the protocol must be configured on ISA Server. ISA Server comes pre-configured with a number of protocol definitions for commonly used protocols that can be used for server publishing rules. You can also create additional protocols.

Server publishing configuration options

When you configure server publishing rules, you need to configure the components listed in the following table.

Configuration option	Explanation
Action	Enables a server publishing rule to be configured to allow network traffic that matches the publishing rule.
Traffic	Defines the protocol that is allowed by this server publishing rule. One server publishing rule can enable only one protocol. To enable more protocols, you must configure multiple server publishing rules.
Traffic source	Defines the network objects that can access the published server. You can limit access to the published server based on networks, network sets, computers, computer sets, address ranges, or subnets.

(*continued*)

Configuration option	Explanation
Traffic destination	Defines the IP address of the published server. You can also configure whether the client requests will appear to come from the client computer or from ISA Server. On a server publishing rule, the default is that the client requests appear to come from the original client.
Networks	Defines the network on which ISA Server will listen for connections on the protocol port. You can also configure ISA Server to listen on all IP addresses on the specified network, or only on specific IP addresses.
Schedule	Defines when the server publishing rule will be active.

Port override options

When you create a server publishing rule, ISA Server listens for client requests on the default port for that protocol. However, you can modify the ports used by ISA Server. You can configure ISA Server to publish on a port other than the default port. For example, you can configure the server publishing rule for FTP services to listen for client connections on port 2211 rather than on port 21. You can also specify that ISA Server redirect the client request to an alternate port number on the internal server. You could configure ISA Server to send all FTP requests to port 2121 on the internal server (assuming that the internal FTP server has been modified to provide FTP services on that port). In either case, ISA Server receives client requests for the published service on the firewall port specified, and then forwards requests to the designated port on the published server.

The port override option can be useful when multiple services are using the same default port number on one ISA Server. For example, you can publish one FTP server on the default port for one set of users, and publish another FTP server on another, nonstandard, port for a different set of users.

SSL for server publishing

Server publishing rules use SSL in essentially the same way that Web publishing rules use SSL tunneling. When a client connects to ISA Server using SSL, ISA Server simply redirects the SSL connection to the internal server. The client computer will establish the SSL connection directly with the internal server, not with ISA Server.

There is little configuration required on ISA Server to enable secure publishing. All you need to do to enable secure server publishing is to configure the server publishing rule to use a secure protocol. For example, to enable SSL access to an Internet Mail Access Protocol (IMAP) server, you just configure the server publishing rule to allow the IMAPS Server protocol rather than the IMAP4 Server protocol. This means that ISA Server will listen for client connections on port 993 rather than on 143. You do not need to configure a server certificate on ISA Server, but you do need to configure a server certificate on the internal server providing this service.

How Server Publishing Works

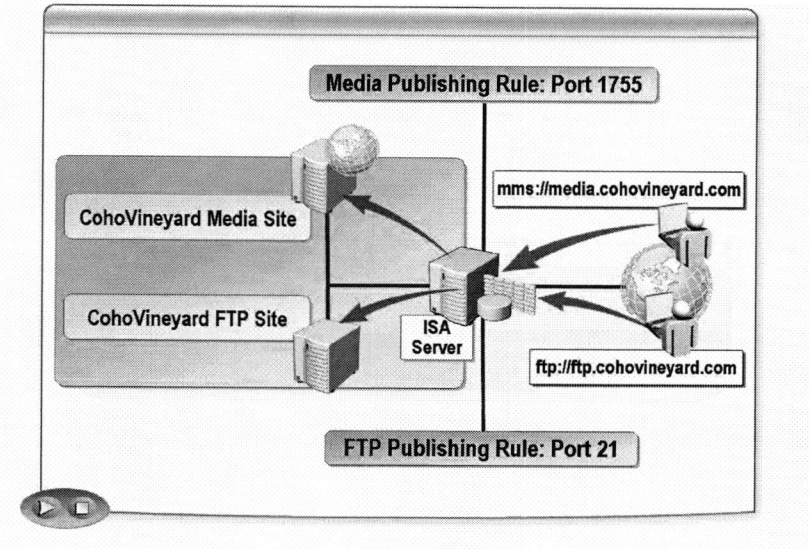

How server publishing works

A server publishing rule for a particular protocol is essentially a reverse NAT mapping. With a server publishing rule, ISA Server maps a port number on an external interface to an internal IP address. When ISA Server receives a request on the external IP address for a specific port, it passes the request to the internal server based on the port number.

ISA Server performs the following steps during server publishing:

1. A client computer on the Internet requests an object from the IP address that is known to provide that service. For example, if an organization wants to configure a media server that will be available to Internet clients, the organization needs to ensure that the correct host information is available on the Internet DNS servers. The IP address provided to the clients is the IP address of the external network interface of the computer running ISA Server. The client request is sent to the IP address.

2. The computer running ISA Server processes the request. It checks the destination port number and then uses the server publishing rule to map the IP address to an internal IP address of an internal server. The request is forwarded to the internal server.

3. The internal server returns the object to the computer running ISA Server, which passes it on to the requesting client.

How to Configure a Server Publishing Rule

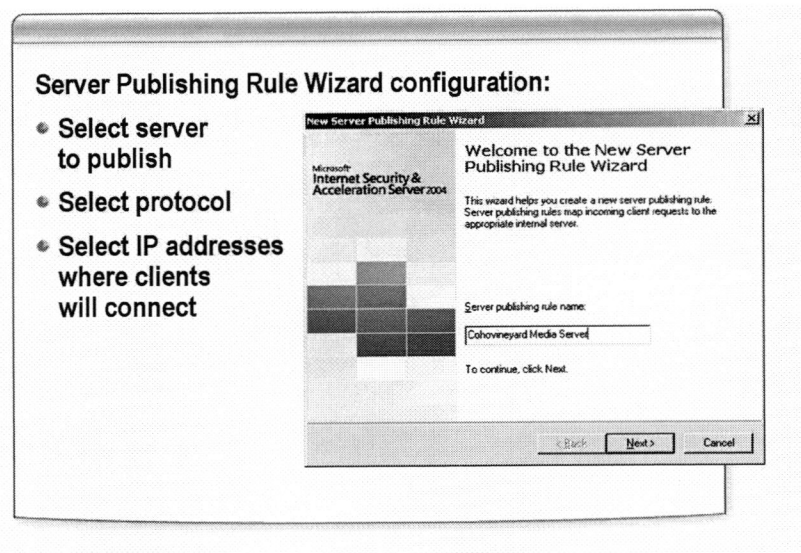

Server Publishing Rule Wizard configuration:

- Select server to publish
- Select protocol
- Select IP addresses where clients will connect

Configuring a server publishing rule

The following steps provide a high-level overview of the process of creating a new server publishing rule; the detailed steps are included in the subsequent practice.

1. Configure the internal server that you are publishing. The server must be configured as a SecureNAT client and have the required service installed and configured.

2. On ISA Server, run the **New Server Publishing Rule** wizard. When you run the wizard, you can configure what ports ISA Server will use. To do this, click **Ports** on the **Select Protocol** page. The port configuration options are listed in the following table.

Category	Configuration option	Use this option to:
Firewall ports	Publish using the default port defined in the protocol definition.	Configure ISA Server to listen for connections on the default protocol port.
Firewall ports	Publish on this port instead of on the default port.	Configure ISA Server to listen for connections on an alternative port.
Published server ports	Send requests to the default port on the published server.	Configure ISA Server to forward requests to the default protocol port on the published server.
Published server ports	Send requests to this port on the published server.	Configure ISA Server to forward requests to an alternative port on the published server.
Source ports	Allow traffic from any allowed source port.	Configure ISA Server to accept connection attempts on any port.
Source ports	Limit access to traffic from this range of source ports.	Configure ISA Server to accept connection attempts on a limited range of ports.

Practice: Configuring Server Publishing

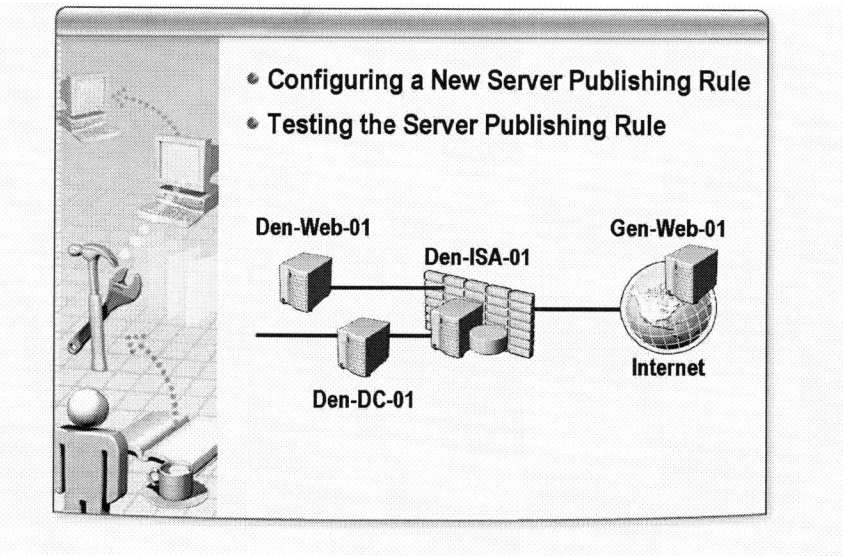

Introduction

In this practice, you will configure a new server publishing rule to publish the ftp.cohovineyard.com site to the Internet. Then you will test the server publishing rule.

▶ **To prepare for this practice**

1. You will need the Den-DC-01 virtual machine, the Den-Web-01 virtual machine, the Den-ISA-01 virtual machine, and the Gen-Web-01 virtual machine for this practice.

2. If necessary, start or resume the required virtual machines and then, on Den-ISA-01, log on to the cohovineyard domain with your user name and password.

Practice

▶ **Configuring a new server publishing rule**

1. If necessary, open **ISA Server Management**, expand the ISA Server computer node, and click **Firewall Policy**.

2. On the **Tasks** tab, click **Create New Server Publishing Rule** to start the **New Server Publishing Rule Wizard**.

3. On the **Welcome to the New Server Publishing Rule Wizard** page, in the **Server publishing rule name** box, type **Coho Vineyard FTP Site** and click **Next**.

4. On the **Select Server** page, in the **Server IP Address** box, type **172.16.1.11**. Click **Next**.

5. On the **Select Protocol** page, in the **Selected Protocol** list, click **FTP Server** and click **Next**.

6. On the **IP Addresses** page, select the check box for **External**. Click **Next**.

7. On the **Completing the New Server Publishing Rule Wizard** page, review the settings and click **Finish**.

8. Click **Apply** to apply the changes and then click **OK** when the changes have been applied.

▶ **Testing the server publishing rule**

1. Switch to the Gen-Web-01 virtual machine.

2. Open **Internet Explorer**. On the **Tools** menu, click **Internet Options**. On the **Advanced** tab, ensure **Enable folder view for FTP sites** is not selected and click **OK**.

3. In the **Address** box, type **ftp://ftp.cohovineyard.com** into the **Address** box.

4. If you receive an **Internet Explorer Security Alert**, click **Yes**.

5. If you receive the **Internet Explorer** warning message, click **Add** twice and then click **Close**. The connection should be successful.

How to Publish Media Services

> **ISA Server includes protocol definitions and application filters for:**
>
> * **Microsoft Media Streaming protocol (MMS)**
>   * Uses either TCP port 80 or TCP and UDP port 1755
>   * Enables access for Windows Media Player client
> * **Progressive Networks protocol (PNM)**
>   * Also called RealNetworks Streaming Media protocol
>   * Uses TCP port 7070
>   * Enables access for RealPlayer 5.0 and earlier clients
> * **Real Time Streaming Protocol (RTSP)**
>   * Uses port 554 for fast access and port 80 for slower access
>   * Enables access to media created and read with RealSystem G2 tools

Introduction

Many organizations need to make multimedia content available to users on the Internet. ISA Server can be used to enable secure access to media servers located on an internal or perimeter network.

Available media formats

ISA Server can enable the following media streaming protocols:

- *Microsoft Media Streaming protocol (MMS)*. MMS can use either TCP port 80 or TCP and User Datagram Protocol (UDP) port 1755. Using port 1755 makes the media traffic faster because it is using pure MMS technology and has no HTTP overhead. MMS uses the Microsoft Windows Media® Player client to access streaming media resources. MMS is the "carrier" of Advanced Streaming Format (ASF), the Microsoft propriety streaming protocol. ISA Server includes the MMS Server protocol definition and an MMS application filter.

- *Progressive Networks protocol (PNM)*. PNM (also called RealNetworks Streaming Media protocol) uses TCP port 7070. This protocol allows for backward compatibility with a RealPlayer 5.0 and earlier client. PNM protocol allows access and server publishing. ISA Server includes the PNM Server protocol definition and a PNM application filter.

- *Real Time Streaming Protocol (RTSP)*. RTSP uses port 554 for fast access and port 80 for slower access. RTSP supports both TCP and UDP connections. RTSP is designed specifically for clips created and read with RealSystem G2 tools. It is an open-standard protocol that supports SureStream files as well as Synchronized Multimedia Integration Language (SMIL), RealText, and RealPix files, which allows RealPlayer G2 and QuickTime 4 client access and server publishing capabilities. ISA Server includes the RTSP Server protocol definition and an RTSP application filter.

How to publish a media server

To publish a media server, create a new server publishing rule. Configure the rule to allow network traffic using the required protocol.

How to Publish Microsoft SharePoint Portal Server

A portal can present different types of information stored on different servers on the internal network

ISA Server can securely publish this information to the Internet using:

- Web publishing to publish the HTTP and HTTPS content using path mapping and link translation to hide the complexity of the internal network configuration
- Flexible authentication to grant only the required level of access
- Server publishing to publish services running protocols other than HTTP or HTTPS
- SSL bridging and tunneling to secure network traffic on the Internet

Introduction

Microsoft SharePoint Portal Server 2003 is a highly effective solution that provides a single interface point to information that comes from many different sources, and enables collaboration among all users who access the portal. SharePoint Portal Server 2003 portals are Web-based and accessible from Internet browsers through the HTTP and HTTPS protocols.

Publishing SharePoint Portal Server portals

ISA Server can be used to securely publish SharePoint Portal Server portals to the Internet. A single portal may contain many different types of information that is located in many different locations on the internal network. ISA Server provides flexible options for publishing all components on the portal to the Internet.

To publish a portal, you may need to use the following ISA Server features.

- *Web publishing*. Web publishing is the best way to make internal Web sites available on the Internet through ISA Server. A single portal may include information from multiple internal sites—using the path-mapping and link-translation features means that all these resources are accessible through a single external URL.

- *Flexible authentication*. A single portal may require many different levels of authentication, especially if the portal is accessible to employees, partner organizations, and customers. ISA Server provides the required authentication flexibility by supporting multiple authentication methods as well as supporting pass-through authentication and delegation of basic authentication.

- *Server publishing*. A portal can also contain content that is not accessible through HTTP or HTTPS. The portal may have links to media servers or FTP servers. To configure access to these resources, you can configure server publishing rules that provide transparent links between the portal page and other types of content.

- *SSL bridging and tunneling*. A portal site could include confidential information that needs to be protected when crossing the network. ISA Server provides flexible options for using SSL to encrypt authentication and data traffic.

Note A SharePoint Portal Server portal can contain may different types of information located on many different servers on the internal network. This can make the ISA Server configuration complex and difficult to implement. For detailed guidance on how to deploy ISA Server to protect SharePoint Portal Server, see the ISA Server 2000 SharePoint Portal Server Deployment Kit located at http://www.isaserver.org/articles/sharepointkit.html.

How to Troubleshoot Web and Server Publishing

To troubleshoot Web and server publishing issues:

- Check the resource availability
- Check the DNS records
- Check the error message
- Check which ports the ISA Server is listening on for connections
- Check the publishing rule configuration
- Check the SSL configuration and certificates

Introduction

By using the ISA Server publishing wizards, you can easily publish internal resources to the Internet. However, there are also many situations in which you may need to troubleshoot connectivity to those published resources.

Troubleshooting Web and server publishing

Use the following guidelines to troubleshoot ISA Server Web and server publishing issues:

- *Check the resource availability.* Can you access the published resource directly? For example, if you are publishing a Web site, try connecting to the Web site from a computer that is located on the same network as the Web server. If the Web site is not available from the same network, then the primary issue is related to the Web server and not to the ISA Server configuration.

- *Check the DNS records.* Does the resource named on the Internet resolve to an IP address on the external network adapter of the computer running ISA Server? If not, then check the zone information on the Internet DNS server that is authoritative for your domain name.

- *Check the error message.* When you fail to connect to the published resource, check the error message that you receive. This is particularly useful when troubleshooting Web publishing rules because HTTP defines a standard set of error messages. For example, if you fail to connect to the Web site and receive an Error 403 page, you know that the connection to the external IP of the computer running ISA Server has succeeded. The issue will therefore be an ISA Server Web publishing issue or an IIS issue. If you receive a 500 Internal Server Error page, there is likely a problem with the SSL certificate on the Web server.

- *Check which ports the ISA Server is listening on for connections.* You can check this by using the netstat utility. To use netstat, type **netstat -an** at a command prompt on the ISA Server computer. If ISA Server is not listening on a port 80 or a port 443, check the Web listener configuration. For other ports, check the server publishing rules configurations.

■ *Check the publishing rule configuration.* When configuring a Web publishing rule, ensure that the public name matches the name that an external user specifies to access the Web site. Also confirm that the internal destination server name or IP address is correct. If you are using a server name for the internal Web server, ensure that ISA Server can resolve the IP address for the server name. You can accomplish this by configuring ISA Server to use an internal DNS server that can provide name resolution, or configuring the server name in the HOSTS file on the computer running ISA Server.

■ *Check SSL configuration and certificates.* If a connection to a secure resource is failing, check the SSL configuration and the installed server certificates. In a secure Web publishing scenario, check the SSL bridging configuration and ensure that ISA Server and the Web server both have certificates if required. Also, check that the name on the certificate matches the FQDN that is used to connect to the certificate. In a server publishing scenario, check the certificate on the published server, and check the server publishing rule to ensure that it is configured to use a secure protocol rather than the nonsecure protocol. Any one of the following problems will result in the Web client receiving a 500 Internal Server Error page:

  • The certificate on the internal Web server is not valid on the date of the request.

  • The certificate authority that issued the Web site certificate for the internal Web server is not trusted by the ISA Server 2004 firewall.

  • The server name provided on the Web publishing rule **To** tab does not match the name on the certificate installed on the published Web site.

Lesson: Configuring ISA Server Authentication

* How Authentication and Web Publishing Rules Work
* ISA Server Web Publishing Authentication Scenarios
* Using RADIUS for Authentication
* How to Implement RADIUS Server for ISA Authentication

Introduction

In many cases, the network resources that are published by Web or server publishing rules are confidential and should be available only to authorized users. To enforce this, you can configure ISA Server 2004 to require authentication for all users accessing a published resource. This lesson describes the types of authentication supported by ISA Server 2004 and how to configure authentication.

Lesson objectives

After completing this lesson, you will be able to:

- Describe how access rules and authentication work together to provide secure Internet access.
- Identify the Web publishing authentication options on ISA Server 2004.
- Describe how RADIUS authentication works.
- Implement a RADIUS server for ISA authentication.

How Authentication and Web Publishing Rules Work Together

ISA Server uses authentication to grant access to publishing rules:

- When the publishing rule specifies a user set other than the All Users group

- Based on the Web listener authentication methods specified for a Web publishing or secure Web publishing rule

- By processing the firewall rules in order of priority. When a firewall rule matches, but requires authentication, ISA Server will prompt for user credentials

Introduction

Authentication is an integral part of any firewall policy. You can limit access to internal resources by limiting access based on the IP address of a computer. However, in most cases, it is much more effective to provide access only to specific users who have authenticated themselves.

How authentication and Web publishing rules work together

Authentication and Web publishing rules work together in the following ways:

- Users can gain access to an internal resource protected by ISA Server only if an access rule or publishing rule grants access to that resource. When you create a publishing rule, you can limit which users can gain access to the resource using the rule. Whenever a rule is configured to grant access to a specific set of users other than the All Users user set, authentication becomes an important part of how the rule is evaluated.

- For Web publishing and secure Web publishing rules, you must configure a Web listener as part of the rule definition. The Web listener defines which authentication methods are enabled. You can configure a Web listener to use more than one authentication mechanism. These authentication mechanisms can be used simultaneously on a Web listener: Basic, Digest, Integrated, and Client Certificate Authentication. When selected, RADIUS, SecurID, or forms-based authentication methods must be the only authentication mechanism configured. Once you have configured the Web listener for a Web publishing or secure Web publishing rule, you can then specify which users can gain access to resources based on the rule.

- When ISA Server receives a request for an internal resource, it processes the firewall policy rules in order. When a firewall rule matches the client request, but ISA Server requires client authentication to validate the match, ISA Server will request that the client authenticate. In other words, if the firewall rule limits access to something other than the All Users user set, then the user must provide credentials to prove his or her identity.

Important By default, Web publishing rules and secure Web publishing rules grant access to the All Users user set, which includes anonymous, or unauthenticated, users. To limit access to a Web publishing rule, remove the All Users user set and add the All Authenticated Users or a specific user set.

ISA Server Web Publishing Authentication Scenarios

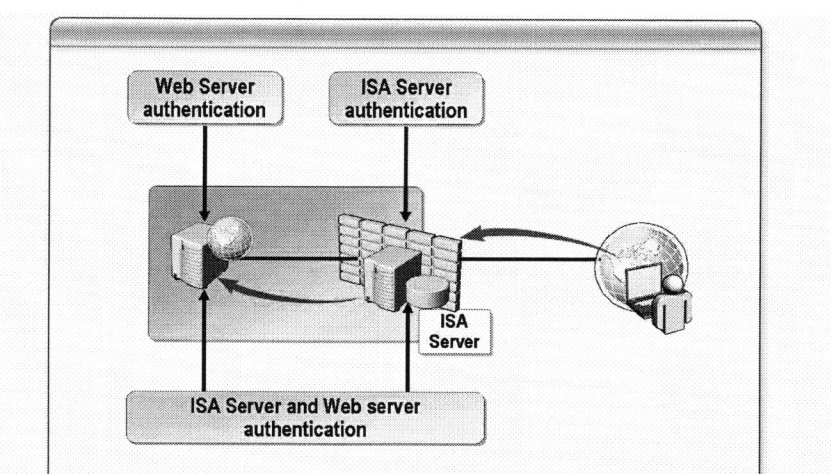

Introduction

When designing an authentication strategy for ISA Server Web publishing or secure Web publishing rules, you have several options. You can configure ISA Server to perform the authentication, or you can configure the published server to perform the authentication. In some cases, you may want to require authentication on both ISA Server and the published server.

Using ISA Server authentication

In some cases, you may want users to authenticate before they reach the internal network. To enable this, you can configure the Web listener associated with the publishing rule to require authentication. Once the users authenticate with ISA Server, they can then access the Web server on the internal network. This is a secure configuration because if the user cannot successfully authenticate with ISA Server, they cannot access anything on the internal network. Use ISA Server authentication if you have fairly simple authentication requirements. For example, if you want to ensure that only authenticated users can access all your published Web servers, then configure the Web listener to allow access to the All Authenticated Users user set. This option also has the added benefit of offloading authentication activity to the ISA Server computer.

Using authentication on the internal Web server

Another option for configuration authentication is to configure the internal resource to require authentication. In this scenario, ISA Server allows anonymous access to the published server, but the server requests authentication. In this configuration, ISA Server uses pass-through authentication to complete the authentication. *Pass-through authentication* refers to the ability of ISA Server to pass a client's authentication information to the destination server. The following steps describe how pass-through authentication works in a Web publishing scenario:

1. The client sends a request for an object on a Web server protected by ISA Server. Because the publishing rule allows anonymous access, ISA Server does not prompt for authentication but passes the request to the Web server.

2. The Web server receives the request and responds that authentication is required.

3. ISA Server passes the authentication-required response to the client.

4. The client returns authentication information to ISA Server.

5. ISA Server passes the client authentication information to the Web server.

6. After successful authentication, the client communicates with the Web server.

This option transfers all authentication activity to the internal server. This is a recommended solution when you have complex authentication requirements. For example, you may be publishing multiple Web sites with some allowing anonymous access, while others requiring authentication. In this scenario, it is easier to configure authentication on the internal Web server.

Important   If you are publishing resources using a server publishing rule, you can only configure authentication on the server hosting the internal resource. You cannot configure authentication on a server publishing rule.

Using ISA Server and internal Web server authentication

You can also design an authentication strategy that requires that users authenticate on ISA Server as well as on the internal Web server. You may choose to implement this solution if you have a Web site with varying types of confidential information. For example, you may want to limit access to a private Web site in your organization to only users who have valid domain user accounts. However, the Web site may also contain a confidential area that should be accessible only to executives. In this case, you could enable ISA Server authentication to limit access to the Web site to the Domain Users group, and then use authentication on the Web server to limit access to confidential information.

When you configure authentication on both servers, the users have to provide their credentials more than once. If you are using basic authentication on both ISA Server and the internal Web server, you can use basic authentication delegation to enable single sign-on for the users. When you enable basic authentication delegation, ISA Server authenticates the users, and then forwards the user credentials to the Web server, allowing the Web server to authenticate users without requesting credentials a second time.

To enable basic authentication delegation, select the check box for **Forward Basic authentication credentials (Basic delegation)** on the **Users** tab of the Web publishing or secure Web publishing rule.

Using RADIUS for Authentication

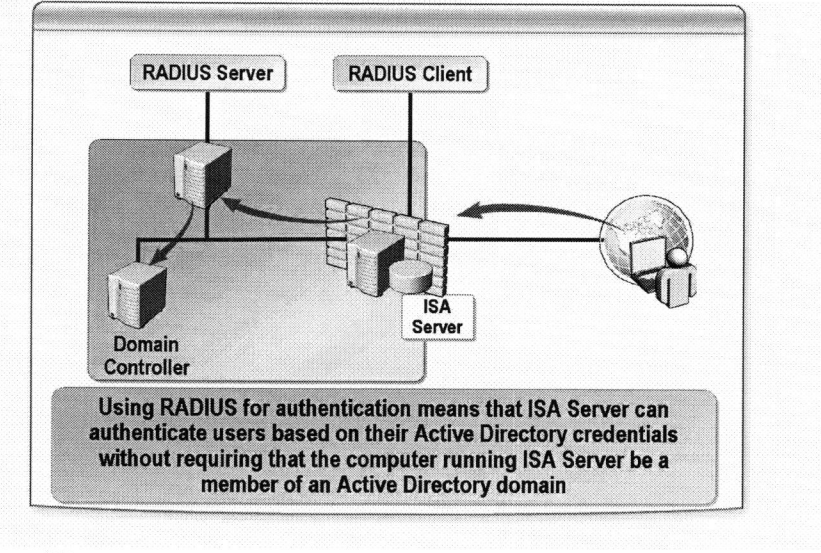

Introduction

ISA Server enables the use of Remote Authentication Dial-In User Service (RADIUS) to authenticate users connecting to resources via the Web proxy filter. These connections include connections from Web proxy clients on protected networks and external clients connecting to resources via Web publishing rules RADIUS is an industry-standard protocol used to provide authentication in heterogeneous environments.

RADIUS infrastructure components

A RADIUS infrastructure includes the following components:

- *RADIUS server*. A RADIUS server has access to all the user accounts within a defined namespace. The RADIUS server passes authentication requests to an authentication server (such as an Active Directory® directory service domain controller) and can also be used to apply policies to user connections. Microsoft includes Internet Authentication Server (IAS) with Windows 2000 and Windows Server 2003. IAS is a Request for Comments (RFC)–compliant RADIUS server.

- *RADIUS client*. A RADIUS client is typically a dial-up server, virtual private network (VPN) server, or wireless access point. The RADIUS client is the server that users connect to when they want to access a network. The RADIUS client collects the user credentials and sends them in the form of a RADIUS message to a RADIUS server. The RADIUS server authenticates the RADIUS client request, and sends back a RADIUS message response.

Using RADIUS for ISA Server authentication

ISA Server can be configured as a RADIUS client. This means that when users connect to ISA Server, ISA Server will send the user logon information to a RADIUS server rather than to an Active Directory domain controller.

Why use RADIUS for ISA authentication?

The most important benefit of using RADIUS for ISA Server authentication is that you can authenticate users based on their Active Directory user names without requiring that the ISA Server computer be a member of the Active Directory domain.

In most organizations that have deployed Active Directory, most user accounts are stored in Active Directory. One of the benefits of using ISA Server as a firewall is that you can use those Active Directory accounts to authenticate user access, for both inbound and outbound access. However, for ISA Server to authenticate Active Directory users, the computer running ISA Server must be a member of the Active Directory domain. Security best practices specify that the firewall should not be located on a server that is a member of a Windows domain. The problem with using a firewall that is a member of a domain is that if an attacker were able to compromise the firewall, the attacker could potentially leverage the firewall's domain member status to launch a successful attack against other internal network servers.

You can use RADIUS to gain the benefit of using the Active Directory domains for authentication without joining the server running ISA Server to the domain. When ISA Server is configured to use RADIUS authentication for incoming Web requests, the firewall forwards the request to a RADIUS server located behind the firewall. The RADIUS server can then forward the authentication request to a server that has the information required to authenticate the user. RADIUS can forward the authentication requests to an Active Directory domain controller, another RADIUS server, or a directory server created by a third party that accepts RADIUS authentication messages.

How to Implement RADIUS Server for ISA Authentication

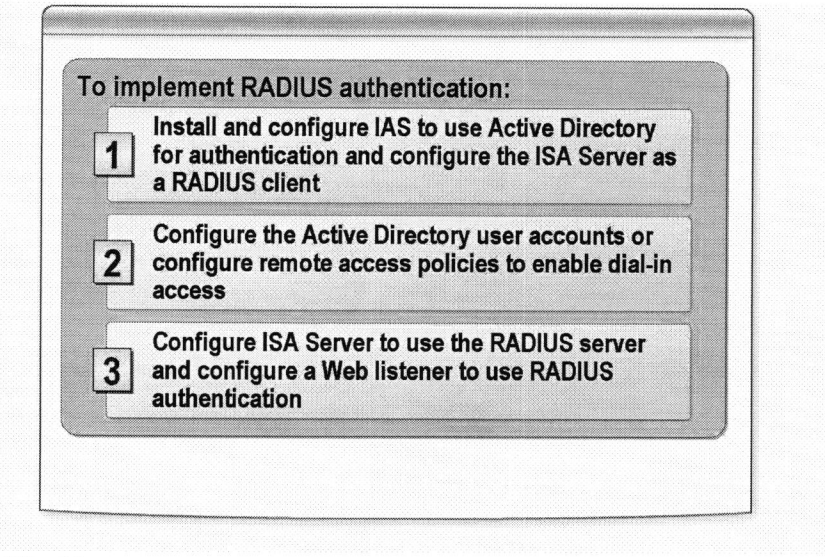

How to implement RADIUS authentication

Configuring ISA Server to use RADIUS for authentication requires several steps. The high-level steps are described here.

1. Install and configure Internet Authentication Server (IAS). IAS is one of the Networking Services installed by using Add or Remove Programs from the Control Panel. To configure IAS, you must complete the following steps:

   a. Configure ISA Server as a RADIUS client. This configuration includes configuring a secret that will be used to create a secure channel between IAS and ISA Server.

   b. Configure IAS to use Active Directory for its user account database. To do this, you must register the IAS server in the Active Directory domain.

2. Configure the Active Directory user accounts and remote access policies. When the user attempts to authenticate on a RADIUS server, the RADIUS server checks the user account properties and the remote access policies to determine if the user can authenticate. The user account must be configured to allow dial-in access. The account can also be configured so that dial-in access is controlled by a remote access policy. If this option is enabled, then a remote access policy must be created that will allow the user dial-in access.

3. Configure ISA Server to use RADIUS for authentication. To enable this, you must configure a Web listener to use RADIUS authentication and configure ISA Server with the server name and shared secret that it will use to connect to the RADIUS Server.

Lab: Configuring Access to Internal Resources

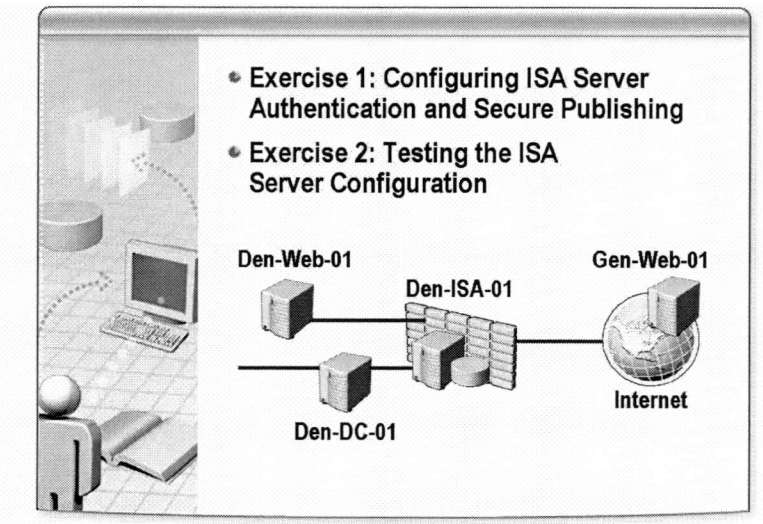

Objectives

After completing this lab, you will be able to:

- Configure Secure Sockets Layer (SSL) bridging from Microsoft Internet Security and Acceleration (ISA) Server to an internal Web site.

- Configure a secure publishing rule to require authentication.

- Configure ISA Server to use Remote Authentication Dial-In User Service (RADIUS) server for authentication.

Note This lab focuses on the concepts in this module and as a result might not comply with Microsoft security recommendations. For example, the Administrator passwords are not as complex as recommended. Additionally, most of the actions performed in this lab are performed while logged in as an Administrator. A better security practice would be to log in as a normal user and use the Runas option to start administrative applications.

Scenario

You have deployed ISA Server at Coho Vineyard and started making internal resources available to the Internet. You have deployed the cohovineyard.com Web site and a secure Web site for online purchases. You have also deployed a File Transfer Protocol (FTP) site. However, because of security concerns, you need to make some changes. You have deployed a RADIUS server and removed Den-ISA-01 from the cohovineyard.com Web site in preparation for making these changes.

The corporate security policy specifies the following settings that need to be modified:

■ ISA Server needs to be configured as a RADIUS client. All authentications must use the RADIUS server.

■ The Store Web site is not ready to be deployed. During the testing phase, only members of the Managers group and the Sales group should be able to access the Web site.

■ The connection between ISA Server and the internal Web server for the Store Web site must be secured using SSL. You have already installed a Web server certificate on Den-Web-01. The certificate name is Den-Web-01.cohovineyard.com.

To prepare for this lab:

1. You will need the Den-DC-01 virtual machine, the Den-ISA-01 virtual machine, the Den-Web-01 virtual machine, and the Gen-Web-01 virtual machine for this lab.

2. If necessary, start or resume the required virtual machines and then, on Den-ISA-01, log on to the cohovineyard domain with your user name and password.

3. On Den-DC-01, log on to the cohovineyard domain with a user name of **Administrator** and a password of **P@ssw0rd**.

Estimated time to complete this lab: 45 minutes

Exercise 1
Configuring ISA Server Authentication and Secure Publishing

In this exercise, you will complete the configuration of ISA Server as a RADIUS client. You will also configure authentication on the store.cohovineyard.com Web site so that only members of the Managers and Sales groups can access the site. Then you will modify the connections between ISA Server and the Store Web site, and between ISA Server and the internal FTP server.

Tasks	Detailed steps
1. Configure Internet Authentication Services on Den-DC-01 to accept Den-ISA-01 as a RADIUS client.	a. On Den-DC-01, open **Internet Authentication Services** from the **Administrative Tools** folder. b. Right-click **Internet Authentication Service (Local)** and click **Register Server in Active Directory**. c. Read the notice explaining that IAS will be able to read users' dial-in settings, and click **OK**. d. When you receive the **Server registered** message, click **OK**. e. Right-click **RADIUS Clients** and click **New RADIUS Client**. f. In the **New RADIUS Client** dialog box, in the **Friendly Name** text box, type **Den-ISA-01**. In the **Client Address (IP or DNS)** text box, type **192.168.1.1**. Click **Next**. g. In the **Additional Information** dialog box, in the **Client-Vendor** list, ensure that **RADIUS Standard** is selected. Type **P@ssw0rd** for the **Shared secret** and the **Confirm shared secret**. Click **Finish**. h. Close **Internet Authentication Service**.
2. Configure Den-ISA-01 as a RADIUS client.	a. Switch to Den-ISA-01. b. In **ISA Server Management**, expand **Configuration** and then click **General**. c. Under **Additional Security Policy**, click **Define RADIUS Servers**. d. In the **RADIUS Servers** dialog box, click **Add**. e. In the **Add RADIUS Server** dialog box, in the **Server** name box, type **Den-DC-01.cohovineyard.com**. f. Click **Change** to change the **Shared secret**. g. In the **Shared Secret** dialog box, type **P@ssw0rd** as the **New Secret** and **Confirm New Secret** and then click **OK**. h. In the **Add RADIUS Servers** dialog box, click **OK**. i. In the **RADIUS Servers** dialog box, click **OK**.

(continued)

Tasks	Detailed steps
3. Modify the configuration of the Coho Vineyard Store Site to use RADIUS for authentication and to limit access to only authenticated users.	a. Open the **Coho Vineyard Store Site Properties** dialog box. b. On the **Listener** tab, access the **Properties** of the **HTTPS Listener**. c. On the **Preferences** tab, click **Authentication**. d. Configure the **Authentication** settings to allow only RADIUS authentication and to require all users to authenticate. e. Ensure Den-DC-01 is configured as the RADIUS Server. Click **OK** to close the **Authentication** dialog box, and click **OK** to close the **HTTPS Listener Properties** dialog box. f. In the **Coho Vineyard Store Site Properties** dialog box, on the **Users** tab, remove **All Users**. Add the **All Authenticated Users** user set. g. Click **Apply** to apply the changes and then click **OK** when the changes have been applied.
4. Create a remote access policy used to authenticate Web requests. Configure the remote access policy to allow access to the Sales and Managers global group.	a. Switch to Den-DC-01 and open **Internet Authentication Services** from the **Administrative Tools** folder. b. Right click **Remote Access Policies** and click **New Remote Access Policy**. c. On the **Welcome to the New Remote Access Policy Wizard** page, click **Next**. d. On the **Policy Configuration Method** page, click **Set up a custom policy**, and type **Store Site Access Policy** in the **Policy name:** text box and click **Next**. e. On the **Policy Conditions** page, click **Add**. f. In the **Select Attributes** dialog box, click **Windows-Groups** and click **Add**. g. In the **Groups** dialog box, click **Add**. h. In the **Enter the Object Names to Select** text box, type **Sales; Managers**. Click **OK**. i. In the **Group** dialog box, click **OK**. j. On the **Policy Conditions** page, click **Next**. k. On the **Permissions** page, click **Grant remote access permission**, and then click **Next**. l. On the **Profile** page, click **Edit Profile**. m. In the **Edit Dial-in Profile** dialog box, click the **Authentication** tab. n. Select **Unencrypted Authentication (PAP,SPAP)**. Click **OK**. o. In the **Dial-in Settings** box, click **No** and then click **Next**. p. On the **Completing to the New Remote Access Policy Wizard** page, click **Finish**.

(*continued*)

Tasks	Detailed steps
5. Configure the Coho Vineyard Secure Web Site to use the certificate issued to Den-Web-01.cohovineyard.com and configure the Web site to require SSL connections.	**a.** Switch to Den-Web-01. **b.** Open **Internet Information Services (IIS) Manager**. **c.** Expand **Den-Web-01** and then expand **Web Sites**. **d.** Right click **Cohovineyard Secure Web Site** and click **Properties**. **e.** On the **Directory Security** tab, click **Server Certificate**. **f.** On the **Welcome to the Web Server Certificate Wizard** page, click **Next**. **g.** On the **Server Certificate** page, click **Assign an existing certificate** and then click **Next**. **h.** On the **Available Certificates** page, click the certificate issued to Den-Web-01.cohovineyard.com. Click **Next**. **i.** On the **SSL Port** page, accept the default and click **Next**. **j.** On the **Certificate Summary** page, click **Next**. **k.** On the **Completing to the Web Server Certificate Wizard** page, click **Finish**. **l.** Under **Secure Communications**, click **Edit**. Click **Require Secure Channel** and then click **OK** twice. **m.** Close all open windows.
6. Configure SSL bridging between Den-ISA-01 and Den-Web-01.	**a.** Switch to Den-ISA-01 and open **ISA Server Management**. **b.** Click **Firewall Policy**, and then double-click **Coho Vineyard Store Site**. **c.** On the **Bridging** tab, clear the check box for **Redirect requests to HTTP port** and click **Redirect requests to SSL port**. Click **OK**. **d.** Click **Apply** to apply the changes and then click **OK** when the changes have been applied.

Exercise 2
Testing the ISA Server Configuration

In this exercise, you will test your ISA Server configuration to ensure that the modifications you implemented were successful and that they meet the company requirements. Use the following information to test the configuration:

- Complete your testing from Gen-Web-01. Log on as Administrator with a password of P@ssw0rd.

- Shu Ito (logon name: Shu, password: P@ssw0rd) is a member of the Domain Users group.

- Jay Adams (logon name: Jay, password: P@ssw0rd) is a member of the Managers group.

- Martin Weber (logon name: Martin, password: P@ssw0rd) is a member of the Sales group.

Tasks	Detailed steps
1. Confirm that only members of the Managers group and the Sales group should be able to access the store Web site.	a. Can Martin Weber access https://secure.cohovineyard.com? b. Can Jay Adams access https:// secure.cohovineyard.com? c. Can Shu Ito access https:// secure.cohovineyard.com? d. Can you access https:// secure.cohovineyard.com using your user name?

To Prepare for the Next Lab

As you finish this lab, shut down all of the virtual machines that you used in the lab. As the virtual machines shut down, select the option to **Commit changes to the virtual hard disk**.

Important You must save the virtual machine changes that you made in this module because later practices and labs require these changes.

After shutting down the virtual machines, restart the Den-ISA-01 virtual machine, the Den-DC-01 virtual machine, the Den-Web-01 virtual machine, and the Gen-Web-01 virtual machine in preparation for the next module.

Module 6: Integrating ISA Server 2004 and Microsoft Exchange Server

Contents

Overview

- Issues in E-Mail Security
- Configuring ISA Server to Secure SMTP Traffic
- Configuring ISA Server to Secure Web Client Connections
- Configuring ISA Server to Secure Client Connections

Introduction

The e-mail messaging service provided by Microsoft® Exchange Server is a critical network service in many organizations. In many organizations, e-mail is also one of the network services that is accessible to the Internet. This means that securing Exchange Server is a critical component in configuring security for the organization's network. Microsoft Internet Security and Acceleration (ISA) Server 2004 provides several options for securing Exchange Server, including securing client connections to Exchange Server.

Objectives

After completing this module, you will be able to:

- Describe the issues in e-mail security.
- Configure ISA Server to secure Simple Message Transfer Protocol (SMTP) traffic.
- Configure ISA Server to secure Web client connections.
- Configure ISA Server to secure client connections.

Lesson: Issues in E-Mail Security

- E-Mail Security Threats Overview
- E-Mail Access Using Web Clients
- E-Mail Access Using Outlook Clients
- E-Mail Access Using POP3, IMAP4, and NNTP Clients
- SMTP Protocol-Level Exploits
- Unwanted and Malicious E-Mail
- How ISA Server 2004 Secures Exchange Server

Introduction

Many of the recent security attacks have been launched by malicious code attached to e-mail messages. At the same time, many organizations need to provide access to the internal e-mail infrastructure to users who are not located on the internal company network. If this access to e-mail is not secure, the e-mail messages may be compromised while crossing the Internet, and providing access to the internal servers may compromise network security. This lesson provides an overview of the security threats exposed by using e-mail.

Lesson objectives

After completing this lesson, you will be able to:

- Describe the e-mail-based security threats.
- Describe how clients access e-mail using Web clients.
- Describe how clients access e-mail using Microsoft Outlook® clients.
- Describe how clients access e-mail using Internet protocol clients.
- Describe SMTP protocol-level exploits.
- Recognize the security threat posed by unwanted and malicious e-mail.
- Describe how ISA Server can be used to secure access to Exchange Server.

E-Mail Security Threats Overview

> ### Ensuring the security of e-mail includes:
>
> - Ensuring that all e-mail client connections to the e-mail server are secure
> - Protecting the e-mail servers from SMTP exploits
> - Preventing unwanted or malicious e-mails from entering the organization's network

E-mail security threats

The security threats related to e-mail fall into the following categories:

- *Securing client connections.* In many organizations, users need access to their e-mail both while they are in and out of the office. Computers running Exchange Server enable several different options for providing access to the user mailboxes from the Internet. By default, many of these client connections are not secure. For example, when the client logs on, the user name and password may be sent in clear text, or the message contents may be sent in clear text across the network.

- *SMTP exploits.* Almost all Internet e-mail is sent using SMTP. To receive e-mail from the Internet, you must expose an SMTP server to the Internet. Like most other protocols, SMTP can be vulnerable to protocol-level strikes such as buffer-overflow attacks. These types of attacks can disable the SMTP server, or enable the attacker to run commands on the server. Another SMTP exploit is mail relay, where an attacker relays e-mail through your server.

- *Malicious or unwanted e-mails.* Malicious e-mails are e-mails that contain viruses or worms. Although some viruses simply replicate and then display messages or images, many viruses can cause extensive damage to hardware, software, or data. A worm is a program that can replicate itself automatically by taking advantage of automatic file sending and receiving. Unwanted e-mails include unsolicited commercial e-mails, also known as spam or junk e-mail. These e-mails waste users' time and also use the e-mail system resources, consuming network bandwidth.

E-Mail Access Using Web Clients

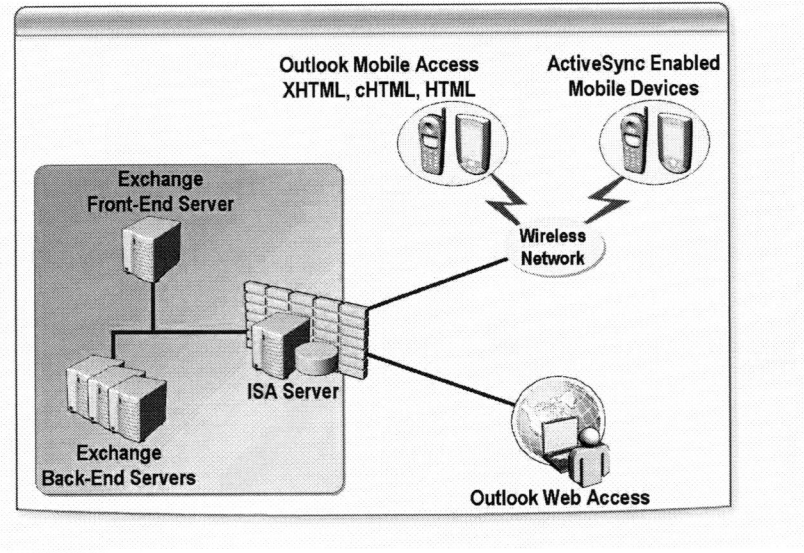

Introduction

Part of securing access to e-mail is providing secure access to Exchange mailboxes for Web-based e-mail clients. The most popular options for providing Web-based client access to Exchange mailboxes are using Outlook Web Access (OWA) and Outlook Mobile Access (OMA) and Microsoft Exchange ActiveSync®.

Outlook Web Access features

Outlook Web Access provides access to a computer running Exchange Server through a Web browser. OWA does not require any client software or client configuration other than a Web browser. Although OWA does not provide all of the functionality provided by a full Outlook client, the fact that it is easy to deploy and does not require any special client makes OWA an attractive option for providing remote access.

By default, all servers running Exchange 2000 and Exchange Server 2003 are OWA servers. To install Exchange, Internet Information Services (IIS) must be installed on the computer. When the user connects to a computer running Exchange Server from the Web browser, the request is passed from IIS to the computer running Exchange Server. The requested content is returned to the IIS server where it is forwarded to the Web browser.

OWA is frequently deployed using front-end and back-end servers. In this scenario, the front-end server must be running Exchange 2000 Server Enterprise Edition or Exchange Server 2003 Enterprise Edition or Standard Edition. In this configuration, clients connect to the front-end servers. This server authenticates the user, and then queries Active Directory® directory service to determine which back-end computer running Exchange Server hosts the user mailbox. The front-end server then forwards the request to the back-end server. The back-end server replies to the front-end server, which replies to the client.

OWA security issues

The use of OWA raises several issues with e-mail security, including:

- *Securing the user logon.* By default, OWA is configured to use Hypertext Transfer Protocol (HTTP). This means that all user logon information is passed in clear text to the computer running Exchange Server. This issue can be easily addressed using Secure Sockets Layer (SSL) to encrypt all user sessions. However, some clients may cache the user logon credentials so that if the user does not close all Web browser sessions, another user may be able to access the user's e-mail without logging on.

- *Securing e-mail contents.* Because all messages are sent in clear text using HTTP, the e-mail contents may not be secure while crossing the Internet. You can use Hypertext Transfer Protocol Secure (HTTPS) to secure the e-mail. However, some Web browsers may cache the e-mail contents on the local computer. For example, when you open an attachment using OWA, it is stored in the temporary Internet files on the computer. Another user may be able to gain access to the files.

Exchange Server 2003 wireless device support

Exchange Server 2003 allows users of wireless and small devices, such as mobile phones, personal digital assistants (PDAs), or smart phones (hybrid devices that combine the functionality of mobile phones and PDAs), access to Exchange data. Exchange ActiveSync and Outlook Mobile Access (OMA) are two of the mobile service components that are built into Exchange Server 2003.

Exchange ActiveSync is a service provided in Exchange Server 2003 that allows users to synchronize their Exchange information (inbox, subfolders, calendar, contacts, and tasks) with their ActiveSync-enabled mobile device (such as Pocket PC 2002, Smartphone 2002, and Microsoft Windows Mobile™ 2003 or later devices).

OMA is a service provided in Exchange Server 2003 that allows users to access their Exchange mailbox by using a browser-enabled mobile device. Devices such as mobile phones and PDAs that use Extensible Hypertext Markup Language (XHTML), compact HTML (cHTML), or standard HTML browsers allow your users to connect to their inbox, calendar, contacts, and tasks, and perform global address list (GAL) searches. In addition to mobile phones, Windows Mobile™ devices using Microsoft Pocket Internet Explorer and desktop personal computers using Internet Explorer 6.0 or later also support OMA.

Like OWA, OMA or ActiveSync requires that the computer running Exchange Server 2003 be accessible from the Internet using HTTP. When accessing a mailbox using OMA, the wireless device connects to a wireless access point that provides access to the Internet. Then the Web browser on the wireless device is used to access the computer running Exchange Server.

Wireless client security issues

The use of wireless clients raises similar security issues to OWA including:

- *Securing the user logon.* By default, OMA is configured to use HTTP. This means that all user logon information is passed in clear text to the computer running Exchange Server. In addition, authentication to the SMTP server is passed in clear text. This issue can be easily addressed using SSL to encrypt all user sessions.

- *Securing e-mail contents.* Because all messages are sent in clear text using HTTP or SMTP, the e-mail contents may not be secure while crossing the Internet or an unprotected Wireless LAN. SSL can secure the e-mail in this case.

E-Mail Access Using Outlook Clients

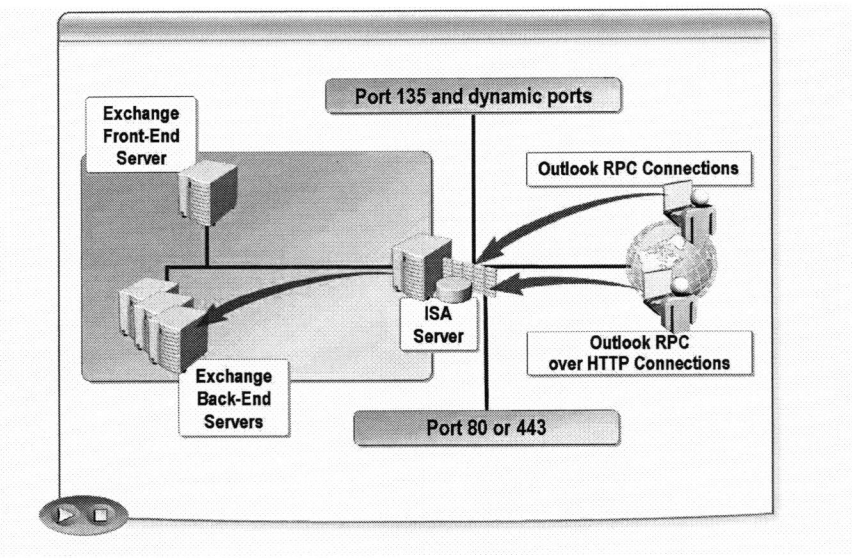

Introduction

Another option for providing remote access to e-mail on a computer running Exchange Server is to use an Outlook client configured to use Messaging Application Programming Interface (MAPI) to communicate with Exchange. The Outlook client provides the most functionality, but also introduces some security risks when used to provide access from the Internet.

Outlook client features

Outlook clients can use MAPI to communicate with Exchange Server stores. Connecting with a MAPI client provides the highest level of functionality that is available using Exchange. One of the most significant benefits of using Outlook compared to OWA is that Outlook provides offline access. With Outlook, you can perform most e-mail tasks while you are not connected to the network, and then automatically synchronize with Exchange Server when connected to the network.

Because it has the highest level of functionality, most users prefer to use their Outlook client not only at work, but also from home and while traveling. However, MAPI requests are sent as a remote procedure call (RPC) to the computer running Exchange Server, and using RPC across the Internet raises some significant security concerns.

Outlook client security issues

The most significant security issue with using MAPI Outlook clients to provide remote access has to do with the nature of RPC communications. When an RPC client initiates a connection with a server, the client request uses port 135. However, after the initial connection, the server and client negotiate which ports to use for subsequent connections. These ports could be any ports above 1024. By default, the actual ports used for the RPCs are not predictable, so all ports above 1024 need to be available for client connections. In most cases, leaving this many ports unsecured is not acceptable.

Another potential security risk for MAPI Outlook clients is that the encoding used for RPC is not secure. If an attacker captures the packets sent using RPC, they will be able to decode the packets and read the messages. Additional security can be enabled by configuring the Outlook client to use encrypted RPC connections.

Using RPC over HTTP

Outlook 2003 with Exchange 2003 running on Microsoft Windows Server™ 2003 supports RPC over HTTP, which simplifies the network and firewall configuration needed to support a MAPI client. Using RPC over HTTP provides all the benefits of using an Outlook client without needing multiple ports open on the firewall. Users running Outlook 2003 can connect directly to a computer running Exchange Server 2003 over the Internet by using HTTP or HTTPS—even if both the computer running Exchange Server and Outlook are behind firewalls and located on different networks. Only the HTTP and HTTPS ports need to be opened on the firewall.

RPC over HTTP can be deployed using front-end and back-end servers. The front-end server is an RPC proxy server that converts the RPC over HTTP packets into normal RPC packets, which are forwarded to the back-end computer running Exchange Server. The back-end server replies to the front-end server, which converts the response back into HTTP packets and replies to the client. In this case, the RPC proxy server does not need to be running Exchange. RPC over HTTP can also be deployed in a single server configuration where the Exchange Server is also configured as the RPC proxy server. In either case, RPC over HTTP requires the use of SSL to encrypt the traffic between the Outlook client and the RPC proxy server.

E-Mail Access Using POP3, IMAP4, and NNTP Clients

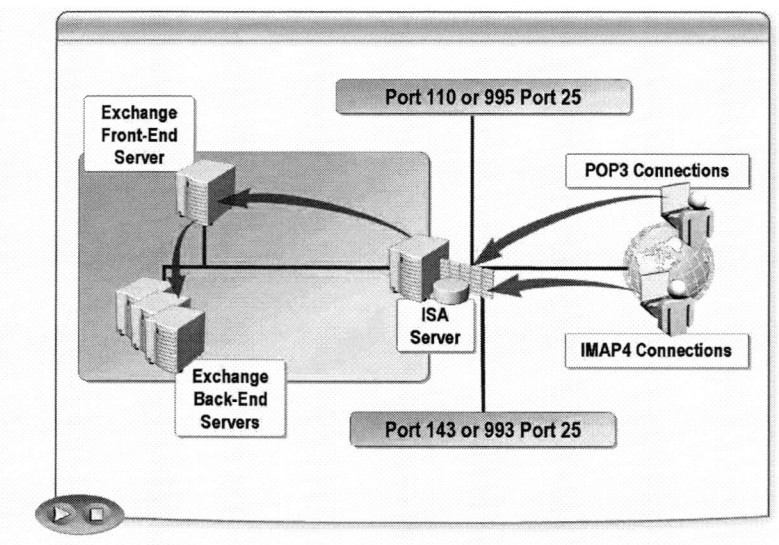

Introduction

Another option for providing remote access to computers running Exchange Server is to use POP3, IMAP4, or NNTP clients. These clients have more limited functionality than either OWA or MAPI Outlook clients but can be used to access Exchange servers from almost any client computer.

Exchange Server Internet protocol support

POP3, IMAP4, and NNTP clients do not provide the full functionality provided by MAPI clients. However, these clients do provide a fast and reliable means to obtain e-mail messages. Exchange Server supports the following protocols to access mailboxes.

- *Post Office Protocol 3 (POP3)*. POP3 is a simple mail retrieval protocol with a limited command set. A POP3 client provides the most basic access to Exchange, allowing a user to access messages in their Inbox only. However, e-mail access is the only feature. Calendaring, task lists, or public folders are not available.

- *Internet Message Access Protocol Version 4 (IMAP4)*. IMAP4 is a more complex mail retrieval protocol with a more advanced command set. IMAP4 enables you to store and manage your messages on the server instead of downloading and managing them on the client (as with POP3). By using IMAP4, you can organize your messages on the server by creating folders. You can also move messages from folder to folder and preview the contents of messages before you download either the entire message or a selected portion of a message such as an attachment.

- *Network News Transfer Protocol (NNTP)*. NNTP is used for accessing newsgroups.

Microsoft Outlook Express supports POP3, IMAP4, and NNTP, as do the majority of other mail readers that are available on the market today. All of these clients use POP3 or IMAP4 to retrieve messages but must use SMTP to send messages.

Frequently, support for these clients in Exchange is deployed using front-end and back-end servers that are similar to the OWA configuration. Both types of servers must be running Exchange 2000 or Exchange Server 2003. In this configuration, clients connect to the front-end servers. This server authenticates the user, and then queries Active Directory to determine which back-end computer running Exchange Server hosts the user mailbox. The front-end server then forwards the request to the back-end server. The back-end server replies to the front-end server, which replies to the client.

Internet protocol client security issues

The most significant security issue with using POP3, IMAP4, and NNTP clients to provide remote access to computers running Exchange Server is the fact that these protocols do not encrypt the network traffic. By default, the user logon traffic is not encrypted, and messages sent and received are not encrypted. However, these messaging protocols can be configured to use SSL to encrypt all traffic sent to the Exchange Server.

A second security issue with Internet protocol clients is the fact that each protocol requires another port to be opened on the firewall. Most firewall administrators resist opening additional ports because this creates another potential attack point. For this reason, many organizations do not support Internet protocols other than HTTPS for e-mail access.

SMTP Protocol-Level Exploits

SMTP servers can be vulnerable to:

- Buffer overflow attacks when SMTP commands are sent with more than expected data, causing memory buffer overflows
- Mail relay attacks when an SMTP server is used to forward unwanted e-mail to Internet recipients
- SMTP command attacks where SMTP commands are used to compromise the server or gain information about the server or recipients on the server

Introduction

In addition to security concerns dealing with clients accessing Exchange from the Internet, the SMTP servers can also be vulnerable to attack at a protocol level.

Buffer-overflow attacks

SMTP servers are vulnerable to several types of attacks. One type of attack is a buffer overflow attack, which can be used to disable the SMTP servers. Attackers use buffer overflow exploits to disable specific server services with the intent of creating a denial of service—either by disabling a specific service on the target computer or by taking the entire machine offline. More elaborate buffer overflow exploits can be used to disable key security features and allow the attacker to run commands of his choice on the targeted machine.

A buffer overflow attack is when a program or process tries to store more data in a memory buffer than the buffer is designed to hold. The extra information can overflow into adjacent buffers, corrupting or overwriting the valid data held in them. In buffer overflow attacks, the extra data may contain code designed to trigger specific actions, in effect sending new instructions to the attacked computer. Buffer overflow attacks can be mounted against an organization's SMTP server by sending large SMTP commands. The best way to prevent a buffer overflow attack against the SMTP server is to stop the attacker at the network perimeter, before the exploit ever finds its way into the corporate network.

Mail relay attacks

Another common type of attack is a mail relaying attack. SMTP relaying means that the mail server permits users to forward e-mail through the server to users in external organizations. In some situations, Exchange Server may need to be configured to support relaying, but this configuration can also cause your computer running Exchange Server to be used for forwarding unwanted e-mail. If your computer running Exchange Server allows anyone to relay, junk e-mailers can use your server to forward these messages to other users. This gives the appearance of your mail server originating the delivery of the messages and may lead to other organizations blocking all message delivery from your server. If possible, you should prevent all mail relaying. However, if you allow Internet protocol clients, who must use SMTP to send mail, then you must allow relaying for those clients. At the minimum, only authenticated users should be allowed to relay and only when they use secure SMTP.

SMTP command attacks

SMTP servers must support a standard set of commands that are used to send and receive SMTP messages. Attackers can use the commands to perform buffer overflow attacks or to send malformed commands that the system programmers did not anticipate. Command-manipulation attacks can lead to total system compromise by giving an attacker access to key files, the ability to overwrite files, or to inject Trojan horse programs onto a mail server.

Some SMTP commands are optional. Some commands such as EXPN and VRFY, if configured incorrectly, can be used to find a list of recipients on the server. If these commands are not required, they can be disabled at the firewall so that the SMTP server does not receive them.

Unwanted and Malicious E-Mail

> **Unwanted e-mail is unsolicited commercial e-mail that:**
> - Consumes server and network resources
> - Reduces user productivity and increases administrative effort
> - Can be filtered using an application-level filter
> - May result in exposure to legal liability
>
> **Malicious e-mails contain viruses or worms that:**
> - Damage data or computers or consume network and computer resources
> - Increase administrative cost and effort
> - Increase the risk of an information leak

Introduction

The most prominent security issue related to e-mail is the number of unwanted and malicious e-mails that are sent across the Internet. These types of e-mails can be grouped in two categories: unwanted junk e-mail that uses up computer resources and user time but does not cause harm to the computer, and malicious e-mails that contain viruses, worms, or Trojan horse programs.

Unwanted e-mail

It has been estimated that unwanted e-mail messages consume over 50 percent of total bandwidth usage on the Internet today. Unwanted e-mail leads to the following problems:

- Wasted bandwidth on both internal and Internet networks, which may lead to increased Internet bandwidth cost, and increased non-productive traffic on the corporate network

- Increased resource usage, including disk space, processor, and memory use on mail servers

- Decreased employee productivity due to reading and deleting unwanted e-mail

- Increased administrative costs as network administrators attempt to reduce the negative effects of unwanted e-mail

- Increased exposure to legal liability to users who may view offensive unwanted e-mail messages

Most organizations attempt to filter unwanted e-mail before it gets to the e-mail servers. The challenge is to determine which e-mail messages are unwanted e-mail while still allowing valid e-mail messages into your mail systems. To filter junk e-mail, you must use an application-layer filter. These filters can inspect the SMTP messages transporting the unwanted e-mail and filter out messages based on factors such as source e-mail address, keywords in the subject line or message body, and attachment name or extension.

Malicious e-mail

Viruses and worms sent by e-mail can cause a tremendous amount of damage to corporate networks. Viruses and worm attacks are responsible for:

- Destruction of data on servers and workstations

- Denial-of-service attacks on servers and workstations

- Lost employee productivity because a workstation or network server is unavailable

- Distribution of corporate secrets by means of mass-mailing worms

- Increased administrative costs due to repairing damaged workstations and servers

- Increased bandwidth use on the corporate network and Internet connection secondary to mass-mailing worms and denial-of-service attacks

The most common way that viruses and worms get into an organization's network is by e-mail. Virus writers realize that e-mail is a critical service in most organizations and they take advantage of this fact by crafting viruses and worms that spread by e-mail. When users open e-mail attachments that contain dangerous code, the code is released to the user's computer and then spreads to the rest of the network. A single infected host can damage virtually every networked device in a short period of time.

To effectively prevent the spread of viruses and worms, organizations need to deal with the viruses at multiple levels. Antivirus programs should be installed on the e-mail servers as well as on the client computers. Another level in the defense is to block all e-mail attachments at the perimeter. An SMTP application filter on the network perimeter can then examine all e-mail attachments and scan the attachment for viruses, worms, and other dangerous code. Based on the results of the scan and its rule configuration, the application filter can delete the message, quarantine the network for further inspection, or forward the message to the e-mail server.

How ISA Server 2004 Secures Exchange Server

Introduction

Exchange Server is a full-featured e-mail server that provides many options for users to access their e-mail, calendar, tasks, and contacts from the Internet. Like all Internet-compatible e-mail servers, Exchange Server also supports SMTP to exchange e-mail with other SMTP servers.

ISA Server 2004 and Exchange Server

ISA Server 2004 is designed to provide a secure perimeter protecting all access to computers running Exchange Server. ISA Server enables secure and highly accessible remote access to Microsoft Exchange services for users and can be used to filter SMTP traffic as it enters or leaves the organization.

ISA Server 2004 provides the following features to help secure the Exchange infrastructure:

- Mail Server and Outlook Web Access Publishing Wizards that can be used to easily and securely configure access to computers running Exchange Server. The wizards are used to configure all access to the computers running Exchange Server, including for Internet protocol clients.

- Support for Outlook Web Access publishing including forms-based authentication. ISA Server also supports OMA and ActiveSync server publishing. In all cases, the ISA Server HTTP filter can apply application-layer filtering to the client connections.

- Support for MAPI connections from Outlook clients where ISA Server manages the mapping of the dynamic RPC ports.

- Protection against SMTP mail server attacks with the SMTP and POP3 application filters.

- Application filtering for unwanted e-mail with the SMTP Message Screener.

Lesson: Configuring ISA Server to Secure SMTP Traffic

* How ISA Server Secures SMTP Traffic
* How to Configure ISA Server to Secure SMTP Traffic
* How SMTP Filtering Works
* How to Configure the SMTP Application Filter
* How SMTP Message Screener Works
* How to Implement SMTP Message Screener
* Integrating ISA Server and Exchange Server to Secure SMTP Traffic

Introduction

One of the ways that ISA Server can secure Exchange Server is by providing enhanced options for filtering all SMTP messages sent to the computers running Exchange Server from the Internet. This lesson explains how to publish SMTP servers and how to configure SMTP filtering.

Lesson objectives

After completing this lesson, you will be able to:

- Describe how ISA Server secures SMTP traffic.
- Configure ISA Server to secure SMTP traffic.
- Describe how the SMTP application filter works.
- Configure the SMTP application filter.
- Describe how the SMTP message screener works.
- Implement the SMTP message screener.
- Describe how to integrate ISA Server and Exchange Server to secure SMTP traffic.

How ISA Server Secures SMTP Traffic

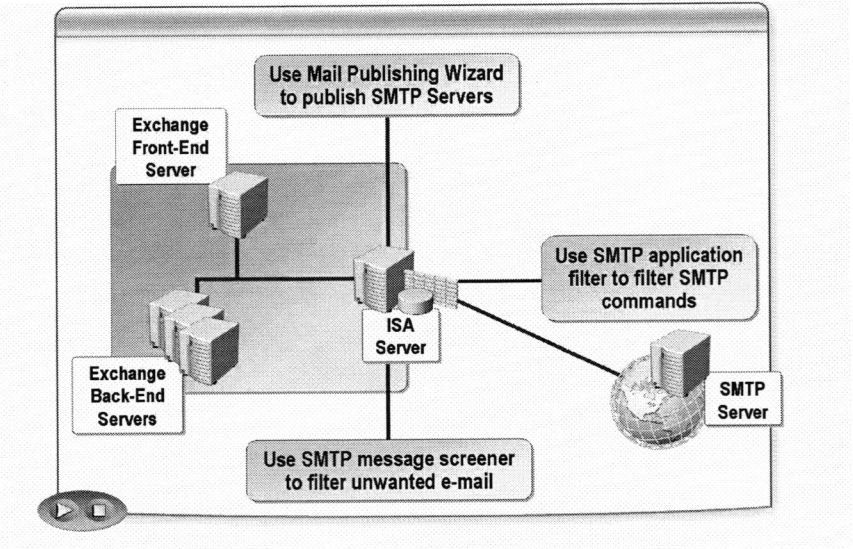

Introduction

ISA Server provides three components for securing SMTP traffic. The first is the Mail Server Wizard, which can be used to publish the SMTP server to the Internet. The second component is the SMTP message screener, which can help reduce the amount of unwanted e-mail entering the organization. The third component is the SMTP application filter, which can be used to block buffer overflow attacks or SMTP command-based attacks on Exchange Server.

Mail Server Wizard

You can use the Mail Server Wizard to make Exchange Server available to Internet clients. The Mail Server Wizard includes several options, one of which is publishing an SMTP server.

SMTP application filter

ISA Server 2004 provides intelligent application-layer filtering to help prevent Internet attackers from using buffer overflow commands to disable or take control of your computer running Exchange Server. The SMTP application-layer filter inspects the commands included in all incoming SMTP communications. You can configure the SMTP filter to limit the size of the SMTP command sequences as well to block specific commands.

SMTP message screener

The ISA Server 2004 SMTP Message Screener can be used to control incoming SMTP mail by performing application-layer inspection of all SMTP messages. The message screener can scan the messages and examine the attachments and then block or hold messages for later inspection.

You can configure the SMTP Message Screener to block or hold incoming or outgoing e-mail using the following parameters:

- Source or destination e-mail domain
- Source or destination e-mail address
- Attachment size, file extension, or file name
- Keywords in the mail subject or body

The Message Screener can block or hold messages leaving the internal network in the same way that it does for messages entering the network.

How to Configure ISA Server to Secure SMTP Traffic

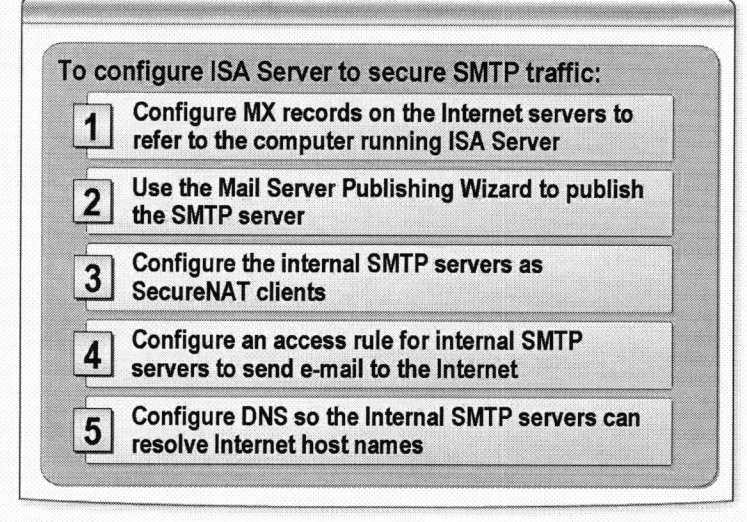

To configure ISA Server to secure SMTP traffic:

1. Configure MX records on the Internet servers to refer to the computer running ISA Server

2. Use the Mail Server Publishing Wizard to publish the SMTP server

3. Configure the internal SMTP servers as SecureNAT clients

4. Configure an access rule for internal SMTP servers to send e-mail to the Internet

5. Configure DNS so the internal SMTP servers can resolve Internet host names

Configuring ISA Server to publish an SMTP server

The following steps provide a high-level overview of the process of configuring ISA Server to publish an SMTP server; the detailed steps are included in the subsequent practice.

1. Configure the Mail Exchange (MX) records on the Internet Domain Name Service (DNS) servers to point to a Host record that uses the IP address of the external network adapter on the computer running ISA Server. When an SMTP server on the Internet needs to deliver a message to a recipient in a specific DNS domain, the SMTP server attempts to locate the MX records for the domain by querying the DNS server that is authoritative for that domain.

2. Use the Mail Server Publishing Wizard to publish the SMTP server located on the internal network.

3. If the internal SMTP servers will also send e-mail to the Internet, then configure the internal SMTP servers as Secure Network Address Translation (SecureNAT) clients by configuring the default gateway on the SMTP server to point to the IP address of the internal network interface card on the server running ISA Server.

4. Configure an access rule that enables internal SMTP servers to send e-mail to the Internet. If your current Internet access rule allows all computers on the internal network to use any protocol to connect to Internet resources, then you do not need to configure this access rule. However, if you have limited access to the Internet to specific protocols or specific computers, you must configure an access rule that allows only the explicitly defined the SMTP servers to send e-mail to the Internet.

5. Configure DNS so that the internal SMTP servers can locate the MX records and resolve DNS host names for SMTP servers on the Internet.

Practice: Publishing an SMTP Server

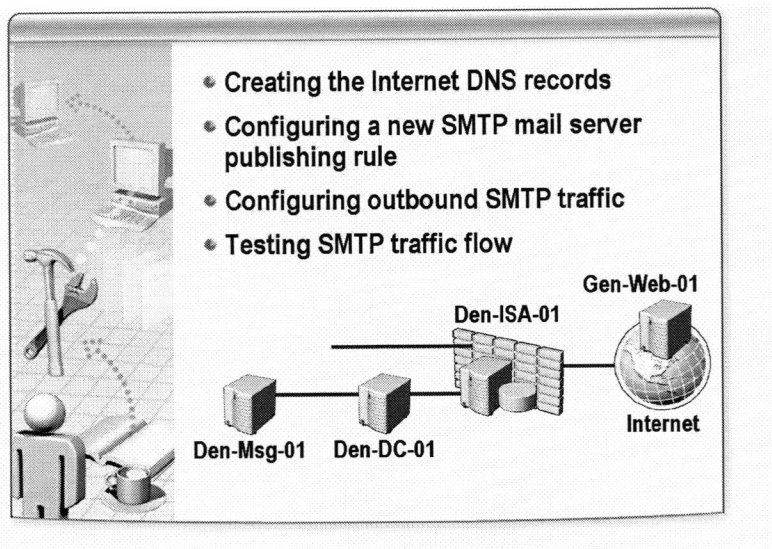

- Creating the Internet DNS records
- Configuring a new SMTP mail server publishing rule
- Configuring outbound SMTP traffic
- Testing SMTP traffic flow

Gen-Web-01
Den-ISA-01
Internet
Den-Msg-01   Den-DC-01

Introduction

In this practice, you will configure the lab environment to enable Internet e-mail to flow between the Coho Vineyard organization and other organizations on the Internet. To do this, you will configure the required DNS records on the Internet DNS servers. Next, you will configure ISA Server to publish the internal SMTP server at Coho Vineyard and also configure it to allow the internal SMTP servers to send e-mail to the Internet. Then you will test the configuration to ensure that SMTP e-mail can flow through ISA Server.

▶ **To prepare for this practice**

1. You will need the Den-DC-01 virtual machine, the Den-Msg-01 virtual machine, the Den-ISA-01 virtual machine, and the Gen-Web-01 virtual machine for this practice.

2. If necessary, start or resume the required virtual machines and then, on Den-ISA-01, log on to the cohovineyard domain with your user name and password.

Practice

▶ **Creating the Internet DNS records**

1. Switch to the Gen-Web-01 virtual machine.

2. Log on to Gen-Web-01 using a user name of **Administrator** and a password of **P@ssw0rd**.

3. Open the **DNS** management console from the **Administrative Tools** folder.

4. Expand **Forward Lookup Zones**, and then expand **cohovineyard.com**.

5. Right-click **cohovineyard.com** and click **New Host (A)**.

6. In the **New Host** dialog box, in the **Name** text box, type **Mail**. Configure the **IP address** as 131.107.1.100. Click **Add Host**, click **OK**, and then click **Done**.

7. Right-click **cohovineyard.com** and click **New Mail Exchanger (MX)**.

8. In the **New Resource Record** dialog box, in the **Fully qualified domain name (FQDN) of mail server** field, type **mail.cohovineyard.com**. Click **OK**.

9. Expand contoso.com, and then right-click **contoso.com** and click **New Mail Exchanger (MX)**.

10. In the **New Resource Record** dialog box, in the **Fully qualified domain name (FQDN) of mail server** field type **www.contoso.com**. Click **OK**.

11. Close the **DNS** management console.

▶ **Configuring a new SMTP mail server publishing rule**

1. Switch to the Den-ISA-01 virtual machine.

2. Open **ISA Server Management**, expand **Den-ISA-01** if necessary, and click **Firewall Policy**.

3. On the **Firewall Policy** task pane **Tasks** tab, select **Publish a Mail Server**.

4. On the **Welcome to the New Mail Server Publishing Wizard** page, type **Coho Vineyard Mail** as the rule name, and then click **Next**.

5. On the **Select Access Type** page, click **Server-to-Server communication: SMTP, NNTP**, and then click **Next**.

6. On the **Select Services** page, select **SMTP**. Click **Next**.

7. On the **Select Server** page, type **192.168.1.12** as the **Server IP address** of the computer running Exchange Server, and then click **Next**.

8. On the **IP Addresses** page, select **External**, and then click **Next**.

9. On the **Completing the New Mail Server Publishing Rule Wizard** page, review the configuration, and then click **Finish**.

▶ **Configuring outbound SMTP traffic**

1. On **Tasks** tab, click **Create New Access Rule**.

2. On the **Welcome to the New Access Rule Wizard**, type **SMTP Outbound** as the name for the access rule, and then click **Next**.

3. On the **Rule Action** page, select **Allow**, and then click **Next**.

4. On the **Protocols** page, in the **This rule applies to list**, click **Selected protocols**, and then click **Add**.

5. In the **Add Protocols** dialog box, expand **Mail**, and then select **SMTP**. Click **Add**, and then click **Close to close the Add Protocols** dialog box. On the **Protocols** page, click **Next**.

6. On the **Access Rule Sources** page, click **Add to open the Add Network Entities** dialog box, expand **Networks**, select **Internal**, click **Add**, and then click **Close**. On the **Access Rule Sources** page, click **Next**.

7. On the **Access Rule Destinations** page, click **Add to open the Add Network Entities** dialog box, click **Networks**, select the **External network** (representing the Internet), click **Add**, and then click **Close**. On the **Access Rule Destinations** page, click **Next**.

8. On the **User Sets** page, accept the default user set of **All Users** and click **Next**.

9. On the **Completing the New Access Rule Wizard** page, review the configuration, and then click **Finish**.

10. Click **Apply** to apply the changes and then click **OK** when the changes have been applied.

▶ **Testing SMTP traffic flow**

1. Switch to the Gen-Web-01 virtual machine.

2. On the **Start** menu, point to **All Programs**, and then click **Outlook Express**.

3. The Internet Connection Wizard starts. On the **Your Name** page, in the **Display name** field, type **Contoso Administrator**. Click **Next**.

4. On the **Internet E-mail Address** page, in the **E-mail address** field, type **administrator@contoso.com**, and then click **Next**.

5. On the **E-mail Server Names** page, enter **Gen-Web-01** as both the **Incoming mail (POP3, IMAP, or HTTP)** server and the **Outgoing mail (SMTP)** server. Click **Next**.

6. On the **Internet Mail Logon** page, type **P@ssw0rd** in the **Password** field, and then select **Log on using Secure Password Authentication (SPA)**. Click **Next**.

7. On the **Congratulations** page, click **Finish**.

8. Create a new e-mail and send it to **jay@cohovineyard.com**. Use a subject of Test1.

9. Switch to the Den-Msg-01 virtual machine.

10. Log on to the cohovineyard domain with a user name of **Administrator** and a password of **P@ssw0rd**.

11. Open **Internet Explorer**. If you receive an Internet Explorer message, click **In the future, do not show this message** and click **OK**.

12. In the **Address** box, type **http://den-msg-01/exchange/jay/inbox**. Press **Enter**.

13. In the **Connect to den-msg-01.cohovineyard.com** dialog box, log on using **cohovineyard\jay** and a password of **P@ssw0rd**.

14. If you receive an Internet Explorer warning message, click **Add**, and then click **Add** again and click **Close**.

15. Expand **Inbox** and double-click the message from Contoso Administrator. Click **Reply**, type a short message, and then click **Send**.

16. Switch to the Gen-Web-01 virtual machine.

17. In Outlook Express, click **Send/Recv** and review the message from Jay Adams.

18. Close all open windows on both Gen-Web-01 and Den-Msg-01.

How SMTP Filtering Works

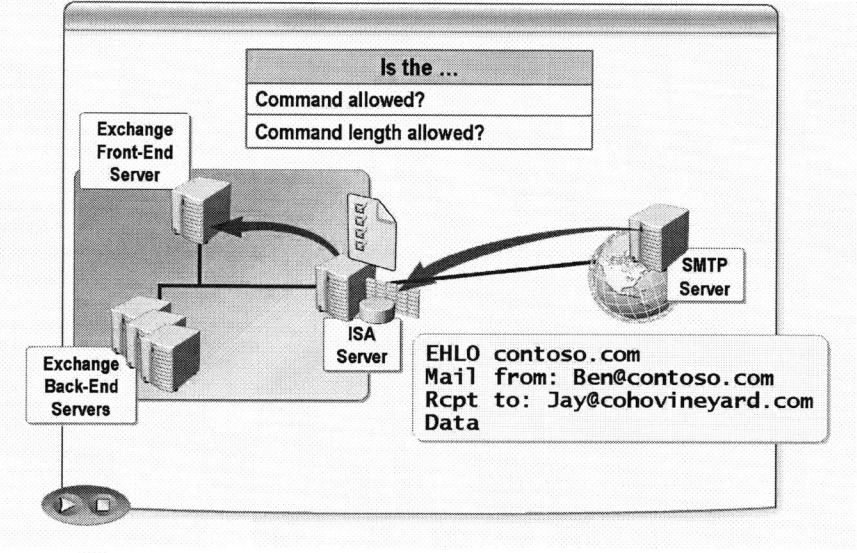

Introduction

When ISA Server is configured to publish an SMTP server, it intercepts all SMTP traffic that arrives on port 25 of the external interface card of the ISA Server computer. The SMTP filter on ISA Server accepts the traffic, inspects it, and forwards it to internal SMTP servers only if the SMTP filter allows it.

SMTP command filtering

The SMTP filter examines the SMTP commands sent by Internet SMTP servers and clients. This application-layer filter checks to see if the commands are allowed and if they are larger than they should be. SMTP commands that are larger than the limits you configure in the SMTP filter are assumed to be attacks against the SMTP server and are stopped by the SMTP filter.

The SMTP filter can be configured to disable specific SMTP commands. When an SMTP server or client uses a command that is defined but disabled, the filter stops the command and closes that connection. For example, if you disable the VRFY command, ISA Server will block all SMTP connections that use this command. When a client uses a command that is not recognized by the SMTP filter, the connection is also denied. For example, the SMTP filter does not define the TURN command, so TURN commands will be blocked by the SMTP filter.

Each SMTP command also has a maximum length that specifies the number of bytes allowed for each command. If an attacker sends a command that exceeds the number of bytes allowed for the command, ISA Server drops the connection and prevents the attacker from communicating with the corporate mail server. For example, the default maximum length for the RCPT TO command is 266 bytes. If a SMTP connection uses a longer RCPT TO command than this limit, the connection is dropped.

Note The SMTP request for comments (RFC) considers the AUTH command as part of the MAIL FROM command. For this reason, the SMTP filter blocks MAIL FROM commands only when they exceed the length of the MAIL FROM and AUTH commands issued (when AUTH is enabled). For example, if you specify the maximum length of MAIL FROM as 266 bytes and AUTH as 1024 bytes, the message will be blocked only if the MAIL FROM command exceeds 1290 bytes.

If an SMTP command is blocked because it violates one of the SMTP filter's conditions, the blocked message will only be logged when the SMTP Filter event alert is enabled. This alert is disabled by default.

The SMTP filter must be located on the computer running ISA Server. All SMTP traffic that passes through ISA Server is analyzed by the SMTP filter and forwarded if allowed.

How to Configure the SMTP Application Filter

Introduction

The SMTP filter is installed and enabled by default. When you publish an SMTP mail server, or enable an SMTP access rule, all SMTP messages are filtered using the default policy.

Configuring the SMTP filter

To modify the default configuration of the SMTP filter, complete the following procedure:

1. In ISA Server Management, click Add-ins.

2. In the details pane, on the **Applications Filters** tab, double-click **SMTP Filter**.

3. On the **SMTP Commands** tab, click the applicable command, and then click **Edit**.

4. In the **SMTP Command Rule** dialog box, you can disable the command by clearing the **Enable SMTP command** check box.

5. To modify the maximum length for the SMTP command, type the maximum length of the command line (in bytes) for the command in the **Maximum Length** field.

6. Click **OK** to close the **SMTP Command Rule** dialog box.

7. To add an additional SMTP command to the filter, on the **SMTP Commands** tab, click **Add**.

8. In the **SMTP Command Rule** dialog box, in **Command Name**, type the name of the command.

9. In **Maximum Length**, type the maximum length of the command line (in bytes).

10. Click **OK** to close the **SMTP Command Rule** dialog box.

11. Click **OK** to close the **SMTP Filter Properties** page.

How SMTP Message Screener Works

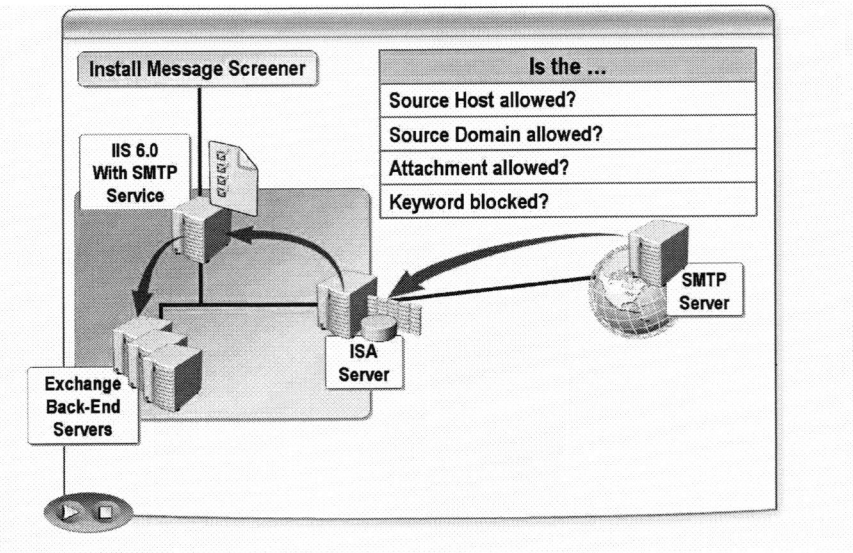

Introduction

SMTP message screener works together with the SMTP filter to intercept and filter all SMTP traffic. Message screener is designed for filtering unwanted and malicious e-mail.

How message screener filters messages

The message screener must be installed on a server running the IIS 5.0 or 6.0 SMTP service. The message screener component can be installed on the computer running ISA Server, on a computer running Exchange Server, or on any other IIS 5.0 or IIS 6.0 SMTP server in the internal network or in a perimeter network.

SMTP message screener can be configured to filter incoming mail based on:

- *The information in the MAIL FROM SMTP command.* The MAIL FROM command specifies the source SMTP address for the e-mail message. This is used for sender and domain name filtering.

- *The information in the Content-Disposition header field for each attachment.* This field commonly contains the attachment file name and extension. Message Screener can filter attachments by extension, by name, or by size.

- *Keywords in the message subject or body.* This is used for filtering the message subject and the body, either text/plain or text/html content type.

SMTP Message Screener can be configured to delete e-mail messages, hold e-mail messages for later inspection, or forward e-mail messages to a specific e-mail account for further examination and analysis.

Important   If Message Screener is installed but not enabled and configured, Message Screener will drop all messages.

How to Implement SMTP Message Screener

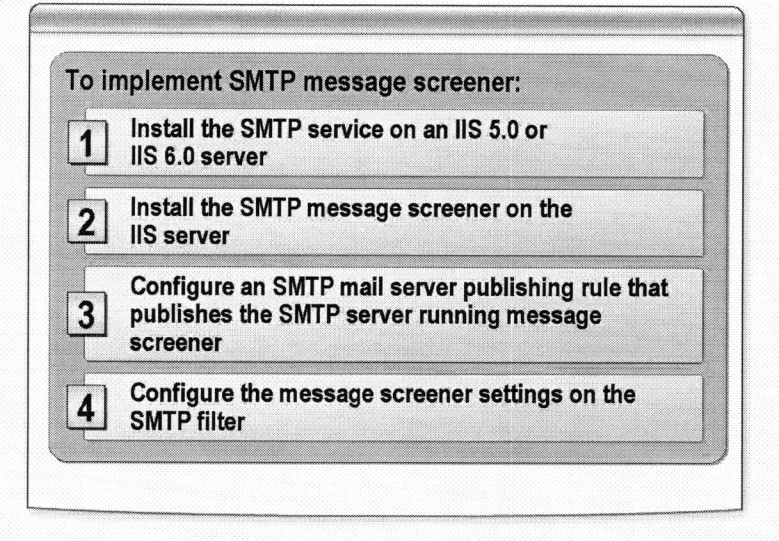

To implement SMTP message screener:

1. Install the SMTP service on an IIS 5.0 or IIS 6.0 server

2. Install the SMTP message screener on the IIS server

3. Configure an SMTP mail server publishing rule that publishes the SMTP server running message screener

4. Configure the message screener settings on the SMTP filter

---

To implement SMTP message screener

SMTP message screener is an optional component that is included with ISA Server. This component is unique in that it does not need to be installed on a server running ISA Server but can be installed on any server running the SMTP service included with IIS 5.0 or IIS 6.0.

The following steps provide a high-level overview of how to implement SMTP message screener; the detailed steps are included in the subsequent practice.

1. Install the SMTP service on the IIS server where you are going to install the SMTP message screener. Only the SMTP service and the default components included with this service are required.

2. Install the SMTP message screener on the IIS server. To install the message screener, run setup from the ISA Server CD-ROM and choose a custom installation. Install only the message screener component.

3. Configure a user account on the message screener computer with access to the ISA Server computer. Do this by running the SMTPCred.exe program from the FPC\Program Files\Microsoft ISA Server directory on the ISA Server 2004 CD. When you run SMTPCred.exe, enter the username, domain, and password of a user who has administrative permissions on ISA Server.

4. Configure an SMTP mail server publishing rule that publishes the SMTP server running message screener.

5. Configure the message screener properties on the SMTP filter. To configure the message screener properties in **ISA Server Management**, expand **Configuration**, and then click Add-ins.

6. On the **Application Filters** tab, double click **SMTP Filter**. You can configure the settings listed in the following table:

Tab	Use this setting to:
Keywords	Provide a string that the message screener will look for in e-mails. You can select whether the action is applied if the keyword is found in the message header, the body, or both. You can also specify an action for when a message meets the keyword criteria. You can configure the message screener to delete the message, hold the message, or forward the message to a specified mailbox.
Users/Domains	Add the names of senders or of entire domains for which e-mail will be blocked. When the SMTP sender address matches the blocked senders or domains list, the message will be deleted.
Attachments	Configure how message screener will filter attachments. You can configure message screener to filter attachments based on attachment name, attachment extension, or attachment size limit. You can also specify an action for when a message meets the attachment criteria. You can configure the message screener to delete the message, hold the message, or forward the message to a specified mailbox.

Practice: Implementing SMTP Message Screener

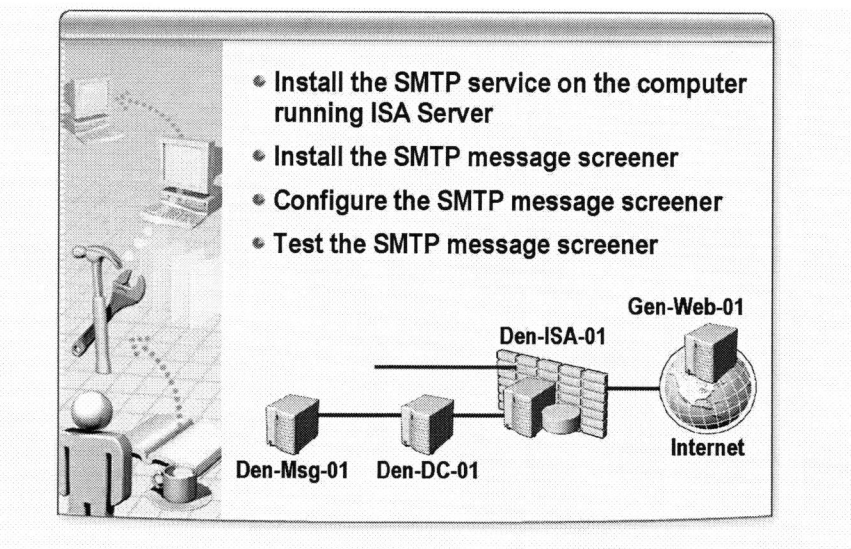

- Install the SMTP service on the computer running ISA Server
- Install the SMTP message screener
- Configure the SMTP message screener
- Test the SMTP message screener

Introduction

In this practice, you will install the SMTP service on the server running ISA Server, and then install the SMTP message screener on that server. Then you will configure and test the message screener.

Practice

▶ **To prepare for this practice**

1. You will need the Den-DC-01 virtual machine, the Den-Msg-01 virtual machine, the Den-ISA-01 virtual machine, and the Gen-Web-01 virtual machine for this practice.

2. If necessary, start or resume the required virtual machines and then, on Den-ISA-01, log on to the cohovineyard domain with your user name and password.

▶ **Installing the SMTP service on the computer running ISA Server**

1. Open **Add or Remove Programs** from the **Control Panel**.

2. Click **Add/Remove Windows Components**.

3. In the **Windows Components** dialog box, click **Application Server**, and then click **Details**.

4. In the **Application Server** dialog box, click **Internet Information Services (IIS)**, and then click **Details**.

5. In the **Internet Information Services (IIS)** dialog box, click the **SMTP Service** check box, and then click **OK**.

6. Click **OK** in the **Internet Information Services (ISS)** dialog box, and then click **OK** to close the **Application Server** dialog box. In the **Windows Components** dialog box, click **Next**.

7. If you see an **Insert Disk** dialog box, click **OK**. Then click **Browse** and browse to **c:\win2k3\i386**. Click **Open** and then click **OK**.

8. When the installation finishes, click **Finish**. Minimize **Add or Remove Programs**.

Note Because the SMTP message screener component is installed on the same server as ISA Server, you must configure the SMTP server to listen only on the internal IP address of the computer running ISA Server. Then you will configure ISA Server to publish that IP address as the SMTP server. You also need to configure the SMTP server to relay messages for the internal domain, cohovineyard.com.

---

9. Open **Internet Information Services (IIS)** from the **Administrative Tools** folder.

10. Expand **DEN-ISA-01(local computer)**, then right-click **Default SMTP Virtual Server** and click **Properties**.

11. On the **General** tab, in the **IP address** list, click **192.168.1.1**.

12. On the **Access** tab, click **Relay**. In the **Relay Restrictions** dialog box, ensure that **Only the list below** is selected, and that **Allow all computers which successfully authenticate to relay regardless of the list above** is selected. This configuration means that authenticated users can relay through this server, but no one else can. Click **OK**, and then click **OK** again to close the **Default SMTP Virtual Server Properties**.

13. Expand **Default SMTP Virtual Server**, then right-click **Domains** and point to **New**, and then click **Domain**.

14. On the **Welcome to the New SMTP Domain Wizard** page, accept the default of **Remote**, and then click **Next**.

15. On the **Domain Name** page, type **cohovineyard.com** and click **Finish**.

16. Expand **Domains**, right-click **cohovineyard.com**, and click **Properties**.

17. On the **General** tab, click **Allow incoming mail to be relayed to this domain**. Under **Route domain**, click **Forward all mail to smart host** and type **[192.168.1.12]**. Click **OK**.

18. Right-click **Default SMTP Virtual Server** and click **Stop**. Right-click **Default SMTP Virtual Server** again and click **Start**.

19. Close Internet Information Services (IIS) Manager.

▶ **Installing the SMTP message screener**

1. In the **Add or Remove Programs** dialog box, click **Microsoft ISA Server 2004**. Click **Change/Remove**.

2. On the **Welcome to the Installation Wizard for Microsoft ISA Server 2004** page, click **Next**.

3. On the **Program Maintenance** page, click **Modify**, and then click **Next**.

4. On the **Custom Setup** page, click the icon next to **Message Screener** and select **This feature will be installed on local hard drive**. Click **Next**.

5. On the **Services** page, click **Next**.

6. On the **Ready to Modify the Program** page, click **Install**.

7. On the **Installation Wizard Completed** page, click **Finish**. If an Internet Explorer dialog box appears, click **In the future, do not show this message** and click **OK**. Close all open Windows.

▶ **Configure the message screener**

1. Open **ISA Server Management**. In the console tree, click **Firewall Policy**.

2. Right-click **Coho Vineyard Mail SMTP Server**, and click **Properties**. On the **To** tab, change the server IP address to **192.168.1.1**. Click **OK**.

3. Expand **Configuration**, and then click **Add-ins**. On the **Application Filters** tab, right click **SMTP Filter** and click **Properties**.

4. On the **Keywords** tab, click **Add** to open the **Mail Keyword Rule** dialog box. In **Keyword**, type **test**. In the **Action** drop-down list, click **Forward message to**. In **E-mail address**, type **administrator@cohovineyard.com**. Click **OK**.

5. Click **OK** to close the **SMTP Filter Properties** dialog box.

6. Click **Apply** to apply the changes and then click **OK** when the changes have been applied.

▶ **Test the SMTP message screener configuration**

1. Switch to the Gen-Web-01 virtual machine.

2. Open **Outlook Express**.

3. Create a new e-mail and send it to **jay@cohovineyard.com**. Use a subject of **Test**.

4. Switch to the Den-Msg-01 virtual machine.

5. Open **Internet Explorer** and type **http://den-msg-01/exchange/jay/inbox** in the **Address** bar. Press **Enter**.

6. In the **Connect to den-msg-01.cohovineyard.com** dialog box, log on using **cohovineyard\jay** and a password of **P@ssw0rd**.

7. Expand **Inbox** and confirm that Jay did not receive the e-mail with the subject of Test.

8. In the Address bar, type **http://den-msg-01/exchange/administrator/inbox**. Press **Enter**.

9. In the **Connect to den-msg-01.cohovineyard.com** dialog box, log on using **cohovineyard\administrator** and a password of **P@ssw0rd**.

10. Expand **Inbox** and confirm that the administrator received the e-mail that was sent to Jay Adams with the subject of test.

11. Close **Internet Explorer**.

Integrating ISA Server and Exchange Server to Secure SMTP Traffic

You can deploy message screener:

- On the computer running ISA Server. This option is the easiest to configure but least secure
- On an IIS server in the internal or perimeter network. Using a server in the perimeter network is most complicated to configure, but most secure
- To filter only inbound messages. Configure ISA Server to publish the message screener server, and configure access rules for the internal SMTP servers to send e-mail to the Internet
- To filter inbound and outbound messages. Configure ISA Server to publish the message screener server, and configure the internal SMTP servers to route messages to the message screener server

Introduction

ISA Server and Exchange server can be used together to ensure the most secure SMTP server configuration. There are several options available for integrating these two products.

Message screener deployment options

The SMTP filter must be installed on the ISA Server that is used to publish SMTP servers and used to configure access rules for sending SMTP messages to the Internet. However, because message screener does not need to be installed on a computer running ISA Server, you have several options for deploying message screener. One of the questions that you need to answer when deploying SMTP message screener, is where to install the message screener component. You have two options:

- *Install message screener on ISA Server.* You can install message screener on the server running ISA Server and configure it to filter inbound messages. In this configuration, ISA Server Firewall services forwards all messages to the SMTP service which scans the messages. This configuration is less secure than installing message screener on another server because message screener requires that the SMTP service be installed on the ISA Server computer. As well, this configuration is not scalable for larger organizations. For these reasons, installing the message screener component on ISA Server is recommended only for situations where no additional servers are available, and where ISA Server is not operating as an Internet Edge firewall.

- *Install message screener on another IIS server.* This is the more secure configuration because the IIS server running the SMTP service is not directly accessible from the Internet. The ISA Server can filter the SMTP commands, and only allowed packets will reach the SMTP message screener server. This option is also scalable because the Firewall service and SMTP message screener are separated. For maximum security, the IIS server running message screener should be located in a perimeter network and the server should not be a member server in the internal domain. However, if the SMTP server is not a member of the internal domain and is also configured as the SMTP relay server for POP3 or IMAP4 clients, users will not be able to authenticate to this server to relay messages. Installing the message screener component on a server in the perimeter network requires additional ISA Server configuration because you need to configure server publishing rules or access rules between the perimeter network and the internal network, but this option is more secure.

The second design question is whether to scan inbound messages only or both inbound and outbound messages.

- *Use message screener for inbound messages only.* In this configuration, you configure ISA Server to publish the server running message screener, and configure message screener to forward all allowed messages to the computers running Exchange Server on the internal network. You also configure the access rule on ISA Server to allow the internal computers running Exchange Server to send SMTP messages to the Internet. Use this configuration if your organization does not have any requirement to scan outbound message contents.

- *Use message screener for inbound and outbound messages.* In this configuration, you configure ISA Server to publish the server running message screener, and configure message screener to forward all approved messages to the computers running Exchange Server on the internal network. You also configure the internal computers running Exchange Server to send all SMTP messages to the server running message screener. Message screener scans outbound messages and then forwards the messages through ISA Server to the Internet. In this scenario, the server running message screener must be able to use DNS to locate the mail servers for both the internal and external DNS domains. Use this configuration to ensure the security of outbound e-mail. For example, you can use message screener to scan outbound messages for specific content or to block messages with specified attachments.

Lesson: Configuring ISA Server to Secure Web Client Connections

* How Does ISA Server Secure OWA Connections?
* How to Configure ISA Server to Enable OWA Access
* How to Configure Forms-Based Authentication
* How to Configure ISA Server to Enable Access for Other Web Clients

Introduction

Many organizations have chosen to use Web-based clients to give remote users access to their Exchange mailboxes. One of the most popular ways to provide access to e-mail for users outside the internal network is to deploy an Outlook Web Access (OWA) server so that users can access their mailboxes from any computer with an Internet connection and a Web browser. In addition, Exchange Server 2003 also enables access to mailboxes for wireless mobile clients, including Outlook Mobile Access (OMA) and Microsoft ActiveSync clients. This lesson describes how to use ISA Server to secure Web client connections.

Lesson objectives

After completing this lesson, you will be able to:

- Describe how ISA Server secures OWA connections.
- Configure ISA Server to enable OWA access.
- Configure OWA forms-based authentication.
- Configure ISA Server to enable other Web client connections.

How Does ISA Server Secure OWA Connections?

Introduction

Outlook Web Access provides access to user mailboxes and public folders on a computer running Exchange Server for Web browser clients. OWA is a popular way to access e-mail remotely because it does not require any specific e-mail client or client configuration.

Mail Server Wizard

You can use the Mail Server Wizard to make the Outlook Web Access server available to Internet clients. When you publish Outlook Web Access servers through computers running ISA Server, you are protecting the Outlook Web Access server from direct external access because the name and IP address of the Outlook Web Access server are not accessible to the user. The user accesses the computer running ISA Server, which then forwards the request to the Outlook Web Access server according to the conditions of your mail server publishing rule.

When you configure a mail server publishing rule for OWA, you can choose the SSL bridging configuration for the OWA rule. To maximize security, you should configure secure connections for both the connection between the OWA client and the computer running ISA Server and between the computer running ISA Server and the OWA server.

Note You can also use the Mail Server Wizard to publish Outlook Mobile Access and Exchange ActiveSync.

Forms-based authentication

To provide another level of security, ISA Server also enables the option of enforcing forms-based authentication for all OWA clients. Forms-based authentication is a type of Microsoft ASP.NET-based authentication in which an unauthenticated user is directed to an HTML form. After the user provides credentials, the system issues a cookie containing a ticket. On subsequent requests, the system first checks the cookie to see if the user was already authenticated, so that the user does not have to supply credentials again.

After a user has been authenticated using forms-based authentication, the credential information is not cached on the client computer. This is particularly important in a scenario in which users are connecting to your Outlook Web Access server from public computers, where you would not want user credentials to be cached. Users are required to re-authenticate if they close the browser, log off from a session, or navigate to another Web site. Also, you can configure a maximum idle session time-out, so that if a user is idle for a prolonged period of time, re-authentication is required.

Note ISA Server supports forms-based authentication for Exchange Server 5.5, Exchange 2000 Server, and Exchange Server 2003. Exchange Server 2003 also supports forms-based authentication. You must not configure Exchange Server 2003 for forms-based authentication if you plan to implement this by using ISA Server.

Controlling attachment availability

Another option available on computers running ISA Server for securing OWA access is the option to control the user's ability to view and save attachments. By default, if a user views an attachment on a public computer, the attachment is saved in the Temporary Internet Files on that computer. The users may also be able to save an attachment to the local hard drive. In both cases, confidential company data may be stored on the client computer where other users may be able to access the information. ISA Server provides a mechanism for blocking e-mail attachments for users on public/shared computers or users on private computers (or both). This prevents users from opening or saving attachments, although the users can see that the message has an attachment.

How to Configure ISA Server to Enable OWA Access

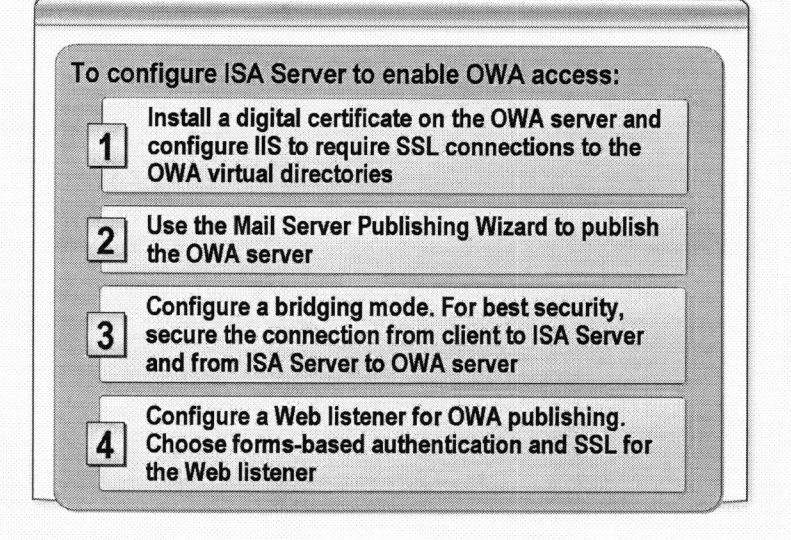

To configure ISA Server to enable OWA access:

1. Install a digital certificate on the OWA server and configure IIS to require SSL connections to the OWA virtual directories

2. Use the Mail Server Publishing Wizard to publish the OWA server

3. Configure a bridging mode. For best security, secure the connection from client to ISA Server and from ISA Server to OWA server

4. Configure a Web listener for OWA publishing. Choose forms-based authentication and SSL for the Web listener

Introduction

For the most part, publishing Outlook Web Access is similar to publishing any other Web server. The easiest way to publish an Outlook Web Access server is to use the Mail Server Publishing Wizard on ISA Server 2004 to make an internal OWA server accessible to Internet clients.

Configuring ISA Server to enable OWA access

The following steps provide a high-level overview of how to configure ISA Server to enable OWA access; the detailed steps are included in a subsequent practice.

1. Install a certificate on the OWA server and on the computer running ISA Server. On the OWA server, configure IIS to require SSL connections for the /Exchange, /Exchweb, and the /Public virtual servers.

2. Start the Mail Server Publishing Rule Wizard from the ISA Server Management console. Configure the publishing rule to provide access to Web Clients and, specifically, to Outlook Web Access. When you configure an OWA mail server publishing rule, it automatically creates a path that maps to the /Exchange, /Exchweb, and /Public virtual folders on the OWA Server.

3. Choose a bridging mode. You have three options when choosing a bridging mode:

    a. **Secure connection to clients**. Specifies that ISA Server establish a secure connection with the client computers and a standard connection to the mail server.

    b. **Secure connection to clients and mail server**. Specifies that ISA Server establish a secure connection with both the mail server and the clients.

    c. **Standard connections only**. Specifies that ISA Server establish a standard connection with both the mail server and the clients.

    The most secure option is to require a secure connection from both ISA Server to the clients and ISA Server to the OWA server. This option enables HTTP application filtering on the computer running ISA Server and secures the network traffic both on the Internet and on the protected network.

4. Choose a Web listener for Outlook Web Access publishing. The Web listener for Outlook Web Access publishing should be configured to use forms-based authentication. If you have configured secure connections to the clients, be sure that the listener listens for requests on an HTTPS port.

How to Configure Forms-Based Authentication

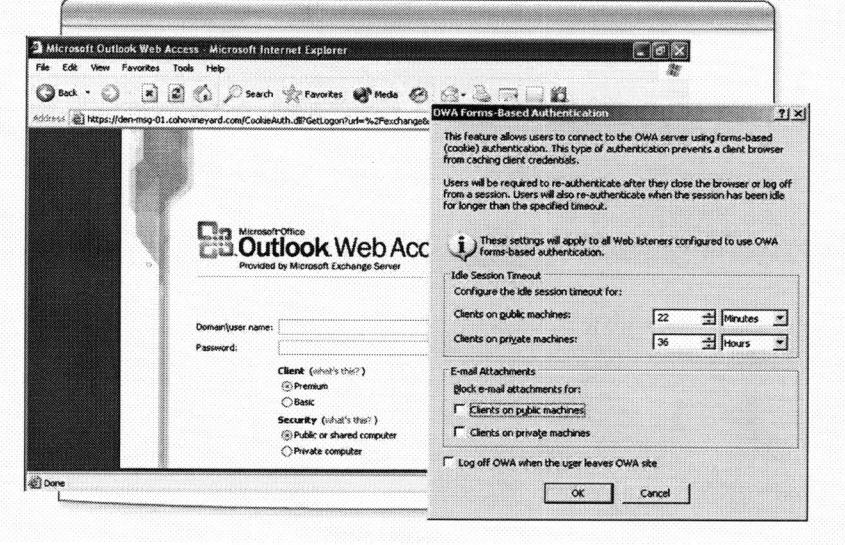

Introduction

One of the important advances in ISA Server 2004 is OWA forms-based authentication. Forms-based authentication ensures that the user credentials are not cached on the client computer after the user logs off, or after a time-out period expires.

Idle session time-outs

When you configure forms-based authentication, you can configure how long a user's credentials will remain on the client computer after a period of inactivity. When a user logs on using forms-based authentication, a cookie stores the OWA user credentials. When the user logs off from OWA, the cookie is cleared and it is no longer valid for authentication.

You can also limit how long the credentials are stored if the user does not log off. The logon page enabled by forms-based authentication allows the user to select the security option that best fits the client they are connecting from. The two options available are:

- *Public or shared computer*. Public or shared computer is the default setting. It provides a short default time-out option of 22 minutes of user inactivity before the cookie times out.

- *Private computer*. The private computer option allows for a longer period of inactivity before automatically ending the session—its internal default value is 36 hours. This option should be used if the user is the only operator of the computer, and the computer adheres to the security policies of the user's company.

The automatic time-out is valuable for keeping a user account secure from unauthorized access. Although this time-out does not completely eliminate the possibility that an unauthorized user may access an account if an Outlook Web Access session is accidentally left running on a public computer, the time-out greatly reduces this risk.

Blocking e-mail attachments

Another option that is enabled with forms-based authentication is the option to prevent users from opening or saving attachments. You can configure attachment blocking for public computers, private computers, or both. Blocking attachments, particularly on public computers, is recommended.

Configuring Forms-Based Authentication

To configure ISA Server to require forms-based authentication for OWA connections, complete the following steps.

1. In **ISA Server Management**, click **Firewall Policy**.

2. In the task pane, on the **Toolbox** tab, in the **Network Objects** pane, expand **Web Listeners**, right-click the Web Listener that is used for OWA connections, and then click **Properties**.

3. In the **Web listener** properties dialog box, on the **Preferences** tab, click **Authentication**.

4. In the **Authentication** dialog box, in the **Method** list, enable **OWA Forms-Based**, and then click **Configure**.

5. On the **OWA Forms-Based Authentication** dialog box, you can configure the **Idle Session Timeout** setting for public and private computers as well as configure whether users will be allowed to open e-mail attachments box on private and public computers. If you select **Log off OWA when the user leaves the OWA site**, the user will be logged off when they connect to a Web site other than the OWA site.

How to Configure ISA Server to Enable Access for Other Web Clients

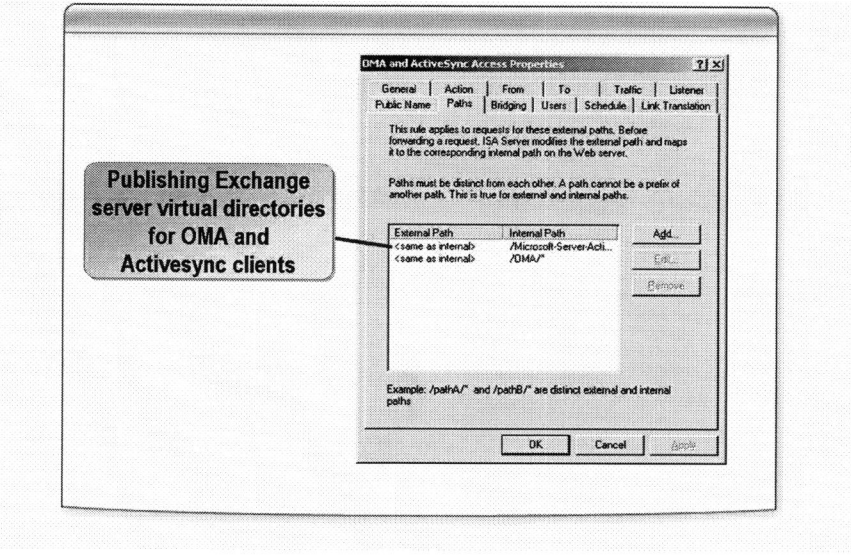

Introduction

ISA Server can also be configured to publish Outlook Mobile Access and Exchange ActiveSync services to the Internet. These services are available only with Exchange Server 2003.

Configuring OMA and ActiveSync access

Configuring access to OMA and ActiveSync on ISA Server is almost identical to enabling access to Outlook Web Access. When you run the Mail Server Publishing Wizard, you can choose to enable the Outlook Mobile Access and Exchange ActiveSync Web client mail services. When you choose these options, the /Microsoft-Server-ActiveSync virtual directory and the /OMA virtual directories are mapped to the OWA server. If you have forms-based authentication configured for the Web listener used for OWA, you must use a different Web listener for OMA and ActiveSync access. OMA and ActiveSync do not support forms-based authentication.

Practice: Configuring ISA Server for Secure OWA Connections

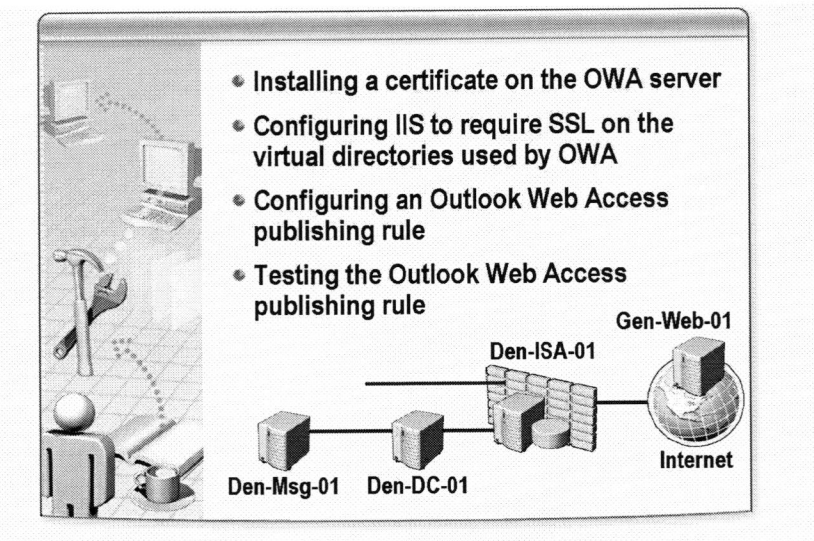

Introduction

In this practice, you will use the New Mail Server Publishing Wizard to configure a new publishing rule for Outlook Web Access clients. You will then test the publishing rule.

▶ **To prepare for this practice**

1. You will need the Den-DC-01 virtual machine, the Den-Msg-01 virtual machine, the Den-ISA-01 virtual machine, and the Gen-Web-01 virtual machine for this practice.

2. If necessary, start or resume the required virtual machines and then, on Den-Msg-01, log on to the cohovineyard domain with a user name of **Administrator** and a password of **P@ssw0rd**.

Practice

▶ **Install a certificate on the OWA server**

1. On **Den-Msg-01** and open **Internet Information Services (IIS) Manager**.

2. Expand **Den-Msg-01**, and then expand **Web Sites**.

3. Right-click **Default Web Site** and click **Properties**.

4. On the **Directory Security** tab, click **Server Certificate**.

5. On the **Welcome to the Web Server Certificate Wizard** page, click **Next**.

6. On the **Server Certificate** page, click **Create a new certificate**. Click **Next**.

7. On the **Delayed or Immediate Request** page, click **Send the request immediately to an online certification authority** and click **Next**.

8. On the **Name and Security Settings** page, accept the defaults and click **Next**.

9. On the **Organization Information** page, type **Coho Vineyard** as the **Organization** name and **Messaging** as the **Organizational unit** name. Click **Next**.

10. On the **Your Site's Common Name** page, type **Den-msg-01.cohovineyard.com** as the **Common name**. Click **Next**.

11. On the **Geographic Information** page, accept the default for the **Country/Region**, type **Colorado** as the **State/province** and type **Denver** as the **City/locality**. Click **Next**.

12. On the **SSL Port** page, accept the default and click **Next**.

13. On the **Choose a Certification Authority** page, accept the default and click **Next**.

14. On the **Certification Request Submission** page, review the settings, and then click **Next**.

15. On the **Completing to the Web Server Certificate Wizard** page, click **Finish**. Click **OK**.

▶ **Configuring IIS to require SSL on the virtual directories used by OWA**

1. In the **IIS Manager** console, expand **Default Web Site**, right-click **Exchange**, and then click **Properties**.

2. In the **Exchange Properties** dialog box, on the **Directory Security** tab, in the **Secure communications** box, click **Edit**.

3. In the **Secure Communications** box, enable **Require secure channel (SSL)**, and then click **OK**.

4. Click **OK** to close the **Exchange Properties** dialog box.

5. Right-click **ExchWeb**, and then click **Properties**.

6. Repeat steps 2–4 on the **ExchWeb** virtual directory properties.

7. Right-click **Public**, and then click **Properties**.

8. Repeat steps 2–4 on the **Public** virtual directory properties.

9. Close the **IIS Manager** console.

▶ **Configuring an Outlook Web Access publishing rule**

1. Switch to Den-ISA-01 and, if necessary, log on to the cohovineyard domain with your user name and password.

2. Open **ISA Server Management** and click **Firewall Policy**.

3. On the **Firewall Policy** tasks pane, on the **Tasks** tab, click **Publish a Mail Server**.

4. On the **Welcome to the New Mail Server Publishing Rule Wizard** page, type **OWA Access Rule**, and then click **Next**.

5. On the **Select Access Type** page, select **Web client access: Outlook Web Access (OWA), Outlook Mobile Access, Exchange Server ActiveSync**, and then click **Next**.

6. On the **Select Services** page, ensure that **Outlook Web Access** is selected. Click **Next**.

7. On the **Bridging Mode** page, accept the default to create a **Secure connection to clients and mail server** and click **Next**.

8. On the **Specify the Web Mail Server** page, in the **Web mail server** text box, type **den-msg-01.cohovineyard.com**. Click **Next**.

9. On the **Public Name Details** page, ensure that **This domain name (type below)** is configured in the **Accept request for drop-down list**. In the **Public name** box, type **secure.cohovineyard.com** and click **Next**.

10. On the **Select Web Listener** page, in the **Web Listener** drop-down list, click **HTTPS Listener**. Click **Edit**.

11. On the **HTTPS Listener Properties** page, on the **Preferences** tab, click **Authentication**. Clear the options to use RADIUS authentication. Click **OK** when the warning message appears.

12. Click **Basic**, and click **Yes**. Click **OK** and then, in the **HTTPS Listener** dialog box, click **OK** again.

13. On the **Select Web Listener** page, click **Next**.

14. On the **User Sets** page, accept the default and click **Next**.

15. On the **Completing the New Mail Server Publishing Rule Wizard** page, click **Finish**.

16. Double click **OWA Access Rule**. On the **Users** tab, click **Forward Basic authentication credentials (Basic delegation)**. Click **OK**.

17. Ensure that the **OWA Access Rule** is listed before the **Coho Vineyard Store Site** rule. If it is not, click **OWA Access Rule** and click **Move Selected Rule Up**.

18. Click **Apply** to apply the changes and then click **OK** when the changes have been applied.

▶ **Testing the Outlook Web Access publishing rule**

1. Switch to Gen-Web-01.

2. Open **Internet Explorer** and type **https://secure.cohovineyard.com/ exchange** in the **Address** bar. Press **Enter**.

3. In the **Security Alert** dialog box, click **OK**.

4. In the **Connect to secure.cohovineyard.com** dialog box, log on using **cohovineyard\jay** and a password of **P@ssw0rd**.

5. If you receive an **Internet Explorer** warning message, click **Add**, then click **Add** again, and click **Close**.

6. Ensure that you can access the computer running Exchange Server using OWA.

▶ **To prepare for the next practice**

1. You will need the Den-DC-01 virtual machine, the Den-Msg-01 virtual machine, the Den-ISA-01 virtual machine, and the Den-Clt-01 virtual machine for the next practice.

2. Shut down the Gen-Web-01 virtual machine without saving the changes and start the Den-Clt-01 virtual machine.

Lesson: Configuring ISA Server to Secure Client Connections

* **Multimedia: Connecting MAPI Clients to Exchange Server Through a Firewall**
* **How ISA Server Secures Outlook RPC Connections**
* **About RPC over HTTP**
* **How to Configure RPC over HTTP**
* **Enabling E-Mail Access for POP3 and IMAP4 Clients**

Introduction

The full Outlook messaging client provides the highest level of functionality of any messaging client. However, because the Outlook client requires RPC connectivity to the computer running Exchange Server, it is difficult to provide secure access to the computers running Exchange Server from the Internet for Outlook clients. ISA Server can be used to secure the Outlook RPC connections as well as support RPC over HTTP connections. This lesson describes how ISA Server can be used to secure the Outlook connections to computers running Exchange Server. It also describes how ISA Server can be used to secure connections from Internet protocol e-mail clients.

Lesson objectives

After completing this lesson, you will be able to:

- Describe how Outlook clients connect to computers running Exchange Server through a firewall.

- Describe how ISA Server secures Outlook RPC connections.

- Describe how RPC over HTTP is implemented.

- Configure ISA Server to provide RPC over HTTP access to Exchange.

- Configure ISA Server to provide e-mail access for POP3 and IMAP4 clients.

Multimedia: Connecting MAPI Clients to Exchange Server Through a Firewall

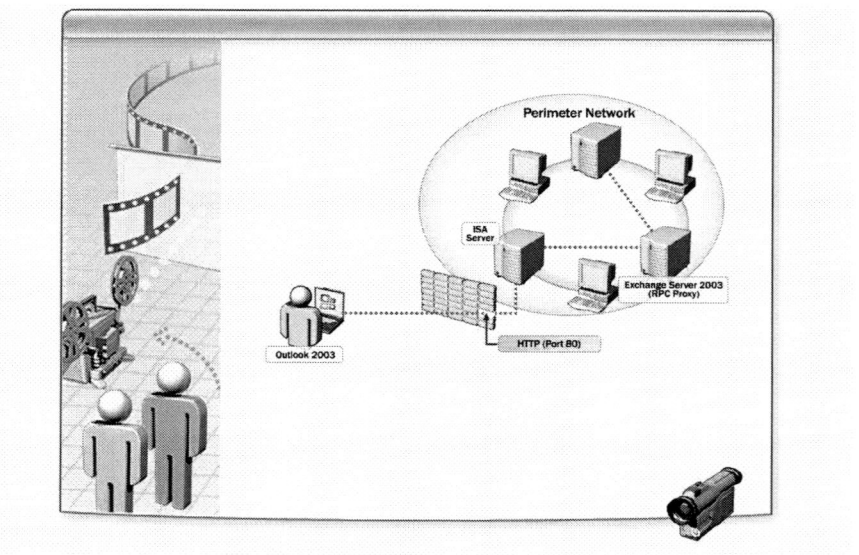

Outlook clients can be configured as MAPI clients. This presentation shows how MAPI mail clients use RPC to connect through a firewall to servers running Exchange Server 2003.

Tip To view the presentation *Connecting MAPI Clients to Exchange Server Through a Firewall* later on your own, open the Web page on the Student Materials compact disc, click **Multimedia**, and then click the title of the presentation.

How ISA Server Secures Outlook RPC Connections

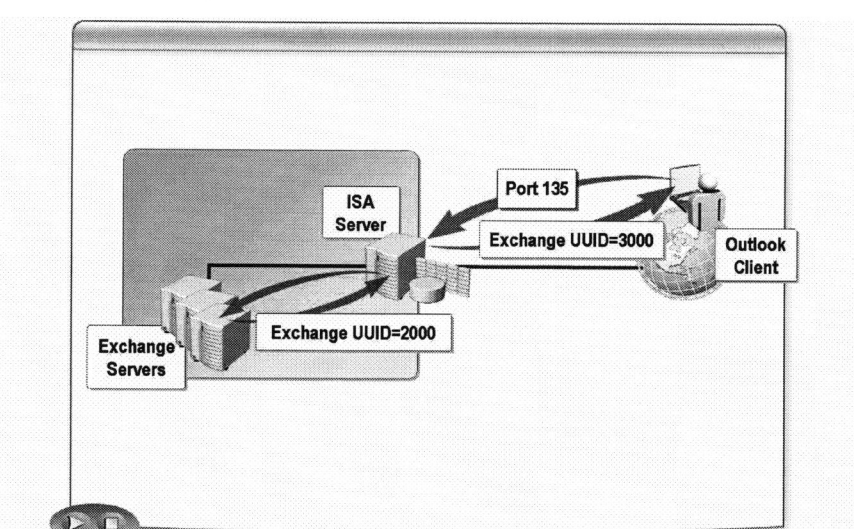

Introduction

The ISA Server RPC filter enables secure Outlook MAPI connections from the Internet with the corporate computer running Exchange Server. When this feature is enabled, connection requests from remote Outlook MAPI clients must be done through a secure encrypted channel. If the connection is not secured, ISA Server drops the client request. This allows ISA Server, instead of users, to control the level of security.

How the RPC application filter works

When an Outlook MAPI client from the Internet connects to a computer running Exchange Server through ISA Server, the RPC application filter works as follows:

1. The Outlook client issues a request over port 135 (Transmission Control Protocol [TCP]) through ISA Server to the computer running Exchange Server to find the service port number associated with the Exchange RPC universally unique identifier (UUID).

2. The computer running Exchange Server sends a response back with a port number on which the client can communicate. The response includes all the UUIDs and associated port numbers that the client will use to connect to the required Exchange services.

3. ISA Server uses the RPC application filter to capture this information, and maintains it in a table. ISA Server allocates a new port on the ISA Server computer, and changes the response that it sends to the Outlook client to reflect this change. This information is also maintained in the table.

4. The Outlook MAPI client establishes a connection to the MAPI ports that ISA Server instructed it to use. ISA Server screens the RPC commands to ensure that no exploits are contained within the channel.

5. Information sent by the Outlook MAPI client is forwarded by ISA Server to the computer running Exchange Server.

6. The computer running Exchange Server responds to the Outlook MAPI client and ISA Server intercepts the responses. The RPC filter screens these responses and changes the source port number.

7. ISA Server forwards the responses to the Outlook MAPI client.

Practice: Configuring ISA Server to Secure Outlook RPC Connections

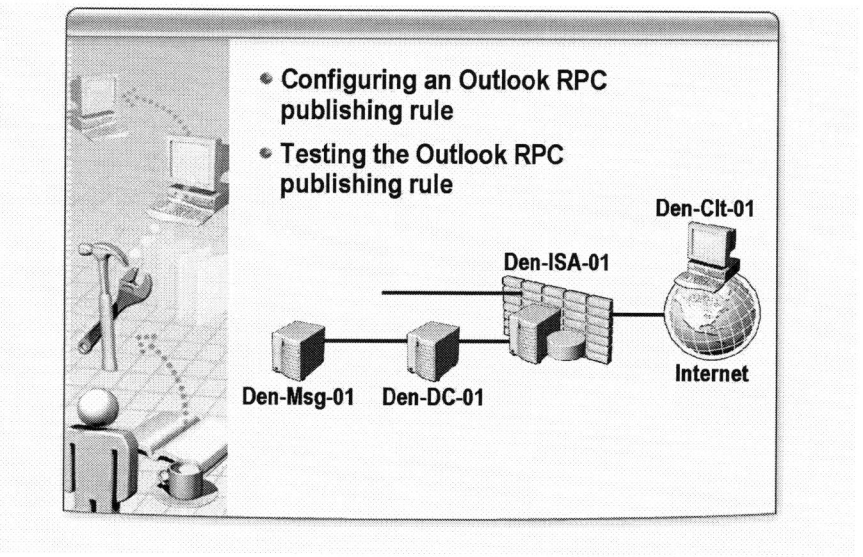

Introduction

In this practice, you will use the New Mail Server Publishing Wizard to configure a new publishing rule for Outlook RPC clients. You will then test the publishing rule.

Practice

▶ **To prepare for this practice**

1. You will need the Den-DC-01 virtual machine, the Den-Msg-01 virtual machine, the Den-ISA-01 virtual machine, and the Den-Clt-01 virtual machine for this practice.

2. If necessary, start or resume the required virtual machines and then, on Den-ISA-01, log on to the cohovineyard domain with your user name and password.

▶ **Configuring an Outlook RPC publishing rule**

1. In **ISA Server Management**, click **Firewall Policy**.

2. On the **Firewall Policy** task pane, on the **Tasks** tab, select **Publish a Mail Server** to start the **New Mail Server Rule Wizard**.

3. On the **Welcome to the New Mail Server Publishing Rule Wizard** page, type **Outlook Client Access** as the name for the rule, and then click **Next**.

4. On the **Select Access Type** page, click **Client access: RPC, IMAP, POP3, SMTP**, and then click **Next**.

5. On the **Select Services** page, select **Outlook (RPC)**, and then click **Next**.

6. On the **Select Server** page, type **192.168.1.12**, and then click **Next**.

7. On the **IP Addresses** page, click **External**, and then click **Next**.

8. On the **Completing the New Mail Server Publishing Rule Wizard** page, review the configuration, and then click **Finish**.

9. Click **Apply** to apply the changes and then click **OK** when the changes have been applied.

▶ **Testing the Outlook RPC publishing rule**

1. Switch to Den-Clt-01 and log on to the cohovineyard domain with a user name of **Administrator** and a password of **P@ssw0rd**.

2. Open the **Control Panel**. Click **Network and Internet Connections**, and then click **Network Connections**.

3. Right-click **Local Area Connection**, and then click **Properties**.

4. Click **Internet Protocol (TCP/IP)** and click **Properties**.

5. Click **Use the following IP address** and enter the following information:

   a. IP address: **131.107.1.10**

   b. Subnet mask: **255.255.255.0**

   c. Default gateway: blank

   d. Preferred DNS server: blank

6. Click **OK**, and then click **Close**.

7. Because the Internet DNS server (Gen-Web-01) is offline, you must create a HOSTS file entry for the Cohovineyard mail server. To do this, open **Notepad**, and open **c:\windows\system32\drivers\etc\hosts**. Click at the end of the file and type **131.107.1.100 den-msg-01.cohovineyard.com secure.cohovineyard.com** and press **Enter**. Save the file and close **Network Connections**.

8. Open **Microsoft Office Outlook** from the **Start** menu.

9. On the **Outlook 2003 Startup** page, click **Next**.

10. On the **E-mail Accounts** page, click **Next**.

11. On the **Server Type** page, click **Microsoft Exchange Server**, and then click **Next**.

12. On the **Exchange Server Settings** page, in the **Microsoft Exchange Server** field, type **Den-MSG-01.cohovineyard.com**. In the **User name** field, type **Jay Adams**, and then click **Next**.

13. On the **Congratulations** page, click **Finish**.

14. In the **Connect to den-msg-01.cohovineyard.com** dialog box, log on as **cohovineyard\Jay** with a password of **P@ssw0rd**.

15. On the **User Name** dialog box, click **OK**.

16. Confirm that you can access the computer running Exchange Server through ISA Server.

About RPC over HTTP

RPC over HTTP requires:

- Exchange Server 2003 running on Windows Server 2003 and Windows Server 2003 global catalog servers

- Outlook 2003 running on Windows XP

- Windows Server 2003 server running RPC proxy server with the Exchange and domain controller service port numbers defined in the registry

- A modified Outlook profile that connects to the Exchange server using HTTPS

Introduction

Outlook 2003 with Exchange 2003 running on Windows Server 2003 supports RPC over HTTP, which provides MAPI client access to the computer running Exchange Server without using the RPC ports. Instead, users running Outlook 2003 can connect directly to a computer running Exchange Server over the Internet by using HTTP or HTTPS.

Requirements for RPC over HTTP

The requirements for RPC over HTTP and the computers and servers to which those requirements apply are shown in the following table.

These computers	Must meet these requirements
Clients	• Outlook 2003
	• Windows XP with Service Pack 1 with Windows XP update Q331320
	• Windows XP with Service Pack 2
Servers	• Exchange 2003 on Windows Server 2003 for front-end servers (if front-end servers are deployed)
	• Exchange 2003 on Windows Server 2003 for back-end servers
	• Exchange 2003 on Windows Server 2003 for public folders
	• Exchange 2003 on Windows Server 2003 for system folders
	• Windows Server 2003 for the global catalog server

To configure Exchange 2003 for RPC over HTTP

When you deploy RPC over HTTP, you need to configure a computer running Windows Server 2003 as an RPC proxy server. The RPC proxy server accepts the RPC over HTTP or HTTPS connections and translates them into regular RPCs. In a scenario in which you have deployed Exchange front-end and back-end servers, the Exchange front-end servers should be configured as RPC proxy servers. If the RPC proxy server is on a different protected network than the back-end Exchange servers, then you also need to enable RPC communications between the servers through the ISA Server firewall.

The high-level steps to configure Exchange 2003 for RPC over HTTP are as follows; the detailed steps for configuring this option are included in the lab:

1. Configure the Exchange front-end server as an RPC proxy server by adding the **RPC over HTTP** subcomponent to the **Windows Networking Services** component. If you have Exchange Server 2003 Service Pack 1 installed, then use **Exchange System Manager** to configure the server as a RPC front-end server.

2. Configure the **Authentication Method** in the RPC virtual directory in Internet Information Services (IIS) to use **Basic authentication**. Also configure the virtual directory to require SSL connections.

3. Modify the registry on the RPC proxy server and global catalog server to use specified port numbers. To communicate with the domain controllers and computers running Exchange Server, the RPC proxy server specifies which ports to use to communicate with the domain controllers, global catalog servers, and all the computers running Exchange Server that the RPC client must communicate with. If you have Exchange Server 2003 Service Pack 1 installed, you can avoid editing the registry by using the **Exchange System Manager** to configure the back-end servers as RPC back-end servers.

After you have completed these steps, your Exchange environment is configured to accept and respond to requests from clients that are using RPC over HTTP.

To configure Outlook 2003 for RPC over HTTP

If you want your users to be able to use RPC over HTTP to connect to their mailboxes, your users must create an Outlook profile on their computers that contains the necessary settings for RPC over HTTP. These settings enable SSL communication with Basic authentication, which is necessary when using RPC over HTTP.

The steps to configure Outlook 2003 for RPC over HTTP are as follows:

1. Create an Outlook profile for your users to use with RPC over HTTP.

2. Configure the Outlook profile to connect to a computer running Exchange Server and to use cached mode.

3. Configure the Outlook profile to connect to the mailbox by using HTTP.

4. Configure the profile's Exchange proxy settings with the fully qualified domain name (FQDN) of the RPC proxy server, and then configure the SSL options.

How to Configure RPC over HTTP

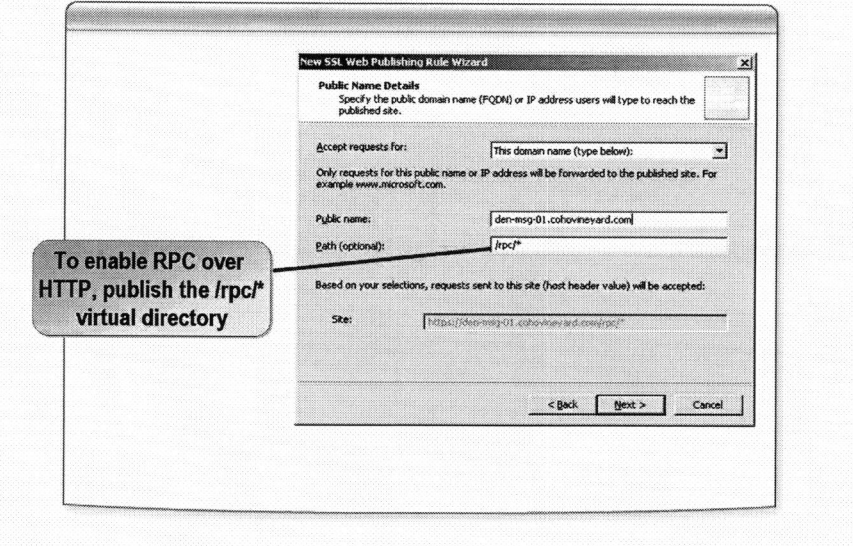

Introduction

After configuring the computers running Exchange Server and Outlook clients to support RPC over HTTP, you must configure ISA Server to support this feature. To enable this, you need to publish the \rpc virtual directory on your RPC proxy server through ISA Server.

Configuring ISA Server for RPC over HTTP

You can configure ISA Server to enable RPC over HTTP by using a Web publishing rule to publish the \rpc virtual directory on the RPC proxy server. To make the connection more secure, you should use a Web listener configured for SSL and configure SSL bridging to encrypt the client connection to ISA Server and the connection from ISA Server to the RPC proxy server.

To publish the \rpc virtual directory, create a secure Web publishing rule:

1. Open ISA Server Management and click **Firewall Policy**.

2. In the task pane, on the **Tasks** tab, click **Publish a Web Server** to start the **New Web Publishing Rule Wizard**.

3. On the **Welcome to the New Secure Web Publishing Rule Wizard** page, in the **Name** field, type a name for the rule and click **Next**.

4. On the **Select Rule Action** page, ensure that the default **Allow** is selected, which will allow requests to reach your Web server according to the conditions set by the rule. Click **Next**.

5. On the **Select Web Site to Publish** page, in Web server, specify the RPC proxy server that you want to publish. This can be the computer name or the IP address of the computer. Select **Send the original host header**. Click **Next**.

6. On the **Select Public Domain Name** page, provide information regarding what requests will be received by the ISA Server computer and forwarded to the Web server. Because you want to publish a specific virtual folder on the RPC proxy server, you should specify the server name and include the \rpc folder.

7. On the **Select Web Listener** page, specify the Web listener that will listen for Web page requests that should be redirected to your Web server, and then click **Next**. If you have not defined a Web listener, click **New** and use the **New Web Listener Wizard** to create a new Web Listener.

8. On the **User Sets** page, make sure the default, **All users**, is displayed. This will allow any computer in the external network to access the published Web pages. To restrict the access to specific users, use the **Remove** button to remove **All users**, and the **Add** button to access the **Add Users** dialog box. Click **Next**.

9. On the **Completing the New Web Publishing Rule Wizard** page, review the configuration and click **Finish**.

10. In the **ISA Server** details pane, click **Apply** to apply the changes you have made.

Enabling E-Mail Access for POP3 and IMAP4 Clients

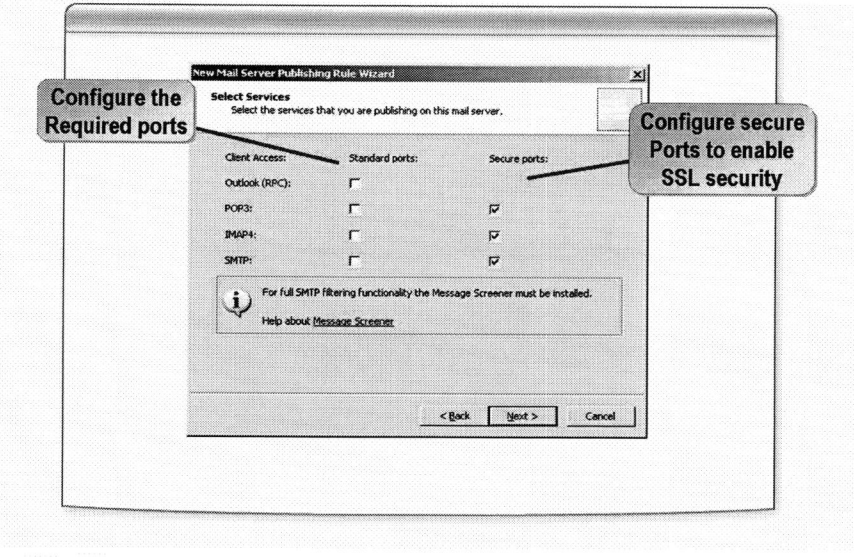

Introduction

In addition to publishing computers running Exchange Server so they can be accessed using Outlook as a MAPI client, ISA Server can also be used to publish Exchange Server for clients such as Outlook Express. These clients use POP3 or IMAP4 to read messages in the Exchange Server mailboxes and use SMTP to send messages to the computers running Exchange Server. Alternatively, these clients can be configured to use POP3S, IMAP4S, and SMTPS.

Configuring e-mail access for Internet clients

You can use the New Mail Server Publishing Rule Wizard to create a new server publishing rule for Internet protocol clients. When running the wizard, choose to create a client access rule, and then choose IMAP4 or POP3 as the client access protocols. If no publishing rule is configured allowing access to an SMTP server, then you also need to configure the publishing rule to support SMTP.

When you configure the publishing rule, you can choose to enable the POP3, IMAP4, and SMTP secure ports. If you choose to use secure ports, all user logon and message transfer traffic is encrypted using SSL. This means that you must have a server certificate configured on the computer running Exchange Server.

If you configure access for multiple protocols using the mail server publishing wizard, the wizard automatically creates a server publishing rule for each protocol that you published.

Lab: Integrating ISA Server 2004 and Microsoft Exchange Server

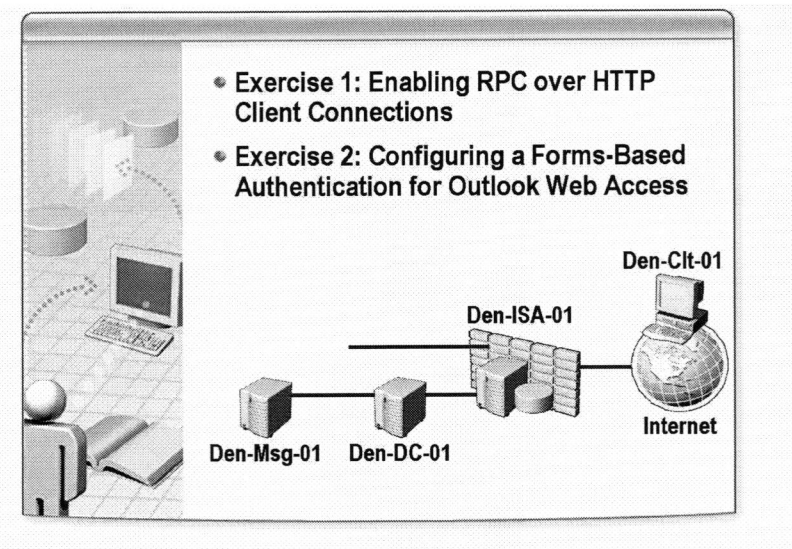

Objectives

After completing this lab, you will be able to:

- Configure ISA Server to enable RPC over HTTP Outlook client connections.

- Configure ISA Server to use forms authentication for OWA connections.

Note This lab focuses on the concepts in this module and as a result might not comply with Microsoft security recommendations. For example, the Administrator passwords are not as complex as recommended. Additionally, most of the actions performed in this lab are performed while logged on as an Administrator. A better security practice would be to log on as a normal user and use the Runas option to start administrative applications.

Scenario

You have deployed computers running Microsoft Internet Security and Acceleration (ISA) Server at Coho Vineyard. You have also deployed computers running Exchange Server on the internal network and configured ISA Server to publish the computer running Exchange Server for Simple Mail Transfer Protocol (SMTP), Microsoft Outlook Web Access (OWA) and Microsoft Exchange Server remote procedure call (RPC) connections. However, the organization's requirements have changed. You now need to enable RPC over Hypertext Transfer Protocol Secure (HTTPS) connections to the computer running Exchange Server. And you need to enable forms-based authentication for Outlook Web Access.

To prepare for this lab:

1. You will need the Den-DC-01 virtual machine, the Den-ISA-01 virtual machine, the Den-Clt-01 virtual machine, and the Den-Msg-01 virtual machine virtual machine for this practice.

2. If necessary, start or resume the required virtual machines and then, on Den-Msg-01, log on to the cohovineyard domain with a user name of **Administrator** and a password of **P@ssw0rd**.

Estimated time to complete this lab: 60 minutes

Exercise 1
Enabling RPC over HTTP Client Connections

In this exercise, you will configure the computer running Exchange Server and the domain controller to support RPC over HTTPS. Then you will configure the computer running ISA Server to support RPC over HTTPS connections from Outlook clients on the Internet. Last, you will configure an Outlook profile on a client computer to support RPC over HTTPS and test the connection.

Tasks	Detailed steps
1. On the Den-Msg-01 computer, install the **RPC over HTTP Proxy** network service.	a. On the Den-Msg-01 computer, on the **Start** menu, click **Control Panel**, and then click **Add or Remove Programs**.
	b. In the **Add or Remove Programs** window, click **Add/Remove Windows Components**.
	c. On the **Windows Components** page, select the **Networking Services** component, and then click **Details**.
	d. In the **Networking Services** dialog box, select the **RPC over HTTP Proxy** check box, and then click **OK**.
	e. On the **Windows Components** page, click **Next**.
	f. If you see an **Insert Disk** dialog box, click **OK**. Then click **Browse** and browse to **c:\win2k3\i386**. Click **Open** and the click **OK**.
	g. On the **Completing the Windows Components Wizard** page, click **Finish**.
	h. Close the **Add or Remove Programs** window.
2. Configure the **/Rpc** virtual directory: Anonymous access: **No** Authentication method: **Basic authentication** only Require SSL: **Yes**	a. Open the **Internet Information Services (IIS) Manager**.
	b. In the **IIS Manager** console, expand **Den-Msg-01**, expand **Web Sites**, expand **Default Web Site**, and then in the left pane, select **Rpc**.
	c. Right-click **Rpc** and then click **Properties**.
	d. In the **Rpc Properties** dialog box, on the **Directory Security** tab, in the **Authentication and access control** dialog box, click **Edit**.
	e. In the **Authentication Methods** dialog box, enable **Basic authentication**.
	f. In the **IIS Manager** warning message box, click **Yes** to confirm that you want to continue.
	g. In the **Authentication Methods** dialog box, clear the options for **Enable anonymous access** and **Integrated Windows authentication** and then click **OK**.
	h. On the **Directory Security** tab, in the **Secure communications** box, click **Edit**.
	i. In the **Secure communications** box, enable **Require secure channel (SSL)**, and then click **OK**.
	j. Click **OK** to close the **Rpc Properties** dialog box.
	k. Close the **IIS Manager** console.

(continued)

Tasks	Detailed steps
3. Configure Den-Msg-01 as an RPC back-end server.	**a.** Click **Start**, point to **All Programs**, point to **Microsoft Exchange**, and then click **System Manager**. **b.** In **Exchange System Manager**, expand the **Servers** object, right-click **Den-Msg-01**, and then click **Properties**. **c.** On the **Den-Msg-01 Properties** dialog box, click the **RPC-HTTP** tab, and then select the option next to **RPC-HTTP back-end server**. **d.** In the **Exchange System Manager** warning message, click **OK**. **e.** Click **OK** in the **Den-Msg-01** dialog box. **f.** Close **Exchange System Manager**.
4. Configure the **RPC Proxy** network service to communicate with the Exchange Server (**Den-Msg-01.cohovineyard.com**) on the following ports: **6001**, **6002**, and **6004** Because we do have only one Exchange Server rather than a front-end and back-end server, we must still edit the registry to configure the Exchange server to use the required ports.	**a.** Open a **Command Prompt** window. **b.** At the command prompt, type **cd c:\program files\windows resource kits\tools**, and then press **ENTER**. **c.** Type **rpccfg.exe /hd**. **d.** The output of the command displays which ports on which computer the RPC Proxy service is allowed to create an RPC connection to. The default setting is: Den-Msg-01 100-5000. **e.** Type **rpccfg.exe /hr Den-Msg-01**. **f.** This removes the current port range settings for Den-Msg-01. **g.** The next commands add the required port ranges for both the NetBIOS name and the fully qualified domain name (FQDN) of the (back-end) computer running Exchange Server and the Global Catalog server. The RPC connections to the computer running Exchange Server are done at ports 6001, 6002, and 6004. **h.** Type **rpccfg.exe /ha Den-Msg-01 6001-6002 6004**. **i.** Type **rpccfg.exe /ha Den-Msg-01.cohovineyard.com 6001-6002 6004**. **j.** Type **rpccfg.exe /hd**. **k.** Close the Command Prompt window.
5. Restart the Den-Msg-01 computer.	**a.** On the **Start** menu, click **Shut Down**. **b.** In the **Shut Down Windows** dialog box, type the following information: • What do you want the computer to do: **Restart** • Option: **Other (Planned)** (default) • Comment: **Changed RPC Proxy settings** and then click **OK**.

(*continued*)

Tasks	Detailed steps
6. On the Den-ISA-01 computer, disable the existing rule that publishes the computer running Exchange Server by using RPC.	a. On the Den-ISA-01 computer, in the **ISA Server** console, in the left pane, select **Firewall Policy**. b. In the right pane, right-click **Outlook Client Access Exchange RPC Server**, and then click **Disable**. c. Click **Apply** to apply the changes and then click **OK** when the changes have been applied.
7. Create a secure Web publishing rule. Name: **Publish RPC over HTTPs** Web server: **Den-Msg-01. cohovineyard.com/rpc** Send host headers: **Yes** Public name: **Secure.cohovineyard.com/rpc/*** Web listener: **Https Listener** Forward basic authentication: **Yes**	a. In the task pane, on the **Tasks** tab, click **Publish a Secure Web Server**. b. In the **New SSL Web Publishing Rule Wizard** page, in the **SSL Web publishing rule name** text box, type **Publish RPC over HTTPS**, and then click **Next**. c. On the **Publishing Mode** tab, accept the default of **SSL Bridging**, and then click **Next**. d. On the **Select Rule Action** page, accept the default of **Allow**, and then click **Next**. e. On the **Bridging Mode** tab, accept the default of **Secure connection to clients and Web server**, and then click **Next**. f. On the **Define Web Site to Publish** page, type the following information: • Computer name or IP address: **Den-Msg-01.cohovineyard.com** • Forward the original host header: **Enable** • Folder: **rpc/*** and then click **Next**. g. On the **Public Name Details** page, type the following information: • Public domain (list box): **This domain name (type below):** • Public domain (text box): **secure.cohovineyard.com** • Folder: **/rpc/*** (default) and then click **Next**. h. On the **Select Web Listener** page, in the **Web Listener** list box, select **HTTPS Listener**, and then click **Next**. i. On the **User Sets** page, click **Next**. j. On the **Completing the New Web Publishing Rule Wizard** page, click **Finish**. k. In the right pane, right-click **Publish RPC over HTTPs**, and then click **Properties**. l. In the **Publish RPC over HTTPS Properties** dialog box, on the **Users** tab, enable **Forward Basic authentication credentials (Basic delegation)**, and then click **OK**. m. Click **Apply** to apply the changes and then click **OK** when the changes have been applied.

(*continued*)

Tasks	Detailed steps

8. Configure the Jay Adams Outlook profile to use RPC over HTTP:
 	
URL:**secure.cohovineyard.com**
 	
Use SSL only: **Yes**
 	
Principal name:
msstd: secure.cohovineyard.com
 	
On fast/slow networks, use HTTP first: **Yes**
 	
Proxy authentication: **Basic**
	a. Switch to Den-Clt-01.
	b. On the **Start** menu, right click **E-mail**, and then click **Properties**.
	c. In the **Mail Setup - Outlook** dialog box, click **E-mail Accounts**.
	d. In the **E-mail Accounts** dialog box, select **View or change existing e-mail accounts**, and then click **Next**.
	e. On the **E-mail Accounts** page, click **Change**.
	f. On the **Exchange Server Settings** page, click **More Settings**.
	g. In the **Microsoft Exchange Server** dialog box, on the **Connection** tab, enable **Connect to my Exchange mailbox using HTTP**, and then click **Exchange Proxy Settings**.
	h. In the **Exchange Proxy Settings** dialog box, type the following information:
	  • Use this URL (https://): **secure.cohovineyard.com**
	  • Connect using SSL only: **enable** (default)
	  • Mutually authenticate the session: **enable**
	  • Principal name for proxy server: **msstd: secure.cohovineyard.com**
	  • On fast networks, connect using HTTP first: **enable**
	  • On slow networks, connect using HTTP first: **enable** (default)
	  • Proxy authentication setting: **Basic Authentication**
	  and then click **OK**.
	i. Click **OK** to close the **Microsoft Exchange Server** dialog box.
	j. On the **Exchange Server Settings** page, click **Next**.
	k. On the **E-mail accounts** page, click **Finish**.
	l. Click **Close** to close the **Mail Setup - Outlook** dialog box.

9. Send an e-mail to Jay Adams to test the RPC over HTTP connection to ISA Server.	a. Open **Outlook** from the **Start** menu. and log on as **cohovineyard\Jay** with a password of **P@ssw0rd** b. Send an e-mail to Jay Adams. After a few seconds, Outlook sends the message from the Outbox. It will then appear in the Inbox. This results shows that Outlook successfully connected to the Exchange Server on Den-Msg-01 by using secure RPC over HTTP connections to ISA Server. c. Close **Outlook**.

Exercise 2
Configuring a Forms-Based Authentication for Outlook Web Access

In this exercise, you will modify the existing Outlook Web Access publishing rule to support forms-based authentication. You will then modify the time-out settings and attachment settings for public computers and test the configuration.

Tasks	Detailed steps
1. On the Den-ISA-01 computer, configure the **HTTPS Listener** Web listener to use **OWA Forms-Based** authentication.	a. Switch to the Den-ISA-01 virtual machine. b. In the **ISA Server Management** console, in the left pane, select **Firewall Policy**. c. In the task pane, on the **Toolbox** tab, in the **Network Objects** pane, expand **Web Listeners**, right-click **HTTPS Listener**, and then click **Properties**. d. In the **HTTPS Listener Properties** dialog box, on the **Preferences** tab, click **Authentication**. e. In the **Authentication** dialog box, in the **Method** list, disable **Basic**. f. In the warning message box, click **OK** to confirm that (currently) a request that requires authentication will fail. g. In the **Authentication** dialog box, in the **Method** list, enable **OWA Forms-Based**, and then click **Configure**. h. On the **OWA Forms-Based Authentication** dialog box, in the **Idle Session Timeout** box, configure the **Clients on public machines** time-out setting to be **2 minutes**. i. In the **E-mail attachments** box, click **Clients on public machines**. j. Click **Log off OWA when the user leaves the OWA site**. k. Click **OK** to close the **OWA Forms-Based Authentication** dialog box. l. Click **OK** to close the **Authentication** dialog box. m. Click **OK** to close the **HTTPS Listener Properties** dialog box. n. Click **Apply** to save the changes and then click **OK** when the changes have been applied.

(*continued*)

Tasks	Detailed steps
2. On the Den-Clt-01 computer, log on to the OWA Web site, and test the client settings.	**a.** Switch to Den-Clt-01.
	b. Open **Internet Explorer** and type **https://secure.cohovineyard.com/exchange** in the **Address** bar. Press **Enter**. In the **Security Alert** dialog box, click **OK**. Confirm that the **Public or Shared computer** is selected under **Security**.
	c. In the **Outlook Web Access** page, log on using **cohovineyard\jay** and a password of **P@ssw0rd**.
	d. Ensure that you can access the Exchange server using OWA.
	e. Test the public computer configuration by sending Jay Adams a message containing an attachment. Can you open the attachment?
	f. Browse to **www.cohovineyard.com**. Do you need to authenticate before returning to OWA?
	g. With the Jay Adams mailbox open, wait for two minutes. Do you need to re-authenticate before getting access to mailbox contents?
	h. Log off OWA and log on again. This time, select the option to log on from a **Private computer**.
	i. Can you open the message with an attachment?
	j. Browse to **www.cohovineyard.com**. Do you need to authenticate before returning to OWA?
	k. With the Jay Adams mailbox open, wait for two minutes. Do you need to re-authenticate before getting access to mailbox contents?
	l. Close all open windows.

To Prepare for the Next Lab

As you finish this lab, shut down all of the virtual machines that you used in the lab. To shut down the virtual machines, click **Close** from the **Action** menu. **Select Turn off and delete changes** and click **OK**.

After shutting down the virtual machines, restart the Den-DC-01 virtual machine, the Den-ISA-01 virtual machine, the Den-Web-01 virtual machine and the Gen-Web-01 virtual machine in preparation for the next module.

Microsoft®

Module 7: Advanced Application and Web Filtering

Contents

Overview

- Advanced Application and Web Filtering Overview
- Configuring HTTP Web Filters
- Additional Application and Web Filters

Introduction

Some of the most important features available in Microsoft® Internet Security and Acceleration (ISA) Server 2004 are application and Web filters. By implementing these filters, ISA Server administrators can configure very specific filtering of the traffic that flows through the computer running ISA Server. The filtering occurs at the application layer. For example, Hypertext Transfer Protocol (HTTP) filters can be configured to allow or block traffic based on file extensions or specific virus signatures. An ISA Server administrator needs to be able to configure application and Web filtering to provide advanced protection for the organization's network.

Objectives

After completing this module, you will be able to:

- Describe how application filtering and Web filtering work.
- Configure HTTP Web filters.
- Configure other application and Web filters.

Lesson: Advanced Application and Web Filtering Overview

- **What Is an Application Filter?**
- **What Is a Web Filter?**
- **Why Use Application and Web Filters?**
- **Application and Web Filter Architecture**

Introduction

A primary advantage of ISA Server over traditional firewalls is its ability to filter the application data in the network packets as they enter or leave the network. Application and Web filters provide this functionality. This lesson provides an overview of how application and Web filters work in ISA Server 2004.

Lesson objectives

After completing this lesson, you will be able to:

- Define what an application filter is.
- Define what a Web filter is.
- Describe why to use application and Web filters.
- Describe the ISA Server 2004 application and Web filter architecture.

What Is an Application Filter?

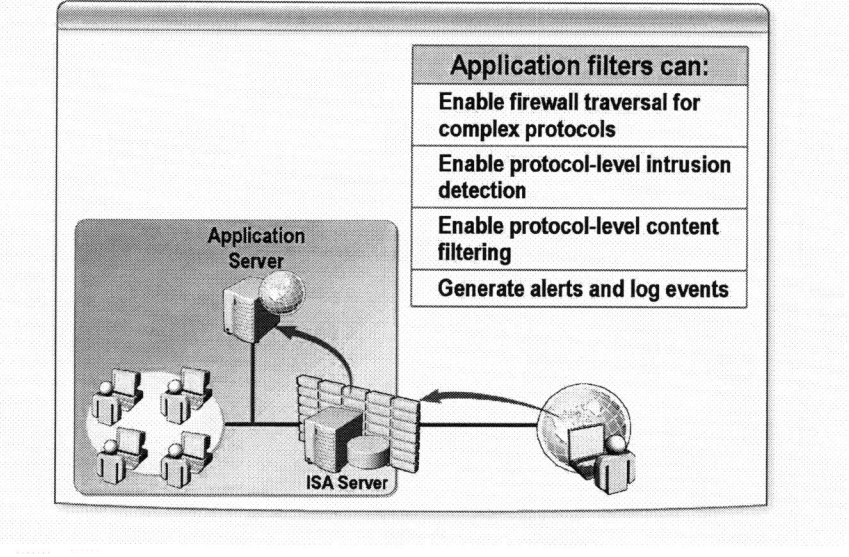

Introduction

Application filters work with the firewall service in ISA Server to intercept and process network packets as they pass through ISA Server. Application filters examine the application-level data within those packets and then filter the packets based on firewall rules.

What is an application filter?

ISA Server application filters are implemented as Component Object Model (COM)–server dynamic link libraries (DLLs) in the process space of the firewall service. The firewall service in ISA Server 2004 runs in user mode. When the firewall service starts, all application filters that are registered with the firewall service are also loaded.

Application filters are add-ons to the firewall service. When a packet arrives, the firewall service uses firewall rules defined in the rules engine to check the packet. One check is to see if an application filter is associated with the protocol used by the packet. If there is, the firewall service passes the packet to the application filter for further inspection. An application filter can perform protocol-specific or system-specific tasks such as authentication and checking for viruses.

ISA Server includes many application filters, but also provides the application-filter application programming interface (API) that can be used to build custom application filters.

Application filter functionality

Application filters can be used in several different ways on ISA Server, including:

- *Enabling firewall traversal for complex protocols.* Application filters can extend the ability of ISA Server to handle complicated protocols that require more than a single transmission control protocol (TCP) connection. Some applications, such as file transfer protocol (FTP) or media streaming applications, initiate a connection with a server using a specified port number. However, once the initial connection has been established, the server and client negotiate one or more dynamic ports that will be used for further communications. An application filter can enable the firewall traversal of these protocols. The application filter enables ISA Server to track the negotiation between the client and server as they determine the secondary connections, and then ISA Server can dynamically configure the ports required for the secondary connections. An example of such a filter is the built-in FTP application filter that handles all aspects of configuring a firewall to automatically allow a secondary FTP data channel.

- *Enabling protocol-level intrusion detection.* Application filters can examine the contents of application packets to check for protocol-level intrusion detection. A common example of this type of filtering is based on filtering commands to protect against buffer overflow attempts. ISA Server provides Post Office Protocol 3 (POP3), Simple Mail Transport Protocol (SMTP), and Domain Name System (DNS) application filters that provide this type of functionality.

- *Enabling protocol-level content filtering.* Application filters can parse high-level application protocols, look for actual data (the payload), and apply rules and processing based on the content. For example, you can use the feature to provide protocol-level syntax validation, antivirus scanning on file transfers, or scans of the content based on defined strings. The SMTP filter provided with ISA Server is an example of these types of application filters.

- *Generating alerts and log events.* Application filters can also be used to create alerts and log events based on the activity discovered by the application filter. For example, if a DNS application filter detects repeated attack attempts, the filter can create an alert or log the information.

Note Many third-party vendors use application filters to implement features such as content filtering, access control, specialized authentication methods, and intrusion detection. For a listing of many of the third-party products that are compatible with ISA Server, see http://www.isaserver.org and the Partners Web site at http://www.microsoft.com/isaserver/partners.

What Is a Web Filter?

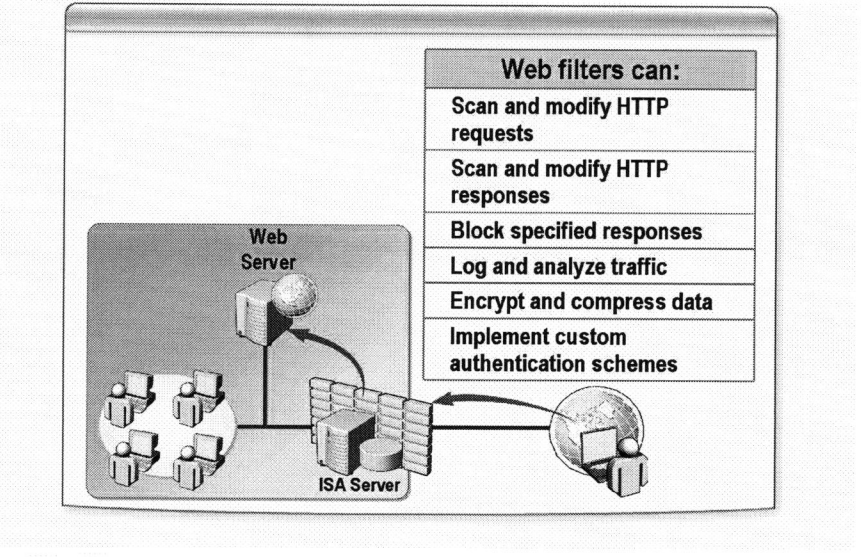

Introduction

Web filters also extend the functionality of the firewall service in ISA Server by providing advanced filtering capability for hypertext transfer protocol (HTTP) packets as they pass through ISA Server.

What is a Web filter?

Web filters are DLLs that are based on the Internet Information Server (IIS) Internet Server Application Programming Interface (ISAPI) model. The Web filters are loaded by the Web proxy filter, which is an application filter. When a Web filter is loaded, it passes information to the Web proxy filter that specifies the types of events that the filter is configured to monitor. Each time one of those events occurs, the Web filter is notified.

Web filter functionality

Web filters can be used to perform a number of different tasks, including:

- *Request scanning and modification.* A Web filter can scan HTTP client requests and modify or add a header to a request. For example, you could use a Web filter to add a cookie header to the request, or remove a header sent by the client.

- *Response scanning and modification.* Web filters can scan and modify the server responses. For example, during link translation, ISA Server substitutes the externally accessible server names for the internal names. The link translation filter included with ISA Server is a Web filter.

- *Block specific responses.* Web filters can be used to block access to particular sites based on the content of the server response. These features can also be used to scan HTTP packets for viruses.

- *Traffic logging and analysis.* Web filters can be used to log specific information about HTTP traffic and to create reports based on the logged information.

- *Data encryption or compression.* Web filters can be used to apply custom data encryption or compression schemes to HTTP packets.

- *Custom authentication schemes.* Microsoft Office Outlook® Web Access (OWA) forms-based authentication, RSA SecurID authentication, and Remote Authentication Dial-In User Service (RADIUS) authentication are all implemented as Web filters in ISA Server. Third-party vendors can use Web filters to implement additional authentication schemes.

Why Use Application and Web Filters?

> **Application and Web filters provide:**
>
> - Protection against malicious code by blocking packets that have worm or virus characteristics
> - Protection against user actions by blocking the download of harmful programs or ensuring that some types of data do not leave the network
> - Protection against specific network connections by blocking connection attempts by specific applications
> - Integration with third-party or custom filters that have been developed using the application filter API or the Web filter API

Introduction

Application and Web filters provide an extra layer of security for a network. These filters can examine every packet that flows through ISA Server and filter the packets based on the results of that inspection. This ensures that the packets, which may be exploit attempts or just unwanted information, never reach the target computer.

Benefits of using application and Web filters

Application and Web filters provide many benefits including:

- *Protection against malicious code.* You can use application-layer filters to stop random attacks from sources such as viruses and worms. When a new worm or virus is released, you can identify the characteristics by which the worm or virus spreads and then use an application or Web filter to block the virus. For example, if a worm uses a particular file extension in its attack, you can configure the SMTP filter or the HTTP filter to block this extension.

- *Protection against user actions.* You can also use application-layer filtering to protect your network and systems from the harmful actions of unaware employees. For example, you can configure filters that prevent potentially harmful programs from being downloaded via the Internet or ensure that critical customer data does not leave the network in an e-mail. Internal security issues such as these are as critical as external threats to your organization's network.

- *Protection against specific network communication.* Application-layer filtering can also more broadly limit employee actions on the network. ISA Server 2004 includes filtering capability that can restrict common types of inappropriate communication on your network such as peer-to-peer file-exchange services. The filtering capabilities of ISA Server can limit these and other types of undesirable network communication.

- *Integration with third-party or custom filters.* ISA Server 2004 includes an application programming interface (API) that can be used by your in-house programmers or third-party vendors to create custom filters that can deal with almost any new attack.

Application and Web Filter Architecture

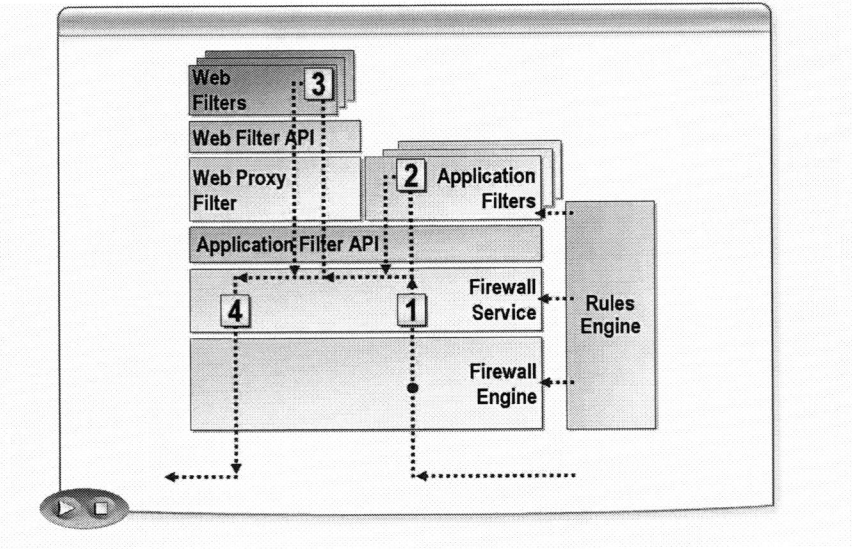

Introduction

Application and Web filters run in user mode within the firewall service on ISA Server 2004. The application- and Web-filtering architecture is designed to provide high performance as well as easy extensibility.

Application and Web filter architecture

The application- and Web-filtering architecture includes the following components:

- *Application filter API*. This API is located above the firewall service and is used by the firewall services to pass packets to the application filters. This API provides a layer of abstraction between the firewall service and the application filters, which enables developers to write additional application filters that will operate on specific application-layer protocols.

- *Web proxy filter*. The Web proxy filter manages all HTTP and Hypertext Transfer Protocol Secure (HTTPS) protocol requests and replies. In ISA Server 2000, the Web proxy is implemented as a service, but in ISA Server 2004, it is implemented as an application filter. This change provides a unified architecture for the proxy filter, which enables it to use the services of the firewall service, including caching.

- *Web filter API*. This API is located above the Web proxy filter and is implemented at a higher level than the application filter API. The application filter is concerned with support for TCP and User Datagram Protocol (UDP) sessions, connections, and sockets; the Web filter API deals only with the specifics of managing HTTP (and HTTPS) requests. The Web proxy filter takes care of the application filter issues for the Web filters. The Web filter API is similar to the IIS ISAPI filter API.

How application and Web filters work

The following steps describe how a client request flows through a computer running ISA Server, including the application and Web filters.

1. A client connects to the computer running ISA Server and requests a resource located on another network. The firewall engine performs packet filtering on the request and, if the request is allowed at that level, a connection is created and the packet is passed to the firewall service. The firewall service also examines the packet, including determining the application protocol used by the packet. The firewall service then checks the firewall rules to see if an application or Web filter is associated with the protocol used by the packet.

2. If an application filter is associated with the protocol, the firewall service passes the request to the application filter. The application filter evaluates the request based on the filter configuration and either rejects or accepts the request.

3. If the request is using HTTP or HTTPS, the firewall service checks to see if a Web proxy filter is registered for this traffic. If it is, the firewall service passes the request to the Web proxy filter, where the request is evaluated based on the Web filter configuration. The Web filter either accepts or rejects the request.

4. If the request is accepted by either the application filter or the Web filter, it is passed back to the firewall service and out the network interface to the destination server.

Lesson: Configuring HTTP Web Filters

* HTTP Web Filtering Overview
* How to Configure HTTP Web Filter General Properties
* How to Configure HTTP Web Filter Methods
* How to Configure HTTP Web Filter Extensions
* How to Configure HTTP Web Filter Headers
* How to Configure HTTP Web Filter Signatures
* How to Identify an HTTP Application Signature
* Best Practice: HTTP Filter Configuration for Web Publishing

Introduction

Almost all organizations allow users on the internal network to use HTTP to access Web resources. Most organizations also allow HTTP traffic into the network as Internet users access internal Web resources. The fact that HTTP is so widely used means HTTP-based attacks have become increasingly popular and sophisticated. It is, therefore, critical to examine all HTTP traffic entering or leaving the organization's network. This lesson describes how to implement and manage HTTP filtering in ISA Server 2004.

Lesson objectives

After completing this lesson, you will be able to:

- Describe how HTTP filtering works.
- Configure the HTTP filter general properties.
- Configure the HTTP filter methods.
- Configure the HTTP filter extensions.
- Configure the HTTP filter headers.
- Configure the HTTP filter signatures.
- Identify an HTTP signature.
- Describe the best practices for configuring HTTP filtering.

HTTP Web Filtering Overview

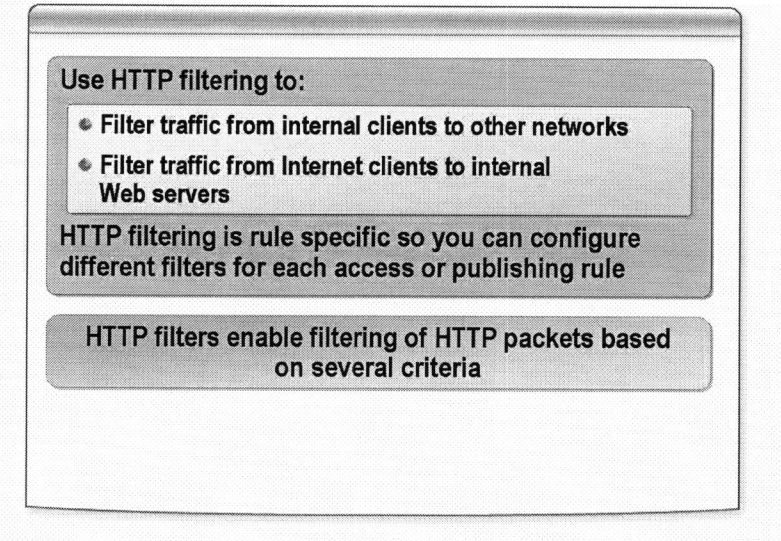

Use HTTP filtering to:

- Filter traffic from internal clients to other networks
- Filter traffic from Internet clients to internal Web servers

HTTP filtering is rule specific so you can configure different filters for each access or publishing rule

HTTP filters enable filtering of HTTP packets based on several criteria

Introduction

One of the most important Web filters included with ISA Server 2004 is the HTTP filter. Many Internet applications now use HTTP to tunnel the application traffic. For example, Microsoft MSN® Messenger uses HTTP as the application-layer protocol. The only way to block these types of applications without blocking all HTTP traffic is to use HTTP filtering.

HTTP filtering scenarios

HTTP filtering can be applied in two general scenarios:

- Clients on an internal network accessing HTTP objects on another network through ISA Server. This access is controlled by ISA Server access rules, to which an HTTP policy can be applied using the HTTP filter.

- Clients on the Internet accessing HTTP objects on a Web server that is published through ISA Server. This access is controlled by ISA Server Web publishing rules, to which an HTTP policy can be applied using the HTTP filter.

HTTP filtering is rule specific, so that you can apply different levels and types of filtering depending on the specific requirements of your firewall policy. For example, you can use HTTP filtering to block the use of a particular peer-to-peer file-sharing service for one set of users, but allow it for another set, or you can allow Internet users to use specific methods such as POST for one Web publishing rule, but deny the method on another Web publishing rule.

Note HTTP filters can also filter HTTPS traffic in a Web publishing Secure Sockets Layer (SSL) bridging scenario. In this case, ISA Server decrypts the packet and inspects it before re-encrypting the packet. HTTP filters cannot filter HTTPS traffic in an SSL tunneling scenario. For more details on configuring SSL bridging and tunneling, see Module 5, "Configuring Access to Internal Resources," in Course 2824, *Implementing Microsoft Internet Security and Acceleration Server 2004.*

HTTP filter options   The HTTP filter can block HTTP requests based on the following options:

- *Length of request headers and payload.* Limits the maximum HTTP header size and request body size for a client request.

- *Length of Uniform Resource Locator (URL).* Limits the maximum URL size for client requests.

- *HTTP request method.* Specifies the HTTP method, such as POST, GET, or HEAD, that will be blocked.

- *HTTP request file name extension.* Prevents the downloading of any content using HTTP based on file extensions such as .exe, .asp, or .dll.

- *HTTP request or response header.* Specifies how server headers will be returned or forwarded when the server responds to the client. For example, the request or response header may be Location, Server, or Via.

- *Signature or pattern in the requester response headers or body.* Specifies HTTP access based on specific strings in the response header or body.

The HTTP filter is initially configured with defaults that help ensure secure HTTP access. However, depending on the specific deployment scenario, these options should be customized.

Note   To fully understand how the HTTP filter works, you need to understand how HTTP works. For more information on the HTTP protocol, see Request for Comments (RFC) 2616: Hypertext Transfer Protocol HTTP/1.1, located at http://www.ietf.org/rfc/rfc2616.txt.

How to Configure HTTP Web Filter General Properties

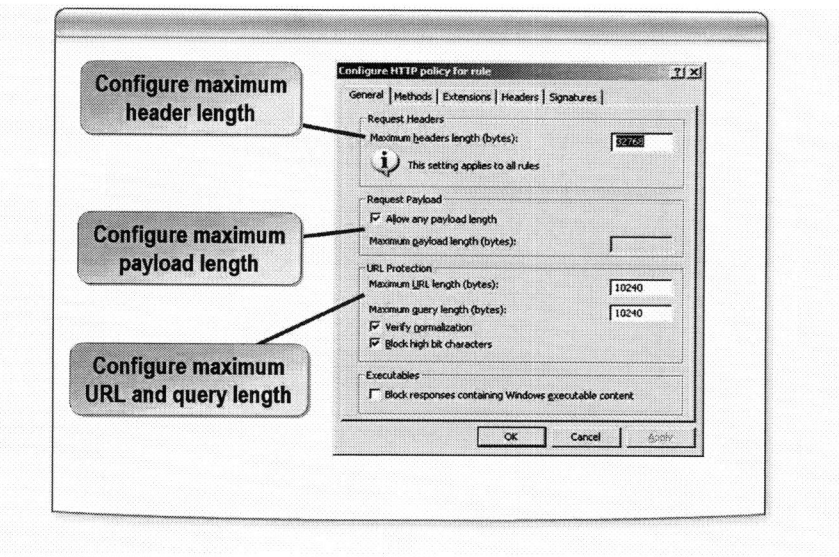

Introduction

HTTP filters are applied on a per-rule basis. To configure the HTTP filters on a particular access rule or Web publishing rule, modify the HTTP policy for that rule.

Important   The one exception to the per-rule application of the HTTP filter is the **Maximum headers length** setting on the **General** tab of the **Configure HTTP policy for rule** dialog box. This setting is applied to all rules globally, which means that if you change it in one rule, it is changed in all rules.

Configuring HTTP policy general properties

To access the HTTP policy associated with a specific rule, right-click the rule in **ISA Server Management** and select **Configure HTTP**.

The following table describes the configuration options available on the **General** tab of an HTTP policy.

Setting	Configuration options	Explanation
Request Headers, Maximum headers length (bytes)	Specify the maximum number of bytes that a request can have in its headers (URL and headers) before it is blocked.	Reducing the allowed header size mitigates the risk of attacks that require complex and long headers, such as buffer overflow attacks and some denial-of-service attacks. If you set the maximum header length too low, it could break some legitimate applications that use long headers. It is recommended that you start with a limit of 10,000 bytes, and increase it only if you find that needed applications are being blocked.
Request Payload, Allow any payload length	To block requests exceeding a specified maximum payload length, clear the **Allow any payload length (bytes)** check box. Then, in **Maximum payload length (bytes)**, specify the maximum number of bytes.	By limiting the request payload you can restrict the amount of data a user can POST to your Web site in a Web publishing scenario. To determine what limit to set, estimate the maximum size of a file that would constitute a legitimate POST based on your site usage and use that as the allowed payload length.

(*continued*)

Setting	Configuration options	Explanation
URL Protection, Maximum URL length (bytes)	Specify the maximum URL length allowed.	Use this option to limit the length of URLs used in a request. You may want to limit the URL length if you learn of an attack based on a long URL string. By default the maximum query length is set to 10240.
URL Protection, Maximum query length (bytes)	Specify the maximum query length allowed in a request.	The query is the part of a URL that follows "?". You may want to limit the query length if you learn of an attack based on a long query string. By default the maximum query length is set to 10240.
URL Protection, Verify normalization	Use this to block requests with URLs containing escaped characters after normalization.	Web servers receive requests that are URL encoded. This means that certain characters may be replaced with a percent sign (%) followed by a particular number. For example, %20 corresponds to a space. Normalization is the process of decoding URL-encoded requests.

Because the percent sign (%) itself can be URL encoded, an attacker can submit a URL request to a server that is basically double-encoded. When you select Verify Normalization, the HTTP filter normalizes the URL twice. If the URL after the first normalization is different from the URL after the second normalization, the filter rejects the request. |
| URL Protection, Block high-bit characters | Specify that URLs with high-bit characters will be blocked. | When you select Block high-bit characters, URLs that contain double-byte character sets (DBCS) or Latin 1 characters will be blocked. These are typically characters from languages that require more than 8 bits to represent the characters of the language, and therefore use 16 bits. |
| Executables, select Block responses containing Microsoft Windows® executable content | Specify that responses containing Windows executable content are to be blocked. | This option blocks all Windows executable content (responses that begin with MZ). In most cases, it is recommended to use file extensions to block specific types of files instead of this option. |

How to Configure HTTP Web Filter Methods

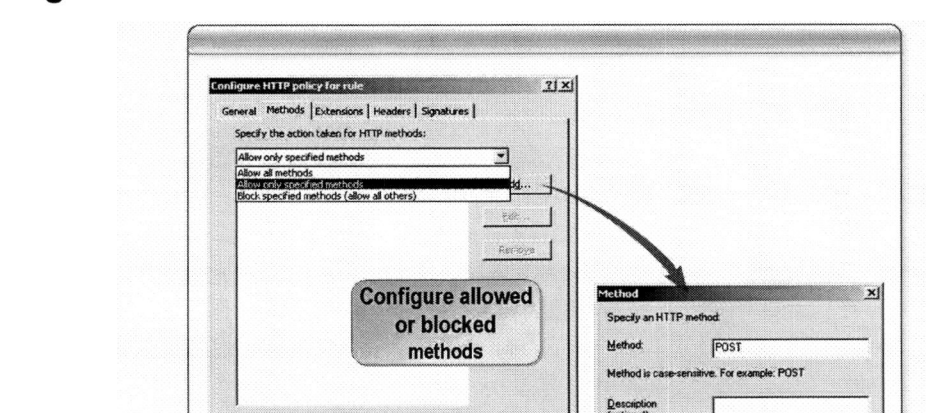

HTTP Methods

An HTTP method (also known as an *HTTP verb*) is an instruction sent in a request message that notifies an HTTP server of the action to perform on the specified resource. For example, "GET" specifies that a resource is being retrieved from the server. The following table lists the HTTP 1.1 methods defined in RFC 2616.

Method	Description
GET	Retrieves the specified Uniform Resource Identifier (URI)
HEAD	Retrieves only the header of the specified URI
POST	Asks the server to accept the enclosed information, such as a bulletin board message of form data
PUT	Asks the server to accept the enclosed information as the specified URI
DELETE	Asks the server to delete the specified URI
TRACE	Asks the server to return the request message (used for diagnostics)
CONNECT	Reserved for requesting a proxy tunnel

Configuring HTTP policy methods

To configure HTTP methods, follow this procedure.

1. To access the HTTP policy associated with a specific rule, right-click the rule in **ISA Server Management** and select **Configure HTTP**.

2. To modify the HTTP methods settings on the HTTP policy, click the **Methods** tab.

3. In **Specify the action taken for HTTP methods**, select one of the following:

    a. **Allow all methods**. No blocking according to method will be applied.

    b. **Allow selected methods**. All requests will be blocked except those with the specified methods.

    c. **Block specified methods (allow all others)**. All requests will be allowed except those with methods specified in the list.

4. If you have selected either of the last two options, click **Add** to add a method to the list.

5. When you click **Add**, the **Method** dialog box opens. Provide the method (case-sensitive) and a description, and then click **OK**.

An example of blocking by method would be to block PUT so that internal clients cannot post data to an external Web page. This is useful in a secure network scenario where you want to prevent sensitive information from being posted on a Web site. This can also be useful in Web publishing, to prevent attackers from posting malicious material to your Web site.

How to Configure HTTP Web Filter Extensions

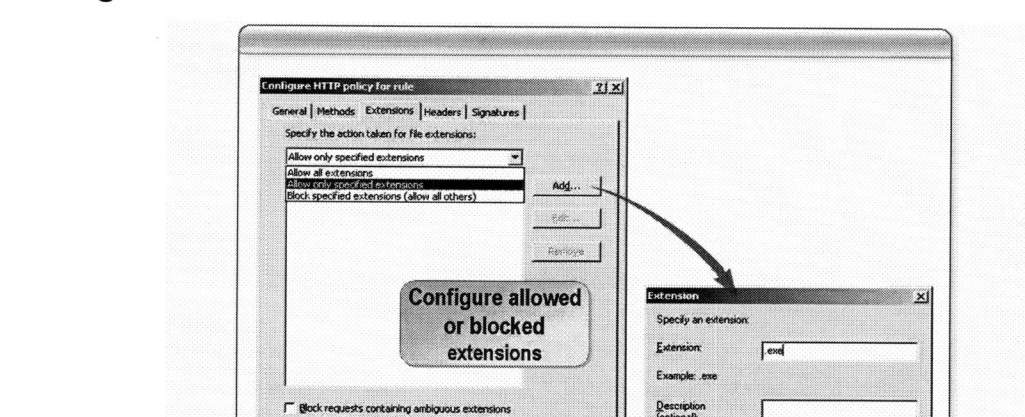

How ISA Server determines extensions

You can configure ISA Server to allow or deny HTTP downloads based on file extensions. When the HTTP filter is configured in this way, it analyzes each HTTP request to see if the request includes a configured extension. ISA Server considers an extension to be any character or characters that fall after the last period (.) of a URL and that end with a slash (/) or question mark (?) or the end of the URL if there is no slash or question mark.

In addition, if ISA Server identifies characters following a period that seem to be an extension (for example, .exe, .dll, or .com), the HTTP filter uses those as the extension. If there are multiple entries that appear to be extensions, ISA Server evaluates just the first extension.

The following table lists some examples of client requests and how ISA Server evaluates the extensions.

Client request	Extension
http://server/path/file.ext	.ext
http://server/path/file.htm/additional/path/info.asp	.asp
http://server/Path.exe/file.ext	.exe

In the last example listed in the table, if the HTTP filter allows .exe extensions, the request will be allowed (even if the filter does not allow .ext extensions). To work around this issue, configure a signature setting that denies the .ext signature in the URL.

Configuring HTTP policy for extensions

To specify file extensions, follow this procedure.

1. To access the HTTP policy associated with a specific rule, right-click the rule in **ISA Server Management** and select **Configure HTTP**.

2. To modify the HTTP extensions settings on the HTTP policy, click the **Extensions** tab.

3. In **Specify the action taken for file extensions**, select one of the following:

   a. **Allow all extensions**. No blocking according to requested file extensions will be applied.

   b. **Allow selected extensions**. All requests will be blocked except those with specified requested file extensions.

   c. **Block specified extensions (allow all others)**. All requests will be allowed except those with requested file extensions specified in the list.

4. Click **Add** to add an extension to the list.

5. When you click **Add**, the **Extension** dialog box opens. Provide the extension (case-sensitive) and a description, and then click **OK**.

6. Select **Block requests containing ambiguous extensions** if you want to block content when ISA Server cannot determine the extension.

A typical use of extension blocking is to block executable files such as .exe, .bat, or .cmd files. Another example is to use extension blocking to prevent worm attacks. For example, the Code Red Worm uses a header that included "GET http://<ipaddress>/default.ida?" so you could stop the worm from entering the network by blocking .ida extensions. You can also use file extensions to enforce organizational policies that restrict the types of data that can be downloaded.

How to Configure HTTP Web Filter Headers

HTTP Headers

When a client sends a request to a Web server, or when the server responds, the first part of that response is always the HTTP request or response.

- The HTTP request from the client includes the client's HTTP method (such as GET) as well as the URI that the client is requesting and the protocol version.

- The server HTTP response contains the protocol version followed by a numeric status code and its associated textual phrase. For example, if the server responds with a 2xx code, the server is indicating that the request was successfully received, understood, and accepted. A 4xx code is a client error that indicates that the request contains bad syntax or cannot be fulfilled.

After the HTTP request or response, the client and server send an HTTP header. The request-header fields allow the client to pass additional information about the request, and about the client itself, to the server. Headers contain information about the client, including browser and operating system data, authorization information, and the format types that client supports for the server response. The client header can also use the User-Agent to indicate the specific application that is making the request.

You can use this header information to block HTTP packets.

Configuring HTTP policy for headers

To configure how the HTTP filter will manage headers, follow this procedure.

1. To access the HTTP policy associated with a specific rule, right-click the rule in **ISA Server Management** and select **Configure HTTP**.

2. To modify the HTTP headers settings on the HTTP policy, click the **Headers** tab.

3. In **Headers**, list the headers that will be blocked. Click **Add** to add a header to the list. When you click **Add**, the **Header** dialog box opens. Specify whether the response or request header will be checked, provide the header, and then click **OK**.

4. In **Server Header**, specify how the server header will be returned in the response. The server header is a response header that contains information such as the name of the server application and software version information, for example, **HTTP: Server = Microsoft-IIS/6.0**. The possible settings are:

   a. **Send original header**. The original header will be returned in the response.

   b. **Strip header from response**. No header will be returned in the response.

   c. **Modify**. A modified header will be returned in the response. If you select this option, in **Change to**, type the value that will appear in the response.

5. In **Via Header**, specify how the Via header will be forwarded in the request or returned in the response. Via headers provide a way for proxy servers in the path of a request to ensure that they are also included in the path of the response. Each server along the request's path can add its own Via header. Each sender along the response path removes its own Via header and forwards the response to the server specified in the next Via header on the stack. For example, you can use this feature to avoid disclosing the name of your computer running ISA Server in a response. The possible settings are:

   a. **Send default**. The default header will be used.

   b. **Modify header in request and response**. The Via header will be replaced with a modified header. If you select this option, in the **Change too** box, type the header that will appear instead of the Via header.

How to Configure HTTP Web Filter Signatures

HTTP signatures

An HTTP signature can be any string of characters in the HTTP header or body. To block an application based on signatures, you need to identify the specific patterns the application uses in request headers, response headers, and body, and then modify the HTTP policy to block packets based on that string.

One of the difficulties in configuring the HTTP policy to block packets based on the signature is ensuring that the signature contains the specific information you need to block the chosen HTTP packet while not blocking other packets. For example, if you create an HTTP policy to block the word "Mozilla," you would block most Web browsers as well as other applications. This is because most Web browsers are Mozilla compatible and include this term in HTTP headers. In most cases, you should use a more application-specific string. For example, to block MSN Messenger, configure the rule to block User-Agent: MSN Messenger in the request header.

Configuring HTTP policy for signatures

To configure how the HTTP filter will manage signatures, follow this procedure.

1. To access the HTTP policy associated with a specific rule, right-click the rule in **ISA Server Management** and select **Configure HTTP**.

2. To modify the HTTP signatures settings on the HTTP policy, click the **Signatures** tab. The **Signatures** tab shows the signatures that will be blocked.

3. Click **Add** to add a signature to the list. In the **Signature** dialog box, in the **Name** text box, type a name for the signature search.

4. Under **Signature search criteria**, in the **Search in** drop-down list, select the part of the client request or server response you want the Web filter to search. Then, in the **Signature** text box, type the string that you want to filter.

5. When you have added signatures to the list on the Signatures tab, you can enable or disable specific signatures using the check boxes next to the signature names.

Note   When you configure the HTTP policy to search the HTTP request body or response body, you can also specify how much of the body will be scanned for the signature and what format to use when scanning. By default, the filter will scan only the first 100 bytes of the request or response body. Increasing this number can negatively impact the server performance. You can also specify whether to search using text or binary format.

You can use HTTP signatures to block access to specific applications or to specific content. For example, if you configure the policy to block User-Agent: MSN Messenger in the request header, users will not be able to use MSN Messenger through the firewall. You can also block access to sites that might contain malicious code if you are aware of common malicious code. For example, a Web page containing <iframe src="?"/> will cause Internet Explorer to use up central processing unit (CPU) resources in an infinitely nested iframe element. To prevent access to Web pages containing this code, use a signature that searches in the response body for the text <iframe src="?"/>.

HTTP signature filtering assumes that all HTTP requests and responses are Uniform Transformation Format-8 (UTF-8, a transformation of Unicode character encoding) encoded. If a different encoding scheme is used, signature blocking cannot be performed.

How to Identify an HTTP Application Signature

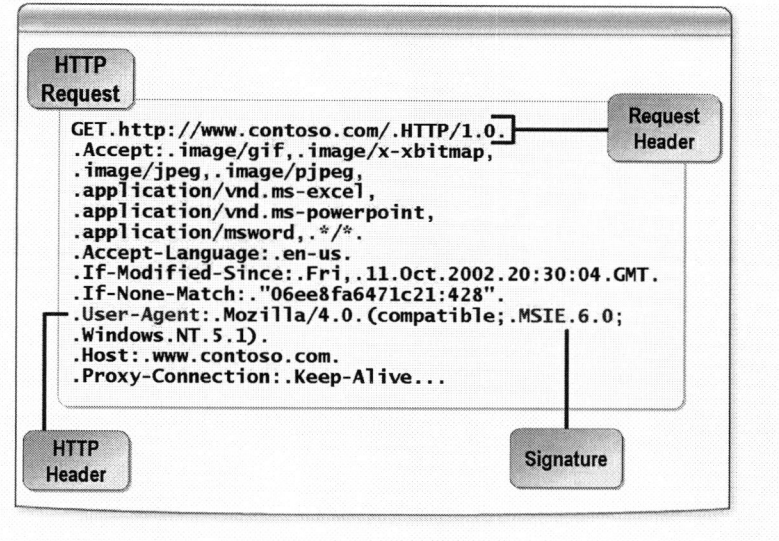

Introduction

One of the benefits of using the HTTP filter is that you can use it to block applications that tunnel through HTTP. The best way to block these applications is to configure the HTTP policy to block the application based on the application signature.

Identifying a HTTP application signature

In some cases, you may not know the specific signature used by an application and may need to identify the signature before you can configure the filter. To identify the signature used by the application, follow these steps:

1. Configure Network Monitor or another packet capture tool to capture all network packets on the computer running ISA Server. If the application client is on the internal network, configure the packet capture tool to monitor the internal network interface. If the client is on the Internet, configure the tool to capture packets on the external interface.

2. Start the network capture tool and then start the application. Capture the network packets as they pass through the network interface on the computer running ISA Server.

3. Examine the captured packets. Locate the packets that have the client's source address and the server's destination address. In most cases, the fourth packet (after the handshake packets SYN, SYNACK, and ACK) will be an HTTP request packet from the client computer. This packet usually contains the application signature. In some cases, you may have to look for the signature in later packets.

The following table shows some of the signatures used by common HTTP-based applications.

Application	Search in	HTTP header	Signature
MSN Messenger	Request headers	User-Agent:	MSN Messenger
Windows Messenger	Request headers	User-Agent:	MSMSGS
Netscape 7	Request headers	User-Agent:	Netscape/7
Netscape 6	Request headers	User-Agent:	Netscape/6
AOL Messenger (and all Gecko browsers)	Request headers	User-Agent:	Gecko/
Yahoo Messenger	Request headers	Host:	msg.yahoo.com
Kazaa	Request headers	P2P-Agent:	Kazaa Kazaaclient:
Kazaa	Request headers	User-Agent:	KazaaClient
Kazaa	Request headers	X-Kazaa-Network:	KaZaA
Gnutella	Request headers	User-Agent:	Gnutella Gnucleus
Edonkey	Request headers	User-Agent:	e2dk
Internet Explorer 6.0	Request headers	User-Agent:	MSIE 6.0
Morpheus	Response header	Server:	Morpheus
Bearshare	Response header	Server:	Bearshare
BitTorrent	Request headers	User-Agent:	BitTorrent
Simple Object Access Protocol (SOAP) over HTTP	Request headers Response headers	User-Agent:	SOAPAction

Best Practice: HTTP Filter Configuration for Web Publishing

To configure a baseline HTTP filter:

- Configure maximum header, payload, URL and query lengths
- Verify normalization and do not block high-bit characters
- Allow only GET, HEAD, and POST
- Block executable and server side includes extensions
- Block potentially malicious signatures

Use the httpfilterconfig.vbs script from the ISA Server CD to import and export HTTP filter configurations

Introduction

Each organization will need to determine the optimal HTTP filtering policy according to company security requirements and new exploits or attacks. However, there are some specific settings that can be configured in most Web publishing scenarios.

Baseline Web publishing HTTP policy

For Web publishing, create an HTTP policy with the parameters shown in the following table.

Tab	Parameter
General	Maximum headers length is 32768.
	Allow any payload length is selected.
	Maximum URL length is 260.
	Maximum query length is 4096.
	Verify normalization is selected.
	Block high-bit characters is not selected.
Methods	Allow only specified methods:
	GET
	HEAD
	POST

(*continued*)

Tab	Parameter
Extensions	Block specified extensions (allow all others):
	.exe
	.bat
	.cmd
	.com
	.htw
	.ida
	.idq
	.htr
	.idc
	.shtm
	.shtml
	.stm
	.printer
	.ini
	.log
	.pol
	.dat
Headers	No changes from the default.
Signatures (Request URL)	Block content containing these signatures
	..
	./
	\
	:
	%
	&

Importing the baseline Web publishing policy

You can use the httpfilterconfig.vbs script to export and import an HTTP filter script. To do this, follow these steps.

1. Create an HTTP policy using a text editor such as Notepad, and save as an .xml file.

2. On the ISA Server CD, browse to the folder **\sdk\samples\admin**. Locate the script **HttpFilterConfig.vbs**.

3. From a command line, run the script **HttpFilterConfig.vbs** using the following syntax:

```
\ScriptDirectory\HTTPFilterConfig.vbs import RuleName
\file directory\HTTPPollicyXmlFileName
```

where *ScriptDirectory* is the location of the script, either the \sdk\samples\admin folder on the CD, or a location on the local hard drive if you copy the script to there. *RuleName* is the name of the Web publishing or Outlook Web Access publishing rule to which you want to import the HTTP Policy configuration, *filedirectory* is the location where the HTTP policy .xml file is stored, and *HTTPPolicyXmlFileName* is the name of the .xml file.

For example, to import the CohoHTTPPolicy.xml file and apply it to the Coho Vineyard Web Publishing Rule, type the following at a command prompt:

```
F:\sdk\samples\admin\HTTPFilterConfig.vbs import Coho Vineyard
Web Publishing Rule c:\ISAServerXml\CohoHTTPPolicyXmlFile
```

To export an HTTP policy file, type the same command but use the command export rather than import.

Practice: Configuring HTTP Filtering

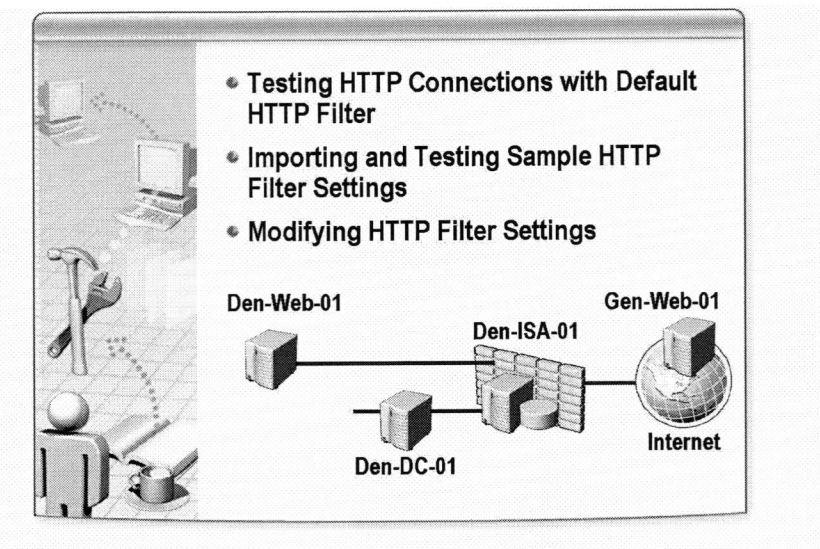

Introduction

In this practice, you will test the default HTTP filtering policy on the computer running ISA Server. Then you will import the sample HTTP filter configuration included with ISA Server 2004 and test the results. Finally, you will modify the baseline HTTP filter, import it again, and test the results.

▶ **To prepare for this practice**

1. You will need the Den-DC-01 virtual machine, the Den-Web-01 virtual machine, the Den-ISA-01 virtual machine, and the Gen-Web-01 virtual machine for this practice.

2. If necessary, start or resume the required virtual machines and then log on Gen-Web-01 with a user name of **Administrator** and a password of **P@ssw0rd**.

▶ **Testing HTTP connections with the Default HTTP filter**

1. On Gen-Web-01, open **Internet Explorer** and, in the **Address** box, type **http://www.cohovineyard.com/abc** and then press **Enter**. Internet Explorer displays the HTTP error 404 (File not found). HTTP Filtering allowed the request, and the error message was returned from the Den-Web-01 Web server because the requested object does not exist.

2. In Internet Explorer, in the **Address** box, type **http://www.cohovineyard.com/%252e** and then press **Enter**. The HTTP request that you typed contains a double-encoded hexadecimal representation, which is often used in Unicode canonicalization attacks. The HTTP filter blocked the request and returned an internal server error that indicates that the attempt was blocked by the HTTP Security filter.

3. In Internet Explorer, in the **Address** box, type
   http://www.cohovineyard.com/scripts/root.exe?/dir+c and then press
   Enter. Internet Explorer displays the HTTP error 404 (File not found).
   HTTP Filtering allowed the request, and the error message was returned
   from the Den-Web-01 Web server because the requested object does not
   exist.

▶ **Importing the Sample HTTP filter settings**

1. Switch to the Den-ISA-01 virtual machine and log on to the cohovineyard
   domain with your user name and password.

2. Open a command prompt and type **CD C:\Program Files\
   Microsoft Learning\2824\setup\sdk\samples\admin** and press **Enter**.

3. Type **HTTPFilterConfig.vbs import "Coho Vineyard Web Site"
   httpfiltersampleconfig.xml**.

4. Click **OK** in the **Windows Script Host** dialog box. Close the command
   prompt.

▶ **Testing HTTP connections with the Baseline HTTP filter**

1. Switch to the Gen-Web-01 virtual machine.

2. Open **Internet Explorer** and, in the **Address** box, type
   http://www.cohovineyard.com/abc and then press **Enter**. Internet Explorer
   displays the HTTP error 404 (File not found). HTTP Filtering allowed the
   request, and the error message was returned from the Den-Web-01 Web
   server because the requested object does not exist.

3. In Internet Explorer, in the **Address** box, type
   http://www.cohovineyard.com/%252e and then press **Enter**. The HTTP
   filter blocked the request and returned an internal server error that indicates
   that the attempt was blocked by the HTTP Security filter.

4. In Internet Explorer, in the **Address** box, type
   http://www.cohovineyard.com/scripts/root.exe?/dir+c and then press
   Enter. Again, the HTTP filter blocked the request because of the .exe file
   extension in the request header.

▶ **Modifying baseline HTTP settings**

1. Switch to the Den-ISA-01 virtual machine.

2. Open **ISA Server Management**, expand **Den-ISA-01** and click **Firewall
   Policy**.

3. In the details pane, right-click the **Coho Vineyard Web Site** Web
   publishing rule and click **Configure HTTP**. This will bring up the
   Configure HTTP Policy for rule dialog box.

4. On the **Signatures** tab, click **Add**.

5. In the **Signature** dialog box, in the **Name** text box, type **Block ABC
   signature**.

6. In the **Signature** text box, type **abc**. Click **OK**.

7. Click **OK** to close the **Configure HTTP Policy for rule** dialog box.

8. Click **Apply** to apply the changes and then click **OK** when the changes have been applied.

▶ **Testing HTTP connections with the modified HTTP filter**

1. Switch to the Gen-Web-01 virtual machine.

2. Open **Internet Explorer** and, in the **Address** box, type **http://www.cohovineyard.com/abc** and then press **Enter**. HTTP Filtering blocked the request and returned an internal server error that indicates that the attempt was blocked by the HTTP filter.

▶ **To prepare for the lab**

1. You will need the Den-DC-01 virtual machine, the Den-ISA-01 virtual machine, the Den-Clt-01 virtual machine, and the Gen-Web-01 virtual machine for this practice.

2. Shut down the Den-Web-01 virtual machine without saving the changes and start the Den-Clt-01 virtual machine.

Lesson: Additional Application and Web Filters

* About the FTP Application Filter
* About the SOCKS V4 Application Filter
* Other Application and Web Filters
* How to Develop Application and Web Filters

Introduction

ISA Server 2004 includes several other application and Web filters. Much of ISA Server's functionality, such as SMTP filtering, link translation, OWA forms-based authentication, and DNS filtering are implemented using application or Web filters. This lesson describes the functionality provided by several other application filters and provides a summary of the application and Web filters available in ISA Server. This lesson also provides an overview of how application and Web filters can be developed using the ISA Server Software Development Kit (SDK).

Lesson objectives

After completing this lesson, you will be able to:

- Describe how the FTP application filter works.
- Describe how the SOCKS V4 application filter works.
- List the application and Web filters included with ISA Server.
- Describe how application and Web filters can be developed using the SDK.

About the FTP Application Filter

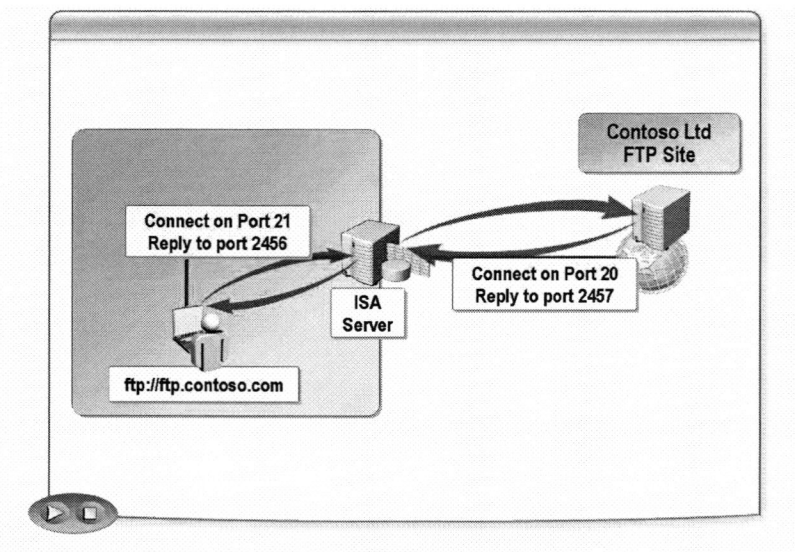

Introduction

Enabling the file transfer protocol (FTP) at the firewall can be a very complex process for administrators because FTP uses multiple ports and connections to transfer data. The FTP Access Filter is specially designed to ease the administrative burden by handling this complexity and securely managing all needed connections.

How FTP works

The following steps describe how an FTP connection is set up.

1. The FTP client creates a connection to an FTP server using port 21. As part of the request, the FTP client also indicates on which port it will be listening for a response. This port will be a random port over 1023.

2. The server responds on the port indicated by the client, and the client and server complete the three-way handshake.

3. Once the three-way handshake is complete, the server initiates a connection with the client on port 20. This port will be used for the data channel to actually transmit the data. The server also indicates a port greater than 1023 that the client should respond to.

4. The client and server complete a three-way handshake on the new ports and then begin to transmit data.

The first two steps in the process are similar to most protocol connections. However, when the FTP server initiates a connection back to the client on port 20, the connection is not part of any existing TCP session and so would normally be blocked because the connection was not initiated from the internal network.

How the FTP filter works

The FTP filter enables the FTP connections to allow client computers secure access to FTP servers without requiring complex access rules on the firewall. The FTP filter monitors the initial FTP connection between the FTP client and server and enables the server connection attempt to set up the data channel. The FTP filter also translates the client's internal Internet Protocol (IP) address into an address that can be accessed by the FTP server from the Internet.

This filter can be used to protect your organization's FTP server or servers. A computer running ISA Server placed between the user requesting a file and the FTP server can limit and block access requests. All incoming requests are passed through the computer running ISA Server before they reach the company's FTP server, thus maximizing its security.

Whether the FTP filter is used for incoming or outgoing FTP traffic, you can specify the level of access allowed. You can configure the FTP filter to:

- Block all access to FTP servers.

- Allow read-only access to information on FTP servers.

- Allow full access to the information on the FTP server.

Configuring the FTP filter

There are several different configuration options available with the FTP filter:

- You can disable the FTP filter on any access rule or server publishing rule. By default, the FTP filter is enabled on all rules that enable FTP. If you want to disable the FTP filter on a particular rule, access the protocol properties on the rule and disable the FTP filter.

- You can disable the FTP filter for all rules. To disable the FTP filter, access the **Add-ins** container in **ISA Server Management**. Right-click **FTP Access Filter** and select **Disable**.

- You can configure the FTP filter to allow read-only access or read-write access for each rule using FTP. By default, the FTP filter allows only read access to FTP servers. If you want to enable write access, locate the access rule in the **Firewall Policy** container. Right-click the rule and click **Configure FTP**. Clear the **Read Only** check box.

About the SOCKS Version 4 Application Filter

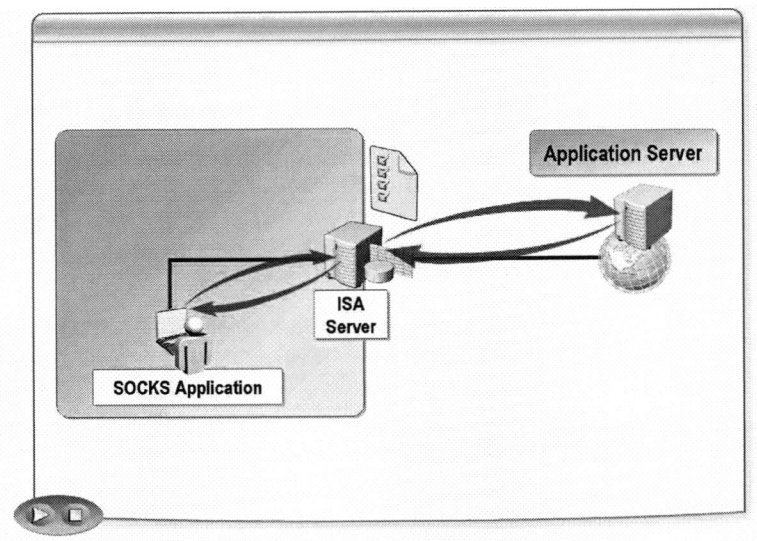

Introduction

The SOCKS network communication method is an alternative to the WinSock proxy service enabled by the Firewall Client and the Firewall Service on ISA Server. SOCKS can support almost any client platform, including Microsoft Windows, UNIX/Linux, Macintosh, and even nonstandard devices. It is most commonly used on non-Windows machines in a mixed computing environment.

How SOCKS works

WinSock proxy provided by the Firewall Client is transparent to applications. That is, the application does not need to be aware that the network request is being forwarded to a proxy server because the Firewall Client makes this transparent. However, to use SOCKS-based communications, your client applications must be SOCKS compatible and your firewall must support SOCKS connections. The following steps describe how a SOCKS application connects to a server on another network.

1. The SOCKS client application sends a request packet to a SOCKS-compliant firewall. The request includes information such as the IP address and port number for the destination server, and the user's identification.

2. The SOCKS server examines the request and determines whether it has any rule allowing the type of access requested by the client.

3. If the request is allowed, the server proxies the request to the server on the Internet.

4. The Internet server replies to the proxy server, which proxies the reply to the client.

The SOCKS filter on ISA Server

With the SOCKS Version 4 filter, administrators can allow or block SOCKS communications through a computer running ISA Server. When enabled, the filter will dynamically manage connections to ensure smooth communications for this complex protocol.

The SOCKS filter provided with ISA Server forwards requests from SOCKS applications to the Microsoft Firewall service. ISA Server checks the access policy rules to determine if the SOCKS client application can communicate with the Internet. ISA Server 2004 supports SOCKS Version 4–compliant communication.

When you install ISA Server, the SOCKS filter is disabled for all networks. You can configure ISA Server to listen for SOCKS requests on any network and on any port. SOCKS applications typically send requests to port 1080, but you can modify the default port on the SOCKS filter if the SOCKS applications are configured to use a different port.

Because client computers running Windows can use the Firewall Client instead of a SOCKS client, you normally do not need to enable the SOCKS filter on ISA Server if you have only Windows clients. This filter should be enabled only if your network includes clients who require the use of a SOCKS proxy.

Other Application and Web Filters

ISA Server 2004 includes:

- Application filters that enable complex and secure client to server connections while hiding the complexity of the firewall configuration from the administrator

- Web filters to implement features such as special authentication mechanisms and link translation

ISA Server application filters

When you configure a server publishing rule, many of the available protocols include an application filter that enables complex client-to-server connections while hiding the complexity from the administrator. ISA Server 2004 includes the application filters listed in the following table.

Application Filter	Functionality
DNS filter	The DNS filter allows an organization to screen incoming DNS communications for malicious commands and data before they reach the DNS server.
MMS filter	Microsoft Media Server (MMS) protocol is the primary streaming media technology used by Microsoft products. MMS is a very sophisticated protocol and ISA Server 2004 provides the MMS filter to assist administrators with managing its complexity.
PNM filter	The PNM (Progressive Networks Metafile) filter enables media streams to either be sent or received using RealNetworks, Inc. products. The PNM filter manages the multiple ports and connections used by this protocol.
POP intrusion detection filter	The POP intrusion detection filter is designed to protect POP e-mail servers on your company's network from buffer overflow attacks.
PPTP Filter	ISA Server 2004 can be used to secure both inbound and outbound Point-to-Point Tunneling Protocol (PPTP) communications. With ISA Server 2004, a PPTP server can easily be placed behind the computer running ISA Server on the internal network. The PPTP filter simplifies the configuration of the firewall rules for managing this type of communication.

(continued)

Application Filter	Functionality
RPC Filter	The Remote Procedure Call (RPC) filter enables clients from one network to access RPC servers on another network. The RPC filter manages the complex port number-to-universally unique identifier (UUID) translation.
RTSP Filter	Real Time Streaming Protocol (RTSP) is a streaming media format that is used by Apple QuickTime technology. Using the RTSP filter, administrators can allow or restrict incoming or outgoing RTSP connections. The filter also manages RTSP connections.
SMTP Filter	The SMTP filter uses content inspection to examine SMTP commands and ensure that they are not harmful to your organization's e-mail server.

ISA Server Web filters

When you configure a Web publishing rule, the computer running ISA Server uses Web filters to implement features such as special authentication mechanisms and link translation. ISA Server 2004 includes the Web filters listed in the following table.

Web Filter	Functionality
OWA forms-based authentication filter	OWA forms-based authentication is enabled by this filter. When this filter is enabled on a Web publishing rule, the filter intercepts authentication requests and performs all authentication, and disconnects the session when the session times out or the user logs off.
SecurID Filter	The SecurID filter implements the third-party authentication scheme provided by RSA Data Security, Inc. SecurID requires that users provide a second means of proving their identities.
RADIUS Authentication Filter	The RADIUS authentication filter also enables ISA Server 2004 to support non-Windows-based user authentication using RADIUS technology.
Link Translation Filter	The link translation filter enables the translation of internal server names to server names that are accessible from the Internet.

How to Develop Application and Web Filters

ISA Server filters that can be developed include:

- Protocol-enabling filters
- Protocol-scanning filters
- Redirection filters
- NAT supporting filters
- Intrusion detection filters
- Content filtering filters

Use the ISA Server SDK to create custom filters

Introduction

ISA Server 2004 ships with the ISA Server Software Development Kit (SDK). The SDK can be used by developers to create application and Web filters.

Filter types

The SDK enables the creation of many different filter types, including:

- *Protocol-enabling filters*. These application filters enable the usage of complicated protocols that require more than a single TCP connection to flow through the Microsoft Firewall service. These filters dynamically configure the ISA Server to allow future secondary connections. The FTP access filter is an example of a protocol-enabling filter that is included with ISA Server 2004. The SDK can be used to create custom filters for managing any protocol connections.

- *Protocol-scanning filters*. These filters scan data from specific protocols for items such as an intrusion or virus. Examples of protocol-scanning filters included with ISA Server 2004 are the POP intrusion detection filter and the DNS intrusion detection filter that are based on technology from Internet Security Systems, Inc. (ISS), and are provided with ISA Server.

- *Redirection filters*. A redirection filter may cause specific connections to be redirected into its control. The filter can then act as a server.

- *NAT-supporting filters*. Many protocols pass IP addresses of internal servers as part of their data. In a network address translation (NAT) environment, these internal IP addresses are hidden and need to be translated to externally visible addresses. An application filter can monitor the traffic and modify the relevant fields within a message to include the correct external addresses according to existing publishing rules, or according to some other criteria. For example, using the FTP access filter, an FTP client behind the computer running ISA Server may direct an FTP server to connect to it, passing its address and port information as part of the protocol. The FTP access filter translates this information to an externally visible listening socket, enabling the file transfer to take place without disclosing the internal address.

- *Intrusion-detection filters.* Application filters can examine traffic going through the computer running ISA Server and look for known attack signatures. ISA Server provides two such filters, which detect known intrusion signatures for DNS and POP3.

- *Content-filtering filters.* Application filters can parse high-level application protocols, look for actual data (the payload), and apply rules and processing based on the content. Examples include applying protocol-level syntax validation, antivirus scanning on file transfers, SOAP or eXtensible Markup Language (XML) filtering, and content categorization. The firewall-service HTTP and SMTP filters demonstrate this capability. In these scenarios, the overall structure of the application filter is the same. It typically attaches itself to each connection and implements the specifications and RFCs relevant to the protocols it represents to handle the traffic and apply rules to it. The filter should keep a session state and use it to control the data transfer through the computer running ISA Server. It may modify the data flow, change the session payload, stop sessions that seem to violate the policy, or call ISA Server APIs to automatically configure allow or deny rules for expected future traffic. Content filtering for HTTP traffic is accomplished by developing an ISAPI filter, called a Web filter in the context of ISA Server and the Firewall service.

Developing application filters

To develop an application filter for ISA Server, the application filter must have the following characteristics:

- The application filter must use the IFWXFirewall interface. The IFWXFirewall interface provides access to all Firewall service functions.

- An application filter must include a COM object that implements the IFWXFilter interface. Filters must be registered as COM servers and as extensions of the Microsoft Firewall service in the ISA Server configuration. When the Firewall service starts, it creates an instance of the filter object for each application filter that is installed on the computer running ISA Server and enabled.

- The application filter must be invoked by an event that is registered with the Firewall service. When a client connects to the Firewall service, the Firewall service examines the connection to see if it matches an event for which an application filter is registered.

- Application filters follow an active data-pumping programming model in which an application filter that registers itself on a connection takes full ownership of the connection and actively pipes the data through from one side to the other.

- Application filters can be chained so that the same protocol is handled by more than one filter. When an application filter pumps data through a socket interface, it can be a virtual socket that is actually connected to the next filter, or it can be a real network socket that actually writes and reads data from the network.

Note For detailed information on how to develop application filters, see Developing Application Filters, located at http://msdn.microsoft.com/library/default.asp?url=/library/en-us/isa/isafireflt_42lv.asp, and Developing an Application Filter for Microsoft Internet Security and Acceleration Server 2004 at http://msdn.microsoft.com/msdnmag/issues/04/03/ISAServer2004/default.aspx. For information on developing Web filters, see Developing Web (ISAPI) Filters for ISA, located at http://msdn.microsoft.com/library/default.asp?url=/library/en-us/isa/isaisapi_09sx.asp.

Lab: Configuring the HTTP Web Filter

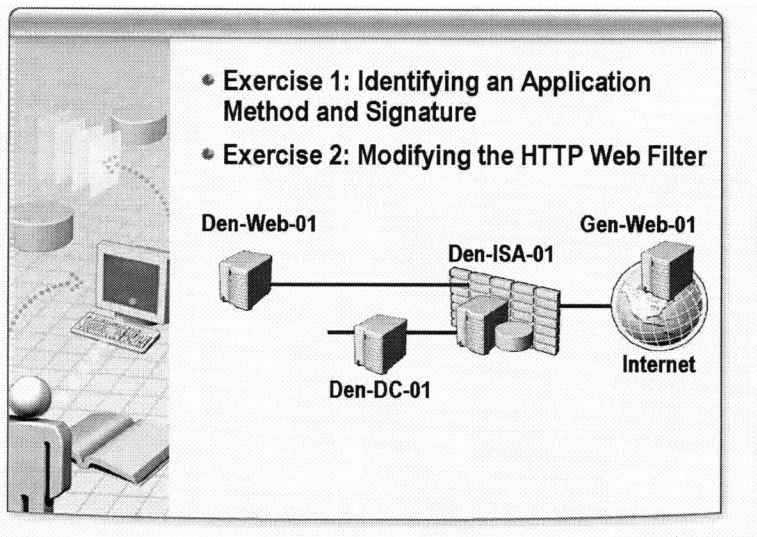

Objectives

After completing this lab, you will be able to:

- Identify an application-layer signature.
- Configure Microsoft Internet Security and Acceleration (ISA) Server to block an application based on methods and signatures.

Note This lab focuses on the concepts in this module and as a result might not comply with Microsoft security recommendations. For example, the Administrator passwords are not as complex as recommended. Additionally, most of the actions performed in this lab are performed while logged on as an Administrator. A better security practice would be to log on as a normal user and use the Runas option to start administrative applications.

Scenario

You have deployed ISA Server at Coho Vineyard. You have configured ISA Server to publish internal Web sites as well as internal servers running Microsoft Exchange Server. The internal users can use Hypertext Transfer Protocol (HTTP), Hypertext Transfer Protocol Secure (HTTPS), and File Transfer Protocol (FTP) to access the Internet. During a routine security review, you notice that several users are copying internal company documents to a server on the Internet. The users then connect to the same server on the Internet from home and download the documents. As far as you can tell, the users are only doing this as an efficient means of moving documents. However, this practice is against the corporate security policy and the security officer has asked you to prevent users from using this means of moving files.

You investigate and determine that the users are using a Web folder on their local desktop to connect to the remote server. The users are using Web Distributed Authoring and Versioning (WebDAV) over HTTP to transfer the folders. To block this type of access, you must prevent users from using WebDAV through the firewall. You will do this by modifying the HTTP filter setting on the access rule that allows users to access resources on the Internet.

To prepare for this lab:

1. You will need the Den-DC-01 virtual machine, the Den-ISA-01 virtual machine, the Den-Clt-01 virtual machine, and the Gen-Web-01 virtual machine for this practice.

2. If necessary, start or resume the required virtual machines and then, on Den-ISA-01, log on to the cohovineyard domain with your user name and password.

Estimated time to complete this lab: 30 minutes

Exercise 1
Identifying an Application Method and Signature

In this exercise, you will use Network Monitor to capture the packets used by a WebDAV client when accessing files on another server. In preparation for blocking the client access, you will then examine the packets to identify the HTTP method and signature used by the WebDAV client.

Tasks	Detailed steps
1. Prepare Network Monitor on Den-ISA-01 to capture packets on the internal network interface.	a. On the Den-ISA-01 computer, open **Network Monitor** from the **Administrative Tools** folder. b. A Network Monitor message will remind you to select a network. Click **OK** to close the message. c. In the **Select a Network** dialog box, expand **Local Computer**. Click **Internal** and then click **OK**.
2. Configure Den-Clt-01 to use a Web Folder to access the HTTP://www.contoso.com/ uploads folder.	a. On Den-Clt-01, log on to the cohovineyard domain using a user name of **Jay** with a password of **P@ssw0rd**. b. Open the **Control Panel**. Click **Network and Internet Connections**. c. In the **Network and Internet Connections** dialog box, click **My Network Places**. d. Under **Network Tasks**, click **Add a network place**. e. On the **Welcome to the Add Network Place Wizard** page, click **Next**. f. On the **Where do you want to create this network place?** page, click **Next**. g. On the **What is the address of this network place** page, in the **Internet or network address** box, type **http://www.contoso.com/uploads** and then click **Next**. h. On the **What do you want to name this place** page, click **Next**. i. On the **Completing the Add Network Place Wizard** page, click **Finish**. j. Wait till the Web folder opens and then close all open Windows.

(*continued*)

Tasks	Detailed steps
3. Capture and examine the packets from Den-Clt-01 accessing the Web folder.	**a.** Switch to Den-ISA-01.
	b. From the **Network Monitor** menu, click **Capture** and select **Start** (or press F10).
	c. Switch to Den-Clt-01.
	d. Open **My Network Places** from the **Start Menu**.
	e. Double-click **uploads on www.contoso.com**.
	f. Switch to Den-ISA-01.
	g. From the **Network Monitor** menu, click **Capture** and select **Stop and View** (or press SHIFT+F11).
	h. Inspect the packets that were captured by clicking on the first packet in the top window. Look for a packet sent from Den-Clt-01 to Den-ISA-01 with an ACK value of 0 in the Transmission Control Protocol (TCP) header.
	i. Examine the next two packets sent between Den-Clt-01 and Den-ISA-01; these packets are the packets used for the three-way handshake.
	j. Examine the first packet after the three-way handshake is complete. What HTTP method is used in this packet?
	k. What is the value of the User-Agent field?
	l. Document your answers and close Network Monitor without saving the changes.

Exercise 2
Modifying the ISA Server System Policy

In this exercise, you will configure the HTTP filter on the access rule that enables Internet access for Coho Vineyard users to block the WebDAV application. First, you will block the Method used by the WebDAV application, and then you will use a signature to block the application.

Tasks	Detailed steps
1. Configure the HTTP filter on the Web Access Only rule to block the WebDAV method.	a. On Den-ISA-01, start **ISA Server Management**. Click **Firewall Policy**. b. Right-click the **Web Access Only** access rule and click **Configure HTTP**. c. In the **Configure HTTP policy for rule** dialog box, click the **Methods** tab. d. Change the action taken for HTTP methods to **Block specified methods (allow all others)**. e. Add the WebDAV method that you identified in the previous exercise. f. Close the **Method** tab and the **Configure HTTP policy for rule** dialog box. g. Click **Apply** to apply the changes and then click **OK** when the changes have been applied.
2. Test whether you have successfully blocked WebDAV access.	a. Switch to Den-Clt-01. b. Close **uploads on www.contoso.com**. Open **My Network Places** from the **Start Menu**. c. Double click **uploads on www.contoso.com**. d. Confirm that you cannot access the Web folder and close the open Window.
3. Remove the HTTP filter configuration on the Web Access Only rule that is blocking the WebDAV method. Configure the filter to block WebDAV access based on signature.	a. On Den-ISA-01, in **ISA Server Management**, click **Firewall Policy**. b. Right-click the **Web Access Only** access rule and click **Configure HTTP**. c. In the **Configure HTTP policy for rule** dialog box, click the **Methods** tab. d. Change the action taken for HTTP methods to **Allow all methods**. e. Click the Signature tab. Click **Add**. f. In the **Name** text box, type **WebDAV block**. g. In the **Search in** list, click **Request Headers**. h. In the **HTTP header** box, type **User-Agent**. i. In the **Signature** box, type the signature that you discovered in the previous exercise. j. Click **OK** to close the **Signature** box and then click **OK** to close the **Configure HTTP policy for rule** dialog box. k. Click **Apply** to apply the changes and then click **OK** when the changes have been applied.

(continued)

Tasks	Detailed steps
4. Test whether you have successfully blocked WebDAV access.	a. Switch to Den-Clt-01. b. Open **My Network Places** from the **Start** menu. c. Double-click **uploads on www.contoso.com**. d. Confirm that you cannot access the Web folder and close the open window.

To Prepare for the Next Lab

As you finish this lab, shut down all of the virtual machines that you used in the lab. To shut down the virtual machines, click **Close** from the **Action** menu. **Select Turn off and delete changes** and click **OK**.

After shutting down the virtual machines, restart the Den-DC-01 virtual machine, the Den-ISA-01 virtual machine, and the Den-Clt-01 virtual machine in preparation for the next module.

Module 8: Configuring Virtual Private Network Access for Remote Clients and Networks

Contents

Overview

* Virtual Private Networking Overview
* Configuring Virtual Private Networking for Remote Clients
* Configuring Virtual Private Networking for Remote Sites
* Configuring VPN Quarantine Control Using ISA Server 2004

Introduction

Organizations require secure access to the internal network for remote users. Many organizations also need a secure means to connect to multiple locations. Implementing a virtual private network solution is the solution for both of these requirements. Microsoft® Internet Security and Acceleration (ISA) Server 2004 provides a VPN solution that provides full VPN functionality combined with the secure filtering of a firewall.

Objectives

After completing this module, you will be able to:

- Describe how virtual private networks (VPNs) work and the components required to configure VPNs.
- Configure ISA Server to enable VPNs for remote clients.
- Configure ISA Server to enable VPNs for remote sites.
- Configure ISA Server to enable VPN quarantine service.

Lesson: Virtual Private Networking Overview

* **What Is Virtual Private Networking?**
* **VPN Protocol Options**
* **VPN Authentication Protocol Options**
* **VPN Quarantine Control**
* **Virtual Private Networking Using Routing and Remote Access**
* **Virtual Private Networking Using ISA Server 2004**
* **Benefits of Using ISA Server for Virtual Private Networking**

Introduction

This lesson provides an overview of virtual private networking. It discusses the protocols and authentication methods available when using Microsoft Windows Server™ 2003 or ISA Server 2004 to implement virtual private networking and explains how the VPN quarantine control works. This module also provides an overview of how VPNs are implemented using Routing and Remote Access in Windows 2000 Server or Windows Server 2003 and using ISA Server 2004 and the benefits of using ISA Server to implement VPNs.

Lesson objectives

After completing this lesson, you will be able to:

- Describe what a VPN is and when to use it.

- Identify VPN protocol options.

- List VPN authentication options.

- Describe the way that VPN quarantine control works.

- Describe how to use Windows Routing and Remote Access service to implement VPNs.

- Describe how to use ISA Server 2004 to implement VPNs.

- State the benefits of using ISA Server 2004 to enable VPNs.

What Is Virtual Private Networking?

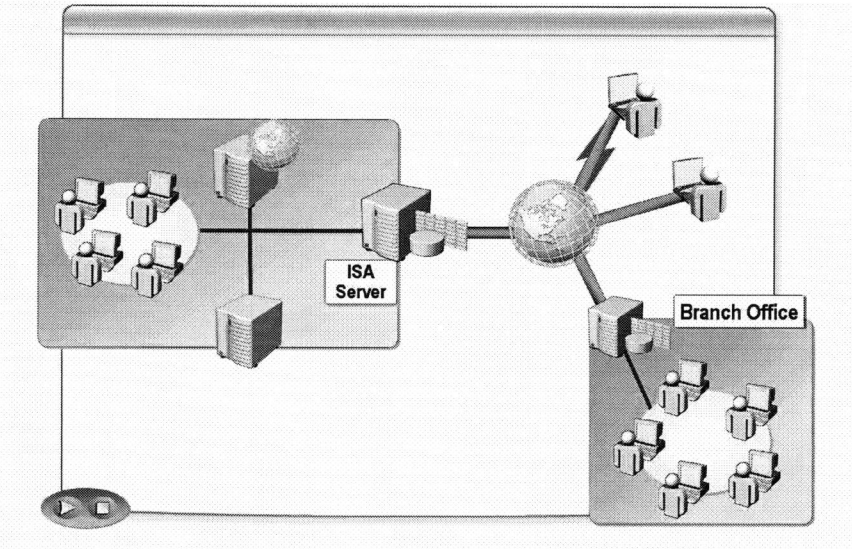

Introduction

Virtual private networking allows secure remote access to resources on an organization's internal network that would otherwise be available only if the user were directly connected to the corporate local area network (LAN).

What is a VPN?

A virtual private network (VPN) is an extension of the internal network located behind the computer or device configured as a VPN server. The VPN is a virtual network that enables communication between a remote access server and computers on the internal network or between two remote sites even though the computers might be in different locations and separated by a public network such as the Internet.

When you configure a VPN, you create a secured, point-to-point connection across a public network such as the Internet. A VPN client uses special Transmission Control Protocol/Internet Protocol (TCP/IP)–based protocols called *tunneling protocols* to connect to a virtual connection port on a VPN server. The tunneling protocols use encryption protocols to provide data security as the data is sent across the public network. The two VPN protocols supported by ISA Server are Microsoft Point-to-Point Tunneling Protocol (PPTP) or the Layer 2 Tunneling Protocol (L2TP).

PPTP and L2TP create "virtual" direct connections between a VPN client and VPN remote access server, or between two VPN gateways. This virtual network connection allows a computer connected over the virtual network to send and receive TCP/IP messages in the same way it does on other directly connected networks, such as computers located on the same Ethernet LAN. The actual network connection is transparent to the applications running on the client computer.

PPTP and L2TP use encryption protocols ensure that the connection is private or secure by encrypting all traffic sent across a public network. The PPTP VPN protocol uses the Microsoft Point-to-Point Encryption protocol (MPPE) to protect data moving through the PPTP virtual networking connection. The L2TP/IPSec VPN protocol uses Internet Protocol Security (IPSec) to encrypt data moving through the L2TP virtual network.

VPN scenarios

VPNS are used in two primary scenarios:

- *Network access for remote clients.* In this scenario, a remote user establishes a connection to the Internet and then creates a tunneling protocol connection to the VPN remote access server. The remote user can use any available technology to connect to the Internet, including dial-up connection to an Internet service provider (ISP) or a direct connection such as a cable or digital subscriber line (DSL) connection. Once connected to the Internet, the VPN client makes a virtual private network connection to the VPN remote access server that is also connected to the Internet. The remote access server authenticates the user and possibly the remote computer, establishes a secure connection and transfers encrypted data between the virtual private networking client and the organization's network.

- *Site-to-site VPNs.* A site-to-site VPN connection connects two or more networks in different locations using a VPN connection over the Internet. In this scenario, each site requires a VPN gateway and an Internet connection. When the gateways establish a VPN connection with one another, the site-to-site VPN link is established. Users can then communicate with other networks over the VPN site-to-site link. The VPN gateways act as VPN routers that route the packets to the appropriate network. In most cases, a site-to-site VPN connection is made between branch office and main office networks.

Benefits of using VPNs

The primary benefits of using VPNs are:

- *Reduced costs.* Using the Internet as a connection medium saves long-distance phone expenses and requires less hardware than a dial-up networking solution. In the case of a site-to-site VPN, using the Internet as a wide area network (WAN) is also less expensive than using a dedicated WAN connection.

- *Security.* Authentication prevents unauthorized users from connecting to the VPN servers. Strong encryption methods make it extremely difficult for a hacker to interpret the data sent across a VPN connection.

- *Flexibility.* By using VPNs, the organization does not need to manage Internet connections or dial-up servers for remote users. The users only need to be able to connect to the Internet using whatever technology is available.

- *Transparency to applications.* One of the significant advantages of using a VPN connection, rather than an alternative solution such as a client/server Web application, is that VPN users at remote locations can potentially access all protocols and servers on the corporate network. The remote access VPN user does not need special software to connect to each of these services, and the network and firewall administrator does not need to create special proxy applications to connect to these resources.

VPN Protocol Options

Factor	PPTP advantages and disadvantages	L2TP/IPSec advantages and disadvantages
Client operating systems supported	• Windows 2000, Windows XP, Windows Server 2003, Windows NT Workstation 4.0, Windows ME, or Windows 98	• Windows 2000, Windows XP, or Windows Server 2003
Certificate support	• Requires a certificate infrastructure only for EAP-TLS authentication	• Requires a certificate infrastructure or a pre-shared key
Security	• Provides data encryption • Does not provide data integrity	• Provides data encryption, data confidentiality, data origin authentication, and replay protection
NAT support	• To locate PPTP-based VPN clients behind a NAT, the NAT should include an editor that can translate PPTP	• To locate L2TP/IPSec-based clients or servers behind a NAT, both client and server must support IPSec NAT-T

Introduction

VPN security is based on the tunneling and authentication protocols that you use and the level of encryption that you apply to VPN connections. ISA Server 2004 supports two VPN tunneling protocols for remote access clients: Point-to-Point Tunneling Protocol (PPTP) and Layer Two Tunneling Protocol with Internet Protocol security (L2TP/IPSec).

PPTP

PPTP uses Point-to-Point Protocol (PPP) user authentication methods and Microsoft Point-to-Point Encryption (MPPE) to encrypt IP traffic. PPTP supports the use of Microsoft Challenge Handshake Authentication Protocol Version 2 (MSCHAP V2) for password-based authentication. For stronger authentication for PPTP connections, you can implement a public key infrastructure (PKI) using smart cards or certificates and Extensible Authentication Protocol–Transport Level Security (EAP-TLS).

PPTP is widely supported and easily deployed, and it works with most network address translators (NATs). Although it is not considered as secure as IPSec, a PPTP-based VPN solution is less complex to administer and can reduce costs associated with implementing a certificate infrastructure.

L2TP/IPSec

L2TP/IPSec is the more secure of the two VPN protocols—it uses PPP user authentication methods and IPSec encryption to encrypt IP traffic. This combination uses certificate-based computer authentication to create IPSec security associations in addition to PPP-based user authentication. L2TP/IPSec provides data integrity, data origin authentication, data confidentiality, and replay protection for each packet.

Support for L2TP/IPSec is provided with Windows Server 2003, and also with Microsoft Windows® 2000 and Windows XP. To use L2TP/IPSec with Microsoft Windows 98, Windows Millennium Edition, or Microsoft Windows NT® Workstation 4.0, download and install Microsoft L2TP/IPSec VPN Client (Mls2tp.exe).

Note For information about Mls2tp.exe, see the Microsoft L2TP/IPSec VPN Client link on the Web Resources page at http://www.microsoft.com/ windows2000/server/evaluation/news/bulletins/l2tpclient.asp.

L2TP/IPSec and PPTP considerations

When implementing a VPN solution, keep in mind the benefits and limitations of supported protocols. The table in the illustration lists factors that you should consider as you plan and implement a VPN solution. It also describes the advantages and disadvantages of using PPTP or L2TP/IPSec.

Note For the highest level of security, implement a VPN solution that uses L2TP/IPSec with certificate-based IPSec authentication and Triple-DES (3DES) for encryption. Both the VPN remote access server and the remote access clients must be configured to support this level of security.

VPN Authentication Protocol Options

Authentication protocol	Considerations
PAP	• Uses plaintext passwords and is the least secure authentication protocol
SPAP	• Uses a reversible encryption mechanism employed by Shiva
CHAP	• Requires passwords stored by using reversible encryption • Compatible with Macintosh and UNIX-based clients • Data cannot be encrypted
MS-CHAP	• Does not require that passwords be stored by using reversible encryption • Encrypts data
MS-CHAPv2	• Performs mutual authentication • Data is encrypted by using separate session keys for transmitted and received data
EAP-TLS	• Most secure remote authentication protocol • Enables multifactor authentication

Introduction

Before you choose any remote access authentication protocol, be sure you understand the security implications of the protocols.

PAP

Password Authentication Protocol (PAP) uses plaintext passwords and is the least secure authentication protocol. It is typically used if the remote access client and remote access server cannot negotiate a more secure form of authentication.

SPAP

The Shiva Password Authentication Protocol (SPAP) is a reversible encryption mechanism employed by Shiva. When a computer running Windows XP Professional connects to a Shiva LAN Rover, it uses SPAP, as does a Shiva client that connects to a server running Routing and Remote Access. This form of authentication is more secure than plaintext but less secure than CHAP or MS-CHAP.

CHAP

The Challenge Handshake Authentication Protocol (CHAP) is a challenge–response authentication protocol. It uses the Message Digest 5 (MD5) algorithm to hash the response to a challenge that the remote access server issues. CHAP is used by various vendors of dial-in servers and client computers, including Macintosh and UNIX. Data cannot be encrypted when you use the CHAP protocol. Therefore, CHAP is not considered a secure option.

MS-CHAP

Microsoft CHAP (MS-CHAP) is similar to CHAP, but can also use MPPE to encrypt data. MS-CHAP is more secure than CHAP, but use MS-CHAP only if you run earlier Microsoft operating systems that require it. Both CHAP and MS-CHAP are only as secure as the strength of the user's password.

MS-CHAP version 2   MS-CHAP version 2 was designed to fix many of the security issues with MS-CHAP, including the lack of mutual authentication. MS-CHAP version 2 uses mutual authentication so both the client and the server are authenticated. As well, data is encrypted by using separate session keys for transmitted and received data, which makes it more difficult for an attacker to sniff the traffic and use a brute force attack on the key. The session-key generation is not entirely based on the user's password, so a weak password will not necessarily leave the session vulnerable. MS-CHAPv2 is supported by VPN clients running Windows XP, Windows Server 2003, Windows 2000, Windows NT Workstation 4.0 with Service Pack 4 (SP4) and later, Windows Millennium Edition or Windows 98.

EAP   Extensible Authentication Protocol (EAP) is the most secure remote authentication protocol. It uses certificates on both the client and the server to provide mutual authentication, data integrity, and data confidentiality. It negotiates encryption algorithms and secures the exchange of session keys. Use EAP if you are implementing multifactor authentication technologies such as smart cards or universal serial bus (USB) token devices.

Guidelines for selecting authentication protocols   Consider the following factors when choosing an authentication protocol for VPN connections:

- If you use smart cards or have a certificate infrastructure that issues user and computer certificates, use the EAP authentication protocol for both PPTP and L2TP connections to provide the most secure authentication.

- If you do not have the infrastructure or budgetary means to support an EAP authentication strategy, use a password-based authentication protocol such as MS-CHAPv2. If you use password-based authentication, ensure that you enforce strong passwords by using Group Policy.

- Always use the most secure protocols that your network access servers and clients can support and configure the remote access server and the authenticating server to accept only secure authentication protocols. However, you may have to configure the authenticating server to accept less secure authentication protocols for compatibility with older VPN clients.

Pre-shared keys   ISA Server 2004 allows you to use pre-shared keys in place of certificates when creating remote access and gateway-to-gateway VPN connections. All VPN client machines running updated L2TP/IPSec VPN client software can use a pre-shared key to create an L2TP/IPSec remote access VPN client connection with the ISA Server 2004 firewall/VPN server. Windows 2000 and Windows Server 2003 VPN gateways can also be configured to use a pre-shared key to establish site-to-site links.

Pre-shared key support for IPSec-based VPN connections should be used with care. The preferred method is to use certificates. A single remote-access server can use only one pre-shared key for all L2TP/IPSec connections requiring a pre-shared key for authentication. This means that you must issue the same pre-shared key to all L2TP/IPSec VPN clients connecting to the remote access server using a pre-shared key. Unless you distribute the pre-shared key within a Connection Manager profile, each user must manually enter the pre-shared key into the VPN client software settings. This reduces the security of the L2TP/IPSec VPN deployment and increases the probability of user error and the number of support calls related to L2TP/IPSec connection failures.

VPN Quarantine Control

VPN Quarantine Control:

* Enables screening of VPN client machines before granting them access to the organization's network

* Uses a client script that analyzes the security configuration of the remote access client

* VPN clients connecting to ISA Server with approved security configurations are moved from the VPN Quarantine network to the VPN Clients network

Introduction

In most cases, a VPN remote access server can only validate the credentials of remote access users. If the remote access users successfully authenticate, they can access all resources on the internal network. However, the remote access client may not comply with corporate network policies. VPN quarantine control can delay normal remote access to a private network until a client-side script validates the remote access client configuration.

What is VPN quarantine control?

VPN quarantine control allows you to screen VPN client machines before allowing them access to the organization's network. To enable VPN quarantine, you create a Connection Manager Administration Kit (CMAK) package that includes a VPN client profile and a VPN-quarantine client-side script. This script runs on the client and checks the security configuration of the remote access client and reports the results to the VPN server. If the client passes the security configuration check, the client is granted access to the organization's network.

If you are using ISA Server as the VPN server, and the script reports that the client meets the software requirements for connecting to the network, the VPN client is moved from the VPN Quarantine network to the VPN Clients network. You can set different access policies for hosts on the VPN Quarantine network compared to the VPN Clients network.

Although quarantine control does not protect against attackers, computer configurations for authorized users can be verified and, if necessary, corrected before they can access the network. A timer setting is also available, which you can use to specify an interval at which the connection is dropped if the client fails to meet configuration requirements.

Quarantine-capable remote access clients

The following clients can use VPN quarantine:

- Microsoft Windows Server 2003
- Microsoft Windows XP Home Edition and Windows XP Professional
- Windows 2000
- Windows Millennium Edition
- Windows 98 Second Edition

Virtual Private Networking Using Routing and Remote Access

> **RRAS supports:**
>
> * Remote access policies that define remote access connections and connection parameters
> * Connection Manager components to simplify the configuration of remote access clients
> * RADIUS servers for authentication and the centralization of remote access policies
> * VPN quarantine control to restrict network access to quarantined clients
> * Packet filtering for securing VPN and network quarantine connections

Introduction

Windows 2000 Server and Windows Server 2003 include the Routing and Remote Access Service (RRAS), which can be used as dial-up or VPN remote access server. RRAS includes several features that can be implemented to manage a VPN solution.

RRAS remote access policies

One of the tools used to manage remote access in RRAS is remote access policies. Remote access policies are an ordered set of rules that define how remote access connections are either authorized or rejected. You can use remote access policies to specify the groups or individuals that are allowed remote access and to set different types of connection constraints. A remote access policy consists of the following three components:

- *Conditions*. The conditions of remote access policies are a list of parameters, such as the time of day, user groups, caller IDs, or IP addresses, that are matched to the parameters of the client that is connecting to the server. The first set of policy conditions that match the parameters of the incoming connection request are processed for access permission and configuration. If none of the condition sets are matched, the access attempt will fail.

- *Remote access permission*. Remote access connections are permitted based on a combination of the dial-in properties of a user account and remote access policies. The permission setting on the remote access policy works with the user's dial-in permissions in Active Directory® directory service.

- *Profile*. Each policy includes a profile of settings, such as authentication and encryption protocols, that are applied to the connection. The settings in the profile are applied to the connection immediately and may cause the connection to be denied. For example, if the profile settings for a connection specify that the user can only connect for 30 minutes at a time, the user will be disconnected from the remote access server after 30 minutes. Where applicable, connection restrictions for a user account override the connection restrictions for the remote access policy profile.

Connection Manager

The Connection Manager group of programs is a set of optional components used to create a managed remote access solution. Connection Manager enables a network administrator to pre-configure remote access clients, add custom settings and a custom appearance, and provide a phone book that can be updated and that enables users to find the most convenient dial-up access number. The Connection Manager product includes:

- *Connection Manager client.* The Connection Manager client provides a simplified way to connect to a remote network. Once the connection manager client is installed, the user only needs to enter a user name and password and select a phone number, if applicable. The administrator configures all other settings before distributing the service profile.

- *Connection Manager Administration Kit (CMAK).* CMAK allows the administrator to create and configure the service profile. This service profile is then distributed to remote access clients as a small, self-installing package. CMAK also allows the administrator to customize Connection Manager features, such as branding, custom actions, and custom Help files, in addition to enhanced security features.

- *Connection Point Service (CPS).* CPS allows you to create and maintain phone books. It consists of a Phone Book Administrator (PBA) that is used to create and publish phone book files, and the Phone Book Service (PBS) that is used to distribute phone books to Connection Manager clients on request.

Support for RADIUS servers

RRAS supports the use of Remote Authentication Dial-In User Service (RADIUS) servers for authentication and remote access policy configuration. In this configuration, the RRAS server is configured as a RADIUS client that forwards all authentication requests to a RADIUS.

Packet filtering for VPN connections using RRAS

RRAS supports the use of PPTP or L2TP/IPSec input and output filters on the interface that is connected to the Internet to limit network traffic to these VPN protocols. When you configure a VPN server, IP routing is enabled between the internal network interface and the Internet-facing network interface. This provides a connection between your internal network and possible attackers on the Internet. To protect your intranet so that the only traffic that is forwarded to the internal network is the traffic sent and received over secure VPN connections, you must block all network packets except PPTP or L2TP/IPSec traffic on the Internet interface.

Support for VPN quarantine control

RRAS supports the use of quarantine control to restrict client access to the network. RRAS uses IP filters to limit the resources that a client can access while in quarantine and also provides a time-out setting for disconnecting quarantined clients if they do not meet the security requirements.

Virtual Private Networking Using ISA Server 2004

> **ISA Server enables VPN access:**
>
> * Including remote client VPN access for individual clients and site-to-site VPN access to connect multiple sites
> * By enabling VPN-specific networks including:
>   * VPN Clients network
>   * Quarantined VPN Clients network
>   * Remote-site networks
> * By using network and access rules to limit network traffic between the VPN networks and the other networks with servers running ISA Server
> * By extending RRAS functionality

Introduction

ISA Server 2004 can also be used as a VPN server. ISA Server 2004 depends on and enhances the basic VPN functionality provided by Routing and Remote Access, available with Microsoft Windows Server 2003 and Windows 2000.

ISA Server VPN connection types

ISA Server supports two types of VPN connections:

■ *Remote-client access VPN connection.* A remote access client makes a remote access VPN connection that connects to a private network. ISA Server provides access to the internal network to which the VPN server is attached. To configure remote-client VPN access on ISA Server, you configure the computer running ISA Server to accept VPN connections and define the parameters for what types of connections will be accepted.

■ *Site-to-site VPN connection.* A VPN gateway server makes a site-to-site VPN connection that connects two private networks. To configure site-to-site VPN connections, you configure a remote-site network on the computer running ISA Server and then define how the VPN connection to the remote network will be created. You also define access rules that determine what types of traffic will be allowed to flow from the remote network to the other networks protected by ISA Server.

ISA Server and VPN networks

ISA Server assigns computers to networks and then uses network rules, network access rules, and publishing rules to restrict the movement of network traffic between networks. These concepts are also used by ISA Server to manage VPN connections. ISA Server uses the following networks for VPN connections:

- *VPN Clients network.* This network contains the IP addresses of all of the VPN clients that have connected using VPN client access.

- *Quarantined VPN Clients network.* This network contains the IP addresses of all of the VPN clients that have connected using VPN client access but have not yet cleared quarantine.

- *Remote-site network.* This network contains the IP addresses of all of the computers in a remote site when a site-to-site VPN connection is configured. Additional remote-site networks are created for each remote-site connection.

ISA Server uses these networks just like it uses any other directly connected networks. That means that you can use network rules and access rules to define the conditions under which network packets will be passed from one network to another.

RRAS and ISA Server VPNs

ISA Server uses RRAS to provide some of the VPN functionality, so the RRAS service must be running on ISA Server to enable VPN access. While most VPN configuration is done by using ISA Server Management, you can also configure some advanced settings using Routing and Remote Access; however, you must be careful not to override specific settings that should be configured only in ISA Server. In particular, note the following:

- If you use RRAS to enable network address translation (NAT), some ISA Server features may not function properly.

- Do not use RRAS to enable or disable IP routing. ISA Server always synchronizes RRAS settings, but RRAS does not check how ISA Server configures this functionality.

- RRAS packet filters are not applied when ISA Server is running. It is recommended that you copy the functionality defined by the packet filters used for quarantine in RRAS to ISA Server.

Benefits of Using ISA Server for Virtual Private Networking

Benefits	Explanation
Connection security	• ISA Server uses firewall access policies to inspect and filter all traffic from VPN clients
Performance	• ISA Server is optimized to enforce complex security requirements on VPN connections
Quarantine control for Windows 2000	• VPN quarantine is not available in Windows 2000 RRAS but can be enabled with ISA Server 2004 on Windows 2000
Logging and monitoring	• ISA Server can log all VPN connections and enables live monitoring of VPN connections
IPSec tunnel-mode stateful inspection	• Enables stateful inspection to enforce user/group, site, computer, protocol, and application-layer access controls for IPSec tunnel-mode traffic
Enhanced protection	• ISA Server is protected via firewall access policy on all interfaces

Benefits of using ISA Server for VPN access

ISA Server 2004 provides a number of benefits as a VPN server that are not available with RRAS. The features and benefits are listed in the following table.

Feature	Benefits
Connection control and security	VPN integration with ISA Server 2004 allows for greater access control over VPN connections. Information sent through ISA Server 2004 from VPN clients can be controlled using firewall access policies. This ensures that the traffic can be statefully inspected, and then forwarded or rejected, based on a wide range of criteria including who sent it, where it is going, what application it is coming from or going to, and time of day. All this is possible because ISA Server 2004 treats the VPN virtual interface like any other network interface on the firewall computer and applies firewall policies to it.
Performance	Windows Server 2003 RRAS is optimized for VPN connectivity performance and not for applying protective mechanisms.
	ISA Server 2004 includes significant performance enhancements for the enforcement of security and access control–related policies. This enables ISA Server 2004 to provide high-performance VPN connectivity, even when configured to enforce complex enterprise-level security requirements.
Ability to quarantine VPN connections using Windows 2000	VPN quarantine is not available in Windows 2000 RRAS. The addition of ISA Server 2004 enables Windows 2000 VPN servers to enforce VPN quarantine policies.

(continued)

Feature	Benefits
Logging and monitoring	Windows Server 2003 only allows rudimentary database and text-based logging of VPN connections. When the Windows Server 2003 RRAS VPN capabilities are integrated with ISA Server 2004, VPN logging can include not only all VPN remote access and site-to-site connections, but also the related application traffic. The ability to log and review the actual traffic is essential in allowing administrators to identify problematic VPN-based communication. This traffic can be viewed in real time and recorded to a text file, Microsoft Data Engine (MSDE) database, or SQL database for enhanced analysis and reporting. ISA Server also lets administrators view the connection state and the active sessions in the connections.
Stateful inspection of IPSec tunnel-mode site-to-site links	The Windows 2000 and Windows Server 2003 RRAS VPN is able to establish site-to-site VPN links with other VPN routers using IPSec tunnel mode to the VPN-routed connection. However, the RRAS VPN service can not statefully inspect traffic moving through the IPSec site-to-site link. In contrast, ISA Server can be used to set strong user/group, site, computer, protocol, and application-layer-specific access controls over connections moving through the site-to-site link. Users are able to access only allowed content on the remote network, and remote network users are allowed to access only local network resources that they are explicitly allowed to access.
Enhanced protection of VPN server resources	The Windows Server 2003 RRAS VPN includes a basic network firewall that prevents unsolicited non-VPN connections to the external interface of the VPN server computer. This basic firewall functionality provides a level of security against Internet-based attackers. However, the basic firewall does not provide any level of protection against attacks on the internal or VPN interfaces of the RRAS VPN server.
	ISA Server extends this level of protection by applying firewall policy to all interfaces. ISA Server enforces firewall access policy on all interfaces, including the internal, perimeter, and VPN interfaces. ISA Server is protected via firewall access policy on all interfaces installed on the ISA Server 2004 firewall and VPN server computer.

Lesson: Configuring Virtual Private Networking for Remote Clients

- VPN Client Access Configuration Options
- How to Enable and Configure VPN Client Access
- Default VPN Client Access Configuration
- How to Configure VPN Address Assignment
- How to Configure VPN Authentication
- How to Configure Authentication Using RADIUS
- How to Configure User Accounts for VPN Access
- How to Configure VPN Connections from Client Computers

Introduction

Providing a remote access solution for remote or mobile clients is one of the most common deployment scenarios for VPNs. A VPN is a cost-effective and secure alternative to using dial-up networking for many companies. This lesson describes how to enable VPNs for remote clients using ISA Server 2004.

Lesson objectives

After completing this lesson, you will be able to:

- Identify the VPN client access configuration options.
- Enable and configure VPN client access.
- Describe the default ISA Server configuration for VPN client access.
- Configure VPN address assignment.
- Configure VPN authentication.
- Configure authentication using RADIUS.
- Configure user accounts for VPN access.
- Configure VPN connections from client computers.

VPN Client Access Configuration Options

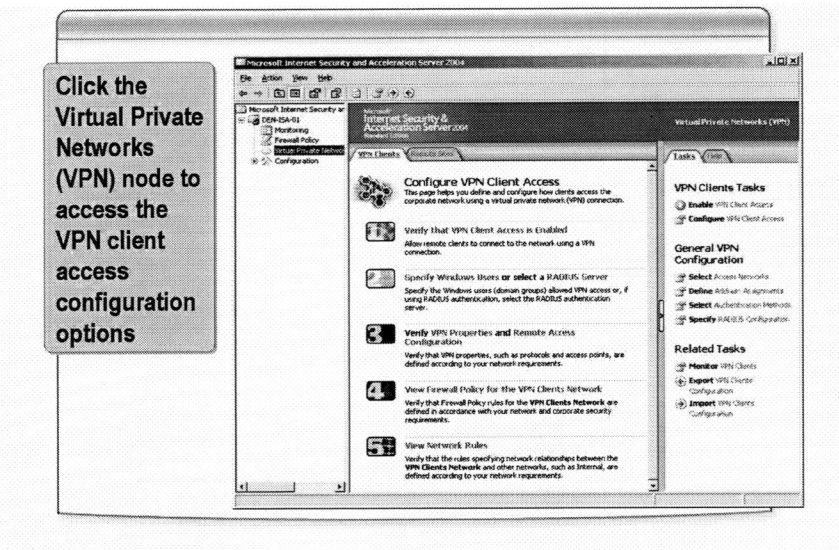

Click the Virtual Private Networks (VPN) node to access the VPN client access configuration options

Introduction

To enable remote access clients to access the internal network using VPN, you need to configure the VPN client access settings on ISA Server.

VPN client configuration options

When you configure VPN client access, you need to configure the components listed in the following table:

Configuration option	Explanation
Enable VPN client access	By default, VPN access is disabled on ISA Server. To allow remote clients to use VPNs, you must enable this option.
Configure the user accounts for users that can connect to the network using a VPN	ISA Server supports Windows-based authentication and RADIUS authentication. You need to configure which groups in Active Directory or which RADIUS server to use to assign remote access permissions. For users that do not use Windows authentication, you can also configure user mapping.
Configure VPN protocols	ISA Server supports PPTP and L2TP/IPSec remote access protocols. You can configure one or both.
Configure the remote access configuration	You can configure the network(s) that ISA Server will listen to for VPN connections, how ISA Server will assign IP addresses to VPN clients, and the authentication options available for VPN clients.
Configure network rules	You can also configure network rules for the network relationship between the VPN Clients network and the internal or external networks.
Configure the firewall access rules for the VPN Clients network	All VPN clients are placed in the VPN Clients network. You can use firewall access rules between the VPN Clients network and the internal network to limit user access to internal network resources. You can also configure firewall access rules to configure VPN user access to the Internet.

How to Enable and Configure VPN Client Access

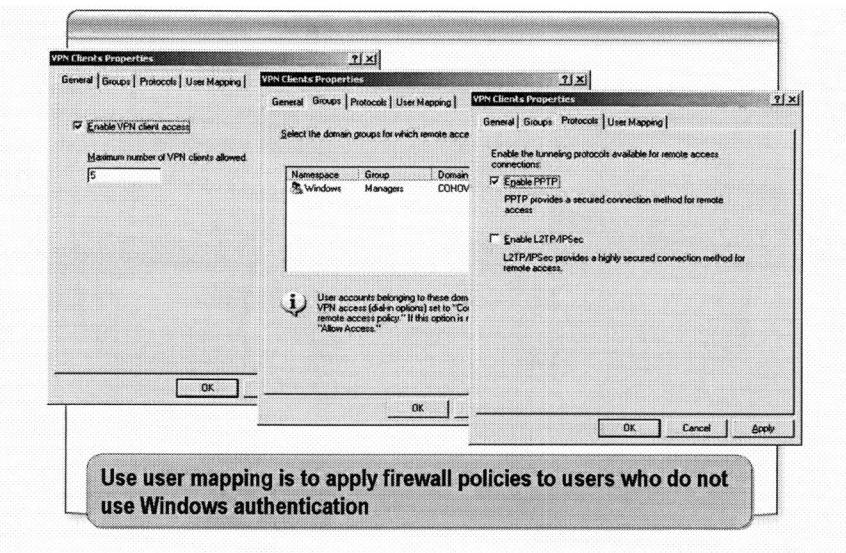

Use user mapping is to apply firewall policies to users who do not use Windows authentication

Introduction

Before any users can access ISA Server using a VPN, you must enable VPN client access. When you enable this option, ISA Server enables VPN access using a default configuration that you can modify to meet your organization's requirements.

Enabling VPN client access

Most of the VPN client access configuration is managed using the **Configure VPN Client Access** dialog box in **ISA Server Management**. To access this dialog box, open **ISA Server Management** and click **Virtual Private Networks (VPN)**.

To enable VPN client access, click **Enable VPN Client Access** in the **Tasks** pane, and then click **Apply** to apply the changes to the ISA Server configuration.

Configuring VPN client access

To configure VPN client access, complete these steps:

1. In ISA Server Management, click **Virtual Private Networks (VPN)**.

2. Click **Configure VPN Client Access** in the **Tasks** pane.

3. On the **General** tab, you can enable or disable VPN client access as well as change the value for the **Maximum number of VPN clients allowed**.

4. Click the **Groups** tab. By default, no groups are allowed to access ISA Server using a VPN. To assign this permission to a group, click **Add**. If the computer running ISA Server is configured to use an Active Directory domain for authentication, then add the Active Directory groups. Click **OK**.

5. On the **Protocols** tab, select the protocols that you want to enable for VPN access. Click **OK**.

6. On the **User Mapping** tab, click the **Enable User Mapping** check box if you want to enable user mapping. If you want to use a domain to authenticate users who do not enter a domain name when they authenticate, click the **When username does not contain a domain, use this domain** check box and then enter the domain name in the **Domain Name** text box. Click **OK**.

What is user mapping?

User mapping is used to map VPN clients connecting to the ISA Server using an authentication method that is not based on "Windows authentication" (such as RADIUS or EAP authentication) to the Windows namespace. When user mapping is enabled and configured, firewall policy access rules specifying user sets for Windows users and groups are also applied to authenticated users that do not use Windows authentication. If you do not define user mapping for users from namespaces that are not based on Windows, default firewall policy access rules will not be applied to them.

User mapping allows you to use RADIUS authentication of domain users and apply user/group based-access control over VPN clients who authenticated using RADIUS. Without the user mapping feature, you would not have access to strong user/group-based access control.

When user mapping is enabled and a user tries to create a VPN connection, the user is prompted for his or her credentials. The credentials are passed to the RADIUS server and the user name and domain supplied by the user are mapped to the same user name and domain in Active Directory and the user is authenticated as if Windows credentials had been presented.

Default VPN Client Access Configuration

Component	Default Configuration
System policy rules	• System policy rule that allows the use of PPTP, L2TP, or both is enabled
VPN access network	• ISA Server will listen for VPN client connections only on the External network
VPN protocols	• Only PPTP is enabled for VPN client access
Network rules	• A route relationship between the VPN Clients network and the Internal network • A NAT relationship between the VPN Clients network and the External network
Firewall access rules	• No firewall access rules are enabled
Remote access policy	• Default policy requires MS-CHAP v2 authentication

Default VPN client access configuration

When you enable VPN client access, the following default settings are applied:

- *System policy rules.* When VPN client access is enabled, a system policy rule named **Allow VPN client traffic to ISA Server** is enabled. Depending on which protocols are configured for remote-client access, the system policy rule allows the use of PPTP, L2TP, or both, from the external network to the computer running ISA Server (Local Host network).

- *VPN access network.* By default, ISA Server will listen for VPN client connections only on the external network. This property can be modified. When this property is modified, the system policy rule is changed automatically to apply to the additional or changed networks.

- *VPN protocol.* By default, only PPTP is enabled for VPN client access. This can be modified to include L2TP/IPSec only or both protocols. When this setting is modified, the system policy rule is updated to allow the appropriate protocol.

- *Network Rules.* Enabling VPN client access does not modify the network rules configured on ISA Server. When you install ISA Server, two network rules are created that include the VPN Clients network, one specifying a route relationship between the VPN Clients network and the internal network, and one specifying a NAT relationship between the VPN Clients network and the external network. The second rule is part of the Internet access rule that also defines the relationship between the internal network and external network.

■ *Firewall access rules.* By default, clients on the VPN Clients network cannot access any resources on any other network. You can manually configure a firewall access rule that enables this access, or you can use a network template to configure the rule. If you use a network template, a firewall access rule named **VPN Clients to Internal Network** is created. This rule allows access from the VPN Clients network to the internal network using all protocols. The VPN Clients network is also included in any rule that you create using a network template to grant Internet access. For example, if you use a network template to enable Internet access using all protocols, clients on the VPN Clients network will be able to access the Internet using that rule.

■ *Remote access policy.* When you enable ISA Server for VPN client access, a remote access policy named **ISA Server Default Policy** is created in Routing and Remote Access. This default policy denies access to all VPN connections except those explicitly allowed by the remote access profile. The remote access profile for the default policy enables MS-CHAPv2 authentication and requires authentication for all VPN connections.

How to Configure VPN Address Assignment

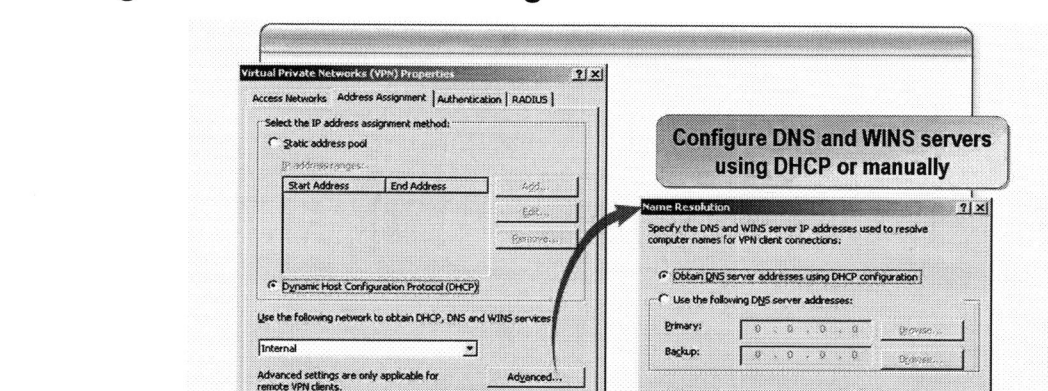

Introduction

When VPN clients connect to the VPN server, they must be assigned an IP address configuration that enables them to access the resources on the internal network or other networks. ISA Server can be configured to assign the IP address configuration directly, or to use a Dynamic Host Configuration Protocol (DHCP) server to assign the addresses.

IP addressing for VPN clients

In most cases, VPN clients are assigned IP addresses that are part of the internal network subnet. The advantage of this addressing scheme is that you do not need to create special routing table entries to support the VPN clients and all VPN clients will automatically be able to access the internal network and the Internet (using the protocols specified in the access rules). In this configuration, ISA Server acts as an Address Resolution Protocol (ARP) proxy for VPN clients. For example, when addresses assigned to the VPN Clients network are part of the internal network segment, computers from the internal network will send ARP queries to VPN clients. ISA Server will intercept the queries and reply on behalf of the connected VPN client.

Assigning IP addresses to VPN clients

When VPN clients connect to ISA Server, the client must be assigned an IP address. There are two ways that ISA Server can assign the addresses:

- *Dynamic address assignment.* To enable dynamic address assignment, a DHCP server must be accessible from the computer running ISA Server. Any computer running Windows Server 2003 or Windows 2000 Server on the internal network can serve as the DHCP server. If you use a DHCP server for address assignment, ISA Server retrieves a group of available IP addresses from the DHCP server. When a VPN client connects, ISA Server assigns one of these addresses to the VPN client. As part of the IP address assignment, ISA Server also assigns other TCP/IP properties such as the Domain Name System (DNS) servers and Windows Internet Naming Service (WINS) servers. The IP address assigned to the client is automatically moved from the internal network to the VPN Clients network (or Quarantined VPN Clients network if quarantine is enabled and the client is quarantined).

■ *Static address assignment*. You can also configure ISA Server with a static pool of addresses to assign to VPN clients. In this configuration, you do not need a DHCP server; rather, you configure the IP addresses on the computer running ISA Server. When a client connects, ISA Server assigns one of the IP addresses to the VPN client. If you use a static address pool for address assignment, the addresses that you want to assign to the pool must first be removed from other defined networks, because overlapping of IP addresses between networks is not allowed. You must also provide one more IP address in the static address pool than the expected number of remote VPN connections because the VPN interface on ISA Server requires an IP address.

Configuring IP address assignment

To configure ISA Server to assign IP addresses, use the following procedure:

1. In **ISA Server Management**, click **Virtual Private Networking**.

2. On the **Tasks** tab, click **Define Address Assignment**.

3. On the **Address Assignment** tab, select one of the following options:

   a. **Static address pool**. To assign static addresses to the remote VPN gateway or the remote VPN clients. If you select Static address pool, click **Add** to specify the IP address range. In the **IP Address Range Properties** dialog box, in **Starting address**, type the first address in the range of addresses to assign to the VPN clients. In **Ending address**, type the last address in the range of addresses to assign to the VPN clients.

   b. **Dynamic Host Configuration Protocol**. To dynamically assign addresses to the remote VPN gateway or the remote VPN clients.

4. In **Use the following network to obtain DHCP, DNS, and WINS services**, select the network on which the name-resolution servers are located. In most cases, this will be the internal network.

5. To configure the DNS and WINS server IP addresses that will be assigned to VPN clients, click **Advanced**. By default, the DNS and WINS servers assigned by DHCP are also assigned to VPN clients, but you can modify this so that ISA Server assigns alternate DNS and WINS server addresses.

How to Configure VPN Authentication

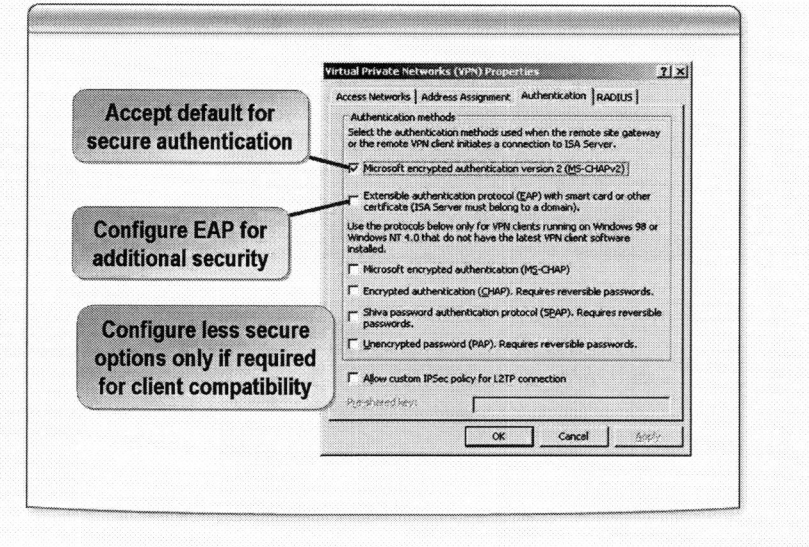

Introduction

ISA Server supports multiple authentication protocols for VPN clients. You can enable one or all of the authentication protocols. As a best practice, you should enable only the most secure protocols that are supported by your remote access clients.

Configuring VPN authentication

To configure ISA Server authentication, use the following procedure:

1. In **ISA Server Management**, click **Virtual Private Networking**.

2. On the **Tasks** tab, click **Select Authentication Methods**.

3. On the **Authentication** tab, select the authentication methods you want to enable.

4. To enable a pre-shared key for L2TP/IPSec connections with ISA Server 2004, click **Allow custom IPSec policy for L2TP connection**. Then type the pre-shared key into the **Pre-shared key** text box.

Note If you configure ISA Server to use a pre-shared key for L2TP connections, all L2TP clients must use that pre-shared key. These clients will not be able to use certificates for authentication.

How to Configure Authentication Using RADIUS

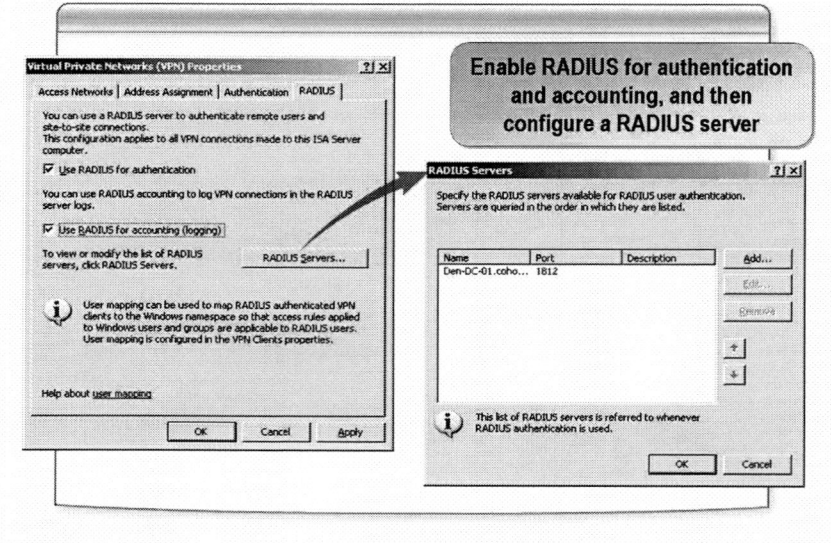

Introduction

Just like ISA Server can be configured to use RADIUS to enable authentication for Web publishing rules, it can also use RADIUS to authenticate VPN users. ISA Server can use IAS servers or any other RADIUS-compliant server.

Why use RADIUS for authentication?

Windows 2000 Server and Windows Server 2003 both include Internet Authentication Service, which is a RADIUS-compliant server. When ISA Server is configured to use the IAS server for authentication, the VPN server component forwards the credentials presented to it by the VPN client to the IAS server on the internal network. The IAS server forwards these credentials to a domain controller that authenticates the user.

The most important advantage for using RADIUS to authenticate VPN clients is so that you can use domain credentials for authentication when the server running ISA Server is not a member of the network domain. This adds a layer of security to the ISA Server firewall/VPN server solution because, if the firewall is compromised in any way, the machine's domain membership cannot be leveraged to attack the internal network.

A second advantage for using RADIUS for authentication is that this configuration allows you to centralize Remote Access Policy administration. For example, you could have five servers running ISA Server configured as VPN remote access servers configured in a network load balancing (NLB) array. You could configure the settings manually on each server, or you could configure each of the servers to use an IAS server for authentication and then configure the Remote Access Policies once on the IAS server. By doing this, the same remote access policies are automatically applied to each computer running ISA Server.

Configuring ISA Server for RADIUS authentication

To configure ISA Server authentication, use the following procedure:

1. In **ISA Server Management**, click **Virtual Private Networking**.

2. On the **Tasks** tab, click **Specify RADIUS Configuration**.

3. On the **RADIUS** tab, click **Use RADIUS for authentication** to configure ISA Server to forward authentication requests to the RADIUS server. Click **Use RADIUS for accounting (logging)** to configure RADIUS logging to log VPN connections on the RADIUS server.

4. Click **RADIUS Servers**. In the **RADIUS Servers** dialog box, click **Add**.

5. In the **Add RADIUS Servers** dialog box, enter the following information:

   a. **Server name**. The host name or IP address of the Internet Authentication Service (IAS) server.

   b. **Secret**. The server running Routing and Remote Access and the IAS server share a secret that is used to encrypt messages sent between them. You must configure both the remote access server and the IAS server to use the same shared secret.

   c. **Port**. The remote access server must send its authentication requests to the User Datagram Protocol (UDP) port on which the IAS server is listening. The default value of 1812 does not need to be changed when you are using an IAS server. The default port for RADIUS accounting is 1813.

Note   In addition to configuring ISA Server to use a RADIUS server for authentication, you must also configure the RADIUS server to accept ISA Server as a RADIUS client.

How to Configure User Accounts for VPN Access

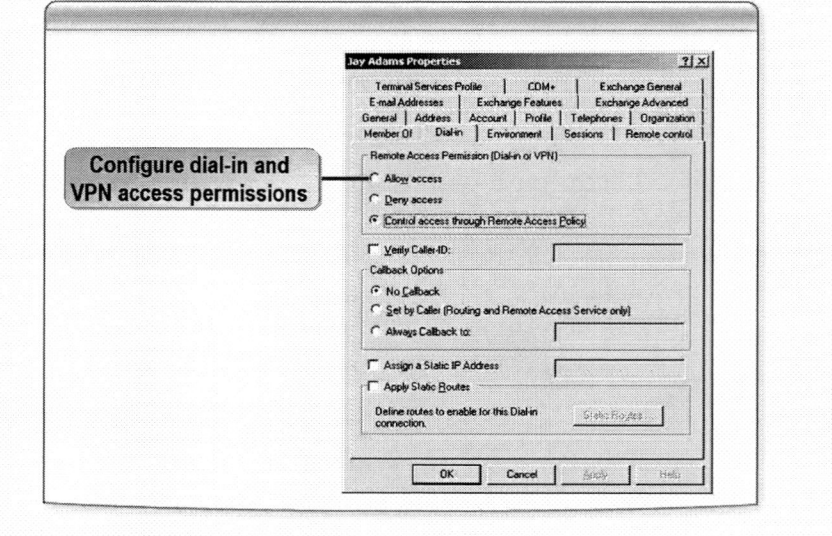

Configure dial-in and VPN access permissions

Introduction

In addition to configuring ISA Server to enable VPN connections, you must also configure Active Directory user accounts to enable dial-in permissions for those accounts. Until this is configured, no users will be able to connect to ISA Server using a VPN.

Configuring user accounts

The default user account configuration varies depending on the domain being used to authenticate users.

- In Windows 2000 mixed-mode domains, or in Windows Server 2003 domains at the Windows 2000 mixed functional level, all user accounts have dial-in access disabled by default. You must enable dial-in access on a per-account basis for these Active Directory domains.

- In Windows 2000 native mode domains, or in Windows Server 2003 domains at the Windows 2000 native or Windows Server 2003 functional levels, all user accounts have dial-in access controlled by Remote Access Policy by default. You can control dial-in access by just modifying the remote access policy.

- Windows NT 4.0 domains always have dial-in access controlled on a per-user account basis.

Perform the following steps to modify the user account properties for dial-in access.

1. Open **Active Directory Users and Computers** from the **Administrative Tools** folder.

2. Locate the user account you want to modify, and access the user account properties.

3. On the **Dial-in** tab, choose one of the following options:

   - **Deny access**. If you choose this option, the user will not be able to connect using VPN regardless of the remote access policy configuration.

   - **Allow access**. This option will override permissions set on the remote access policy, so the user will have permission to connect to the VPN server even when they are not granted permission in a remote access policy. Other settings in the remote access policy profile may still prevent the user from connecting.

   - **Control access through Remote Access Policy**. Use the option to configure remote access permissions using remote access policies. This option is available only when the domain is at the Windows 2000 or Windows Server 2003 functional level.

How to Configure VPN Connections from Client Computers

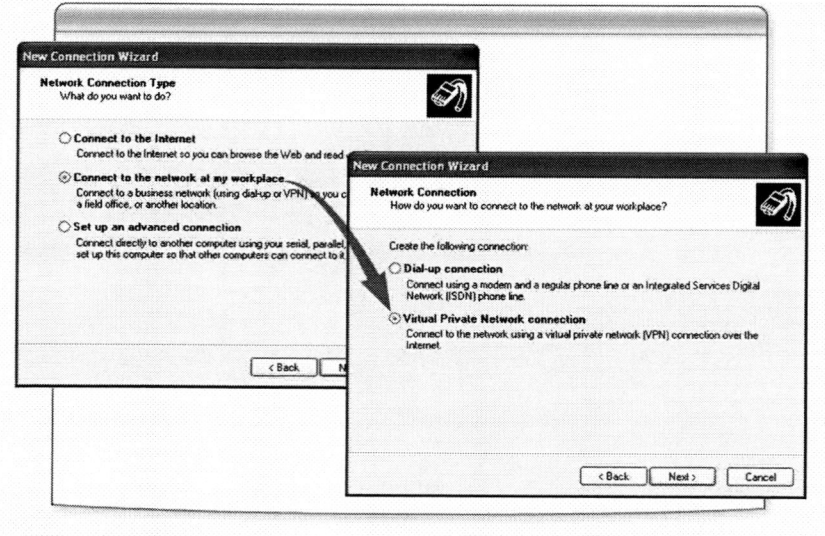

Introduction

After configuring ISA Server to enable VPN client access, you need to configure VPN connections on the remote access clients. The exact steps to enable VPN connections will vary depending on the client operating system.

Configuring VPN client connections

To configure a client computer running Windows XP as a VPN client, perform the following steps to connect to the VPN remote access server:

1. On the **Start** menu, click **Control Panel**, right-click **Network Connections**, and then click **Open**. The **Network Connections** window opens.

2. In the **Network Connections** window, click **Create a new connection**.

3. In the **Welcome to the New Connection Wizard** dialog box, click **Next**.

4. On the **Network Connection Type** page, click **Connect to the network at my workplace**, and then click **Next**.

5. On the **Network Connection** page, click **Virtual Private Network connection**, and then click **Next**.

6. On the **Connection Name** page, in the **Company Name** text box, type a name for the connection, and then click **Next**.

7. On the **VPN Server Selection** page, in the **Host name or IP address** text box, type the server name or IP address for the VPN access server, and then click **Next**.

8. On the **Connection Availability** page, click **Next**.

9. On the **Completing the New Connection Wizard** page, click **Finish**.

10. The wizard creates a new connection in the **Network Connections** window.

Note To configure a PPTP connection, you only need to supply a user name and password to connect. To configure an L2TP/IPSec connection, you also need to install a client certificate on the client computer or configure a pre-shared secret.

Practice: Configuring VPN Access for Remote Clients

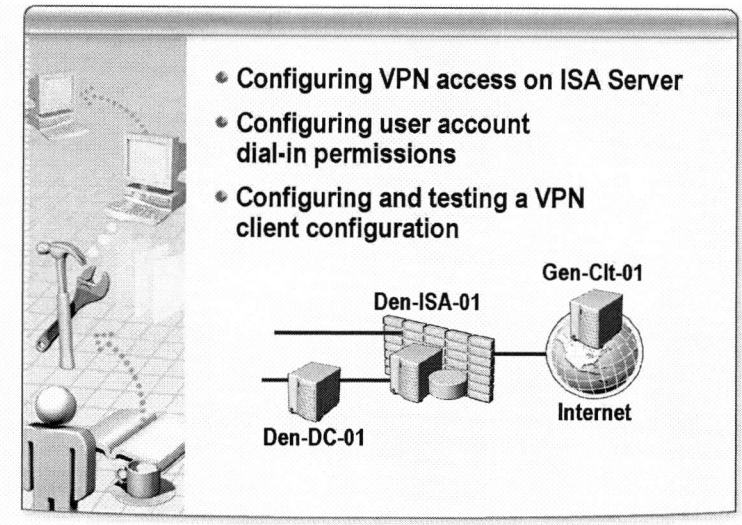

Introduction

In this practice, you will enable VPN client access on ISA Server 2004. You will then configure a VPN client connection on a client computer running Windows Server 2003 and test the VPN connection.

► **To prepare for this practice**

1. You will need the Den-DC-01 virtual machine, the Den-Clt-01 virtual machine, and the Den-ISA-01 virtual machine for this practice.

2. If necessary, start or resume the required virtual machines and then, on Den-ISA-01, log on to the cohovineyard domain with your user name and password.

3. On Den-DC-01, log on to the cohovineyard domain with a user name of **Administrator** and a password of **P@ssw0rd**.

4. On Den-Clt-01, log on to the cohovineyard domain with a user name of **Administrator** and a password of **P@ssw0rd**.

To complete this practice, you need to configure Den-Clt-01 as a client computer on the Internet.

1. On Den-Clt-01, click **Start**, click **Control Panel**, and click **Network and Internet Connections**. Then click **Network Connections**.

2. Right-click **Local Area Connection** and click **Properties**.

3. Click **Internet Protocol (TCP/IP)** and click **Properties**.

4. Configure the network connection with an IP address of 131.107.1.10, with a subnet mask of 255.255.255.0. Click **OK** and then click **Close**. Close all open windows.

Practice

▶ **Configuring VPN client access on ISA Server**

1. On Den-DC-01, open **Active Directory Users and Computers** from the **Administrative Tools** folder.

2. Click **Users**, and double-click **RAS and IAS Servers**. On the **Members** tab, click **Add**.

3. In the **Select Users, Contacts, Computers or Groups** dialog box, click **Object Types**.

4. On the **Object Types** dialog box, click **Computers**, and then click **OK**.

5. In the **Enter the object names to select** text box, type **den-isa-01**. Click **OK**.

6. Click **OK** to close the **RAS and IAS Servers Properties** dialog box.

7. Switch to Den-ISA-01.

8. Open **ISA Server Management**, expand **Den-ISA-01**, and then select **Virtual Private Networks (VPN)**.

9. In the task pane, on the **Tasks** tab, click **Enable VPN Client Access**.

10. On the **Tasks** tab, click **Configure VPN Client Access**.

11. In the **VPN Client Properties** dialog box, on the **Groups** tab, click **Add**. In the **Select Groups** dialog box, click **Locations**.

12. In the **Locations** dialog box, click **cohovinyard.com** and then click **OK**.

13. In the **Enter the object names to select** field, type **Managers**. Click **OK**.

14. On the **Protocols** tab, ensure that only **Enable PPTP** is selected.

15. Click **OK** to close the **VPN Clients Properties** dialog box.

16. In the left pane, right-click **Virtual Private Networks (VPN)**, and then click **Properties**.

17. In the **Virtual Private Networks (VPN) Properties** dialog box, on the **Access Networks** tab, notice that ISA Server is configured to only accept incoming VPN connections from the **External** network.

18. On the **Address Assignment** tab, notice that ISA Server is configured to use DHCP to assign IP addresses.

19. On the **Authentication** tab, notice that ISA Server is configured to allow only MS-CHAPv2 authentication for incoming VPN connections.

20. Click **OK** to close the **Virtual Private Networks (VPN) Properties** dialog box.

21. Click **Apply** to apply the changes and then click **OK** when the changes have been applied.

22. Restart Den-ISA-01.

▶ **Configuring and testing a VPN client connection**

1. While Den-ISA-01 reboots, switch to the Den-Clt-01 computer.

2. On the **Start** menu, click **Control Panel**, and then click **Network and Internet Connections**.

3. Click **Create a connection to the network at your workplace**.

4. On the **Network Connection** page, click **Virtual Private Network** connection and then click **Next**.

5. On the **Connection Name** page, in the **Company Name** text box, type **Coho Vineyard VPN**, and then click **Next**.

6. On the **VPN Server Selection** page, in the **Host name or IP address** text box, type **131.107.1.100**, and then click **Next**.

7. On the **Connection Availability** page, click **Next**.

8. On the **Completing the New Connection Wizard** page, click **Finish**.

9. Wait until Den-ISA-01 finishes rebooting. Once the server is back online, click **My Network Places** in the left pane, and then click **View Network Connections**.

10. Double-click **Coho Vineyard VPN**.

11. In the **Connect Cohovineyard VPN** dialog box, log on as **cohovineyard\jay** with a password of **P@ssw0rd**, and then click **Connect**.

12. After creating the VPN connection to the computer running ISA Server, an icon that represents the established connection appears in the System tray. Right-click the icon and click **Disconnect**.

▶ **To prepare for the next practice**

1. You will need the Den-DC-01 virtual machine and the Den-ISA-01 virtual machine for the next practice.

2. You can pause, but do not shut down the Den-Clt-01 virtual machine.

Lesson: Configuring Virtual Private Networking for Remote Sites

- Site-to-Site VPN Access Configuration Components
- About Choosing a VPN Tunneling Protocol
- How to Configure a Remote-Site Network
- Network and Access Rules for Site-to-Site VPNs
- How to Configure the Remote-Site VPN Gateway Server
- How to Configure Site-to-Site VPNs Using IPSec Tunnel Mode

Introduction

Another common deployment scenario for VPNs is to provide a secure connection between company locations through a public network such as the Internet. A VPN is often a cost-effective and secure alternative to using a dedicated wide area network (WAN) connection between company locations. This lesson describes how to enable VPNs between remote sites using ISA Server 2004.

Lesson objectives

After completing this lesson, you will be able to:

- Describe remote-site VPN access configuration options.
- Choose a VPN tunneling protocol.
- Configure a remote-site network on ISA Server.
- Configure network and access rules for site-to-site VPNs.
- Configure the remote-site VPN gateway server.
- Configure a site-to-site VPN using IPSec tunnel mode.

Site-to-Site VPN Access Configuration Components

Component	Default Configuration
Choose a VPN protocol	• Choose the appropriate protocol-based security requirements and the VPN gateway servers
Configure a remote-site network	• The remote-site network includes all IP addresses in the remote site
Configure VPN client access	• VPN client access must be enabled in order to enable site-to-site access
Configure network rules and access rules	• Use access rules or publishing rules to make internal resources accessible to remote office users
Configure the remote-site VPN gateway	• Configure the remote office VPN server to connect ISA Server and to accept connections from ISA Server

Site-to-site VPN configuration components

When you configure site-to-site VPNs, you need to configure the components listed in the following table:

Configuration Components	Explanation
Determine the tunneling protocol to use	ISA Server supports several tunneling protocols. You need to choose the appropriate protocol based your organization's security requirements and the VPN gateway servers that you will deploy in each site.
Configure a remote-site network	To enable site-to-site VPNs, you need to create a remote-site network on ISA Server. All of the client computers in the remote site are located in this network. ISA Server uses this network as it does any other network.
Configure VPN client access	When a remote VPN gateway server connects to ISA Server, the remote server is treated like any other VPN client. This means that you must enable VPN client access to enable site-to-site access.
Configure network rules and firewall access rules	Because ISA Server sees the remote-site network just like it sees any other network, you need to configure the VPN client access settings on ISA Server to enable remote access clients to access the internal network or any other network. You can use access rules or publishing rules to make internal resources accessible to remote office users.
Configure the remote-site VPN gateway	Once you have configured ISA Server in the head office, you also need to configure the remote office VPN server. This remote-office VPN gateway server could be another computer running ISA Server, a computer running Windows Server that runs RRAS, or a third-party VPN gateway server. The exact configuration of this server will depend on the type of server used in the remote site.

About Choosing a VPN Tunneling Protocol

Protocol	Use to	Comments
IPSec Tunnel Mode	• Connect to non-Microsoft VPN gateways	• Only option if you are connecting to a non-Microsoft VPN server • Requires certificates or pre-shared keys
L2TP over IPSec	• Connect to ISA Server or Windows RRAS VPN gateways	• Requires user name and password and certificates or pre-shared keys for authentication
PPTP	• Connect to ISA Server or Windows RRAS VPN gateways	• Requires user name and password for authentication • Less secure than L2TP over IPSec

Introduction

ISA Server supports several tunneling protocols. You need to choose the appropriate protocol based your organization's security requirements and the VPN gateway servers that you will deploy in each site.

What is a tunneling protocol?

A *tunneling protocol* is a protocol that encapsulates a network packet inside a new packet. This new packet might have new addressing and routing information, which enables it to travel through a network. Often, tunneling is combined with encryption to provide data confidentiality—in this case, the original packet data (as well as the original source and destination) is encrypted so that the packets cannot be captured and read. After the encapsulated packets reach their destination, the encapsulation is removed, and the original packet header is used to route the packet to its final destination.

VPN protocol options

ISA Server supports the following three protocols for site-to-site VPN connections:

■ *Point-to-Point Tunneling Protocol (PPTP)*. Point-to-Point Tunneling Protocol (PPTP) is a network protocol that enables the secure transfer of data between remote sites. PPTP-based VPNs can be encrypted by using Microsoft Point-to-Point Encryption (MPPE). The primary advantage of using PPTP to create a site-to-site VPN connection is that PPTP connections require only user-level authentication through a PPP-based authentication protocol. This means that the VPN gateway servers do not need any certificates or other authentication mechanism.

■ *Layer Two Tunneling Protocol (L2TP) over Internet Protocol security (IPSec)*. Layer Two Tunneling Protocol (L2TP) is an industry-standard Internet tunneling protocol that provides encapsulation for sending Point-to-Point Protocol (PPP) across IP networks. The Microsoft implementation of the L2TP protocol uses Internet Protocol security (IPSec) encryption to protect the data stream from the VPN client to the VPN server. L2TP/IPSec connections require user-level authentication and, in addition, computer-level authentication using computer certificates or a pre-shared key.

- *IPSec tunnel mode.* When Internet Protocol security (IPSec) is used in tunnel mode, IPSec itself provides encapsulation for IP traffic only. The primary reason for using IPSec tunnel mode is interoperability with other routers, gateways, or end systems that do not support L2TP over IPSec or PPTP VPN tunneling.

Comparing tunneling protocols

The following table compares the three tunneling protocols supported by ISA Server.

Protocol	When to use	Security level	Comments
IPSec tunnel mode	Connecting to third-party VPN server	High if certificates are used for authentication, moderate if pre-shared keys are used	This is the only option you can use if you are connecting to a server running a non-Microsoft VPN. Requires certificates or pre-shared keys.
L2TP over IPSec	Connecting to a computer running ISA Server 2000 or ISA Server 2004r, or a server running Windows RRAS	High	Requires that the remote VPN server be a computer running ISA Server or a server running a Windows VPN. Requires user name and password and certificates or pre-shared keys for authentication.
PPTP	Connecting to a computer running ISA Server 2000 or ISA Server 2004, or a server running Windows RRAS	Moderate	Requires that the remote VPN server be a computer running ISA Server or a server running a Windows VPN. Requires only a user name and password for authentication.

How to Configure a Remote-Site Network

Configuration Option	Explanation
VPN protocol	• Choose the tunneling protocol that you will use to connect to the remote site
Remote VPN server	• Enter the server name or IP address for the VPN gateway server in the remote site
Remote authentication	• Enter a user name and password that will be used to initiate a VPN connection to the remote-site VPN gateway server
L2TP/IPSec authentication	• If required, configure a pre-shared key that will be used to authenticate the computers when creating the tunnel
Network address	• Configure the IP address range for all of the computers in the remote-site network

Introduction

To configure ISA Server to support site-to-site VPNs, you must configure one or more remote-site networks. A remote-site network will contain the IP addresses for all computers connecting from the remote office.

Configuring remote-site networks

To configure a site-to-site VPN in ISA Server, you need to create a new remote-site network. To create a new remote site:

1. Open **ISA Server Management** and click **Virtual Private Networks (VPN)**.

2. In the details pane, click the **Remote Sites** tab.

3. On the **Tasks** tab, click **Add Remote Site Network** to start the **New Network Wizard**. When you run the wizard you are presented with the configuration options listed in the following table:

Configuration option	Explanation
VPN protocol	Choose the tunneling protocol you will use to connect to the remote site.
Remote VPN server	Enter the server name or IP address for the VPN gateway server in the remote site.

(continued)

Configuration option	Explanation
Remote authentication	When you configure a site-to site VPN, you can configure which VPN gateway can initiate the VPN connection. For example, you may want to allow only the remote-site VPN gateway to initiate the VPN connection. You can configure the VPN so that one or both servers can initiate the connection. If you want the server that you are configuring to initiate the connection, then you need to enter a user name and password on the Remote Authentication page. This user account will be used to initiate the connection on the destination VPN gateway server, so this account must be created on the destination server or in the domain in which the destination server is a member. This user account name must also exactly match the name of the VPN network you will be creating on the destination VPN gateway.
L2TP/IPSec Authentication	If you choose to use L2TP/IPSec as the tunneling protocol, you have the option of configuring a pre-shared key that will be used to authenticate the computers when creating the tunnel. By default, L2TP/IPSec tunnels will use digital certificates to authenticate the servers. Pre-shared key authentication does not require the hardware and configuration investment of a public key infrastructure (PKI), which is necessary for using computer certificates for IPSec authentication. Pre-shared keys are simple to configure on a local VPN server. However, pre-shared keys are not as secure as certificates. If you want a long-term, strong authentication method, you should consider using certificates.
Network Address	You need to configure the IP address range for all of the computers in the remote-site network.

Note If you have not enabled VPN client access on ISA Server, you must enable this before the remote office VPN gateway servers will be able to connect to the ISA Server VPN service. The reason for this is that ISA Server considers the remote VPN gateway server connection to be the same as any other VPN client connection.

Network and Access Rules for Site-to-Site VPNs

To enable network traffic across a site-to-site VPN:

- Two system policy rules are enabled:
  - Allow VPN site-to-site traffic to ISA Server
  - Allow VPN site-to-site traffic from ISA Server
- Create a network rule for remote-site networks
- Configure access rules or publishing rules enabling or restricting network access
  - For full access, allow all protocols through ISA Server
  - For limited access, configure access rules or publish rules that define allowed network traffic

Introduction

When you configure a site-to-site VPN in ISA Server, a new network is established. This network is created for the remote site, but it is treated by ISA Server in the same way that any directly attached network is treated.

System policies for site-to-site networks

When a remote network is created, the VPN site-to-site connection is enabled. When this happens, ISA Server enables two system policy rules. One of the rules, named **Allow VPN site-to-site traffic to ISA Server**, allows access from all external networks to the computer running ISA Server (Local Host network), using the VPN tunneling protocols. One or more networks from which VPN clients can connect to ISA Server can be specified. When this is modified, the system policy rule is changed automatically to apply to the additional or changed networks.

The second system policy rule that is created is **Allow VPN site-to-site traffic from ISA Server**. This policy allows all VPN tunneling protocols from the Local Host network to the external network and to a computer set named **IPSec Remote Gateways**. IPSec Remote Gateways is a predefined computer set, which cannot be modified. When an IPSec site-to-site network is added, the IP address configured as the remote tunnel endpoint is added to the IPSec Remote Gateways computer set.

Configuring network rules for remote-site networks

After you have created the remote-site network, ISA Server views it as it does any other network connected to the computer running ISA Server. This means that you need to create a network rule establishing whether the network has a network address translation (NAT) or route relationship with the other networks connected to the computer running ISA Server. You should establish a route relationship between the remote-site network and the internal network if two-way communication is required. If the computers that must communicate across the various networks have public IP addresses, a route relationship can be created without concern about address duplication, because public IP addresses are unique. When the computers have private IP addresses, there is a risk that there will be duplicate addresses across the VPN networks. You must ensure that there is no duplication of IP network numbers between the computers that have to connect across the two VPN networks, so that a route relationship can be established.

Configuring access rules for remote-site networks

After you create the remote-site networks, you also need to configure access rules to regulate traffic between the remote site and the other networks connected to your computer running ISA Server. You can use any access rule or publishing rule to configure relationship. There are two high-level options:

- *Open communication between networks.* One option is to configure the branch office to have full access to the internal network. To enable full access, create an access rule allowing all traffic from the remote-site network to the internal network.

- *Controlled communication between networks.* In this scenario, you do not want the branch office users to have complete access to the internal network but want to limit access based on users, computers, or traffic destination. For example, you may want to create a firewall policy that allows the following types of communication:

  - Some users will have full access to the internal network of the main office, while others have limited access.

  - Specific users will have access to an application server on the internal network of the main office.

  - All users will have access to the computer running Microsoft Exchange Server on the internal network of the main office.

  - The domain controller in the branch office will communicate with the domain controller in the main office, so that users from the branch office can be authenticated for access to the computer running Exchange Server in the main office.

  Follow these general steps to create this firewall access policy:

  - Create computer sets representing the groups of users who will have differing access rights. Where there is only one computer, such as a single domain controller, you can create a computer object rather than a computer set.

  - Create computer objects representing the computers that users will have access to on the internal network of the main office. In this example, you will need computer objects for the application server, one for the computer running Exchange Server, and one for the internal domain controller. Where there is more than one server, such as two computers running Microsoft SQL Server™, create a computer set rather than a computer object.

- Create an access rule allowing all traffic for the users who need full access to the internal network of the main office.

- Create an access rule allowing application-specific network traffic from the application user computer set to the application server on the internal network of the main office.

- Publish Exchange Server on the internal network of the main office, using the Exchange Server remote procedure call (RPC) protocol.

- Create an access rule allowing Lightweight Directory Access Protocol (LDAP), LDAP (UDP), LDAPS, LDAP GC, LDAPS GC, DNS, Kerberos (TCP), and Kerberos (UDP) traffic from the remote-site domain controller to the internal domain controller of the main office.

How to Configure the Remote-Site VPN Gateway Server

To configure the remote site VPN gateway server:

- Configure the remote-site VPN gateway to use the same tunneling protocol
- Configure the connection to the main-site VPN gateway
- Configure network routing rules that enable or restrict the flow of network traffic between networks

Introduction

After configuring one of the VPN gateways, you also need to configure the other VPN gateway. The specific steps in configuring the VPN gateway for the remote site will depend on the type of VPN gateway used in the remote office.

Remote gateway configuration components

ISA Server can support a variety of VPN gateway servers in the remote site, including:

- ISA Server 2004 or ISA Server 2000 configured as a VPN gateway server
- Windows Server 2003 or Windows 2000 Server with RRAS configured as a VPN gateway server
- Non-Microsoft VPN gateways that support IPSec tunnel–mode VPN connections

Regardless of what type of VPN gateway you use in the remote site, you need to configure the components listed in the following table:

Configuration Components	Explanation
Configure the VPN gateway to use the same tunneling protocol	The remote site gateway must use the same protocol as the main office gateway. If you are using L2TP/IPSec or IPSec tunneling protocols, ensure that the two gateways are configured with the same pre-shared key or have digital certificates that are trusted by the other VPN gateway.
Configure the connection to the main site VPN gateway	If you are using ISA Server as the remote office VPN gateway, then configure a remote site network for the main office. If you are using RRAS or a non-Microsoft VPN gateway, then configure the connection to the main office VPN gateway. As part of this configuration, create a user account that will be used by the computer running ISA Server at the main office to initiate connections to the remote office, and configure the remote office VPN gateway to initiate connections to the main office.
Configure network routing	If you are using ISA Server as the remote office VPN gateway, then you need to network rules and access rules or publishing rules to make network resources accessible to main office users. If you are using RRAS or a non-Microsoft VPN gateway, then configure the routing rules that you want to apply for traffic from the main office network.

Note   In some cases, the remote office may use a dial-up connection to the Internet rather than a dedicated connection. You can configure both ISA Server and RRAS on a Windows Server to initiate the dial-up connection when the VPN gateway detects traffic intended for the main office. If you are using ISA Server, access the dial-up settings on the **General** tab in **ISA Server Management**.

How to Configure Site-to-Site VPNs Using IPSec Tunnel Mode

To configure site-to-site VPNs using IPSec tunnel mode:

- Configure a local VPN gateway IP address used by the computer running ISA Server to listen for VPN connections
- Configure the VPN gateways to use a certificate or a pre-shared key for authentication
- Configure advanced IPSec settings to optimize VPN security

Creating an IPSec tunnel-mode VPN

There are only two differences between configuring a site-to-site VPN using IPSec tunnel mode and configuring a PPTP or L2TP/IPSec-based VPN.

- When you configure the remote VPN gateway IP address, you must also configure a local VPN gateway IP address used by the computer running ISA Server to listen for VPN connections.

- You can configure the VPN gateways to use a certificate for authentication or a pre-shared key for authentication.

Advanced IPSec protocol configuration

After you configure the remote-site network, you can also configure advanced IPSec settings. The settings specify the settings IPSec will use when creating the VPN tunnel and can be used to maximize VPN security. To access the advanced IPSec configuration, open the properties dialog box for the remote-site network that is using IPSec tunneling mode. On the **Connection** tab, click **IPSec Configuration**.

In the **IPSec Configuration** dialog box, you can configure the **Phase I** or **Phase II** tabs. On the **Phase I** tab, you can configure the main mode settings of the Internet Key Exchange protocol. This protocol is used to create an initial secure channel between the VPN gateway servers to secure authentication traffic and the traffic that is used to negotiate the encryption settings for the other traffic that will be sent between the gateways.

On the **Phase II** tab, you can configure the quick mode settings of the Internet Key Exchange protocol. This protocol defines the configuration settings for the encryption of network traffic using Encapsulating Security Payload (ESP).

Note For more information about the configuration of advanced IPSec configuration options, see "Configure IPSec Networks" in the ISA Server documentation. For more information on IPSec, see the IPSec Technical Reference, which is one of the technical reference documents located at http://www.microsoft.com/resources/documentation/WindowsServ/2003/all/techref/en-us/Default.asp?.

Practice: Configuring VPNs for Remote Sites

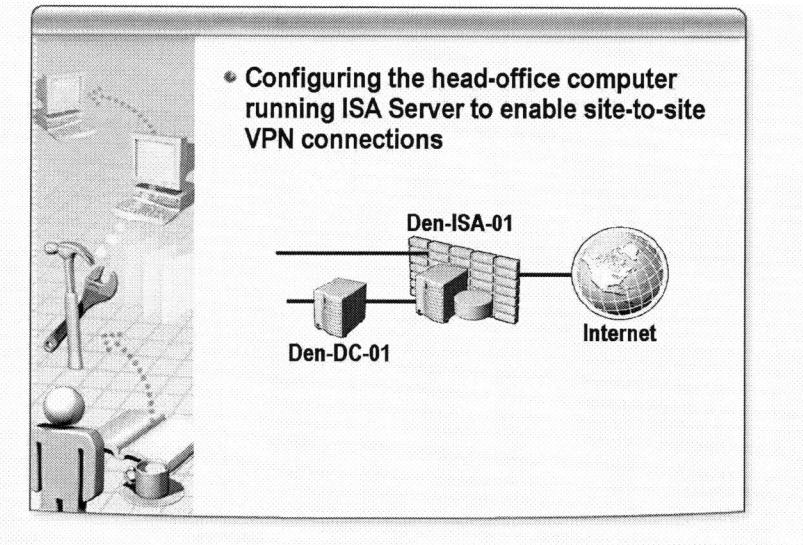

Introduction

In this practice, you will configure one side of a site-to-site VPN solution using ISA Server 2004. You will configure the computer running ISA Server in one site to create a PPTP tunnel and configure the network rules to allow full access between the two networks.

▶ **To prepare for this practice**

1. You will need the Den-DC-01 virtual machine, and the Den-ISA-01 virtual machine for this practice.

2. If necessary, start or resume the required virtual machines and then, on Den-ISA-01, log on to the cohovineyard domain with your user name and password.

3. On Den-DC-01, log on to the cohovineyard domain with a user name of **Administrator** and a password of **P@ssw0rd**.

Practice

▶ **Configuring the head-office computer running ISA Server to enable site-to-site VPN connections**

1. On Den-DC-01 and open **Active Directory Users and Computers**.

2. In the **Users** container, create a new user account named **BranchOfficeVPN**. Assign a password of **P@ssw0rd**. Clear the check box for **User must change password at next logon**.

3. Do not create a mailbox for the user. Open the user properties. On the **Dial-in** tab, configure **Remote Access Permissions** as **Allow Access**. Click **OK** and close **Active Directory Users and Computers**.

4. Switch to the Den-ISA-01 machine and open **ISA Server Management**.

5. Expand **Den-ISA-01**, and then click **Virtual Private Networks (VPN)**.

6. Click the **Remote Sites** tab.

7. In the tasks pane, on the **Tasks** tab, click **Add Remote Site Network** to start the **New Network Wizard**.

8. On the **Welcome to the New Network Wizard** page, type **BranchOfficeVPN**, and then click **Next**.

9. On the **VPN Protocol** page, click **Point-to-Point Tunneling Protocol (PPTP)**, and then click **Next**.

10. On the **Remote Site Gateway** page, type **131.107.1.101** as the IP address for the remote VPN server, and then click **Next**.

11. On the **Remote Authentication** page, click **Local site can initiate connections to remote site using these credentials**. Fill in the following information.

    a. User Name: **HeadOfficeVPN**

    b. Domain: **Den-ISA-02**

    c. Password and confirm password: **P@ssw0rd**

    Click **Next**.

12. The **Local Authentication** page provides a reminder that a user with dial-in properties must be configured on the local network for the remote network to be able to initiate a connection to the local network. This user must have the same name as the remote network. Click **Next**.

13. On the **Network Addresses** page, click **Add**.

14. In the **IP Address Range Properties** dialog box, type **192.168.2.0** as the **Starting Address** and **192.168.2.255** as the **Ending Address**. Click **OK** and then click **Next**.

15. On the **Completing the New Network Wizard** page, review the configuration, and then click **Finish**.

16. Read the ISA Server 2004 warning message and click **OK**.

17. Click **Apply** to apply the changes and then click **OK** when the changes have been applied.

After you have created the remote VPN, ISA Server views it as it does any other network connected to the computer running ISA Server. You now need to create network rules and access rules enabling access from the remote-office network to the internal network.

1. On the Den-ISA-01 virtual machine, in **ISA Server Management**, expand **Configuration**, and then click **Networks**.

2. Click the **Network Rules** tab in the **Details** pane. On the **Tasks** tab, click **Create a New Network Rule**.

3. On the **Welcome to the New Network Rule Wizard** page, type **Branch Office VPN** in the **Network rule name** text box. Click **Next**.

4. On the **Network Traffic Sources** page, click **Add**.

5. In the **Add Network Entities** dialog box, click the **Networks** folder. Double-click on the **Internal** network. Click **Close**.

6. Click **Next** on the **Network Traffic Sources** page.

7. On the **Network Traffic Destinations** page, click **Add**.

8. In the **Add Network Entities** dialog box, click **Networks**, then double-click the **BranchOfficeVPN** network. Click **Close**.

9. Click **Next** on the **Network Traffic Destinations** page.

10. On the **Network Relationship** page, click **Route**, and then click **Next**.

11. Click **Finish** on the **Completing the New Network Rule Wizard** page.

12. Click **Apply** to apply the changes and then click **OK** when the changes have been applied.

Coho Vineyard has decided that the clients on both the main and branch office networks need to have full access to all resources on each network. Therefore, you must create access rules to allow traffic from the main office to the branch office and from the branch office to the main office.

1. Click **Firewall Policy**. On the **Tasks** tab, click **Create New Access Rule**.

2. On the **Welcome to the New Access Rule Wizard** page, type **Head Office to Branch Office** in the **Access Rule name** text box. Click **Next**.

3. On the **Rule Action** page, click **Allow**, and click **Next**.

4. On the **Protocols** page, select **All outbound traffic** in the **This rule applies to** list. Click **Next**.

5. On the **Access Rule Sources** page, click **Add**.

6. In the **Add Network Entities** dialog box, click the **Networks** folder, and double-click the **Internal** network. Click **Close**.

7. Click **Next** on the **Access Rule Sources** page.

8. On the **Access Rule Destinations** page, click **Add**.

9. In the **Add Network Entities** dialog box, click the **Networks** folder, and then double-click on the **BranchOfficeVPN** network. Click **Close**.

10. Click **Next** on the **Access Rule Destinations** page.

11. On the **User Sets** page, accept the default entry **All Users**, and click **Next**.

12. Click **Finish** on the **Completing the New Access Rule Wizard** page.

13. Repeat steps 1-12, creating another remote access rule. The access rule name is Branch Office to Head Office and the access rule allows traffic from the BranchOfficeVPN network to the Internal Network.

14. Click **Apply** to apply the changes and then click **OK** when the changes have been applied.

15. Restart Den-ISA-01.

▶ **To prepare for the next practice**

- You will need the Den-DC-01 virtual machine, the Den-ISA-01 virtual machine, and the Den-Clt-01 virtual machine for the next practice.

Lesson: Configuring Quarantine Control Using ISA Server 2004

* How Does Network Quarantine Control Work?

* About Quarantine Control on ISA Server

* How to Prepare the Client-Side Script

* How to Configure VPN Clients Using Connection Manager

* How to Prepare the Listener Component

* How to Enable Quarantine Control

* How to Configure Internet Authentication Service for Quarantine Control

* How to Configure Quarantine Access Rules

Introduction

Windows Server 2003 provides a quarantine service that is used to confirm the security configuration of a remote client before granting the client full access to the internal network. ISA Server 2004 provides an integrated solution for VPN quarantine. This lesson describes what the quarantine service is, how it works, and how to implement ISA Server 2004 to support VPN quarantine.

Lesson objectives

After completing this lesson, you will be able to:

■ Describe how network quarantine control works.

■ Describe how to implement quarantine control on ISA Server.

■ Prepare the client-side script for quarantine control.

■ Configure VPN clients using Connection Manager.

■ Prepare the listener component for quarantine control.

■ Enable quarantine control on ISA Server.

■ Configure Internet Authentication Server for quarantine.

■ Configure access rules for quarantine control.

How Does Network Quarantine Control Work?

Introduction

The VPN quarantine control feature allows you to screen VPN client machines before allowing them access to the organization's network. VPN quarantine control can delay normal remote access to a private network until the remote access client configuration has been validated by a client-side script.

Network quarantine control overview

The following process describes how ISA Server quarantine control works when the remote listener and remote client component provided with Windows Server 2003 Resource Kit and ISA Server policies are used to implement quarantine control:

1. The user on the quarantine-compatible remote access client uses the installed quarantine Connection Manager (CM) profile to connect with the computer running ISA Server with quarantine control enabled.

2. The remote access client passes its authentication credentials to the computer running ISA Server. The computer running ISA Server validates the authentication credentials of the remote access client and, assuming that the credentials are valid, checks its remote access policies.

3. If the connection attempt matches the quarantine policy, the connection is accepted with quarantine restrictions, and the client is assigned an IP address and placed in the Quarantined VPN Clients network. At this point, the remote access client can only connect to resources that are enabled by the firewall policy for the Quarantined VPN Clients network. The client has up to the number of seconds specified in the ISA Server quarantine properties to notify the computer running ISA Server that the script has run successfully.

4. After connecting, the CM profile on the VPN client runs the quarantine script. The quarantine script verifies that the remote access client computer's configuration complies with network policy requirements.

5. If all the tests for network policy compliance pass, the script runs Rqc.exe with its command-line parameters, one of which is a text string for the version of the quarantine script included within the CM profile. Rqc.exe sends a notification to the computer running ISA Server, indicating that the script was successfully run.

6. The notification is received by the listener component (Rqs.exe) on ISA Server. The listener component verifies the script version string in the notification message with those configured in the registry and sends back either a message indicating that the script version was valid or a message indicating that the script version was invalid. If the script version was valid, the listener component informs ISA Server that the client has been accepted, which causes ISA Server to move the client from the Quarantined VPN Clients network to the VPN Clients network. The client can now access all resources that are accessible from the VPN Clients network.

About Quarantine Control on ISA Server

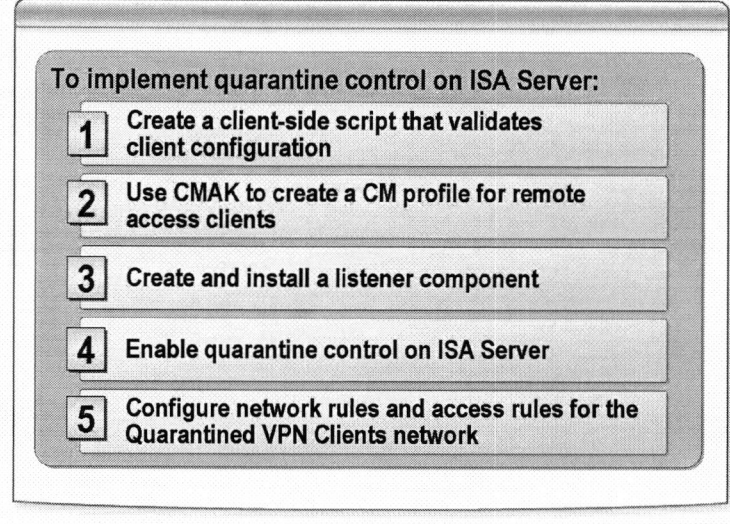

To implement quarantine control on ISA Server:

1. Create a client-side script that validates client configuration

2. Use CMAK to create a CM profile for remote access clients

3. Create and install a listener component

4. Enable quarantine control on ISA Server

5. Configure network rules and access rules for the Quarantined VPN Clients network

Implementing quarantine control overview

Configuring quarantine control on ISA Server requires a number of configuration steps. Before you enable quarantine mode, you must complete the following steps:

1. Create a client-side script that validates client configuration information.

2. Use CMAK to create a CM profile that includes a notification component and the client-side script. The notification component provides verification to the computer running ISA Server that the script has successfully run. If you do not want to create your own notification component, you can use Rqc.exe from the Windows Server 2003 Resource Kit. Distribute the CM profile to all users who need to access your network through the VPN connection.

3. Create and install a listener component on the ISA Server. The listener component is installed on the computer running ISA Server, and receives notification from the notifying component that the script on the client has successfully performed all configuration checks. After the listener component receives notification, it removes the client from quarantine mode, and the computer running ISA Server applies standard remote access policy to the client. If you do not want to create your own listener component, you should use the Rqs.exe sample that can be downloaded from the ISA Server 2004 Web site at http://www.microsoft.com/isaserver/downloads/2004.asp.

4. Enable quarantine control on ISA Server. After completing all of the previous steps, you can then implement quarantine control on ISA Server. When you enable quarantine for ISA Server, you can configure a time-out setting that specifies the amount of time a client attempting to create a VPN connection is allowed to remain in quarantine mode and an exception list of users to whom quarantine is not applied. Users in this list are automatically joined to the VPN Clients network.

5. Configure network rules and access rules for the Quarantined VPN Clients network. Before a client computer clears quarantine, the client's IP address is added to the Quarantined VPN Clients network. For the client to have access to any network resources, you need to configure network and access rules so that clients on this network to gain access to the internal network. At a minimum, you should configure the firewall policy so that the client can perform name resolution using DNS, obtain the latest version of the CM profile, or access instructions and components needed to make the remote access client comply with network policies.

How to Prepare the Client-Side Script

> **The client-side script:**
> - Can be an executable file, a script, or a simple command file
> - Contains a set of tests to ensure that the remote access client complies with network policy
> - Runs Rqc.exe if all of the tests specified in the script are successful
>
> **Command for running Rqc.exe**
>
> rqc *ConnName TunnelConnName TCPPort Domain UserName ScriptVersion*

Introduction

The quarantine script or program that you create to validate client configuration during remote access can be an executable file (*.exe), a script file (*.vbs) or a simple command file (*.cmd or *.bat). In the script, perform a set of tests to ensure that the remote access client complies with network policy.

Running Rqc.exe

If all of the tests specified in the script are successful, the script must run Rqc.exe with the following parameters:

```
rqc ConnName TunnelConnName TCPPort Domain UserName
ScriptVersion
```

The command-line parameters of Rqc.exe are as follows:

- *ConnName*. The name of the remote access connection on this host. The value of this parameter can be inherited from the Connection Manager profile %DialRasEntry% variable (also known as a macro).

- *TunnelConnName*. The name of the tunnel connection on this host. The value of this parameter can be inherited from the Connection Manager profile %TunnelRasEntry% variable.

- *TCPPort*. The TCP port used to send the notification message. The default TCP port used by Rqs.exe is 7250. If you configure Rqs.exe to use a TCP port other than 7250, you must specify that TCP port number here.

- *Domain*. The domain of the connecting user. The value of this parameter can be inherited from the Connection Manager profile %Domain% variable.

- *UserName*. The user name of the connecting user. The value of this parameter can be inherited from the Connection Manager profile %UserName% variable.

- *ScriptVersion*. A text string that contains the script version. You can specify a text string using keyboard characters, except the /0 character sequence.

If the remote access computer fails to pass the network policy compliance tests, the script can direct the remote access user to a Web page that contains instructions about how to comply with the security policy.

Note For more information on creating quarantine control scripts and a sample script, see Network Access Quarantine Control in Windows Server 2003 located at http://www.microsoft.com/windowsserver2003/techinfo/overview/ quarantine.mspx.

How to Configure VPN Clients Using Connection Manager

To configure VPN clients using Connection Manager:

- **Configure a quarantine VPN client profile that includes:**
    - A post-connect action that runs the client-side script
    - A client-side script that checks the client security configuration
    - A notification component
- **Distribute and install the client profile on all remote clients that require quarantined VPN access**

Introduction

The Connection Manager family of programs is a set of optional components used to create a managed remote access solution. Connection Manager enables a network administrator to pre-configure remote access clients. The Connection Manager family of products includes the Connection Manager client, the Connection Manager Administration Kit (CMAK), and Connection Point Services (CPS).

Configuring a quarantine CM profile

To enable clients to use quarantine mode, you must configure a Connection Manager profile using the Connection Manager Administration Kit. The profile contains the following components:

- *A post-connect action that runs a network policy requirements script.* This functionality is configured when the CM profile is created with CMAK.

- *A network policy requirements script.* This script performs validation checks on the remote access client computer to verify that it conforms to network policies. It can be a custom executable file or a simple command file (also known as a *batch file*). When the script has run successfully and the connecting computer has satisfied all of the network policy requirements (as verified by the script), the script runs a notification component (an executable) with the appropriate parameters.

> **Note** If the script does not run successfully, it can direct the remote access user to a quarantine resource, such as an internal or external Web page, that describes how to install the components that are required for network policy compliance.

- *A notification component.* The notification component sends a message that indicates a successful execution of the script to the quarantine-compatible remote access server. You can use your own notification component or you can use Rqc.exe, which is provided with the Windows Server 2003 Resource Kit.

To configure the quarantine CM profile, run the Connection Manager Administration Kit wizard. Only two parts of the configuration process are specific to creating a quarantine CM profile:

1. *Define a custom action.* You can use the Connection Manager Administration Kit wizard to define a custom action. This action can occur before the client connects, or at any stage during or after the connection. To create a profile that will enable quarantine control, you must configure a custom action that will run the quarantine requirements script after the client connects.

2. *Add the notification component as an additional file.* As part of the CM profile, you can install additional files on the client computer. To enable a quarantine profile, you need to add the rqc.exe or a custom notification component to the profile.

Distributing the CM profile

After you create the quarantine Connection Manager profile, it must be distributed and installed on all your remote access client computers. The profile itself is an executable file that must be run on the remote access client to install the profile and configure the quarantine network connection.

There are many methods to distribute and run the profile on remote access client computers:

- Send the profile executable file, or a link to the profile, to your remote access users with instructions to run the profile that installs the quarantine connection.

- Place the profile executable file on a Web page and instruct your users to run the profile that installs the quarantine connection.

- Have the profile run as part of a startup script or as part of the domain logon script.

- Put the executable file on a CD or a floppy disk.

In addition to distributing the profile to your remote access users, place the profile on a file share or Web site that is accessible from the Quarantined VPN Clients network. If the profile is placed on a share or a Web site, you can instruct remote access clients who do not have the current profile installed and are in quarantine mode to install the latest profile and then reconnect.

How to Prepare the Listener Component

Command for running ConfigureRQSforISA.vbs

*Cscript ConfigureRQSForISA.vbs /install
SharedKey1\0SharedKey2 pathtoRQS.exe*

ConfigureRQSforISA.vbs:

* Installs RQS as a Network Quarantine Service

* Creates an access rule that allows communication on
  port 7250 from the VPN Clients and Quarantined VPN
  Clients networks to the Local Host network

* Modifies registry keys on the computer running ISA
  Server so that RQS will work with ISA Server

* Starts the RQS service

Introduction

The Network Quarantine Service (Rqs.exe) provides the listener service for computers running ISA Server to support VPN Quarantine. This component must be installed on all computers running ISA Server that will provide quarantine services. In addition, the computer running ISA Server must be configured to enable network traffic intended for the listener service.

Configuring the Network Quarantine Service

The easiest way to install the Network Quarantine Service and configure ISA Server to support listener network traffic is to use the ConfigureRQSForISA.vbs script provided with ISA Server 2004.

The syntax to use this script is:

```
Cscript ConfigureRQSForISA.vbs /install SharedKey1\0SharedKey2
pathto RQS.exe
```

- The /install command line switch installs the listener service. To uninstall the listener service, use /remove.

- The SharedKey value is the key that the notification component will send to the listener component. The notification message sent by Rqc.exe contains a text string that indicates the version of the quarantine script being run. This string is configured for Rqc.exe as part of its command-line parameters, as run from the quarantine script. Rqs.exe compares this text string to a set of text strings stored in the registry of the computer running ISA Server. If there is a match, the quarantine conditions are removed from the connection. If the client provides a shared key that is not in the allowed set, it will be disconnected. There can be more than one shared key, separated by "\0".

- The path to RQS.exe defines where the listener executable is located.

The script performs the following actions:

■ Installs RQS as a service and sets it to run in the security context of the local system account. The service name is Network Quarantine Service.

■ Creates an ISA Server access rule that allows communication on the RQS port (7250) from the VPN Clients and Quarantined VPN Clients networks to the Local Host network. This is necessary so that the computer running ISA Server can receive notice that the client has met the connection requirements.

■ Modifies registry keys on the computer running ISA Server so that RQS will work with ISA Server.

■ Starts the RQS service.

Using a custom listener component

If you create your own listener component, it must be designed to listen for a message from the notification component and use the MprAdminConnectionRemoveQuarantine application programming interface (API) to remove the quarantine restrictions from the remote access connection. The API must call Vpnplgin.dll (in the ISA Server installation directory), rather than Mprapi.dll, which is used for Routing and Remote Access.

How to Enable Quarantine Control

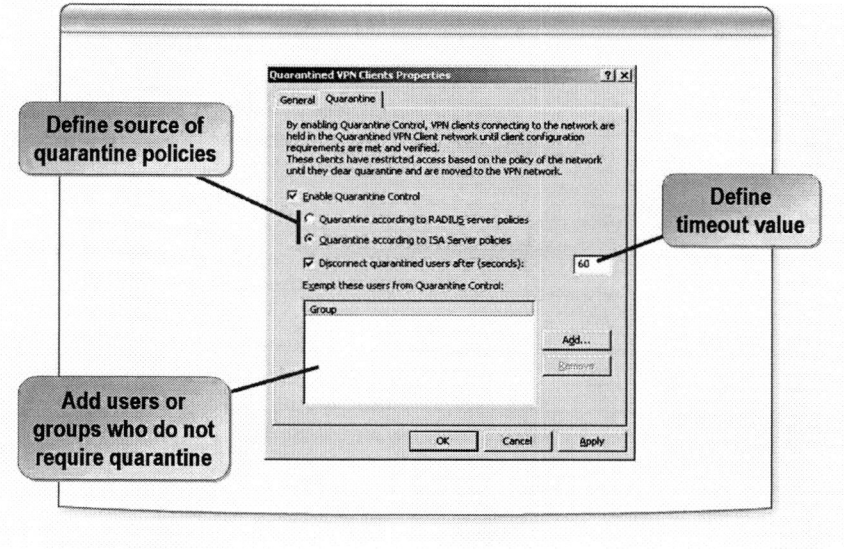

Introduction

After configuring all the other components, you are finally ready to enable quarantine service on ISA Server. To enable quarantine service, complete the following steps.

1. In the console tree of **ISA Server Management**, click **Networks**.

2. In the details pane, click the **Networks** tab, and then select the **Quarantined VPN Clients** network.

3. On the **Tasks** tab, click **Edit Selected Network**.

4. On the **Quarantine** tab, click **Enable Quarantine Control**, and then select one of the following options:

   a. **Quarantine according to RADIUS server policies**. When a VPN client attempts to connect, Routing and Remote Access policy determines whether the connection request is passed to ISA Server. After Routing and Remote Access policy has been verified, the client unconditionally joins the VPN Clients network. To use this option, you must configure ISA Server to use RADIUS for authentication and configure the quarantine policies on the RADIUS server.

   b. **Quarantine according to ISA Server policies**. When a VPN client attempts to connect to the computer running ISA Server, Routing and Remote Access unconditionally passes the request to ISA Server. ISA Server places the connecting client in the Quarantined VPN Clients network, subjecting the client to the firewall policy defined for that network. When the client clears quarantine, it moves into the VPN Clients network.

5. If quarantined clients should be disconnected after a specified time, select **Disconnect quarantine users after (seconds)** and type the number of seconds that will pass before a client will be removed from the Quarantined VPN Clients network and disconnected from ISA Server.

6. If specific users should be exempted from quarantine control, click **Add** under **Exempt these users from Quarantine Control**. Add the user sets that represent the users who are not required to go through quarantine control.

Important Note that when quarantine mode is disabled, all remote VPN clients with appropriate authentication permissions are placed in the VPN Clients network and will have the access you have allowed the VPN Clients network in your firewall policy. However, once you enable quarantine mode, all client connections will be forced to use the quarantine mode. If a client does not support quarantine mode, they will not be able to connect. If the Network Quarantine Service is not running, users will not be able to connect. The only exception to this is if you configure a user set in the **Exempt these users from Quarantine Control**.

How to Configure Internet Authentication Service for Quarantine Control

To configure IAS for quarantine control:

- Install the listener component on the server running IAS
- Configure a remote access policy that configures the quarantine settings
  - MS-Quarantine-IPFilter setting
  - MS-Quarantine-Session-Timeout setting

Introduction

If you are running ISA Server on Windows Server 2003, you can enable quarantine by using RADIUS policy or by using ISA Server policy. When you run ISA Server on Windows 2000 Server, you can only enable quarantine using ISA Server policy. If you enable quarantine using RADIUS policy, you can use Internet Authentication Service on Windows Server 2003 or Windows 2000 Server to act as the RADIUS server.

Using IAS for quarantine control

In a situation in which you have several branch offices, each running ISA Server 2004, you may want to enable quarantine using RADIUS policy to centralize the quarantine control in a single RADIUS server that serves all of the branches.

If you use RADIUS to manage the quarantine settings, you must install the listener component on the RADIUS server and then configure a remote access policy that configures the quarantine settings. RADIUS uses two settings in a remote access policy to enforce the quarantine:

- *MS-Quarantine-IPFilter setting.* This setting is used to configure the packet filters that quarantine the remote access client until the notifying component on the remote access client indicates that the computer is in compliance with quarantine policies. You can use the MS-Quarantine-IPFilter attribute to configure input and output packet filters to allow the client computer to connect using TCP port 7250 (for the notification component to connect to the RADIUS server) and other traffic needed to access the quarantine resources. This includes filters that allow the remote access client to access name resolution servers (such as DNS servers), file shares, or Web sites.

- *MS-Quarantine-Session-Timeout.* You can use the MS-Quarantine-Session-Timeout attribute to specify how long the remote access server must wait to receive the notification that the script has run successfully before terminating the connection.

After you configure IAS and ISA Server to use RADIUS, VPN client requests are passed by ISA Server to the IAS server. The remote access policy on IAS determines whether the connection request is passed to ISA Server. After Routing and Remote Access policy has been verified, the client unconditionally joins the VPN Clients network.

How to Configure Quarantine Access Rules

> **To configure the access rules for VPN quarantine:**
>
> * Create access rules with the Quarantined VPN Clients network as the source and appropriate servers or networks as the destination
> * Configure access rules that:
>   * Enable the notification component to communicate with the listener component
>   * Enable access to required network services such as domain controllers or DNS
>   * Enable access to resources that are needed to meet the quarantine requirements on the VPN clients

Introduction

The final step in configuring quarantine control for VPN clients is to configure the access rules for the Quarantined VPN Clients network to access required resources on other networks.

Configuring access rules for quarantine clients

To allow access to a resource, create an access rule with the Quarantined VPN Clients network as the source and the server to which access is required as the destination. To configure this rule, create a computer rule element for each server, so that it can be used in access rules. Alternatively, you can create a computer set containing all of the computers to which the quarantined clients require access, and create an access rule with the Quarantined VPN Clients network as the source and the computer set as the destination.

The following are some examples of the types of access you may want to allow the Quarantined VPN Clients network.

- For Rqc.exe-notification traffic, use destination TCP port 7250. (This is the default TCP port used by Rqs.exe.)
- Allow queries to LDAP servers on the internal network.
- Allow traffic to domain controllers or RADIUS servers.
- Allow quarantined VPN clients to issue DNS queries to DNS servers.
- Allow quarantined VPN clients to access WINS servers.
- Allow quarantined VPN clients to use Hypertext Transfer Protocol (HTTP) to access internal Web servers. Use this option if you have a Web page that explains how the user can configure his or her computer so that it meets the quarantine security requirements, or if the Web page contains any other resource that can be used to configure the quarantined VPN client.
- Allow quarantined VPN clients to use NetBIOS over TCP/IP using destination TCP port 139 to enable access to file shares on the internal network. Use this option to enable client access to a share that contains resources that can be used to configure the quarantined VPN client.

Another option is to design your network so that all of the servers to which access is required are on a subnet, and define a Subnet rule element for use in the access rule. In this configuration, you may enable access using all protocols to the specific subnet, or limit access to only the required protocols.

Practice: Configuring ISA Server to Support VPN Quarantine

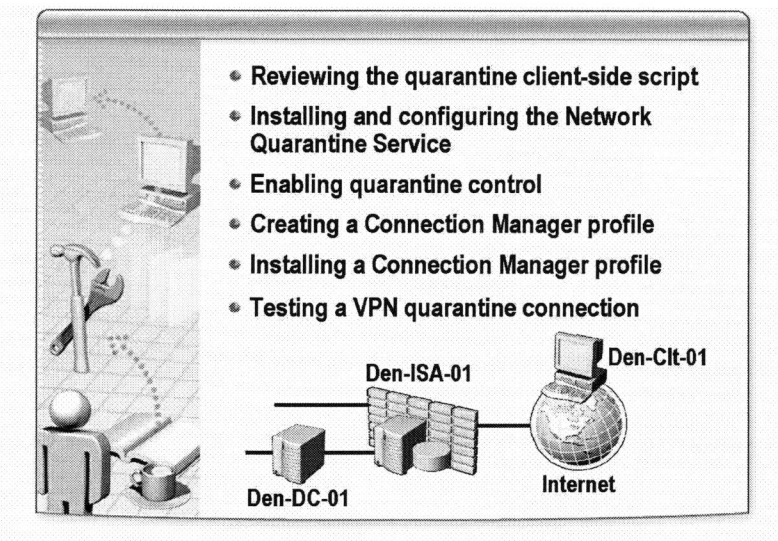

- Reviewing the quarantine client-side script
- Installing and configuring the Network Quarantine Service
- Enabling quarantine control
- Creating a Connection Manager profile
- Installing a Connection Manager profile
- Testing a VPN quarantine connection

Den-ISA-01   Den-Clt-01

Den-DC-01   Internet

Introduction

In this practice, you will enable quarantine VPN client access on ISA Server 2004. You will then use Connection Manager Administration Kit to create a remote access profile. Then you will install the profile on a remote access client to test the quarantine policy.

▶ **To prepare for this practice**

1. You will need the Den-DC-01 virtual machine, the Den-Clt-01 virtual machine, and the Den-ISA-01 virtual machine for this practice.

2. If necessary, start or resume the required virtual machines and then, on Den-ISA-01, log on to the cohovineyard domain with your user name and password.

Practice

▶ **Reviewing the quarantine client-side script**

1. On the Den-ISA-01 virtual machine, use **Windows Explorer** to open the **C:\Program Files\Microsoft Learning\2824** folder.

2. The RQScript.vbs script file in the **2824** folder is the script that this practice uses to check the security configuration of the VPN client computer.

3. Right-click the **RQScript.vbs** file and then click **Edit** (do not click Open).

4. The RQScript.vbs script file checks whether Internet Connection Firewall (ICF) is enabled on the network connections of the VPN client computer. If this is the case, it passes the script identifier (RQScript_ID) RQVersion3 back to the remote access server (ISA Server), which will remove the quarantine restrictions.

5. Close **Notepad**.

▶ **Installing and configuring the Network Quarantine Service using ConfigureRQSForISA.vbs**

1. Open a command prompt and switch to the **C:\Program Files\ Microsoft Learning\2824** directory.

2. At the command prompt, type Cscript configurerqsforisa.vbs /install RQVersion3 "c:\program files\windows resource kits\tools" and press **ENTER**.

3. Wait until the script finishes running and then close the command prompt.

▶ **Confirming the ISA Server configuration**

1. On the **Start** menu, click **Run**.

2. In the **Run** dialog box, type **regedit.exe**, and then press ENTER.

3. In the **Registry Editor** window, select the **HKEY_LOCAL_MACHINE\ SYSTEM\CurrentControlSet\Services\rqs** key.

4. Confirm that the **AllowedSet** key was created and configured with a value of **RQVersion3**. RQVersion3 is the identifier of the script (RQScript.vbs) that this practice uses to check the security configuration of the client computer.

5. Confirm that the **Authenticator** key was created and configured with a value of **C:\Program Files\Microsoft ISA Server\vpnplgin.dll**.

6. Close the **Registry Editor** window.

7. On the **Start** menu, click **Administrative Tools**, and then click **Services**.

8. In the **Services** console, in the right pane, right-click **Network Quarantine Service**, and then click **Properties**.

9. In the **Network Quarantine Service Properties** dialog box, in the **Startup type** list box, select **Manual**, and then click **OK**. Then click **Stop** to stop the service. The **Network Quarantine Service** is started later in this lab.

10. Close the **Services** console.

When the security configuration of the VPN client computer meets the security policy, the RQC.exe application on the client computer notifies the RQS.exe service on ISA Server that the quarantine restrictions can be removed. This requires an access rule to allow communication (using TCP port 7250) from the **Quarantined VPN Clients** network to the **Local Host** network (ISA Server).

11. In the **ISA Server Management**, click **Firewall Policy**.

12. In the task pane, on the **Toolbox** tab, click **Protocols** and expand **User-Defined**.

Note   If the RQS protocol is not visible, refresh the ISA Server Management view.

---

13. Double-click **RQS** and on the **Parameters** tab, confirm that the configuration matches the following settings:

   a. Protocol type: **TCP**

   b. Direction: **Outbound**

   c. Port Range From: **7250**

   d. Port Range To: **7250**

14. Click **OK**.

   A new firewall access rule is required that allows RQS communication from a VPN client computer on the Quarantined VPN Clients network to ISA Server.

15. In the task pane, on the **Firewall Policy** tab, double-click **Network Quarantine (RQS)**.

16. On the **Action** tab, confirm that **Allow** is selected.

17. On the **Protocols** tab, confirm that the access rule applies to the **RQS** protocol only.

18. On the **From** tab, confirm that the rule accepts traffic from the **Quarantined VPN Clients, VPN Clients** networks.

19. On the **To** tab, confirm that the rule applies to traffic sent to the **Local Host** network.

20. Click **OK**.

▶ **Enabling quarantine control**

1. In the **ISA Server** console, in the left pane, expand **Configuration** and select **Networks**.

2. In the right pane, on the **Networks** tab, right-click the **Quarantined VPN Clients** network, and then click **Properties**.

3. In the **Quarantined VPN Clients Properties** dialog box, on the **Quarantine** tab, select **Enable quarantine control**.

4. In the message box, click **OK** to confirm that enabling quarantine requires configuration on both the computer running ISA Server and VPN client computers.

5. Ensure that **Quarantine according to ISA Server policies** is selected.

6. Click **Disconnect quarantine users after (seconds)** and type **60** in the text box. Click **OK**.

7. Click **Apply** to apply the changes and then click **OK** when the changes have been applied.

▶ **Creating a Connection Manager profile**

1. On the Den-ISA-01 virtual machine, on the **Start** menu, click **Control Panel**, and then click **Add or Remove Programs**.

2. In the **Add or Remove Programs** window, click **Add/Remove Windows Components**.

Note   If Windows Setup starts but it does not display the Windows Component Wizard, use Task Manager to stop Windows Setup. Then restart Windows Setup by clicking Add/Remove Windows Components.

---

3. On the **Windows Components** page, select the **Management and Monitoring Tools** component, and then click **Details**.

4. In the **Management and Monitoring Tools** dialog box, select the **Connection Manager Administration Kit** check box, and then click **OK**.

5. On the **Windows Components** page, click **Next**.

6. In the **Insert Disk** dialog box, click **OK**. Click **Browse** and browse to **C:\win2k3\i386**. Click **Open** and then click **OK**.

7. On the **Completing the Windows Components Wizard** page, click **Finish**.

8. Close the **Add or Remove Programs** window.

9. On the **Start** menu, click **Administrative Tools**, and then click **Connection Manager Administration Kit**.

10. On the **Welcome to the Connection Manager Administration Kit Wizard** page, click **Next**.

11. On the **Service Profile Selection** page, accept the default of **New profile**, and then click **Next**.

12. On the **Service and File Names** page, type the following information:

    a. Service name: **VPN to Cohovineyard**

    b. File name: **VPN_RQ**

    Click **Next**.

13. On the **Realm Name** page, click **Next**.

14. On the **Merging Profile Information** page, click **Next**.

15. On the **VPN Support** page, click the check box for **Phone book from this profile**. Under **Always use the same VPN server**, type **131.107.1.100** and then click **Next**.

16. On the **VPN Entries** page, click **Next**.

17. On the **Phone Book** page, clear the **Automatically download phone book updates** check box, and then click **Next**.

18. On the **Dial-up Networking Entries** page, click **Next**.

19. On the **Routing Table Update** page, click **Next**.

20. On the **Automatic Proxy Configuration** page, click **Next**.

21. On the **Custom Actions** page, click **New**.

22. In the **New Custom Action** dialog box, enter the following information:

    a. Description: **Quarantine policy checking**

    b. Program to run: **c:\Program Files\Microsoft Learning\ 2824\RQScript.vbs**

    c. Parameters: **%DialRasEntry% %TunnelRasEntry% %Domain% %UserName%**

    d. Action type: **Post-connect**

    e. Run this custom action for: **All connections** (accept default)

    f. Include the custom action program with this service profile: **enable**

    g. Program interacts with the user: **enable** (accept default)

    Click **OK**.

23. On the **Custom Actions** page, click **Next**.

24. On the **Logon Bitmap** page, click **Next**.

25. On the **Phone Book Bitmap** page, select Default graphic, and then click **Next**.

26. On the **Icons** page, select **Default icons**, and then click **Next**.

27. On the **Notification Area Shortcut Menu** page, click **Next**.

28. On the **Help File** page, select **Default Help file**, and then click **Next**.

29. On the **Support Information** page, click **Next**.

30. On the **Connection Manager Software** page, select **Install Connection Manager 1.3**, and then click **Next**.

31. On the **License Agreement** page, click **Next**.

32. On the **Additional Files** page, click **Add**.

33. In the **Browse** dialog box, in the **C:\Program Files\Windows Resource Kits\Tools** folder, select the **rqc.exe** file and then click **Open**.

34. On the **Additional Files** page, click **Next**.

35. On the **Ready to Build the Service Profile** page, click **Next**. A Command Prompt window opens and closes as the new Connection Manager profile (VPN_RQ.exe) is created in the C:\Program Files\Cmak\Profiles\VPN_RQ folder.

36. On the **Completing the Connection Manager Administration Kit Wizard** page, click **Finish**.

37. Open **Windows Explorer** and browse to **C:\Program Files\ Cmak\Profiles**. Copy the **VPN_RQ** folder to the desktop of the host computer.

▶ **Installing a Connection Manager Profile**

1. Switch to Den-Clt-01.

2. Copy the **VPN_RQ** folder from the desktop of the host computer to the Den-Clt-01 desktop.

3. Open the **VPN_RQ** folder, right-click **VPN_RQ** (the Win32 Cabinet Self-Extractor file), and then click **Open**.

4. In the **VPN to Coho Vineyard** message box, click **Yes** to confirm that you want to install the Connection Manager profile.

5. In the next **VPN to Coho Vineyard** dialog box, accept the default of **My use only**, and then click **OK**.

6. The **Connection Manager** profile is installed on the Den-Clt-01 computer. After the installation is completed, the Network Connections window opens, and the **VPN to Coho Vineyard** connection dialog box is shown.

▶ **Testing a VPN quarantine connection**

1. In the **VPN to Coho Vineyard** connection dialog box, type the following information:

   a. User name: **Jay**

   b. Password: **P@ssw0rd**

   c. Logon domain: **cohovineyard**

   d. Save password: **ENABLE**

   e. Connect automatically: **disable** (accept default)

   Click **Connect**.

2. The quarantine script displays a message box to indicate that the security configuration of the client computer does not meet the security policy (ICF is not enabled on the network connections).

3. Click **OK** to close the **Remote Access Quarantine** message box.

4. The connection stays in quarantine mode and is dropped after 60 seconds. Wait for the connection to be dropped. In the **Reconnect** dialog box, click **No**.

5. In the **Network Connections** window, right-click **Local Area Connection**, and then click **Properties**.

6. In the **Local Area Connection Properties** dialog box, on the **Advanced** tab, enable **Protect my computer and network**, and then click **OK**. Internet Connection Firewall (ICF) is enabled for the local area connection. This is the security configuration that the RQScript.vbs script file verifies.

7. In the **Network Connections** window, under **Connection Manager**, right-click **VPN to Cohovineyard**, and then click **Connect**.

8. In the **VPN to Cohovineyard** connection dialog box, ensure that the **User name** and **Password** information is still present, and then click **Connect**. This time the quarantine script displays a message box to indicate that the security configuration of the client computer does meet the security policy. However, the RQC.exe notifying component on the client computer is not able to contact the RQS.exe service on ISA Server to remove the quarantine restrictions. The RQS.exe service cannot be contacted, because the service is not started yet in this exercise.

9. Click **OK** to close the **Remote Access Quarantine** message box.

10. The connection stays in quarantine mode and is dropped after 60 seconds. Wait for the connection to be dropped. In the **Reconnect** dialog box, click **No**.

11. Switch to Den-ISA-01 virtual machine. On the **Start** menu, click **Administrative Tools**, and then click **Services**.

12. In the **Services** console, in the right pane, right-click **Network Quarantine Service**, and then click **Start**. The **Network Quarantine Service** (RQS.exe) is now started and listens on TCP port 7250.

13. Close the **Services** console.

14. Switch to the Den-Clt-01 virtual machine.

15. On the Den-Clt-01 virtual machine, in the **Network Connections** window, under **Connection Manager**, right-click **VPN to Coho Vineyard**, and then click **Connect**.

16. In the **VPN to Coho Vineyard** connection dialog box, ensure that the **User name** and **Password** information is still present, and then click **Connect**. The quarantine script successfully notifies the RQS.exe service. ISA Server removed the quarantine restrictions by moving the VPN client computer from the Quarantined VPN Clients network to the VPN Clients network.

17. Click **OK** to close the **Remote Access Quarantine** message box.

18. At the command prompt, type **ping 192.168.1.10**, and then press ENTER. Four ping replies are returned from the Den-DC-01 virtual machine (192.168.1.10) on the internal network.

19. Close the **Command Prompt** window.

20. In the **Run** dialog box, type **\\192.168.1.10** and then press ENTER. A Windows Explorer window opens for \\192.168.1.10. These results show that the VPN client computer can now connect to resources on the internal network.

21. Close the **\\192.168.1.10** window.

22. Right-click the connection icon in the system tray area, and then click **Disconnect**.

23. In the **Network Connections** window, under **Virtual Private Network** (not under Connection Manager), right-click **Coho Vineyard VPN**, and then click **Connect**.

24. In the **Connect Coho Vineyard VPN** dialog box, type the following information:

    a. User name: **Jay**

    b. Password: **P@ssw0rd**

25. Click **Connect**. Den-Clt-01 successfully establishes a VPN connection to ISA Server.

26. Open a command prompt and type **ping 192.168.1.10**, and then press ENTER. The ping attempt times out. This VPN connection does NOT use the Connection Manager profile, and does not start the post-connect script to verify the security configuration of the VPN client computer. ISA Server will place the client computer in the Quarantined VPN Clients computers network, awaiting a notification from the RQC.exe notifying component on the client computer. Even though the client computer meets the security requirements (ICF is enabled), the notification is never sent to the ISA Server, and the connection is dropped after 60 seconds.

27. Close the **Command Prompt** window.

28. Close the **Network Connections** window.

▶ **To prepare for the next practice**

1. As you finish this practice, shut down all of the virtual machines that you used in the practice. To shut down the virtual machines, click **Close** from the **Action** menu. **Select Turn off and delete changes** and click **OK**.

2. After shutting down the virtual machines, restart the Den-DC-01 virtual machine and the Den-ISA-01 virtual machine in preparation for the next module.

Module 9:
Implementing Caching

Contents

Overview

- ● Caching Overview
- ● Configuring General Cache Properties
- ● Configuring Cache Rules
- ● Configuring Content Download Jobs

Introduction

One of the benefits of using Microsoft® Internet Security and Acceleration Server 2004 to provide access to the Internet is that ISA Server can cache much of the content that clients request from the Internet. By caching the information, ISA Server provides quicker responses to clients requesting information from the Internet. Caching is an important feature in ISA Server 2004 and the administrator needs to know how to configure this feature for maximum efficiency.

Objectives

After completing this module, you will be able to:

- ■ Describe how caching is implemented on ISA Server 2004.

- ■ Configure caching properties on ISA Server 2004.

- ■ Configure cache rules on ISA Server 2004.

- ■ Configure content download jobs on ISA Server 2004.

Lesson: Caching Overview

- What Is Caching?
- How Caching Works for Requests for New Objects
- How Caching Works for Requests for Cached Objects
- How Content Download Jobs Work
- How Caching Is Implemented in ISA Server 2004
- Web Proxy Chaining and Caching

Introduction

To configure caching to provide the fastest client response and make the most efficient use of server resources, it is important to know how ISA Server 2004 implements caching. This lesson provides an overview of how caching works, and also describes how ISA Server 2004 implements caching.

Lesson objectives

After completing this lesson, you will be able to:

- Describe what caching is.
- Describe how caching works for requests for new objects.
- Describe how caching works for requests for cached objects.
- Describe how content download jobs work.
- Explain how caching is implemented in ISA Server 2004.
- Describe how caching works with Web chaining.

What Is Caching?

> **ISA Server caching stores a copy of requested Web content in the server memory or on the hard disk**
>
> **ISA Server caching provides:**
>
> - Improved performance — information is stored on the computer running ISA Server
> - Reduced bandwidth usage — no additional Internet network traffic
>
> **ISA Server caching scenarios include:**
>
> - Forward caching — Internet Web servers
> - Reverse caching — internal Web servers

Introduction

One of the primary deployment scenarios for ISA Server 2004 is as a Web proxy server in which ISA Server retrieves information from the Internet for internal clients. ISA Server supports Web caching as a way to improve the speed with which this information is returned to Web clients.

What is caching?

Caching stores Web content on the computer running ISA Server in the server random access memory (RAM) or on the hard disk. The next time a user requests the same information, the ISA Server cache provides it, enabling a quicker response to the client. ISA Server 2004 can be configured to enable the caching of Hypertext Transfer Protocol (HTTP) and File Transfer Protocol (FTP) objects.

Benefits of using caching

ISA Server 2004 caching provides several benefits:

- *Improved performance*. Web caching provides quicker client response for Internet access by bringing the cache closer to the user. When a user behind the ISA Server 2004 firewall requests Web content, ISA Server checks to see if the content is contained in its cache. If it is, the cached content is returned to the user. Accessing Web content from a cache on the corporate network is faster than requiring a connection to a remote Web server located on the Internet. ISA Server stores cached content on the server hard disk or in RAM memory. Recently accessed information is stored in memory and remains in memory as long as that content continues to be accessed by users.

- *Reduced bandwidth usage*. Web caching can help reduce the overall bandwidth usage on the organization's Internet connection. When users request Web content already contained in cache, that content is returned to the user immediately from the cache. No bandwidth hit is generated on the Internet connection.

Caching scenarios

ISA Server supports both forward and reverse caching:

■ *Forward Caching*. Forward caching occurs when a user on the corporate network makes a request for Web content located on an Internet Web server. The user initiates an HTTP, Hypertext Transfer Protocol Secure (HTTPS), or FTP request to an Internet Web server and the request is intercepted by ISA Server. ISA Server retrieves the content from the Internet Web server, stores it in its cache and returns the content to the user.

■ *Reverse Caching*. Reverse caching takes place when users on the Internet request Web content located on the corporate network and accessible through a Web publishing rule. When an Internet user requests content from the internal server, ISA Server forwards the request to the Web server. The Web server sends the requested content to ISA Server, which then returns the content to the Internet user who made the request. In this scenario, ISA Server will cache a copy of the requested information so that the next request for the same information can be provided from the ISA Server cache rather than accessing the internal Web server again.

How Caching Works for Requests for New Objects

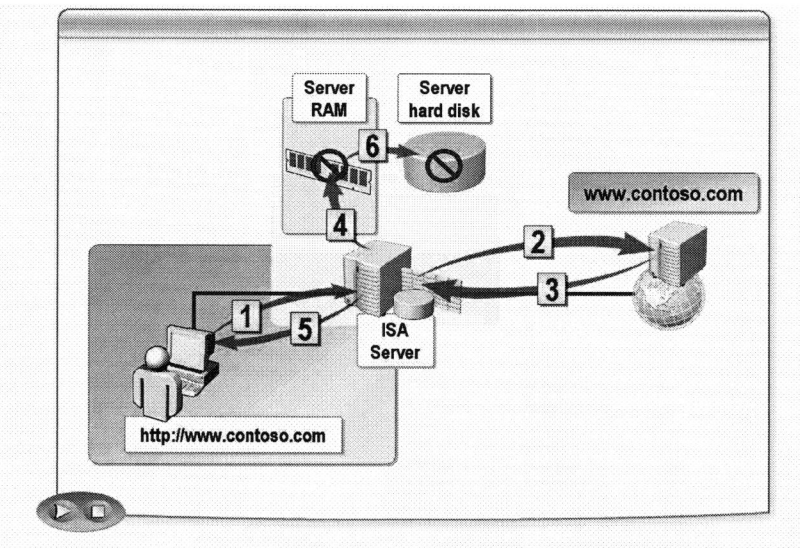

How caching works

When a user requests an HTTP or FTP object, the Web proxy client sends the request to the Web proxy component on ISA Server. In a forward caching scenario, the following actions occur to complete the client request:

1. The Web proxy client sends a request for content located on an Internet Web server. The Web request is intercepted by ISA Server and forwarded to the Web proxy filter.

2. ISA Server checks if the requested content is contained in its cache. If the content is not in the cache, or if the content has expired (that is, the header information in the content indicates that it should no longer be served from a cache), then ISA Server forwards the request to the Web server on the Internet.

3. The Web server on the Internet returns the information requested.

4. The ISA Server Web proxy filter places the Web content in its in-memory cache. ISA Server uses an in-memory cache to store the most frequently requested content.

5. After placing the Web content in the in-memory cache, ISA Server 2004 Web caching server returns the content to the user who requested it.

6. After a period of time, the ISA Server Web proxy filter will copy the contents of the in-memory cache to the disk-based cache. If the content is not frequently accessed, the in-memory cache will flush the content and the only copy of the content on ISA Server will be in the disk-based cache.

Note By default, the Microsoft Firewall service forwards HTTP requests from Firewall clients and SecureNAT clients to the Web proxy service. This means that when caching is enabled, all Web content can be cached.

How Caching Works for Requests for Cached Objects

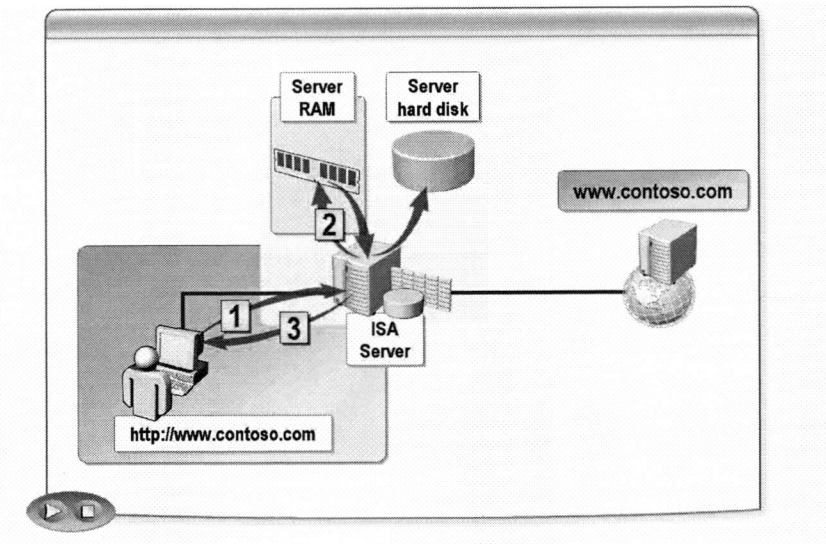

How caching works for cached objects

When a user requests an HTTP or FTP object that is stored in the Web proxy cache, ISA Server returns that object to the user from the cache. Whether the Web proxy service retrieves the object from RAM or from the hard disk, the client receives the object quickly and no Internet traffic occurs.

When a user requests an HTTP or FTP object that ISA Server has in its cache, the following actions occur:

1. The host on the internal network sends the request to the server running ISA Server. The Firewall service passes the request to the Web proxy filter.

2. The ISA Server Web proxy filter checks to see if it has cached this content and whether the content has expired. If the content is still valid, ISA Server retrieves the content from the in-memory cache.

3. Content retrieved from cache is returned to the user who requested it.

How Content Download Jobs Work

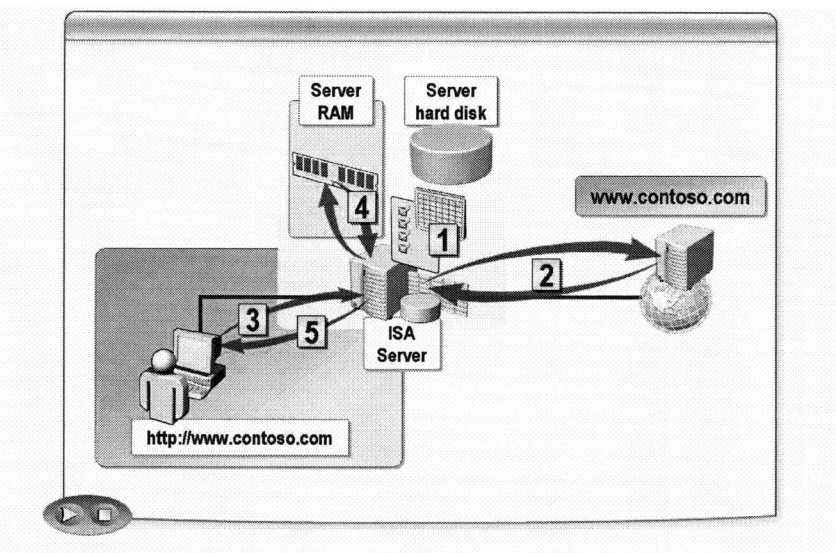

Introduction

ISA Server extends caching performance by enabling content download jobs. By monitoring and analyzing Internet access, you can determine which Web content will be needed by internal clients. You can then create a content download job to download the Web content to the ISA Server cache before any client ever requests the object.

Benefits of using content download jobs

Content download jobs are useful if you can predict what Web content users will need to access frequently and when that Web content is updated and required. For example, if you know that many users in your organization need access to a partner organization's Web site that is updated every night, you can create a content download job that downloads the Web site content to the ISA Server cache after it has been updated every night. This means that the content can be downloaded at night and all the content on the Web site will be in the ISA Server cache when the users need it the next day.

You can also use content download jobs to optimize Web server publishing. You can configure ISA Server to periodically retrieve the Web content from the internal Web server so that all requests from Internet clients are served from the ISA Server cache rather than directly from the internal Web server.

How content download jobs work

When you enable content download jobs, the following actions occur:

1. You create a content download job based on your analysis of client Web activity. The content download job specifies which Web content will be retrieved from the Internet as well as when.

2. At the scheduled time, ISA Server uses a background process to retrieve the content from the Web server.

3. A user on the internal network sends a request for the Web content to the server running ISA Server. The Firewall service passes the request to the Web proxy filter.

4. The ISA Server Web proxy filter determines that the content is in the Web cache, so ISA Server retrieves the content from the cache.

5. Content retrieved from cache is returned to the user who requested it.

How Caching Is Implemented in ISA Server 2004

> ISA Server caching optimizes Web caching performance by:
>
> - Using RAM and disk caching
> - Maintaining the RAM cache in physical memory
> - Maintaining a directory of cached items
> - Using a single cache file
> - Providing quick recovery
> - Using efficient cache updates
> - Providing automatic cleanup

Introduction

When you enable Web caching, you configure ISA Server to store Web objects in its cache. ISA Server keeps the object in its cache for an amount of time that is specific to the object.

How long is content cached?

The time for an object to remain in the cache is called Time-to-Live (TTL). When ISA Server places an object into its cache, it sets a TTL for the object. ISA Server returns the HTTP object that is stored in its cache to clients until the TTL has expired.

ISA Server can set the TTL based on the creation date and the modification date of the object or by using the settings that you configure when you enable Web caching or configure caching rules.

Many Web pages use metatags to set expiration dates for content. When a Web page has an expiration date, ISA Server sets the TTL of the object to match the Web page's expiration date.

ISA Server caching features

ISA Server includes the following features that optimize cache performance:

- *RAM and disk caching*. ISA Server allocates RAM for caching popular objects and caches other objects on disk. When caching an object, ISA Server places an object into the RAM cache first and then writes objects to disk. RAM and disk caching help to improve access speed for users to popular Web sites. By default, ISA Server 2004 uses 10 percent of the RAM on the server to cache Web content.

- *Maintaining the RAM cache in physical memory*. ISA Server optimizes the cache stored in RAM by keeping most of the memory that is used for caching in RAM instead of paging it to disk.

- *Directory of cached objects*. ISA Server maintains a directory of cached objects in RAM to optimize the process of determining whether the server has an object in its cache.

■ *Single cache file*. ISA Server maintains a single cache file per disk partition to hold cached objects so that gaining access to objects does not use additional system resources that would be needed for opening and closing multiple files. The cache file size can be configured for each disk partition.

■ *Quick recovery*. ISA Server quickly rebuilds the directory of cached objects on startup, even after an abnormal termination.

■ *Efficient cache updates*. ISA Server automatically determines which objects to keep in the RAM cache. This decision is based on the likelihood of a user requesting the same object again, which is determined by how recently and how frequently an object is accessed.

■ *Automatic cleanup*. ISA Server removes objects that have not been accessed recently or frequently when the disk space that is allocated to the cache starts to fill up.

How ISA Server restricts content

ISA Server does not cache all content that is requested by Web clients. The following table describes the way ISA Server restricts the content that it caches:

Restriction	Description
ISA Server does not cache responses to requests that contain the following HTTP response headers.	• Cache-control: no-cache • Cache-control: private • Pragma: no-cache • www-authenticate • Set-cookie
ISA Server does not cache responses to requests that contain the following HTTP request headers.	• Authorization, unless the origin server explicitly allowed this by including the "cache-control: public" header in the response • Cache-control: no-store

Note For more information about Web pages and caching, see the article "HOW TO: Prevent Caching in Internet Explorer," in the Microsoft Knowledge Base at http://support.microsoft.com/support/kb/articles/Q234/0/67.asp.

Web Proxy Chaining and Caching

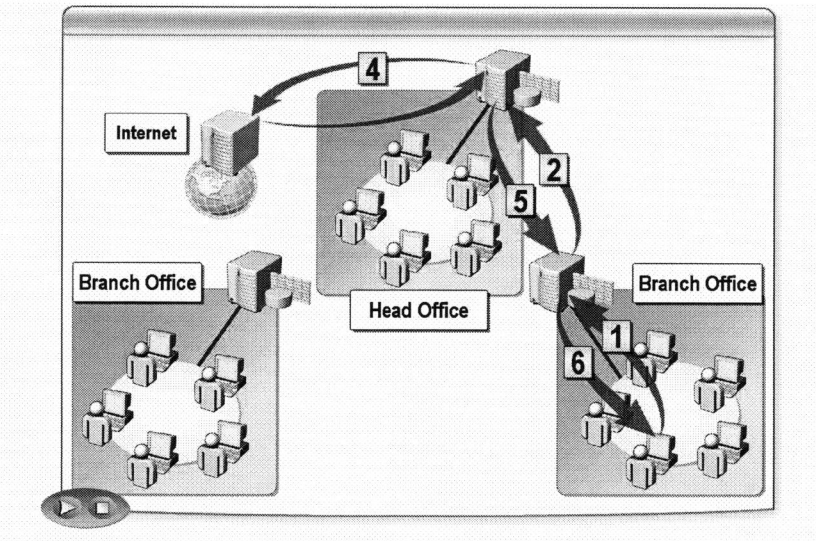

Introduction

Some organizations include multiple locations with computers running ISA Server deployed in each location. In this scenario, you can combine caching with Web proxy chaining to optimize caching performance.

Web proxy chaining and caching

You might use Web proxy chaining when your organization has multiple branch office locations, but all Internet requests are routed through one location at the head office. In this scenario, you can install ISA Server in each office and then configure ISA Server at the branch offices to route all Internet requests to the server running ISA Server at the head office.

One of the benefits of using Web chaining is the accumulated caching on ISA Server. If all the servers running ISA Server in the branch offices are configured to forward their requests to the head-office ISA Server, the head-office ISA Server will develop a large cache that contains many requested items. The combination of caching at the local branch office and at the head office increases the chances that the Internet content can be delivered to the client without downloading it again from the Internet.

The following steps describe how Web proxy chaining works in this branch office/main office scenario:

1. The Web client sends a request for Web content to the Web caching server at the branch office. If the Web caching server at the branch office contains a valid version of the Web content in its cache, it will return the content to the user who requested it.

2. If the content the branch office user requested is not contained in the branch office server's cache, the request is forwarded to an upstream Web caching server in the Web proxy chain.

3. If the upstream Web caching server has a valid copy of the requested content in cache, the content is returned to the branch office Web caching server. The branch office Web caching server places the content in its own Web cache and then returns the content to the branch office user who requested the content.

4. If the upstream Web caching server at the main office does not contain the requested content in its cache, it will forward the request to the Web server on the Internet. The Internet Web server returns the requested content to the main office Web caching server. The Web caching server at the main office places the content in cache.

5. The main office returns the content to the branch office Web caching server. The branch office Web caching server places the content in its cache.

6. The branch office Web caching server returns the content from its cache to the user who requested it.

Lesson: Configuring General Cache Properties

● Caching Configuration Components
● How to Enable Caching and Configure Cache Drives
● How to Configure Cache Settings

Introduction

The first step in configuring caching on ISA Server 2004 is to configure the general caching properties. This includes enabling caching by configuring cache drives and configuring additional cache settings. This lesson details how these settings are configured.

Lesson objectives

After completing this lesson, you will be able to:

■ Describe what is required to configure caching on ISA Server 2004.

■ Enable caching and configure cache drives.

■ Configure cache settings.

Caching Configuration Components

Component	Explanation
Define cache drives	• Enables caching by configuring a cache drive for storing the cached content
Configure caching settings	• Modifies the default TTL and types of cached content
Configure caching rules	• Enables unique caching policies for specific Web content
Configure content download jobs	• Enables the prefetch of content before clients request the content

Introduction

By default, caching is disabled on ISA Server 2004. If your ISA Server is being used as a Web proxy server, you should enable caching on ISA Server to optimize Web access performance.

Configuring caching

To configure caching on ISA Server 2004, you need to complete the following components:

Component	Explanation
Define cache drives	To enable caching on ISA Server, you must specify the drive the ISA Server will use for caching.
Configure caching settings	When you enable caching, ISA Server begins to cache requested Web content based on a default configuration. You can modify the cache settings to modify the TTL the ISA Server will use for caching objects, and to modify what types of content will be cached.
Configure caching rules	Caching rules are used to apply caching policies to specific Web content. If users in your organization have unique caching requirements for a Web site, use caching rules to configure the settings.
Configure content download jobs	Content download jobs can prefetch content from the Internet before a user even requests the content. Use content download jobs when you know that users will require updated content from a specific Web site.

How to Enable Caching and Configure Cache Drives

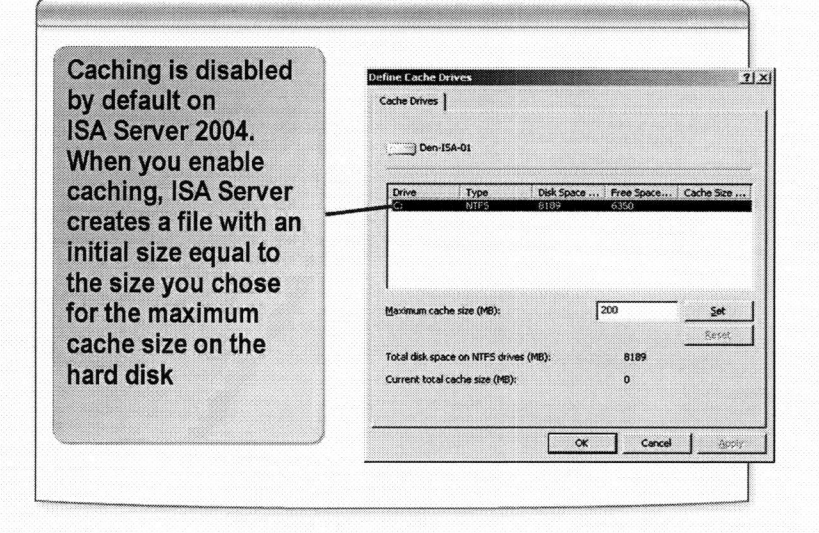

Introduction

By default, a new installation of ISA Server is configured with a maximum cache size of 0 MB, which means that ISA Server will not cache any content. To enable caching, you need to define a cache drive.

Defining a cache drive

To define a cache drive, follow these steps:

1. Open **ISA Server Management** and, in the console tree, click **Cache**.

2. In the details pane, click the **Cache Rules** tab.

3. On the **Tasks** tab, click **Define Cache Drives**.

4. In the **Define Cache Drives** dialog box, select one of the drives listed in the list box.

5. In **Maximum cache size**, type the amount of space on the selected drive to allocate for caching.

6. Click **Set** to configure the cache drive.

Note The drive you use for caching must be a local drive that is formatted using NTFS. To optimize performance, use a drive different from the one on which the main ISA Server system, the operating system and the page file are installed.

When you configure a drive to be used for caching, ISA Server creates a file with a .cdat extension in the \urlcache folder on that drive. The .cdat file is as large as the amount of space you dedicated for caching on that drive. As ISA Server caches the objects, it places the objects into the .cdat file. If the .cdat file is too full to hold a new object, ISA Server removes older objects from the cache by using a formula that evaluates age, popularity, and size. The .cdat file can only be accessed by the Web proxy service.

How to Configure Cache Settings

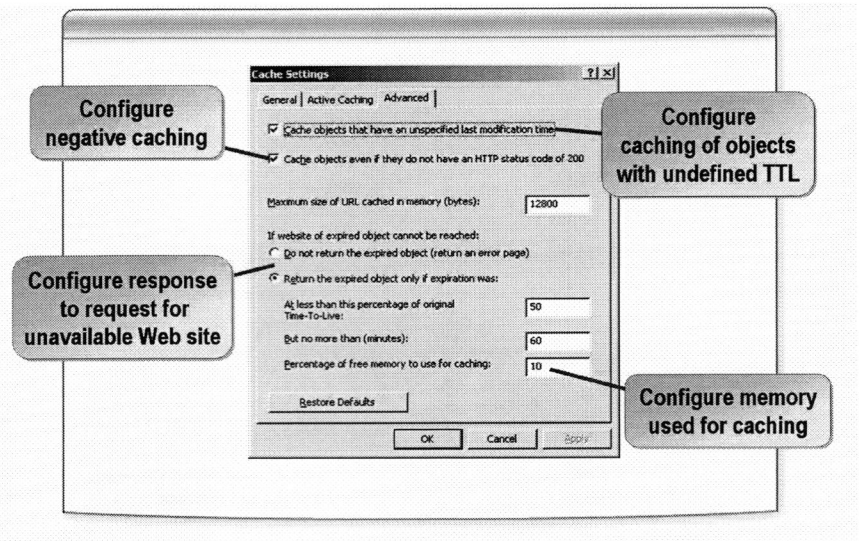

Introduction

After you define the cache drives, ISA Server will begin caching Web content based on the default caching configuration. This default configuration can be modified to meet your organization's requirements.

Configuring cache settings

You can configure how ISA Server caches specific types of HTTP objects. By limiting certain types of content, you can improve the efficiency of the caching process. For example, you can configure ISA Server to limit the size of cached objects to reserve cache space for additional smaller objects.

To configure content settings for caching:

1. In **ISA Server Management**, in the console tree, click **Cache**, and then in the details pane, click **Configure Cache Settings**.

2. In the **Cache Settings** dialog box, on the **Advanced** tab, configure the settings listed in the following table.

Configuration Option	Use this option to:
Cache objects that have an unspecified last modification time	Configure ISA Server to cache objects that do not have a TTL defined in the page header. If you select this option, ISA Server will cache these objects and clean them up based on the parameters defined by the cache rule that applies to content retrieved from the specific Web site.
Cache objects even if they do not have an HTTP status code of 200	Configure responses by ISA Server to requests that failed to return an object. This type of caching is referred to as negative caching. When you configure negative caching, ISA Server returns error messages to clients and caches the negative results, even if the Web site is only temporarily unavailable. Until the TTL for the negative response expires, clients may receive an error message from ISA Server even if the object is available again. When you configure negative caching, HTTP objects with the following status codes are cached: • 203 Partial information • 300 Redirection • 301 Object has moved permanently • 410 Object is gone
Maximum size of URL cached in memory (bytes)	Configure the Uniform Resource Locators (URLs) that ISA Server will store in memory. When you increase the amount of memory that a single object may occupy, ISA Server will store fewer Web objects. ISA Server will cache objects larger than this limit on disk.
If Web site of expired object cannot be reached: Do not return the expired object (return an error page)	Configure ISA Server to never return an expired item to a user. For example, ISA Server may have a cached copy of a Web page that has expired. Normally, when a user requests the same page, ISA Server would retrieve a fresh page from the Internet Web server. However, if the Internet Web server is not available and this option is selected, ISA Server will return an error message to the user.
If Web site of expired object cannot be reached: Return the expired object only if expiration was:	Configure ISA Server to retrieve an object from its cache when the object is not accessible on the Internet, even if the TTL for the object has expired. If this option is selected, ISA Server will respond to the user with the expired Web page. You should enable this setting only if viewing an expired version of an object is preferable to not viewing the object at all.
At less than this percentage of original Time-To-Live	Configure the time period for when ISA Server will return an expired object based on the original TTL. For example, if a Web page has a TTL of 100 minutes and this option is set at 50 percent, ISA Server will return the page for 50 minutes after it expires.
But no more than (minutes)	Configure the maximum time period for when ISA Server will return an expired object. For example, if a page has a TTL of 24 hours, and the percentage value is set at 50 percent, but this value is set at 60 minutes, ISA Server will respond with an error message to all requests for objects that have been expired for more than 60 minutes.
Percentage of free memory to use for caching	Configure the amount of RAM the computer running ISA Server will use for caching. If this server is used primarily as a caching server, you should increase this number. If you are using ISA Server for reverse caching, you should configure the RAM cache to be equal to your internal Web site size so that all client requests can be provided from the RAM cache.

Note The ISA Server Management interface provides the option to configure active caching, but the functionality has been disabled in ISA Server 2004. Review the Readme.htm file on the ISA Server CD-ROM.

Practice: Configuring General Cache Properties

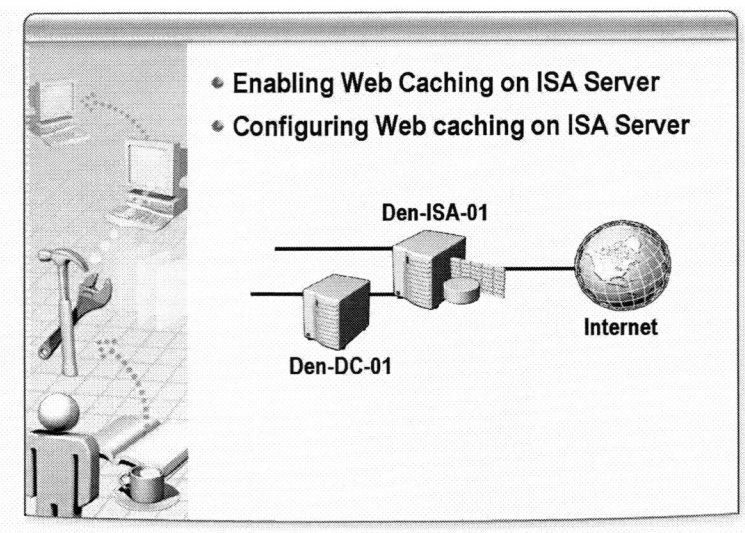

Introduction

In this practice, you will enable Web caching on ISA Server by defining a cache drive. Then you will configure Web caching.

▶ **To prepare for this practice**

1. You will need the Den-DC-01 virtual machine and the Den-ISA-01 virtual machine for this practice.

2. If necessary, start or resume the required virtual machines and then, on Den-ISA-01, log on to the cohovineyard domain with your user name and password.

Practice

▶ **Enabling Web caching on ISA Server**

1. Open **ISA Server Management**. Expand **Den-ISA-01**, expand **Configuration**, and then click **Cache**.

2. In the details pane, click **Cache Rules** tab.

3. On the **Tasks** tab, click **Define Cache Drives**.

4. In the **Define Cache Drives** dialog box, ensure that the C: drive is selected.

5. In **Maximum cache size**, type **50**. Click **Set** to configure the cache drive.

6. Click **OK** and then click **Apply**. In the **ISA Server Warning** dialog box, click **Save the changes and restart the services** and then click **OK**.

▶ **Configuring Web caching on ISA Server**

1. After the changes are applied, click **OK**.

2. Click **Configure Cache Settings**.

3. In the **Cache Settings** dialog box, on the **Advanced** tab, clear the check box for **Cache objects even if they do not have an HTTP status code of 200.** Click **OK**.

4. Click **Apply** to apply the changes and then click **OK** when the changes have been applied.

Lesson: Configuring Cache Rules

- What Are Cache Rules?
- How to Create a Cache Rule
- Managing Cache Rules

Introduction

Cache rules are used to specify the types of content stored in the cache and how objects are served from the cache. This lesson explains how cache rules are configured.

Lesson objectives

After completing this lesson, you will be able to:

- Describe what cache rules are.
- Create and configure cache rules.
- Manage cache rules.

What Are Cache Rules?

Cache rule options	Default cache rule
Define the destination set that the rule applies to	• Applies to all Web content
Define how content is returned to the user	• Returns non-expired content to the user
Define whether content is stored in the cache	• Caches the default cacheable objects
Define whether to cache HTTP, FTP, or both types of content	• Enables caching of both HTTP and FTP content
Define the maximum size for cached objects	• Does not apply any size restrictions to cached objects
Define whether to cache SSL content	• Caches SSL content

Introduction

In some cases, you may have different caching requirements for specific Web content. You can use *cache rules* to define the types of Web content that is stored in the cache and how Web content is stored and returned to users from the cache.

Cache rule settings

When you enable caching on ISA Server, a default cache rule is enabled. You can also configure a wide variety of settings that enable you to fine-tune caching performance on ISA Server. The following table describes the default cache rule and the ways you can change options to fine tune caching performance.

Cache rule options	The default cache rule
Apply to content retrieved from all Internet locations, or limit the rule to apply to specific destination sets. You can also configure the rule to apply to all Internet content except specific destination sets.	Applies to content requested from all network locations
Define how Web content is returned to the user. For example, you can define a cache rule that will always return the content from the cache, whether the information has expired or not.	Will return non-expired content to a Web user who requests the content. If the content has expired, ISA Server will route the request to the Web server
Define whether Web content is stored in the cache. You can configure the cache rule so that the Web content is never cached, or so that specific parameters are applied defining what type of content is cached.	Will cache the default cacheable objects

(continued)

Cache rule options	The default cache rule
Define whether HTTP content, FTP content, or both types of content are cached and configure the caching configuration for each protocol.	Enables both HTTP and FTP caching with a default TTL setting. You can enable or disable HTTP or FTP caching on the default rule, or modify the default TTL settings. These settings are the only settings that you can modify on the default cache rule
Define the maximum size for cached objects.	Does not set limits on the maximum size of cached objects
Define whether Secure Socket Layer (SSL) content will be cached.	Caches SSL responses

Why use cache rules?

The default caching configuration, including the cache settings and the default cache rule, will be sufficient for many organizations. If these settings are not modified, the default settings apply to all Web content cached in the ISA Server cache for both forward and reverse caching scenarios.

However, in some cases, you may also need to configure a more specific caching configuration. For example, users in your organization may frequently access a Web site, so you may want to configure the cache so that all content from that Web site is cached on the computer running ISA Server. If the Web site contains critical information that changes frequently, you may need to implement the opposite solution, that is, configure the Web site to never be cached.

How to Create a Cache Rule

Cache Rule Wizard Page	Configuration Options
Cache Rule Destinations	• Use destination sets to define the Web content that this rule applies to
Content Retrieval	• Defines how ISA Server responds to client requests if the content is or is not in cache
Cache Content	• Defines the types of content ISA Server will cache
Cache Advanced Configuration	• Defines maximum size for caching objects and SSL response caching
HTTP Caching	• Enables and configures TTL settings for HTTP content
FTP Caching	• Enables and configures TTL settings for FTP content

Configuring a new cache rule

The following steps provide a high-level overview of the process of configuring caching rules on ISA Server 2004; the detailed steps are included in the subsequent practice.

To create a new caching rule, complete the following steps.

1. In **ISA Server Management**, choose the option to **Create a Cache Rule**.

2. The **New Cache Rule Wizard** will start. All the cache rule settings can be configured using the wizard.

3. The first option you have is to define the **Cache Rule Destination**. The cache rule destination uses destination sets to define which Web content this rule applies to. You can use any destination set that is available on ISA Server, or create a new destination set. For example, if you want to apply this rule to a specific Web site, you can use or create a URL set or a domain name set and apply the rule only to that destination set.

4. The second option you need to define is the **Content Retrieval** settings. The settings are described in the following table:

Content Retrieval Options	Choose this option to:
Only if a valid version of the object exists in the cache. If no valid version exists, route the request to the server.	Configure ISA Server to retrieve the requested object from the cache if it has not expired. If the object has expired, ISA Server will retrieve the content from the Internet.
If any version of the object exists in the cache. If none exists, route the request to the server.	Configure ISA Server to retrieve the requested object from its cache if any version exists, even if the version is expired. If no version exists, ISA Server will retrieve the content from the Internet.
If any version of the object exists in the cache. If none exists, drop the request (never route the request to the server).	Configure ISA Server to retrieve the requested object from its cache if any version exists, even if the version is expired. If no version exists, ISA Server will return an error to the client.

5. You can also configure what content will be stored in the cache on the **Cache Content** page. The options are listed in the following table:

Cache Content options	Choose this option to:
Never, no content will ever be cached	Configure ISA Server to not cache any of the requested content but to always retrieve it from the Internet.
If source and request headers indicate to cache	Configure ISA Server to cache all content that is marked as cacheable.
In addition, also cache: Dynamic content	Configure ISA Server to also cache dynamic content that would normally not be cached.
In addition, also cache: Content for offline browsing (302, 307 responses)	Configure ISA Server to cache content with 302 and 307 response codes. These response codes indicate that the content has been temporarily relocated or the client has been temporarily redirected.
In addition, also cache: Content requiring user authentication for retrieval	Configure ISA Server to cache content that may require authentication to be accessed.

6. On the **Cache Advanced Configuration** page, you can configure the settings listed in the following table:

Advanced caching options	Choose this option to:
Do not cache objects larger than:	Limit the size of objects that ISA Server will cache.
Cache SSL responses	Configure ISA Server to cache SSL content. ISA Server can only cache SSL content in an SSL bridging configuration.

7. On the **HTTP Caching** page, you can configure the settings listed in the following table:

HTTP caching options	Choose this option to:
Enable HTTP caching	Enable or disable the caching of HTTP content.
Set TTL of objects (percent of the content age)	Configure the TTL for HTTP content. The time is expressed as a percentage of the TTL provided by the content.
TTL time boundaries	Configure the minimum and maximum amount of time that the content should be cached.
Also apply these TTL boundaries to sources that specify expiration	Configure the ISA Server TTL settings to override the expiration data included with the content.

8. On the **FTP Caching** page, you can configure the settings listed in the following table:

FTP caching options	Choose this option to:
Enable FTP caching	Enable or disable the caching of FTP content.
TTL for FTP objects	Configure how long the TTL is for FTP content.

Managing Cache Rules

> **Managing cache rules includes:**
>
> - Modifying the cache rule configuration after creating the rule
>
> - Modifying the cache rule order to evaluate cache rules for specific Web sites before cache rules for all Web sites
>
> - Disabling or deleting cache rules that are no longer required
>
> - Exporting the cache rule configuration before modifying the cache rules in case the modification is not successful

Introduction

After you configure caching rules, you may need to modify the cache rule settings or manage the cache rules.

Managing cache rules

There are several possible actions that you may need to perform to manage cache rules. These include:

- *Modifying settings.* You may need to modify a cache rule after creating it. To modify the cache rule settings, open **ISA Server Management**, expand the **Cache** container, and click the cache rule on the **Cache Rules** tab. Then click **Edit Selected Rule**. The configuration options when modifying the rule are the same as the options when creating the rule, with one additional option. When you modify the cache rule properties, you can use destination sets to configure exceptions to the network entities that the rule applies to. For example, if you need to configure a rule that applies to all Web sites except one, you can configure a destination set for the Web site's URL and add it to the **Exceptions** list.

- *Managing rule order.* Just like firewall access rules, you may need to modify the cache rule order to achieve a desired result. When ISA Server receives a Web request, it evaluates the cache rules in order. The first cache rule that matches the client request is applied. For example, you may have a cache rule that specifies the caching criteria for all Internet Web sites and another rule that specifies different caching requirements for a specific Web site. If the caching rule controlling caching for all Web sites is listed before the more specific rule, the more specific rule will never be applied. In general, you should configure the more specific rules so that they are evaluated first. The default caching rule will always be the last rule to be applied. To modify the rule order, click the rule you want to reorder and click either **Move Selected Rules Up** or **Move Selected Rules Down**.

- *Disabling or deleting cache rules.* If a cache rule is no longer required, you can disable or delete the rule. To do this, click the rule you want to modify and then click **Disable Selected Rules** or **Delete Selected Rules**.

- *Export and import cache rules.* Just like any other ISA Server configuration setting, you can export the cache rule configuration to an .xml file and import cache rule settings. Use this option to create a backup copy of your cache rules before modifying the configuration.

Practice: Configuring Cache Rules

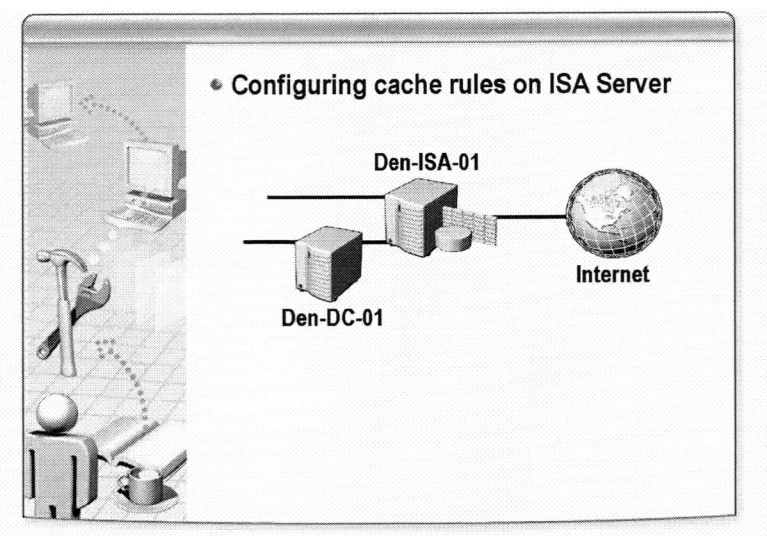

Introduction

In this practice, you will configure a cache rule on ISA Server.

▶ **To prepare for this practice**

1. You will need the Den-DC-01 virtual machine, and the Den-ISA-01 virtual machine for this practice.

2. If necessary, start or resume the required virtual machines and then, on Den-ISA-01, log on to the cohovineyard domain with your user name and password.

Practice

▶ **Configuring cache rules on ISA Server**

1. Open **ISA Server Management**. Expand **Configuration**, and then click **Cache**. Click the **Cache Rules** tab.

2. On the **Tasks** tab, click **Create a Cache Rule**.

3. On the **Welcome to the New Cache Rule Wizard** page, type **Tailspin Toys Cache Rule** as the name for the rule and click **Next**.

4. On the **Cache Rule Destination** page, click **Add** to open the **Add Network Entities** dialog box. Click **New**, and then click **URL Set**.

5. In the **New URL Set Rule Element** dialog box, in the **Name** text box, type **Tailspin Toys URL**. Click **New**.

6. Type **http://www.tailspintoys.com/***, and then click **OK**.

7. In the **Add Network Entities** page, expand **URL Sets** and click **Tailspin Toys URL**. Click **Add**, and then click **Close**.

8. On the **Cache Rule Destination** page, click **Next**.

9. On the **Content Retrieval** page, click **Next**.

10. On the **Cache Content** page, click **Next**.

11. On the **Cache Advanced Configuration** page, click **Next**.

12. On the **HTTP Caching** page, ensure that HTTP caching is enabled and then click **Next**.

13. On the **FTP Caching** page, disable FTP caching and then click **Next**.

14. On the **Completing the New Cache Rule Wizard** page, review the settings and then click **Finish**.

15. Click **Apply** to apply the changes and then click **OK** when the changes have been applied.

▶ **To prepare for the next practice**

1. You will need the Den-DC-01 virtual machine, the Den-ISA-01 virtual machine, and the Gen-Web-01 virtual machine for the next practice.

2. Start the Gen-Web-01 virtual machine.

Lesson: Configuring Content Download Jobs

* What Are Content Download Jobs?
* How to Create a Content Download Job
* Managing Content Download Jobs

Introduction

ISA Server 2004 enables the option to schedule content downloads from the Internet. With this option, ISA Server can prefetch content from the Internet prior to any user request for the content and store the content in the cache. This lesson explains how scheduled content downloads are configured.

Lesson objectives

After completing this lesson, you will be able to:

■ Describe content download jobs.

■ Configure content download jobs.

■ Manage content download jobs.

What Are Content Download Jobs?

Content download jobs:

* Allow you to schedule content for download at a specific time even if no user on the network has requested the content

* Improve Internet access performance

* Can be used to download content to the branch office during nonworking hours

* Can be used to ensure access to critical Internet content even when the Internet connection is not available

What are content download jobs?

Passive caching depends on a user initiating a request for Web content. Passive caching takes place when the first user makes a request for Web content.

In addition to passive caching, ISA Server also enables *content download jobs*. Content download jobs allow you to schedule content for download at a specific time or recurring times. You can schedule ISA Server 2004 to automatically download content that no user on the network has yet requested, or schedule content to be downloaded from a particular site and configure the cached content to remain in cache for a specific amount of time.

Why use content download jobs?

Just like passive caching, the main reasons for using content download jobs are to improve Internet access performance and decrease the use of bandwidth to the Internet. There are several possible scenarios in which content download jobs can provide this functionality. For example, you can create a content download job at a branch office ISA Server so that the entire main office intranet site is downloaded from the main office Web server. The content download job can be configured to take place during non-working hours so that the branch office link to the main office is not utilized for the download during working hours. When branch office users arrive at the office, the main office Web site's content is stored in the branch office cache. Branch office users can quickly download even large files from cache, while at the same time freeing up the branch office link to the main office during work hours for other business-related network activity.

You can also use content download jobs to update information from Internet Web sites. For example, users may frequently request a price list from the Web site of a business partner. You can configure a scheduled content download so that ISA Server retrieves the price list each night. By using a scheduled content download, the most recent version of the price list will be in the cache each morning.

You can also use scheduled content downloads to ensure that Web content is always available to users even when they are unable to connect to the Internet. For example, users may need access to a particular Web site at all times, and any disruption in that access may disrupt business processes. In this case, you can configure ISA Server to download the content and provide the content for users even when the Internet connection is not available.

To determine the Web sites for which to create scheduled download jobs, review the ISA Server reports for the most frequently accessed Web sites. You can create scheduled download jobs so that ISA Server will retrieve content from these Web sites when there is the most available bandwidth.

How to Create a Content Download Job

Content Download Job Wizard Page	Configuration Options
Download Frequency	• Defines a schedule for when the content download will occur
Content Download	• Defines the content that will be downloaded • Includes maximum links, objects, and concurrent connections used for downloads
Content Caching	• Defines what types of content to cache • Defines the TTL for cached content

Configuring a new content download job

The following steps provide a high-level overview of the process of configuring content download jobs on ISA Server 2004; the detailed steps are included in the subsequent practice.

To create a new content download job, complete the following steps.

1. In **ISA Server Management**, access the **Content Download Jobs** under the **Cache** heading.

2. Click **Schedule a Content Download Job**. If this is the first time you are enabling a content download job, you will receive a message stating the requirements for enabling schedule download jobs. The following two requirements must be met to enable content download jobs:

   a. The Local Host network must be configured to listen for Web proxy client requests. This option is enabled by default.

   b. The Scheduled Download Job configuration group must be enabled. This option is not enabled by default but can be enabled from the warning screen or by editing system policy.

3. After applying the change, click **Schedule a Content Download Job** again. The **New Scheduled Content Download Job Wizard** starts.

4. The first setting is **Download Frequency**. The options are described in the following table:

Download Frequency Options	Choose this option to:
One time only, on the completion of this wizard	Configure ISA Server to download the content once, immediately after you apply the changes made by the wizard.
One time only, scheduled	Configure ISA Server to download the content once, based on a schedule that you configure.
Daily	Configure ISA Server to download the content every day at a configured time.
Weekly	Configure ISA Server to download the content on a weekly schedule. You can configure the schedule to download on specific day(s) during the week and at particular times.

5. The next page in the wizard depends on the choice you made in the previous step. If you chose any option other than the first option, you use this page to configure the download schedule.

6. Next, on the **Content Download** page, you configure the content download job. You have the following options:

Content download options	Choose this option to:
Download content from this URL:	Specify the URL that will be downloaded to the ISA Server cache.
Do not follow link outside the specified URL domain name	Specify that only content from the domain name in the URL will be downloaded. If this option is not selected, ISA Server will download content from all links up to the maximum depth-of-links setting.
Maximum depth of links per page	Specify the number of links ISA Server will follow to download content.
Limit number of objects retrieved to maximum of:	Specify the maximum number of Web objects that will be downloaded by this job.
Maximum number of concurrent TCP connections to create for this job	Specify the maximum number of connections that will be used to download content at the same time.

7. On the **Content Caching** page, you can choose how the content is cached on ISA Server. You have the following options:

Content caching options	Choose this option to:
Cache all content.	Specify that all content will be cached even if the source and request headers indicate that the content is not cacheable.
If source and request headers indicate to cache, or if content is dynamic, then the content will be cached.	Specify that all content will be cached if the source and request headers indicate that the content is cacheable, or if the content is dynamic.
If source and request headers indicate to cache, then the content will be cached.	Specify that all content will be cached if the source and request headers indicate that the content is cacheable.
Expire content according to the cache rule.	Specify that the content will expire based on the cache rule that applies to this content.
Set TTL if not defined in response.	Specify that the content will expire based on the TTL defined in the response header and the associated cache rule. If there is no TTL defined in the response header, configure the TTL based on the value configured in the **Mark downloaded objects with a new TTL (minutes)** text box.
Override object's TTL.	Specify that the content will expire based on the TTL value configured in the **Mark downloaded objects with a new TTL (minutes)** text box.

Managing Content Download Jobs

Managing content download jobs includes:

* Modifying the content download job configuration after creating the job

* Starting content download jobs outside the scheduled time or stopping content download jobs that are running

* Disabling or deleting content download jobs that are no longer required

Introduction

After you configure content download jobs, you may need to modify the job setting or configure other content download job settings.

Managing content download jobs

There are several possible actions that you many need to perform to manage content download jobs. These include:

- *Modifying settings.* You may need to modify a content download job after creating it. To modify the cache rule settings, open **ISA Server Management**, expand the **Cache** container, and click the content download job on the **Content Download Jobs** tab. Then click **Edit the Selected Job**. The configuration options when modifying the job are the same as the options when creating the job.

- *Starting and stopping content download jobs.* Regardless of the schedule configured for the content download job, you can force the job to start immediately or stop a currently running job. To start a content download job, click the job you want to start and click **Start the Selected Job**. To stop a currently running job, click the job you want to stop and click **Stop the Selected Job**.

- *Disabling or deleting content download jobs.* If a content download job is no longer required, you can disable or delete the job. To do this, click the job you want to modify, and then click **Disable the Selected Jobs** or **Delete the Selected Jobs**.

Practice: Configuring Content Download Jobs

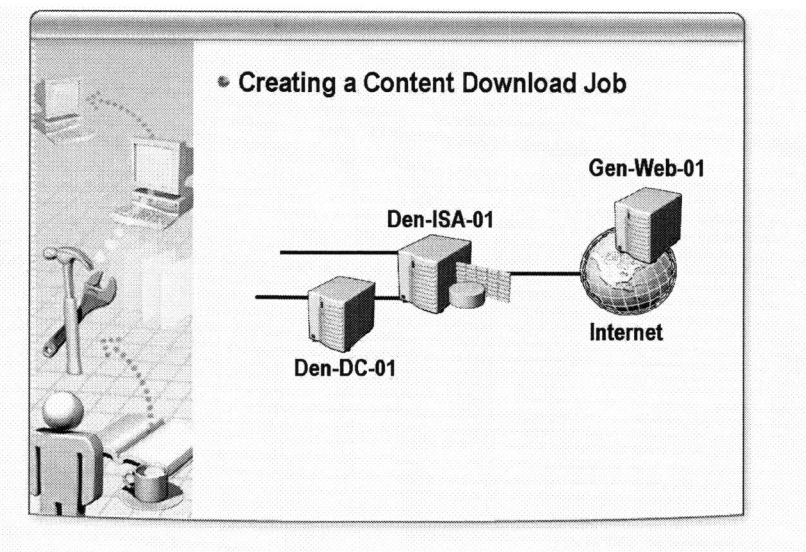

Introduction

In this practice, you will create a content download job on ISA Server 2004.

▶ **To prepare for this practice**

1. You will need the Den-DC-01 virtual machine, the Den-ISA-01 virtual machine, and the Gen-Web-01 virtual machine for this practice.

2. If necessary, start or resume the required virtual machines and then, on Den-ISA-01, log on to the cohovineyard domain with your user name and password.

Practice

▶ **Creating a content download job on ISA Server**

1. In **ISA Server Management**, click **Cache**, and then click the **Content Download Jobs** tab.

2. On the **Tasks** tab, click **Schedule a Content Download Job**.

3. On the **Enable Schedule Content Download Jobs** dialog box, click **Yes**.

4. Click **Apply** to apply the changes and then click **OK** when the changes have been applied.

5. On the **Content Download Jobs** tab, click the **Tasks** tab, and then click **Schedule a Content Download Job**.

6. On the **Welcome to the New Scheduled Content Download Job Wizard** page, type **Download Contoso Ltd** as the name for the rule and click **Next**.

7. On the **Download Frequency** page, click **Daily**, and then click **Next**.

8. On the **Daily Frequency** page, configure a **Job start date** with today's date, and a **Job start time** of five minutes from now. Click **Next**.

9. On the **Content Download** page, in the **Download content from this URL** text box, type **http://www.contoso.com**. Click **Next**.

10. On the **Content Caching** page, click **Next**.

11. On the **Completing the New Scheduled Content Download Job Wizard** page, review the configuration and click **Finish**.

▶ **To prepare for the lab**

1. You will need the Den-DC-01 virtual machine, the Den-ISA-01 virtual machine, the Den-Clt-01 virtual machine and the Gen-Web-01 virtual machine for the next practice.

2. Start the Den-Clt-01 virtual machine.

Lab: Configuring Caching

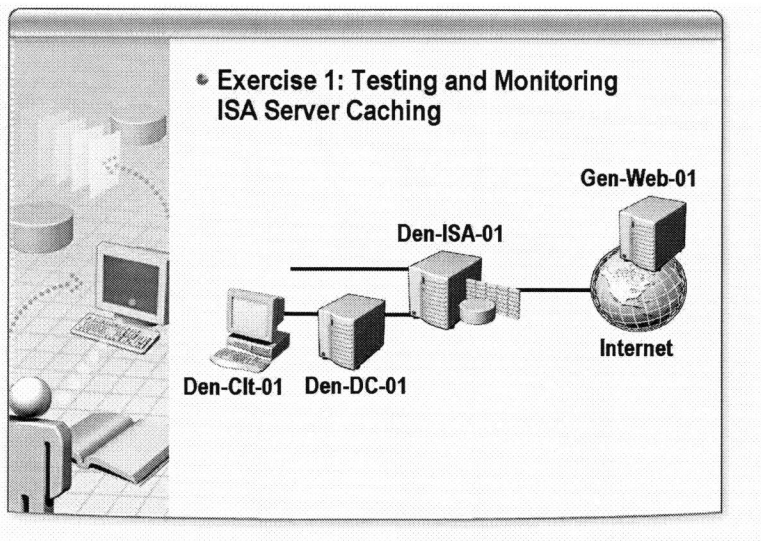

Objectives

After completing this lab, you will be able to:

- Test and monitor Microsoft Internet Security and Acceleration (ISA) Server caching.

Note This lab focuses on the concepts in this module and as a result might not comply with Microsoft security recommendations. For example, the Administrator passwords are not as complex as recommended. Additionally, most of the actions performed in this lab are performed while logged on as an Administrator. A better security practice would be to log on as a normal user and use the Runas option to start administrative applications.

Scenario

You have deployed ISA Server at Coho Vineyard and configured it as a cache server. You have configured caching rules and content download jobs. Now you need to test and monitor caching on ISA Server.

To prepare for this lab:

1. You will need the Den-DC-01 virtual machine, the Den-ISA-01 virtual machine, the Den-Clt-01 virtual machine, and the Gen-Web-01 virtual machine for this practice.

2. If necessary, start or resume the required virtual machines and then, on Den-ISA-01, log on to the cohovineyard domain with your user name and password.

**Estimated time to complete this lab:
30 minutes**

Exercise 1
Testing and Monitoring ISA Server Caching

In this exercise, you will configure ISA Server to monitor caching performance. You will then test the caching configuration enabled in the practices in this lab and monitor the caching performance.

Tasks	Detailed steps
1. Configure Internet Explorer on Den-Clt-01 to not retain cached files.	a. On the Den-Clt-01 computer, log on to the cohovineyard domain using a user name of **Jay** and a password of **P@ssw0rd**. b. Click **start** and then right-click **Internet**. Click **Internet Properties**. c. On the **Advanced** tab, under **Security**, select the check box for **Empty Temporary Internet Files when browser is closed**. d. Click **OK**.
2. Configure ISA Server to log caching information. By default, ISA Server does not log caching information. To enable logging, add the **Cache Information** field to the log file.	a. On Den-ISA-01, in **ISA Server Management**, click **Monitoring**. b. Click the **Logging** tab. On the **Tasks** tab, click **Configure Web Proxy Logging**. c. In the **Web Proxy Logging Properties** dialog box, on the **Fields** tab, select the check box for **Cache Information**. Click **OK**. d. Click **Apply** to apply the changes and then click **OK** when the changes have been applied. e. On the **Logging** tab, click **Start Query**. f. Right-click **Log Time** and click **Add/Remove Columns**. g. In the **Add/Remove Columns** dialog box, click **Cache Information** and then click **Add** to add the column to the **Displayed Columns** list. h. Click **Cache Information** in the **Displayed Columns** list and move it up so that it is second in the list. i. Click **URL** in the **Displayed Columns** list and move it up so that it is third in the list. j. Click **OK**.
3. Configure **Performance Monitor** on ISA Server to monitor caching performance.	a. On Den-ISA-01, open the **Performance** console from the **Administrative Tools** folder. b. Ensure that the **Pages/sec** counter is selected and press DELETE. Press DELETE two more times, deleting all the performance counters. c. Click the **Add (+)** button on the **Performance** console tool bar. d. In the **Add Counters** dialog box, in the **Performance Object** list, click **ISA Server Cache**. e. Click **All counters**, and then click **Add**. f. Click **Close** to close the **Add counters** dialog box. g. Press **Ctrl-R** to switch the performance view to a report view.

(*continued*)

Tasks	Detailed steps
4. Test the ISA Server caching configuration when no pages have been cached on the server. 5. For a complete listing of the cache information log values, search ISA Server Online Help for the **Cache info log values** article.	a. Switch to Den-Clt-01. b. Open **Internet Explorer** and access **www.tailspintoys.com**. c. Click each of the links listed on the left side of the page. d. Close **Internet Explorer**. e. Switch to Den-ISA-01 and click **Stop Query**. f. Review information in the **Cache Information** and **Destination IP** columns for each of the Tailspin Toys URLs. A cache information value of 800000 means that the content was retrieved from the Internet, but that the content is cacheable and that the response included the **Last-Modified** header. A destination Internet Protocol (IP) that is the actual IP address of the server on the Internet also indicates that the page was retrieved from the Internet. g. Review the Cache Information value for the http://131.107.10.200/ intranet_orgchart.htm page. A value of 40840000 indicates that this content should not be cached because it contains the **Cache-Control: No-Cache** header or the **Pragma: No-Cache** header. h. Review the Cache Information value for the http://131.107.10.200/ intranet_locations.htm page. A value of a00000 indicates that this content should be cached but it has a time limit defined. i. Switch to the **Performance Console**. Notice that ISA Server has cached six URLs.
6. View the source page for the http://131.107.10.200/ intranet_orgchart.htm page.	a. Switch to Den-Clt-01. b. Open **Internet Explorer** and access **www.tailspintoys.com**. c. Click **Executive Organization Chart** on the left side of the page. d. On the **View** menu, click **Source**. e. Notice that the page header includes the **<META http:-equiv= "Pragma" content="no-cache">** line. Close the source file. f. Close **Internet Explorer**.
7. View the Internet Information Server (IIS) Server configuration for the Tailspin Toys Web pages.	a. Switch to Gen-Web-01. b. Log in as the local **Administrator** with a password of **P@ssw0rd**. c. Open **Internet Information Services (IIS) Manager** from the **Administrative Tools** folder. d. Expand **Web Sites**, and then click **Tailspin Toys Web Site**. e. Right-click **index.html** and click **Properties**. On the **HTTP Headers** tab, notice that **Enable content expiration** is not enabled. Click **OK**. f. Right-click **intranet_locations.htm** and click **Properties**. On the **HTTP Headers** tab, notice that **Enable content expiration** is enabled and that the content is set to expire after five minutes. Click **OK**. g. Right-click **intranet_orgchart.html** and click **Properties**. On the **HTTP Headers** tab, notice that **Enable content expiration** is enabled and that the content is set to expire immediately. Click **OK**.

(continued)

Tasks	Detailed steps
8. Test the ISA Server caching configuration when the content has been cached on the server	a. Switch to Den-ISA-01, and in **ISA Server Management**, click **Start Query**. b. Switch to Den-Clt-01. c. Open **Internet Explorer** and access www.tailspintoys.com. d. Click on each of the links listed on the left side of the page. e. Close **Internet Explorer**. f. Switch to Den-ISA-01 and click **Stop Query**. g. Review information in the **Cache Information** and **Destination IP** columns for each of the Tailspin Toys URLs. A cache information value of 0 means that the content was retrieved from the ISA Server cache. A destination IP of 0.0.0.0 also indicates that the page was retrieved from the ISA Server cache. h. Switch to the **Performance** console. Notice that the **Total URLs Retrieved from Memory Cache** and the **Total Bytes Retrieved from Memory Cache(KB)** counters show that ISA Server retrieved the cached content from the memory cache.
9. Test the ISA Server caching configuration for Web sites downloaded using a content download job.	a. In **ISA Server Management**, click **Cache**. b. On the **Content Download Jobs** tab, right-click **Contoso Download Ltd** and click **Start**. c. Click **Monitoring** and click **Start Query**. d. Switch to Den-Clt-01. e. Open **Internet Explorer** and access **www.contoso.com**. f. Click on each of the links listed on the left side of the page. g. Close **Internet Explorer**. h. Switch to Den-ISA-01 and click **Stop Query**. i. Review information in the **Cache Information** and **Destination IP** columns for each of the Contoso.com URLs. Notice that all the pages were retrieved from the ISA Server cache.

To Prepare for the Next Lab

As you finish this practice, shut down all of the virtual machines that you used in the practice. To shut down the virtual machines, click **Close** from the **Action** menu. **Select Turn off and delete changes** and click **OK**.

After shutting down the virtual machines, restart the Den-ISA-01, Den-DC-01, and Den-Clt-01 virtual machines in preparation for the next module.

Module 10: Monitoring ISA Server 2004

Contents

Overview

- Monitoring Overview
- Configuring Alerts
- Configuring Session Monitoring
- Configuring Logging
- Configuring Reports
- Monitoring Connectivity
- Monitoring Services and Performance

Introduction

One of the critical components of managing Microsoft® Internet Security and Acceleration (ISA) Server 2004 is monitoring the activity on the server. Monitoring includes real-time monitoring and configuring alerts that provide immediate information of the current activity on the computer running ISA Server. Monitoring also includes configuring logging and reports that provide complete or summary information on the activity on ISA Server. The ISA Server administrator needs to be able to configure monitoring on the computer running ISA Server.

Objectives

After completing this module, you will be able to:

- Describe the reasons for monitoring ISA Server and which components can be monitored.

- Configure alerts.

- Configure session monitoring.

- Configure logging.

- Configure reporting.

- Configure connectivity monitoring.

- Configure service and performance monitoring.

Lesson: Monitoring Overview

- Why Implement Monitoring?
- ISA Server Monitoring Components
- Designing a Monitoring and Reporting Strategy
- Using the ISA Server Dashboard for Monitoring

Introduction

ISA Server 2004 provides several monitoring options that can be accessed through the ISA Server Management administration tool. This lesson provides an overview of what components can be monitored on ISA Server and how to design a monitoring and reporting strategy.

Lesson objectives

After completing this lesson, you will be able to:

- Describe the reasons to implement monitoring.
- List the components that can be monitored in ISA Server.
- Design a monitoring and reporting strategy.
- Use the ISA Server Dashboard for monitoring.

Why Implement Monitoring?

Use monitoring to:

- Monitor traffic between networks to ensure that only legitimate traffic passes between networks
- Troubleshoot network connectivity between ISA Server clients, servers, and networks
- Collect information about attacks and to detect attacks as they occur
- Plan future modifications to the ISA Server or Internet access infrastructure

Introduction

ISA Server is a critical component in an organization's network infrastructure. If ISA Server is deployed as an Internet edge firewall, it is operating as a firewall securing the internal network. It may also be providing secure access to Internet resources for internal clients and access to specified internal resources for Internet clients. If ISA Server is not available, this functionality is disrupted. If the ISA Server is being attacked from the Internet, the internal network may be at risk.

Why monitor ISA Server?

There are many reasons for monitoring ISA Server. Some of these include:

- *Monitoring traffic flow between networks.* You need to monitor traffic between networks to ensure that your access rules are configured correctly and that only the expected traffic is passing through ISA Server. You also need to monitor ISA Server regularly to identify normal and legitimate traffic passing through the server. After you identify a typical traffic pattern, you can detect any variation that might indicate a potential problem.

- *Troubleshooting network connectivity.* Monitoring ISA Server is a critical component of troubleshooting network connectivity issues. For example, if users report that they cannot access resources on the Internet, you can connect to ISA Server to help locate the problem. In this scenario, the problem could be with the client configuration, the ISA Server configuration, or the availability of the Internet resource. By monitoring ISA Server, you can identify the option most likely to be the source of the problem and begin troubleshooting it.

■ *Investigating attacks*. If ISA Server is operating as a firewall, it is inevitable that it will be exposed to attacks from the Internet. If ISA Server is configured correctly, it can detect and block most attacks. However, even if ISA Server is successfully blocking the attacks, you should still be aware that the attacks are occurring and be aware of any variations in the normal attack patterns.

If a new attack is launched against ISA Server, you need to be alerted as quickly as possible that the attack is occurring so that you can determine how to respond to an attack. After the attack is finished, you should also have enough information logged on ISA Server to investigate the attack. If the attack was successful, investigate why the attack succeeded so that you can configure ISA Server to block similar attacks in the future. Even if the attack is not successful, investigate the attack pattern to detect possible patterns that may lead to additional attacks.

■ *Planning*. By monitoring the computer running ISA Server, you can also gather information you can use for planning modifications to the current ISA Server infrastructure. By collecting performance data over a period of time, you can identify trends and use this information for planning future deployments of ISA Server.

ISA Server Monitoring Components

Components	Explanation
Alerts	Monitors ISA Server for configured events and then performs actions when the specified events occur
Sessions	Provides information on the current client sessions
Logging	Provides detailed archived information about the Web Proxy, Microsoft Firewall service, or SMTP Message Screener
Reports	Summarizes information about the usage patterns on ISA Server
Connectivity	Monitors connections from ISA Server to any other computer or URL on any network
Performance	Monitors server performance in real time, create a log file of server performance or configure performance alerts

Monitoring options

ISA Server Management provides many components to that can be used to monitor the computer running ISA Server. ISA Server provides the monitoring options listed in the following table.

Monitoring components	Explanation
Alerts	Monitors ISA Server for configured events and then performs actions when the specified events occur. The alert service is configured with many events that are monitored by default. You can also configure additional alert definitions.
Sessions	Provides information on all of the current client sessions on ISA Server. ISA Server lists sessions of the following types: Firewall client, SecureNAT, virtual private network (VPN) client, VPN site-to-site, and Web proxy.
Logging	Provides detailed information about the Web proxy, Microsoft Firewall service, or Simple Mail Transfer Protocol (SMTP) Message Screener. You can use the logs to monitor the activity on ISA Server in real time, or you can review the log files for earlier activity.
Reports	Summarizes information about the usage patterns on ISA Server. For example, you can create reports that summarize information about the users who access the most sites through ISA Server and what sites are accessed, as well as about what protocols and applications are being used most often. You can also use reports to monitor the security of your network. For example, you can generate reports that track malicious attempts to access internal resources.

(*continued*)

Monitoring components	Explanation
Connectivity	Enables regular monitoring of connections from the computer running ISA Server to any other computer or Uniform Resource Locator (URL) on any network. For example, you can use connectivity options to monitor connections to domain controllers, Domain Name System (DNS) servers, published Web servers, and external Web servers. This feature provides advance warning when the connection to any required service or network fails.
Performance	Collects performance data on the computer running ISA Server. You can monitor server performance in real time, create a log file of server performance over a longer period of time for detailed analysis, or configure performance alerts to create an event as a result of counters reaching certain values.

Designing a Monitoring and Reporting Strategy

When:	Determine:
Monitoring real-time information	• Which events should trigger an alert • The event threshold before the alert is triggered • The information that you need to monitor server performance
Collecting long-term information	• The information you need to monitor server performance over time • The information you need to monitor server usage • The information you need to monitor security events
Developing a response strategy	• How to respond to the critical events that occur on the ISA Server

Introduction

If you were to configure ISA Server to collect all of the possible types of information, it would be difficult to analyze or understand the data collected on a busy computer running ISA Server. You need to develop a monitoring strategy to locate the important information for your organization.

Monitoring real-time information

You can monitor real-time information by configuring alerts that are raised when specific events occur. You can also collect real-time information about client connections, server performance, and connectivity on ISA Server. Consider the following points when you create a monitoring and reporting strategy:

- *Decide the events you need to be alerted to in real time.* ISA Server can raise alerts based on almost any event that occurs. In most cases, you do not need to be alerted in real time about every alert. For example, if ISA Server blocks a single spoofing attack, you probably do not need to receive an alert. However, if the connection between ISA Server and a business-critical published Web server fails, you might decide that you need to receive an alert.

- *Determine the threshold for the alert.* As part of deciding which events will raise alerts, you also need to determine the threshold for when ISA Server will raise the alerts. If ISA Server detects hundreds of spoofing attacks within minutes, then you probably do want to receive an alert. If a single VPN client fails to authenticate once, you are probably not interested, but if the same client tries to authenticate many times, you may want to be alerted.

- *Monitor ISA Server using the ISA Server Management or Performance monitor.* You can also collect real-time information from ISA Server using ISA Server Management and the Performance monitor. In many cases, you might use these tools for real-time analysis only when a problem is reported. For example, if users report that the Internet connection is slower than usual, you can use these tools to determine why. If you use the Performance monitor, use the pre-configured ISA Server Performance monitor to monitor the most important counters on ISA Server.

Collecting long-term information

In addition to the real-time information that you can collect on ISA Server, you should also develop a strategy to collect longer-term information on ISA Server. Categories of information that you should collect include:

■ *Performance-related information.* To prepare for future modifications to the ISA Server infrastructure, regularly collect information about ISA Server performance. As a best practice, collect information about the performance to establish a baseline and then regularly collect the same types of information to determine how the performance on ISA Server is changing.

■ *Usage information.* Regularly collect usage reports. This is useful for future planning and to monitor the current activity on the server.

■ *Security-related information.* Collect information about security-related events. This information allows you to develop a baseline of the normal security events, which makes it easier to detect an anomaly to that regular pattern.

As part of collecting long-term information, also develop a strategy for archiving and regularly reviewing the information. The time line for reviewing this information will depend on the types of information collected. For example, you may want to review the security-related information on a daily basis, the usage information on a weekly basis, and the performance data only once per month.

Developing a response strategy

As part of your monitoring strategy, create a strategy for how to respond to critical events on ISA Server. These events could include:

■ Network security breaches.

■ Denial-of-service attacks.

■ Unusual usage patterns.

In each case, develop a strategy for how you will detect these types of activities and then how you will respond when the event is detected. As part of this strategy, create an immediate-response plan (such as isolating servers or networks, or shutting down services) and a longer-term plan for investigating and mitigating the attacks.

Using the ISA Server Dashboard for Monitoring

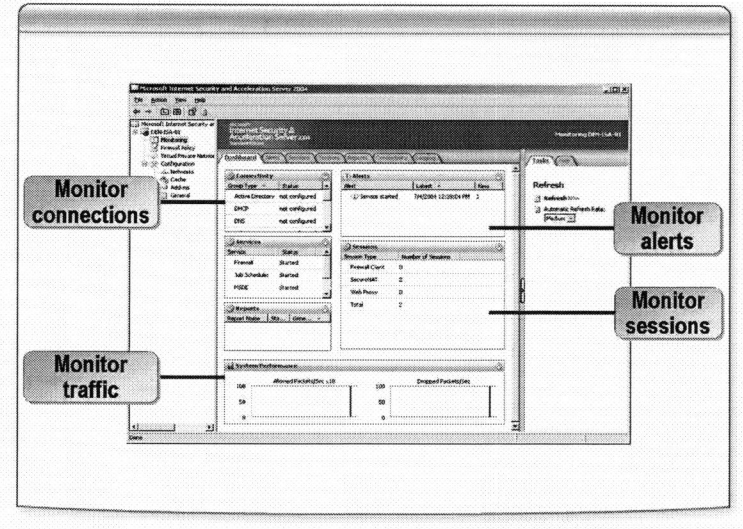

Dashboard components   The Dashboard view in ISA Server Management displays a summary of the information that is available for real-time monitoring on ISA Server. Most of the nodes in the Dashboard display a summary of the information that is available on the other views under the Monitoring node. In addition, the system performance information displays the **Allowed Packets/sec** and the **Blocked Packets/sec** performance counters for the computer running ISA Server.

In each of the nodes, Dashboard provides visual information on the status of each monitoring component. An X in a red circle indicates a potential problem, a yellow icon indicates a warning, a blue i in a white circle on the Alerts box indicates there are unacknowledged alerts, and a check mark in a green circle indicates that everything is okay.

Lesson: Configuring Alerts

- What Is an Alert?
- How to Configure Alert Definitions
- How to Configure Alert Events and Conditions
- How to Configure Alert Actions
- Alert Management Tasks

Introduction

ISA Server 2004 can be configured to create an alert when specific server-related events occur. You can also configure the alert to perform several different actions when the specified event occurs. This lesson explains how to configure and manage ISA Server 2004 alerts.

Lesson objectives

After completing this lesson, you will be able to:

- Describe an alert.
- Configure alert definitions.
- Configure alert events and conditions.
- Configure alert actions.
- Manage alerts.

What Is an Alert?

An alert is:

- A notification of an event or action that has occurred on ISA Server

- Triggered according to the conditions and trigger thresholds specified for the event associated with the alert

When a server event takes place and records an alert:

- The ISA Server Management console displays the alert in the Alerts view

- An entry appears in the alerts view that lists column headings such as type of alert, the date and time, status, and category

---

Introduction

To maintain the functionality and security of ISA Server and the networks protected by ISA Server, you need to know when specific events take place on ISA Server. For example, you need to know if an ISA Server service stops responding, or if a specific type of intrusion is being detected. You can use the ISA Server alert service to notify you when specific events occur, as well as to configure alert definitions to trigger a series of actions when an event occurs.

What is an alert?

An *alert* is a notification of an event or action that has occurred on ISA Server. When the event occurs, an alert is triggered according to the conditions and trigger thresholds specified for the event. Some examples of default events that trigger alerts include:

- *Service Started*. This informational event provides an alert concerning the proper startup of a specific ISA Server–related service.

- *IP Spoofing*. This warning event provides an alert that indicates that an Internet Protocol (IP) packet source address is not valid.

- *Intrusion Detected*. This warning event provides an alert that indicates that ISA Server has detected an external user attempting an intrusion attack.

- *DNS Intrusion*. This warning event provides an alert that indicates that a host-name overflow, length overflow, zone high port, or zone transfer attack occurred.

Note For a complete list of events available when configuring alerts in ISA Server 2004, see "Alerts" in ISA Server 2004 Help.

As a response to a specific event, you can configure an alert to send an e-mail notification, run a program, report to the Microsoft Windows® event log, or start and stop a service. For example, you can configure ISA Server to send you an e-mail message when a specified number of intrusion attempts have occurred.

You can also use scripts to configure advanced responses to the alerts. For example, you can create a program that scans the logs for the IP address of an intruder and then creates a filter that blocks connections from the intruder's IP address. You can then configure the alert to run the program whenever ISA Server generates an alert that is based on an intrusion attempt.

Alert structure

When a server event takes place and records an alert, the ISA Server Management console displays the alert in the Alerts view of the Monitoring node. A summary of all of the most recent alerts is also listed in the Alerts area of the Dashboard view.

When an alert is triggered, an entry appears in the Alerts view that lists the following information in column format:

- *Alert.* The **Alert** column indicates the type of alert that has occurred based on a predefined list of configured alerts and events. As alerts occur, all identical alerts are grouped together by category for ease of use. You can expand or collapse a category to display or hide each individual alert within each category.

- *Latest.* The **Latest** column shows the date and time that an alert took place. If multiple alerts are grouped together, the main category heading illustrates the latest date and time of the most current alert.

- *Status.* The **Status** column illustrates the status of the alert. Valid status entries include:

  - *New.* These are the most recent alerts. Any alert that has a New status is also displayed in the Dashboard Alerts snapshot pane.

  - *Acknowledged.* You can acknowledge an alert to remove the notification entry in the Dashboard snapshot pane. When an alert is acknowledged, the entry is not removed from the Alerts view; only the status is changed to reflect the state.

- *Category.* The **Category** column illustrates the category that the alert belongs to. Valid categories include **Security, Cache, Routing, Firewall, Service,** and **Other**.

Accessing the **Add/Remove Columns** command from the **View** menu provides the ability to add other columns to the Alerts view, including:

- *Severity.* Valid severity categories include **Information, Warning,** and **Error**.

- *Server.* The **Server** column lists the name of the ISA Server that has generated the alert.

- *Count.* The **Count** column lists the number of times a specific alert has been recorded.

When you click each registered alert, the bottom of the **Alerts** view provides **Alert Information**, which contains a detailed description of the selected alert.

How to Configure Alert Definitions

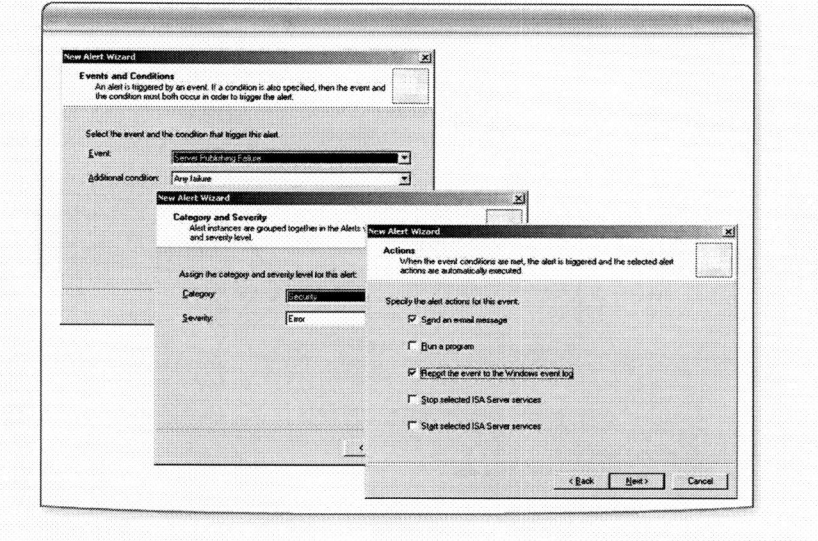

What is an alert definition?

An *alert definition* lists the specific actions or notifications that occur when an event takes place on the computer running ISA Server. During ISA Server installation, alert definitions are defined for a number of built-in general events. Several of these events allow you to define a more specific alert by configuring conditions related to the event. For example, ISA Server includes the pre-configured **Intrusion Detected** event. The associated alert is configured to report on any intrusion detected. You may want to redefine this general alert to provide additional specific notifications related to all port-scan attacks, ping-of-death attacks, or other conditions.

Configuring new alert definitions

The following steps provide a high-level overview of the process of configuring alert definitions:

1. In **ISA Server Management**, click **Monitoring** and then click the **Alerts** view.

2. In the Task pane, click **Configure Alert Definitions**.

3. To enable or disable an **Alert Definition** that is already configured, click the check box next to the desired alert.

4. To add a new **Alert Definition**, click **Add** in the **Alerts Properties** dialog box to open the **New Alert Wizard**. When you configure a new alert definition, provide the following information:

   a. Provide an **Alert name**.

   b. Choose a specific **Event** and additional condition that will trigger the alert. You cannot add any event that is already configured as an alert and that does not have any additional conditions.

c. Assign the **Category** and **Severity** level for the alert that you are configuring. These options provide a way to group together alert instances in the **Alerts** view according to category type and severity level.

d. Specify an alert action for the event. Your choices include **Send an email message**, **Run a program**, **Report the event to the Windows event log**, **Stop selected ISA Server Services**, and **Start selected ISA Server Services**.

e. Depending on which alert actions you have selected, you may have additional steps such as SMTP server and e-mail configuration settings, program startup parameters, or the selection of ISA Server services to stop or start.

How to Configure Alert Events and Conditions

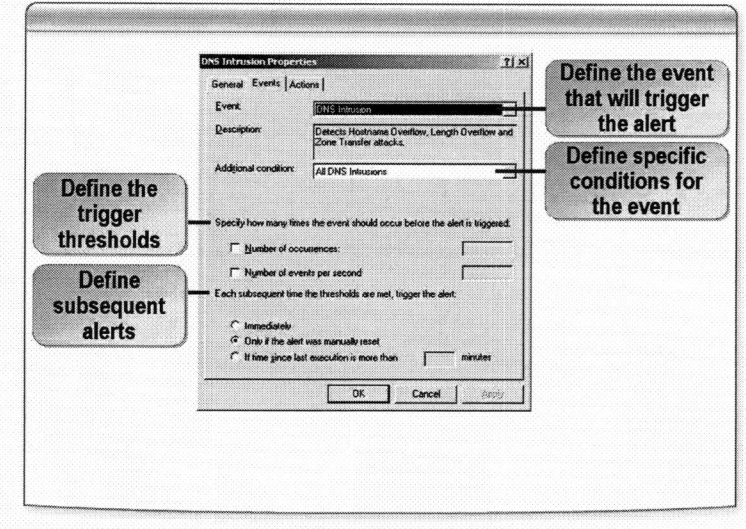

What are alert events and conditions?

Alert events define actions that occur on the computer running ISA Server that can raise alerts. Alert conditions are additional criteria applied by ISA Server when alert events happen. For example, Domain Name System (DNS) intrusion is an alert event. Additional conditions that you can apply to the alert event include raising an alert when any DNS intrusion attempt is detected, or raising an alert only when specific DNS intrusion attempts are detected. You can also modify the event trigger-threshold limits. The trigger threshold refers to how many times the event should occur before the alert is triggered and how long to wait before issuing the alert again.

Configuring alert events and conditions

To configure alert events and conditions, complete the following steps.

1. In **ISA Server Management**, click **Monitoring** and then click the **Alerts** view.

2. In the Task pane, click **Configure Alert Definitions**.

3. Select the **Alert Definition** you want to configure and then click **Edit**.

4. On the **General** tab, you can edit the name, **Description**, **Category**, or **Severity** of the alert definition. You can also enable or disable the alert by clicking the **Enable** check box.

5. On the **Events** tab, you can configure the options described in the following table:

Events tab options	Choose this option to:
Event	Configure the event that is to be associated with the selected Alert definition. The Description text box explains what each event refers to.
Additional condition	Configure specific conditions for events that have additional conditions available.

(continued)

Events tab options	Choose this option to:
Alert Action Trigger Threshold/Number of occurrences	Specify how many times the event should occur before the alert is triggered.
Alert Action Trigger Threshold/Number of events per second	Specify how many times per second an event should occur before the alert is triggered.
Immediately	Specify that a subsequent alert is sent immediately when a threshold is met after the initial alert is triggered.
Only if the alert was manually reset	Specify that a subsequent alert is sent when a threshold is met and the initial alert was manually reset.
If time since last execution is more than	Specify that a subsequent alert is sent when a threshold is met after a specified amount of time.

How to Configure Alert Actions

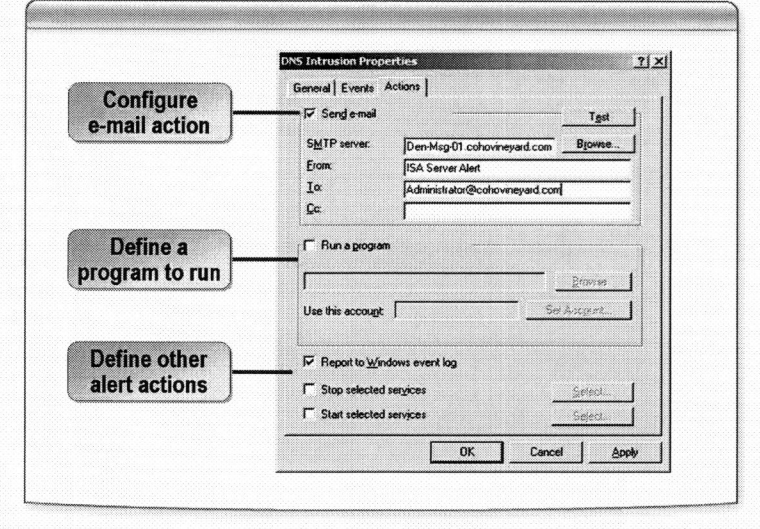

What is an alert action?

An alert action is an optional task that takes place when an alert condition is met. Actions that can be configured are:

- Send an e-mail message.
- Run a program.
- Log the event in the Windows event log.
- Stop or start the Microsoft Firewall service or the Microsoft ISA Server Job Scheduler.

Configuring alert actions

To configure alert actions, complete the following steps:

1. In **ISA Server Management**, click the **Alerts** view under the **Monitoring** node.
2. In the Task pane, click **Configure Alert Definitions**.
3. Select the **Alert Definition** you want to configure and then click **Edit**.
4. Click the **Actions** tab.

5. The options on the **Actions** tab are described in the following table:

Actions tab options	Choose this option to:
Send e-mail	Specify that an e-mail message be sent when the alert conditions are met.
SMTP Server	Provide the IP address or name of the Simple Mail Transfer Protocol (SMTP) server.
	If you configure an SMTP server located on the internal network, you must enable the system policy rule that allows the Local Host network to access the internal network using the SMTP protocol. In the **System Policy Editor**, in the **Remote Monitoring** configuration group, select **SMTP**, and then click **Enable**. The **Allow SMTP protocol from firewall to trusted servers** rule is enabled.
	If you configure an e-mail action to use an external SMTP server, you must create an access rule that allows the Local Host network to access the external network (or the network on which the SMTP server is located), using the SMTP protocol.
From	Provide the e-mail address of the sender.
To	Provide the e-mail address of the recipient.
Cc	Provide the e-mail address of the person who receives a copy of the e-mail alert.
Test	Send a test e-mail message to the recipient.
Run Program	Specify that a program will be executed when the alert conditions are met.
Use this account	Configure the name of a specific user account or local system account that will be used to run the specified program. The specified user must have Logon as batch-job permissions.
Report to Windows event log	Specify that the event will be written to the Windows event log when the alert conditions are met.
Stop selected services	Specify that the selected services will be stopped when the alert conditions are met. The two services that can be stopped are the Microsoft Firewall service or the Microsoft ISA Server Job Scheduler.
Start selected services	Specify that the selected services will be started when the alert conditions are met. The two services that can be started are the Microsoft Firewall service or the Microsoft ISA Server Job Scheduler.

Alert-Management Tasks

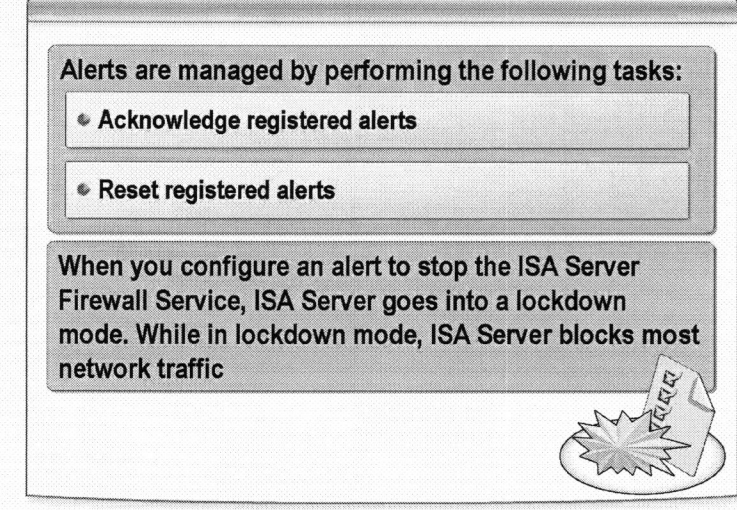

Introduction

After you configure alert definitions, you need to manage the list of alerts. You can manage the alerts both in the Dashboard and Alerts views. It is important to manage this list to easily recognize the most recent alerts as well as to purge alerts that are no longer relevant.

Managing alerts

Alerts are managed by performing two types of tasks. These tasks include:

- *Acknowledge registered alerts*. You can indicate that you have addressed a specific alert by acknowledging the event. When you mark an event as acknowledged, the status for the event is changed in the Alerts view and the event is no longer displayed on the Dashboard. To acknowledge an event, right-click the alert and then click **Acknowledge**. You can also click **Acknowledge Selected Alerts** from the Task pane.

- *Reset registered alerts*. To reset an alert means to remove it from the Alerts view. To reset an alert, right-click the alert and then click **Reset**. You can also click **Reset Selected Alerts** from the Task pane.

Note All alerts are reset when ISA Server reboots.

You can reset or acknowledge an entire group of alerts by selecting the group heading and specifying the desired task.

Lockdown mode

When you configure an alert to stop the ISA Server Firewall Service, or when you manually stop the service, ISA Server goes into a lockdown mode. When ISA Server is in lockdown mode, the following restrictions apply:

- The following system policy rules are still applicable:

  - Allow ICMP (Ping) requests from selected computes to ISA Server.

  - Allow remote management from selected computers using MMC.

  - Allow DHCP replies from DHCP servers to ISA Server.

  - Allow remote management from selected computers using Terminal Server.

- Outgoing traffic from the Local Host network to all networks is allowed. If an outgoing connection is established, that connection can be used to respond to incoming traffic. For example, a DNS query can receive a DNS response on the same connection.

- No incoming traffic is allowed.

- VPN remote access clients cannot access ISA Server, and access is denied to remote site networks in site-to-site VPN scenarios.

- Any changes to the network configuration while ISA Server is in lockdown mode are applied only after the Firewall Service restarts and ISA Server exits lockdown mode.

- ISA Server does not trigger any alerts.

Troubleshooting ISA Server when the Firewall Service is not running is difficult because of these restrictions. However, you can access the ISA Server computer by using an MMC from a remote computer, or you can log on directly to the ISA Server computer. After you have access to the ISA Server Management Console, review the alerts and logs to see what triggered the lockdown mode.

Practice: Configuring and Managing Alerts

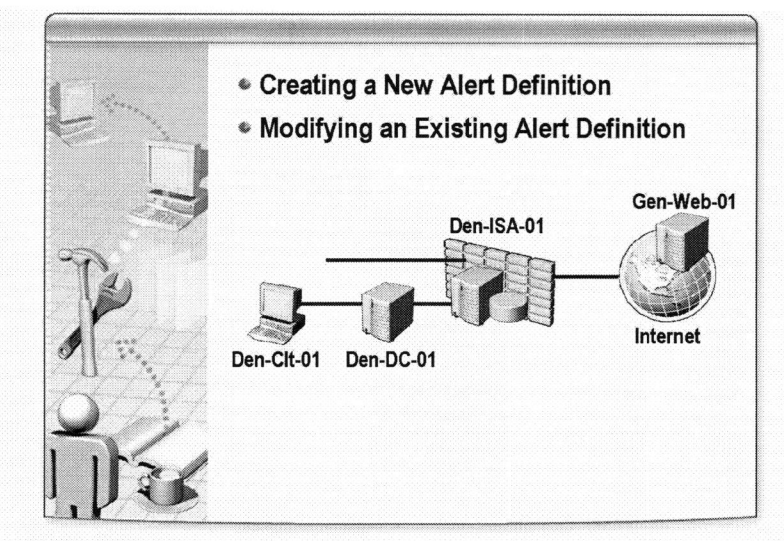

Introduction

In this practice, you will enable adding a new alert definition as well as modify an existing alert definition in ISA Server.

▶ **To prepare for this practice**

1. You will need the Den-DC-01 virtual machine, the Den-Clt-01 virtual machine, the Gen-Web-01 virtual machine, and the Den-ISA-01 virtual machine for this practice.

2. If necessary, start or resume the required virtual machines and then, on Den-ISA-01, log on to the cohovineyard domain with your user name and password.

Practice

▶ **Creating a new alert definition**

1. In **ISA Server Management**, expand **Den-ISA-01**, click **Monitoring** and then click the **Alerts** view.

2. In the Task pane, click **Configure Alert Definitions**.

3. Click **Add** in the **Alerts Properties** dialog box to open the **New Alert Wizard**.

4. On the **Welcome to the New Alert Configuration Wizard** page, type **Network Configuration Change** as the **Alert name**. Click **Next**.

5. On the **Events and Conditions** page, in the **Event** list, choose **Network configuration changed**. In the **Additional condition** list, choose **NIC Disabled**. Click **Next**.

6. On the **Category and Severity** page, in the **Category** list, click **Routing**. In the **Severity** list, click **Warning**. Click **Next**.

7. On the **Actions** page, click **Send and e-mail message** and **Report the event to the Windows event log**. Click **Next**.

8. On the **Sending E-mail Messages** page, fill in the following information:

   a. SMTP server: **den-msg-01.cohovineyard.com**

   b. From: **ISAServerAlert**

   c. To: **administrator@cohovineyard.com**

   Click **Next**.

9. On the **Completing the New Alert Configuration Wizard** page, review the configuration and then click **Finish**.

10. On the **Alert Definitions** tab, enable the new alert definition by clicking the check box for **Network configuration changed**.

▶ **Modifying an existing alert definition**

1. On the **Alerts Properties** page, click **VPN connection failure** and then click **Edit**.

2. On the **Events** tab, click the check box for **Number of occurrences**. In the text box, type **3**. Click **Apply**.

3. On the **Actions** tab, click **Send e-mail** and fill in the following information:

   a. SMTP server: **den-msg-01.cohovineyard.com**

   b. From: **ISAServerAlert**

   c. To: **administrator@cohovineyard.com**

4. Click **OK**. Click **OK** on the **VPN Connections Failure Properties** page. Click **OK** on the **Alerts Properties** page.

5. Click **Apply** to apply the changes and then click **OK** when the changes have been applied.

Lesson: Configuring Session Monitoring

- **What Is Session Monitoring?**
- **About Managing Sessions**
- **How to Configure Session Filtering**

Introduction

ISA Server 2004 provides the ability to monitor real-time information about the current sessions open on the server. This lesson describes how to configure and manage session monitoring on ISA Server.

Lesson objectives

After completing this lesson, you will be able to:

- Describe session monitoring.
- Manage sessions.
- Configure session filtering.

What Is Session Monitoring?

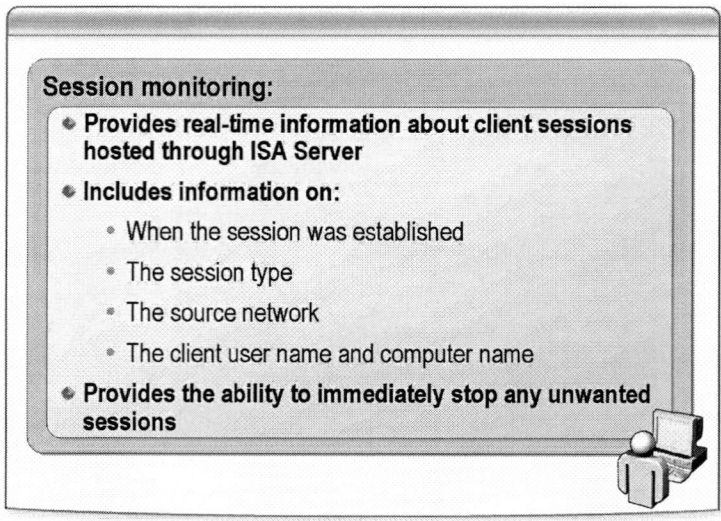

Session monitoring:

- Provides real-time information about client sessions hosted through ISA Server
- Includes information on:
  - When the session was established
  - The session type
  - The source network
  - The client user name and computer name
- Provides the ability to immediately stop any unwanted sessions

Introduction

Session monitoring enables you to identify the users or computers that are maintaining a session on the computer running ISA Server.

What is session monitoring?

Session monitoring provides real-time information about client sessions being hosted through ISA Server. The type of information that is presented includes:

- *Activation*. This column shows the date and time that the session has been established.

- *Session Type*. This column shows the type of session that has been established. Session types include SecureNAT, Firewall client, VPN client, VPN site-to-site, and Web proxy.

- *Client IP*. This column displays the IP address of the client initiating the session.

- *Source Network*. This column displays the network from which the session has been initiated.

- *Client Username*. This column displays the name of the client that has initiated the session.

- *Client Host Name*. This column displays the name or IP address of the client host computer.

You can add two other column headings to provide additional information about the server and application. To add the headings, click **Add/Remove Columns** from the **View** menu of the **ISA Server Management** console. You can also right-click the headings in the **Sessions** view and then select the columns you want to view.

These additional headings are:

- *Server Name*. This column displays the name of the computer running ISA Server that is hosting the session.

- *Application Name*. This column displays the name of any application maintaining a session through ISA Server.

All session details are listed in the **Sessions** view of the **ISA Server Management** console. A summary of total Firewall client, SecureNAT, and Web proxy sessions is displayed on the Dashboard.

Note   When IP Routing is disabled, traffic from users and IP addresses is listed in the Sessions view. When IP Routing is enabled, only sessions from traffic that passes via an application filter is listed.

About Managing Sessions

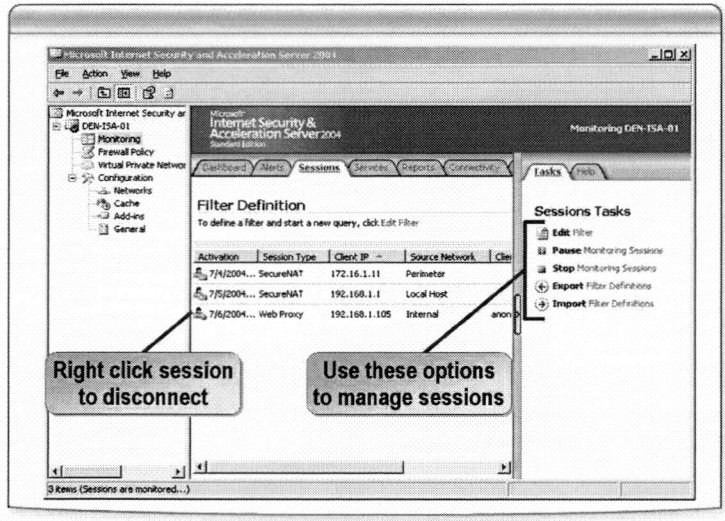

Managing sessions

In addition to viewing session information, you can also perform several tasks on the session entries. These tasks include:

■ *Disconnecting the session*. This task allows you to stop all unwanted sessions immediately. When you stop a session, all associated connections are closed. Note that this does not prevent a client from reactivating the session. If you want to prevent the client from reconnecting, you must change the firewall policy configuration so that it specifically denies access to the unwanted client.

■ *Pausing monitoring sessions*. This task allows you to pause monitoring. Any sessions that are currently displayed in the Sessions view are not removed; however, new sessions are not added to the view. When you resume session monitoring, ISA Server updates the view with the relevant, new session information.

■ *Stopping monitoring sessions*. This task allows you to stop session monitoring, which clears the sessions view. When session monitoring is stopped, all information about any monitored session is lost. When you restart session monitoring, ISA Server starts to collect all information about active sessions.

Disconnecting sessions

You may want to disconnect a session to stop unwanted connections immediately. The following steps provide an overview of the process of viewing and disconnecting sessions.

To view and disconnect sessions, complete the following steps.

1. In **ISA Server Management**, click **Monitoring**.
2. Click the **Sessions** tab.
3. Identify the current sessions that are listed in the **Sessions** view.
4. To disconnect a specific session, click the session and then click **Disconnect Session** in the Task pane. You can also right-click the session and then click **Disconnect Session**.

Pausing session monitoring

To pause session monitoring, complete the following steps.

1. In **ISA Server Management**, click **Monitoring**.
2. Click the **Sessions** tab.
3. Click **Pause Monitoring Sessions**, which can be found in the Task pane or by right-clicking a session and clicking **Pause Monitoring Sessions**.
4. To resume Session Monitoring, click **Resume Monitoring Sessions**.

Note When you pause session monitoring, the items displayed in the Sessions view are not removed.

Stopping session monitoring

To stop session monitoring, complete the following steps.

1. In **ISA Server Management**, click **Monitoring**.
2. Click the **Sessions** tab.
3. Click **Stop Monitoring Sessions**, which can be found in the Task pane or by right-clicking a session and clicking **Stop Monitoring Sessions**.
4. To resume Session Monitoring, click **Start Monitoring Sessions**.

Note When you stop monitoring sessions, ISA Server loses information about any sessions that had been monitored.

How to Configure Session Filtering

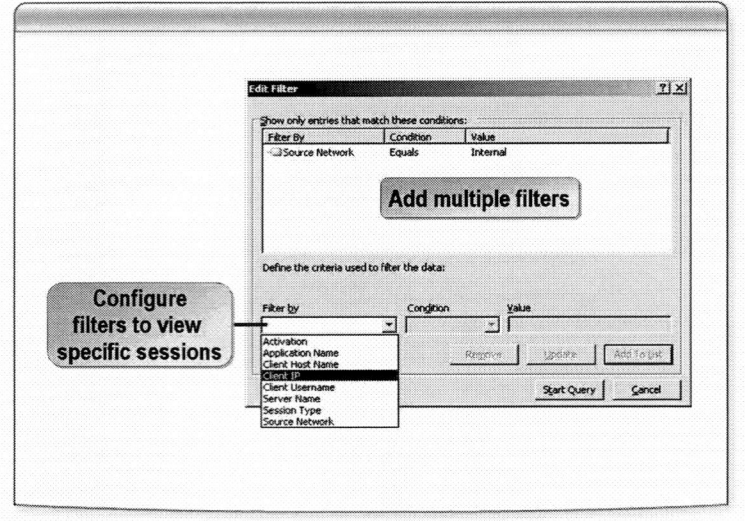

What is a filter definition?

If you have a large number of users in your organization, you can use a filter definition to determine the sessions to display in the Sessions view. You can create a filter on a set of conditions to focus on specific issues. For example, if you want to view sessions only by a specific client, you can create a filter to view only sessions initiated by that specific client.

Configuring session filtering

The following steps provide an overview of how to configure session filtering.

1. In **ISA Server Management**, click **Monitoring**.

2. Click the **Sessions** tab.

3. Click **Edit Filter**, which can be found in the Task pane or as a link under the **Filter Definition** heading.

4. Select filter criteria from the following sections:

   • *Filter By*. Select a specific heading to filter, such as Session Type, Client IP, Client Username, or others.

   • *Condition*. Select a specific condition to apply to the filtered heading. Some examples of conditions include Equals, Contains, Not Contains, and Not Equal.

   • *Value*. The Value field provides a text box for you to enter a specific value to filter. For example, if you are filtering by session type, you are able to select the various session types available in ISA Server 2004.

5. Click **Add to List** to add it to the filter list.

6. Continue to add additional filters as required.

After creating a filter definition, you can save it for future use. To save a filter definition, click **Save Filter Definition** in the Task pane.

Practice: Configuring Session Monitoring

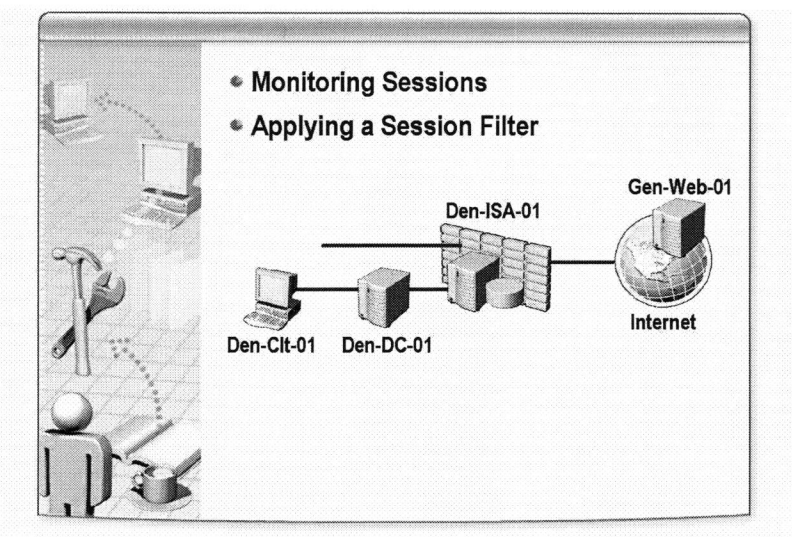

Introduction

In this practice, you will enable session monitoring on ISA Server and use a session filter to limit the information displayed in the Sessions view in ISA Server Management.

▶ **To prepare for this practice**

1. You will need the Den-DC-01 virtual machine, the Den-Clt-01 virtual machine, the Gen-Web-01 virtual machine, and the Den-ISA-01 virtual machine for this practice.

2. If necessary, start or resume the required virtual machines and then, on Den-ISA-01, log on to the cohovineyard domain with your user name and password.

3. On Den-Clt-01, log on to the cohovineyard domain with a user name of **Jay** and a password of **P@ssw0rd**.

4. On Den-DC-01, log on to the cohovineyard domain with a user name of **Administrator** and a password of **P@ssw0rd**.

Practice

▶ **Monitoring sessions**

1. Switch to Den-Clt-01. Open Microsoft **Internet Explorer** and connect to **http://www.contoso.com**.

2. Switch to Den-DC-01. Open **Internet Explorer** and connect to **http://www.tailspintoys.com**.

3. Switch to Den-ISA-01. In **ISA Server Management**, click **Monitoring**.

4. Click the **Sessions** tab.

5. Click **Edit Filter**. In the **Filter by** drop down list, click **Source Network**. In the **Condition** drop down list, click **Equals**. In the **Value** drop down list, click **Internal**. Click **Add to List**, then click **Start Query**.

6. Notice the current sessions.

7. Right-click the session from Den-Clt-01, and then click **Disconnect Session**. In the warning dialog box, click **Yes**.

8. Switch to Den-Clt-01. Refresh the page for http://www.contoso.com.

9. Switch to Den-ISA-01. Notice that the Den-Clt-01 session has been reestablished.

▶ **Using a session filter**

1. On the **Tasks** tab, click **Edit Filter**.

2. On the **Edit Filter** page, in the **Filter by** list, click **Client IP**. In the **Condition** list, click **Greater or Equal**. In the **Value** box, type **192.168.1.101**. Click **Add to List**.

3. On the **Edit Filter** page, in the **Filter by** list, click **Session Type**. In the **Condition** list, click **Equals**. In the **Value** box, click **Web Proxy**. Click **Add to List**.

4. Click **Start Query**. Notice that only the Web Proxy client session from Den-Clt-01 is listed.

▶ **To prepare for the next practice**

1. You will need the Den-DC-01 virtual machine, the Den-Msg-01 virtual machine, the Gen-Web-01 virtual machine, and the Den-ISA-01 virtual machine for the next practice.

2. Shut down Den-Clt-01 without saving any changes and start the Den-Msg-01 virtual machine.

Lesson: Configuring Logging

* What Is Logging?
* Log Storage Options
* How to Configure Logging
* How to View ISA Server Logs
* How to Configure Log Filter Definitions

Introduction

ISA Server provides the option to log all activity related to the Firewall service, Web proxy service, and the SMTP message screener. These logs can be used to provide usage information and also to provide information about malicious or inappropriate activity on the server. This lesson describes how to configure logging on ISA Server 2004.

Lesson objectives

After completing this lesson, you will be able to:

- Define logging.
- Identify log storage formats.
- Configure logging of services.
- View ISA Server logs.
- Configure log filter definitions.

What Is Logging?

The logging feature:

● Provides extended log storage to generate reports, analyze trends, or investigate security issues

● Can be configured to provide Firewall logging, Web proxy logging, and SMTP message screener logging

● Provides a log viewer to assist in monitoring and analyzing server activity for MSDE-based logs

Introduction

You can monitor ISA Server activity by configuring logging. By default, when ISA Server 2004 is installed, logging is enabled for all components. The main benefit of ISA Server logging is that, in addition to viewing log information from within the ISA Server Management console, you can also configure extended log storage to generate reports, analyze trends, or investigate security issues.

Which components can be logged?

ISA Server 2004 provides the ability to monitor activity and perform the following types of logging tasks:

■ *Firewall Logging*. Records attempts to communicate by using the Firewall service.

■ *Web Proxy Logging*. Records attempts to communicate by using the Web proxy service.

■ *SMTP Message Screener Logging*. Records SMTP Message Screener events and status information.

Viewing log entries

You can use the ISA Server log viewer to monitor and analyze server activity. Each time an event is logged, it is displayed in the log viewer if the log viewer is active. You can also filter the data displayed in the log viewer to only show data that meets specific criteria. You can view the online logs or you can run a query against a repository to see archived log information.

You can also copy and paste data displayed in the log viewer to a text file for further analysis as required.

Note The SMTP Message Screener log information is not displayed in the log viewer because the information is stored in a text log file. Only logs that are stored in Microsoft Data Engine (MSDE) format can be viewed using the log viewer.

Log Storage Options

Log storage option:	Explanation:
MSDE	• Logs can be viewed in the log viewer • Default format for Web proxy and Firewall Service logs
SQL database	• Logs can be stored on separate server • Logs can be analyzed by using database tools
File	• Logs can be stored in W3C or ISA Server format • Only available format for SMTP message screener logs

The MSDE and log files are stored by default in the ISALogs folder, which is located in the ISA Server installation folder

Introduction

To meet your security and trend analysis requirements, it is important to understand your options for storing ISA Server log information. You can store ISA Server log information in one of the following:

- Microsoft Data Engine (MSDE) database
- SQL database
- File

Storing logs in MSDE format

Storing a log in MSDE format provides the ability for events to be viewed in the log viewer. MSDE databases are limited to two gigabytes in size. When a log exceeds the size limit, ISA Server automatically creates a new database. Also, at the beginning of each day a new log-file database is created. However, the log viewer displays the data as if it were in a single database.

Note By default, the log information for Web proxy and Firewall Service logs are saved in MSDE format.

Storing logs in a SQL database

You can store log information in a SQL database to provide advanced storage and analysis capabilities. The use of a SQL database also provides the ability to store the logs on a remote server or storage location.

Note The system policy rule named **Allow remote logging using NetBIOS transport to trusted servers** must be enabled to log to a SQL database.

Saving logs to a file format

You can save ISA Server logs to a file in one of the following formats:

- *World Wide Web Consortium (W3C) format.* W3C logs contain both data and directives describing the version, date, and logged fields. The tab character is used as a delimiter. Date and time are in Coordinated Universal Time (UTC) format.

- *ISA Server format.* ISA Server format contains only data with no directives. All fields are always logged and the comma character is used as a delimiter. The date and time fields are in local time.

ISA Server log files are limited to two gigabytes in size. When a log exceeds the size limit, ISA Server automatically creates a new file. Also, at the beginning of each day a new log file is automatically created.

Note The SMTP Message Screener log information is saved by default in file format. It cannot be saved to a database format.

Log maintenance

The MSDE and log files are stored by default in the ISALogs folder, which is located in the ISA Server installation folder.

When you configure ISA Server to use an MSDE database or use a file for logging, you can configure how long log information should be stored on the local disk as well as how much disk space should be allocated for logging.

ISA Server checks every 10 minutes that logs do not exceed the specified limits.

How to Configure Logging

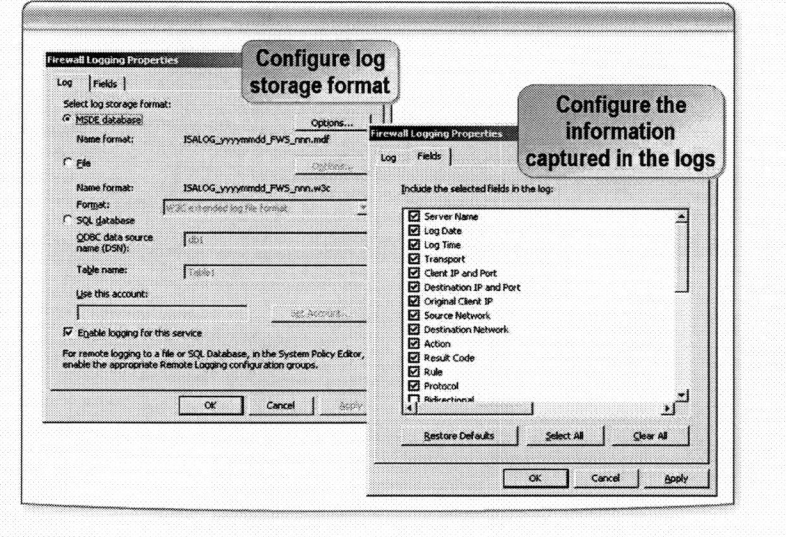

Configuring logging of ISA services

To configure logging for the Firewall service, Web proxy service, or the SMTP Message Screener, complete the following steps.

1. In ISA Server Management, click **Monitoring**.

2. Click the **Logging** view.

3. On the **Tasks** tab, choose one of the following tasks, depending on which service you are configuring:

   - Configure Firewall Logging

   - Configure Web Proxy Logging

   - Configure SMTP Message Screener Logging

4. Configure the **Log** options. The options are described in the following table:

Log option	Choose this option to:
MSDE database	Configure the log to use the MSDE format. Click the **Options** button to configure additional settings such as the log file storage location and log file storage limits.
File	Configure the log to be stored in a file format. You can choose to save the file in either the W3C extended log file format or the ISA Server file format. Click the **Options** button to configure additional settings such as the storage location of the log file and log file storage limits.
SQL Database	Configure the log file to be stored in an Open Database Connectivity (ODBC)-compliant database. Additional settings include the ODBC data source name, the table name, and the account name to use when logging on to the log database.
Enable logging for this service	Specify whether logging is enabled for this service. If not selected, no events are recorded in the log.

5. Click the **Fields** tab to configure the fields to include in the log.

How to View ISA Server Logs

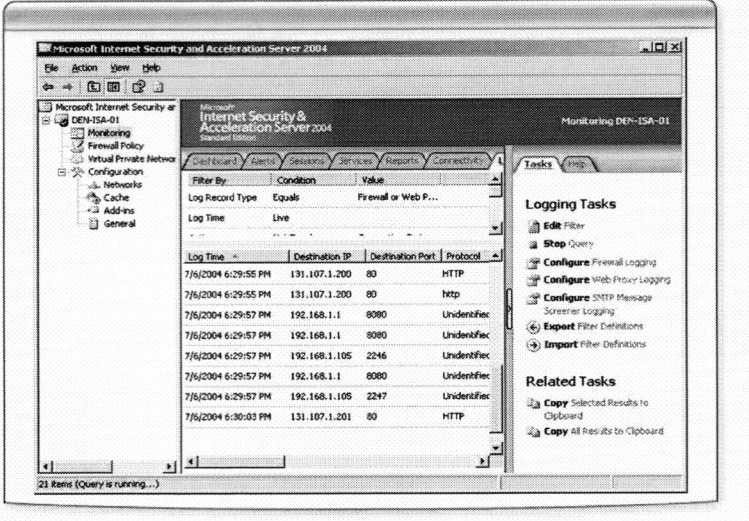

Introduction

The method you use to view an ISA Server log depends on the type of log and the storage format. Any log stored in the MSDE format can be viewed using the log viewer. Logs that are stored in the file format can be viewed with a standard text editor such as Notepad. Logs that are stored in a SQL database can be viewed using SQL reporting software such as Microsoft SQL Server™ 2000 Reporting Services, located at http://www.microsoft.com/sql/reporting/default.asp.

Viewing log files stored in the file format

To view a log file stored in the file format, browse to C:\Program Files\ Microsoft ISA Server\ISALogs or an alternate location if you moved the log files. Use Notepad to open one of the following file types:

- ISALOG_*yyyymmdd*_FWS_*nnn*.w3c. This file type refers to the W3C format. *yyyy* represents the year, *mm* represents the month, *dd* represents the day, and *nnn* represents multiple log files created on the same day.

- ISALOG_*yyyymmdd*_FWS_*nnn*.iis. This file type refers to the ISA Server file format. *yyyy* represents the year, mm represents the month, *dd* represents the day, and *nnn* represents multiple log files created on the same day.

Note FWS refers to the Firewall service, WEB refers to the Web proxy service, and EML refers to the SMTP Message Screener.

Viewing log files stored in the MSDE format

To view a log file stored in the MSDE format, complete the following steps.

1. In **ISA Server Management**, click **Monitoring**.

2. Click the **Logging** tab.

3. To view the information being logged at the current time, click **Start Query**.

4. To view archived information or to limit the number of entries in the log viewer, configure a filter to view specific information contained within the log files.

How to Configure Log Filter Definitions

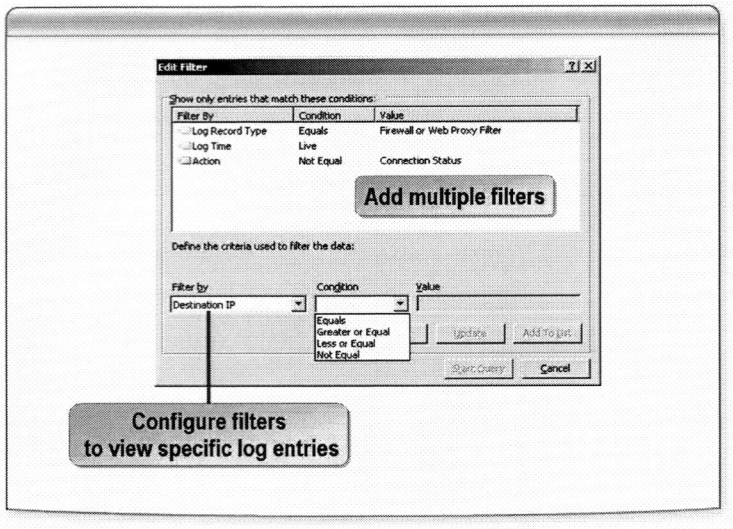

Introduction

The log filter is used to limit the number of entries displayed in the log viewer to entries matching specified criteria. The log filter can be configured to view live data or historical data stored in the MSDE database.

Configuring log filter definitions

To configure log filter definitions, complete the following steps.

1. In **ISA Server Management**, click **Monitoring**.

2. Click the **Logging** tab.

3. In the Task pane, click **Edit Filter**.

4. Configure the **Log Record Type** with one of the following values:

   • Firewall

   • Firewall or Web Proxy Filter

   • Web Proxy Filter

5. Configure the **Log Time** to provide the appropriate **Condition**, consisting of date and time ranges with which to filter the data. Choose **Live** to show current activity.

Note   When you create a filter, you must specify exactly one **Log Time** and one **Log Record Type**. These two categories cannot be removed. Also, the log viewer displays log data only if it matches all of the expressions included in the filter. The filter expressions are combined using the logical AND operator.

---

6. Add additional **Categories**, **Conditions**, and **Values** as needed.

7. Click **Start Query** to begin viewing the results of the filter.

Tip   You can save the filter by clicking **Save Filter Definitions** in the Task pane. To recall a saved filter, click **Load Filter Definitions** and then select the saved file.

Lesson: Configuring Reports

* What Are Reports?
* How to Configure the Report Summary Database
* How to Generate a Report
* How to Create a Recurring Report Job
* How to View Reports
* How to Publish Reports

Introduction

ISA Server can be configured to produce reports that provide summary information about activity that occurs on the server. These reports can be created on an on-demand basis, or can be scheduled to be created on a recurring scheduled basis. This lesson describes how to configure and use the reports on ISA Server.

Lesson objectives

After completing this lesson, you will be able to:

- Describe reports and the information included in the reports.
- Configure the report summary database.
- Create a report.
- Create a recurring report job.
- View a report.
- Publish a report.

What Are Reports?

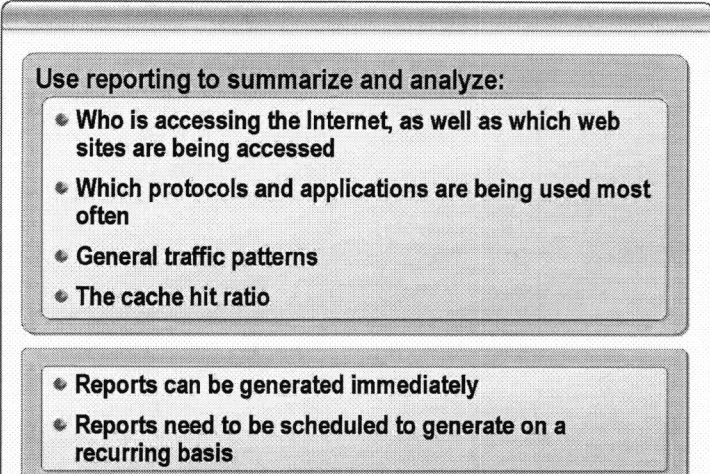

Use reporting to summarize and analyze:

- Who is accessing the Internet, as well as which web sites are being accessed
- Which protocols and applications are being used most often
- General traffic patterns
- The cache hit ratio

- Reports can be generated immediately
- Reports need to be scheduled to generate on a recurring basis

---

What are reports?

ISA Server 2004 provides extensive reporting capabilities to assist you in analyzing ISA Server activities. *Reports* are collections of information generated from data collected from the ISA Server log files. You can use the reporting feature to summarize and analyze common usage patterns such as:

- Internet users and the Web sites that are accessed.

- The protocols and applications most often used.

- General traffic patterns.

- The cache hit ratio.

You can also use reports to monitor the security of your network, such as attempts to access internal resources or the number of connections to a published server.

Generating reports

You can generate a report immediately or you can schedule reports to generate on a recurring basis. The report can include daily, weekly, monthly, or yearly data.

Report contents

ISA Server provides the following report content options:

- *Summary Reports*. Summary reports include a set of statistics about ISA Server usage. Summary reports combine data from the Web proxy service logs and Firewall service logs.

- *Web Usage Reports*. Web usage reports include a set of reports that display top Web users, common responses, and Web browsers. These reports show how an organization uses the Web and are based on the Web proxy service logs.

- *Application Usage Reports*. Application usage reports display Internet application usage, including incoming and outgoing traffic, top users, client applications, and destinations. Application usage reports can help you to plan network capacity and determine bandwidth policies. Application usage reports are based on the Firewall service logs.

■ *Traffic and Utilization Reports*. Traffic and utilization reports display total Internet usage by application, protocol, and direction; average traffic and peak simultaneous connections; cache hit ratios; errors; and other statistics. Traffic and utilization reports can help you plan and monitor network capacity and determine bandwidth policies. Traffic and utilization reports combine data from the Web proxy service logs and the Firewall service logs.

■ *Security Reports*. Security reports list attempts to breach network security. Security reports can help identify attacks or security violations after they have occurred. Security reports are based on the Web proxy service logs and the Firewall service logs.

You can modify the information that is displayed for each of these logs. To do this, access the **Reports** tab in **ISA Server Management**, and then click the appropriate report under **Customize Reports**.

How reporting works

ISA Server reports are based on the Web proxy and Microsoft Firewall service logs. Each summary log from ISA Server is combined into a database which, by default, resides in the ISASummaries folder. When a report is created, all relevant summary databases are combined into a single report database. The report is then created based on the combined summaries. At a specific time, an application called DailySum.exe summarizes the Web proxy and Firewall service log information. DailySum.exe always runs on the computer running ISA Server regardless of whether you create or schedule reports. Two log summaries are saved; one with a daily summary and one with a monthly summary. At the beginning of each month, Dailysum.exe creates another monthly summary that summarizes all the past month's daily summaries.

Note   For information on what log fields are included in the reports, see "How the report mechanism works," in Microsoft ISA Server Help.

How to Configure the Report Summary Database

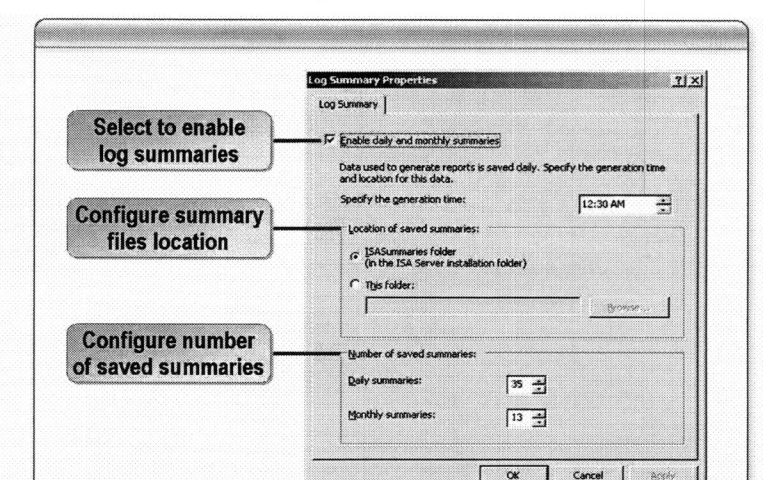

Configuring the log summary database

The report summary database contains the report information created daily from the ISA Server log files. By default, daily and monthly log summaries are generated automatically at 12:30 A.M. You can change these parameters to fit your organization's needs. To configure the log summary database settings, complete the following steps.

1. In **ISA Server Management**, click **Monitoring**.

2. Click the **Reports** tab.

3. In the Task pane, scroll to the **Related Tasks** section and then click **Configure Log Summary**.

4. The **Log Summary Properties** dialog box contains the following options:

Log Summary options	Choose this option to:
Enable daily and monthly summaries	Click the check box to enable or disable the creation of the daily and monthly log summaries.
Specify the generation time	Specify the time that the log summaries are generated.
Location of saved summaries	Specify a location to save the summary database information. By default, the ISASummaries folder is used.
Number of saved summaries	Specify the number of saved daily and monthly summaries to save.

How to Generate a Report

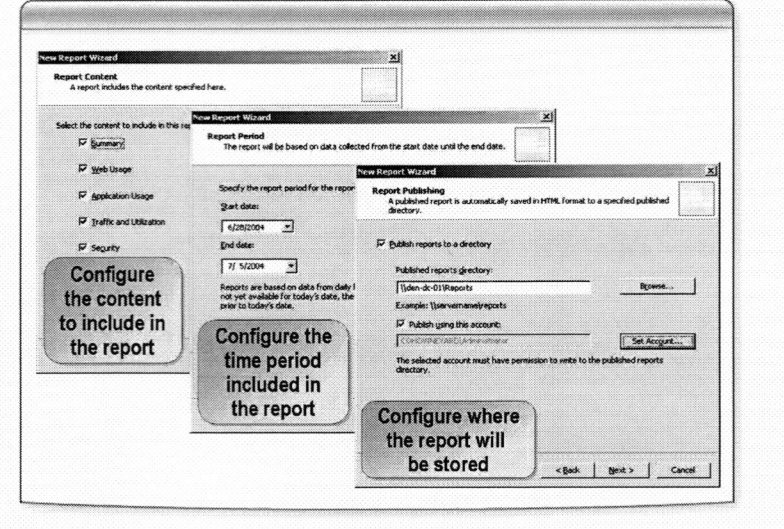

Introduction

You can generate a new report at any time using the ISA Server Management console. When you generate a new report, ISA Server displays the information that you select from the summary logs.

Note Because ISA Server reports are based on the log summary information, any information that is added to the logs after the log summary is created is not included in the report. This means that, in most cases, the reports do not contain the current day's information.

Generating a report

The following steps provide an overview of how to generate a report. To generate a new report, complete the following steps.

1. In **ISA Server Management**, click **Monitoring**.

2. Click the **Reports** tab.

3. In the Task pane, click **Generate a New Report**. The New Report Wizard starts.

4. On the **Welcome to the New Report Wizard** page, type a name for the report.

5. On the **Report Content** page, select the check box next to the content you want to include in the report. The content choices are:

- *Summary*. This section includes summarized information about network traffic usage, sorted by application.

- *Web Usage*. This section includes information about top Web users, common responses, and browsers.

- *Application Usage*. This section includes Internet application usage information about top users, client applications, and destinations.

- *Traffic and Utilization*. This section includes total Internet usage by application, protocol, and direction. These reports also show average traffic and peak simultaneous connections, cache hit ratio, errors, and other statistics.

- *Security*. This section lists attempts to breach network security.

6. On the **Report Period** page, specify the start and end dates for the report.

7. The **Report Publishing** page enables you to publish reports to a directory. You have the following options for report publishing:

Report Publishing option	Choose this option to:
Publish reports to a directory	Click the check box to enable or disable report publishing to a directory.
Published reports directory	Type a path or click **Browse** to enter a location to store the published reports.
Publish using this account	Click the check box and enter an account name that has permission to write to the published reports directory.

The **Send E-mail Notification** page provides the option to configure e-mail notification for when a report is generated.

8. Click **Finish** to close the wizard.

The new report is shown in the Report view. The status column shows the report as Generating. When the generation is complete, the status will show as Completed.

Note   The Microsoft ISA Server Job Scheduler service must be running to create a report.

How to Create a Recurring Report Job

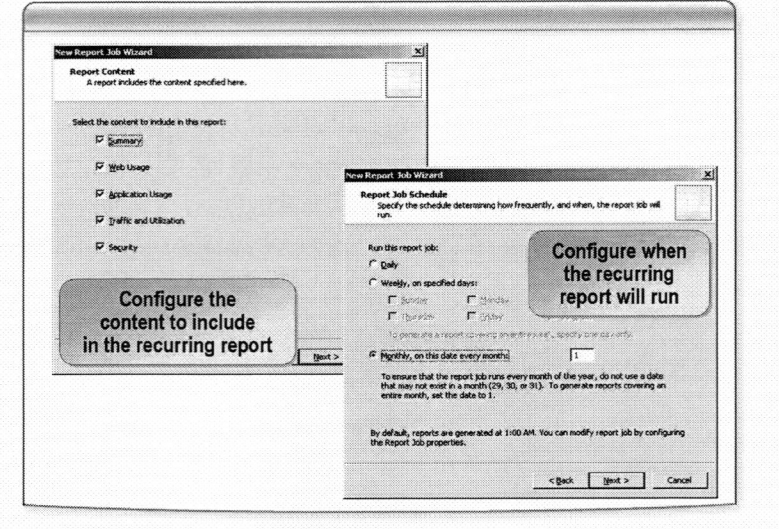

Creating recurring report jobs

Your organization may need weekly or monthly reports for auditing and trend analysis requirements. Instead of manually creating reports, a recurring report job can be configured that will automatically create the reports for you.

To create a recurring report job, complete the following steps.

1. In **ISA Server Management**, click **Monitoring**.

2. Click the **Reports** tab.

3. Click **Create and Configure Report Jobs**.

4. In the **Report Jobs Properties** dialog box, click **Add**. The **New Report Job Wizard** starts.

5. On the **Welcome to the New Report Job Wizard** page, type a name for the report job.

6. On the **Report Content** page of the wizard, choose the option to customize the report content. Select the check box next to the content you want to include in the report.

7. On the **Report Job Schedule** page, specify the schedule. The schedule determines how frequently the report job will run. The options include:

   - Daily.

   - Weekly, or on specified days.

   - Monthly, or on a specific date of every month.

Note By default, reports are generated at 1:00 A.M. You can change the report job by configuring the Report job properties.

8. On the **Report Publishing** page, choose the option to publish reports to a directory.

9. On the **Send E-mail Notification** page, choose the option to configure e-mail notification for when a report is generated.

10. Click **Finish** to close the wizard.

The report job is listed in the **Report Job** page of the **Report Jobs Properties** dialog box. The only way to view this dialog box is to click the **Create and Configure Report Jobs** link in the Task pane.

After the scheduled report job runs, a new report appears in the Reports view of ISA Server Management.

How to View Reports

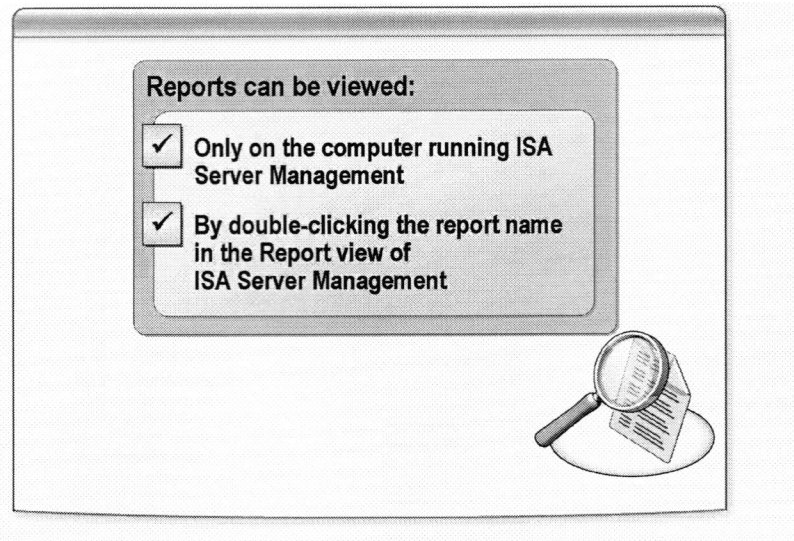

Viewing Reports

After a report is generated, it can be viewed only on the computer running ISA Server Management. On any other computer, the report shows either empty data, or a page with empty frames and a message that the "Page cannot be displayed."

As each report is generated, the report is displayed in the Reports view. The following columns are displayed by default:

- *Report Name*. This column displays the name of the report.

- *Period*. This column displays how frequently the report is generated.

- *Start Date*. This column displays the start date of the report. Information is shown only from this start date.

- *End Date*. This column displays the end date of the report. Information is shown only up to this end date.

- *Status*. This column displays whether the report is being generated or completed.

An additional column is available to be displayed if required:

- *Generation Date*. This column displays the date on which the report was created.

You can view a report by double-clicking the report name in the Report view of ISA Server Management. You can also select the report and then click **View Selected Report** in the Task pane. The report is displayed in Microsoft Internet Explorer.

How to Publish Reports

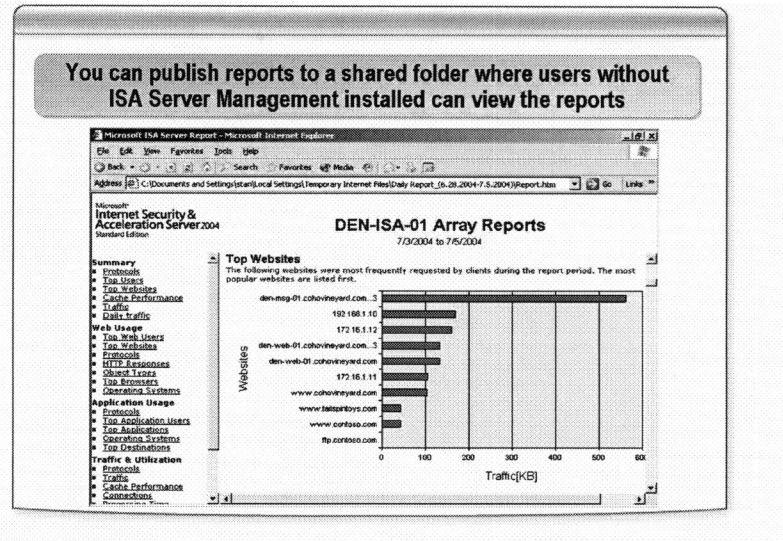

Publishing reports

To make reports more available, you can publish them to a shared folder. Any individual who needs access to the reports needs to have Read permissions to this folder. Users do not need to have ISA Server Management installed on their computers to view the reports.

To successfully publish a report, the IsaRepGen.exe process must have Write permissions to the publishing folder. If you manually publish a report, the IsaRepGen.exe process uses the credentials of the user publishing the report. When you publish a recurring report, you need to configure the credentials IsaRepGen.exe uses to publish the reports.

To publish reports, complete the following steps.

1. In **ISA Server Management**, click **Monitoring**.
2. Click the **Reports** tab and then click the applicable report.
3. On the Tasks tab, click **Publish Selected Report**.
4. In the **Browse for** folder, select the folder in which the published reports folder should be created.

To view the published report, browse to the folder where the report was published and open the Report.htm file. This file contains links to all the other information in the report.

Practice: Configuring Reports

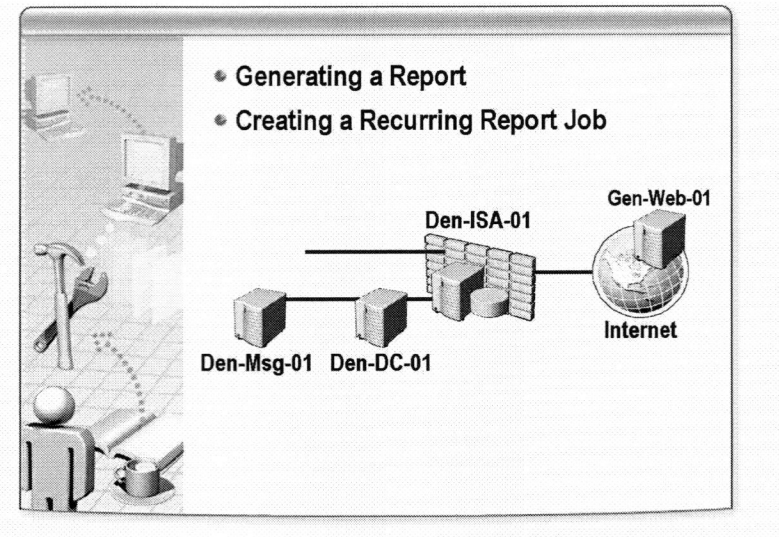

Introduction

In this practice, you will generate a report in ISA Server Management. In addition, you will create a recurring report job that will create and publish a monthly report.

▶ **To prepare for this practice**

1. You will need the Den-DC-01 virtual machine, the Den-Msg-01 virtual machine, the Gen-Web-01 virtual machine, and the Den-ISA-01 virtual machine for this practice.

2. If necessary, start or resume the required virtual machines and then, on Den-ISA-01, log on to the cohovineyard domain with your user name and password.

Practice

▶ **Generating a report**

1. In **ISA Server Management**, click **Monitoring**.

2. Click the **Reports** tab.

3. In the Task pane, click **Generate a New Report**. The **New Report Wizard** starts.

4. On the **Welcome to the New Report Wizard** page, type **Daily Report** and click **Next**.

5. On the **Report Content** page, ensure that all the check boxes for the report content are selected. Click **Next**.

6. On the **Report Period** page, in the **Start date** box, select the date on which this course started. Click **Next**.

7. On the **Report Publishing** page, click **Next**.

8. On the **Send E-mail Notification** page, click **Next**.

9. Click **Finish** to close the wizard.

10. Wait until the **Daily Report** status is **Completed** and then double-click the report. In the **Internet Explorer** dialog box, click **Close**.

11. In the **Internet Explorer** warning dialog box, click **In the future, do not show this message** and click **OK**.

12. View the information that is provided in the report and then close the report.

▶ **Creating a recurring report job**

1. Switch to Den-DC-01 and create a folder on the C: drive named WebReports. Share the folder. Configure the **Share Permissions** on the folder to grant **Change** and **Read** permission to the ISA Admins group. Modify the **Security** settings on the folder to grant the ISA Admins **Modify** permissions.

2. On Den-ISA-01, in **ISA Server Management**, click **Create and Configure Report Jobs**.

3. In the **Report Jobs Properties** dialog box, click **Add**. The **New Report Job Wizard** starts.

4. In the **Welcome to the New Report Job Wizard** page, type **Monthly Report** and click **Next**.

5. On the **Report Content** page, ensure that all the check boxes for the report content are selected. Click **Next**.

6. On the **Report Job Schedule** page, click **Monthly, on this date every month**. In the text box, enter today's date. Click **Next**.

7. On the **Report Publishing** page, click **Publish reports to a directory**. In the Published reports directory text box, type **\\den-dc-01\webreports**.

8. Click **Publish using this account** and then click **Set Account**. Enter cohovineyard*yourusername* and password and click **OK**.

9. On the **Report Publishing** page, click **Next**.

10. On the **Send E-mail Notification** page, click **Send e-mail notification for completed reports** and fill in the following information:

    a. SMTP server: **den-msg-01.cohovineyard.com**

    b. From: **ISAServerReports**

    c. To: **administrator@cohovineyard.com**

    d. Message: **The monthly report has been generated.**

    e. Click **Include a link to the completed report in the message**.

    f. Click **Test** and click **OK**.

11. Click **Next**. On the **Finishing the New Report Job Wizard**, review the configuration and then click **Finish**.

12. On the **Report Jobs** tab, click **Monthly Report** and click **Edit**.

13. On the **Schedule** tab, set the **Generation hour:** value to a time five minutes from now.

14. Click **OK** twice.

Lesson: Monitoring Connectivity

* How Does Connectivity Monitoring Work?
* Configuring Connectivity Monitoring

Introduction

One of the monitoring components available in ISA Server 2004 is connectivity monitoring. This feature can be used to monitor connectivity between the computer running ISA Server 2004 and both internal and external network resources. This lesson describes how to configure connectivity monitoring on ISA Server 2004.

Lesson objectives

After completing this lesson, you will be able to:

- Understand how connectivity monitoring works in ISA Server 2004.
- Configure connectivity monitoring.

How Does Connectivity Monitoring Work?

Connectivity monitoring:

- **Uses connectivity verifiers to monitor connections from ISA Server to other servers or URLs**
- **Can be configured to use any of the following in connection methods:**
  - Ping to check for simple network connectivity
  - TCP connection to verify that a service is running on the destination server
  - HTTP GET request to verify that a Web server is running on the destination server

Introduction

In addition to monitoring activity directly on the computer running ISA Server, you can also use connectivity monitoring to monitor the availability of connections between ISA Server and other servers on the network.

What is connectivity monitoring?

When you use connectivity monitoring, you can verify connectivity with other computers by regularly monitoring connections from the computer running ISA Server to any specific computer or URL on any network. When you configure a connectivity verifier, you can configure the method the verifier will use to determine connectivity. The following options are available:

- *Ping.* When you configure a connectivity verifier to use this method, ISA Server sends an ICMP ECHO_REQUEST to the specified server and waits for an ICMP ECHO_REPLY. This test checks for simple network connectivity.

- *TCP connection.* When you configure a verifier to use this method, ISA Server tries to establish a Transmission Control Protocol (TCP) connection using a specified port number on the specified server. For example, if you are testing connectivity with a domain controller, ISA Server will try to establish a connection using the Lightweight Directory Access Protocol (LDAP) port (number 389). This test not only checks for network connectivity but also verifies that a specific service is running on the server and can be reached by ISA Server.

- *HTTP GET request.* When you configure a verifier to use this method, ISA Server sends an HTTP GET command to the specified server or URL and waits for the reply. This tests for network connectivity and verifies that a Web server is running on the destination server and can be reached by ISA Server. When a connectivity verifier that issues an HTTP request to check connectivity is created, ISA Server enables a system policy rule that allows HTTP and HTTPS traffic from the Local Host network to All Networks, named **Allow HTTP/HTTPS from ISA Server to selected servers for connectivity verifiers**.

When you configure a connectivity verifier, it is categorized into one of the following groups: Active Directory® directory service, Dynamic Host Configuration Protocol (DHCP), DNS, Published Servers, Web, and others. The server group status for each group is displayed on the Dashboard view so you can quickly identify if there is a problem with a particular service.

Configuring Connectivity Monitoring

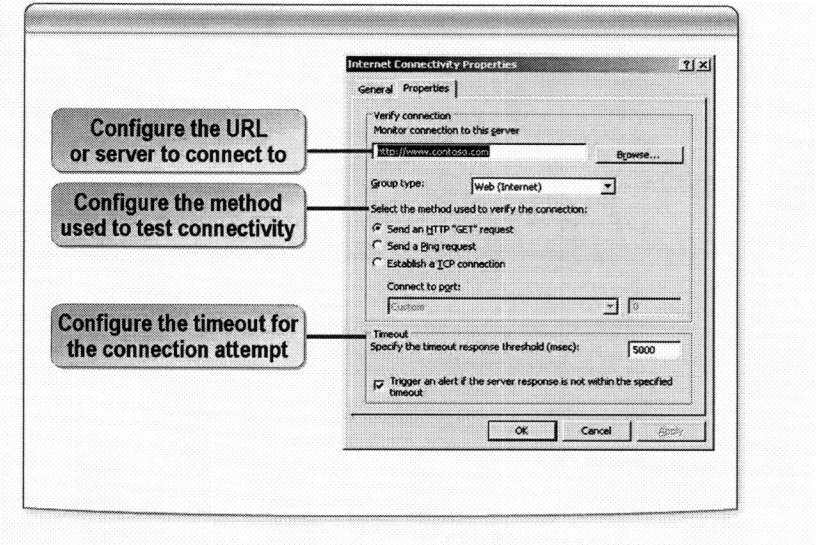

Introduction

To configure connectivity monitoring, complete the following steps.

1. In **ISA Server Management**, click **Connectivity**.

2. On the **Tasks** tab, click **Create New Connectivity Verifier**.

3. On the **Welcome to the New Connectivity Verifier Wizard** page, type a name and then click **Next**.

4. On the **Connectivity Verification Details** page, fill in the information listed in the following table:

Configuration Option	Use this option to:
Monitor connectivity to this server or URL	Type the name or URL of the server that the connectivity is verifying.
Group used to categorize this connectivity verifier	Select the group this verifier belongs to.
Verification method	Choose the verification method used for this verifier. You can choose to use an HTTP GET request, Ping request, or a TCP connection. If you choose the TCP connection method, you can also choose the protocol and port number used to create the TCP connection.

5. Click **Next**, and then **Finish** to complete the wizard.

6. By default, the connectivity verifier will test connectivity with the specified server every 5,000 milliseconds. You can modify this setting by right-clicking the verifier in the **Connectivity** view and clicking **Properties**. On the **Properties** page, modify the value for **Specify the timeout response (msec)**. At the same time, you can also configure whether the verifier will trigger an alert if the connection fails.

Practice: Configuring Connectivity Monitoring

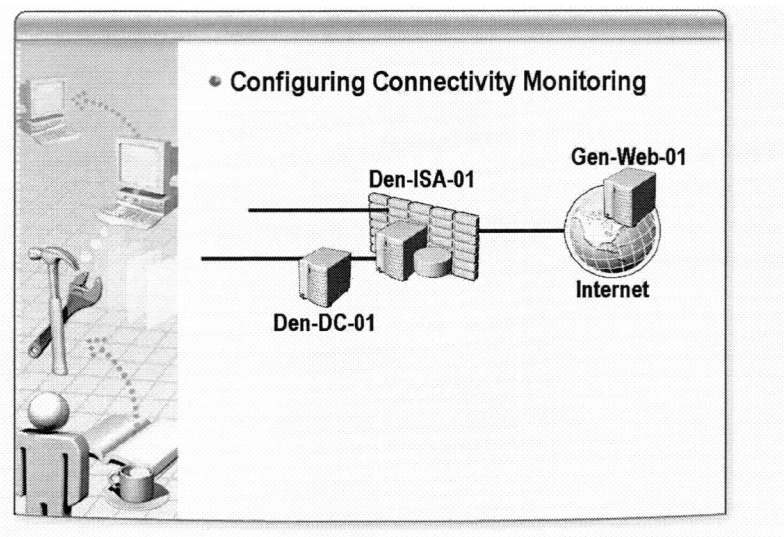

Introduction

In this practice, you will configure connectivity monitoring in ISA Server Management.

▶ **To prepare for this practice**

1. You will need the Den-DC-01 virtual machine, the Gen-Web-01 virtual machine, and the Den-ISA-01 virtual machine for this practice.

2. If necessary, start or resume the required virtual machines and then, on Den-ISA-01, log on to the cohovineyard domain with your user name and password.

Practice

▶ **Configuring connectivity monitoring**

1. In **ISA Server Management**, click **Connectivity**.

2. On the **Tasks** tab, click **Create New Connectivity Verifier**.

3. On the **Welcome to the New Connectivity Verifier Wizard** page, type **Internet Connection Test** and then click **Next**.

4. On the **Connectivity Verification Details** page, fill in the following information:

   a. Monitor connectivity to this server or URL: **www.tailspintoys.com**

   b. Group used to categorize this connectivity verifier: **Web (Internet)**

   c. Verification Method: **Send an HTTP GET request**

   Click **Next**.

5. On the **Completing the New Connectivity Verifier Wizard** page, review the configuration and then click **Finish**.

6. In the **Enable HTTP Connectivity Verification** dialog box, click **Yes**.

7. Double-click **Internet Connection Test**. On the **Properties** page, under **Timeout**, change the response threshold to 10000 milliseconds. Click **OK**.

8. Create another connectivity verifier with the following configuration:

   a. Connectivity Verifier Name: **DC Connection Test**

   b. Monitor connectivity to this server or URL:
      den-dc-01.cohovineyard.com

   c. Group used to categorize this connectivity verifier: **Active Directory**

   d. Verification Method: **Establish a TCP connection using this protocol: LDAP.**

9. Create another connectivity verifier with the following configuration:

   a. Connectivity Verifier Name: **DNS Connection Test**

   b. Monitor connectivity to this server or URL:
      den-dc-01.cohovineyard.com

   c. Group used to categorize this connectivity verifier: **DNS**

   d. Verification Method: **Establish a TCP connection using this protocol: DNS**

10. Create another connectivity verifier with the following configuration:

    a. Connectivity Verifier Name: **Network Connection Test**

    b. Monitor connectivity to this server or URL: **192.168.1.10**

    c. Group used to categorize this connectivity verifier: **Others**

    d. Verification Method: **Send a Ping request**

11. Click **Apply** to apply the changes and then click **OK** when the changes have been applied.

Lesson: Monitoring Services and Performance

* Monitoring ISA Server Services
* Performance Monitoring with ISA Server

Introduction

ISA Server enables two additional monitoring options, including monitoring the services on the computer running ISA Server and monitoring the server performance. This lesson explains how to implement these monitoring components.

Lesson objectives

After completing this lesson, you will be able to:

* Monitor and manage ISA Server services.
* Identify the performance components to monitor by using ISA Server.

Monitoring ISA Server Services

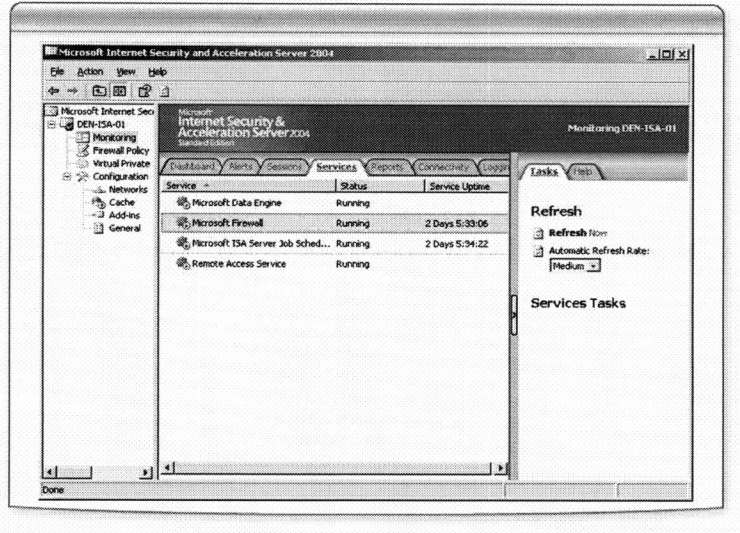

Introduction

When ISA Server 2004 is installed, the following Windows operating system services are also installed:

- Microsoft Firewall service
- Microsoft ISA Server Control service
- Microsoft ISA Server Job Scheduler service
- Microsoft Data Engine (MSDE)
- Microsoft ISA Server Storage

Monitoring and managing services

You can use the **Services** view in **ISA Server Management** to view and control the status of some of the ISA Server services. By default, the Microsoft Firewall, Microsoft ISA Server Job Scheduler, and Microsoft Data Engine services are listed in the Services view. As additional services are installed or enabled on ISA Server, these services may also appear in the Services view. For example, when ISA Server is configured as a VPN server, the Remote Access Service is added to the Services view.

The services listed in the Services view can be monitored or managed in ISA Server Management. Other services, such as the ISA Server Control service and the Microsoft ISA Server Storage service, must be managed using the Services console from the Administrative Tools folder, or by using a command line.

Performance Monitoring with ISA Server

Performance Objects	Explanation
ISA Server Firewall Engine	Includes performance counters to monitor connections and throughput for the firewall engine
ISA Server Cache	Includes performance counters to monitor the memory, disk, and URL activity associated with the cache as well as cache performance
ISA Server Firewall Service	Includes counters to monitor Firewall service connections and associated services such as DNS. This object monitors only Firewall client connections
ISA Server Web Proxy Service	Includes counters to monitor the number of users and the rate at which ISA Server transfers data for Web Proxy clients to remote and upstream servers

Monitoring the ISA Server counters as well as other performance counters to determine server performance and bottlenecks

Introduction

ISA Server 2004 also uses the Windows 2000 or Microsoft Windows Server™ 2003 Performance Monitor to monitor server performance. You can use the default ISA Server Performance monitor or create a custom view of server performance.

ISA Server performance objects

The ISA Server installation configures several new performance objects that you can use to monitor system performance on the computer running ISA Server. You view the performance objects and their associated performance counters in real time in System Monitor. System Monitor is a monitoring tool that is included with Windows 2000 and Windows Server 2003. You can also log performance data and create alerts from the data by using Performance Log and Alerts.

The ISA Server performance objects are listed in the following table:

Object	Explanation
ISA Server Firewall Engine	Includes performance counters to monitor connections and throughput for the Firewall engine. Use these counters to monitor the number of client connections, the number of allowed and dropped packets, and the number of bytes passed through the Firewall engine. For example, use the **Active Connections** counter to monitor the number of clients currently connected to ISA Server.
ISA Server Cache	Includes performance counters to monitor the memory, disk, and URL activity associated with the cache. Use these performance counters to monitor the effectiveness of the cache for clients. For example, you can use the **Disk URL Retrieve Rate** performance counter to determine the rate at which URLs are retrieved from the disk cache.
ISA Server Firewall Service	Includes performance counters to monitor Firewall service connections and associated services such as DNS. This object monitors only Firewall client connections. For example, you can use the **Active Sessions** performance counter to monitor the number of Firewall client sessions that are running simultaneously.
ISA Server Web Proxy Service	Includes counters to monitor the number of users and the rate at which ISA Server transfers data to remote and upstream servers. For example, you can use the **Total Users** performance counter to monitor the total number of users that are connected to the Web proxy service.

When you install ISA Server, a pre-configured Performance monitor is created to monitor the most critical ISA Server performance counters. To access this Performance monitor, click **ISA Server Performance Monitor** in the **Microsoft ISA Server** menu on the **Start** menu.

In addition to monitoring the ISA Server–specific performance counters, also monitor the other performance counters such as memory usage, CPU usage, and disk usage. Use the combination of ISA Server performance information and the Windows server performance information to detect potential performance issues and bottlenecks on the computer running ISA Server.

Lab: Monitoring ISA Server 2004

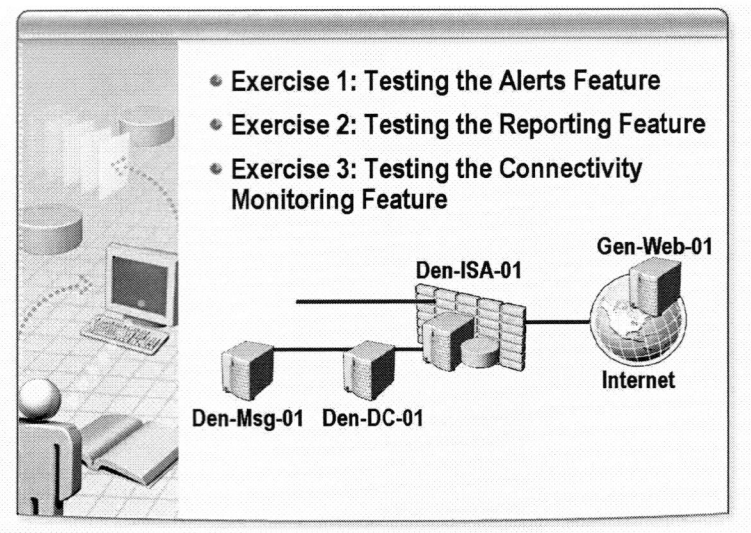

Objectives

After completing this lab, you will be able to:

■ Test the alerts feature in Microsoft Internet Security and Acceleration (ISA) Server 2004.

■ Test the reporting feature in ISA Server 2004

■ Test the connectivity feature in ISA Server 2004.

Note This lab focuses on the concepts in this module and, as a result, might not comply with Microsoft security recommendations. For example, the Administrator passwords are not as complex as recommended. Additionally, most of the actions performed in this lab are performed while logged on as an Administrator. A better security practice would be to log on as a normal user and use the Runas option to start administrative applications.

Scenario

You have deployed ISA Server at Coho Vineyard. You have configured ISA Server to publish internal Web sites as well as internal servers running Microsoft Exchange Server. You are now implementing a monitoring procedure on ISA Server. You are concerned about attack attempts on the computer running ISA Server, so you want to create an alert when it is under attack. As well, you have configured a recurring report job to publish usage reports every month. You have also configured a connectivity monitoring policy by which ISA Server monitors connectivity to several internal and external servers. You would now like to test these monitoring features on ISA Server.

To prepare for this lab:

1. You will need the Den-DC-01 virtual machine, the Den-ISA-01 virtual machine, the Den-Msg-01 virtual machine, and the Gen-Web-01 virtual machine for this practice.

2. If necessary, start or resume the required virtual machines and then, on Den-ISA-01, log on to the cohovineyard domain with your user name and password.

Estimated time to complete this lab: 30 minutes

Exercise 1
Testing the Alerts Feature

In this exercise, you will test the alerts feature in ISA Server 2004 by performing actions that will trigger the alerts. You will test network configuration change alert that you created in the module practice.

Tasks	Detailed steps
1. Test the Network Configuration Change that you created in the practice by performing a port scan of the well-known port numbers on ISA Server.	a. On Den-ISA-01, click **Start**, point to **Control Panel**, then point to **Network Connections**, and then click **Perimeter**. b. On the **Perimeter Status** dialog box, click **Disable**. c. Open **ISA Server Management**, click **Monitoring**, and then click the **Alerts** tab. Press **Refresh Now**. d. When the alert appears, click the alert and read the alert description. Notice that there are two Network Configuration alerts; one is the default alert, while the other is the custom alert that you created. e. Right-click both alerts, and then click **Acknowledge**. f. Open **Event Viewer** and then open the **Application Log**. Notice the event created by Microsoft Firewall. g. Re-enable the Perimeter interface.
2. Confirm that the e-mail message associated with the alert has been sent to the Administrator account.	a. Log on to Den-Msg-01 using **cohovineyard\administrator** with a password of **P@ssw0rd**. b. Open Internet Explorer. In the **Internet Explorer** dialog box, click **In the future, do not show this message** and click **OK**. c. Connect to http://den-msg-01/exchange. d. Log on using **cohovineyard\administrator** with a password of **P@ssw0rd**. e. In the Internet Explorer warning message, click **Add**, and then click **Add** again and click **Close**. f. Confirm that the e-mail messages from ISAServerAlerts have arrived.

Exercise 2
Testing the Reporting Feature

In this exercise, you will confirm that the recurring report job ran successfully and that the Administrator received the e-mail message associated with the recurring report. You will also view the generated report.

Tasks	Detailed steps
1. Confirm that the e-mail message associated with the recurring report has arrived. View the report.	a. In Outlook Web Access on Den-Msg-01, confirm that a message from ISAServerReports has arrived. Open the message.
	b. Select the report location information in the clipboard and then paste it into a **Run** command.
	c. Click **OK**. Click **Close** to close the Internet Explorer warning page and view the report.

Exercise 3
Testing the Connectivity Monitoring Feature

In this exercise, you will test the connectivity monitoring feature in ISA Server 2004 by performing actions that will trigger the connectivity monitoring alerts. You will test all of the connectivity verifiers that you created in the practices in this module.

Tasks	Detailed steps
1. Test the **Internet Connection Test**.	a. On Den-ISA-01, reset all of the connectivity alerts. b. Switch to Gen-Web-01 and open **Internet Information Services (IIS) Manager**. c. Stop the **Tailspin Toys Web Site**. d. Switch back to Den-ISA-01 and wait for the **No connectivity** alert to appear. Review the contents of the alert and then right-click the alert. Click **Reset**. e. Switch to Gen-Web-01 and start the **Tailspin Toys Web Site**.
2. Test the **DNS Connection Test**.	a. Switch to Den-DC-01 and open a command prompt. b. Type **sc stop DNS**. c. Switch back to Den-ISA-01 and wait for the **No connectivity** alert to appear. Review the contents of the alert and then right-click the alert. Click **Acknowledge**. d. Switch back to Den-DC-01 and type **sc start DNS** in the command prompt window.
3. Test the **DC Connection Test** and the **Network Connection Test**.	a. Switch to Den-DC-01. b. Disable the **Local Area Connection**. c. Switch back to Den-ISA-01 and wait for the **No connectivity** alert to appear. Review the contents of the alert. Notice that all three alerts associated with Den-DC-01 report an error. Right-click the alert and click **Acknowledge**. d. Switch back to Den-DC-01 and re-enable the **Local Area Connection**.

To Prepare for the Next Lab

As you finish this lab, shut down all of the virtual machines that you used in the practice. To shut down the virtual machines, click **Close** from the **Action** menu. **Select Turn off and delete changes** and click **OK**.

Module 11: Implementing ISA Server 2004 Enterprise Edition

Contents

Overview

- Overview of ISA Server 2004 Enterprise Edition
- Planning an ISA Server 2004 Enterprise Edition Deployment
- Implementing ISA Server 2004 Enterprise Edition

Introduction

Microsoft® Internet Security and Acceleration (ISA) Server 2004 Standard Edition is an advanced firewall and proxy server. However, ISA Server Standard Edition is limited in its scalability because each ISA Server computer must be managed individually, and Standard Edition does not provide a means for load sharing or redundancy. This module explores the differences between ISA Server 2004 Standard Edition and ISA Server 2004 Enterprise Edition and then provides details about the Enterprise Edition features that enhance scalability. This module also includes details about how to install and manage ISA Server 2004 Enterprise Edition.

Objectives

After completing this module, you will be able to:

- Describe the features that are unique to ISA Server 2004 Enterprise Edition.

- Plan an ISA Server 2004 Enterprise Edition deployment.

- Install, configure, and manage ISA Server 2004 Enterprise Edition.

Lesson: Overview of ISA Server 2004 Enterprise Edition

- Animation: Comparing ISA Server 2004 Enterprise Edition and Standard Edition
- Why Deploy ISA Server Enterprise Edition?
- What Is Active Directory Application Mode?
- What Is a Configuration Storage Server?
- What Are Enterprise Policies?
- What Are Enterprise Networks?
- What Are Arrays and Array Policies?
- What Are Effective Policies?
- How Enterprise Edition Integrates with Network Load Balancing
- How Enterprise Edition Enables Virtual Private Networking
- How Enterprise Edition Enables Distributed Caching Using CARP

Introduction

This lesson summarizes the differences between ISA Server 2004 Standard Edition and Enterprise Edition. The primary difference between the two editions is that Enterprise Edition is designed to provide scalability for organizations that will deploy multiple ISA Server computers. The lesson then goes into more detail in describing the features of Enterprise Edition.

Lesson objectives

After completing this lesson, you will be able to:

- Describe the differences between ISA Server 2004 Enterprise Edition and ISA Server 2004 Standard Edition.

- Describe the benefits of deploying ISA Server Enterprise Edition.

- Describe how Active Directory® Application Mode is used by ISA Server 2004 Enterprise Edition.

- Describe a Configuration Storage server.

- Describe what enterprise policies are.

- Describe what enterprise networks are.

- Describe what array policies are.

- Describe what effective policies are.

- Describe how ISA Server 2004 integrates network load balancing (NLB).

- Describe how to enable virtual private networking using ISA Server Enterprise Edition.

- Describe how distributed caching is enabled using Cache Array Routing Protocol (CARP).

Animation: Comparing ISA Server 2004 Enterprise Edition and Standard Edition

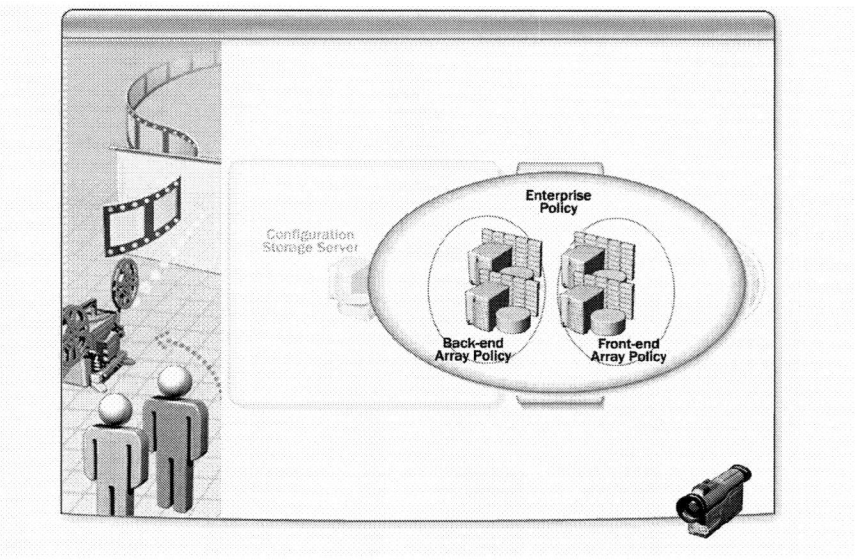

Introduction

This animation presents a high-level overview of the difference between ISA Server 2004 Standard Edition and ISA Server 2004 Enterprise Edition. ISA Server 2004 Enterprise Edition provides enhanced scalability thorough the use of a centralized Configuration Storage Server and centralized policies, through NLB integration, and through distributed caching using CARP.

Tip To view the Comparing ISA Server 2004 Enterprise Edition and Standard Edition presentation later on your own, open the Web page on the Student Materials compact disc, click **Multimedia**, and then click the title of the presentation.

Why Deploy ISA Server Enterprise Edition?

ISA Server 2004 Enterprise Edition enables:

- Easier management of multiple-server deployments
- More scalable Web proxy caching
- More scalable and fault-tolerant deployments

ISA Server 2004 Enterprise Edition deployment scenarios:

- Deploying multiple ISA Server computers with the same configuration
- Deploying ISA Server computers in a distributed administration scenario
- Deploying ISA Server computers without Active Directory

Introduction

ISA Server Standard Edition and ISA Server Enterprise Edition provide similar functionality. The most significant difference between the two versions is that Enterprise Edition provides enhanced scalability. ISA Server Standard Edition provides firewall and proxy server services on a single computer while Enterprise Edition provides the same services on multiple servers.

Easier to manage multiple servers

One of the primary differences between Standard Edition and Enterprise Edition is how the two versions store their configuration information. Standard Edition stores its configuration information in the local computer registry. ISA Server Enterprise Edition stores its configuration information in a separate directory located on one or more Configuration Storage servers. The Configuration Storage servers use Active Directory Application Mode (ADAM) to store the configuration information.

On the Configuration Storage server, you can configure enterprise policies, arrays, and array policies. Then you can install ISA Server on multiple computers and assign each of them to a specific array. All the enterprise and array policies will be assigned automatically to each ISA Server computer in the array. To change the ISA Server configuration, simply change the information on the Configuration Storage server. You can also configure array-level permissions so that you can delegate the management and monitoring of ISA Server computers in each array.

More scalable Web proxy caching

ISA Server 2004 Enterprise Edition also enhances scalability by enabling shared Web caching across an array of multiple servers. With Enterprise Edition, multiple ISA Server computers can be configured as a single logical cache so that the caching capacity for all the ISA Server computers is combined. To enable this feature, ISA Server uses CARP, which is used to manage the distribution and retrieval of Web information across multiple ISA Server computers.

Scalable and fault-tolerant deployments

The third feature available with Enterprise Edition is the integration of NLB with ISA Server. With NLB, several computers can be clustered so that the entire group of servers shares a single IP address. When client computers connect to the NLB cluster, they connect to that shared IP address. NLB delivers high availability by redirecting incoming network traffic to working cluster members if one of the servers in the cluster fails or is offline. Any connections to the failed computer are lost, but the services remain available.

With ISA Server 2004 Standard Edition, you can configure NLB manually and manage it using the Microsoft Windows® management tools. With Enterprise Edition, NLB is integrated so that NLB can be managed using the ISA Server Management Console. This means that NLB configuration is performed through ISA Server management. ISA Server also provides NLB health monitoring and manages the failover from one ISA Server computer in the cluster to another.

Enterprise deployment scenarios

These Enterprise Edition features mean that you can deploy ISA Server Enterprise Edition in many scenarios, including:

- *Deploying multiple ISA Server computers that require the same configuration.* Some organizations require multiple ISA Server computers with the same configuration. For example, a large organization may want to deploy multiple servers in a large office to provide scalable access to Internet resources, or to provide fault-tolerant publishing access to public Web sites. This organization can configure an array, and enable NLB and CARP on the array. The organization can then install as many ISA Server computers as needed into the array, and all servers will have the same configuration.

- *Deploying ISA Server computers in a distributed administration scenario.* Some organizations require the option to enable distributed administration. For example, an organization with multiple branch offices or divisions may require the ability to configure some configuration settings at an organization level, while delegating some administrative rights to other administrators. ISA Server Enterprise Edition enables this configuration by using enterprise policies for the organizationwide configuration and allowing for the delegation of administrative rights at an array level.

- *Deploying ISA Server computers without Active Directory.* ISA Server 2000 Enterprise Edition uses Active Directory directory service to store its configuration information. This means that each ISA Server computer must be a member of an Active Directory domain. Because ISA Server 2004 uses ADAM, deploy Enterprise Edition without storing any information in Active Directory. You can deploy the Configuration Storage Server and ISA Server computers as domain members or as workgroup members.

What Is Active Directory Application Mode?

Active Directory Application Mode:

- Is a special mode of the Active Directory directory service
- Is an LDAP-compatible directory that does not require DNS or domains
- Enables multiple-master replication between ADAM servers

- ADAM is installed when you install Configuration Storage server
- You use ISA Server Management to manage the directory information stored in ADAM

Introduction

The Configuration Storage server uses ADAM to store and replicate configuration data for all the ISA Server computers in an ISA Server enterprise. When you install the Configuration Storage server, you also automatically install ADAM on the computer.

Note An *ISA Server enterprise* is a collection of ISA Server 2004 computers that use the same Configuration Storage directory.

What is ADAM?

ADAM is a special mode of the Active Directory directory service that is designed for directory-enabled applications. ADAM is a Lightweight Directory Access Protocol (LDAP)–compatible directory service that runs on servers running Microsoft Windows Server™ 2003. ADAM is designed to be a stand-alone directory service; it does not require the deployment of Domain Name System (DNS), domains, or domain controllers.

You can run multiple instances of ADAM concurrently on a single computer, with an independently managed schema for each ADAM instance. ADAM also enables replication of data between multiple servers using a multiple-master replication model. This means that when ADAM servers are configured as replication partners, changes to the directory data can be made on any server and the data will be replicated to all other replication partners.

Note ADAM also runs on computers running Windows XP Professional, but this deployment is not supported with ISA Server. For detailed information about ADAM, see the Windows Server 2003 Active Directory Application Mode site at http://www.microsoft.com/windowsserver2003/adam/default.mspx

Although ISA Server 2004 Enterprise Edition uses ADAM to store its configuration information, you need not install ADAM directly. Instead, it is installed when you install a Configuration Storage server. Moreover, you will rarely directly access the directory information using the ADAM tools. Instead, you will use ISA Server Management to modify the directory data.

What Is a Configuration Storage Server?

Introduction

A Configuration Storage server stores the configuration for all the arrays in the enterprise. There can be multiple configuration storage servers in the enterprise, with each replicating to the rest any updates to enterprise configuration. Configuration Storage servers store the configuration in ADAM. Hence, there is no centralized master copy of directory information. Instead, any change committed on any Configuration Storage server is replicated to every other Configuration Storage server within the enterprise.

Deploying Configuration Storage servers

You can deploy multiple Configuration Storage servers in an enterprise. When you deploy the first Configuration Storage server, you must choose the option to create a new enterprise. For subsequent installation, you should choose to join an existing enterprise.

When you create an array, you must specify a Configuration Storage server from which the array will receive updates. After you create an array, you will be able to change the array's Configuration Storage server. In addition to a primary Configuration Storage server, an array may be assigned a backup Configuration Storage server.

Note If your Configuration Storage Server is a member of a workgroup rather than a domain, you can deploy only one Configuration Storage server in your enterprise.

ISA Server communication

When the ISA Server Firewall Service starts, it initiates a connection to its designated Configuration Storage server. If the Configuration Storage server is available, the latest configuration is downloaded and applied to the registry of the ISA Server computer. If a Configuration Storage server is not available, the Firewall Service software will initiate a connection to its backup Configuration Storage server, if one has been designated for use. If the backup Configuration Storage server is unavailable or has not been designated, the Firewall Service will use its last known configuration. Any updates to the ISA Server configuration are not applied until the ISA Server computer can connect to the Configuration Storage server.

Whenever you change a configuration in the ISA Server Management Console, the change is replicated to available Configuration Storage servers. The configuration changes are retrieved by the ISA Server computers and applied to the local registry. By default, ISA Server computers will check for configuration changes every 15 seconds. This setting can be modified for each array.

The servers in an array use the following protocols to communicate with each other and with the Configuration Storage server:

- *MS Firewall Storage.* This protocol is an inbound LDAP-based protocol. It uses port 2172 for Secure Sockets Layer (SSL) connections and port 2171 for non-SSL connections. Array members communicate with the Configuration Storage server using the MS Firewall Storage protocol. Computers running ISA Server Management also use the MS Firewall Storage protocol to read from and write to the Configuration Storage server.

- *MS Firewall Storage Replication.* This protocol is an outbound Transmission Control Protocol (TCP), which is defined on port 2173. MS Firewall Storage Replication is used for configuration replication between Configuration Storage servers.

- *MS Firewall Control.* This is another outbound TCP protocol and is defined on port 3847. It is used for communications between ISA Server Management and computers running ISA Server services.

- *Remote Procedure Call (RPC).* To monitor server performance, the ISA Server Management computer requires remote procedure call (RPC) connectivity to the ISA Server computers.

What Are Enterprise Policies?

Definition

- An ordered set of access rules and policy elements defined at the enterprise level

Options

- Unless you configure enterprise policies, only array policies apply
- You can configure enterprise polices to be applied before or after the array policy
- Configure policy elements that can be used when configuring enterprise or array rules

Introduction

An ISA Server enterprise is a collection of all ISA Server 2004 computers that use the same Configuration Storage server directory to store configuration information. When you configure an enterprise, you can also configure enterprise policies.

What is an enterprise policy?

An enterprise policy is a policy defined at the enterprise level that can be applied to any array. Like any other firewall policy, an enterprise policy contains an ordered set of access rules. The enterprise policy can also include policy elements such as computer sets, Uniform Resource Locator (URL) sets, or subnets.

How to use enterprise policies

When you create an enterprise, an enterprise policy named Default Policy is created. This policy does not contain any access rules other than a final access rule named Default Deny Rule, which denies all network traffic. Because this enterprise policy does not contain any additional policy rules, if you apply this rule to an array, only the array policy rules will be applied on that array. You cannot modify the Default Policy.

As an enterprise administrator, you can define enterprise policies. In most cases, you would define enterprise policies that can be applied across the entire enterprise. For example, you could define an enterprise policy that blocks the downloading of executables using Hypertext Transfer Protocol (HTTP), or an enterprise policy that allows HTTP and Hypertext Transfer Protocol Secure (HTTPS) access to the Internet for all users.

The enterprise policy rules, together with the array policy rules, make up the rule base for ISA Server computers in the array. When you define the enterprise policy, you can define the enterprise policy rules so that they are applied before or after the array policy rules. Because ISA Server processes the rules in order, the rule order and the placement of enterprise rules affect the final policy. The first rule to match a request received by ISA Server will be used to determine access, and subsequent rules will not be checked.

In addition to enterprise rules, you can also define enterprise policy elements, such as networks, URL sets, or schedules. These policy elements can be used when configuring rules for any enterprise policy and when creating array-level rules.

After you create the enterprise policies, you can assign the enterprise policies to the arrays in the enterprise. Only one enterprise policy can be assigned to each array.

What Are Enterprise Networks?

Definition

- A range of enterprise-level IP addresses that do not cross a security boundary

To use enterprise networks, you can:

- Use the predefined enterprise networks, which are associated with array networks of the same name
- Define enterprise rules using enterprise networks
- Use enterprise networks to enable communication between arrays
- Manage the IP address space in the organization

Introduction

In addition to creating enterprise policies, you can also create enterprise networks. Enterprise networks can be used when configuring other policy rules.

What is an enterprise network?

An enterprise network is a range of IP addresses defined on the enterprise level. When you create an enterprise network, the only configuration option you have is to configure the IP address range. For example, you can create an enterprise network named Internal that includes all the IP addresses that are internal to your organization, but you cannot configure options such as Web Proxy client or Firewall client settings.

The IP addresses assigned to an enterprise network cannot cross any security boundary, such as a firewall or a virtual private network (VPN) connection. However, you can create an enterprise network that contains the IP addresses in a perimeter network, or the IP addresses for a remote site. An IP address can be included in only one enterprise network.

Predefined enterprise networks

ISA Server includes predefined enterprise networks that act as a placeholder for array-level networks of the same name. Predefined enterprise networks cannot be explicitly used when creating array-level firewall policy rules. Instead, they are typically used in the enterprise policy. Any rule applied by the enterprise administrator to the predefined enterprise network will be applied to the array-level network of the same name. For example, an enterprise rule that allows HTTP access to the external network will be applied to the external network for each array. ISA Server includes the following predefined enterprise networks:

- External
- Local Host
- Quarantined VPN Clients
- VPN Clients

How to use enterprise networks

Enterprise networks can be used in several different scenarios:

- Enterprise networks can be used to create enterprise-level rules. For example, you can create an enterprise network named Internal Network that includes all the IP addresses for computers on your network. Then you can create an enterprise-level rule that controls Internet access. This rule applies to any computer on any internal network. If you add an array, the rule automatically applies to the internal network of that array, so long as it is within the IP address range of the enterprise network.

- Enterprise networks enable communication between arrays. When an array's networks are defined as part of an enterprise network, ISA Server can recognize the communication between the networks as internal traffic. Otherwise, ISA Server will consider the request to be from an external source, and the request will be rejected by the ISA Server spoof-detection feature.

- Enterprise networks allow the enterprise administrator to manage the IP address space of the enterprise, so that if a network is added on one array, there is no need to configure every other array to recognize that new network. So long as the new network is in an enterprise network, and the other arrays have built their networks based on the IP ranges defined in the enterprise networks, the new network will be recognized by all the arrays in the enterprise. To enable this, the array administrator must define the array networks using the enterprise networks. For example, if there is an enterprise network called Internal Network, the array administrator can create an array network and choose the Internal Network enterprise network as the IP range for that array network.

What Are Arrays and Array Policies?

Array definition

* A group of ISA Server 2004 computers that share the same configuration
* Includes a Configuration Storage server and ISA Server Management computers
* Requires that ISA Server computers have a similar server configuration

Array policy definition

* A set of access rules and publishing rules applied to all array members
* An array policy definition includes:
  * Policy elements that can define array rules
  * Array networks that define network configuration options

Introduction

An ISA Server enterprise includes one or more arrays. Each array contains one or more ISA Server computers and has a specific array policy applied to it.

What is an array?

An array is a group of ISA Server 2004 computers that share the same configuration. An array includes:

- One or more Configuration Storage servers, which store the configuration information for the array.

- One or more array members, which are computers on which ISA Server services are installed.

- One or more remote management computers, which are computers with the ISA Server Management Console installed.

All ISA Server computers in an array must have the same server configuration, including:

- The same number of network adapters connected to array-level networks.

- The same time-zone configuration, with synchronized clocks (for logging).

- The same hard-disk partitions (for logging).

- The same certificates installed on each array member (for SSL communications).

- The same network services available to each array member (for example, the servers must use the same DNS servers and the same servers for certificate revocation-list checking and have access to the same Active Directory domain controllers).

- The same language version of ISA Server and Windows Server 2003 installed, with the same locale set for the computer and for the logged-on user.

- The same ISA Server updates installed.

- The same domain and site configuration (or belong to a workgroup).

You cannot move a server from one array to another after you install ISA Server services. To move the server, uninstall ISA Server services, and then reinstall ISA Server services.

What is an array policy?

An array policy is a set of rules that is defined on the array level and is specific to the array. These rules include access rules, publishing rules, and policy elements, in addition to array networks.

Tip The array configuration displayed in ISA Server Manager is almost exactly the same as the configuration displayed in ISA Server Manager when connected to a computer running ISA Server 2004 Standard Edition. The only new item in the interface is a Servers container that lists all the servers in the array. However, many of the objects in an array have additional configuration options related to Enterprise Edition features such as NLB and CARP.

You can define any access rules or publishing rules at the array level. These rules will be applied to all array members. You can also create array-policy elements that can be used to create array-level rules.

You can also define array networks for each array. The IP addresses of an array network can contain IP ranges as well as enterprise networks, including more than one enterprise network. You can configure all network level settings on the array networks except for the VPN Clients network and the Quarantined VPN Clients network.

What Are Effective Policies?

Definition

- The resultant policy applied to an array member after the system policy, enterprise policy and the array policy rules are evaluated based on rule order

Example:

- Enterprise policy rules applied before array firewall policy
  - *Allow HTTP and HTTPS access to the Internet for all users.*
- Branch office array firewall policy rules
  - *Allow all protocol access from the Internal network to the Internet for all authenticated users*
  - *Allow DNS protocol traffic from branch-office DNS servers*
- Enterprise policy rules applied after array firewall policy
  - *Enable DNS protocol traffic from main-office DNS servers*

Introduction

You can define ISA Server policies at both the enterprise and array levels. Each ISA Server computer configuration is affected by policies at both levels. The end result of all the policies applied to the ISA Server computer is the effective policy.

What is the effective policy?

The effective policy for an array is a combination of system, enterprise and array policies. The system policy rules are always applied first. When you define enterprise policy rules, you can configure the rules to be applied before the array policy rules are applied, or you can configure the enterprise rules to be applied after the array rules. The order in which you place the rules determines how the rules are applied.

Just like ISA Server Standard Edition, ISA Server Enterprise Edition always evaluates the policy rules shown in the Firewall Policy list in a specified order. When the ISA Server computer receives a client request, ISA Server starts evaluating all the policy rules. The first rule that applies to the client request is applied, whether the rule explicitly allows or explicitly denies access. For example, if an access rule that allows all HTTP access to the Internet is evaluated before an access rule blocking access to a particular Web site, access to the Web site will be allowed.

When ISA Server 2004 Enterprise Edition evaluates the policy rules, it begins by evaluating the enterprise rules that are applied before the array policy rules. Then the array firewall policy rules are evaluated, followed by the enterprise rules that apply after the array policy. Finally, if no other rules apply to the client request, the final default deny rule is applied.

Effective policy example   To understand how the effective policy works, consider the following example of an enterprise policy and a branch-office array policy configuration:

- Enterprise Policy Rules Applied Before Array Firewall Policy
  - Allow HTTP and HTTPS access from all protected networks to the Internet for all users.
- Branch-Office Array Firewall Policy Rules
  - Allow all protocol access from the array's internal network to the Internet for all authenticated users.
  - Allow DNS protocol traffic from a computer set that includes all DNS servers at the branch office to the Internet.
- Enterprise Policy Rules Applied After Array Firewall Policy
  - Enable DNS protocol traffic from a computer set that includes all DNS servers at the main office to the Internet.

With this rule configuration, the following actions would occur:

- When a user from the branch office tries to access the Internet using HTTP, the user is granted access without requiring authentication.
- When a user from the branch office tries to access the Internet using any protocol other than HTTP or HTTPS, the user will be required to authenticate.
- The DNS servers in the branch office are configured to forward DNS queries directly to the Internet. This is enabled using the array DNS rule. If the DNS servers in the branch office were configured to forward all queries to the DNS servers at the main office, the array DNS rule would not be required, because the enterprise rule enables the main-office DNS servers to send queries to the Internet.

How Enterprise Edition Integrates with Network Load Balancing

Enterprise Edition integrates with network load balancing (NLB) by:

* NLB configuration is performed using ISA Server Management
* ISA Server provides NLB health monitoring
* Each network in an array can be configured for NLB
* ISA Server enables single affinity so clients always connect to the same ISA Server computer
* ISA Server supports bi-directional affinity for front-end/back-end firewall scenarios

Introduction

NLB is a Windows network component that is used to create a cluster of computers that can be addressed by a single-cluster IP address. NLB provides load balancing and high availability for IP-based services. ISA Server Enterprise Edition integrates with NLB so that you can configure and manage the NLB functionality using the ISA Server Management tools.

Benefits of network load balancing

NLB provides the following benefits:

■ NLB delivers high availability by redirecting incoming network traffic to working cluster members if one of the servers in the cluster fails or is offline. Any connections to the failed computer are lost, but the services remain available.

■ NLB delivers scalability by distributing the incoming network traffic among one or more virtual IP addresses (the cluster IP addresses) assigned to the cluster.

■ NLB employs an algorithm for statistically mapping incoming clients to the cluster hosts based on their IP address. So long as the number of computers in the NLB cluster does not change, the same cluster member will always respond to the same client.

■ NLB maintains existing Point-to-Point Tunneling Protocol (PPTP) and Internet Protocol Security (IPSec) tunnel connections.

■ Clients accessing the NLB cluster are unable to distinguish the cluster from a single server, so no client configuration is required.

Integrating NLB with ISA Server

ISA Server NLB is based on Windows Server 2003 Network Load Balancing. When you configure NLB through ISA Server, NLB is integrated with ISA Server functionality. This provides important functionality that is not available in Windows NLB alone:

- NLB configuration is performed through the ISA Server Management Console.

- ISA Server provides NLB health monitoring and discontinues NLB on a particular computer if the server is not available or if the Firewall Service on the server has stopped.

- When NLB integration is enabled, each network in an array can be configured as an NLB cluster. Because NLB is enabled per network and configured at an array level, you can configure how a specific network is load-balanced.

- ISA Server enables single affinity by default. When you enable NLB on an array network, the network is configured for single affinity. This means that all connections from the same client to the same array will always be handled by the same ISA Server computer in the array. This will continue indefinitely until a host is either added or removed from the array or one of the host members is not available, at which time the connections originating from that IP address may be mapped to a different host in the array.

- ISA Server enables bi-directional affinity. In some cases, single affinity does not provide sufficient functionality. For example, you can configure a secure Web publishing rule that is publishing an internal server that is located behind an NLB cluster. In this scenario, NLB can be configured on both the external interface facing the Internet and the internal interface facing the published servers. Because the internal published servers are configured as secure network address translation (SecureNAT) clients, they must use the shared IP address for the NLB cluster as their default gateway. However, NLB has to ensure that the response from the published server is always routed to the same ISA Server computer that handled the request from the Internet client because this is the only ISA Server computer in the array that has the security context for that particular session. ISA Server enables this functionality by using bi-directional affinity.

How Enterprise Edition Enables Virtual Private Networking

> **Network load balancing can be integrated with virtual private networking to enable:**
>
> * **Network load balancing for remote access VPNs**
>   * The VPN clients must connect to the shared IP address
> * **Network load balancing for site-to-site VPNs**
>   * The remote-site VPN server must connect to the shared IP address
>   * Client requests are automatically directed to the VPN tunnel owner
>   * Tunnel failover is automatically enabled
>
> **Deploying a Site-to-Site VPN without NLB will disable automatic failover**

Introduction

Just as ISA Server Standard Edition does, ISA Server Enterprise Edition supports remote-access VPNs, including network quarantine control and site-to-site VPNs. The added feature that is available in Enterprise Edition is the option to use NLB for VPN connections.

Remote-access VPN and NLB

When you enable NLB for an array and configure the array policy to enable remote-access VPNs, the VPN client must be configured to connect to the NLB shared IP address. When a remote access client initiates a VPN connection to an array, one of the array members establishes the VPN connection and allocates an IP address for that client. From then on, that array member maintains the VPN connection, and all traffic for that remote client passes through that array member.

Site-to-site VPN and NLB

To enable NLB for site-to-site VPNs, the remote-site network must be configured to connect to the shared IP address for the NLB cluster in the destination site. When NLB is enabled on a remote site network, ISA Server automatically assigns one array member to handle the VPN tunnel. In this way, parallel tunnels between two sites are not created.

Moreover, when a client on one network tries to access resources on another remote-site network, the client request is automatically directed to the array member that hosts the VPN connection.

If the server that owns a site-to-site VPN connection fails, ISA Server automatically shifts the connection to another ISA Server array member.

Site-to-site VPN without NLB

You can also enable site-to-site VPNs without integrating the VPN service and NLB. In this scenario, the administrator must select one of the array members as the ISA Server computer that will initiate the VPN connection to the remote site, and the remote-site ISA Server computer must be configured to use the specified ISA Server computer as the tunnel destination. This scenario does not provide any fault tolerance; if the server designated as the VPN tunnel owner fails, the administrator must configure another ISA Server computer to manage the connection.

How Enterprise Edition Enables Distributed Caching Using CARP

CARP enables distributed caching:

- Without duplication of cache content
- Without network traffic between ISA Server computers
- That can adjust to the addition or removal of array members
- That evenly distributes the cache or distributes the cache based on load factors

CARP works by:

- Using a script on the Web client that selects the ISA Server computer that will cache the Web content
- Using a script on the ISA Server computer to redirect client requests to the ISA Server compute that will cache the Web content

CARP does not use the shared IP address assigned to a NLB cluster

---

Introduction

ISA Server provides distributed caching through the use of CARP. CARP distributes the cache used by Web proxies across an array of ISA Server computers. Although CARP assigns each ISA Server computer a unique set of cached data, the array of computers functions as a single, logical cache.

How CARP works

CARP is used by Web browsers and by ISA Server to increase performance in operations accessing a Web proxy cache that is distributed across multiple ISA Server computers. CARP uses hash-based routing to determine which ISA Server computer will respond to a client request and cache specific Web content.

CARP provides the following benefits:

- CARP eliminates the duplication of cache contents across multiple ISA Server computers. The result is a faster response to queries and a more efficient use of server resources.

- Because CARP determines which ISA Server computer will cache any specific content, no traffic is required among ISA Server computers to determine which server is caching the content.

- CARP automatically adjusts when array members are added or removed. The hash-based routing means that, when a server is either taken offline or added, only minimal reassignment of URL caches is required.

- CARP ensures that the cache objects are either distributed evenly between all servers in the array or by the load factor that is configured for each server.

How CARP works

The CARP process provides efficient routing for Web requests on the client side and on the server side.

When client-side CARP is enabled, the Web browser downloads the Array.dll?Get.Routing.Script from an ISA Server computer in the array. When a user types a URL into a Web browser, the URL is handed off to the script, which calculates which ISA Server computer in the array will be used to cache the content. The script always returns the same server list for a given URL, ensuring that each URL is cached on one array server only.

The script generated by ISA Server implements the CARP algorithm. The script includes information about the configuration and current status of the array. The script ensures that the URL space is distributed evenly across the available ISA Server computers. You can also configure a load factor for each array member that allows you to distribute the cache based on server configuration.

ISA Server also enables server-side CARP for those Web clients that do not use client-side CARP. In this situation, when a client sends a Web request to an array member, the server runs the CARP script with the requested URL and determines which array member can best serve the request. The request is forwarded to that server.

CARP and NLB

NLB can be used to load-balance all types of network traffic going into the array. When clients connect to an NLB cluster, they use the shared IP address for the cluster.

CARP cannot use the shared IP address, however, because the client requests must be sent to a specific ISA Server computer. Because of this, CARP does not include the virtual IP address in the script sent to clients or when server-side requests are forwarded to other array members. Instead, CARP uses the specific IP address for the ISA Server computer in its script.

Lesson: Planning an ISA Server 2004 Enterprise Edition Deployment

- ● ISA Server Enterprise Edition Deployment Scenarios
- ● Planning the Configuration Storage Server Deployment
- ● Planning Enterprise and Array Policy Configuration
- ● Planning for Centralized Monitoring and Management
- ● Migrating from ISA Server 2000 Enterprise Edition Overview

Introduction

ISA Server 2004 Enterprise Edition can be deployed in a variety of scenarios that require a scalable configuration. As you prepare to deploy Enterprise Edition in these scenarios, you will find that some aspects of planning the ISA Server Enterprise Edition deployment are quite different from planning a Standard Edition deployment. This lesson provides an overview of the ISA Server Enterprise Edition deployment scenarios and the planning components for deploying ISA Server in each scenario.

Lesson objectives

After completing this lesson, you will be able to:

- Describe the ISA Server 2004 Enterprise Edition deployment scenarios.
- Plan the Configuration Storage server deployment.
- Plan enterprise- and array-policy deployments.
- Plan for centralized monitoring and management.
- Describe the process of migrating from ISA Server 2000 Enterprise Edition to ISA Server 2004 Enterprise Edition.

ISA Server Enterprise Edition Deployment Scenarios

Deploy multiple ISA Server computers in identical roles to:
- Use centralized management using arrays
- Implement Network Load Balancing
- Implement CARP
- Use centralized monitoring

Deploy ISA Server computers in a workgroup to:
- Isolate the ISA Server computers from the domain
- Implement flexible ISA Server computer configurations

Deploy ISA Server computers in a branch office to:
- Use multiple ISA Server computers for each role
- Deploy a Configuration Storage server in each office

Introduction

ISA Server 2004 Enterprise Edition can be deployed for the same scenarios in which ISA Server Standard Edition can be deployed. However, there are some scenarios in which ISA Server Enterprise Edition offers maximum benefit.

Multiple ISA Server computers in an identical role

One of the deployment scenarios in which Enterprise Edition offers the most benefit is where you require multiple ISA Server computers to perform identical roles. In this scenario, Enterprise Edition offers the following benefits:

- *Centralized management using arrays.* Because you deploy multiple ISA Server computers in the same role, you can create an array for each role and configure the array policies. You can then add as many ISA Server computers as required for that role.

- *Network load balancing.* If the ISA Server computers are being used to provide access to Internet resources, or to publish internal resources to the Internet, you can take advantage of NLB.

- *CARP.* If the ISA Server computers are being used to provide access to Internet resources and you require caching, you can take advantage of the caching scalability provided by CARP.

- *Centralized monitoring.* You can monitor multiple ISA Server Enterprise Edition computers using a single ISA Management workstation.

Note   Module 4, "Configuring ISA Server as a Firewall," of Course 2824, *Deploying and Managing Microsoft Internet Security and Acceleration Server 2004*, discusses the option of using network templates to apply an ISA Server configuration. You can still use network templates to configure ISA Server Enterprise Edition; however, you will configure the network template at the array level, and the settings will be applied to all array members.

Workgroup scenario

A workgroup is a grouping of computers that do not share a common directory. Although workgroups do not offer the centralized user accounts and authentication offered by domains, you may choose to deploy your ISA Server computers in a workgroup rather than in a domain for additional security. In this scenario, even if an attacker gains access to the ISA Server computer, the hacker will have no access to any domain account. Moreover, workgroup computers do not need to connect to domain controllers, so you can reduce the number of system policy rules and access rules that need to be enabled.

ISA Server Enterprise Edition supports three domain and workgroup configurations:

- A simple installation of an ISA Server array in a workgroup, where the Configuration Storage server is a member of a domain but the ISA Server computers are not. In this scenario, you can deploy multiple Configuration Storage servers and implement certificate authentication between the Configuration Storage servers and the ISA Server computers.

- Installation of both the Configuration Storage server and the ISA Server array in a workgroup, creating an isolated enterprise. In this scenario, you can only deploy a single Configuration Storage server for the enterprise and must implement certificate authentication between the Configuration Storage servers and the ISA Server computers.

- A mixed installation of multiple ISA Server arrays, where the Configuration Storage server is a member of a domain, and some of the ISA Server computers are also domain members, but some ISA Server computers are not. In this scenario, you can create one or more arrays that include ISA Server computers that are domain members and one or more arrays that contain ISA Server computers that are within a workgroup.

Note For more information about configuring ISA Server in workgroup configurations, see Module 12, "Implementing ISA Server 2004 Enterprise Edition: Back-to-Back Firewall Scenario," of Course 2824, *Deploying and Managing Microsoft Internet Security and Acceleration Server 2004*.

Branch-office scenario

ISA Server Enterprise Edition can also optimize the ISA Server deployment in a branch-office scenario if you require multiple ISA Server computers in each branch. In this scenario, you can take advantage of NLB for site-to-site VPNs as well as CARP if you require caching.

In this scenario, the ISA Server computers at the main office can be deployed as domain members, while the branch-office ISA Server computers can be in the same domain as the main office, in a child domain, in a separate domain with trust between the domains, or in a workgroup.

In a branch-office scenario, you can deploy a Configuration Storage server in each branch office so that the ISA Server computers can always access a local copy of the ISA Server configuration.

Note For more information about configuring ISA Server servers in a branch-office scenario, see Module 13, "Implementing ISA Server 2004 Enterprise Edition: Site-to-Site VPN Scenario," of Course 2824, *Deploying and Managing Microsoft Internet Security and Acceleration Server 2004*.

Planning the Configuration Storage Server Deployment

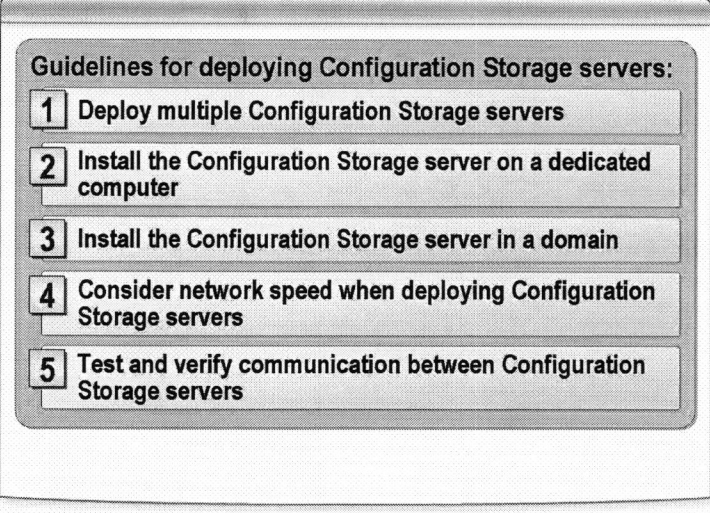

Guidelines for deploying Configuration Storage servers:

1. Deploy multiple Configuration Storage servers
2. Install the Configuration Storage server on a dedicated computer
3. Install the Configuration Storage server in a domain
4. Consider network speed when deploying Configuration Storage servers
5. Test and verify communication between Configuration Storage servers

Introduction

Because the ISA Server enterprise configuration information is stored in the Configuration Storage server directory, it is critical that you plan the Configuration Storage server implementation carefully.

Configuration Storage server deployment options

You have the following options when planning your Configuration Storage server deployment:

- *Deploy a single Configuration Storage server to manage the entire enterprise.* You must deploy at least one Configuration Storage server to create an ISA Server enterprise. If you deploy only one server, that server will be used by all ISA Server computers when requesting configuration information.

- *Deploy multiple Configuration Storage servers in the same enterprise.* You can also deploy multiple Configuration Storage servers. In this configuration, each server will store the configuration information for the entire enterprise, but you can configure each array to use a different Configuration Storage server to obtain configuration updates. You can also deploy the Configuration Storage servers across multiple offices. ADAM multiple-master replication means that you can perform updates on any Configuration Storage server and the changes will be replicated to all other servers.

- *Deploy multiple Configuration Storage servers in different ADAM sites.* If your organization has multiple locations and you are deploying Configuration Storage servers in each location, you can create multiple ADAM sites for each location. When you create a site, you can configure how frequently replication occurs between the sites. You can use this option to manage the bandwidth between organization locations.

- *Install the Configuration Storage server in a domain or workgroup.* You can deploy Configuration Storage server in either a domain or workgroup. If you deploy Configuration Storage server in a workgroup, you can deploy only one server in your ISA Server enterprise and will need to use certificates to authenticate between the ISA Server computers and the Configuration Storage server. If you deploy the Configuration Storage server in a domain, you can use domain authentication and deploy multiple servers.

- *Install the Configuration Storage server as a dedicated server.* You can install Configuration Storage server on a dedicated server that does not have any other ISA Server components installed on the server.

- *Install the Configuration Storage server on a server also running ISA Server services.* You can also install Configuration Storage server on a computer that is also running the ISA Server services. In this configuration, the server can operate as a firewall as well as a Configuration Storage server.

Configuration Storage server design guidelines

Use the following guidelines when planning your Configuration Storage server deployment:

- Deploy multiple Configuration Storage servers.

  Configuration Storage servers provide redundancy for each other so that, if one server fails, the other server is still available for the ISA Server computers. The Configuration Storage servers also provide redundancy through replication. If you make a change on one server, that change will be replicated to the other Configuration Storage servers so that, even if the first server fails, the change is retained. You should back up all your Configuration Storage servers on a regular basis, but if you do not have multiple Configuration Storage servers, the backup is much more critical because it will be the only means to recover the enterprise information in the event of a server failure.

- Install the Configuration Storage server on a dedicated computer on which no other ISA Server services are running.

  This is particularly important if the ISA Server computer is being deployed at the edge of the network. You should place the Configuration Storage server on the internal network.

- Install the Configuration Storage server in a domain.

  To take advantage of domain authentication, you must join the computer running as the Configuration Storage server to the domain member. Doing so allows you to use domain accounts to configure administrative delegation and user sets.

- Consider network speed when deploying Configuration Storage servers.

  You should ensure that every ISA Server computer has a fast LAN network connection to a Configuration Storage server. The ISA Server Management computer also should have a fast network connection to the Configuration Storage server. Usually this means that you should deploy at least one Configuration Storage server per office location.

- Test and verify communication between each Configuration Storage server, and between each Configuration Storage server and other computers:

  - ISA Server computers

  - ISA Server Management computers

- If your Configuration Storage servers are separated by firewalls, ensure that the firewall configuration enables the required LDAP/LDAPS ports.

Planning Enterprise and Array Policy Configuration

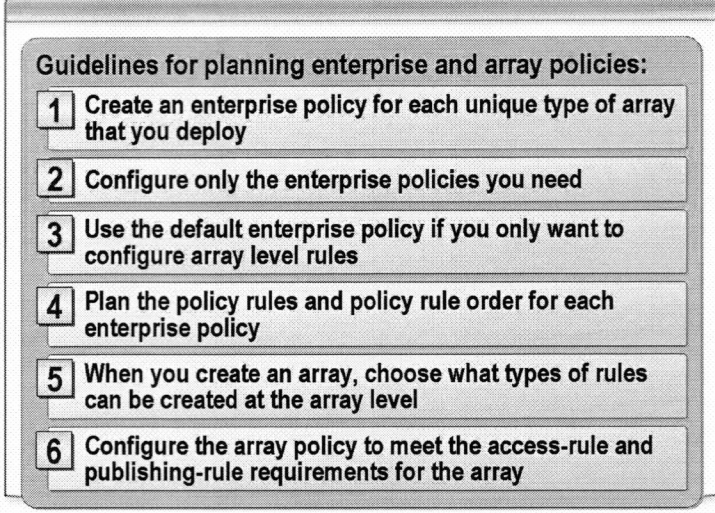

Guidelines for planning enterprise and array policies:

1. Create an enterprise policy for each unique type of array that you deploy

2. Configure only the enterprise policies you need

3. Use the default enterprise policy if you only want to configure array level rules

4. Plan the policy rules and policy rule order for each enterprise policy

5. When you create an array, choose what types of rules can be created at the array level

6. Configure the array policy to meet the access-rule and publishing-rule requirements for the array

Introduction

Because ISA Server Enterprise Edition supports both enterprise and array policies, you need to plan the implementation of policies at both levels, in addition to planning for the interaction between the two different policies.

Planning enterprise policies

You can create one or more enterprise policies and then apply that enterprise policy to the arrays that you create in your ISA Server enterprise. Each array can have only one enterprise policy applied to it.

When you create enterprise policies, start by considering what types of arrays you will be deploying. If you are deploying only one array, or if all the arrays that you will be deploying are similar, then you should create a single enterprise policy. For example, if you need to define similar access and publishing rules for all your arrays, you should configure a single enterprise policy and apply it to all arrays.

However, if you deploy arrays with different requirements, you may need to implement multiple enterprise policies. For example, if you deploy several front-end firewall arrays, several back-end firewall arrays, and an array for site-to-site VPN servers, you may want to configure an enterprise array for each type of array.

Note If you are deploying just one array of each type, consider not using enterprise policies at all and configuring all the policies at the array level. There is little benefit in configuring an enterprise policy if each array requires a unique policy.

You can also create no enterprise polices and just use the default enterprise policy. If you want to configure all policy rules at the array level, you can apply the default enterprise policy to each array.

After you have determined how many enterprise policies you will need, you can define the policy rules for each policy. The enterprise policy rules should apply to all the arrays.

After creating the policy rules, determine the order in which the rules will be applied. Each rule in the policy can be defined so that it applies either before or after the array policy. If a rule must always be applied to the array, configure the rule so that it is applied before the array policy. If you want to give the array administrator the option of applying the rule, or of overriding the rule by creating an array-level rule, configure the enterprise rule to be configured after the array rule.

Arrays are created by an enterprise administrator. When you create an array, you configure which enterprise policy will be applied to the array. Also, you can configure what types of policy rules can be created for the array. You can choose whether deny-access rules, allow-access rules, and publishing rules can be created for the array. You could choose this option when you want to apply only enterprise policies to the array.

Note If you do not allow the creation of a particular type of rule for an array, no one, not even an enterprise administrator, can create that type of rule. You can modify this setting after you deploy the array.

Planning array policies

Planning array policies is similar to planning the configuration of a single ISA Server Standard Edition computer. The array policy defines the networks, network elements, access rules, and publishing rules that apply to all the ISA Server computers in the array just like these components can be used to apply a policy to a single ISA Server computer. When planning these policies, you must consider the organization's security policies, business requirements, and publishing requirements.

The only additional factor that you need to consider when planning the array policy is how the policy will interact with the enterprise policy. You need to consider which access rules are applied before the array policy because you cannot override those rules at the array level. You also need to consider the rules applied after the array policy and choose either to use those rules or to override them by configuring an array-policy rule.

Planning for Centralized Monitoring and Management

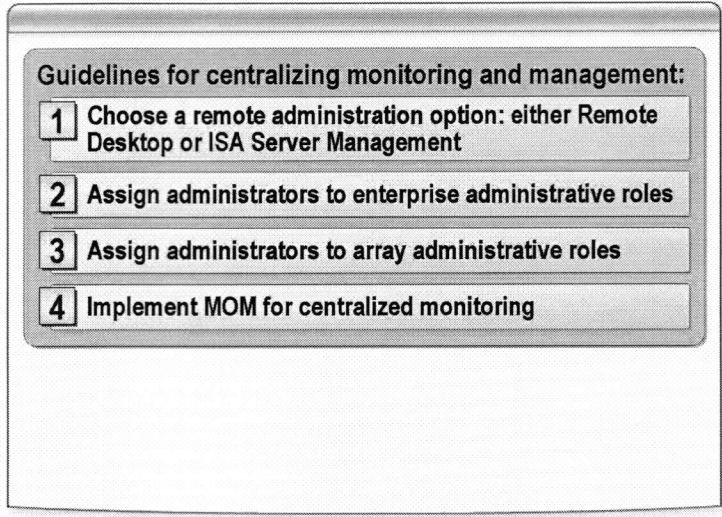

Guidelines for centralizing monitoring and management:

1 Choose a remote administration option: either Remote Desktop or ISA Server Management

2 Assign administrators to enterprise administrative roles

3 Assign administrators to array administrative roles

4 Implement MOM for centralized monitoring

Introduction

One benefit of deploying ISA Server Enterprise Edition is that you can manage and monitor multiple ISA Server computers from a central location.

Remote management options

In most organizations, the Configuration Storage server and ISA Server computers will be located in a secured server room. If your organization includes multiple locations, the servers may be located in a different office location than where you are. In either case, you will need to use remote administration to administer ISA Server. Like ISA Server Standard Edition, you have two options that you can use for remote administration:

- *Remote administration using Remote Desktop or Terminal Services.* Use this approach when you need to configure Windows Server settings or when you need to restart ISA Server services that may interfere with Microsoft Management Console (MMC) connectivity.

- *Remote administration through ISA Server Management.* ISA Server Management can be installed on an administrator workstation. The Enterprise Edition version of ISA Server Management is similar to the Standard Edition version but also displays the enterprise-level information. When you use the monitoring tools in the Enterprise Edition, the monitoring information for all ISA Server computers in the array is displayed.

Regardless of which solution you choose, you should deploy a client computer that you will use to manage the ISA Server configuration. Install ISA Server Management on this computer. If you are going to use this client computer to manage all ISA Server computers in the enterprise, add the computer to the Enterprise Remote Management Computers computer set defined in the enterprise policy. If you are going to administer only ISA Server computers in a particular array, add the client computer to the Remote Management Computers set defined for each array.

Define enterprise administrators

ISA Server Standard Edition enables administrative roles that can be configured on each server. ISA Server Enterprise Edition also enables role-based administration, but it does so at the enterprise and array levels. ISA Server provides the following roles for enterprise administration.

- *ISA Server Enterprise Administrator*. Users and groups assigned this role have full control over the enterprise and all array configurations. The Enterprise Administrator can also assign roles to other users and groups.

- *ISA Server Enterprise Auditor*. Users and groups assigned this role can view the enterprise configuration and all array configurations but cannot modify settings.

In addition, ISA Server includes an Enterprise Policy Editor role that can be assigned to a specific enterprise policy. A user assigned to this role can create policy rules for the enterprise policy.

Note For detailed information about the specific rights assigned to each role, see the topic Administrative Roles in ISA Server Online Help.

Define array administrators

You can also organize your array-level administrators into separate, defined-in-advance roles, each with its own set of tasks. ISA Server provides the following roles for array administrators:

- *ISA Server Array Monitoring Auditor*. Users and groups assigned this role can monitor the ISA Server computer and network activity, but they cannot configure specific monitoring functionality.

- *ISA Server Array Auditor*. Users and groups assigned this role can perform all monitoring tasks, including log configuration, alert-definition configuration, and all monitoring functions available to the ISA Server Basic Monitoring role.

- *ISA Server Administrator*. Users and groups assigned this role can perform any ISA Server task, including rule configuration, applying of network templates, and monitoring.

Important If the computer running the ISA Server services belongs to a workgroup, but the Configuration Storage server belongs to a domain, then user accounts configured on the domain should be used to access the Configuration Storage server. However, you will need to create mirrored accounts on each ISA Server computer to facilitate intra-array communication and administration.

Using MOM to monitor ISA Server

Microsoft Operations Manager (MOM) is the event and performance management tool that can be used to centralize monitoring for multiple Windows servers. MOM provides comprehensive event management, monitoring, reporting, and trend analysis. MOM provides management packs that are used to monitor specific applications and services.

To enable ISA Server monitoring by using MOM, you must install the MOM management pack available for ISA Server 2004 on the MOM server. Then install the MOM management agent on each ISA Server computer. Agents are used to collect data and execute MOM commands for the specific service or application. As well, you need to create an access rule that uses the Microsoft Operations Manager Agent protocol and allows traffic between the MOM server and the ISA Server array. The protocol enables outbound TCP traffic on port 1270 and send-and-receive UDP traffic on port 1270.

Migrating from ISA Server 2000 Enterprise Edition Overview

> **Steps to migrate the ISA Server 2000 configuration to ISA Server 2004:**
>
> - Use the ISA Server Migration Wizard to export the ISA Server 2000 configuration to an .xml file
> - Install Configuration Storage server
> - Import the .xml configuration file into the Configuration Storage server
>
> ---
>
> You can also upgrade individual ISA Server 2000 computers to ISA Server 2004 after you deploy the Configuration Storage server

Introduction

ISA Server 2004 supports an upgrade path from ISA Server 2000 Enterprise Edition to ISA Server 2004 Enterprise Edition. Most ISA Server 2000 configuration information will be upgraded to ISA Server 2004.

Migrating the enterprise configuration information

ISA Server 2000 Enterprise Edition stores its configuration information in Active Directory. When ISA Server 2000 Enterprise Edition is installed as an array member, ISA Server setup modifies the Active Directory schema to include ISA Server–specific classes and attributes. Because ISA Server 2004 stores the same information in ADAM, you cannot upgrade the ISA Server 2000 infrastructure merely by upgrading the ISA Server computers. Instead, you must migrate the ISA Server 2000 configuration to ISA Server 2004. To do this, complete these steps:

1. Run the ISA Server Migration Wizard on the ISA Server 2000 computer. The wizard creates an .xml file with the configuration information.

2. Install Microsoft ISA Server 2004 Enterprise Edition, selecting the option to install the Configuration Storage server.

3. Import the .xml file to the ISA Server 2004 computer.

Best Practice   Before importing the .xml file, perform a full backup of the current settings on the ISA Server 2004 computer.

Upgrading an ISA Server computer

After you migrate the ISA Server configuration to the Configuration Storage server, you can start deploying servers running ISA Server 2004 services. You can also perform an in-place upgrade of the individual ISA Server 2000 computers to ISA Server 2004. When you perform the upgrade, you will need to choose the Configuration Storage server to use for configuration information and the ISA Server 2004 array of which the server will be a part.

Note For detailed information about how to upgrade an ISA Server 2000 Enterprise Edition infrastructure to ISA Server 2004 Enterprise Edition and on how each specific item is upgraded, see the *Upgrading to Microsoft Internet Security and Acceleration (ISA) Server 2004 Enterprise Edition* guide that is included on the ISA Server 2004 Enterprise Edition CD-ROM. To access the guide, run isaautorun.exe from the CD-ROM and then click **Read Migration Guide**.

Lesson: Implementing ISA Server 2004 Enterprise Edition

- Requirements for Installing Enterprise Edition
- ISA Server Enterprise Edition Implementation Overview
- How to Install Configuration Storage Server
- How to Configure Enterprise Policies and Networks
- How to Configure Arrays and Array Policies
- How to Install ISA Server 2004 Enterprise Edition
- How to Configure an ISA Server Management Computer

Introduction

Once you have completed the planning for your ISA Server Enterprise Edition deployment, you are ready to start deploying ISA Server. To start deployment, first review the requirements for installing ISA Server Enterprise Edition and understand how to install and configure the ISA Server components. In this lesson, you will install a Configuration Storage server, create enterprise and array policies, and prepare to install ISA Server 2004 Enterprise Edition.

Lesson objectives

After completing this lesson, you will be able to:

- List the requirements for installing Enterprise Edition.
- Install the Configuration Storage server.
- Configure enterprise policies and networks.
- Configure array policies.
- Install ISA Server 2004 Enterprise Edition.
- Configure an ISA Server management computer.

Requirements for Installing Enterprise Edition

Server component or service	Capable of running on:		
	Windows Server 2003	Windows 2000 Server	Windows XP
Configuration Storage Server	✓		
ISA Server services	✓		
Message Screener	✓	✓	
Firewall Client Share	✓	✓	✓
ISA Server Management	✓	✓	✓

Hardware requirements:

- A network adapter for each connected network
- A network adapter for intra-array communication is recommended if you implement NLB
- 150 MB of disk space plus space for caching and logging

Introduction

The requirements for installing ISA Server Enterprise Edition are similar to the requirements for Standard Edition.

Operating system requirements

ISA Server 2004 Enterprise Edition requires the following Windows operating systems:

- The ISA Server Enterprise Edition Configuration Storage Server and ISA Server services must be installed on a computer running Microsoft Windows Server 2003. Enterprise Edition is not supported on Windows 2000 Server.

- You can install the Message Screener component on computers running Windows Server 2003 or Microsoft Windows 2000 Server.

- You can install the Firewall Client Share and ISA Server Management on computers running Windows Server 2003, Windows 2000 Server, or Microsoft Windows XP.

Additional requirements

ISA Server 2004 Enterprise Edition also has the following additional requirements:

- At least one network adapter for each network connected to the ISA Server computer.

- If you plan to configure NLB, add an additional network adapter for intra-array communication. Load balancing should not be configured for this network.

- One local hard-disk partition that has at least 150 MB of available hard-disk space. The disk should be formatted with the NTFS file system.

- In addition, you will need to allow additional disk space for logging or Web caching. At a minimum, allow an additional 4 gigabytes (GB) of disk space.

ISA Server Enterprise Edition Implementation Overview

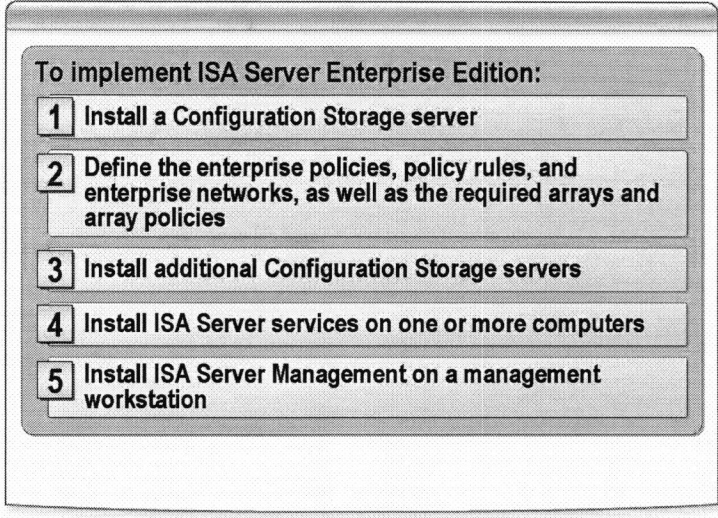

To implement ISA Server Enterprise Edition:

1. Install a Configuration Storage server
2. Define the enterprise policies, policy rules, and enterprise networks, as well as the required arrays and array policies
3. Install additional Configuration Storage servers
4. Install ISA Server services on one or more computers
5. Install ISA Server Management on a management workstation

Introduction

The ISA Server Enterprise Edition deployment requires more steps than a Standard Edition deployment. With Standard Edition, you can just install ISA Server on a server and complete the configuration after deployment. With ISA Server Enterprise Edition, actually installing the ISA Server services is one of the last steps you will take.

Installation overview

To implement ISA Server 2004 Enterprise Edition, complete these high-level steps:

1. Install a Configuration Storage server. The Configuration Storage server must be available to install the ISA Server 2004 component. When you install a Configuration Storage server, you can join the server to an existing enterprise or create a replica of an existing enterprise. If this is your first Configuration Storage server, choose to create a new enterprise.

2. On the Configuration Storage server, define the enterprise policies, policy rules, and enterprise networks. Also create the required arrays and array policies. This step is optional: you can create the arrays when you install the ISA Server services, but if you configure the arrays before installing array members, you can join the servers to arrays that already exist and where the array policies are already configured.

3. If required, install additional Configuration Storage servers. By default, when you choose to install a replica of an existing configuration, ADAM replication will immediately begin to populate the configuration information on the new server.

4. Install ISA Server services on one or more computers. When you install a computer running ISA Server services as the first member of a new array, you need to specify addresses for the Internal network.

5. Install ISA Server Management on the workstations that you will use to administer the ISA Server Configuration Storage server and ISA Server computers.

How to Install Configuration Storage Server

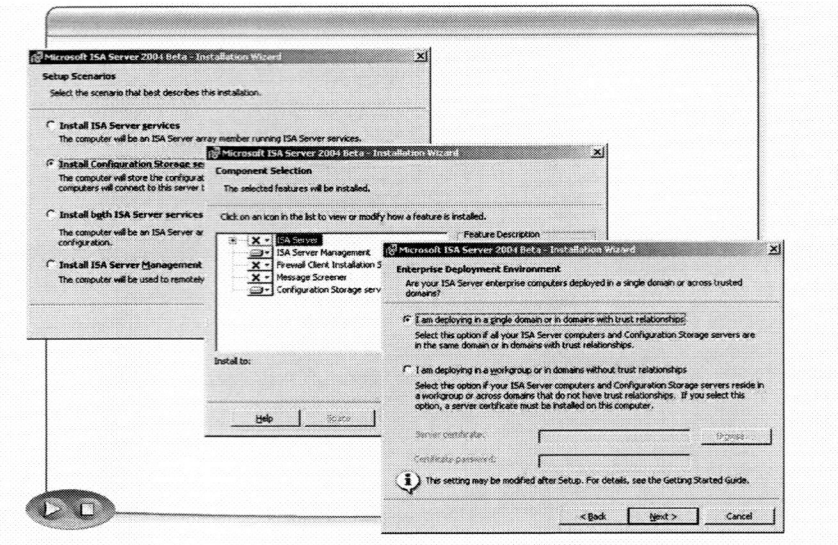

Introduction

The Configuration Storage server stores the configuration information for the entire enterprise so the first step in implementing ISA Server Enterprise Edition is to install and configure this server.

Installing Configuration Storage server

To install Configuration Storage server, complete the following high-level steps on the computer that you have designated as the Configuration Storage server.

1. Access the ISA Server Enterprise Edition installation files and start the installation by running Isaautorun.exe and clicking **Install ISA Server**.

2. Accept the terms and conditions stated in the user license agreement.

3. Enter your customer information.

4. On the **Setup Scenarios** page, you are given four options:

   - **Install ISA Server services**

   - **Install Configuration Storage server**

   - **Install both ISA Server services and Configuration Storage server**

   - **Install ISA Server Management**

   Click **Install Configuration Storage server**, and then click **Next**.

5. On the **Component Selection** page, you are given a choice about what components to install. You have the following options:

   - **ISA Server**

   - **ISA Server Management**

   - **Firewall Client Installation Share**

   - **Message Screener**

   - **Configuration Storage Server**

   Depending on your selection in the previous dialog box, the required components will be selected. On the **Enterprise Installation Options** page, click **Next**, select **Create a new ISA Server Enterprise**, and then click **Next**.

6. On the **New Enterprise Warning** page, click **Next**. This page warns you not to install more than one enterprise. Because you are creating a new enterprise, you can ignore the warning.

7. On the **Create a New Enterprise** page, enter a name and description for the enterprise. Click **Next**.

8. On the **Enterprise Deployment Environment** page, you can choose what type of enterprise you are creating. You have two options:

   - **I am deploying in a single domain or in domains with trust relationships**. If you choose this option, then you will use Windows authentication between all the computers in the enterprise.

   - **I am deploying in a workgroup or in domains without trust relationships**. If you choose this option, then you can use either Windows authentication or choose a certificate that will be used to authenticate computers in the enterprise.

9. On the **Service Account Selection** page, you can choose to have Configuration Storage server service run under the Network Service account or choose another service account.

10. On the **Ready to Install the Program** page, click **Install** to begin the installation.

Configuration Storage Server service accounts

When you install Configuration Storage server on a computer that is not a domain controller, the service will run in the security context of the Network Service account. However, when you install Configuration Storage server on a domain controller, you must create a separate service account. One option is to use an account that is a member of the Domain Admins group, but this is not a security best practice. As an alternative, create a regular user account and then run the .bat file created during the Configuration Storage server installation to configure the account with the required permissions. The .bat file is named *Yourdnsdomainname.bat* and is located in the C:\Program Files\Microsoft ISA Server\ADAMData directory. The .bat file adds the account that you chose as a service principal name in the ADAM directory.

Practice: Installing Configuration Storage Server

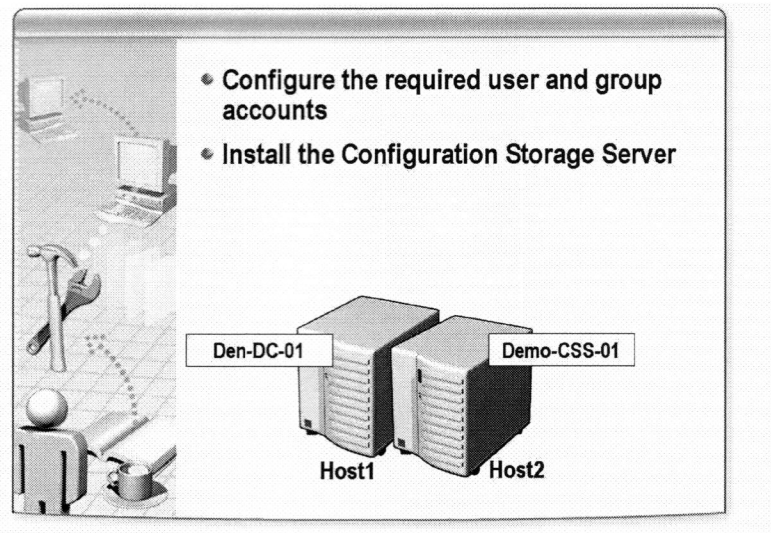

Introduction

In this practice, you will install Configuration Storage server to begin an ISA Server Enterprise Edition deployment. You will also configure user accounts that can be used to delegate administrative rights for multiple arrays.

To prepare the lab environment, you need to:

- Configure administrative user accounts for ISA Server management.

- Install Configuration Storage server on Demo-CSS-01.

▶ **To prepare for this practice**

1. You will need the Den-DC-01 virtual machine and the Demo-CSS-01 virtual machine.

2. Start or resume the required virtual machines, if necessary.

Note   You can complete both parts of this exercise at the same time.

Practice

▶ **Configure the required user and group accounts**

1. On Den-DC-01, log on to the cohovineyard.com domain with a user name of **Administrator** and a password of **P@ssw0rd**.

2. Open **Active Directory Users and Computers** from the **Administrative Tools**.

3. Right-click the **Users** container. Point to **New**, and then click **User**.

4. In the **New Object – User** dialog box, type **EntAdmin** in the **First name** and **User Logon Name** box. Click **Next**.

5. Type a **P@ssw0rd** in the **Password** and **Confirm Password** boxes. Clear the **User must change password at next logon** check box. Click **Next**.

6. Clear the **Create an Exchange mailbox** check box, click **Next**, and then click **Finish**.

7. Right-click the **Users** container. Point to **New**, and then click **Group**.

8. In the **Group Name** box, type **ISA EntAdmins**. Click **Next** twice and then click **Finish**.

9. Select **EntAdmin**, then right-click **EntAdmin**, and click **Add to a group**. In the **Enter the object name to select** box, type **ISA EntAdmins** and then click **OK** twice.

10. Repeat step 9 to add **EntAdmin** to the **Domain Admins** group for the cohovineyard.com domain.

11. Repeat steps 3-9 to create a user account named **ArrAdmin** and a group named **ISA ArrAdmins**. Add **ArrAdmin** to the **ISA ArrAdmins** group.

12. Close **Active Directory Users and Computers**.

► **Install the Configuration Storage Server on Demo-CSS-01**

1. On Demo-CSS-01, log on to the cohovineyard.com domain with a user name of **Administrator** and a password of **P@ssw0rd**.

2. On the virtual PC menu, click **CD**, and then click **Capture ISO Image**.

3. Browse to **C:\Program Files\Microsoft Learning\2824\LabFiles**, and click **ISAEEInstall.iso**. Click **Open**.

4. In **Microsoft ISA Server 2004 120-Day Evaluation Setup**, click **Install ISA Server**.

5. After the setup program prompts that it has completed determining the system configuration, on the **Welcome** page, click **Next**.

6. Review the terms and conditions stated in the user license agreement, click **I accept the terms in the license agreement**, and then click **Next**.

7. On the **Customer Information** page, click **Next**.

8. On the **Setup Scenarios** page, select **Install Configuration Storage server**, and then click **Next**.

9. On the **Component Selection** page, review the settings, and then click **Next**.

10. On the **Enterprise Installation Options** page, select **Create a new ISA Server Enterprise**, and then click **Next**.

11. On the **New Enterprise Warning** page, click **Next**. This page warns you not to install more than one enterprise. Because you are creating a new enterprise, you can ignore the warning.

12. On the **Create New Enterprise** page, type **Coho Vineyards Enterprise** as the **Enterprise name**. Click **Next**.

13. On the **Enterprise Deployment Environment** page, click **I am deploying in a single domain or in domains with trust relationships**, and then click **Next**.

14. On the **Ready to Install the Program** page, click **Install** to begin the installation.

15. After the installation is complete, click **Finish**.

16. In the **Internet Explorer** warning, click **In the future, do not show this message** and click **OK**.

17. Close all open windows.

How to Configure Enterprise Policies and Networks

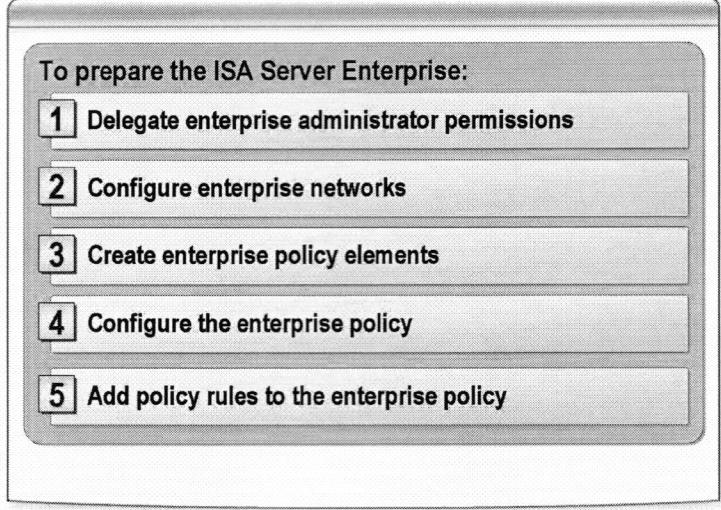

To prepare the ISA Server Enterprise:

1 Delegate enterprise administrator permissions

2 Configure enterprise networks

3 Create enterprise policy elements

4 Configure the enterprise policy

5 Add policy rules to the enterprise policy

Introduction

After you install the Configuration Storage server, the next step in the implementation is to configure the enterprise permissions and configure enterprise networks and enterprise policies and rules.

Delegate enterprise administrator permissions

After installing the Configuration Storage server, you should delegate the enterprise administrative permissions. By default, the user account used to create the enterprise is the only account that has enterprise administrator permissions. To assign enterprise administrator permissions to a group, complete the following procedure:

1. In **ISA Server Management**, right-click **Enterprise**, and click **Properties**.

2. In the **Enterprise Properties** dialog box, on the **Assign Roles** tab, click **Add**.

3. In the **Administration Delegation** dialog box, in the **Group or User** box, type the name of the group you are assigning permissions to.

4. Under **Role**, select the appropriate role, and click **OK**.

Configuring an enterprise network

An enterprise network is a range of IP addresses defined on the enterprise level. This network can then be used to create enterprise rules or added to array network objects. When you create an enterprise network, the only configuration option you have is to configure the IP address range. To configure an enterprise network, complete these steps:

1. In **ISA Server Management**, expand the **Enterprise** node, and click **Enterprise Networks**.

2. In the task pane, on the **Tasks** tab, select **Create a New Network** to start the **New Network Wizard**.

3. Provide a name for the new network, and then click **Next**.

4. On the **Network Addresses** page, click **Add Range** to open the **IP Address Range Properties** dialog box. In **Start address**, type the low end of the IP address range, and in **End address**, type the high end of the IP address range. Click **OK**. On the **Network Addresses** page, click **Next**.

5. On the summary page, review the properties of the enterprise network you are creating, and then click **Finish**.

Create enterprise policy elements

In addition to creating an enterprise network, you can also create enterprise policy elements such as computer sets, URL sets, and domain name sets. To configure enterprise policy elements, complete these steps:

1. In **ISA Server Management**, click **Enterprise Policy**. On the **Toolbox** tab, click the type of policy element that you are creating.

2. Click **New**, and then click the appropriate element type.

3. Complete the information required for the element.

Creating an enterprise policy

The next step is to create an enterprise policy that can be applied to arrays. To configure an enterprise policy, complete these steps:

1. In **ISA Server Management**, expand **Enterprise**, and click **Enterprise Policies**.

2. In the task pane, on the **Tasks** tab, click **Create New Enterprise Policy** to start the **New Enterprise Policy Wizard**.

3. On the **Welcome** page, provide a name for the new policy, and click **Next**.

4. On the **Completing The New Enterprise Policy Wizard** page, click **Finish**.

Adding policy rules to the enterprise policy

The enterprise policy is essentially just a container object; to make it effective, you need to configure policy rules that comprise the policy. When you configure the policy rules, you can choose to apply the rules before or after the array policy rules are applied. To configure an enterprise policy rule, complete these steps:

1. In **ISA Server Management**, expand **Enterprise**, expand **Enterprise Policies**, and then expand an existing enterprise policy.

2. In the task pane, on the **Tasks** tab, select **Create New Access Rule** to start the **New Access Rule Wizard**.

3. On the **Welcome** page of the wizard, enter the name for the access rule, and then click **Next**.

4. On the **Rule Action** page, select **Allow** or **Deny**, and then click **Next**.

5. On the **Protocols** page, configure the protocols that apply to this rule, and then click **Next**.

6. On the **Access Rule Sources** page, select the network or network object from which the access requests will come, and click **Next**.

Note If you are creating an access rule that will enable Internet access for all arrays in the enterprise, choose **All Protected Networks** as the source. The advantage of using **All Protected Networks** as the source, rather than listing specific networks, is that this rule will include any future networks that are added to your enterprise, without requiring you to modify the rule.

7. On the **Access Rule Destinations** page, select the network or network object to which the traffic will flow, and then click **Next**.

8. On the **User Sets** page, choose the appropriate user set, and then click **Next**.

9. Review the information on the wizard summary page, and then click **Finish**.

10. By default, the access rule is created in the post-array enterprise policy. You can move the access rule to the pre-array enterprise policy by right-clicking the rule and selecting **Move up**. Continue to do this until the rule is in the correct location in the pre-array enterprise policy.

How to Configure Arrays and Array Policies

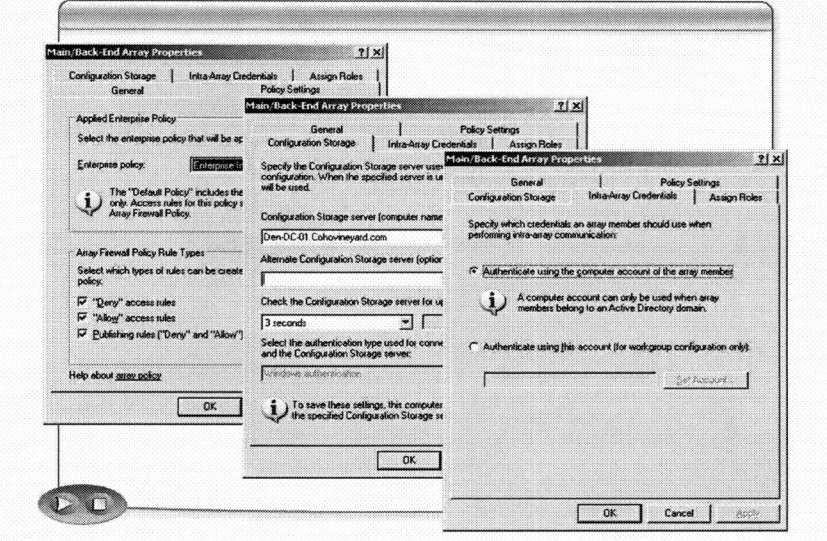

Introduction

After you create an enterprise policy and enterprise policy rules, the next step is to create one or more arrays and then assign array policy rules.

Creating an array

An array is a group of computers running the ISA Server services that share the same configuration. Although you can create an array when you install ISA Server services, as a best practice, you should configure the array first, and then install ISA Server computers into the array. To create an array, complete the following procedures:

1. In **ISA Server Management**, expand **Arrays**.

2. In the task pane, on the **Tasks** tab, click **Create New Array** to start the **New Array Wizard**.

3. On the **Welcome** page of the wizard, provide a name for the new array, and then click **Next**.

4. On the **Array Enterprise Policy** page, from the drop-down menu, select the enterprise policy that will be applied to the new array. You can choose to either apply the default policy or any other enterprise policy that you have created. Click **Next**.

5. On the **Array Policy Rule Types** page, select the types of rules that can be configured for the array. You can choose to enable or disable allow access rules, deny access rules, and publishing rules. Click **Next**.

6. On the summary page of the wizard, review the array configuration and then click **Finish**.

Configuring an array

After you create the array, you can modify the array configuration by completing the following procedure:

1. In **ISA Server Management**, expand **Arrays**.

2. Right-click the array that you are configuring and click **Properties**.

3. On the **Policy Settings** tab, configure the enterprise policy that will apply to the array, and modify the types of firewall policy rules that can be configured for the array.

4. On the **Configuration Storage** tab, configure which Configuration Storage server will be used by the ISA Server computers that are members of the array. You can also configure an alternate Configuration Storage server and configure how frequently the ISA Server computers will check for updates. You can also modify the authentication type.

5. On the **Intra-Array Credentials** tab, configure the account that will be used to authenticate for intra-array communication.

Delegate array administrator permissions

After configuring the array, you may choose to delegate the array administrative permissions. By default, the enterprise administrators have full administrative rights to the array. To assign array administrator permissions to a group, complete the following procedure:

1. In **ISA Server Management**, right-click the array and click **Properties**.

2. In the array **Properties** dialog box, on the **Assign Roles** tab, click **Add**.

3. In the **Administration Delegation** dialog box, in the **Group or User** box, type the name of the group to which you are assigning permissions.

4. Under **Role**, select the appropriate role, and click **OK**.

Creating array policy rules

The next step in configuring the array is to create the policy rules for the array policy. To create the access rules, click the **Firewall Policy** container under the array name and, on the **Tasks** tab, click **Create Array Access Rule**, or click the option to click one of the publishing rules.

Note   The procedures for creating array access rules or publishing rules in an array are identical to creating these rules on an ISA Server Standard Edition computer.

Practice: Configuring Enterprise and Array Policies

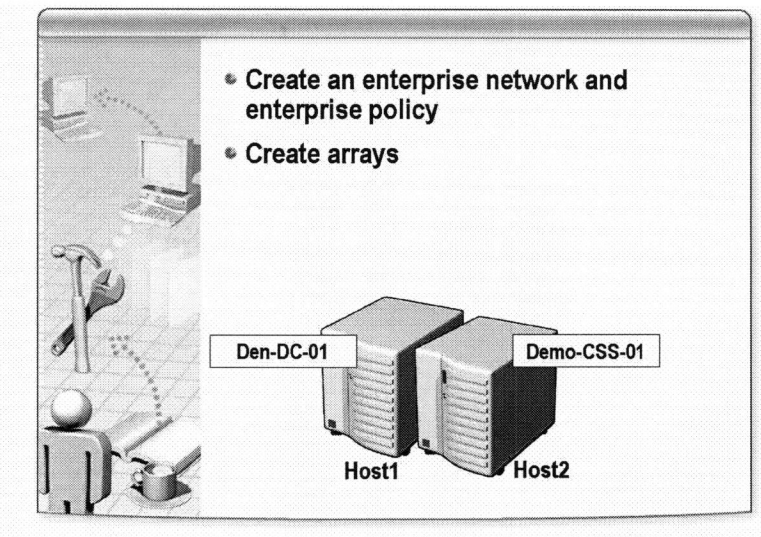

- Create an enterprise network and enterprise policy
- Create arrays

Introduction

In this practice, you will prepare your ISA Server environment for the deployment of ISA Server Enterprise Edition computers by configuring an enterprise network and enterprise policy. Then you will create two arrays: the main-office and back-end array, and the branch-office and front-end array.

▶ **To prepare for this practice**

1. You will need the Den-DC-01 virtual machine and the Demo-CSS-01 virtual machine.

2. Start or resume the required virtual machine, if necessary.

Practice

▶ **Configure an enterprise network and enterprise policy**

1. On Den-CSS-01, if required, log on to the cohovineyard.com domain using a user name of **Administrator** and a password of **P@ssw0rd**.

2. Open **ISA Server Management**.

3. Expand **Enterprise**, and then click **Enterprise Networks**.

4. In the task pane, on the **Tasks** tab, click **Create a New Network** to start the **New Network Wizard**.

5. In **Network** name, type **Main Office Internal** as the network name, and then click **Next**.

6. On the **Network Addresses** page, click **Add Range** to open the **IP Address Range Properties** dialog box. In **Start address**, type **192.168.0.0** and in **End address**, type **192.168.1.255** and then click **OK**.

7. On the **Network Addresses** page, click **Next**.

8. On the summary page of the wizard, review the properties of the enterprise network you are creating, and then click **Finish**.

9. In **ISA Server Management**, click **Enterprise Policies**. On the **Toolbox** tab, click **Network Objects**.

10. Click **New**, and then click **Computer**.

11. In the **New Computer Rule Element** dialog box, under **Name**, type **Den-DC-01**. In **Computer IP Address** type **192.168.1.10**. Click **OK**.

12. Expand **Computer Sets**. Double click **Enterprise Remote Management Computers**. Click **Add**, and then click **Computer**.

13. In the **New Computer Rule Element** dialog box, under **Name**, type **Demo-CSS-01**. In **Computer IP Address** type **192.168.1.22**. Click **OK** twice.

14. On the **Tasks** tab, click **Create New Enterprise Policy** to start the **New Enterprise Policy Wizard**.

15. On the **Welcome** page, type **Enterprise Internet Access Policy** as the name for the new policy. Click **Next**.

16. On the **Completing the New Enterprise Policy Wizard** page, click **Finish**.

17. Expand **Enterprise Policies** and click **Enterprise Internet Access Policy**. On the **Tasks** tab, click **Create Enterprise Access Rule** to start the **New Access Rule Wizard**.

18. On the **Welcome** page of the wizard, type **HTTP and HTTPS Access Rule** as the name for the access rule. Click **Next**.

19. On the **Rule Action** page, select **Allow**, and then click **Next**.

20. On the **Protocols** page, in **This rule applies to**, select **Selected protocols**. Click **Add** to open the **Add Protocols** dialog box.

21. Expand **Web**, click **HTTP**, click **Add**, click **HTTPS**, and then click **Add**. Click **Close** to close the **Add Protocols** dialog box. On the **Protocols** page, click **Next**.

22. On the **Access Rule Sources** page, click **Add** to open the **Add Network Entities** dialog box, expand **Network Sets**, select **All Protected Networks**, click **Add**, and then click **Close**. On the **Access Rule Sources** page, click **Next**.

23. On the **Access Rule Destinations** page, click **Add** to open the **Add Network Entities** dialog box, expand **Enterprise Networks**, select **External**, click **Add**, and then click **Close**. On the **Access Rule Destinations** page, click **Next**.

24. On the **User Sets** page, because your rule applies to all users, you can leave the user set **All Users** in place, and then click **Next**.

25. Review the information on the summary page of the wizard, and then click **Finish**.

26. The rule is created under **Enterprise Policy Rules Applied After Array Firewall Policy**. To move **HTTP and HTTPS Access Rule** under **Enterprise Policy Rules Applied Before Array Firewall Policy**, right-click the rule, and select **Move up**.

27. Create another access rule with the following properties:

   a. Access rule name: **DNS Access Policy**

   b. Rule action: **Allow**

   c. Selected protocol: **DNS**

   d. Access Rule Sources: **Den-DC-01 computer object**

   e. Access Rule destination: **External**

   f. User sets: **All Users**

28. If necessary, move the rule so that it is listed under **Enterprise Policy Rules Applied After Array Firewall Policy**.

29. Click **Apply** to apply the changes, and click **OK** when the changes have been applied.

▶ **Creating the arrays**

1. In **ISA Server Management**, click **Arrays**. On the **Tasks** tab, click **Create New Array** to start the **New Array Wizard**.

2. On the **Welcome** page of the wizard, type **Main/Back-End Array** as the name for the new array, and then click **Next**.

3. On the **Array DNS Name** page, click **Next**.

4. On the **Assign Enterprise Policy** page, from the drop-down menu, select **Enterprise Internet Access Policy**, and then click **Next**.

5. On the **Array Policy Rule Types** page, accept the default. Click **Next**.

6. On the summary page of the wizard, review the array configuration, and then click **Finish**. When the array is created, click **OK**.

7. In the task pane, on the **Tasks** tab, click **Create New Array** to start the **New Array Wizard**.

8. On the **Welcome** page, type **Branch/Front-End Array** as the name for the new array, and then click **Next**.

9. On the **Array DNS Name** page, click **Next**.

10. On the **Assign Enterprise Policy** page, accept the default, and click **Next**.

11. On the **Array Policy Rule Types** page, accept the default, and click **Next**.

12. On the **Summary** page, review the array configuration, and then click **Finish**. When the array has been created, click **OK**.

13. Click **Apply** to apply the changes, and then click **OK** when the changes have been applied.

To prepare for the next lab

When you finish this practice, shut down all the virtual machines that you used in the lab. As the virtual machines shut down, select the **Commit changes to the virtual hard disk** option.

Important You must save the virtual machine changes that you made in this module because later practices and labs require these changes.

How to Install ISA Server 2004 Enterprise Edition

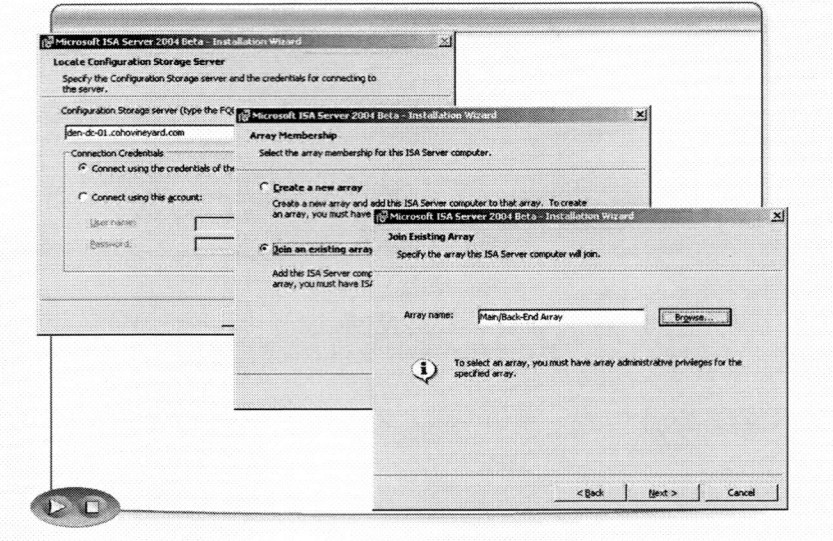

Introduction

Once you have prepared the enterprise and created the required arrays, you are ready to start installing the ISA Server services. Installing the ISA Server services enables the servers to operate as firewall servers.

Installing the ISA Server services

To install ISA Server services, complete the following steps on a Windows Server 2003 computer:

1. Access the ISA Server Enterprise Edition installation files and start the installation by running **Isaautorun.exe** and clicking **Install ISA Server**.

2. Accept the terms and conditions stated in the user license agreement.

3. Enter your customer information.

4. On the **Setup Scenarios** page, you are given four options:

   - **Install ISA Server services**

   - **Install Configuration Storage server**

   - **Install both ISA Server services and Configuration Storage server**

   - **Install ISA Server Management**

   Click **Install ISA Server Services**, and then click **Next**.

5. On the **Component Selection** page, you are given a choice about what components to install. You have the following options:

   - **ISA Server**

   - **ISA Server Management**

   - **Firewall Client Installation Share**

   - **Message Screener**

   - **Configuration Storage Server**

   Depending on your selection in the previous dialog box, the required components will be selected. You can choose to add additional components such as the Firewall Client Installation Share. Click **Next**.

6. On the **Locate Configuration Storage Server** page, type the fully qualified domain name (FQDN) of a Configuration Storage server. Click **Next**.

7. On the **Array Membership** page, select **Join an Existing Array**, or **Create a New Array**, and then click **Next**.

8. If you selected **Join an Existing Array** page, then you will get the **Join an Existing Array** page. Click **Browse**, and then click the array that the ISA Server computer will join. Click **OK**, and then click **Next**.

9. On the **Configuration Storage Server Authentication Options** page, you can choose how the ISA Server services computer will authenticate with the Configuration Storage server. Click **Next**.

10. On the **Internal Network** page, click **Add** to open the **Addresses** dialog box.

11. You can configure the Internal Network either by adding an enterprise network, adding an IP address range, or selecting an adapter address range.

12. On the **Internal Network** page, click **Next**.

13. On the **Services Warning** page, review the list of services that will be stopped or disabled during installation of ISA Server. To continue the installation, click **Next**.

14. On the **Ready to Install the Program** page, click **Install**.

15. After the installation is complete, click **Finish**.

16. You will be prompted to restart the computer. Click **Yes** to restart the computer.

Note   A Configuration Storage server must be available to install the ISA Server services component. This is because each computer running ISA Server services and ISA Server Management retrieves its configuration information from a Configuration Storage server.

Performing an unattended setup

You can install ISA Server 2004 by using the unattended server setup command. The files listed in the following table are located in the FPC folder on the ISA Server CD. The files contain the configuration information that can be used by server setup in unattended mode.

File name	Description
InstallJoinedServer.ini	Install a computer running ISA Server services, and join it to a specific array.
InstallNewArrayAndServer.ini	Install a computer running ISA Server services, and create a new array named ARRAY_NAME.
InstallNewManagementServer.ini	Install a Configuration Storage server.
InstallStandaloneServer.ini	Install ISA Server services and Configuration Storage server.
Uninstallserver.ini	Uninstall a server.

Note   For detailed information about how to modify the configuration files for your installation, see ISA Server Online Help.

How to Configure an ISA Server Management Computer

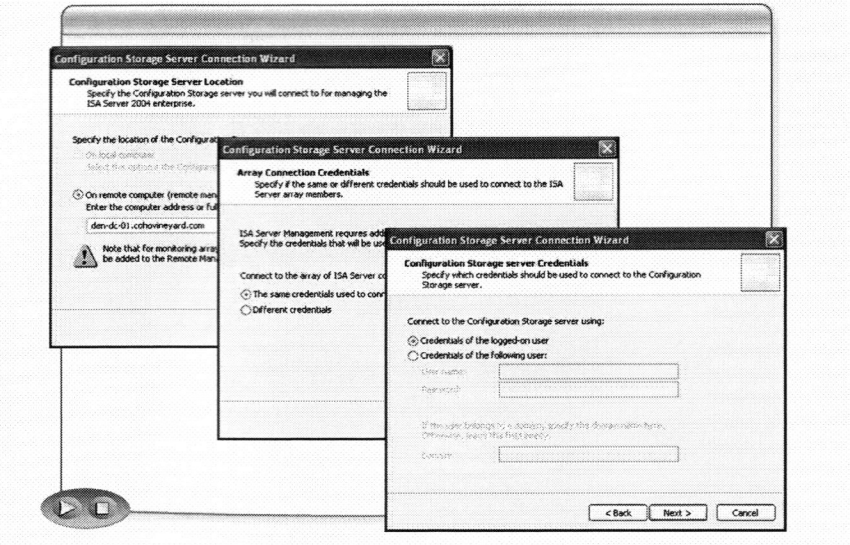

Introduction

After deploying the computers running ISA Server services, you need to continue to manage and monitor the computers. To do this, install the ISA Server Management Tools on an administrator workstation so that you can manage and monitor the ISA Server enterprise.

Install ISA Server Management on an administrator workstation

You can install ISA Server Management on a computer running Windows XP, Windows 2000 Server, or Windows Server 2003.

To install ISA Server Management, start the ISA Server installation from the ISA Server CD-ROM. On the **Setup Scenarios** page, select **ISA Server Management**, and then complete the installation.

Connect to a Configuration Storage server

After you complete the installation, you can connect to a Configuration Storage server in the enterprise. To do this, complete the following procedure:

1. Start **ISA Server Management** from the Microsoft ISA Server folder on the **Start Menu**.

2. On the **Task** tab, click **Connect to Configuration Storage Server**. The **Configuration Storage Server Connection Wizard** starts.

3. On the **Welcome** page of the wizard, click **Next**.

4. On the **Configuration Storage Server Location** page, type the FQDN of the Configuration Storage server.

5. On the **Configuration Storage server Credentials** page, select the option to connect to the Configuration Storage server using the credentials of the logged-on user, or specify alternate credentials. Click **Next**.

6. On the **Array Connection Credentials** page, select the option to use the same credentials to connect to the array as you use to connect to the Configuration Storage server, or specify different credentials.

7. On the **Completing the Connection Wizard** page, review the settings, and click **Finish**. You are connected to the Configuration Storage server and can view the ISA Server Configuration.

8. To monitor the ISA Server computers in an array, you must add the administrator workstation to the **Remote Management Computers** computer set. To do so, expand the array, and click **Firewall Policy**.

9. On the **Toolbox** tab, click **Network Objects**, then double-click **Remote Management Computers**.

10. In the **Remote Management Computers Properties** dialog box, click **Add**, and then click **Computer**.

11. In the **New Computer Rule Element** dialog box, type a name for the computer, and then type the computer IP address. Click **OK** twice.

12. Click **Apply** to apply the changes, and click **OK** when the changes have been applied.

Course Evaluation

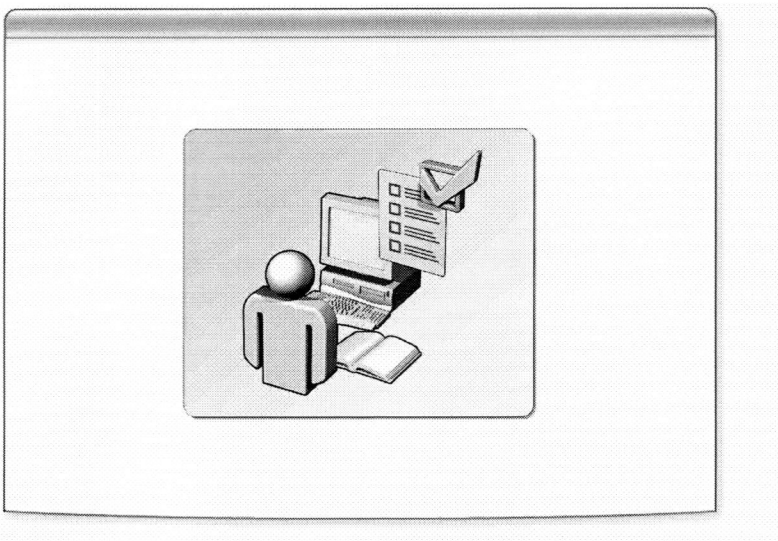

Your evaluation of this course will help Microsoft understand the quality of your learning experience.

At a convenient time before the end of the course, please complete a course evaluation, which is available at http://www.CourseSurvey.com.

Microsoft will keep your evaluation strictly confidential and will use your responses to improve your future learning experience.

Module 12: Implementing ISA Server 2004 Enterprise Edition: Back-to-Back Firewall Scenario

Contents

Overview

* Implementing a Back-to-Back Firewall Scenario
* Lab: Implementing a Back-to-Back Firewall Scenario

Introduction

One of the deployment scenarios for Microsoft® Internet Security and Acceleration (ISA) Server 2004 Enterprise Edition is a back-to-back firewall configuration. ISA Server provides flexibility in securing the perimeter and internal networks while enabling access to published resources in both the perimeter and the internal networks. This module introduces the complexities of implementing a back-to-back firewall configuration and then provides guidelines for deploying this configuration. In the lab, the students will implement and test a back-to-back firewall scenario.

Objectives

After completing this module, you will be able to:

■ Describe the issues involved with deploying ISA Server Enterprise Edition in a back-to-back firewall scenario, and describe possible solutions to those issues.

■ Implement ISA Server 2004 in a back-to-back firewall scenario.

Lesson: Implementing a Back-to-Back Firewall Scenario

- Issues in Deploying a Back-to-Back Firewall Solution
- Guidelines for Configuring ISA Servers in a Workgroup
- Guidelines for Implementing Network Load Balancing
- Guidelines for Configuring a Front-End Firewall Array
- Guidelines for Configuring a Back-End Firewall Array

Introduction

This lesson examines the concepts related to deploying ISA Server in a back-to-back firewall scenario. The lesson describes the problems of deploying this solution and then describes possible solutions to solve those problems.

Lesson objectives

After completing this lesson, you will be able to:

- Describe the issues in deploying a back-to-back firewall solution.
- Configure ISA Server in a workgroup.
- Configure integrated network load balancing.
- Configure the front-end firewall.
- Configure the back-end firewall.

Issues in Deploying a Back-to-Back Firewall Solution

Issues in deploying a back-to-back firewall configuration include:

- Using public or private IP addresses in the perimeter network
- Deploying the ISA Server computers in a domain or workgroup
- Configuring network load balancing
- Configuring name resolution and network routing
- Configuring access to Configuration Storage servers
- Configuring configure publishing rules and access rules
- Configuring SSL connections
- Configuring user authentication

Introduction

Deploying a back-to-back firewall solution is significantly more complex than deploying a single Internet-edge firewall. In a back-to-back firewall scenario, you must ensure that both the front-end and the back-end firewalls are configured correctly to ensure security and functionality.

Deployment considerations

When you prepare to deploy a back-to-back firewall solution using ISA Server 2004 Enterprise Edition, there are several considerations that must be included in your planning. These include:

- *Using public or private IP addresses in the perimeter network.* You can use either public or private Internet Protocol (IP) addressing for the perimeter network, but your decision has implications for how you will configure access to resources on other networks. You must define a route or a network-address translation (NAT) relationship between the internal network and the perimeter network, and between the perimeter network and the external network.

- *Deploying the ISA Servers in a domain or workgroup configuration.* ISA Server Enterprise Edition Configuration Storage server and ISA Server services can be installed on a computer that is a member of a domain, or on a computer that is a member of a workgroup. If you deploy ISA Server on a domain member, it is easier to configure authentication, and you can use the Firewall Client for authenticating outbound access. Deploying ISA Server on computers that are not domain members means that no domain information is stored on the ISA Server computer. But this increases the complexity of configuring communication between ISA Server computers and the Configuration Storage server. You can deploy ISA Server in one array on domain members, and deploy ISA Server in another array on members of a workgroup.

- *Configuring network load balancing.* In a back-to-back firewall configuration, you can configure network load balancing (NLB) on either the front-end array, the back-end array, or both. You can also define NLB on any network that is attached to any of the networks attached to the array. For example, on the back-end array, you can configure NLB for the internal network, the perimeter network, or both.

- *Configuring name resolution and network routing.* Deploying a back-to-back firewall configuration can significantly complicate name resolution and routing configuration. The ISA Server computers, the ISA Server clients, and the published servers must all be able to resolve computer names to IP addresses. However, the computers may be using different IP addresses to access other computers, depending on whether the servers are located in the perimeter network, on the internal network, or on the Internet. Not all the computers will be able to use the same Domain Name System (DNS) server, so you may have to use a split DNS or Hosts files to enable name resolution. The ISA Server computers must also be able to route network packets to networks that are not directly attached. Computers in the perimeter network may need to route network traffic to both the internal and the external network. To enable network routing, you must plan the default gateway configuration carefully, and possibly configure static routes on specific computers.

- *Configuring access to the Configuration Storage servers.* All ISA Server computers must have access to a Configuration Storage server. In most cases, you should deploy the Configuration Storage server on the internal network. You then need to configure firewall rules on the back-end array to enable network traffic between the Configuration Storage servers and the ISA Server computers in the front-end array.

- *Configuring publishing rules and access rules.* In a back-to-back firewall configuration, configuring access rules can also be significantly more complicated. On the front-end array, you may need to configure publishing rules to publish servers in the perimeter network. On the back-end array, you may need to allow access to the same servers in the perimeter network for users on the internal network. In some cases, you may need to enable access to resources on the internal network to computers in the perimeter network. For example, a Web server in the perimeter network may require access to a database server on the internal network, or may require access to a domain controller to authenticate users. You may also need to configure access for Internet users to resources on the internal network, in which case, you must define firewall rules on the front-end array that enable access to the back-end array, and then configure firewall rules on the back-end array that enable access to the published resource.

- *Configuring SSL connections.* With a back-to-back firewall configuration, you can deploy almost any Secure Sockets Layer (SSL) configuration. When you publish a server in the perimeter network, you can choose to use SSL bridging or SSL tunneling on the front-end array. If you publish a resource on the internal network, you can use SSL bridging or tunneling between the front-end array and the back-end array, and use SSL bridging or tunneling on the back-end array.

- *Configuring user authentication.* In a back-to-back firewall configuration, you may require user authentication on the back-end array to restrict access to the Internet or to restrict access to resources published behind the back-end array. You may also require user authentication on the front-end array to restrict access to published resources located in the perimeter network.

Guidelines for Configuring ISA Servers in a Workgroup

ISA Server Enterprise Edition supports the following deployment scenarios:

- Deploying all ISA Server components on domain members

- Deploying all ISA Server components on workgroup members

- Deploying ISA Server components in a mixed configuration

You can change the deployment configuration after deployment

Introduction

ISA Server Enterprise Edition can be deployed in a domain configuration or in a workgroup configuration. In a back-to-back firewall scenario, you have the following deployment options:

- Install the Configuration Storage server or servers and all ISA Server services on computers that are members in a domain or in trusted domains.

- Install the Configuration Storage server or servers and all ISA Server services on computers that are in a workgroup.

- Install the Configuration Storage server or servers on computers that are members in a domain and all or some of the ISA Server services on computers that are in a workgroup. For example, you can install Configuration Storage server on a domain member, install the ISA Server services for the back-end array on domain members, and then install ISA Server services for the front-end array on computers in a workgroup.

Deploying all ISA Server components on domain members

The easiest deployment option is to deploy all ISA Server components on computers that are members of the same domain or in trusted domains. In this scenario, you can use domain authentication for the ISA Server administrators and for all ISA Server clients. In addition, the ISA Server computers can use the domain computer accounts to authenticate with other array members and to authenticate with the Configuration Storage servers. All network traffic between ISA Server computers is encrypted and digitally signed using keys derived from the domain authentication, so you do not need to configure any certificates for ISA Server communication.

The most significant limitation with deploying all ISA Server components on domain members is the concern about deploying a domain member where it can be directly accessed from the Internet. This configuration increases the risk that an attacker can access the domain accounts if the Internet-edge firewall is compromised. Moreover, a domain member requires that additional services be running on the server. If you deploy ISA Server on a domain member in a front-end array, you must also open additional ports on the back-end array for the servers to connect to the domain controllers.

Deploying all ISA Server components on workgroup members

The second option is to deploy all ISA Server components on computers that are members of a workgroup. This configuration has the advantage that no domain accounts are accessible on the ISA Server computer, so even if the server is compromised in an attack, the attacker does not have access to domain resources.

Deploying all the ISA Server components in workgroup complicates the deployment in the following ways:

- You can only deploy one Configuration Storage server in your enterprise. This means that you will not have Configuration Storage server redundancy and all computers running ISA Server services and ISA Server Management must be able to communicate with the single Configuration Storage server.

- Because the workgroup computers cannot access domain user accounts, workgroup clients cannot be authenticated using Microsoft Windows® authentication. You can use Remote Authentication Dial-In User Service (RADIUS) authentication or RSA SecurID authentication to authenticate clients for publishing rules and RADIUS authentication for outbound access rules. Firewall clients depend on access to domain user accounts; therefore, the Firewall Client will not work in a workgroup setting.

- To use centralized administration, you must create mirrored user accounts on all the computers in the array. Mirrored accounts are local users with identical user names and passwords. You will use the credentials of this user when you open ISA Server Management and want to connect to the workgroup array.

- To assign ISA Server roles, you need to create a local user on each workgroup array member that can be assigned to an ISA Server role. If you use the same user account for each role on each computer, you can connect to the Configuration Storage server and each ISA Server computer using the same logon credentials and have access to the same ISA Server administrator role.

- Because the ISA Server computers in a workgroup cannot use domain authentication to create a secure channel between servers, you must configure any array containing workgroup members to use authentication over an SSL-encrypted channel. To enable this option, install a server certificate on the Configuration Storage server and configure the computers running ISA Server services with a root certificate of a mutually trusted certificate authority (CA). You must also configure the array so that a user account is used to authenticate connections between array members, rather than using the domain user account.

Deploying ISA Server components in a mixed configuration

The third deployment option is to install Configuration Storage server on a computer that is a member of a domain, and then to install the ISA Server services on either domain members or workgroup members. This scenario can exploit some of the benefits of deploying ISA Server components on domain members, while enabling the more secure workgroup configuration for workgroup members.

When deploying this configuration, remember the following:

- All members of an array must have the same workgroup or domain configuration. You can deploy an array with domain members, an array with workgroup members, but one array cannot have both types of members.

- For arrays in which the ISA Server computers are members of a domain, you can use domain authentication for the ISA Server administrators, for ISA Server clients as well as for authentication within the array.

- For arrays in which the ISA Server computers are members of a workgroup, you need to consider all the issues of deploying ISA Servers in a workgroup. Configure the array to enable SSL authentication, install a certificate on all Configuration Storage servers, and configure the root certificate on each computer running ISA Server services.

Changing your configuration to allow workgroup arrays

You can modify the ISA Server domain or workgroup configuration after deployment. If you installed the Configuration Storage server without a certificate, you can modify the configuration to support workgroup arrays. To do this, obtain a server authentication certificate for each Configuration Storage server. Then associate the certificate with the appropriate service on the Configuration Storage server. You can do this in two ways:

- *Rerun ISA Server setup*. When you run ISA Server setup, select **Repair** on the **Program Maintenance** page. Then select the option to deploy ISA Server in a workgroup and configure the service to use the certificate.

- Use the ISACertTool tool to install the certificate and associate it with the Configuration Storage service. The ISACertTool is available as part of the ISA Server Resource Kit.

Guidelines for Implementing Network Load Balancing

> **Configuring intra-array addressing:**
>
> - Used by array members to communicate with other array members
> - If not enabling NLB, use the internal network for the intra-array network
> - If enabling NLB, create a separate IP address or a separate network for the intra-array addresses
>
> **When configuring network load balancing:**
>
> - Do not use a layer-2 switch to connect array members
> - If all networks are enabled for NLB, add an additional network adapter and create a separate network for intra-array traffic

Introduction

ISA Server 2004 enables NLB integration whereby you can configure NLB for an array, and then use ISA Server Management to manage NLB for the array.

Configuring intra-array addressing

Before implementing NLB for an array, configure the intra-array communication between the ISA Server computers in each array. The ISA Server computers that are part of an array must be able to communicate with each other to enable features such as Cache Array Routing Protocol (CARP) and NLB.

The servers in the array communicate with each other using the intra-array address. This address is automatically configured during setup and is configured as the first network interface on the internal network. You can modify the intra-array address.

Note   A default system policy, named Allow intra-array communications, permits communication using the MS Firewall Control and remote procedure call (RPC) (all interfaces) protocols to and from all members of the Array Servers computer set. By default, the Array Servers computer set includes the intra-array address of each member server. When you modify the intra-array address, the Array Servers computer set is automatically updated.

When configuring the intra-array address for a server, follow these guidelines:

- If you do not plan to enable NLB for the array, specify the intra-array address as the primary IP address of the first network adapter on the internal network.

- If you plan to enable NLB for the array, use a dedicated network adapter that is located on the internal network for intra-array traffic. Use a different network adapter on the internal network for NLB.

- The best option is to use a dedicated network adapter in a network that is used only for intra-array communication. To do this, configure a network used for intra-array traffic that includes only the intra-array addresses used by all servers in the array.

Configuring network load balancing

After you configure the intra-array addresses for an array, you can enable and configure NLB for the other networks connected to the array. When you configure NLB for a network, you must specify one virtual IP address for the network. The dedicated IP address and the virtual IP address must belong to the same subnet and have the same subnet mask.

When configuring and deploying NLB-enabled networks, follow these guidelines:

- Do not use a layer-2 switch to connect the array members. NLB uses a virtual physical address for the virtual IP address. None of the ISA Server network adapters registers that physical address on the switch, so incoming packets are flooded to all ports on the switch. Instead, connect the network adapters to a hub and uplink that hub to the network switch.

- When load balancing is enabled on all the networks in the array, you must add a network adapter that is dedicated for intra-array traffic. Place this network adapter on a separate network subnet. In this way, all outgoing traffic to other array members will only pass through this network adapter and not through load-balanced networks.

When the Configuration Storage server is installed on an array member, the IP address that the array members use to access the Configuration Storage server should be set to the intra-array address of the Configuration Storage server. Otherwise, the other array members may lose connectivity to the Configuration Storage server.

Guidelines for Configuring a Front-End Firewall Array

> When configuring a back-to-back firewall, begin by defining the Internal and External networks for both arrays
>
> On the front-end firewall array, you need to configure:
> - Network routing
> - The Internal network IP addresses
> - The network relationship
> - Access to resources on the perimeter network
> - Access to resources on the Internal network
> - SSL publishing for perimeter network servers
> - SSL publishing for Internal network servers
> - Authentication

Introduction

When you deploy ISA Server Enterprise Edition in a back-to-back firewall configuration, you must configure both the front-end firewall array and the back-end firewall array.

Defining the ISA Server networks

When configuring the front-end and back-end firewalls in a back-to-back firewall, begin by configuring the ISA Server networks for both arrays. On the back-end array, the Internal network IP addresses includes the network addresses connected to the ISA Server network interface on the internal network. The External network on the back-end array includes the IP addresses in the perimeter network, as well as the IP addresses on the Internet.

On the front-end array, the Internal network includes the IP addresses used in the perimeter network. If you use a NAT relationship between the perimeter network and the Internal network on the back-end array, the Internal network for the front-end array includes only the perimeter network IP addresses. If you define a route relationship between the perimeter network and the Internal network for the back-end array, the Internal network on the front-end array includes the perimeter network IP addresses and the back-end array Internal network IP addresses. On the front-end array, the External network includes only the Internet IP addresses.

Configuring the front-end array

When configuring the front-end firewall array, consider the following guidelines.

- *Configure network routing.* If you define a route relationship between the perimeter network and the Internal network (as defined on the back-end array), the front-end array servers may need to be able to route network traffic to the servers on the back-end Internal network using the actual IP addresses of the Internal servers. In this case, configure network routing before installing ISA Server services on the front-end array servers. In most cases, the front-end array servers need to be configured to use a router connected to the Internet as its default gateway. This means that you must configure a static route on the ISA Server computers so that they can route incoming traffic to the back-end Internal network. If you use a NAT relationship between the perimeter network and the back-end Internal network, the front-end ISA Server computers can route all requests by using the IP address for a network adapter connected to the perimeter network on the back-end ISA Server computers, so no additional routing is required.

- *Configure the Internal network IP addresses for the front-end array.* When you install the first ISA Server computer in the front-end array, you must define the IP addresses that are included on the Internal network for the front-end array. The Internal network IP address range should include the perimeter network IP addresses and, possibly, the IP addresses included in the Internal network on the back-end.

- *Configure the network relationship.* Define a network relationship between the External network on the front-end array and the perimeter network. If you use private IP addresses for the perimeter network, you must configure a NAT relationship between the two networks. If you use public IP addresses for the perimeter network, you can define either a NAT or route relationship.

- *Configure access to resources on the perimeter network.* After you configure the network relationship, begin configuring access to servers or services on the perimeter network. If you configure a NAT relationship, you should use publishing rules to enable access. If you configure a route relationship, you can use either access rules or publishing rules for the same purpose. If you use access rules, external clients must be able to resolve the actual IP address of the servers on the perimeter network. If you use publishing rules, all client connections will use the external IP addresses for the front-end array.

- *Configure access to resources on the back-end array Internal network.* In some cases, you may need to configure access to resources on the Internal network located behind the back-end array. In this case, the front-end ISA Servers will forward the client requests to the back-end array's external IP address. To enable this, configure access or publishing rules that forward the client requests to the appropriate address for the back-end array.

- *Configure SSL publishing for perimeter network servers.* You may also need to configure access to secure Web sites or other resources on the perimeter network. If you use SSL to secure a Web site on the perimeter network, you can use SSL Web publishing to publish the Web site and configure either SSL bridging or SSL tunneling. Similarly, when you publish secure Web sites in an Internet edge firewall scenario or in a 3-Legged firewall scenario, you must ensure that you install all the required server certificates and that the correct Web server names are used for the certificates.

■ *Configure SSL publishing for network servers located on the Internal network behind the back-end array.* You may also need to configure secure access to the resources on the back-end Internal network. In this scenario, you can deploy SSL in the following ways:

● Terminate the SSL connection at the front-end array and enable non-SSL connections to the back-end firewall. To enable this option, you only need server certificates on the front-end array servers. This option is not recommended, because this means that traffic will be sent in clear text across the perimeter network.

● Enable SSL bridging between the front-end array and the back-end array, so that the front-end ISA Servers will decrypt the packet and then re-encrypt the packet before sending it to the back-end array. In this case, you will need certificates on both the back-end and front-end array members.

● Enable SSL tunneling on the front-end array, and use SSL bridging on the back-end array. In this case, you will need certificates only on the back-end array members. This option is not recommended because this means that the front-end ISA Servers cannot apply application filtering to incoming traffic.

● In any case, you may also need server certificates on the server that is being published to provide end-to-end SSL encryption.

Important Before you configure any publishing rules that require SSL termination on the front-end array, you must install the required server certificates on all members of the array. The server certificates must be the same on both servers.

■ *Configuring authentication.* If you publish a Web site on the perimeter network that requires authentication, you can enable authentication on the ISA Server computers or on the published resource. If the ISA Server computers in the front-end array are members of a trusted domain, you can use domain accounts to enable authentication. However, if the front-end servers are in a workgroup, you cannot use domain accounts unless you use RADIUS authentication.

Guidelines for Configuring a Back-End Firewall Array

On a back-end firewall array, you need to configure:

- The internal network IP addresses
- Network routing
- The perimeter network on the internal array
- Network objects
- Access to perimeter network resources
- Access for front-end ISA Server computers
- Access to resources on the Internal network
- Internal network access for domain members

Introduction

In addition to configuring the front-end array, you must also configure the back-end array. The back-end array secures the network traffic between the perimeter network and the Internal network, so the configuration requirements for this network can be quite different from those for the front-end array.

Configuring a back-end array

When configuring a back-end firewall array, consider the following guidelines:

- *Configure the Internal network IP address.* When you install the first ISA Server computer in the back-end array, define the IP address range for the back-end array Internal network. Ensure that the address range includes all addresses located behind the Internal network interface, but does not include the IP addresses for the perimeter network located between the front-end and back-end arrays. You can use an Enterprise network to define the Internal address.

- *Configure routing for the back-end array members.* In most cases, you can just configure the default gateway on the back-end array to use the front-end array servers.

- *Configure the perimeter network on the Internal array.* This network should include only the IP addresses for the perimeter network. After configuring the perimeter network, configure a network rule that defines the relationship between the back-end array's Internal network and the perimeter network. This step is required only if you need to define firewall rules that allow access to or from the entire perimeter network.

- *Configure network objects.* Instead of configuring a network object for the perimeter network, you can configure network objects for the computers in the perimeter network. For example, if you deploy a Web server in the perimeter network and that Web server requires access to the Internal network, configure a computer set for the Web server. Then configure the firewall rule granting access to the back-end Internal network to use the computer set rather than the entire perimeter network. You should also configure a network object for the front-end ISA Server computers that contains the IP addresses for the network adapters connected to the perimeter network (as well as the virtual IP address if NLB is configured). Then use this network object when configuring firewall rules for the front-end servers to access resources such as Configuration Storage servers on the back-end Internal network.

- *Configure access to perimeter network resources.* In some cases, you may need to provide access to servers in the perimeter network for Internal users. To enable this, you can either configure a publishing rule or an access rule.

- *Configure access for ISA Server computers in the front-end array.* For the ISA Server computers in the front-end array to access the Configuration Storage servers on the Internal network, you must configure an access rule that allows the MS Firewall Storage protocol from the front-end array computers to the Configuration Storage server. If you use ISA Server Management on the front-end computers, this rule should also allow access for the MS Firewall Control protocol. To manage the front-end array ISA Server computers, you must also configure an access rule that allows the MS Firewall Control and RPC (all interfaces) protocols from the Configuration Storage server and the ISA Server management workstations to the front-end array computers.

- *Configure access to resources on the back-end array Internal network.* In some cases, you may need to configure access to resources on the Internal network from the Internet or the perimeter network. To enable this, you need configure access or publishing rules that forward the client requests from the perimeter network or the front-end ISA Server computers. You can also enable SSL bridging or SSL tunneling.

- *Configure back-end array Internal network access for domain members.* In some cases, you may also need to provide access to the Internal network for domain member servers located in the perimeter network. For example, you may have a Web server in the perimeter network that is a member of the Internal domain and needs to use domain user accounts to authenticate access to a Web site. Or the front-end ISA Server computers may be members of the Internal domain and may require access to Internal domain controllers. To enable this type of access, you must configure an access rule that allows DNS, Kerberos-Sec (TCP) and Kerberos-Sec (UDP), Lightweight Directory Access Protocol (LDAP), LDAP UDP, and LDAP GC (global catalog) traffic from the domain members to the Internal domain controllers. To join a computer in the perimeter network to the Internal domain, you must also enable RPC (all interfaces) and Microsoft Common Internet File System (CIFS) access.

Caution Deploying domain members in a perimeter network is considered a security risk if anonymous user connections are allowed to the perimeter network.

Practice: Planning a Back-to-Back Firewall Deployment

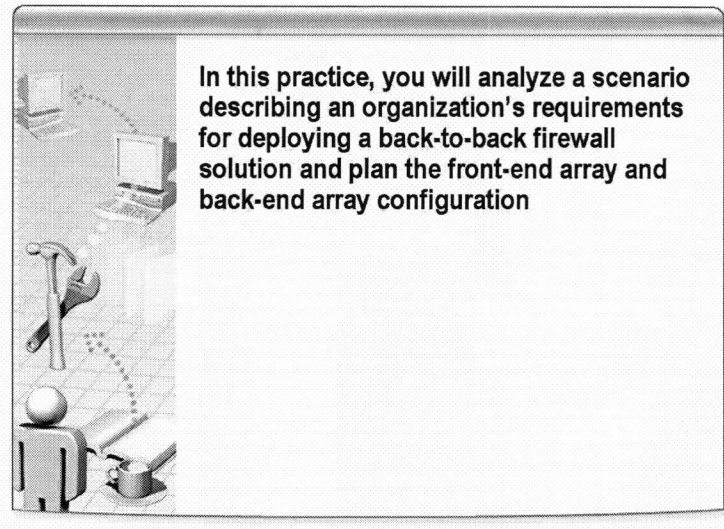

In this practice, you will analyze a scenario describing an organization's requirements for deploying a back-to-back firewall solution and plan the front-end array and back-end array configuration

Introduction

The following scenario describes an organization's requirements for deploying a back-to-back firewall configuration. Determine the firewall configuration that is required for the back-end and front-end arrays, and for the ISA Server computers installed in each array. Discuss your answers with a student partner. When you and your partner have agreed on solutions to the scenario, discuss your solutions with the rest of the class.

Scenario

Coho Vineyard is implementing a back-to-back firewall solution using ISA Server Enterprise Edition as both the front-end and back-end firewall. A Configuration Storage server has been deployed on the Internal network at Coho Vineyard.

Coho Vineyard has the following three IP addresses available to connect to the Internet: 131.107.1.101, 131.107.1.102, and 131.107.1.103.

Coho Vineyard has the following security and functional requirements:

- All users in the organization use Firewall clients to access Internet resources. The organization must be able to restrict access to Internet resources based on domain user accounts.

- The connection to the Internet should not be disrupted if a single ISA Server computer fails.

- The ISA Server computers in the front-end array should not be members of the cohovineyard.com domain.

- Users on the Internal network must be able to access resources on the Internet using Hypertext Transfer Protocol (HTTP), Hypertext Transfer Protocol Secure (HTTPS), and File Transfer Protocol (FTP).

- All users on the Internet must be able to access a company Web site located on a Web server in the perimeter network.

- Users on the Internal network must also be able to access a company Web site located on a Web server in the perimeter network.

- Users on the Internet must be able to access the Microsoft Exchange server on the internal network by using Microsoft Outlook® Web Access (OWA). The connection must be secured from the client to the Exchange server by means of SSL.

- Users on the Internet must be able to access a secure Web site located on a Web server in perimeter network. The connection must be secured from the client to the Web server using SSL. Access to the secure Web site must be restricted to domain user accounts.

Questions

Based on these requirements, how will you configure the Coho Vineyard ISA Server deployment?

1. How will you configure the back-end array and the ISA Server computers that are members of the back-end array?

2. How will you configure the back-end array and the ISA Server computers that are members of the front-end array?

3. What other configurations must you enable?

Lab 12: Implementing a Back-to-Back Firewall Scenario

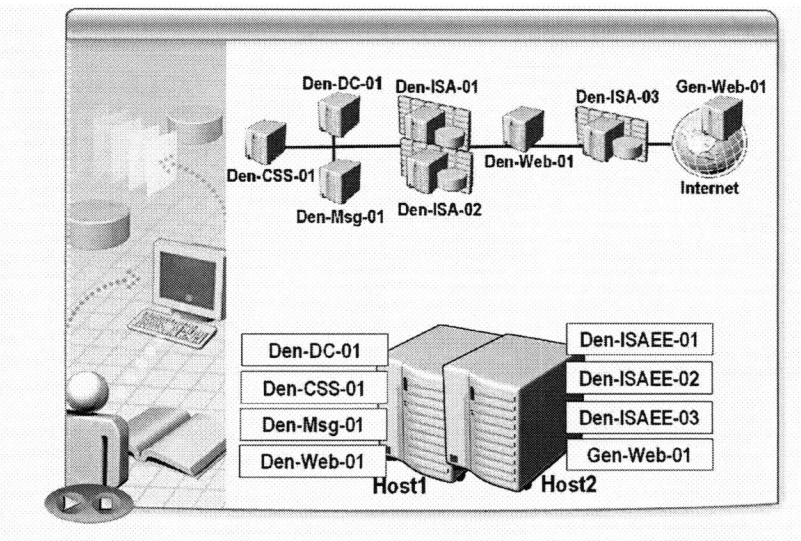

Objectives

After completing this lab, you will be able to:

- Enable network load balancing for an ISA Server array.

- Configure ISA Server services on a computer in a workgroup in a back-to-back deployment scenario.

- Configure firewall policies to enable Internet and internal access in back-to-back firewall configuration.

Note This lab focuses on the concepts in this module and, as a result, may not comply with Microsoft security recommendations. For example, this lab does not comply with the recommendation that users should not be logged in with administrative accounts but should use the **run as** command to perform administrative tasks.

The following diagram illustrates the final lab configuration when the students have completed this lab.

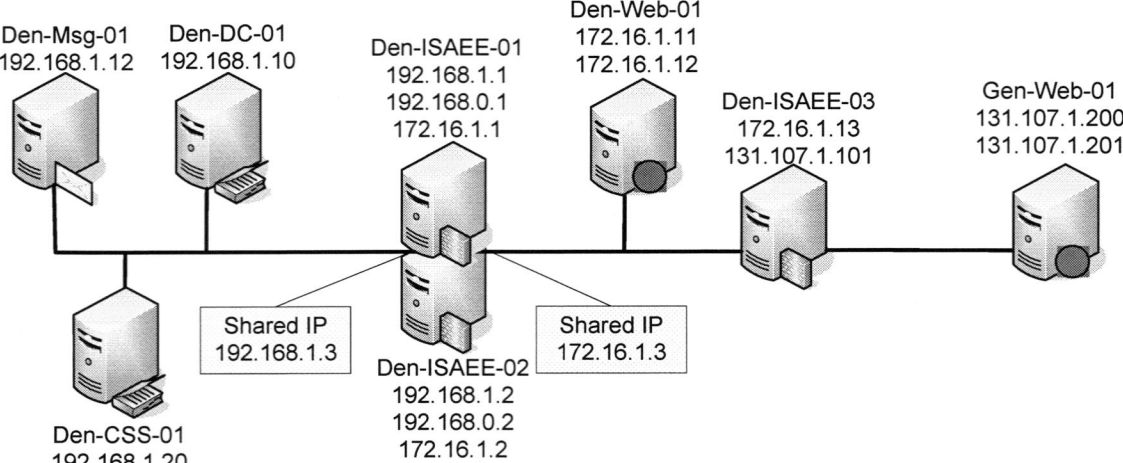

To prepare for this lab:

1. You will need the following virtual machines running for Exercise 1 of this lab:

    On the first student host computer, you will run:

    a. Den-DC-01

    b. Den-CSS-01

    On the second student host computer, you will run:

    c. Den-ISAEE-01

    d. Den-ISAEE-02

    e. Den-ISAEE-03

2. If necessary, start or resume the required virtual machines.

**Estimated time to
complete this lab:
90 minutes**

Exercise 1
Enabling Network Load Balancing for the Main\Front-End Array

In this exercise, you will configure load balancing for the ISA Server computers located in the Main\Front-End Array by enabling network load balancing (NLB).

Scenario

Coho Vineyard wants to ensure that its connection to the Internet is not susceptible to the failure of a single ISA Server computer. To provide this functionality, you will first configure an intra-array network and a perimeter network and configure the required network rules. Then you will configure NLB on the required networks.

Tasks	Detailed steps
1. Configure ISA Server permissions for the ISA Server administrative groups.	a. Perform the following steps on Den-CSS-01. b. Log on to the cohovineyard.com domain with a user account of **Administrator** and a password of **P@ssw0rd**. c. Open **ISA Server Management**. d. Click **Enterprise**, and on the **Tasks** tab, click **Assign Administrative Roles**. e. On the **Assign Roles** tab, click **Add**. f. On the **Administration Delegation** dialog box, in the **Group or User** text box, type **cohovineyard\isa entadmins**. g. From the **Role** drop-down list, select **ISA Server Enterprise Administrator**. Click **OK** twice. h. Right-click **Branch/Front-End Array** and then click **Properties**. i. On the **Assign Roles** tab, click **Add**. j. In the **Administration Delegation** dialog box, in the **Group or User** text box, type **cohovineyard\isa arradmins**. k. From the **Role** drop-down list, select **ISA Server Array Administrator**. Click **OK** twice. l. Click **Apply** to apply the changes and click **OK** when the changes have been applied. m. Log off Den-CSS-01.
2. Create an intra-array network that includes the 192.168.0.0 network.	a. On Den-CSS-01, log on to the cohovineyard.com domain with a user account of **EntAdmin** and a password of **P@ssw0rd**. b. In the **Manage Your Server** dialog box, click **Don't display this page at logon** and then close the page. c. Open **ISA Server Management**. d. Expand **Arrays**, and then expand **Main/Back-End Array**. e. Expand **Configuration**, and then click **Networks**. f. On the **Tasks** tab, click **Create a New Network**. g. On the **Welcome** page of the **Create a New Network Wizard**, type **BE Intra-Array Network** and then click **Next**.

(*continued*)

Tasks	Detailed steps
2. (*continued*)	h. On the **Network Type** page, ensure that **Internal Network** is selected and click **Next**. i. On the **Network Addresses** page, click **Add Adapter**. j. On the **Network Adapters** page, select the check box for the **IntraArray** adapter for **Den-ISAEE-01**, and then click **OK**. k. On the **Network Addresses** page, click **Next**. l. On the **Completing the New Network Wizard** page, review the configuration and then click **Finish**.
3. Configure Den-ISAEE-01 and Den-ISAEE-02 to use the intra-array network for intra-array communication.	a. On Den-CSS-01, in **ISA Server Management**, click **Servers** and then double-click **Den-ISAEE-01**. b. On the **Communication** tab, under **Intra-Array Communication**, select **192.168.0.1** from the drop-down list. c. Click **OK**. d. Double-click **Den-ISAEE-02**. e. On the **Communication** tab, under **Intra-Array Communication**, select **192.168.0.2** from the drop-down list. f. Click **OK**. g. Click **Apply** to apply the changes, then click **OK** when the changes have been applied.
4. Create a perimeter network that includes the 172.16.1.0 network.	a. On Den-CSS-01, under **Main/Back-End Array**, click **Networks**. b. On the **Tasks** tab, click **Create a New Network**. c. On the **Welcome** page of the wizard, type **Perimeter Network** as the network name and then click **Next**. d. On the **Network Type** page, click **Perimeter Network** and then click **Next**. e. On the **Network Address** page, click **Add Adapter**. f. In the **Select Network Adapters** dialog box, select the check box for **Perimeter** on Den-ISAEE-01. Click **OK**. g. On the **Network Addresses** page, click **Next**. h. On the **Completing the New Network Wizard** page, review the configuration and then click **Finish**.
5. Create a network rule between Internal network and the Perimeter network. The network rule will define a route relationship between the two networks.	a. On Den-CSS-01, click the **Network Rules** tab. On the **Tasks** tab, click **Create a Network Rule**. b. On the **Welcome** page of the wizard, type **Internal to Perimeter** as the network rule name, and then click **Next**. c. On the **Network Traffic Sources** page, click **Add**. On the **Add Network Entities** page, expand **Networks**, and then click **Internal**. Click **Add**, then click **Close**, and then click **Next**.

(continued)

Tasks	Detailed steps
5. *(continued)*	d. On the **Network Traffic Destinations** page, click **Add**. On the **Add Network Entities** page, expand **Networks**, and then click **Perimeter Network**. Click **Add**, then click **Close**, and then click **Next**. e. On the **Network Relationship** page, click **Route**, and then click **Next**. f. On the **Completing the New Network Rule Wizard** page, review the configuration, and then click **Finish**. g. Click **Apply** to apply the changes, and then click **OK** when the changes have been applied.
6. Configure Network Load Balancing for the back-end array	a. On Den-CSS-01, click the **Networks** tab, and then on the **Tasks** tab, click **Enable Network Load Balancing Integration**. b. On the **Welcome** page of the wizard, click **Next**. c. On the **Select Load Balanced Networks** page, select the check box for **Perimeter Network**, and then click **Set Virtual IP**. d. In the **Set Virtual IP Address** dialog box, type **172.16.1.3** as the **Virtual IP address** and **255.255.255.0** as the **Mask**. Click **OK**. e. On the **Select Load Balanced Networks** page, select the check box for **Internal**, and then click **Set Virtual IP**. f. In the **Set Virtual IP Address** dialog box, type **192.168.1.3** as the **Virtual IP address** and **255.255.255.0** as the **Mask**. Click **OK**. g. On the **Select Load Balanced Networks** page, click **Next**. h. On the **Completing the Network Load Balancing Integration Wizard** page, review the configuration and then click **Finish**. i. Click **Apply** to apply the changes. j. On the **ISA Server Warning** page, click **Save the changes and restart the services**, and then click **OK**.
7. Configure Den-DC-01 to use the shared IP address for the Internal network as its default gateway.	a. On Den-DC-01, log on to the cohovineyard domain using a user account of **Administrator** and password of **P@ssw0rd**. b. Modify the default gateway for the **Local Area Connection** to use 192.168.1.3.

Exercise 2
Configuring the Front-End Array Server

In this exercise, you will prepare the lab environment for the installation of the ISA Server computer in the front-end array and then complete the installation of ISA Server computer as a front-end array member.

Scenario

Now that you have configured the back-end array, you are ready to continue with the deployment of the front-end array server. To do this, you must configure the back-end array to support the installation and management of the ISA Server computer in the front-end array and then install the ISA Server services on the front-end ISA Server computer.

To prepare for this exercise:

You will need the following virtual machines running for Exercise 2 of this lab:

- On the first student host computer, you will run:

  a. Den-DC-01

  b. Den-CSS-01

- On the second student host computer, you will run:

  c. Den-ISAEE-01

  d. Den-ISAEE-02

  e. Den-ISAEE-03

If necessary, start or resume the required virtual machines.

Tasks	Detailed steps
1. Configure an access rule that enables the MS Firewall Storage and the MS Firewall Control protocols from the front-end ISA Server computers to the Configuration Storage server.	a. Perform these steps on Den-CSS-01. b. In **ISA Server Management**, click **Firewall Policy (Main/Back-End Array)**. c. Click **Create Array Access Rule**. d. On the **Welcome** page of the wizard, type **CSS Access Rule**. Click **Next**. e. On the **Rule Action** page, click **Allow**, and then click **Next**. f. On the **Protocols** page, click **Add**. g. In the **Add Protocols** dialog box, expand **All Protocols**, and then click **MS Firewall Storage**. Click **Add**. h. Click **MS Firewall Control**, click **Add**, and then click **Close**. i. On the **Protocols** page, click **Next**. j. On the **Access Rule Sources** page, click **Add**. k. In the **Add Network Entities** dialog box, click **New**, and then click **Computer**.

(*continued*)

Tasks	Detailed steps
1. (*continued*)	l. In the **New Computer Rule Element** dialog box, type **Den-ISAEE-03** as the name, and type **172.16.1.13** as the **Computer IP Address**. Click **OK**. m. In the **Add Network Entities** dialog box, expand **Computers**, and then click **Den-ISAEE-03**. Click **Add**, and then click **Close**. n. On the **Access Rule Sources** page, click **Next**. o. On the **Access Rule Destinations** page, click **Add**. p. In the **Add Network Entities** dialog box, click **New**, and then click **Computer**. q. In the **New Computer Rule Element** dialog box, type **Den-CSS-01** as the name, and type **192.168.1.20** as the **Computer IP Address**. Click **OK**. r. In the **Add Network Entities** dialog box, expand **Computers**, and then click **Den-CSS-01**. Click **Add**, and then click **Close**. Click **Next**. s. On the **User Sets** page, click **Next**. t. On the **Completing the New Access Rule Wizard** page, review the configuration and then click **Finish**.

2. Configure an access rule that enables the MS Firewall Control and the RPC (all interfaces) protocols from the to the Configuration Storage server to the front-end ISA Servers.	a. On Den-CSS-01, create another array access rule with the following properties.
	  • Access rule name: **ISA Server Access Rule**
	  • Rule Action: **Allow**
	  • Protocols: **MS Firewall Control, RPC (All Interfaces)**
	  • Access Rule Sources: **Remote Management Computers** computer set
	  • Access Rule Destination: **Den-ISAEE-03 computer**
	  • User Sets: **All Users**
	
	b. Click **Apply** to apply the changes, and then click **OK** when the changes have been applied.

3. Configure the Branch/Front-End Array to use SSL authentication.	a. On Den-CSS-01, in **ISA Server Management**, click **Branch/Front-End Array**, and then, on the **Tasks** tab, click **Configure Array Properties**. b. On the **Configuration Storage** tab, click **Select**. c. In the **Select Authentication Type** dialog box, click **Authentication over SSL encrypted channel**, and then click **OK**. d. Click **OK**, and then click **Apply** to apply the changes. Click **OK** when the changes have been applied.

(*continued*)

Tasks	Detailed steps
4. Prepare Den-ISAEE-03 for the installation of ISA Server services.	**a.** Perform these steps on Den-ISAEE-03. **b.** Log on as a local **Administrator** using a password of **P@ssw0rd**. **c.** Open **Computer Management** and create an account named **ArrAdmin** with a password of **P@ssw0rd**. Add the **ArrAdmin** user account to the local **Administrators** group. **d.** Log off and then log on as **ArrAdmin**. **e.** In the **Manage Your Server** dialog box, click **Don't display this page at logon** and then close the page. **f.** Open a **Run** command. In the **Run** box, type **notepad c:\windows\system32\drivers\etc\hosts**. Click **OK**. **g.** At the bottom of the hosts file, type **192.168.1.20 Den-CSS-01.cohovineyard.com**. **h.** Save the file and close **Notepad**. **i.** Open a command prompt and type **route add 192.168.1.0 Mask 255.255.255.0 172.16.1.3 /p**. Press ENTER. **j.** Close the **Command Prompt** window.
5. Install ISA Server Services on Den-ISAEE-03.	**a.** On the Den-ISAEE-03 virtual PC menu, click **CD**, and then click **Capture ISO Image**. **b.** Browse to **C:\Program Files\Microsoft Learning\2824\LabFiles** and click **ISAEEInstall.iso**. Click **Open**. **c.** Click **Install ISA Server 2004**. **d.** On the **Welcome** page of the wizard, click **Next**. **e.** On the **License Agreement** page, click **I accept the terms of the license agreement** and then click **Next**. **f.** On the **Customer Information** page, click **Next**. **g.** On the **Setup Scenarios** page, click **Install ISA Server services**, and then click **Next**. **h.** On the **Component Selection** page, click **Next**. **i.** On the **Locate Configuration Storage Server** page, type **Den-css-01.cohovineyard.com**. Click **Connect using this account**, and then type **cohovineyard\arradmin** as the user name and **P@ssw0rd** as the password. Click **Next**. **j.** On the **Array Membership** page, click **Join an existing array**, and then click **Next**. **k.** On the **Join Existing Array** page, click **Browse**. **l.** Click **Branch/Front-End Array**, click **OK**, and then click **Next**. **m.** On the **Configuration Storage Server Authentication Options**, click **Install a trusted root CA certificate**. Click **Browse** and browse to **C:\Program Files\Microsoft Learning\2824\Labfiles**.

(*continued*)

Tasks	Detailed steps
5. (*continued*)	n. Click **Den-DC-01.cohovineyard.com_CohovineyardCA.crt**, and then click **Open**. Click **Next**. o. On the **Internal Network** page, click **Add**. p. In the **Addresses**, dialog box, click **Add Adapter**. Click **Perimeter**, and then click **OK**. q. Click **OK**, and then on the **Internal Network** page, click **Next**. r. On the **Services Warning** page, click **Next**. s. On the **Ready to Install the program** page, click **Install**. t. When the installation finishes, click **Finish**, and then click **Yes** to restart the computer.
6. Configure Den-ISAEE-03 properties to use the IP address for Configuration Storage Server communication.	a. Perform these steps on Den-CSS-01. b. In **ISA Server Management**, expand **Branch/Front-End Array**, expand **Configuration**, and click **Servers**. c. Double-click **Den-ISAEE-03**. On the **Communication** tab, under Remote Communication, click **Use this IP address or computer name**. d. In the text box, type **172.16.1.13**. Click **OK**. e. Click **Apply** to apply the changes and then click **OK** when the changes have been applied.

Exercise 3
Configuring Firewall Rules for Resource Access

In this exercise, you will configure the firewall rules on both the front-end and back-end arrays to enable access to Internet and Internal resources.

Scenario

Now that you have completed the ISA Server installation, you are ready to configure the firewall rules that will enable access to the required Internet and internal resources. Coho Vineyard has the following access requirements:

- Users on the internal network must be able to access resources on the Internet using HTTP and HTTPS.

- Users on the Internet must be able to access a company Web site located on a Web server in the perimeter network.

- Users on the internal network must also be able to access the company Web site located on a Web server in perimeter network.

- Users on the Internet must be able to access the Exchange server on the internal network using OWA. The connection must be secured from the client to the Exchange server using SSL.

- Users on the Internet must be able to access the secure Web site located on a Web server in perimeter network. The connection must be secured from the client to the Web server using SSL

You will need the following virtual machines running for this exercise:

- On the first student host computer, you will run:

  a. Den-DC-01

  b. Den-CSS-01

  c. Den-Web-01

  d. Den-Msg-01

- On the second host computer; you will run:

  a. Den-ISAEE-01

  b. Den-ISAEE-02

  c. Den-ISAEE-03

  d. Gen-Web-01

If necessary, start or resume the required virtual machines.

Tasks	Detailed steps
1. Enable Internet access for internal users.	a. On Den-ISAEE-01 and Den-ISAEE-02, log on to the cohovineyard.com domain using a user name of **Entadmin** and a password of **P@ssw0rd**.
	b. On both computers, modify the properties of the Perimeter network connection by adding a default gateway of 172.16.1.13.
	c. On Den-ISAEE-03, log on to the local computer as **ArrAdmin**.
	d. In **ISA Server Management**, on the **Tasks** tab, click **Connect to Configuration Storage Server**. The **Configuration Storage Server Connection Wizard** starts.
	e. On the **Welcome** page of the wizard, click **Next**.
	f. On the **Configuration Storage Server Location** page, type **Den-CSS-01.cohovineyard.com**. Click **Next**.
	g. On the **Configuration Storage Server Credentials** page, select **Credentials of the following user**. Type **arradmin** as the user name, **P@ssw0rd** as the Password, and **cohovineyard** as the Domain. Click **Next**.
	h. On the **Array Connection Credentials** page, click **Next**.
	i. On the **Completing the Connection Wizard** page, review the settings and then click **Finish**.
	j. Expand **Arrays**, then expand **Branch/Front-End Array**. Click **Firewall Policy (Branch/Front-End Array)**.
	k. On the **Tasks** tab, click **Create Array Access Rule**.
	l. Create an access rule with the following properties.
	• Access rule name: **Internet Access**
	• Rule action: **Allow**
	• Protocols: **HTTP, HTTPS, DNS**
	• Access Rule Sources: **Internal**
	• Access Rule Destination: **External**
	• User Sets: **All Users**
	m. Click **Apply** to apply the changes, and then click **OK** when the changes have been applied.
2. Test Internet access.	▪ On Den-CSS-01, open **Internet Explorer** and try to access **www.tailspintoys.com** and **www.contoso.com**. The connections should be successful.

(*continued*)

Tasks	Detailed steps
3. Enable access to the Den-Web-01.cohovineyard.com Web server for internal clients.	a. On Den-Web-01, log on as a local **Administrator** with a password of **P@ssw0rd**.
	b. Modify the properties of the **Local Area Connection** to use a default gateway of **172.16.1.13**.
	c. Open a command prompt and type **route add 192.168.1.0 Mask 255.255.255.0 172.16.1.3 /p** and then press ENTER.
	d. Close the command prompt window.
	e. On Den-DC-01, open **DNS** from the Administrative Tools folder and create a host record for **www** in the **cohovineyard.com** domain. Assign an IP address of **192.168.1.3**.
	f. Modify the **Den-Web-01** host record to use an IP address of **172.16.1.11**. Close **DNS**.
	g. On Den-CSS-01, in **ISA Server Management**, click **Firewall Policy (Main/Back-End Array)**.
	h. On the **Tasks** tab, click **Publish a Web Server**.
	i. Create a Web publishing rule with the following properties.
	• Publishing rule name: **Coho Vineyard Web Site**
	• Rule action: **Allow**
	• Web site to publish: **Den-Web-01.cohovineyard.com**
	• Public name: **www.cohovineyard.com**
	• Web Listener: Create a new Web listener named **HTTP Internal** that will listen for HTTP requests on the Internal network.
	• User Sets: **All Users**
	j. Click **Apply** to apply the changes, and then click **OK** when the changes have been applied.
4. Test access to the Coho Vineyard Web site from the internal network.	▪ On Den-CSS-01, open Internet Explorer and try to access www.cohovineyard.com. The connection should succeed.
5. Publish the Cohovineyard Web site for Internet access.	a. On Den-ISAEE-03, add the following entries to the c:\windows\system32\drivers\etc\Hosts file.
	• **172.16.1.12 Secure.cohovineyard.com**
	• **172.16.1.11 www.cohovineyard.com**
	• **192.168.1.12 Den-msg-01.cohovineyard.com**
	b. Save the Hosts file.
	c. On Den-ISAEE-03, in **ISA Server Management**, click **Firewall Policy (Branch/Front-End Array)**.
	d. On the **Tasks** tab, click **Publish a Web Server**.

(*continued*)

Tasks	Detailed steps
5. (*continued*)	e. Create a Web publishing rule with the following properties. • Publishing rule name: **Coho Vineyard Public Web Site** • Rule action: **Allow** • Computer name or IP address: **www.cohovineyard.com** • Public name: **www.cohovineyard.com** • Web Listener: Create a new Web listener named **HTTP Internet** that will listen for HTTP requests on the External network. • User Sets: **All Users** f. Click **Apply** to apply the changes, and then click **OK** when the changes have been applied.
6. Test access to the Coho Vineyard Public Web site.	a. On Gen-Web-01, log on using a user account of **Administrator** and a password of **P@ssw0rd**. b. Open **DNS** and create a host record for **www** in the **cohovineyard.com** domain. Assign an IP address of **131.107.1.101**. c. Modify the host records for secure to use an IP address of **131.107.1.101**. d. Open **Internet Explorer** and try to access **www.cohovineyard.com**. The connection should succeed.
7. Create a Web server certificate request on Den-Web-01.	a. Perform the following steps on Den-Web-01. b. Open **Internet Information Services (IIS) Manager**. c. Expand **Den-Web-01 (local computer)** and expand **Web Sites**. d. Right-click **Cohovineyard Secure Web Site** and click **Properties**. e. On the **Directory Security** tab, click **Server Certificate**. f. On the **Welcome** page, click **Next**. g. On the **Server Certificate** page, click **Next**. h. On the **Delayed or Immediate Request** page click **Next**. i. On the **Name and Security Settings** page click **Next**. j. On the **Organization Information** page, type **Coho Vineyard** as the Organization, and then type **Security** as the Organizational Unit. k. On the **Your Site's Common Name** page, type **Secure.cohovineyard.com** as the Common name. Click **Next**. l. On the **Geographical Information** page, type **Colorado** as the State/province and then type **Denver** as the City/locality. Click **Next**. m. On the **Certificate Request File Name** page, click **Next**. n. On the **Request File Summary** page, click **Next**, and then click **Finish**. o. Close **Internet Information Services (IIS) Manager**. p. Copy the certreq.txt file from the C drive to the host computer desktop.

(*continued*)

Tasks	Detailed steps
8. On Den-DC-01, obtain a Web Server certificate using the certificate request file.	a. On Den-DC-01, copy the certreq.txt file from the host computer desktop to the Den-DC-01 desktop. b. Open the certreq.txt file, select all the file's content, and then press CTRL+C to copy the file into the Clipboard. c. Open **Internet Explorer** and connect to **Http://den-dc-01.cohovineyard.com/certsrv**. Apply for a certificate using the following information. d. Log on as **Administrator** with a password of **P@ssw0rd**. e. Request a certificate using an advanced certificate request. f. Choose to **Submit a certificate request by using a base-64-encoded CMC or PKCS#10file, or submit a renewal request by using a base-64-encoded PKCS#7 file.** g. On the **Submit a Certificate Request or Renewal Request** page, click the **Saved Request** box and then press CTRL+V. h. Under the **Certificate Template**, click **Web Server** and then click **Submit**. i. On the **Certificate Issued** page, click **Download Certificate**. j. In the **File Download** page click **Save**, and then click **Save** to save the file to the Desktop. k. In the **Download Complete Dialog** box, click **Close**. l. Copy the Certnew.cer file to the host computer desktop.
9. On Den-Web-01, install the Secure.cohovineyard.com certificate and configure the secure Web site on Den-Web-01 to require SSL encryption.	a. Copy the Certnew.cer file from the host computer desktop to the Den-Web-01 desktop. b. On Den-Web-01, open **Internet Information Services (IIS) Manager**. c. Expand **Web Sites**, right-click **Cohovineyard Secure Web Site**, and then click **Properties**. d. On the **Directory Security** tab, click **Server Certificate**. e. On the **Welcome Page**, click **Next**. f. On the **Pending Certificate Request** page, click **Next**. g. On the **Process a Pending Request** page, click **Browse** and browse to the Desktop. Click **Certnew** and then click **Open**. Click **Next**. h. On the **SSL Port** page, click **Next**. i. On the **Certificate Summary** page click **Next**, and then click **Finish**. j. Under **Secure Communications**, click **Edit**. k. Click **Require secure channel (SSL)** and then click **OK**.

(*continued*)

Tasks	Detailed steps
10. Export the secure.cohovineyard.com certificate.	**a.** On the **Directory Security** tab, click **View Certificate**. **b.** In the **Certificate** dialog box, click the **Details** tab. On the **Details** tab, click **Copy to File**. **c.** On the **Welcome to the Certificate Export Wizard** page, click **Next**. **d.** On the **Export Private Key** page, click **Yes, export the private key** and then click **Next**. **e.** On the **Export File Format** page, ensure that **Personal Information Exchange – PKCS #12 (.PFX)** is selected. Select **Include all certificates in the certification path if possible** and deselect **Enable strong protection (requires IE 5.0, NT 4.0 SP4 or above)**. Click **Next**. **f.** On the **Password** page, type **P@ssw0rd** in the **Password** and **Confirm Password** boxes. Click **Next**. **g.** On the **File to Export** page, enter **C:\Securecert** in the **File name** box. Click **Next**. **h.** Click **Finish** on the **Completing the Certificate Export Wizard** page. **i.** Click **OK** in the **Certificate** dialog box. **j.** Click **OK** in the **Cohovineyard Secure Web Site Properties** dialog box. **k.** Copy the Securecert.pfx file from the C drive to the host computer desktop.
11. Import the Secure.cohovineyard.com certificate on Den-ISAEE-03.	**a.** On the first student host computer, open a **Run** command and type ***studenthost2*\c$**, where *studenthost2* is the name or IP address of the second student host computer. **b.** Copy the Securecert.pfx file from the first student host desktop to **\\\*studenthost2*\c$**. **c.** On the second host computer, copy the Securecert.pfx file from the C: drive to the Den-ISAEE-03 desktop. **d.** Click **Start** and click the **Run** command. Type **mmc** and click **OK**. In the console, on the **File** menu, click **Add/Remove Snap-in**. **e.** Add the **Certificates**. Configure it to manage certificates on the local computer. **f.** Right-click **Personal** in the left pane of the console, point to **All Tasks** and then click **Import**. **g.** Click **Next** on the **Welcome to the Certificate Import Wizard** page. **h.** Click the **Browse** button. In **Files of type**, select **Personal Information Exchange (*.pfx, *.p12)** and locate the certificate file on the desktop. Click **Open**, and then click **Next**. **i.** On the **Password** page, enter **P@ssw0rd**. Click **Next**. **j.** On the **Certificate Store** page, click **Next**. **k.** Review the settings on the **Completing the Certificate Import** page and then click **Finish**.

(*continued*)

Tasks	Detailed steps
11. (*continued*)	**l.** Click **OK** on the **Certificate Import Wizard** dialog box informing you the import was successful. **m.** Close the Microsoft Management Console (MMC) without saving changes.

12. Configure a secure Web publishing rule to publish the Coho Vineyard Secure Web site for Internet users.	**a.** On Den-ISAEE-03, in ISA Server Management, right-click **Branch/Front-End Array** and click **Refresh**.
	
	b. Click **Firewall Policy (Branch/Front-End Array)**. On the **Tasks** tab, click **Publish a Secure Web Server**.
	
	c. Create **Secure Web Publishing** rule with the following properties.
	  • Access rule name: **Coho Vineyard Secure Web Site**
	  • Publishing Mode: **SSL Bridging**
	  • Rule action: **Allow**
	  • Bridging Mode: **Secure connection to clients and Web server**
	  • Computer name or IP address: **Secure.cohovineyard.com**
	  • Public name: **secure.cohovineyard.com**
	  • Web Listener: Create a Web listener named **HTTPS Internet** that will listen for HTTPS requests on the External network and use the Secure.cohovineyard.com certificate.
	  • User Sets: **All Users**
	
	d. Click **Apply** to apply the changes, and then click **OK** when the changes have been applied.
	
	e. On Gen-Web-01, open Internet Explorer and try to access https://secure.cohovineyard.com. The connection should succeed.

13. On Den-Msg-01, obtain a Web Server certificate for the OWA Web site.	**a.** On Den-Msg-01, log on to the cohovineyard.com domain using a user account of **Administrator** and a password of **P@ssw0rd**. **b.** Open **Internet Information Services (IIS) Manager**. **c.** Expand **Den-Msg-01**, and then expand **Web Sites**. **d.** Right-click **Default Web Site** and then click **Properties**. **e.** On the **Directory Security** tab, click **Server Certificate**. **f.** On the **Welcome to the Web Server Certificate Wizard** page, click **Next**. **g.** On the **Server Certificate** page, click **Create a new certificate**. Click **Next**. **h.** On the **Delayed or Immediate Request** page, click **Send the request immediately to an online certification authority** and then click **Next**. **i.** On the **Name and Security Settings** page, accept the defaults and click **Next**. **j.** On the **Organization Information** page, type **Coho Vineyard** as the Organization and **Messaging** as the Organizational Unit. Click **Next**.

(*continued*)

Tasks	Detailed steps
13. (*continued*)	**k.** On the **Your Site's Common Name** page, type **Den-msg-01.cohovineyard.com** as the Common name. Click **Next**.
	l. On the **Geographic Information** page, accept the default for the **Country/Region**, type **Colorado** as the State/province and then type **Denver** as the City/locality. Click **Next**.
	m. On the **SSL Port** page, click **Next**.
	n. On the **Choose a Certification Authority** page, accept the default and click **Next**.
	o. On the **Certification Request Submission** page, review the settings, and then click **Next**.
	p. On the **Completing to the Web Server Certificate Wizard** page, click **Finish**. Click **OK**.
14. Configure IIS to require SSL on the virtual directories used by OWA.	**a.** In the **IIS Manager** console, expand **Default Web Site**, right-click **Exchange**, and then click **Properties**.
	b. In the **Exchange Properties** dialog box, on the **Directory Security** tab, in the **Secure communications** box, click **Edit**.
	c. In the **Secure Communications** box, enable **Require secure channel (SSL)**, and then click **OK**.
	d. Click **OK** to close the **Exchange Properties** dialog box.
	e. Configure the **ExchWeb** and the **Public** virtual directories to require SSL.
	f. Close the **IIS Manager** console.
15. Configure an access rule on the Main\Back-End Array enabling HTTPS access from the front-end array to Den-Msg-01.	**a.** On Den-CSS-01, in ISA Server Management, click **Firewall Policy (Main/Back-End Array)**.
	b. On the **Firewall Policy** tasks pane, on the **Tasks** tab, click **Create an Array Access Rule**.
	c. Create an access rule with the following properties.
	• Access rule name: **OWA Access**
	• Rule action: **Allow**
	• Protocols: **HTTPS**
	• Access Rule Sources: **Den-ISAEE-03 computer**
	• Access Rule Destination: Create a Computer object named **Den-Msg-01**. Assign an IP address of **192.168.1.12**.
	• User Sets: **All Users**
	d. Click **Apply** to apply the changes, and then click **OK** when the changes have been applied.

(*continued*)

Tasks	Detailed steps
16. Create a secure Web publishing rule on Branch|Front-End Array to publish the OWA site on the back end array.	**a.** On Den-ISAEE-03, in ISA Server Management, click **Firewall Policy (Branch/Front-End Array)**. On the **Tasks** tab, click **Publish a Mail Server**. **b.** Create a mail server publishing rule with the following properties. • Rule name: **Coho Vineyard OWA Site** • Access Type: **OWA** • Services: **OWA** • Bridging Mode: **Secure connections to clients and mail server** • Web Mail Server: **Den-Msg-01.cohovineyard.com** • Public name: **Secure.cohovineyard.com** • Web Listener: **HTTPS Internet** • User Sets: **All Users** **c.** Ensure that the Coho Vineyard OWA Site publishing rule is listed before the Coho Vineyard Secure Web Site rule. If it is not, move the OWA rule up. **d.** Click **Apply** to apply the changes, and then click **OK** when the changes have been applied.
17. Test the Outlook Web Access publishing rule.	**a.** On Gen-Web-01, open Internet Explorer and access **https://secure.cohovineyard.com/exchange**. **b.** In the **Security Alert** dialog box, click **OK**. **c.** In the **Connect to secure.cohovineyard.com** dialog box, log on using **cohovineyard\jay** and a password of **P@ssw0rd**. **d.** You should be able to connect to the OWA site.

To Prepare for the Next Lab

As you finish this lab, shut down all the virtual machines that you used in the lab. To shut down the virtual machines, on the **Action** menu, click **Close**. Select **Turn off and delete changes** and then click **OK**.

Module 13: Implementing ISA Server 2004 Enterprise Edition: Site-to-Site VPN Scenario

Contents

Overview

• Implementing a Site-to-Site VPN Scenario
• Lab: Implementing a Site-to-Site VPN Scenario

Introduction

This module introduces major factors to consider when using a virtual private network (VPN) in a site-to-site deployment to link separate branch offices.

You can use either Microsoft® Internet Security and Acceleration (ISA) Server 2004 Standard Edition or Enterprise Edition to implement a site-to-site VPN. However, deploying a site-to-site VPN using Enterprise Edition introduces additional functionality and increased complexity. For example:

- Enterprise Edition provides network load balancing (NLB) for the VPN connection.

- With Enterprise Edition, your deployment plan must take into account the Configuration Storage server installation in the remote office.

- Your deployment planning must also address enterprise and array policies for the main-office and the branch-office arrays.

In the lab, you will implement and test a site-to-site deployment.

Objectives

After completing this module, you will be able to:

- Describe the issues involved with deploying ISA Server 2004 Enterprise Edition in a site-to-site VPN scenario and describe solutions to those issues.

- Implement ISA Server 2004 in a site-to-site VPN scenario.

Lesson: Implementing a Site-to-Site VPN Scenario

- Issues in Deploying Site-to-Site VPNs
- Guidelines for Implementing Distributed Configuration Storage Servers
- Guidelines for Implementing Network Load Balancing for VPN
- Guidelines for Configuring ISA Server Clients
- Guidelines for Configuring Access Rules for Site-to-Site VPNs

Introduction

This lesson briefly describes the concepts related to deploying ISA Server in a branch-office, site-to-site VPN scenario. The lesson first describes the issues of deploying this solution and then describes possible ways to resolve the issues.

Lesson objectives

After completing this lesson, you will be able to:

- Describe the issues in deploying a site-to-site VPN solution.
- Implement multiple Configuration Storage servers.
- Implement network load balancing for VPN.
- Configure ISA Server clients.
- Configure access rules for site-to-site VPNs.

Issues in Deploying Site-to-Site VPNs

Common site-to-site VPN deployment issues include:

- Choosing a tunneling protocol
- Configuring the remote site VPN gateway server
- Configuring network rules and firewall access rules

ISA Server Enterprise Edition site-to-site deployment issues include:

- Creating a preliminary connection to install the remote Configuration Storage server
- Configuring Configuration Storage server replication between locations
- Implementing NLB for the site-to-site VPN
- Configuring firewall and Web proxy caching

Introduction

Many of the planning issues of deploying a site-to-site VPN using ISA Server Enterprise Edition are similar to those of deploying the VPN using ISA Server Standard Edition. However, ISA Server Enterprise Edition adds levels of functionality and complexity.

Common site-to-site VPN issues

When you deploy a site-to-site VPN using either ISA Server Standard Edition or Enterprise Edition, consider the following planning issues:

- *Choose a tunneling protocol*. ISA Server supports several tunneling protocols. Choose the appropriate protocol based your organization's security requirements and the VPN gateway servers that you deploy in each site.

- *Configure the remote-site gateway server*. The VPN gateway server located remotely could be another computer running ISA Server, a computer running Microsoft Windows Server™ 2003 or Microsoft Windows 2000 Server that runs Routing and Remote Access Service (RRAS), or a third-party VPN gateway server. The exact configuration of this server depends on the type of server used in the remote site.

- *Configure network rules and firewall-access rules*. Because ISA Server implements the remote-site network just like any other network, configure the VPN client-access settings on ISA Server to allow remote-access clients to access the internal network or any other network. You can use access rules or publishing rules to make internal resources accessible to remote-office users.

Note For more information about these planning issues, see Module 8, "Configuring Virtual Private Network Access for Remote Clients and Networks," of Course 2824, *Implementing Microsoft Internet Security and Acceleration Server 2004*.

ISA Server Enterprise Edition deployment issues

ISA Server Enterprise Edition also introduces additional issues that you need to include in your planning for the site-to-site VPN deployment. These issues include:

- *Creating a preliminary connection to install the remote Configuration Storage server.* To deploy ISA Server computers in the remote office, the computers must be able to connect to a Configuration Storage server. Until you deploy the Configuration Storage server in the remote office, however, the ISA Server computers cannot be used to create the site-to-site VPN. You therefore need to deploy a temporary connection between the two sites, deploy the Configuration Storage server in the remote office, and then deploy the ISA Server computers that will be used to deploy the site-to-site VPN.

- *Configuring Configuration Storage server replication between locations.* All Configuration Storage servers in an enterprise store all the configuration information for the entire enterprise. Any change to the configuration is automatically replicated to all other Configuration Storage servers. If you have a large enterprise and a slow network connection between the office locations, you may want to control Configuration Storage server replication between the sites.

- *Implementing NLB for the site-to-site VPN.* ISA Server Enterprise Edition enables the use of NLB for the site-to-site VPN. This configuration provides fault tolerance for the VPN connection, but it also requires additional planning and configuration.

- *Configuring firewall and Web proxy chaining.* Deploying ISA Server Enterprise Edition arrays changes some of the configuration options for ISA Server clients. Using arrays also changes how you will configure firewall and Web proxy chaining.

Guidelines for Implementing Distributed Configuration Storage Servers

To deploy the branch-office Configuration Storage server:

- Use a third-party VPN solution
- Use Routing and Remote Access Service
- Use a server publishing rule
- Use a temporary ISA Server enterprise
- Use an ISA Server backup file

To manage Configuration Storage server replication between office locations, use the ADAMSites tool to create ADAM sites and configure replication between sites

Process overview

As you prepare to deploy a site-to-site VPN, you must first decide how you will deploy a branch-office Configuration Storage server. To do this:

1. Implement a temporary connection between the branch office and the main office. This connection will be used to install the branch-office Configuration Storage server.

2. In the branch office, install a Configuration Storage server.

3. Deploy ISA Server computers that will be used to create the site-to-site VPN.

4. Manage replication between the main-office and the branch-office Configuration Storage servers.

Deploying the branch office Configuration Storage server

One factor that complicates deploying ISA Server Enterprise Edition in a site-to-site VPN configuration is that all the ISA Server configuration information for the enterprise is stored on the Configuration Storage server that is located in the main office. You will not be able to install the ISA Server services or install a Configuration Storage server unless the computers can access configuration information in the main office Configuration Storage server. However, until you deploy the ISA Server computer in the branch office, you cannot use ISA Server to establish the site-to-site VPN that enables communication between the offices.

Options for creating a temporary connection

To address the problem, create a temporary connection between the main office and the branch office and then use this connection to install the Configuration Storage server. You have several options for creating the temporary connection:

- *Use a third-party VPN solution.* If you are using a third party site-to-site VPN solution, use the existing VPN connection to access the Configuration Storage server in the main office. Ensure that the computer on which you will install the components uses the third-party VPN gateway server as its default gateway. After you have installed the ISA Server services in the branch office, remove the third-party VPN solution and create a new connection using ISA Server.

- *Use Routing and Remote Access Service.* You can also use RRAS to establish the VPN tunnel to the main office. In this case, use a computer running Microsoft Windows® 2000 Server or Windows Server 2003 on which ISA Server will not be installed, because the ISA Server installation stops the Routing and Remote Access Service, thereby ending the VPN connection. Once you have created the VPN connection, set it as the default gateway for the computer on which you install the ISA Server components.

Note   You can install a replicate Configuration Storage server in the branch office on the computer that hosts RRAS if it is running Windows Server 2003. Installing Configuration Storage server does not stop RRAS.

- *Use server publishing.* You can publish the Configuration Storage server in the main office to the Internet, and then access the Configuration Storage server from the branch office. If you choose this option, create a computer object for the remote-office computer and enable access to the server publishing rule only to that Internet Protocol (IP) address. The server publishing rule must enable access for the MS Firewall Storage Server and the MS Firewall Storage Replication protocols. After installing the branch-office ISA Server computers, disable the server publishing rule.

- *Use a temporary enterprise.* You can also create a combined ISA Server installation in a separate enterprise in the branch office and use it to establish a VPN connection to the main office. After you have created the VPN connection, install a replicate Configuration Storage server that uses the main Configuration Storage server, and then use that server as the Configuration Storage for the branch array. Finally, remove the combined server.

- *Use an ISA Server backup file.* To deploy this option, use Windows Backup on the Configuration Storage server in the main office to create a backup file (.bkf). When you run Backup, choose to back up only the ADAMData folder, which is located in the Microsoft ISA Server folder. Then, when you install the Configuration Storage server on the computer in the branch office, choose to use the backup file as the replication source. This option is recommended for an environment in which you have many ISA Server computers and the network connection between the branch office and main office is slow because, after you restore the data, only the changes to the enterprise that occurred since the last backup must be replicated rather than the entire configuration.

Managing Configuration Storage server replication

The Configuration Storage servers use multiple-master replication to maintain consistent enterprise information on all Configuration Storage servers within the enterprise. One of the issues with this is that the replication may use up much of the bandwidth between the main office and the branch offices, particularly in a large ISA Server enterprise. In these scenarios, you can optimize the replication by establishing ADAM sites, then configuring how often the configuration information between the sites is replicated.

ADAM is a specialized version of Active Directory® directory service, so it uses the same replication mechanisms as Active Directory. When deploying Active Directory, a main reason for creating sites is to control replication between domain controllers. After you can create the sites, you can also configure site links that define when replication between sites occurs. ADAM works in the same way: you can create ADAM sites, move servers to the appropriate sites, and then configure replication between the sites.

To configure ADAM sites, use the Adamsites.exe tool that is included with the ISA Server 2004 Resource Kit. To move a Configuration Storage server to a different site, perform the following steps:

1. Install the Configuration Storage server on a Windows Server 2003 computer.

2. Use the Adamsites.exe tool to create a site. To do this, open a command prompt, and type **AdamSites Site Create** *NewSite*, where *NewSite* is the name of the new site.

3. Then, use the Adamsites.exe tool to move the server to a new site. At a command prompt, type **AdamSites MoveServer** *ConfigStgServer Site1 NewSite*, where *ConfigStgServer* is the name of the Configuration Storage server, *Site1* is the name of the existing site, and *NewSite* is the name of the new site.

4. You also use the Adamsites.exe tool to configure replication between the sites. At a command prompt, type **AdamSites Sitelink create** *LinkName* **2** *Site1 Site2* **50 480**, where *Linkname* is the name of the link that you are creating, 2 defines the number of sites connected by this link, *Site1* and *Site2* are the site names, 50 defines a site link cost, and 480 defines the replication interval in minutes.

Note By default, the site-link cost is 100 and the replication interval between sites is 180 minutes.

Guidelines for Implementing Network Load Balancing for VPN

When you enable NLB for site-to-site VPNs:

* The connection owner for the VPN connection is automatically assigned with failover in the event of a server failure

* You must assign static IP addresses for VPN clients on each member of a multiple-server array

* You must configure the virtual IP address for the remote array as the VPN tunnel endpoint, and add all the dedicated IP addresses for the array members to the remote site network properties

Introduction

Implementing NLB for site-to-site VPNs requires additional configuration compared with implementing NLB for other networks.

Configuring a connection owner

When a site-to-site VPN is established with an array of ISA Server computers, only one array member is actually the connection owner. The connection owner is the VPN tunnel endpoint for that site.

When NLB is enabled for the network that is accepting the VPN connections, ISA Server automatically assigns the connection owner. ISA Server uses an algorithm to determine which ISA Server computer in the array will be the connection owner, creating as balanced a load as possible on the ISA Server computers. After a tunnel has been established, the connection owner will remain as the VPN tunnel endpoint, even if other array members are added or removed.

ISA Server NLB provides automatic routing of client requests to the array member that hosts the VPN connection. If the server that owns a site-to-site VPN connection fails, ISA Server NLB automatically shifts the connection to another ISA Server array member. When the server fails, the site-to-site VPN will be disconnected, but it will automatically be reconnected using the new connection owner.

When NLB is not enabled, you must assign a connection owner for the remote-site network. If the connection owner becomes unavailable, there is no automatic failover, so the site-to-site VPN will not be re-established until you assign a new connection owner, or until the connection owner is again available.

Assigning IP addresses for VPNs

Implementing VPNs with Enterprise Edition arrays also requires additional configuration for assigning IP addresses to the VPN clients. If you have only one ISA Server computer in an array, you can use a Dynamic Host Configuration Protocol (DHCP) server to assign addresses for VPN connections. If you have more than one server in the array, you must assign addresses using static address pools. When you use static address pools, you must create a static address pool on each computer running ISA Server services that you use for the site-to-site VPN connection. To avoid handing out the same IP address to two different VPN clients, ensure that the address ranges assigned to the array members do not overlap.

Configuring remote-site networks with NLB

When the remote-site network to which you connect is an array with NLB enabled, you must specify the virtual IP address of the NLB-enabled array as the VPN tunnel endpoint.

When the remote-site network is an NLB-enabled array, the initial connection will be to the virtual IP address for the array. However, the tunnel will be established with one of the array members using the dedicated IP address for the ISA Server computer. Because of this, you must specify all the dedicated IP addresses as additional remote-tunnel endpoints for the remote-site network. To specify the additional IP addresses, complete the following steps:

1. In the ISA Server Management Console, select the array that you are configuring.

2. Click **Virtual Private Networks (VPN)**.

3. In the details pane, click the **Remote Sites** tab.

4. In the details pane, select the applicable remote network.

5. On the **Tasks** tab, select **Configure Remote Site**.

6. On the **Remote NLB** tab, click **Add Range**.

7. In **Start address**, type the first address in the range, and, in **End address**, type the last address in the range.

Guidelines for Configuring ISA Server Clients

> **When using ISA Server Enterprise Edition, Web Proxy and Firewall clients must connect to the array DNS name**
>
> * The DNS name is assigned when the array is configured, but can be modified
> * The client must be able to resolve the array DNS name using DNS
> * Configure a DNS host record using the array DNS name and each array member's dedicated IP address if NLB is not enabled and the shared IP address if NLB is enabled
>
> **When configuring Web Proxy or Firewall client chaining, configure the downstream array to use the DNS name for the upstream array**

Introduction

ISA Server Enterprise Edition also changes some options for configuring Web Proxy client and Firewall client connections. These changes also apply to configuring Web Proxy client and Firewall client chaining.

Web Proxy and Firewall client configuration for arrays

When deploying Web Proxy or Firewall clients with ISA Server Standard Edition, you configure the clients to use the IP address or name of the ISA Server computer when connecting to remote resources. However, when deploying Web Proxy or Firewall clients with ISA Server Enterprise Edition, the clients must connect to the array rather than the individual servers.

To enable this, configure the ISA Server clients to use the array DNS name to connect to the array. When you create an array, the array is assigned a DNS name. You can modify the array DNS name after deployment.

For the ISA Server clients to connect to the array DNS name, the clients must be able to resolve the name using DNS. This means that you must add the array DNS name to the DNS zone files used by the ISA Server clients. If the array contains more than one server and you are not using NLB, configure a DNS host record using the dedicated IP address for each array member. If you are using NLB, configure the DNS host record to use the shared IP address for the NLB cluster.

If you have Cache Array Routing Protocol (CARP) enabled for the array, the Web Proxy clients connect to the array using the array DNS name to download the CARP script. The clients use the script to determine which array member to connect to when accessing Web content.

Note The default gateway for the SecureNAT clients should be configured to use the shared virtual IP address for the array if NLB is enabled, and the IP address of one of the array members if NLB is not enabled.

Configuring Web Proxy and Firewall client chaining

When you configure Web Proxy client or Firewall client chaining, you also need to use the DNS name for the upstream array. Just like a client, the ISA Server that forwards the request to the upstream array must be able to resolve the DNS name for the array.

Guidelines for Configuring Access Rules for Site-to-Site VPNs

When configuring access rules for site-to-site VPNs, allow only required network traffic:

- Create computer sets to define specific computers that need access rather than using the entire network
- Configure access rules to allow only required protocols
- Use Web and server publishing rules
- Restrict access based on user sets

When deploying main site domain members or members of a trusted domain in the remote site, you must enable the required protocols between the domain controllers, or between the domain members and domain controllers

Introduction

The final step in deploying the site-to-site VPN connection is to configure the enterprise and array access rules that define what types of network traffic will be allowed to flow between the networks. You have several options when configuring the access rules.

Guidelines for configuring access rules

As a best practice, always configure access rules to allow the least possible access between the two networks. Even if the two networks are considered equally trusted, limiting the network traffic between the two networks can have significant benefits. For example, if the remote-site clients can only use specific protocols to connect to specific computers in the main office, the chances that a virus infection in the branch office can spread to the main office is greatly reduced. Or if a malicious user gains access to the branch-office network, the damage that the attacker can do in the main-office network may be limited.

To limit the level of access between the networks, follow these guidelines:

- Rather than configure access rules that grant access to the entire remote-site network, create computer sets for each type of computer that will be defined in an access rule. For example, if a remote-office DNS server needs to be able to forward DNS queries only to a group of DNS servers in the main office, then configure computer sets for the two groups of computers.

- When creating access rules, limit the access-rule protocols to only the required protocols. If two computer sets only need to communicate using the DNS protocol, then configure the access rule to only use that protocol.

- Use Web and server publishing rules. You can increase the security of the inter-site traffic by using publishing rules. For example, if all users in the branch office require access to the organization's intranet Web site located in the main office, you can publish the Web site to the remote-site network. Then you can implement Hypertext Transfer Protocol (HTTP) filtering to protect the Web server in much the same way as you would protect the Web server from the Internet.

- If you need to restrict access to specific users, create the required user sets, and then configure the access rules to use the user sets.

Deploying domain members in the branch office

One of the complicating factors in deploying a site-to-site VPN solution is whether the computers in the remote site will be members of the same domain as the main-office domain. If the computers in the remote site are members of the same domain and no domain controller is deployed in the remote site, all computers will need to communicate with domain controllers in the main office. If a domain controller is deployed in the remote site, the domain controllers in the two sites need to communicate.

In some cases, the remote-site computers may not be members of the main site domain but may be members of a trusted domain. In this scenario, the domain controllers in the two domains must be able to communicate with each other.

For the domain members to communicate, create an access rule allowing Lightweight Directory Access Protocol (LDAP), LDAP User Datagram Protocol (UDP), secure Lightweight Directory Access Protocol (LDAPS), LDAP Global Catalog (GC), LDAPS GC, DNS, Kerberos (TCP), and Kerberos (UDP) traffic from the remote-site domain controllers to the domain controller of the main office. If there is no domain controller in the remote site, you need to enable these protocols for all domain members in the remote site.

Depending on your network configuration, you may also need to enable additional access rules. For example, if you have Microsoft Windows 98 or Microsoft Windows NT® clients in the remote site, you need to enable an access rule that allows these clients to communicate with the primary domain controller (PDC) or PDC emulator in the main office so that the users can change their passwords. If you use Active Directory but do not have a DNS server in the remote office, configure an access rule enabling DNS queries from the branch office to the main office.

Lab 13: Implementing a Site-to-Site VPN Scenario

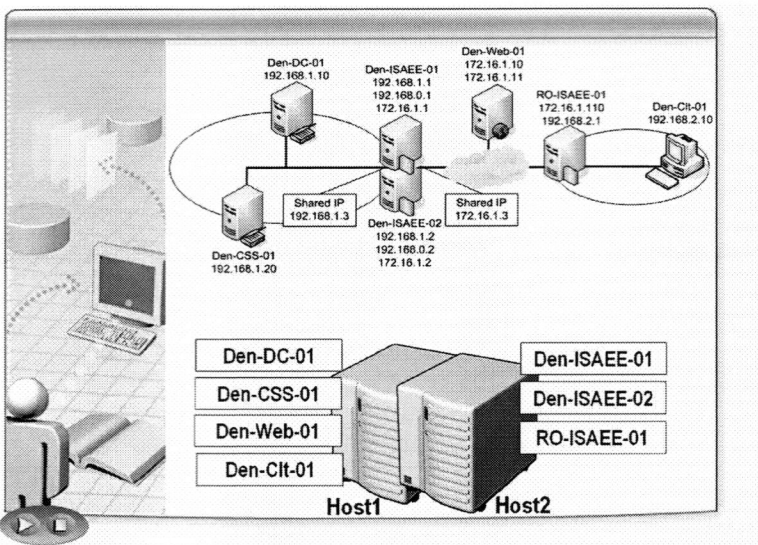

Objectives

After completing this lab, you will be able to:

- Enable NLB and CARP for an array.
- Configure the main office array for a site-to-site VPN.
- Deploy ISA Server services on the remote-site ISA Server computer.
- Configure the branch office array for a site-to-site VPN.

Note   This lab addresses the concepts in this module and, as a result, may not comply with Microsoft security recommendations. For example, this lab does not comply with the recommendation that users should use the **run as** command to perform administrative tasks.

Prerequisites

Before working on this lab, you must have:

- Completed the practices for Module 11 and saved all changes to the virtual machines after the practices.

Estimated time to complete this lab: 90 minutes

▶ **To prepare for this lab**

1. You will need the following virtual machines running for Exercises 1 and 2 of this lab:

   On the first student host computer, you will run:

   a. Den-DC-01

   b. Den-CSS-01

   On the second student host computer, you will run:

   c. Den-ISAEE-01

   d. Den-ISAEE-02

2. If necessary, start or resume the required virtual machines.

Scenario

Coho Vineyard is opening up a new branch office, so you need to configure a site-to-site VPN connection between the main office and the branch office. To do this, you will publish the Configuration Storage server at the main office so that it can be accessed by the server being deployed in the remote office. You will then install ISA Server services on the server at the branch office. Then you will use the branch office ISA Server computer to configure a site-to-site VPN to the main office.

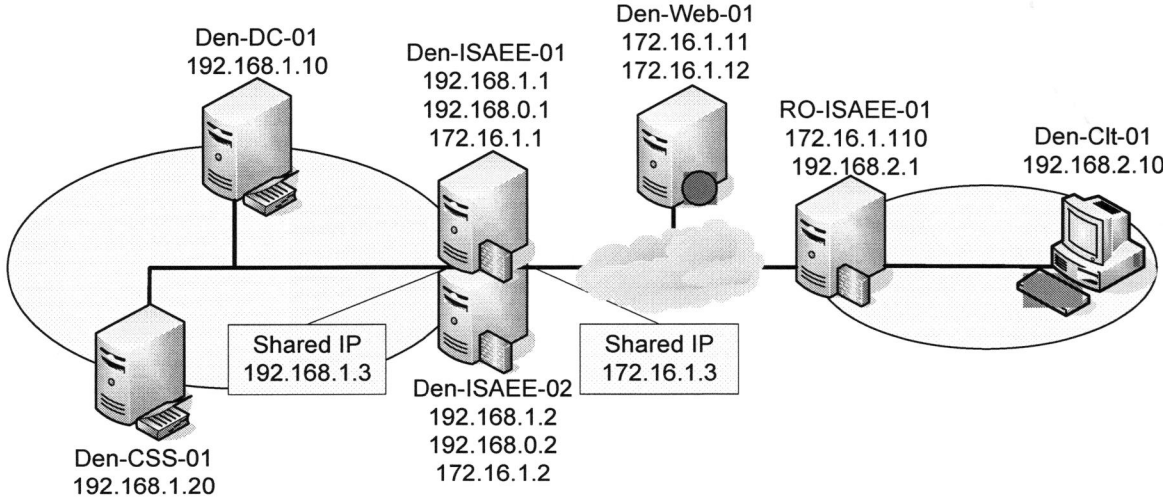

Exercise 1
Enabling NLB and CARP for the Main/Front-End Array

In this exercise, you will configure NLB and CARP for the ISA Server computers located in the Main/Front-End Array.

Scenario

Coho Vineyards wants to ensure that its connection to the Internet is not susceptible to the failure of a single ISA Server computer. To provide this functionality, you will configure an intra-array network. Then you will configure NLB and CARP on the Internal network on the Main/Front-End array.

Tasks	Detailed steps
1. Create an intra-array network that includes the 192.168.0.0 network.	a. Perform the following steps on Den-CSS-01.
	b. Log on to the cohovineyard.com domain with a user account of **Administrator** and a password of **P@ssw0rd**.
	c. Open **ISA Server Management**.
	d. Expand **Arrays**, and then expand **Main/Back-End Array**.
	e. Expand **Configuration**, and then click **Networks**.
	f. On the **Tasks** tab, click **Create a New Network**.
	g. On the **Welcome to the New Network Wizard** page, type **BE Intra-Array Network**, and then click **Next**.
	h. On the **Network Type** page, ensure that **Internal Network** is selected, and then click **Next**.
	i. On the **Network Addresses** page, click **Add Adapter**.
	j. On the **Network Adapters** page, select the check box for the **IntraArray** adapter for **Den-ISAEE-01**, and then click **OK**.
	k. On the **Network Addresses** page, click **Next**.
	l. On the **Completing the New Network Wizard** page, review the configuration, and then click **Finish**.
2. Configure Den-ISAEE-01 and Den-ISAEE-02 to use the intra-array network for intra-array communication.	a. On Den-CSS-01, under **Configuration**, click **Servers**, and then double-click **Den-ISAEE-01**.
	b. On the **Communication** tab, under **Intra-Array Communication**, select **192.168.0.1** from the drop-down list.
	c. Click **OK**.
	d. Double-click **Den-ISAEE-02**.
	e. On the **Communication** tab, under **Intra-Array Communication**, select **192.168.0.2** from the drop-down list.
	f. Click **OK**.
	g. Click **Apply** to apply the changes, and then click **OK** when the changes have been applied.

(continued)

Tasks	Detailed steps
3. Configure network load balancing for the back-end array.	a. On Den-CSS-01, click **Networks**, and then, on the **Tasks** tab, click **Enable Network Load Balancing Integration**. b. On the **Welcome to the Network Load Balancing Integration Wizard** page, click **Next**. c. On the **Select Load Balanced Networks** page, select the check box for **External**, and then click **Set Virtual IP**. d. In the **Set Virtual IP Address** dialog box, type **172.16.1.3** as the **Virtual IP address** and **255.255.255.0** as the **Mask**. Click **OK**. e. On the **Select Load Balanced Networks** page, select the check box for **Internal**, and then click **Set Virtual IP**. f. In the **Set Virtual IP Address** dialog box, type **192.168.1.3** as the **Virtual IP address** and **255.255.255.0** as the **Mask**. Click **OK**. g. On the **Select Load Balanced Networks** page, click **Next**. h. On the **Completing the Network Load Balancing Integration Wizard** page, review the configuration, and then click **Finish**. i. Click **Apply** to apply the changes. j. On the **ISA Server Warning** page, click **Save the changes and restart the services**, and then click **OK**. After the changes have been saved, click **OK**.
4. Enable CARP on the Internal network.	a. On Den-CSS-01, under **Configuration**, click **Cache**. b. Click **Den-ISAEE-01** and click **Define Cache Drives (enable caching)**. c. On the **Cache Drives** tab, in the **Maximum cache size (MB)** box, type **50** and then click **Set**. Click **OK**. d. Click **Den-ISAEE-02** and configure a cache drive of 50 MB. e. Click **Networks**, and then double-click **Internal**. f. On the **CARP** tab, click **Enable CARP on this network**. g. Click **OK**. h. Click **Apply** to apply the changes. i. On the **ISA Server Warning** page, click **Save the changes and restart the services**, and then click **OK**. After the changes have been saved, click **OK**.

5. Configure the default gateway on Den-DC-01 and configure the DNS records required for the front-end and back-end arrays.	a. On Den-DC-01, configure the default gateway for the **Local Area Connection** to use **192.168.1.3**.
	
	b. On Den-DC-01, open **DNS** from the **Administrative Tools** folder and configure the following host records in the cohovineyard.com domain.
	   • MainArray – IP address 192.168.1.3
	   • BranchArray – IP address 192.168.2.1

(continued)

Tasks	Detailed steps
6. Modify the DNS name for the front-end and back-end arrays.	a. On Den-CSS-01, in **ISA Server Management**, right-click **Branch/Front-End Array** and click **Properties**. b. On the **General** tab, change the **DNS Name** to **BranchArray.cohovineyard.com**. Click **OK**. c. Right-click **Main/Back-End Array**, and then click **Properties**. d. On the **General** tab, change the **DNS Name** to **MainArray.cohovineyard.com**. Click **OK**. e. Click **Apply** to apply the changes, and then click **OK** when the changes have been applied.

Exercise 2
Configuring the Main-Office Array for a Site-to-Site VPN

In this exercise, you will configure the user accounts that will be used for authentication when establishing the site-to-site VPN connections. You will also configure the remote-site network on the main-office array.

Scenario

Coho Vineyards is continuing with its deployment of the site-to-site VPN connection. To begin, you must configure the user accounts that the VPN gateway computers will use to authenticate when establishing the VPN connections. You must then configure the remote-site network for the main-office array.

Tasks	Detailed steps
1. Create a user account in the cohovineyard.com domain. The account is called BranchOfficeVPN, and must be granted dial-in permissions.	a. On Den-DC-01, open Active Directory Users and Computers. b. In the **Users** container, create a user account named **BranchOfficeVPN**. Assign a password of **P@ssw0rd**. Clear the check box for **User must change password at next logon**. Do not create a mailbox for the user. c. Open **BranchOfficeVPN** properties. On the **Dial-in** tab, configure **Remote Access Permission** as **Allow Access**. Click **OK**. d. Close **Active Directory Users and Computers**.
2. Enable VPN client access on the Main/Back-End array.	a. Perform the following steps on Den-ISAEE-01. b. Log on to the cohovineyard.com domain with a user account of **Administrator** and a password of **P@ssw0rd**. c. Open **ISA Server Management**, expand **Arrays**, expand **Main/Back-End Array**, expand **Configuration**, and then click **Networks**. d. Double-click **Internal**. e. On the **Addresses** tab, click the listed IP addresses, and click **Remove**. f. Click **Add Network**, click **Main Office Internal**, and click **OK** twice. g. Under **Main/Back-End Array**, click **Virtual Private Networks (VPN)**. h. Click **Define Address Assignments**. In the **Address Assignment** tab ensure that **Static address pool** is selected, and then click **Add**. i. On the **Server IP Address Range Properties** dialog box, select **Den-ISAEE-01** from the drop-down list. In the **Start address** box, type **192.168.3.1**, and in the **End address** box, type **192.168.3.10**. Click **OK**. j. Click **Add** again. On the **Server IP Address Range Properties** dialog box, select **Den-ISAEE-02** from the drop-down list. In the **Start address** box, type **192.168.3.11**, and in the **End address** box, type **192.168.3.20**. Click **OK**.

(continued)

Tasks	Detailed steps
2. *(continued)*	k. Click **Enable VPN Client Access**. If you receive a warning message click **OK**. l. Click **Apply** to apply the changes, and then click **OK** when the changes have been applied.
3. Configure an enterprise network for the remote site IP addresses.	a. On Den-ISAEE-01, expand **Enterprise**, and then click **Enterprise Networks**. b. On the **Tasks** tab, click **Create a New Network**. c. On the **Welcome** page, type **Branch Office Network** as the network name. Click **Next**. d. On the **Network Addresses** page, click **Add Range**. Add the IP address range of 192.168.2.0 to 192.168.2.255 to the network. e. Complete the wizard, click **Apply** to apply the changes, and then click **OK** when the changes have been applied.
4. Configure a remote site network on the Main/Back-End Array.	a. On Den-ISAEE-01, under **Main/Back-End Array**, click **Virtual Private Networks (VPN)**, and then click the **Remote Sites** tab. b. On the **Tasks** tab, click **Add Remote Site Network** to start the **New Network Wizard**. c. On the **Welcome to the New Network Wizard** page, type **BranchOfficeVPN**, and then click **Next**. d. On the **VPN Protocol** page, click **Point-to-Point Tunneling Protocol (PPTP)**, and then click **Next**. e. In the warning dialog box, click **OK**. f. On the **Remote Site Gateway** page, type **172.16.1.110** as the IP address for the remote VPN server, and then click **Next**. g. On the **Remote Authentication** page, click **Local site can initiate connections to remote site using these credentials**. Type in the following information. • User name: **HeadOfficeVPN** • Domain: **RO-ISAEE-01** • Password and confirm password: **P@ssw0rd** Click **Next**. h. On the **Network Addresses** page, click **Add Network**. i. On the **Networks** tab, click the check box for **Branch Office Network**, and then click **OK**. j. On the **Network Addresses** page, click **Next**. k. On the **Completing the New Network Wizard** page, review the configuration, and then click **Finish**. l. Read the ISA Server 2004 warning message, and then click **OK**. If you receive another warning message, click **OK**. m. Click **Apply** to apply the changes, and then click **OK** when the changes have been applied.

(*continued*)

Tasks	Detailed steps
5. Configure a route network relationship between the main office network and the BranchOfficeVPN network.	**a.** On Den-ISAEE-01, in ISA Server Management, under **Main/Back-End Array**, expand **Configuration**, and then click **Networks**. **b.** Click the **Network Rules** tab in the **Details** pane. On the **Tasks** tab, click **Create a New Network Rule**. **c.** On the **Welcome to the New Network Rule Wizard** page, type **Branch Office VPN** in the **Network rule name** box. Click **Next**. **d.** On the **Network Traffic Sources** page, click **Add**. **e.** In the **Add Network Entities** dialog box, click the **Networks** folder. Double-click the **Internal** network. Click **Close**. **f.** Click **Next** on the **Network Traffic Sources** page. **g.** On the **Network Traffic Destinations** page, click **Add**. **h.** In the **Add Network Entities** dialog box, click **Networks**, and then double-click the **BranchOfficeVPN** network. Click **Close**. **i.** Click **Next** on the **Network Traffic Destinations** page. **j.** On the **Network Relationship** page, click **Route**, and then click **Next**. **k.** On the **Completing the New Network Rule Wizard** page, click **Finish**.
6. Configure access rules to allow all network traffic between the main office network and the BranchOfficeVPN network.	**a.** On Den-ISAEE-01, click **Firewall Policy (Main/Back-End Array)**. On the **Tasks** tab, click **Create Array Access Rule**. **b.** On the **Welcome to the New Access Rule Wizard** page, type **Main Office to Branch Office** in the **Access rule name** box. Click **Next**. **c.** On the **Rule Action** page, click **Allow**, and click **Next**. **d.** On the **Protocols** page, select **All outbound traffic** from the **This rule applies to** list. Click **Next**. **e.** On the **Access Rule Sources** page, click **Add**. **f.** In the **Add Network Entities** dialog box, click the **Networks** folder, and then double-click the **Internal** network. Click **Close**. **g.** Click **Next** on the **Access Rule Sources** page. **h.** On the **Access Rule Destinations** page, click **Add**. **i.** In the **Add Network Entities** dialog box, click the **Networks** folder, and then double-click the **BranchOfficeVPN** network. Click **Close**. **j.** Click **Next** on the **Access Rule Destinations** page. **k.** On the **User Sets** page, accept the **All Users** default entry, and then click **Next**. **l.** On the **Completing the New Access Rule Wizard** page, click **Finish**. **m.** Repeat steps a through l, creating another remote access rule. The access rule name is **Branch Office to Main Office** and the access rule allows traffic from the **BranchOfficeVPN** network to the **Internal** network.

(continued)

Tasks	Detailed steps
6. *(continued)*	**n.** Click **Apply** to apply the changes, and then click **OK** when the changes have been applied.
	o. Restart both Den-ISAEE-01 and Den-ISAEE-02.
	p. Wait till both servers have restarted before continuing.

Exercise 3
Deploying ISA Server Services in a Remote Site

In this exercise, you will publish the Configuration Storage server in the main office to enable the ISA Server computer in the branch office to connect to the Configuration Storage server. You will then install ISA Server services on the branch office computer.

Scenario

To begin the branch-office deployment, you must first publish the main office Configuration Storage server for access from the branch office computer. Then you will install and configure ISA Server services on the branch office computer.

To prepare for this lab, you will need the following virtual machines running for Exercise 3 of this lab:

- On the first student host computer, you will run:

  a. Den-DC-01

  b. Den-CSS-01

- On the second student host computer, you will run:

  a. Den-ISAEE-01

  b. Den-ISAEE-02

  c. RO-ISAEE-01

If necessary, start or resume the required virtual machines.

Tasks	Detailed steps
1. Configure the Branch/Front-End Array to use SSL authentication.	a. Perform these steps on Den-ISAEE-01. b. Log on to the cohovineyard domain as **administrator**, with a password of **P@ssw0rd**. c. In **ISA Server Management**, click **Branch/Front-End Array**, and then, on the **Tasks** tab, click **Configure Array Properties**. d. On the **Configuration Storage** tab, click **Select**. e. In the **Select Authentication Type** dialog box, click **Authentication over SSL encrypted channel**, and then click **OK**. f. Click **OK**.
2. Configure a server publishing rule that allows the MS Firewall Storage Server protocol from the branch office ISA Server computer to the Configuration Storage server.	a. On Den-ISAEE-01, in ISA Server Management, click **Firewall Policy (Main/Back-End Array)**. b. Click **Create New Server Publishing Rule**. c. On the **Welcome** page, type **CSS Publishing Rule**. Click **Next**. d. On the **Select Server** page, type **192.168.1.20** as the **Server IP address**, and then click **Next**. e. On the **Select Protocol** page, select **MS Firewall Storage Server** from the **Selected protocol** drop-down list. Click **Next**.

(continued)

Tasks	Detailed steps
2. *(continued)*	**f.** On the **IP Address** page, click **External**, click **Next**, and then click **Finish**. **g.** Double-click the **CSS Publishing Rule**. **h.** On the **From** tab, click **Anywhere**, and click **Remove**. **i.** Click **Add**. **j.** In the **Add Network Entities** dialog box, click **New**, and then click **Computer**. **k.** In the **New Computer Rule Element** dialog box, type **RO-ISAEE-01** as the name, and type **172.16.1.110** as the **Computer IP Address**. Click **OK**. **l.** In the **Add Network Entities** dialog box, expand **Computers**, and then click **RO-ISAEE-01**. Click **Add**, and then click **Close**. Click **OK**. **m.** Click **Apply** to apply the changes, and then click **OK** when the changes have been applied.
3. Prepare RO-ISAEE-01 to operate as the remote office ISA Server computer.	**a.** Perform these steps on the RO-ISAEE-01 virtual machine. **b.** Log on to the local computer using a user name of **Administrator** and a password of **P@ssw0rd**. **c.** Add the following entry to the hosts file on RO-ISAEE-01: **172.16.1.3 Den-CSS-01.cohovineyard.com**. **d.** Create a new user in **Computer Management** named **HeadOfficeVPN**. Assign a password of **P@ssw0rd** and configure the account to allow dial-in permissions.
4. Install ISA Server services on RO-ISAEE-01.	**a.** On the RO-ISAEE-01 virtual machine menu, click **CD**, and then click **Capture ISO Image**. **b.** Browse to **C:\Program Files\Microsoft Learning\2824\LabFiles** and click **ISAEEInstall.iso**. Click **Open**. **c.** In **Microsoft ISA Server Setup**, click **Install ISA Server 2004**. **d.** After the setup program prompts that it has completed determining the system configuration, on the **Welcome to the Installation Wizard for Microsoft ISA Server 2004** page, click **Next**. **e.** Review the terms and conditions stated in the user license agreement, click **I accept the terms in the license agreement**, and then click **Next**. **f.** On the **Customer Information** page, click **Next**. **g.** On the **Setup Scenarios** page, select **Install ISA Server services**, and then click **Next**. **h.** On the **Component Selection** page, review the settings, and then click **Next**.

(*continued*)

Tasks	Detailed steps
4. (*continued*)	i. On the **Locate Configuration Storage Server** page, type **Den-CSS-01.cohovineyard.com** as the **Configuration Storage server**. Click **Connect using this account**, and then type **cohovineyard\administrator** as the user name and **P@ssw0rd** as the password. Click **Next**.
	j. On the **Array Membership** page, click **Join an existing array**, and then click **Next**.
	k. On the **Join an Existing Array** page, click **Browse**.
	l. Click **Branch/Front-End Array**, click **OK**, and then click **Next**.
	m. On the **Configuration Storage Server Authentication Options**, click **Install a trusted root CA certificate**. Click **Browse**, and browse to **C:\Program Files\Microsoft Learning\2824\Labfiles**.
	n. Click **Den-DC-01.cohovineyard.com_CohovineyardCA.crt**, and then click **Open**. Click **Next**.
	o. On the **Internal Network** page, click **Add**.
	p. In the **Addresses** dialog box, click **Add Network**. Click **Branch Office Network** and click **OK**. In the **Addresses** dialog box, click **OK**.
	q. On the **Internal Network** page, click **Next**.
	r. On the **Services Warning** page, click **Next**.
	s. On the **Ready to Install the Program** page, click **Install** to begin the installation.
	t. When the installation completes, click **Finish**. Click **Yes** to restart the computer.
	u. Wait until RO-ISAEE-01 finishes restarting before continuing.

Exercise 4
Configure the Remote Site for a Site-to-Site VPN

In this exercise, you will configure the branch office array to enable a site-to-site VPN with the main office. Then you will test the site-to-site VPN connection.

Scenario

As the final step in preparing the site-to-site VPN, you will configure the remote site network on the branch office array and test the VPN connection.

You will need the following virtual machines running for Exercise 4 of this lab:

- On the first student host computer, you will run:

  a. Den-DC-01

  b. Den-CSS-01

  c. Den-Clt-01

  d. Den-Web-01

- On the second student host computer, you will run:

  a. Den-ISAEE-01

  b. Den-ISAEE-02

  c. RO-ISAEE-01

If necessary, start or resume the required virtual machines.

Tasks	Detailed steps
1. Configure the RO-ISAEE-01 server properties to enable remote administration.	a. Perform these steps on Den-CSS-01. b. In **ISA Server Management**, expand **Branch/Front-End Array**, expand **Configuration**, and then click **Servers**. c. Double-click **RO-ISAEE-01**. On the **Communications** tab, click **Use this IP address or computer name**, and enter **192.168.2.1** in the text box. d. Click **OK**.
2. Configure a remote site network on the Branch/Front-End array.	a. On Den-CSS-01, expand **Arrays**, expand **Branch/Front-End Array**, and click **Virtual Private Networks (VPN)**. b. Click **Define Address Assignments**. In the **Address Assignment** tab, ensure that **Static address pool** is selected, and then click **Add**. c. On the **Server IP Address Range Properties**, select **RO-ISAEE-01** from the drop-down list. In the **Start address** box, type **192.168.3.21**, and in the **End address** box, type **192.168.3.30**. Click **OK** twice. d. Click **Enable VPN Client Access**. e. In the warning message, click **OK**.

(*continued*)

Tasks	Detailed steps
2. (*continued*)	**f.** Click **Apply** to apply the changes, and then click **OK** when the changes have been applied.
	g. Click the **Remote Sites** tab.
	h. On the **Tasks** tab, click **Add Remote Site Network** to start the **New Network Wizard**.
	i. On the **Welcome to the New Network Wizard** page, type **HeadOfficeVPN**, and then click **Next**.
	j. On the **VPN Protocol** page, click **Point-to-Point Tunneling Protocol (PPTP)**, and then click **Next**.
	k. In the warning dialog box, click **OK**.
	l. On the **Connection Owner** page, select **RO-ISAEE-01** from the **Select connection owner** list, and then click **Next**.
	m. On the **Remote Site Gateway** page, type **172.16.1.3** as the IP address for the remote VPN server, and then click **Next**.
	n. On the **Remote Authentication** page, click **Local site can initiate connections to remote site using these credentials**. Type in the following information.
	• User name: **BranchOfficeVPN**
	• Domain: **cohovineyard**
	• Password and confirm password: **P@ssw0rd**
	Click **Next**.
	o. On the **Network Addresses** page, click **Add Network**.
	p. In the **Select Enterprise Networks** dialog box, select **Main Office Internal**. Click **OK**, and then click **Next**.
	q. On the **Completing the New Network Wizard** page, review the configuration, and then click **Finish**.
	r. Read the ISA Server 2004 warning message, and then click **OK**.
	s. Read the second ISA Server 2004 warning message, and then click **OK**.
	t. Click **Apply** to apply the changes, and then click **OK** when the changes have been applied.
3. Configure a route network relationship between the branch office network and the HeadOfficeVPN network.	**a.** On Den-CSS-01, in ISA Server Management, under **Branch/Front-End Array**, click **Virtual Private Networks (VPN)**.
	b. On the **Remote Sites** tab, double-click **HeadOfficeVPN**.
	c. On the **Remote NLB** tab, click **Add Range**.
	d. On the **IP Address Range Properties** dialog box, type **172.16.1.1** as the **Start address**, and **172.16.1.3** as the **End address**. Click **OK** twice.
	e. Under **Branch/Front-End Array**, expand **Configuration**, and then click **Networks**.

(*continued*)

Tasks	Detailed steps
3. (*continued*)	**f.** Click the **Network Rules** tab in the **Details** pane. On the **Tasks** tab, click **Create a Network Rule**.
	g. On the **Welcome to the New Network Rule Wizard** page, type **Main Office VPN** in the **Network rule name** box. Click **Next**.
	h. On the **Network Traffic Sources** page, click **Add**.
	i. In the **Add Network Entities** dialog box, click the **Networks** folder. Double-click the **Internal** network. Click **Close**.
	j. Click **Next** on the **Network Traffic Sources** page.
	k. On the **Network Traffic Destinations** page, click **Add**.
	l. In the **Add Network Entities** dialog box, click **Networks**, and then double-click the **HeadOfficeVPN** network. Click **Close**.
	m. On the **Network Traffic Destinations** page, click **Next**.
	n. On the **Network Relationship** page, click **Route**, and then click **Next**.
	o. On the **Completing the New Network Rule Wizard** page, click **Finish**.
	p. Click **Apply** to apply the changes, and then click **OK** when the changes have been applied.
4. Configure access rules to allow all network traffic between the branch-office network and the HeadOfficeVPN network.	**a.** On Den-CSS-01, click **Firewall Policy (Branch/Front-End Array)**. On the **Tasks** tab, click **Create Array Access Rule**.
	b. On the **Welcome to the New Access Rule Wizard** page, in the **Access rule name** box, type **Main Office to Branch Office**. Click **Next**.
	c. On the **Rule Action** page, click **Allow**, and then click **Next**.
	d. On the **Protocols** page, from the **This rule applies to** list, select **All outbound traffic**. Click **Next**.
	e. On the **Access Rule Sources** page, click **Add**.
	f. In the **Add Network Entities** dialog box, click the **Networks** folder, and then double-click the **HeadOfficeVPN** network. Click **Close**.
	g. On the **Access Rule Sources** page, click **Next**.
	h. On the **Access Rule Destinations** page, click **Add**.
	i. In the **Add Network Entities** dialog box, click the **Networks** folder, and then double-click the **Internal** network. Click **Close**.
	j. Click **Next** on the **Access Rule Destinations** page.
	k. On the **User Sets** page, accept the default entry **All Users**, and then click **Next**.
	l. On the **Completing the New Access Rule Wizard** page, click **Finish**.
	m. Repeat steps a through l, creating another remote-access rule. The access rule name is **Branch Office to Main Office** and the access rule allows traffic from the **Internal** network to the **HeadOfficeVPN** network.

(*continued*)

Tasks	Detailed steps
4. (*continued*)	**n.** Click **Apply** to apply the changes, and then click **OK** when the changes have been applied. **o.** Restart RO-ISAEE-01. Wait until the server has restarted before continuing.

5. Modify the network settings Den-Clt-01 to configure it to operate as a client in the remote site.	**a.** On **Den-Clt-01**, log on to the cohovineyard.com domain using a user account of **Administrator** and a password of **P@ssw0rd**.
	
	b. Modify the network settings for the **Local Area Network** network interface to use:
	
	   • IP address: **192.168.2.10**
	
	   • Subnet mask: **255.255.255.0**
	
	   • Default gateway: **192.168.2.1**
	
	   • DNS Server: **192.168.1.10**

6. Modify the settings for the Branch/Front-End array so that the Enterprise Internet Access Policy is applied to the array.	**a.** On Den-CSS-01, in ISA Server Management, right-click **Branch/Front-End Array**, and then click **Properties**. **b.** On the **Policy Settings** tab, in the **Enterprise policy** list, select **Enterprise Internet Access Policy**. Click **OK**. **c.** Click **Apply** to apply the changes, and then click **OK** when the changes have been applied.
7. Test the site-to-site VPN connection.	**a.** On Den-Clt-01, open a command prompt and type **ping 192.168.1.10**. If the ping is not successful, wait for a minute and try again. The ping attempt should be successful. **b.** Open **Internet Explorer** and attempt to connect to **http://den-web-01.cohovineyard.com**. The connection should be successful.

Course Evaluation

Your evaluation of this course will help Microsoft understand the quality of your learning experience.

To complete a course evaluation, go to http://www.CourseSurvey.com.

Microsoft will keep your evaluation strictly confidential and will use your responses to improve your future learning experience.

Index

Note: Numbers preceding the hyphens indicate the module in which the entry can be found.

Notes

Notes